Essentials of Urban Economics

Essentials of Urban Economics

Arthur O'Sullivan
Department of Economics
Oregon State University

Homewood, IL 60430
Boston, MA 02116

Senior sponsoring editor: Gary Nelson
Editorial coordinator: Beth Bortz
Marketing manager: Ron Bloecher
Project editor: Waivah Clement
Production manager: Mary Jo Parke
Art coordinator: Mark Malloy
Cover designer: Teresa Oeffinger
Compositor: Publication Services, Inc.
Typeface: 10/12 Times Roman
Printer: R. R. Donnelley & Sons Company

Library of Congress Cataloging-in-Publication Data

O'Sullivan, Arthur.
  Essentials of urban economics / by Arthur O'Sullivan.
    p.   cm.
  Includes index.
  ISBN 0-256-12330-6
  1. Urban economics. I. Title.
HT321.088   1993
330.9173⁄2—dc20   92–24424

Printed in the United States of America
1 2 3 4 5 6 7 8 9 0 DOC 9 8 7 6 5 4 3 2

To Conor and Maura

Appleyard and Field
INTERNATIONAL ECONOMICS

Baily and Friedman
MACROECONOMICS, FINANCIAL MARKETS, AND THE INTERNATIONAL SECTOR

Barron and Lynch
ECONOMICS
third edition

Blair
URBAN AND REGIONAL ECONOMICS

Bornstein
COMPARATIVE ECONOMIC SYSTEMS: MODELS AND CASES
sixth edition

Brown and Moore
READINGS, ISSUES, AND PROBLEMS IN PUBLIC FINANCE
third edition

Colander
ECONOMICS

Colander
MICROECONOMICS

Colander
MACROECONOMICS

Denzau
MICROECONOMIC ANALYSIS: MARKETS & DYNAMICS

Hyman
ECONOMICS
second edition

Hyman
MICROECONOMICS
second edition

Hyman
MACROECONOMICS
second edition

Hyman
MODERN MICROECONOMICS: ANALYSIS AND APPLICATIONS
third edition

Katz and Rosen
MICROECONOMICS

Lehmann
REAL WORLD ECONOMIC APPLICATIONS: THE WALL STREET JOURNAL WORKBOOK
third edition

Lindert
INTERNATIONAL ECONOMICS
ninth edition

Maurice and Phillips
ECONOMIC ANALYSIS: THEORY AND APPLICATION
sixth edition

Maurice, Thomas, and Smithson
MANAGERIAL ECONOMICS: APPLIED MICROECONOMICS FOR DECISION MAKING
fourth edition

Nadler and Hansen
MICROCOMPUTER MACROECONOMICS WITH IBM DISK

O'Sullivan
URBAN ECONOMICS
second edition

O'Sullivan
ESSENTIALS OF URBAN ECONOMICS

Peterson
PRINCIPLES OF ECONOMICS: MICRO
eighth edition

Peterson
PRINCIPLES OF ECONOMICS: MACRO
eighth edition

Prager
APPLIED MICROECONOMICS: AN INTERMEDIATE APPROACH

Rima
DEVELOPMENT OF ECONOMIC ANALYSIS
fifth edition

Roger and Daniel
PRINCIPLES OF ECONOMICS SOFTWARE SIMULATION

Rosen
PUBLIC FINANCE
third edition

Schwarz and Van Dyken
MANAGER: MANAGERIAL ECONOMICS SOFTWARE

Seo
MANAGERIAL ECONOMICS: TEXT, SHORT CASES
seventh edition

Sharp, Register, and Leftwich
ECONOMICS OF SOCIAL ISSUES
tenth edition

Shepherd
PUBLIC POLICIES TOWARD BUSINESS
eighth edition

Shugart
THE ORGANIZATION OF INDUSTRY

Slavin
INTRODUCTION TO ECONOMICS
third edition

Streifford
ECONOMIC PERSPECTIVE

Walton and Wykoff
UNDERSTANDING ECONOMICS TODAY
third edition

Preface

This book uses simple economic analysis to explain why cities exist, where they develop, how they grow, and how different activities are arranged within cities. It also explores the economics of urban problems such as poverty, inadequate housing, congestion, pollution, and crime. The text is designed for use in undergraduate courses in urban economics and urban affairs. It has been written for students whose experience with microeconomics is limited to an introductory course in the subject. This book covers more topics than the typical urban economics text, giving instructors several options for a one-semester course in urban economics. A course that emphasizes interurban location analysis would include all the chapters in Part I (Market Forces in the Development of Cities), while other courses might omit Chapter 3 (The Location of Firms and Cities) and Chapter 4 (Market Areas and the Urban Hierarchy). A course emphasizing intraurban location analysis would cover all the chapters in Part II (Land Rent and Urban Land Use Patterns), while other courses might omit Chapter 8 (Land Use Controls and Zoning). A course emphasizing urban problems would incorporate all the chapters in Part III (Urban Problems and the Federal Response) and several of the chapters in Part IV (Urban Problems and Local Government). The chapters on local government could be omitted in a course emphasizing traditional urban problems, but would be an integral part of a course emphasizing urban public finance. The last two chapters deal with education and crime, two urban problems that receive less attention in other urban texts.

Essentials of Urban Economics is a spin-off of *Urban Economics,* second edition, which carries a 1993 copyright date. Although the two books cover the same general topics, this book is written for students with little exposure to economic analysis. This text uses only the most elementary concepts from microeconomics, and applies the concepts in a simple and straightforward fashion. In contrast, *Urban Economics* uses concepts that are not covered in most introductory courses, including the consumer choice model (indifference curves and budget lines), monopolistic competition, the input choice model (isoquants and isocosts), short-run and long-run cost curves, and interactions between markets.

Acknowledgments

I am greatly indebted to my two mentors in urban economics. As an undergraduate at the University of Oregon, I was taught by Ed Whitelaw, whose enthusiasm for urban economics is apparently contagious. He used a number of innovative teaching techniques that made economics understandable, relevant, and even fun. As a graduate student at Princeton University, I was taught by Edwin Mills, one of the founding fathers of urban economics. He refined my mathematical and analytical skills and also provided a steady stream of perceptive insights into urban phenomena. I hope that some of what I learned from these two outstanding teachers is reflected in this book.

I am also indebted to many people who read the book and suggested ways to improve the coverage and the exposition, and to the reviewers who gave me their valuable input: Peter B. Lund, California State University, Sacramento; Richard Marshment, University of Oklahoma/Norman Campus; Herbert Mohring, University of Minnesota/Twin Cities Campus; and Charles Zech, Villanova University.

Arthur O'Sullivan

Contents
in Brief

Contents

14   Local Taxes and Intergovernmental Grants   347

15   Autos and Highways   367

1 Introduction

This book explores the economics of cities and urban problems. Most people have mixed feelings about cities. On the positive side, cities facilitate production and trade, so they increase our standard of living. In addition, they provide consumers with a wide variety of goods and services. Unfortunately, cities also have serious problems such as poverty, congestion, pollution, and crime. Although these problems are truly urban in nature, they could be solved without abandoning our cities. One of the purposes of this book is to show that policies that solve urban problems will increase the vitality of cities, causing cities to grow, not shrink.

Another purpose of the book is to explain some broad changes in the size of cities and the fraction of the population living in cities. In 1990, over 75 percent of the U.S. population lived in urban areas, up from only 6 percent in 1800. This rapid urbanization resulted in large part from the technological changes of the industrial revolution. A number of innovations in production and transportation increased industrial output and trade. Since most firms locate in cities, the increases in output and trade increased the size and number of cities. More recently, however, many northeastern and north-central U.S. cities have actually lost population, a result of migration to the West and the South and a shift away from the traditional manufacturing economy.

Another purpose of the book is to explain some broad changes in the internal spatial structure of cities. In the 19th century, the typical large metropolitan area was monocentric, with the bulk of the city's employment in its central core area. In the typical modern metropolitan area, about half of the jobs are in suburban areas, and many of the suburban jobs are in suburban subcenters. The suburbanization of employment was caused by a number of factors, including changes in transportation and communications technology, the building of highways, and other government policies.

As mentioned in the opening paragraph, this book explores the economics of urban problems. The conventional list of urban problems includes poverty, segregation, inadequate housing, congestion, pollution, inferior education, and crime.

1

This text provides three insights into the analysis of these problems. First, most of these urban problems are related: many of the problems have common roots, and some of the problems are exacerbated by the other problems. For example, poverty contributes to the problems of inadequate housing and crime, and crime contributes to neighborhood deterioration and thus worsens the problem of inadequate housing. Given the common roots and interdependencies of many urban problems, a comprehensive approach to the problems may be more effective than a piecemeal one. The second insight about urban problems is that the economic approach to these problems often differs from the approaches adopted by policymakers. For example, the problems of congestion and pollution occur because some resources (roads and air) are improperly priced; the economic approach is to force travelers and polluters to pay for the resources they use. In contrast, the policy response to these problems often involves regulation or subsidization. The third insight into urban problems is that most of the problems are affected by land-use patterns and also influence land-use patterns. An understanding of the spatial dimension of a particular urban problem is necessary to (1) fully understand the reasons for the problem and (2) predict the spatial responses to a particular public policy.

The remainder of this brief introductory chapter addresses two questions. First, what is urban economics? The answers to this question provide a preview of the material covered in the book. Second, what is a city? The economist's definition of a city differs from the definition used by the U.S. Census Bureau.

What Is Urban Economics?

Urban economics is the study of the location choices of firms and households. Other branches of economics ignore spatial aspects of decision making, adopting the convenient but unrealistic assumption that all production and consumption takes place at a single point. In contrast, urban economics examines the *where* of economic activities. In urban economics, a household chooses where to work and where to live. Similarly, a firm chooses where to locate its factory, office, or retail outlet.

Urban economics explores the spatial aspects of urban problems and public policy. Urban problems such as poverty, segregation, urban decay, crime, congestion, and pollution are intertwined with the location decisions of households and firms: location decisions contribute to urban problems, and urban problems influence location decisions. For example, the suburbanization of employment opportunities contributes to central-city poverty, which causes further suburbanization as wealthy households flee the fiscal problems of the central city. An informed discussion of alternative policy options must take these spatial effects into account.

If urban economics is the study of location choices, why isn't it called *location economics* or *spatial economics?* There are three reasons for the *urban* in urban economics. First, most location decisions have an urban component: over three fourths of the U.S. work force live in cities, meaning that much of location analysis involves urban areas. Second, urban economics is also concerned with location choices within cities. Finally, the most important problems caused by location choices occur in urban areas.

Urban economics can be divided into four related areas, which correspond to the four parts of this book: market forces in the development of cities, land rent and land use within cities, spatial aspects of poverty and housing, and local government expenditures and taxes.

Market Forces in the Development of Cities

The first part of the book shows how the location decisions of firms and households cause the development of cities. A firm chooses the location within a region that maximizes its profit, and a household chooses the location that maximizes its utility. These location decisions generate clusters of activity (cities) that differ in size and economic structure. The questions addressed in this part of the book include the following:

1. Why do cities exist?
2. What is the role of trade in the development of cities?
3. Where do urban areas develop?
4. What is the connection between industrialization and urbanization?
5. Why do cities differ in size and scope?
6. What causes urban economic growth and decline?
7. How do local governments encourage economic growth?
8. How does employment growth affect a city's per capita income?

Land Rent and Land Use within Cities

The second part of the book discusses the spatial organization of activities within cities. In contrast to the first part, which examines location choices from the regional perspective, the second part examines the location choices of firms and households within cities. It shows how land-use patterns are shaped by the interactions between different urban activities. The questions addressed in the second part include the following:

1. What determines the price of land, and why does the price vary across space?
2. Why does the price of housing vary across space?
3. Why are households in U.S. cities segregated with respect to income and race?
4. What factors caused the suburbanization of employment and population?
5. Why was the monocentric city of the 19th century replaced by the multi-centric city of the 20th century?

6. Why do local governments use zoning and other land-use controls to restrict location choices?
7. How does zoning affect the price of land?

Spatial Aspects of Poverty and Housing

The third part of the book examines the spatial aspects of two related urban problems, poverty and housing. Urban poverty has a distinct spatial dimension: the poor are typically concentrated in the central city, far from the expanding employment opportunities in the suburbs. The discussion of poverty addresses the following questions:

1. Who are the poor, and where do they live?
2. What causes poverty?
3. To what extent do market forces diminish racial discrimination in employment?
4. Does residential segregation contribute to poverty?
5. How does the federal government combat poverty?
6. What are the merits of reform proposals such as the negative income tax, workfare, earned-income tax credits, and mandated child support?

The third part of the book also examines the spatial aspects of urban housing problems. Housing choices are linked to location choices because housing is immobile: when a household chooses a dwelling, it also chooses a location. The most important urban housing problems are segregation and the decay of dwellings and entire neighborhoods in the central city. The two housing chapters address the following questions:

1. What makes housing different from other commodities?
2. Why do the poor occupy used housing?
3. What causes racial segregation in housing?
4. Under what conditions will a neighborhood switch from being mostly white to mostly black?
5. How does public policy affect the supply of low-income housing and its price?
6. Should the government build new low-income housing or give money to the poor?
7. How does rent control affect the supply of low-income housing?

Local Government Expenditures and Taxes

The last part of the book explores the spatial aspects of local government policies. Under the fragmented system of local governments, most large metropolitan areas have dozens of local governments, including municipalities, school districts, and special districts. These local governments provide a wide variety of goods, including transportation systems, education, and crime protection. Firms and households "shop" for the jurisdiction that provides the best combination of services and taxes: citizens vote with their feet. Therefore, tax and spending policies affect location choices, thus influencing the spatial distribution of activity within and between cities.

The process of shopping for a local government raises five questions about the fragmented system of local government:

1. Is the fragmented system of government efficient?
2. What is the role of intergovernmental grants in the fragmented system?
3. How do taxpayers respond to local taxes on property, income, and sales?
4. Is the local property tax regressive or progressive?
5. Does the property tax encourage segregation with respect to income and race?

One of the responsibilities of local government is to provide a transportation system. Most cities combine an auto-based highway system with some form of mass transit (bus, light rail, or heavy rail). Since activities are arranged within cities to facilitate interactions between different activities, changes in the transportation system that affect the relative accessibility of different sites also affect land-use patterns. The chapters on transportation address the following questions:

1. What causes congestion, and what are the alternative policy responses?
2. How does congestion affect land-use patterns?
3. What are the alternative policies for dealing with auto pollution?
4. Under what circumstances is a bus system more efficient than a fixed-rail system such as San Francisco's BART or Washington's Metro?
5. What are the costs and benefits of light-rail systems?
6. Should transit be deregulated to allow private firms to compete with transit authorities?

The last two chapters of the book deal with two local public goods: education and crime control. The study of education fits naturally into the scheme of urban economics because education affects location decisions. A household's choice of residence depends in part on the quality of local schools and the taxes required to support the schools. Location choices affect the provision of education: if households segregate themselves with respect to income, per pupil spending is likely to be relatively low in poor districts, so poor children may receive inferior education. In addition, a child's achievement level depends on (1) the income and education level of the child's parents and (2) the achievement level of classmates. Therefore, a child in a poor community may receive an inferior education even if all schools spend the same amount per pupil.

The chapter on education addresses the following questions:

1. Which of the inputs to the education production function are most productive? How do the home environment and the peer group affect educational achievement? Do class size and teachers' qualifications matter?
2. Why does spending per pupil vary across school districts?
3. To what extent do intergovernmental grants decrease spending inequalities?
4. Why does educational achievement vary across school districts?
5. What are the effects of desegregation policies on enrollment in public schools and educational achievement?
6. What are the merits of proposals to use vouchers or tax credits to subsidize education in private schools?

The final chapter of the book explores the economics of crime. Like education, crime affects location decisions: a household's choice of residence depends in part on the local crime rate and the taxes required to support the criminal-justice system. Location decisions affect the provision of crime protection: if households segregate themselves with respect to income, spending on crime protection may be lower in poor areas. In addition, because there is often a relatively large number of potential criminals in poor areas, citizens in poor communities would experience higher crime rates even if spending on crime protection were the same in all communities.

The crime chapter addresses the following questions:

1. Are criminals rational? Is it possible to decrease crime by changing the expected benefits and costs of crime?
2. Why are crime rates relatively high in central cities?
3. What is the optimum amount of crime?
4. How do the police, the courts, and the prison system deter crime?
5. Do policies to control illegal drugs increase property crime?

What Is an Urban Area?

To an urban economist, a geographical area is considered *urban* if it contains a large number of people in a relatively small area. In other words, an **urban area** is defined as an area with a relatively high population density. For example, suppose that the average population density of a particular county is 20 people per acre. If part of the county contains 50,000 people in a 20-square-mile area (i.e., the population density is 2,500 people per square mile), it would be considered an urban area because it has a relatively high population density. This definition accommodates urban areas of vastly different size, from a small town to a large metropolitan area. The economist's definition is stated in terms of population density because the urban economy is based on frequent contact between different economic activities, and such contact is feasible only if firms and households are packed into a relatively small area.

Census Definitions

The Census Bureau defines a number of geographical areas. Since most empirical work in urban economics is based on census data, a clear understanding of these definitions is important.

Municipality or City. A **municipality** is defined as an area over which a municipal corporation provides local government services such as sewage, crime protection, and fire protection. Another census term for municipality is **city**. In this case, *city* refers to the area over which a municipal government exercises political authority. When a census document refers to a *city*, it is referring to the political city, not the economic city. To define the economic city, we would draw boundaries to include all the activities that are an integral part of the area's economy. When using census data, it's important to remember the distinction between the political city and the economic city.

Urbanized Area. An **urbanized area** includes at least one large central city (a municipality) and the surrounding area with population density exceeding 1,000 people per acre. To be an urbanized area, the total population of the area must be at least 50,000. Figure 1–1 shows an urbanized area as the large circle centered on a municipality. The urbanized area outside the central city is called the **urban fringe**. In 1990, there were 396 urbanized areas in the United States, containing 63.6 percent of the nation's population.

FIGURE 1-1   Urbanized Area and Metropolitan Area

Central city
(municipality)

Urbanized area

County

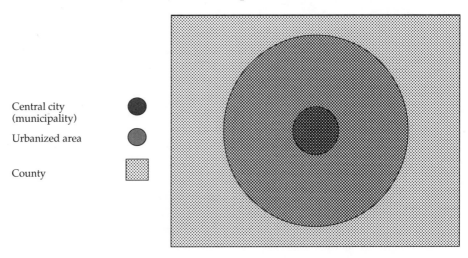

Metropolitan Area. A **metropolitan area (MA)** is defined as the area containing a large population nucleus and the nearby communities that are integrated, in an economic sense, with the nucleus. Each metropolitan area contains either (1) a central city with at least 50,000 people or (2) an urbanized area. In the census definition, the nucleus of a metropolitan area is either the central city or the urbanized area, and the integrated communities are the surrounding counties from which a relatively large number of people commute to the nucleus. To be designated a metropolitan area, the area in and around an urbanized area must have either a central city with population greater than 50,000 or a total population (including the integrated counties) of at least 100,000 (75,000 in New England). This means that some small urbanized areas are not metropolitan areas. For example, consider an urbanized area with 40,000 people in its central city, 60,000 people in the urbanized area, and another 30,000 people in the integrated counties, for a total of 90,000. Because the central city has fewer than 50,000 residents and the entire area has fewer than 100,000 people, the urbanized area is not considered a metropolitan area. In 1990, there were 284 metropolitan areas in the United States, ranging in population from just over 50,000 to just over 18 million.

Figure 1–1 shows the simplest possible arrangement of a metropolitan area. The MA is the county containing the urbanized area. This simple case shows one of the problems with the MA concept. To form a metropolitan area, the Census Bureau takes an urbanized area (or a central city) and tacks on the rest of the county, so the MA includes areas that are essentially rural. Metropolitan areas are defined by counties because the county is the smallest geographical unit for which a wide range of data is collected. In New England, where counties are relatively unimportant, metropolitan areas include the urbanized area and towns that are sufficiently integrated with the urban area.

Most metropolitan areas include more than one county. A **central county** is defined as one in which (1) the majority of the population lives in the urbanized area or (2) at least 2,500 of the area's residents live in the central municipality. An adjacent county is included in the metropolitan area if it is sufficiently integrated with the central county or counties. The degree of integration is measured in terms of commuting flows and population density. For example, the county is included in the MA if over 50 percent of its work force commutes to a central county and its population density exceeds 25 people per square mile. As the commuting percentage drops, the threshold population density increases. For the minimum commuting percentage (15 percent), the county is included if the population density exceeds 50 people per square mile.

Consolidated Metropolitan Statistical Area (CMSA). There are two types of metropolitan areas: consolidated metropolitan statistical areas (CMSAs) and metropolitan statistical areas (MSAs). If the population of a metropolitan area exceeds 1 million, the metropolitan area may be divided into two or more primary metropolitan statistical areas (PMSAs). A PMSA consists of a large urbanized county (or a cluster of counties) that is integrated, in an economic sense, with other portions of the larger metropolitan area. When a metropolitan area is divided into two or more PMSAs, the metropolitan area is called a **consolidated metropolitan statistical area (CMSA)**.

In 1990, there were 20 of these large metropolitan complexes, ranging in population from just over 1 million (Hartford–New Britain–Middletown) to just over 18 million (New York–Northern New Jersey–Long Island). Figure 1–2 shows the maps of two CMSAs, Chicago–Gary–Lake County, and San Francisco–Oakland–San Jose. Each of these CMSAs has six PMSAs.

Metropolitan Statistical Area (MSA).   A **metropolitan statistical area (MSA)** is defined as a metropolitan area that does not qualify as a CMSA. Most MSAs are designated as such because they have less than a million residents. Other MSAs have more than a million residents, but do not have distinct areas within the metropolitan area that can be classified as separate PMSAs. In 1990, there were 264 MSAs, ranging in population from just over 50,000 to just under 2.4 million (Baltimore).

Figure 1–3 shows the maps of two multiple-county MSAs, Sacramento and Atlanta. The urbanized areas are the darkened areas near the centers of the MSAs. There are four counties in the Sacramento MSA, two of which stretch far to the east through rural areas to the Nevada border, about 90 miles from the city of Sacramento. The Atlanta MSA is more compact, with 18 counties surrounding an urbanized area centered on the city of Atlanta.

The Census Bureau recently changed its terminology for metropolitan areas. Before 1983, metropolitan areas were called standard metropolitan statistical areas (SMSAs), and groups of related SMSAs were called standard consolidated statistical areas (SCSAs).

Urban Place and Urban versus Rural.   An **urban place** is defined as a geographical area with at least 2,500 inhabitants in a relatively small area. The Census Bureau defines the nation's **urban population** as all people living in urbanized areas plus people outside urbanized areas who live in urban places. According to this definition, in 1990, about three fourths of the U.S. population lived in urban areas.

Summary: What Is Urban?   In collecting and reporting data, the Census Bureau uses several definitions of *urban*. Table 1–1 shows, for three different urban definitions, the percentage of the U.S. population that is considered urban. The percentage living in urban areas (75.2 percent) exceeds the percentage in urbanized areas (63.6 percent) because the urban-area definition includes people who live in relatively small places (urban places with population between 2,500 and 50,000). The percentage living in metropolitan areas differs from the percentage in urbanized areas for two reasons. First, the metropolitan-area definition excludes

FIGURE 1–2 **Consolidated Metropolitan Statistical Areas**

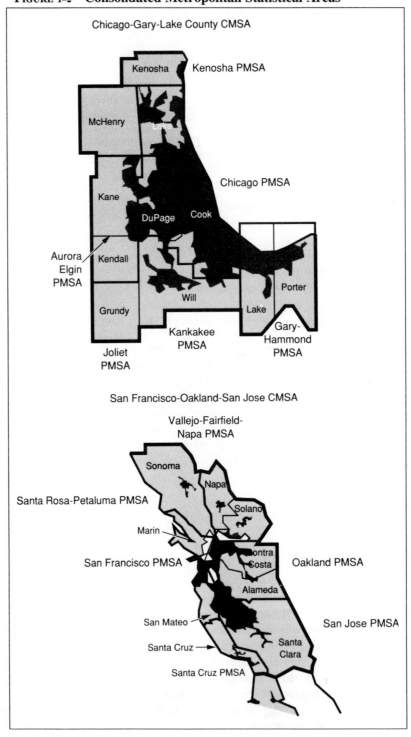

FIGURE 1–3   Metropolitan Statistical Areas

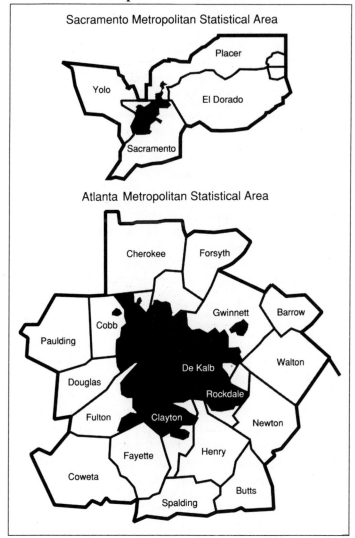

people who live in urbanized areas with either a relatively small central city (less than 50,000) or a relatively small total population (less than 100,000 in the urbanized area and the integrated counties). Second, the metropolitan-area definition includes people who live outside urbanized areas (in the county containing the urbanized area or a county adjacent to the urbanized area). The exclusion of people in small urbanized areas is outweighed by the inclusion of people outside urbanized areas, so the percentage of the population living in metropolitan areas exceeds the percentage in urbanized areas.

TABLE 1-1   **Urbanization of U.S. Population under Different Census Definitions**

Area Definition	Percent of U.S. Population in Area in 1990
Urbanized area: central city and surrounding dense area	63.6%
Metropolitan area: CMSAs and MSAs	77.5
Urban area: urbanized areas and smaller urban places	75.2

Definitions Used in This Book

This book uses three terms to refer to spatial concentrations of economic activity: *urban area, metropolitan area*, and *city*. These three terms, which will be used interchangeably, refer to the economic city (an area with a relatively high population density that contains a set of closely related activities), not the political city. When referring to a political city, the book will use the term *central city* or *municipality*.

Discussion Questions

1. Suppose that you have the power to develop a new set of census definitions for urban and metropolitan areas. How would you define (*a*) a metropolitan area, (*b*) an urban resident, (*c*) a central city, and (*d*) a suburban area?

2. Consider a region in which all urbanized areas have populations of at least 100,000. Will the percentage of the region's population living in urbanized areas be less than or greater than the percentage living in metropolitan areas?

3. Between 1980 and 1990, the gap between the percentage of the population living in urbanized areas and the percentage of the population living in metropolitan areas decreased, from 14.8 percentage points (76.2% − 61.4%) to 13.9 percentage points (77.5% − 63.6%). Provide an explanation for the narrowing of the gap.

4. Which of the three "urban" definitions used by the Census Bureau (urbanized area, urban place, metropolitan area) is closest to the economist's definition of a city?

5. In 1990, 86 percent of the population in the western states lived in urbanized areas, and 85 percent lived in metropolitan areas. In the same year, 79 percent of the population in the northeastern states lived in urbanized areas, and 88 percent lived in metropolitan areas. Why is the West more urbanized than the Northeast under the urbanized-area definition but less urbanized under the metropolitan-area definition?

Reference

U.S. Department of Commerce. "Appendix A: Area Classifications." *1990 Census of Population and Housing: Summary of Population and Housing Characteristics*. Washington, D.C.: U.S. Government Printing Office, 1990. Defines all the geographical entities and concepts that are used in the 1990 census. See pages A-8 to A-13 for definitions of cities and metropolitan areas.

PART I

Market Forces in the Development of Cities

In a market economy, individuals exchange their labor for wage income, which is then used to buy other goods and services. How do these market transactions affect cities? Chapter 2 discusses the fundamental reasons for urbanization, focusing on the effects of comparative advantage and scale economies in production. Chapter 3 shows how the location decisions of firms cause the development of cities in particular locations. Chapter 4 takes a regional perspective, showing how competition among firms leads to the development of a hierarchical system of cities. Chapter 5 explores the reasons for urban economic growth.

2 The Reasons for Urbanization

Between 1800 and 1990, the percentage of the U.S. population living in cities increased from 6 percent to 75 percent. During the same period, the population of the nation's three largest cities increased from an average of about 64,000 to about 3.5 million. This chapter discusses the reasons for the transformation of the United States into a highly urbanized nation. Although the chapter deals exclusively with urbanization in the United States, most other countries experienced the same transformation for the same reasons.

This chapter explores three reasons for urbanization. **Comparative advantage** makes trade between regions advantageous, and interregional trade causes the development of market cities. **Internal scale economies** in production allow factories to produce goods more efficiently than individuals can, and the production of goods in factories causes the development of industrial cities. **Agglomerative economies** in production cause firms to cluster in cities, and this clustering causes the development of large cities.

Figure 2–1 shows the trend in U.S. urbanization from 1800 to 1990. In 1800, as mentioned above, only about 6 percent of the population lived in cities. The share of population in cities increased to 15 percent by 1850, 40 percent by 1900, 64 percent by 1950, and 75 percent by 1990. Except for the period of the Great Depression (the 1930s), the pace of urbanization was fairly steady between about 1840 and 1970. Since then, urbanization has proceeded at a much slower pace.

Comparative Advantage and Commercial Cities

Table 2–1 shows the population trends for the U.S. cities with the largest population in 1930. In 1810, only four cities (New York, Philadelphia, Baltimore, and Boston) had more than 10,000 residents. These relatively large cities existed

17

FIGURE 2–1 **Percentage of U.S. Population Living in Urban Areas, 1800–1990**

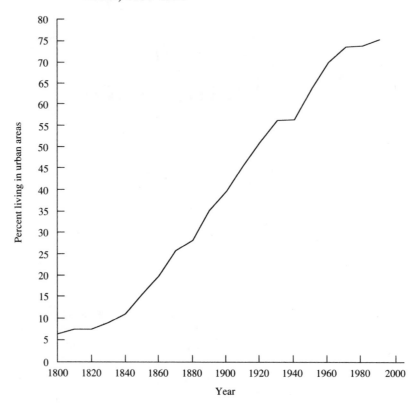

Year

TABLE 2–1 **Population of Largest U.S. Cities, 1810–1930**

City	Rank in 1930	Population in Year (thousands)			
		1810	1850	1890	1930
New York	1	120	696	2,507	6,930
Chicago	2	–	30	1,100	3,376
Philadelphia	3	54	121	1,047	1,951
Detroit	4	–	21	206	1,569
Los Angeles	5	–	2	50	1,238
Cleveland	6	–	17	261	900
Baltimore	7	47	169	434	805
Boston	8	34	137	448	781
Pittsburgh	9	5	47	239	670
Washington	10	8	40	189	487

SOURCE: U.S. Bureau of Census, *Census of Population*.

because of interregional trade. The rapid growth of these cities around the turn of the century was caused in large part by the Napoleonic wars, which tied up the English and French merchant marine and caused a boom in the American shipping industry. In 1850, the four seaports were still the dominant cities in the nation, with the population of the smallest one (Philadelphia) about 2.5 times the population of the next largest city (Pittsburgh).

These large cities of the early 1800s were primarily trading cities. They owed their existence to interregional trade resulting from comparative advantage in production. How does comparative advantage generate trade, and how does trade cause the development of cities?

Comparative Advantage and Trade

The notion of comparative advantage is based on the principle of opportunity cost. Consider a country with two regions, one (West) that is more productive than the other (East) in the production of two goods, wheat and cloth. In Table 2–2, western residents produce twice as much wheat per hour and six times as much cloth per hour. In a one-hour period, a western worker can produce either six yards of cloth or two bushels of wheat, so the opportunity cost of cloth is one third of a bushel of wheat: by producing a yard of cloth (in one sixth of an hour), the household gives up one third of a bushel of wheat. An eastern worker can produce either one bushel of wheat or one yard of cloth, so the opportunity cost of cloth is one bushel of wheat. Because the West has a lower opportunity cost of cloth (one third a bushel versus one bushel), it has a comparative advantage in the production of cloth. Similarly, the East has a comparative advantage in wheat because the opportunity cost is one yard of cloth instead of three.

Comparative advantage may lead to trade between the two regions. To explain the possible advantages of trade, suppose that all households in the country are initially self-sufficient. Suppose that an eastern household and a western household agree to exchange two yards of cloth for every bushel of wheat: the price of wheat is two yards of cloth. If the western household switches one hour of work from wheat production to cloth production, it sacrifices two bushels of wheat to produce six additional yards of cloth. If it exchanges the extra cloth for three bushels of wheat from an eastern household, its gain from trade is one bushel of wheat. If the eastern household switches one hour of work from cloth to wheat production and exchanges the extra bushel of wheat for two yards of cloth, its gain from trade is one yard of cloth. In the absence of transportation costs, both households benefit from trade, so they will make the trade.

What about transportation costs? If transportation costs are large enough, there will be no gains from trade. For example, suppose that it takes an hour to execute the trade between the two households. In this case, the western household gives up four bushels of wheat (two bushels for the extra hour of cloth production and two bushels for the hour of travel time) to get three bushels of wheat in exchange

TABLE 2-2   **Comparative Advantage and Trade**

	Output per Labor Hour		Opportunity Cost of Production	
	East	*West*	*East*	*West*
Wheat	1	2	1 Cloth	3 Cloth
Cloth	1	6	1 Wheat	⅓ Wheat

for the extra cloth it produces, which is obviously a bad deal. For trade to occur, transportation costs must be small relative to the differences in productivity that generate comparative advantage. For example, if it takes only 15 minutes (one quarter of an hour) to execute the trade, the western household gives up two and a half bushels of wheat to get three bushels, so trade is beneficial. If the net gains from trade are positive, western households specialize in cloth production and eastern households specialize in wheat production.

Trade and Cities

Trade will cause the development of a trading city if there are scale economies in transportation. To explain the importance of scale economies in transportation, suppose that there are no scale economies: the transport cost per bushel of wheat (or yard of cloth) per mile is independent of the volume shipped. In this case, households in the two regions engage in direct trade; that is, each eastern household links up with a western household to exchange cloth and wheat. If there are scale economies in transportation, however, the cost per unit per mile decreases as the volume transported increases, so it is cheaper to transport wheat and cloth in bulk. By exploiting these scale economies, trading firms can collect, transport, and distribute the goods at a lower cost than would be incurred by households engaged in direct trade. The trading firms locate at places convenient for the collection and distribution of the goods, causing the development of marketplaces at crossroads, ports, river junctions, and other transshipment points.

The location decisions of traders cause the development of trading cities. People employed by the trading firms live near the marketplace to economize on commuting costs, and the competition for this land increases its price. As the price of land increases, residents economize on land by occupying relatively small lots. In other words, the population density around the marketplace is higher than the population density in the rest of the region. Since a city is defined as a place with a relatively high population density, the combination of comparative advantage and scale economies in transportation causes the development of a market city.

The Industrial Revolution and Scale Economies in Production

As was shown in Figure 2–1, the share of the nation's population living in cities increased from 15 percent in 1850 to over 55 percent in 1930. During the same period, the largest cities in the United States grew dramatically (refer back to Table 2–1). Between 1850 and 1890, the populations of New York, Boston, and Baltimore more than doubled, and the population of Philadelphia increased more than eightfold. Lurking behind these changes were large increases in urban manufacturing activity: the share of employment in manufacturing more than doubled in all of these cities, from about 9 percent of total employment to about 19 percent.

Between 1850 and 1930, industrial cities replaced the commercial cities at the top of the urban hierarchy. During this period, the most dramatic urban growth occurred away from the eastern seaboard, in Chicago, Detroit, Cleveland, Pittsburgh, and Los Angeles. On average, the populations of these cities increased over 18-fold between 1850 and 1890. Again, manufacturing growth led the way: in Chicago and Detroit, the percentage of employment in manufacturing almost quadrupled, from about 5 percent to around 19 percent; in Cleveland, the percentage in manufacturing more than doubled, from 8 percent to 19 percent. Chicago was the first city to displace one of the eastern seaport cities from the top four positions, moving into the second spot by 1890. Between 1890 and 1930, the eastern seaport cities grew at relatively slow rates, allowing other cities to move ahead of them in the ranking. By 1930, most of the nation's largest cities were industrial cities, not commercial cities.

The rapid urbanization between 1850 and 1930 was caused in part by innovations in manufacturing generated by the industrial revolution. New machines, made of iron instead of wood, were developed for the production of most goods. Manual production by skilled artisans was replaced by mechanized production using interchangeable parts, specialized labor, and steam-powered machines. These innovations generated large scale economies in production, causing the development of industrial cities. How do scale economies in production cause the development of industrial cities?

Scale Economies and Factory Production

To explain the role of production scale economies in the development of cities, consider a region in which people consume cloth, a good that can be produced either in the home or in a factory. Suppose that the cost of production (including the cost of materials and the opportunity cost of labor) is $4 per yard in both the home and the factory. In other words, there are no scale economies in production; the unit cost is independent of the volume produced. Because the cost of factory cloth, including the cost of traveling to and from the factory, exceeds the cost of homemade cloth ($4), all the households in the region will produce their own cloth.

Consider the effects of introducing scale economies in the production of cloth. If there are scale economies in the production of cloth, the average cost of cloth decreases as the volume produced increases, so factory cloth costs less than home-made cloth. These scale economies may arise for two reasons:

1. **Factor specialization.** In a large operation, each worker is assigned a single task. The specialization of labor increases productivity because (*a*) workers' skills increase with repetition and (*b*) workers spend less time switching from task to task. The making of woolen cloth has several steps: the raw wool is spun into yarn, the yarn is woven into cloth, and the raw cloth is finished (cleaned, thickened, and dyed). One reason for scale economies in cloth production is that individual workers can specialize in different tasks. A group of 10 specialized workers can produce more than 10 times as much as 10 individuals working in isolation (each of whom performs all the production tasks).

2. **Indivisible inputs.** An input to the production process is indivisible if the input has a minimum efficient scale. If an indivisible input is cut in half, the total output of the two halves is less than the output of the whole. The cloth factory uses equipment (spinning machines, power looms, thickening machines, dyeing vats) that cannot be efficiently scaled down for use by individual clothmakers. As output increases, the factory uses more indivisible inputs, increasing productivity.

Suppose that, given the scale economies in cloth production, the cost of factory cloth is $1 per yard, compared to $4 per yard for homemade cloth. A household will buy factory cloth if the net cost of factory cloth is less than the cost of homemade cloth. As shown in Figure 2–2, there are two components to the net cost of factory cloth. The first is the price paid to the factory ($1). The second is the time required to travel to and from the cloth factory. If the opportunity cost of travel time is 50 cents per round-trip mile, the net cost of factory cloth rises from $1 for a household located next to the factory to $2 for a household located two miles away, and so on. For households located within six miles of the factory, the net cost of factory cloth ($1 paid to the factory and up to $3 in travel costs) is less than the cost of home production. The **market area** of the cloth factory is defined as the area over which the factory underprices home production. In this example, the market area is a circle with a radius of four miles.

The Cloth Factory and the Industrial City

A small urban area develops around the cloth factory. The workers live near the factory to economize on commuting costs and bid up the price of land near the factory. As the price of land increases, workers economize on land by occupying small lots. In other words, the population density around the cloth factory is higher than the population density in the rest of the region. Since a city is defined as a

FIGURE 2–2   **The Market Area of the Cloth Factory**

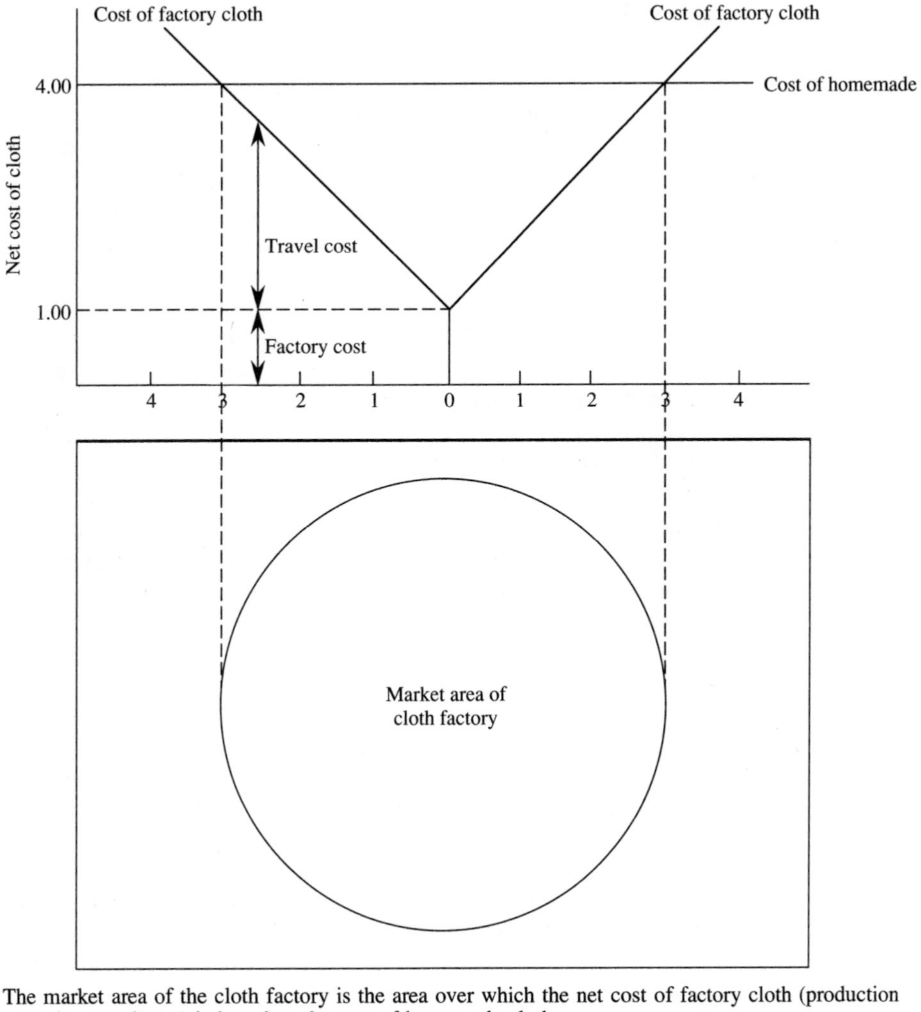

The market area of the cloth factory is the area over which the net cost of factory cloth (production cost plus travel cost) is less than the cost of homemade cloth.

place with a relatively high population density, the factory causes the development of a small factory city.

This simple example demonstrates the effects of scale economies on urban development. The introduction of scale economies decreases the relative cost of factory cloth, causing some households to switch from homemade cloth to factory cloth. The factory workers cluster around the factory, causing the development of a city. The manufacturing innovations generated by the industrial revolution increased scale economies in production and thus contributed to the development of cities.

As an example of an innovation that contributed to urbanization, consider the sewing machine, which was developed in the middle of the 19th century. Around the beginning of the 19th century, about four fifths of the clothing worn in the United States was hand-sewn in the home for a member of the household. The other fifth was hand-sewn by tailors. The sewing machine increased the scale economies in the production of clothing and thus allowed factory producers to underprice home producers. By 1890, $9/10$ of U.S. clothing was being made in factories. As clothing factories sprang up in the United States, new cities developed around the factories.

The sewing machine also contributed to the development of U.S. cities around shoe factories. Before 1700, most shoes were produced in the home or in the local village. The cost of transportation was so high that local production was efficient. Over time, transportation costs decreased, allowing the exploitation of comparative advantage in shoe production. The putting-out system was implemented in the 1700s: shoe producers distributed raw materials to cottage workers, collected their output, and finished the shoes in a central shop. As new shoemaking machines were developed, the number of operations performed in the central shop increased. The McKay sewing machine, which mechanized the process of sewing the soles to the uppers, increased scale economies in shoe production to the point at which the central shop became a genuine factory. Cities developed around the new shoe factories.

Other Innovations from the Industrial Revolution

The industrial revolution generated a number of other innovations that contributed to urbanization. Innovations in agriculture increased productivity and freed up workers for urban factories. Innovations in intercity transportation decreased transportation costs, increasing interregional trade and factory production. Innovations in intracity transportation and construction methods increased the feasible size of cities.

Innovations in Agriculture

The rapid urbanization during the industrial revolution was made possible by innovations that increased agricultural productivity. Farmers substituted machinery for muscle power and simple tools, increasing the output per farmer. For example, using a horse-drawn reaper, two people could harvest the same amount of grain as eight people using traditional harvesting methods. In addition, the development of agricultural science led to innovations in planting, growing, harvesting, and processing. As productivity increased, laborers were freed from food-raising responsibilities, allowing them to pursue other activities in cities. In the United

States, the share of employment in agriculture decreased from 69 percent in 1840 to 2.8 percent in 1988.

Innovations in Intercity Transportation

Innovations in intercity transportation contributed to industrialization and urbanization. The steamship and the railroad decreased the costs of moving goods between cities, decreasing the delivered price of factory goods. Production became more centralized, and factory cities grew. The new transportation modes also decreased the costs of moving agricultural goods, allowing greater regional specialization in agriculture. Agricultural regions were better able to exploit their comparative advantages, so agricultural productivity increased.

Before the railroad linked eastern cities with the western parts of the United States, a large fraction of the food consumed in New England was produced by the region's farmers. Similarly, a large fraction of the goods consumed in the West (for example, shoes) were produced by local craftsmen. The railroad allowed eastern factories to underprice western craftsmen and allowed western farmers to underprice eastern farmers. Trade increased because the railroad allowed both regions to exploit their comparative advantages.

Industrial cities developed at points accessible to the new intercity transportation network. During the steamship era, cities developed along the rivers and lakes served by the steamship. Firms that fueled their steam engines with coal located along rivers served by coal shippers. Later, the development of the railroad caused the development of cities along the rail lines. The cities that developed at transshipment points had commercial jobs (transportation, trade, business services) and manufacturing jobs.

Innovations in Intracity Transportation

Innovations in intracity transportation increased the feasible size of cities. The size of a city is limited by the cost of traveling within the city. One rule of thumb is that the geographical area of the city should be small enough that the typical resident can travel from the edge of the city to the city center in an hour. Before the innovations in intracity transport, most people walked to workplaces and shops, so the radius of the city could be no more than two miles. During the last half of the 19th century, a series of innovations in public transit increased the speed of intracity travel, increasing the potential radius of the city.

The city of Boston provides a good example of the effects of transit innovations on city size. In 1850, Boston was a "walking" city with a radius of about two miles. In the 1860s, the horse-powered railroad (horses pulling cars along rails) was introduced, and the radius of the city increased to 2.5 miles in 1872 and 4.0 miles in 1887. By the 1890s, the horse-powered railroad was replaced by the electric trolley, which traveled at twice the speed and carried three times as many passengers. As a result, the radius of the city increased to about six miles. In the 40 years during which walking was replaced by the trolley, the radius of the city tripled and the land area increased ninefold.

The introduction of the internal-combustion engine had similar effects on the size of cities. This new engine allowed the development of relatively small vehicles for transporting people and goods. The development of the automobile decreased the cost of intracity travel, causing further increases in the feasible radius of the city. In addition, it freed travelers from the old fixed-rail systems that were designed to deliver people from the residential areas along the streetcar lines (the spokes) to the city center (the hub). The automobile increased the accessibility of locations throughout the city: residents could live between the spokes, and firms could locate outside the hub. As the set of feasible locations for residents and firms increased, cities grew.

The introduction of the truck had similar effects. The truck decreased the cost of intercity transportation, increasing the advantages of centralized (urban) production. In addition, the truck freed firms from their dependence on the railroad terminal and the port, allowing firms to locate outside the central city. As the set of feasible production locations increased, the feasible population of the city increased. The development of the truck and the automobile also caused the suburbanization of population within the urban area, a topic to be covered in Chapter 7.

Innovations in Construction Methods

Innovations in construction methods also increased city sizes. The first skyscraper, a 10-story building that housed the Home Insurance Company, appeared in 1885 in Chicago. The building was revolutionary because its frame was made of steel instead of bricks. Because the steel frame was relatively light, the steel-framed building could be taller than the traditional brick building. The development of the elevator decreased intrabuilding travel costs of tall buildings, increasing the feasibility of the skyscraper. The skyscraper increased the intensity of land use, increasing the city's productive capacity and its feasible population.

Agglomerative Economies in Production

This section explores some of the reasons why cities are large. The analysis of scale economies earlier in the chapter suggests that a city develops around a factory. This section explains why most cities have more than one factory. In other words, it explains the development of large industrial cities.

The large industrial city develops because of agglomerative economies in production. By locating close to one another, firms can produce at a lower cost. This is an example of a **positive externality** in production: the production cost of a particular firm decreases as the production of other firms increases. Agglomerative economies occur for three principal reasons: the sharing of suppliers of intermediate inputs, labor market economies, and communication economies.

Scale Economies in Intermediate Inputs

One source of agglomerative economies is the sharing of the suppliers of intermediate inputs. The idea is that firms share input suppliers and locate close to the common input supplier to economize on travel costs. Vernon (1972) uses the Manhattan dressmaking industry as an example of an industry subject to this type of agglomerative economy.

Because the demand for high-fashion dresses is unpredictable, dressmaking firms are relatively small. A firm cannot commit itself to large-scale production of a given type of dress, but instead must be prepared to quickly change to another type of dress if the first dress is a bomb. The firm must employ inputs (capital and labor) that can (1) produce a wide variety of dresses and (2) make the transition from one dress to another quickly. As a result, specialized labor and machinery are not feasible. In addition, the manager of the firm must carefully monitor the dress market, the design process, and the production process. The operation must be kept small enough that the manager can be involved in most decisions.

One of the intermediate inputs to dressmaking is buttons. Suppose that there are scale economies in the production of buttons, and it takes 10 dressmakers to generate sufficient button demand to exhaust the scale economies in button production. By sharing a buttonmaker, the 10 dressmakers can get buttons at a lower cost. Because the scale economies in buttonmaking are large *relative to* the scale economies in dressmaking, the dressmakers share a buttonmaker.

Why should dressmakers cluster around the button firm? They locate near the button producer because they must supervise the production of buttons. Because the buttons for a high-fashion dress are not standardized, they cannot be ordered out of a catalog. The buttons are designed to complement the other features of the dress, and the dressmaker participates in the design and fabrication of buttons to ensure that the buttons match the dress. Given the importance of face-to-face contact, dressmakers locate close to the buttonmaker.

To summarize, agglomerative economies from the sharing of input suppliers occur when three conditions are met:

1. Several firms have a common intermediate input.
2. The input demand of an individual firm is not large enough to exploit the scale economies in the production of the intermediate input.
3. Transportation costs for the intermediate input are relatively high, because (*a*) face-to-face contact between buyer and seller is necessary or (*b*) the intermediate input is bulky, fragile, or must be delivered quickly.

The first two conditions mean that firms will share an input supplier. The third condition means that the firms will all locate close to the supplier.

Other Examples of Sharing of Input Suppliers

There are many other examples of clusters that result from scale economies in the provision of intermediate inputs.

1. **Corporate headquarters.** A corporate headquarters produces a wide variety of outputs. The executive may design an advertising campaign one week, pick a location for a new plant the next week, and develop a strategy to fend off a lawsuit the following week. Most corporations use outside advertising firms because scale economies in the production of advertising campaigns are large relative to the advertising demand of an individual corporation. Corporate executives need to be close to the advertising firm because the executives assist in the design of the advertising campaign. Therefore, face-to-face contact is important. In general, the clustering of corporate headquarters (usually in central business districts) allows corporations to exploit scale economies in the production of intermediate goods (advertising, economic consultants, legal services) for which face-to-face contact is an important part of the production process.

2. **High-technology firms.** Firms producing new high-technology goods face uncertain demand for their products. Instead of producing all of their own components, they purchase electronic parts from firms that can exploit scale economies in production. The firms interact with their suppliers in the design and fabrication of the components, and must locate close enough to facilitate frequent face-to-face contact. Although the high-technology firm need not locate close to its supplier of nuts and bolts (standardized inputs that can be ordered from a catalog), it needs to locate close to the supplier of nonstandardized electronic parts. In addition, high-technology firms exploit scale economies in product testing by sharing firms that provide testing facilities. They locate close enough to tap the testing facilities at top speed.

3. **Publishers.** Newspapers and magazines produce outputs (text and illustrations) that change in unpredictable ways from day to day. In producing their products, publishers call on a wide variety of experts, including information sources and illustrators. If each publisher uses an expert on Armenian history for one story per year, it would be inefficient for each publisher to hire a full-time Armenian expert. Instead, the publishers may share a single expert, sharing the cost of specialized information. Similarly, publishers occasionally need special illustrations and call on graphic design firms to do the illustrations. Publishers cluster around or-

ganizations that provide expert information (libraries, research institutes, universities) and illustrations (graphic design firms).

Business and Public Services as Intermediate Inputs

What is the role of business services in the development of firm clusters? Some industries require specialized financial services such as specialized banking and insurance. There are scale economies in the provision of these services, and firms in a cluster can exploit these scale economies by sharing banks and insurance agencies. Similarly, there are scale economies in the provision of transportation services, and firms can share a transportation firm. For example, a small firm can hire trucks from a trucking firm instead of providing its own truck fleet.

Public services also play a role in the development of firm clusters. The public sector is responsible for the development of the transportation network and the sewage system. If firms in an industry require specialized transport networks or sewage services, public-service costs are lower if the firms cluster. The provision of public education has also played a role in the development of firm clusters. In England, some towns established spinning schools to provide specialized laborers for the textile industry. More recently, the universities and colleges in Silicon Valley turn out a large number of engineers and computer scientists for the computer industry.

Labor Market and Communication Economies

A second reason for agglomerative economies is that firms with rapidly changing demands for labor can share the urban work force. Consider an industry with rapidly changing production processes and product demands. For example, every year, computer firms introduce new products; some are big sellers, and others fail. Eventually, the workers in the unsuccessful firms move to the successful ones. A cluster facilitates the transfer of workers between computer firms for two reasons. First, workers in the cluster have relatively low search costs because (1) information about job openings is spread through informal channels (casual conversation at restaurants, bowling alleys, and baseball games) and (2) prospective employers are nearby, making formal job search relatively easy. Second, because of the physical proximity of employers, moving costs are relatively low: workers can easily switch to a different firm in the same city. Because search costs and moving costs are relatively low, firms in the cluster of computer firms can quickly fill their job vacancies and can quickly increase production.

The television industry also benefits from labor-market economies. In a given season, some television programs are hits and others are failures. When it becomes clear which programs will continue to be produced, actors and technicians move from the unsuccessful programs to the successful ones. The concentrations of the television industry in Los Angeles and New York facilitate the transfer of laborers from one firm to another.

A third reason for agglomerative economies is that a cluster of firms facilitates the rapid exchange of information and the diffusion of technology. Workers from different firms exchange ideas about new products and new production techniques; the larger the number of workers in an industry, the greater the opportunity to exchange ideas. The opportunity to exchange ideas occurs in both formal and informal settings. A cluster of computer makers produces a large concentration of computer scientists and engineers, who can exchange ideas while they work (e.g., the suppliers of intermediate inputs interact with the designers of new products) and play (e.g., the workers from unrelated firms "talk shop" while eating or jogging).

The Incubation Process

Agglomerative economies are responsible for the **incubation process**. A cluster of firms supplies a rich set of intermediate inputs and provides a nurturing environment where firms in an immature industry "incubate," developing new products and production technologies. In the early life of many industries, demand is unpredictable and production techniques are unsettled, so firms cluster to (1) exploit scale economies in the production of intermediate goods, (2) realize labor-market economies, and (3) exploit the opportunities to exchange ideas about products and production processes. As the industry matures, it develops standardized products and production processes, allowing large-scale production. Firms internalize most of the production process and move to locations that provide lower labor and land costs. This is also known as the **product cycle theory** of industrial location: products are developed by small firms in clusters; when the product is standardized and produced on a larger scale, firms move to sites with lower labor and land costs.

As pointed out by Vernon (1972), one example of incubation comes from the radio industry. In the 1920s, the market for radios was unpredictable and firms were experimenting with alternative production processes. Mass production was impractical; the firms didn't know what kind of radio consumers wanted and hadn't developed efficient production techniques. Radio firms were small, agile, and nervous, and they clustered in New York City to exploit scale economies in the production of intermediate goods. In the 1930s and 1940s, products were standardized and radio firms developed efficient methods of mass production. They moved their assembly facilities to the Midwest, which had lower wages and better access to the national markets. Tube producers migrated to the Northeast and the South, where labor costs were lower.

The computer industry is also subject to the incubation process. In the 1970s and early 1980s, the demand for computers was unpredictable and production techniques were being developed. Small computer firms clustered in the Silicon Valley in California and along Route 128 in Boston to exploit agglomerative economies. The standardization of products and production processes allowed firms to set up large production facilities outside the clusters. Why have the clusters survived the exodus of production facilities? New products continue to be developed, and firms continue to cluster to exploit agglomerative economies. Most firms maintain their research and development facilities in the clusters and set up branch plants for manufacturing and assembly.

Empirical Estimates of Agglomerative Economies

How important are agglomerative economies in production? One approach to measuring agglomerative economies is to estimate the effects of changes in total output on labor productivity. If agglomerative economies exist, output per worker for a particular industry should increase with the total industry output and total output of the city. Henderson (1986) estimates that a 10 percent increase in the size of the industry in a particular city increases productivity by between 0.2 percent and 1.1 percent. In another study, Segal (1976) estimates that large metropolitan areas (population exceeding 2 million) are 8 percent more productive than smaller cities.

Recent Trends in Urbanization

As shown in Figure 2–1, the pace of urbanization in the United States has slowed since 1950. Using the new definition of an urban area, the percentage of the population living in cities increased by 4.9 percentage points during the 1950s, 3.6 percentage points during the 1960s, 0.1 percentage point during the 1970s, and 1.5 percentage points during the 1980s.

Figure 2–3 shows the percentages of population living in urban areas for the United States as a whole and four U.S. regions. The western region is the most urbanized, with 86 percent of its population in urban areas. The western region has five of the six most urbanized states: California (93 percent), Hawaii (89 percent), Nevada (88 percent), Arizona (88 percent), and Utah (87 percent). The other highly urbanized states are New Jersey (89 percent), Florida (85 percent), Massachusetts (84 percent), and New York (84 percent). The southern region is the least urbanized, with 69 percent of its population in urban areas.

Metropolitan versus Nonmetropolitan Growth

Figure 2–4 provides a closer look at urbanization between 1960 and 1990. The figure shows the population growth rates for metropolitan areas (areas included in an MSA or a CMSA) and nonmetropolitan areas (counties that are not a part

FIGURE 2–3   **Percentage of U.S. and Regional Populations in Urban Areas**

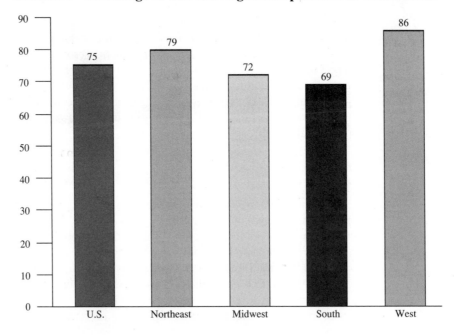

FIGURE 2–4   **Growth Rates in Metropolitan and Nonmetropolitan Areas**

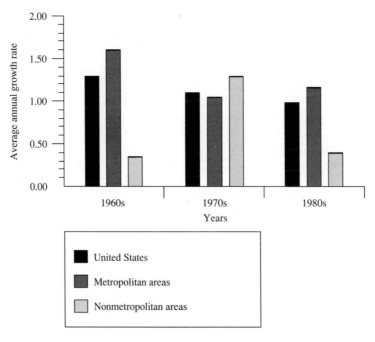

of an MSA or a CMSA). During the 1960s, metropolitan areas grew more than four times faster than nonmetropolitan areas (1.6 percent per year compared to 0.35 percent). In contrast, during the 1970s, nonmetropolitan areas grew about 25 percent faster than metropolitan areas (1.29 percent per year compared to 1.04 percent). During the 1980s, metropolitan areas grew more than three times faster than nonmetropolitan areas (1.29 percent per year compared to 0.39 percent).

Nonmetropolitan areas grew faster than metropolitan areas in the 1970s for a number of reasons:

1. **Dispersion of manufacturing employment.** Improvements in the intercity highway system increased the accessibility of nonmetropolitan locations. Some labor-intensive manufacturers moved from metropolitan areas to low-wage nonmetropolitan areas.

2. **Slow decline in farm employment.** Although total employment in agriculture decreased during the decade, it decreased at a relatively slow rate. Fewer people left farms to move to cities.

3. **Growth in extractive industries.** Increased prices for energy and raw materials increased employment in oil and mining industries. For example, total mining employment increased from 626,000 in 1969 to 957,000 in 1979.

4. **Growth in recreation and retirement activities.** A large number of elderly people moved to retirement communities in nonmetropolitan areas, pulling retail and service jobs to retirement areas. Other urban households moved to nonmetropolitan areas with outdoor recreational opportunities.

5. **Population spillovers.** Some households moved to counties that the Census Bureau inappropriately classifies as "nonmetropolitan." Some of these counties are integrated, in an economic sense, with a nearby MSA but are still considered nonmetropolitan. Alonso (1980) suggests that this statistical problem causes a significant overestimate of the nonmetropolitan growth rate. During the 1970s, many of the fastest growing areas were "nonmetropolitan" counties adjacent to metropolitan areas (MSAs and CMSAs).

During the 1980s, the growth rate for nonmetropolitan areas decreased and the growth rate for metropolitan areas increased, restoring the historical pattern of relatively rapid metropolitan growth. According to Garnick (1988), growth rates in nonmetropolitan areas decreased for three reasons. First, farm employment decreased more rapidly, a result of declining farm prices. Second, the employment in extractive industries decreased, a result of decreasing energy and resource prices. Third, labor-intensive manufacturing employment in nonmetropolitan areas decreased, a result of increased competition from abroad.

TABLE 2–3   **Population and Annual Growth Rates for the 25 Largest U.S. Metropolitan Areas**

Metropolitan Area: CMSA or MSA	1990 Rank	1990 Population	Growth 1980s (%)	Growth 1970s (%)
New York–Northern N.J.–Long Island CMSA	1	18,087	−0.36%	0.31%
Los Angeles–Anaheim–Riverside CMSA	2	14,532	1.42	2.37
Chicago–Gary–Lake County CMSA	3	8,066	0.20	0.16
San Francisco–Oakland–San Jose CMSA	4	6,253	1.22	1.54
Philadelphia–Wilmington–Trenton CMSA	5	5,899	−0.12	0.38
Detroit–Ann Arbor CMSA	6	4,665	−0.07	−0.19
Boston–Lawrence–Salem CMSA	7	4,172	0.08	0.49
Washington, D.C. MSA	8	3,924	0.67	1.90
Dallas–Fort Worth CMSA	9	3,885	2.23	2.86
Houston–Galveston–Brazoria CMSA	10	3,711	3.64	1.82
Miami–Fort Lauderdale CMSA	11	3,193	3.43	1.90
Altanta MSA	12	2,834	2.42	2.86
Cleveland–Akron–Lorain CMSA	13	2,760	−0.57	−0.26
Seattle–Tacoma CMSA	14	2,559	1.31	2.03
San Diego MSA	15	2,498	3.21	2.98
Minneapolis–St. Paul MSA	16	2,464	0.76	1.43
St. Louis MSA	17	2,444	−0.22	0.28
Baltimore MSA	18	2,382	0.51	0.80
Pittsburgh–Beaver Valley CMSA	19	2,243	−0.53	−0.77
Phoenix MSA	20	2,122	4.51	3.47
Tampa–St. Petersburg–Clearwater MSA	21	2,068	3.85	2.51
Denver–Boulder CMSA	22	1,848	2.71	1.34
Cincinnati–Hamilton CMSA	23	1,744	0.29	0.49
Milwaukee–Racine CMSA	24	1,607	−0.03	0.23
Kansas City MSA	25	1,566	0.43	0.89

SOURCE: U.S. Bureau of the Census, *1991 Statistical Abstract of the United States: 1991,* Washington, D. C., 1991.

Population Losses in Some Metropolitan Areas

Another recent trend is the decline of some metropolitan areas. Table 2–3 shows the population growth rates for the 25 largest CMSAs and MSAs. During the 1970s, 7 of the top 25 metropolitan areas lost population: New York, Philadelphia, Detroit, Cleveland, St. Louis, Pittsburgh, and Milwaukee. The largest losses occurred in Cleveland (0.57 percent per year), Pittsburgh (0.53 percent per year), and New York (0.36 percent per year). In the 1980s, Detroit, Cleveland, and Pittsburgh continued to lose population.

Why have some metropolitan areas decreased in size? First, people migrated from the northern states to southern and western states, decreasing the growth rates of northeastern and north-central metropolitan areas. Between 1980 and 1990, the average annual growth rate was close to zero for northeastern and north-central metropolitan areas, compared to over 2 percent for southern and western metropolitan areas. Given this migration pattern, the best a northern metropolitan area could hope for is a small positive growth rate. In some northern metropolitan areas, there were large losses in manufacturing employment, resulting in negative growth rates. Decreases in employment in primary metals, motor vehicles, rubber, and nonelectrical machinery caused population losses in Pittsburgh, Cleveland, and Detroit.

The Postindustrial City

What does the future hold for cities? One economic trend that will affect cities and the urbanization process is the shift in employment from manufacturing to services. Table 2–4 shows the changes in distribution of employment between 1947 and 1988, and Figure 2–5 shows the employment percentages for seven industries (retail and wholesale trade are combined into "trade") in 1947 and 1988. Table 2–4 shows that the percentage of jobs in the goods-producing sector (agriculture, mining, construction, and manufacturing) decreased from around 45 percent in 1947 to around 26 percent in 1988. The percentage in the service

TABLE 2–4   **Distribution of Employment by Industry, 1947 to 1988**

	Percentage of Jobs in Activity				
	1947	*1959*	*1969*	*1979*	*1988*
Goods-Producing Sector					
Agriculture	11.60%	7.40%	4.00%	3.30%	3.01%
Mining	1.70	1.20	0.80	1.00	0.67
Construction	5.20	5.50	5.40	5.90	4.74
Manufacturing	26.90	25.60	25.40	21.98	17.93
Total: goods-producing	45.40	39.60	35.70	32.10	26.35
Service-Producing Sector					
Transportation	7.40	6.40	5.70	5.40	5.13
Wholesale trade	4.60	5.20	5.10	5.60	5.57
Retail trade	14.60	13.90	13.40	14.70	17.66
Finance, insurance, real estate	3.30	4.20	4.60	5.60	6.17
Services	13.00	14.70	16.90	19.70	23.07
Government	11.80	16.10	18.60	16.90	16.05
Total: service-producing	54.60	60.40	64.30	67.90	73.65
Total	100.00	100.00	100.00	100.00	100.00

SOURCE: Daniel H. Garnick, "Local Area Economic Growth Patterns: A Comparison of the 1980s and Previous Decades," *Urban Change and Poverty,* ed. M. G. McGeary and L. E. Lynn (Washington, D.C.: National Academy Press, 1988); U.S. Bureau of the Census, *Statistical Abstract of the United States:* 1991, Washington, D.C., 1991.

FIGURE 2–5   **Percentage of Employment by Industry, 1947, 1969, 1988**

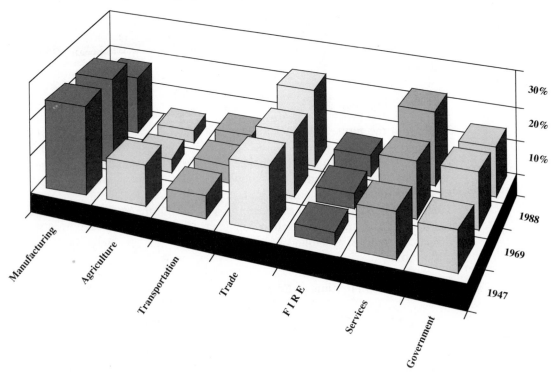

sectors (transportation; wholesale and retail trade; finance, insurance, and real estate; services; and government) increased from around 55 percent in 1947 to around 74 percent in 1988. The largest percentage increases in employment occurred in retail trade; services; finance, insurance, and real estate (FIRE); and government.

How will the decrease in the relative importance of manufacturing affect cities? Most cities in the United States developed as manufacturing centers during the industrial revolution. The shift to a more service-oriented economy will certainly bring dramatic changes to some metropolitan areas. The cities that continue to be dependent on traditional manufacturing activity are likely to decline.

Summary

1. Between 1800 and 1930, the percentage of the U.S. population in cities increased from 6 percent to 56 percent. The pace of urbanization has slowed since World War II, rising from 64 percent in 1950 to 75 percent in 1990.

2. One of the reasons for cities is comparative advantage, which results from differences in productivity. Trade occurs if the differences in productivity are large enough to offset transport costs. Trading firms (and urban areas) develop if there are scale economies in transportation.

3. A second reason for the development of cities is internal scale economies in production, which result from factor specialization and indivisible inputs. If scale economies are large relative to transport costs, goods are produced in factories. Factory workers economize on travel costs by locating near factories, causing the development of factory cities.

4. The rapid urbanization of the 19th and 20th centuries was caused by the industrial revolution and the associated innovations in agriculture, transportation, and manufacturing.

    a. The relative cost of factory goods decreased because transportation costs decreased and scale economies in production were realized. Factory employment increased and cities developed around the factories.

    b. Agricultural productivity increased as farmers substituted machines for laborers, freeing laborers to pursue nonagricultural activities. Transportation costs decreased, allowing greater regional specialization and greater productivity.

    c. Innovations in intracity transportation and construction techniques increased the feasible size of cities.

5. Agglomerative economies occur if the production cost of a particular firm decreases as total output of the industry or the city increases. There are three sources of agglomerative economies:

    a. If there are scale economies in the production of an intermediate good for which transportation costs are relatively high, several firms share a supplier of the intermediate input and form a cluster around the input supplier.

    b. If output per firm varies from year to year, a cluster of firms facilitates the transfer of workers from one firm to another (labor-market economies).

    c. A cluster of firms improves communication, facilitating the rapid exchange of information and the diffusion of innovations (communication economies).

6. Urban areas, with their rich set of intermediate inputs, provide a nurturing environment for immature industries (the incubation process).

7. In the 1970s, nonmetropolitan areas grew faster than metropolitan areas. In the 1980s, the growth rate for nonmetropolitan areas decreased, restoring the historical pattern of more rapid growth in metropolitan areas.

Exercises and Discussion Questions

1. The table below summarizes the productivity of workers in wheat and cloth production in two parts of a region.

	Output per Labor Hour		Opportunity Cost of Production	
	East	*West*	*East*	*West*
Wheat (bushels)	1	12		
Cloth (yards)	1	3		

   a. Complete the table by providing the opportunity costs of producing wheat and cloth in the East and the West.
   b. Assume that transport costs are zero and that the exchange rate is two bushels of wheat for one yard of cloth. If a western household switches one hour from cloth production to wheat production and exchanges half of its additional wheat for cloth, will the household be better-off?
   c. Under what conditions will the differences in labor productivity cause the development of cities?

2. Consider a country with two regions that are separated by a mountain range. Initially, there are no cities in the country. Suppose that a tunnel is bored through the mountain, decreasing travel costs between the two regions. Under what conditions will the tunnel cause the development of trading cities?

3. Consider a region that has a single factory city (a city that developed as a result of scale economies in production). Suppose that the introduction of pump sneakers decreases the cost of travel from 50 cents to 25 cents per round-trip mile. Assume that the new type of shoes sells for the same price as the old type. How will the new footwear affect the size of the region's city? Will its population increase or decrease?

4. Consider a 10-firm industry that produces computer equipment, a set of goods with rapidly changing demand and production technology. The industry has the following characteristics:
   i. The 10 firms produce computer equipment, using labor and raw materials.
   ii. Raw materials are ubiquitous (available at all locations at the same price).
   iii. Each firm produces one new product per year, and each product becomes obsolete after a year.
   iv. Only 3 of the 10 new products will be successful (sell more than a trivial amount).

v. The monetary and time costs of switching a worker from one firm to another are zero, regardless of the spatial distribution of firms.

a. Will the firms in the industry form a cluster? Why or why not?

b. How would your answer to (*a*) change if workers incur moving costs when they switch from one firm to another?

5. Critically appraise the following statement: "Innovation in agriculture during the industrial revolution was a necessary—but not sufficient—condition for the urbanization of society."

References and Additional Readings

Alonso, William. "The Population Factor and Urban Structure." In *The Prospective City,* ed. Arthur Solomon. Cambridge, Mass.: MIT Press, 1980. A discussion of recent trends in urbanization.

Davis, Kingsley. "Urbanization." In *The Urban Economy,* ed. Harold Hochman. New York: W. W. Norton, 1976. A brief history of urbanization.

Garnick, Daniel H. "Local Area Economic Growth Patterns: A Comparison of the 1980s and Previous Decades." In *Urban Change and Poverty,* ed. Michael G. McGeary and Lawrence E. Lynn. Washington, D.C.: National Academy Press, 1988. Discusses growth trends in metropolitan and nonmetropolitan areas from 1959 to 1984, and examines the growth rates of the 50 largest metropolitan areas (MSAs and CMSAs) over this period.

Hall, Peter, and Ann Markusen. *Silicon Landscapes.* Boston: Allen and Unwin, 1985. Discusses the role of external scale economies in the location of high-technology industries.

Henderson, J. V. "Efficiency of Resource Usage and City Size," *Journal of Urban Economics* 19 (1986), pp. 47–90. Estimates the magnitude of agglomerative economies.

Higgs, Robert. "American Inventiveness, 1870–1920." *Journal of Political Economy* 79 (1971), pp. 661–67.

Hohenberg, Paul M., and Lynn H. Lees. *The Making of Urban Europe 1000–1950.* Cambridge, Mass.: Harvard University Press, 1985. Discusses the reasons for the urbanization of Europe.

Hoover, Edgar M. *Location Theory and the Shoe and Leather Industries.* Cambridge, Mass.: Harvard University Press, 1937. Discusses the role of scale economies in the location of shoe and leather industries.

Jacobs, Jane. *The Economy of Cities.* New York: Random House, 1960. Discusses why many innovations are developed in urban areas.

Mumford, Lewis. *The City in History.* New York: Harcourt, Brace, and World, 1961. A lengthy discussion of the history of urbanization, including a discussion of the reasons for the development of the first cities.

Olmstead, Alan, and Eugene Smolensky. *The Urbanization of the United States.* Morristown, N.J.: General Learning Press, 1973.

Rosenberg, Nathan, and L. E. Birdzell. *How the West Grew Rich.* New York: Basic Books, 1986. Discusses the transformation of the Western world from the anarchy and autarchy of the Dark Ages to its present state.

Segal, David. "Are There Returns to Scale in City Size?" *Review of Economics and Statistics* (July 1976), pp. 339–50. Estimates the magnitude of agglomerative economies.

Vernon, Raymond. "External Economies." In *Readings in Urban Economics*. ed. M. Edel and J. Rothenberg. New York: Macmillan, 1972. Discusses the reasons for agglomerative economies.

The Location of Firms and Cities

Chapter 2 showed that cities develop because of comparative advantage, scale economies, and agglomerative economies. Cities develop around the concentrations of employment generated by firms, so the location choices of firms play a role in the location of cities. This chapter explores the location decisions of two types of firms: industrial firms and commercial firms. **Industrial firms** (e.g., sawmills, breweries, manufacturers, and bakeries) process raw materials and intermediate inputs into outputs. **Commercial firms** trade goods rather than producing them. The location decisions of industrial and commercial firms cause the development of various types of cities. This chapter also discusses the role of government in the location of cities.

Commercial Firms and Trading Cities

The location decisions of commercial firms cause the development of trading cities. Trading firms collect goods from suppliers and distribute the goods to consumers, providing employment for salespeople and other intermediaries. Trading firms typically locate at transshipment points (ports, crossroads, railroad junctions, river junctions) because such locations offer convenient points for the collection and distribution of goods. Transportation firms move goods from place to place, providing employment at transshipment points for truckers, sailors, and longshoremen. Firms providing business services (banking, insurance, bookkeeping, machine repair) locate close to the trading and transportation firms that use their services.

The American fur trade was an important force in the development of cities along the Mississippi River. New Orleans, located at the mouth of the Mississippi River, provided a convenient transshipment point for American furs destined for

European markets. In 1764, fur traders from New Orleans established St.Louis, located at the junction of the Missouri and Mississippi rivers, as a central substation for the fur trade. By 1800, there were over 1,000 people in St. Louis, living in the middle of an almost unpopulated continent.

The experience of New York City illustrates the importance of trade in the development of cities. The city, which began as a fur-trading post for the Dutch, was taken over by the British in 1664. The city grew rapidly, along with other eastern cities, as a result of the flour trade with the West Indies. At the time of the war of 1812, New York and Philadelphia were about the same size. Following the war, New York grew rapidly and became the country's dominant city. Why?

The rapid growth of New York was caused by increases in trading activity, which was caused by two factors. First, New York State built the Erie Canal, connecting New York City with the Great Lakes. The Erie Canal opened vast market areas to New York traders. Second, traders in New York developed innovative trading practices, one of which was the auction sale. A British manufacturer consigned his goods to a U.S. auctioneer, who then sold the goods to U.S. merchants. The auction sale decreased prices because it eliminated the British exporter and the traditional U.S. importer. While Philadelphia and Boston passed laws that discouraged auction sales, New York allowed them. U.S. merchants responded by buying more goods from New York traders, so the city grew at the expense of Philadelphia and Boston. New York traders were also the first to establish regularly scheduled shipping across the Atlantic, which attracted more traders and shippers to the city.

Cities also developed as a result of the railroad. The spread of the railroad after 1830 gave merchants in Boston, Philadelphia, and Baltimore access to midwestern markets, so these cities diverted some trading activity from New York. In 1868, Kansas land speculators chose a site for a new city along the Chisholm Trail (the route for cattle drives from Texas to Kansas railheads). They persuaded the railroad company to extend their tracks to the site. By 1872, thousands of carloads of cattle were being shipped from the city, and Wichita was a booming cow town.

Transfer-Oriented Industrial Firms

A **transfer-oriented firm** is defined as one for which transportation cost is the dominant factor in the location decision. The firm chooses the location that minimizes total transport cost, defined as the sum of **procurement cost** and **distribution cost.** Procurement cost is the cost of transporting raw materials from the input source to the factory. Distribution cost is the cost of transporting the firm's output from the factory to the consumer.

The classic model of a transfer-oriented firm has four assumptions:

1. **Single output.** The firm produces a fixed amount of a single good. The output is shipped from the factory to a marketplace at point M.

2. **Single transferable input.** The firm may use several inputs, but only one input is shipped from an input source (point *F*) to the factory. All other inputs are **ubiquitous** (available at all locations at the same price).

3. **Fixed factor proportions.** The firm produces its fixed amount of output with a fixed amount of each input. In other words, firms do not substitute between inputs in response to changes in relative prices, but use a single recipe for producing the good.

4. **Fixed prices.** The firm is so small that it does not affect the prices of its inputs or outputs.

Under these four assumptions, the firm maximizes its profit by minimizing its transportation costs. The firm's profit equals total revenue (price times the quantity of output) less input costs and transport costs. Total revenue is the same at all locations because the firm sells a fixed amount of output at a fixed price. Input costs are the same at all locations because the firm buys a fixed amount of each input at fixed prices. The only costs that vary across space are procurement cost (input transport costs) and distribution cost (output transport costs). Therefore, the firm will choose the location that minimizes its total transport costs.

The firm's location choice is determined by the outcome of a tug-of-war. The firm is pulled toward the input source by low procurement costs and pulled toward the market by low distribution costs. For the **resource-oriented firm,** the pull toward the input source is relatively strong, so the firm locates near its raw-material source. For the **market-oriented firm,** the pull toward the market is relatively strong, so the firm locates near its marketplace.

Resource-Oriented Firms

Table 3–1 shows the transport characteristics of a resource-oriented firm. The firm makes baseball bats, using five tons of wood to produce three tons of bats. The firm is involved in a weight-losing activity in the sense that the output is lighter than the transferable input. The **monetary weight** of the input is defined as the physical weight of the input (five tons) times the transportation rate ($1 per ton per mile, or $5 per mile). Similarly, the monetary weight of the output is three tons times $1,

TABLE 3–1   Physical and Monetary Weights of a Resource-Oriented Firm

	Input (wood)	Output (bats)
Physical weight (tons)	5	3
Transport rate (cost per ton per mile)	$1	$1
Monetary weight (physical weight times rate)	$5	$3

FIGURE 3–1   Total Transport Cost for Resource-Oriented Firm

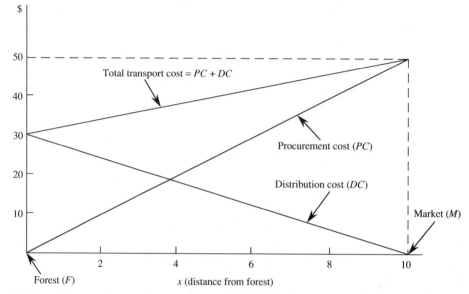

Total transport cost (the sum of procurement cost and distribution cost) is minimized at the forest because the monetary weight of the input ($5) exceeds the monetary weight of the output ($3). The weight-losing activity locates at its source of raw materials.

or $3 per mile. The firm is considered a resource-oriented firm because the monetary weight of its transferable input exceeds the monetary weight of its output.

Figure 3–1 shows the firm's transportation costs. Procurement cost is defined as the cost of shipping the wood from the forest to the factory and equals the monetary weight of the input (weight times rate) times the distance between forest and factory. The slope of the procurement-cost curve is the monetary weight of the input, so procurement cost rises by $5 per mile, from zero at the forest to $50 at the market 10 miles away. Distribution cost is defined as the cost of shipping the output from the factory to the market and equals the monetary weight of the output (weight times rate) times the distance from the factory to the market. The slope of the distribution-cost curve is the monetary weight of the output, so distribution cost decreases by $3 per mile, from $30 at the forest (10 miles from the market) to zero at the market.

Total transport cost is the sum of procurement costs and distribution costs, as shown in Figure 3–1. Total transport cost is minimized at the forest site ($30). If the firm moves one mile away from the forest toward the market, its distribution cost decreases by $3 (the monetary weight of the output) but procurement cost increases by $5 (the monetary weight of the input), so total transport cost increases by $2. The total cost is minimized at the forest site because the monetary weight of the input exceeds the monetary weight of the output. The resource-oriented firm locates near its input source.

Weight-Losing Activities.   The bat firm is resource-oriented because it is a **weight-losing activity,** using five tons of wood to produce only three ton of bats. The cost of transporting wood is large relative to the cost of transporting the finished output, so the firm saves on transport costs by locating near the forest. In this case, the tug-of-war is won by the input source because there is more *physical* weight on the input side.

There are many other examples of weight-losing firms. Beet-sugar factories locate near sugar-beet farms because one pound of sugar beets generates only about 2.7 ounces of sugar. Onion dehydrators locate near onion fields because one pound of fresh onions becomes less than one pound of dried onions. Ore processors locate near mines because the processors use only a fraction of the materials extracted from the ground.

Other Resource-Oriented Activities.   Some firms locate near input sources because inputs are relatively expensive to ship. Suppose that the physical weight of the transferable input equals the physical weight of the output, but the unit cost of shipping the input exceeds the unit cost of shipping the output. The firm will locate near its input source because the monetary weight of the input exceeds the monetary weight of the output. The input will be more expensive to ship if it is more bulky, perishable, fragile, or hazardous than the output. Hoover (1975) provides several examples of such activities:

1. **Cotton baling.** The input (fluffy cotton) is more bulky than the output (baled cotton). Since the cost of shipping a ton of fluffy cotton exceeds the cost of shipping a ton of compacted cotton, the cotton baler is resource-oriented and locates near the cotton fields.
2. **Canning.** The input (raw fruit) is more perishable than the output (canned fruit). Since the cost of shipping one ton of perishable fruits (in refrigerated cars) exceeds the cost of shipping canned goods, canners locate near the fruit farms.
3. **Skunk deodorizing.** The input (fully armed skunks) is more fragile and hazardous than the output (disarmed skunks). Since the cost of shipping a ton of armed skunks exceeds the cost of shipping a ton of disarmed ones, the skunk deodorizer will locate near the skunk source.

A firm with a relatively bulky, perishable, fragile, or hazardous input will locate near its input source. The tug-of-war between input forces and output forces is won by the input source, not because the input is heavier, but because it is more expensive to ship.

**TABLE 3–2   Physical and Monetary Weights
of a Market-Oriented Firm**

	Input (sugar)	Output (soft drinks)
Physical weight (tons)	1	4
Transport rate (cost per ton per mile)	$1	$1
Monetary weight (physical weight times rate)	$1	$4

Market-Oriented Firms

For a market-oriented firm, output transport costs are relatively large, so the firm locates near its output market. Table 3–2 shows the transportation characteristics of a market-oriented firm. The bottling company uses one ton of sugar and three tons of water (a ubiquitous input) to produce four tons of soft drinks.

Figure 3–2 shows the firm's transportation costs. The monetary weight of the output exceeds the monetary weight of the input by $3. As the firm moves toward the market, total transport cost decreases by $3 per mile, dropping from $40 at the sugar plantation (point *F*) to $10 at the market. The firm is market-oriented because the monetary weight of the output exceeds the monetary weight of the input.

The bottling firm is market-oriented because it is a **weight-gaining activity.** The firm adds three tons of local water to one ton of sugar to produce four tons of soft drinks, so output is heavier than the transferable input (sugar). In this case, the tug-of-war is won by the market because there is more *physical* weight on the output side.

Some firms locate near their markets because their output is relatively expensive to ship. If the physical weights are equal but the output is more costly to ship, the monetary weight of the output will exceed the monetary weight of the input, and the firm will locate near its market. The cost of shipping the output will be relatively high if the output is relatively bulky, perishable, fragile, or hazardous. Hoover (1975) provides several examples of such firms:

1. **Automobile assembly.** The output (assembled automobiles) is more bulky than the inputs (metal, plastic, and rubber parts). The cost of shipping one ton of assembled automobiles exceeds the cost of shipping the ton of the metal, plastic, and rubber that goes into the automobiles.

2. **Bakery.** The bakery produces a relatively perishable output. Although flour can be stored for months without spoiling, bread becomes stale after just a few days. A bakery locates near its market because it would be expensive to ship bread from a site near the flour mill to the marketplace in a timely manner.

3. **Weapons.** A weapons producer combines harmless inputs into a lethal output. The firm locates near its output market to avoid transporting the hazardous (or fragile) output long distances.

FIGURE 3–2   Total Transport Cost for a Market-Oriented Firm

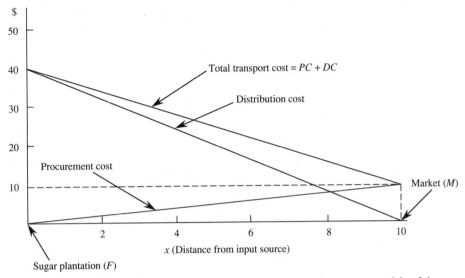

Total transport cost ($PC + DC$) is minimized at the market because the monetary weight of the output ($4) exceeds the monetary weight of the transferable input ($1). The weight-gaining activity locates at its market.

A firm with a relatively bulky, perishable, fragile, or hazardous output will locate near its market. The tug-of-war is won by the output, not because it is heavier, but because it is more expensive to ship.

Implications for the Development of Cities

The analysis of the transfer-oriented firm provides a simple rule for predicting the location choices of firms. If the monetary weight of the input exceeds the monetary weight of the output, the firm will locate at its input source. If the reverse is true, the firm will locate at its market. Of course, this rule is based on a simple model in which the firm has only a single transferable input and a single output. What about more-complex location choices involving a firm with several input sources and markets? The general principles of this section apply to these more realistic cases. The higher the cost of shipping inputs or outputs to a particular location, the greater the pull toward that location.

The analysis of the transfer-oriented firm predicts the development of two types of cities. Resource-oriented firms locate near their raw material sources, causing the development of **resource-based cities**, for example, lumber towns, steel towns, and food-processing towns. The analysis also suggests that as a city grows, it will attract market-oriented firms. The location decisions of these market-oriented firms often generate cities that serve as **regional market centers**.

The Principle of Median Location

The classic model of the transfer-oriented firm assumes that the firm has a single input source and a single market. This section examines the location decisions of firms with several input sources and several markets. The most important concept is the **principle of median location**. According to this principle, the optimum location for a firm with several inputs and outputs is the **median transport location,** the location that splits the total monetary weight of the firm into two equal halves. At the median transport location, half the monetary weight comes from one direction and the other half comes from the other direction.

Location Choice with Multiple Markets

To explain the location choice of a firm with several markets, consider Ann, who makes and delivers pizzas. In choosing a site for her pizza parlor, Ann must consider the following:

1. **Ubiquitous inputs.** All inputs (labor, dough, toppings) are ubiquitous (available at all locations for the same price), so input transport costs are zero.
2. **Pizza consumers.** Ann's customers are located along a highway. The price of pizzas is fixed, and every consumer demands one pizza per day.
3. **Delivery costs.** Ann delivers the pizzas to her customers at no charge, making one trip per customer per day. The delivery cost is 50 cents per pizza per mile.

Ann will choose the location that minimizes total delivery cost.

Figure 3–3 shows the distribution of consumers along the highway. Distances are measured from the western end of the highway (point *W*). There are 2 customers at point *W*, 8 customers at point *X* (one mile from *W*), 1 customer at *Y* (two miles from *W*), and 10 customers at *Z* (nine miles from *W*). Since each customer buys one pizza and the delivery cost is 50 cents per pizza per mile, the the monetary weight of a particular location (the sales volume times the delivery cost per pizza per mile) is half the number of consumers at that location.

According to the principle of median location, Ann will minimize total transport cost at the median location. Since point *Y* divides the monetary weights into two equal halves, it is the median location. The monetary weight of locations to the west is $5 ($1 for *W* plus $4 for *X*), and the monetary weight of locations to the east is $5 ($5 for *Z*). The median location divides Ann's customers into two equal halves: she has 10 customers to the east and 10 to the west.

To show that the median location minimizes total transport cost, suppose that Ann starts at the median location and then moves to point *S*, one mile east of *Y*. As she moves to the east, there is good news and bad news. The good news is that she spends less on delivery to point *Z*: she saves 50 cents per trip to *Z*,

FIGURE 3–3   Pizza Delivery and the Principle of Median Location

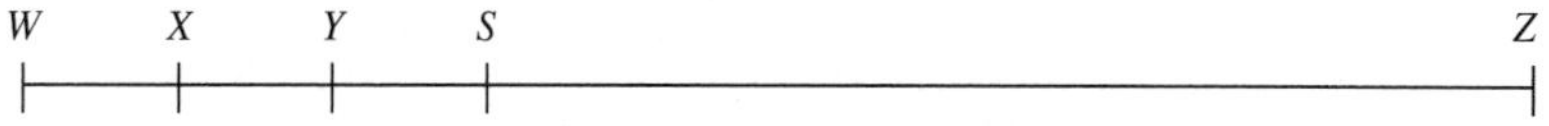

	W	X	Y	S	Z
Distance from W (miles)	0	1	2	3	9
Number of consumers	2	8	1		10
Monetary weight	$1	$4	$0.50		$5

Assumptions:

1. Every consumer purchases one pizza.
2. The delivery cost per pizza per mile is 50¢.
3. The firm delivers one pizza at a time.

Ann locates her pizza parlor at point Y because it is the median location: she delivers 10 pizzas to consumers to the west of Y, and 10 to consumers to the east of Y. A move from Y to S would decrease delivery cost for the 10 consumers at point E (savings of $5) but would increase delivery costs for the 11 consumers at points W, X, and Y (increase in cost of $5.50). Similarly, a move in the oppsite direction would increase total transport cost.

saving a total of $5 in eastward delivery cost. The bad news is that westward delivery cost increases: she pays 50 cents more per trip to points W, X, and Y; since there are 11 customers to the west of S, her westward delivery cost increases by a total of $5.50 ($1 more for W, $4 more for X, and 50 cents more for Y). Since the increase in westward delivery cost exceeds the decrease in eastward cost, the move from Y to S increases total delivery cost. The same is true for a move in the opposite direction: if Ann moves from Y toward W, total delivery cost will increase.

Why does the median location minimize total transport cost? It is the minimum-cost location because it splits pizza consumers into two equal parts. At any location to the east of Y, there will be more consumers to the west of the pizza parlor than to the east. As Ann moves eastward away from Y, she moves farther away from 11 customers but moves closer to only 10 customers. Similarly, a westward move will cause her to move closer to 10 customers, but farther from 11 customers. In general, any move away from the median location will increase delivery costs for *the majority* of consumers, so total costs increase.

It is important to note that the distances between the consumers is irrelevant to the firm's location choice. For example, if the Z consumers were located 100 miles from W instead of 10 miles from W, the median location would still be point Y. Total delivery cost would still be minimized (at a higher level of course) at point Y.

Median Location and Growth of Cities

The principle of median location provides another explanation of why large cities become larger. Suppose that a firm delivers its product to consumers in five different cities. In Figure 3–4, there is one large city at location L, and four small cities at locations S_1, S_2, S_3, and S_4. The firm sells 4 units in each small city and 17 units in the large city. The median location is in the large city, even though the large city is at the end of the line. A one-mile move westward from L would decrease transport cost by $16 (as the firm moved closer to consumers in the small cities), but would increase transport costs by $17 (as the firm moved away from consumers in the large city). The lesson from this example is that the concentration of demand in large cities causes large cities to grow.

Transshipment Points and Port Cities

The principle of median location also explains why some industrial firms locate at transshipment points. A **transshipment point** is defined as a point at which a good is transferred from one transport mode to another. At a port, goods are transferred from trucks or trains to ships. At a railroad terminal, goods are transferred from trucks to the train.

Figure 3–5 shows the location options for a sawmill. The firm harvests logs from locations A and B, processes the logs into lumber, and then sells the lumber in an overseas market at point M. Suppose that because of scale economies in production, a single sawmill is efficient. Highways connect points A and B to the port, and ships travel from the port to point M. The sawmill is a weight-losing activity. The monetary weights of the inputs are $15 for point A and $15 for point B, and the monetary weight of the output is $10.

Where will the firm locate its sawmill? Although there is no true median location, the port is the closest to a median location. If the firm starts at the port (P), it could move either toward one of its input sources or to its market.

1. **Toward input sources A or B**. A one-mile move from P toward point A will cause offsetting changes in the costs of transporting logs from A and B. Because output transport costs increases by $10, the port location is superior to locations between P and A. The same argument applies for a move from P toward B.

FIGURE 3–4   **Median Location in the Large City**

Locations	S_1	S_2	S_3	S_4		L
Demand	4	4	4	4		17

The median location is in the large city (L). Any move to the left of point L will increase travel costs for the majority of consumers, increasing total transportation costs.

FIGURE 3-5   Sawmill Locates at Port

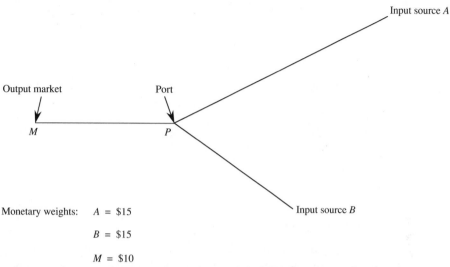

Monetary weights: A = $15

B = $15

M = $10

The firm locates its sawmill at the port (P) because it is the median transport location. A move from P toward either A or B would increase output transport costs by $10 without affecting input transport costs. A move from P toward M would increase input transport costs by $30 but would decrease output transport costs by only $10.

2. **To market (M).** Unless the firm wants to operate a floating sawmill, it would not move to points between the port and the overseas market at M. It could, however, move all the way to the market. A move from P to M would decrease output transport costs by $10 (the monetary weight of output) per mile of distance between M and P and increase input transport costs by $30 per mile (the monetary weight of the inputs). Transport costs would increase by $20 per mile, so the port location is superior to the market location.

Although the sawmill is a weight-losing activity, it will locate at the port, not at one of its input sources. The port location is efficient because it provides a central collection point for the firm's inputs.

There are many examples of port cities that developed as a result of the location decisions of industrial firms. Seattle started in 1880 as a sawmill town: firms harvested trees in western Washington, processed the logs in Seattle sawmills, and then shipped the wood products to other states and countries. Baltimore was the nation's first boomtown; flour mills processed wheat from the surrounding agricultural areas for export to the West Indies. Buffalo was the midwestern center for flour mills, providing consumers in eastern cities with flour produced from midwestern wheat. Wheat was shipped from midwestern states across the Great

Lakes to Buffalo, where it was processed into flour for shipment, by rail, to cities in the eastern United States. In contrast with Baltimore, which exported its output (flour) by ship, Buffalo imported its input (wheat) by ship.

Median Location and Cities

The principle of median location explains the development of several types of cities. If the median transport location is an input source, a resource-based city will form around the input source. If the median location is in the center of the region, a regional market center will develop. If the median location is the transshipment point, a **port city** will develop. If the median location is in an existing city, the city will grow.

Firms Oriented toward Local Inputs

An input is considered local if it cannot be efficiently transported from one location to another. Examples of local inputs are energy, labor, intermediate goods, and local public services. A firm heavily dependent on a local input bases its location decision on the availability of inexpensive local inputs; for example, an energy-intensive firm chooses a site with inexpensive energy, and a labor-intensive firm chooses a site with inexpensive labor. Such firms ignore transportation costs because they are a relatively small part of the total costs.

Energy Inputs

In the first half of the 19th century, energy was a local input. The waterwheel was the first device used to generate nonanimal mechanical energy. The waterwheel was turned by waterfalls and fast-moving streams, providing power for production facilities located along rivers and streams. Textile manufacturers set up factories along small backcountry streams in New England and used waterwheels to power their machinery. Among the cities that developed as a result of the waterwheel are Lowell, Lawrence, Holyoke, and Lewiston.

The development of the steam engine in the second half of the 19th century made energy a transferable input. The steam engine could be operated anywhere, with the only constraint being the availability of coal to fuel the engine. Some energy-intensive manufacturers located near the coal mines in Pennsylvania. Others located along navigable waterways and shipped coal from the mines to their factories. The steam engine allowed New England textile firms to shift from the backcountry waterfall sites to sites along navigable waterways. Production shifted to the Fall River–New Bedford area along the south coast of New England. After the development of the railroad, firms were able to move to production sites connected to the coal fields by rail.

The development of electricity affected the location patterns of manufacturers. Because electricity can be transmitted over distances of several hundred miles, a firm can use the energy generated from water power without locating along a backcountry stream. Similarly, a firm can use coal resources without shipping the bulky fuel from the mine to its factory. In general, the development of electricity decreased the importance of energy considerations in location decisions. The activities for which energy considerations are still important are energy-intensive activities such as the production of aluminum and artificial abrasives. Such activities are attracted to regions that offer inexpensive energy. The Pacific Northwest, with its abundant and inexpensive hydroelectric power, attracts energy-intensive activities.

Labor

There are practical limits on how far laborers are willing to commute, so labor is a local input. A labor-intensive firm, defined as a firm in which labor costs are a large fraction of total cost, chooses a location with low labor costs. Note that the choice is based on labor costs, not simply wages. A high-wage location will be efficient if the labor productivity is high enough to justify the higher wages. In other words, the firm bases its location decision on labor cost *per unit of output*, not simply the hourly wage.

Labor costs differ across space for four reasons. First, firms must compensate their workers for any undesirable features of the local environment. If an area has relatively dirty air or foul weather, workers will demand relatively high wages. Second, areas with strong labor unions generally have higher wages. Third, because households are not perfectly mobile, some areas will have a plentiful supply of labor and thus relatively low wages. In other words, there is disequilibrium in the labor market. Fourth is the phenomenon of **joint labor supply:** households move to locations that provide a job for the household's primary worker, increasing the supply of secondary workers. In colonial Massachusetts, the area north of Boston attracted men to sailing and fishing jobs. The resulting surplus of female workers decreased the wages of jobs held by women. Shoemakers moved to the area to take advantage of its low wages.

There are many examples of firms that base their location decisions primarily on labor costs. When advances in energy technology reduced their dependence on local water power, many textile firms moved from the high-wage New England states to low-wage southern states. More recently, apparel and shoe firms have moved overseas or to sites near the Mexican border to take advantage of inexpensive labor. The location decisions of these labor-intensive industries cause the development of cities in areas where labor is inexpensive.

Amenities, Migration, and Labor Costs

Some firms are indirectly attracted to sites that provide amenities such as good weather, high-quality schools, low crime rates, a clean environment, and cultural opportunities. If workers migrate to locations offering these amenities, the resulting excess supply of labor will decrease wages, attracting labor-oriented firms to the area. In this case, the firm's location choice depends on the location choice of its work force. Instead of workers following firms, firms follow workers. Graves (1979) and Porell (1982) provide empirical support for this phenomenon.

Amenities are most important for firms that employ high-income workers. Since the demands for these amenities are income-elastic, high-income workers are attracted to locations with amenities, and the firms hiring these people follow. For example, research and development firms employ engineers and computer scientists, many of whom place a high value on good weather, high-quality local schools, a clean environment, and cultural opportunities. One explanation for the shift of employment from northern states to the southern and western states is that rising income has increased the demand for certain amenities, causing workers to move to areas that provide these amenities.

Intermediate Inputs: Localization and Urbanization Economies

Some firms are drawn to locations that provide intermediate inputs. As explained in Chapter 2, agglomerative economies generate clusters of firms in the same industry. By sharing the suppliers of intermediate inputs, firms in the cluster exploit scale economies in the production of specialized inputs. The cluster attracts both the demanders of intermediate inputs (dressmakers, corporate headquarters, research and development facilities) and the suppliers of the inputs (buttonmakers, advertising agencies, law firms, testing facilities). Firms in the cluster also exploit scale economies in the provision of specialized business services and local public services.

Agglomerative economies cause firms from different industries to cluster in cities. The firms in cities exploit scale economies in the provision of business services (machine repair, banking, insurance, transportation, employment agencies) and local public services (transportation facilities, schools).

Local Public Services and Taxes

Local governments influence the location decisions of businesses by the provision of public services. The public sector provides some of the inputs used directly by firms (water, roads, ports, and sewers) and provides goods consumed by the city's work force (education, parks, roads, transit systems, public safety). A city can attract firms by providing a set of efficient, high-quality public services. In addition, industrial firms require production sites that (1) are accessible to the intracity and intercity transportation networks and (2) have a full set of public services (water, sewage, electricity). By coordinating its land-use and infrastructure policies to ensure an adequate supply of industrial land, a city can attract new firms and encourage the expansion of existing firms.

The public sector also affects the location decisions of businesses through its tax policies. Taxes on businesses increase production costs and discourage firms from locating in the city. Taxes on residents increase the costs of living in the city and will ultimately result in higher wages and production costs.

Many cities try to attract export firms by offering special subsidies for new firms. Levy (1981) describes several types of subsidy programs, including the following:

1. **Tax abatement.** In some cities, new firms are exempt from local property taxes for a fixed period (e.g., 10 years). Some cities offer tax abatements to all new developments, while others offer abatements only to firms that are particularly sensitive to tax differentials.

2. **Industrial bonds.** Some cities issue tax-free industrial bonds to finance property developments. The local government uses the revenue from the bonds to purchase the land and then leases the property to a private firm. Because the interest income from industrial bonds is not subject to federal taxes, the bond buyer accepts a relatively low interest rate (e.g., 8 percent instead of 12 percent). Therefore, the lessee pays less than the market interest rate on the money borrowed to finance the project. The use of industrial bonds was sharply curtailed by the Tax Reform Act of 1986.

3. **Government loans and loan guarantees.** Some cities loan money directly to developers, and others guarantee loans from private lenders. In both cases, developers borrow money at a relatively low interest rate. Either the city charges an interest rate below the market rate, or the city decreases the risk associated with a private loan, allowing the developer to borrow private money at a relatively low interest rate.

4. **Site development.** Some cities subsidize the provision of land and public services for new development. The city purchases a site, clears the land, builds roads and sewers, and then sells the site to a developer at a fraction of the cost of acquiring and developing the site.

Several Local Inputs

How does a firm with several local inputs choose among the alternative locations? The location choice is determined by the outcome of a tug-of-war between forces pulling the firm toward its different local inputs (labor, energy, intermediate goods, local public services). The strength of the pull toward a particular input source depends on (1) the relative importance of the input to the firm, and (2) the spatial variation in the input price. The greater the importance of the input and the price variation, the stronger the pull toward a particular input source.

Consider a firm that has two local inputs: labor and energy. The firm is pulled toward city L (which has low wages) and city E (which has inexpensive energy).

The forces pulling the firm toward L will win the tug-of-war if (1) the firm's labor consumption is large relative to its energy consumption (i.e., the firm is labor-intensive), and (2) the difference in the wage (controlling for productivity differences) is large relative to the difference in the price of energy.

Transport Costs versus Local-Input Costs

This chapter has divided industrial firms into two types: firms that base their location decisions exclusively on transport costs (transfer-oriented firms), and firms that base their location decisions exclusively on local-input costs (input-oriented firms). Table 3–3 summarizes the results of the chapter, listing the various types of transfer-oriented and input-oriented firms.

In the real world, things are not so tidy. Most firms cannot be easily classified with respect to their locational orientation. For most firms, location decisions are based on both transport costs and local input costs. Since transport costs and input costs vary across space, the typical location choice requires a trade-off between transport costs and input costs. The firm's location decision is determined by the outcome of a complex tug-of-war between the forces pulling the firm toward its local inputs, its nonlocal inputs, and its market.

In the last several decades, many industries have switched from transfer orientation to input orientation. Firms have moved from locations close to input

TABLE 3–3   **Summary of Locational Orientation**

Orientation	Relevant Characteristic	Example
Transfer Orientation	Transport cost is large fraction of total cost	
Resource orientation	Weight loss	Bat factory
	Bulk loss	Cotton baling
	Perishabity loss	Canning
	Hazard (fragility) loss	Skunk deodorizing
Market orientation	Weight gain	Bottling
	Bulk gain	Auto assembly
	Perishability gain	Baking
	Hazard (fragility) gain	Explosives
Local-Input Orientation	Transport cost is small fraction of total cost	
Energy	Energy-intensive production	Aluminum
Labor	Labor-intensive operation	Textiles
Intermediate Inputs		
Specialized inputs	Localization economies	Dressmakers
Business services	Urbanization economies	Corporate headquarters
Amenity orientation	Workers sensitive to weather and recreation	Research and development

sources and markets to locations with inexpensive local inputs. The changes in locational orientation resulted from innovations in transportation and production.

Innovations in Transportation

Improvements in transport technology decreased the cost of transporting both inputs and outputs. For example, the development of fast ocean ships and container technology (shipping freight in large, standardized containers instead of in small bundles) made ocean shipping more efficient, decreasing the unit cost of transportation (cost per ton per mile). Similarly, improvements in rail, trucks, and planes decreased unit freight costs. For some firms, the decrease in transport costs was large enough to cause a switch from a transfer orientation to a local-input orientation. These firms then based their location decisions on access to inexpensive local inputs rather than access to markets or inputs. A recent example is the movement of the assembly operations of many U.S. manufacturers to sites along the Mexican border.

Innovations in Production

Improvements in production techniques decreased the physical weight of inputs. As the weight of inputs decreased, total transport costs decreased, and some transfer-oriented firms became local-input firms. These firms moved from sites with low transport costs to ones with inexpensive local inputs. An example is the U.S. steel industry. Over the last several decades, the amount of coal and ore required to produce one ton of steel has decreased steadily, a result of improved steelmaking methods and the use of scrap metal (a local input) instead of iron ore (a transferable input). As the physical weight of inputs decreased, transport costs decreased relative to labor costs, and some firms became oriented to local inputs. Many steel plants are now located in low-wage countries (Brazil, Korea, Mexico), far from both raw materials and steel markets.

Location Orientation and Growth Patterns

Changes in transport costs affect economic growth patterns. As transport costs decrease, the relative attractiveness of a resource-rich region decreases, causing firms to move to areas with inexpensive local inputs. The steel industry has moved from the eastern United States, with its rich coal and ore deposits, to Japan and Korea, which have neither coal nor ore deposits. The steel industry made the move because the relative importance of transport costs decreased. Steel firms moved to areas with lower wages because the savings in labor costs exceeded the increase in transport costs (for ore, coal, and steel). Similarly, manufacturers have moved from the United States to Asia and Mexico, far from U.S. markets, because the savings in labor costs outweigh the increase in transport costs.

Empirical Work and Case Studies

This section discusses some of the facts about recent location choices. The first two parts examine the location decisions of firms in two branches of the computer industry, semiconductor manufacturers and computer makers. The third part summarizes a study of the factors in the location of the electronic components industry, and the fourth part discusses recent studies of the effects of taxes on location choices. The final part summarizes a case study of the decision to site GM's new Saturn plant near Nashville, Tennessee.

The Semiconductor Industry

The semiconductor industry illustrates some of the complexities of location choices in modern industry. The industry's output is light and compact relative to its value (i.e., it has a low bulk-value ratio), so transport costs are relatively unimportant in location decisions. What matters are localization economies and access to different types of labor.

As explained by Castells (1988), the making of semiconductors involves several distinct operations, requiring three different types of labor:

1. **Research and development.** Engineers and scientists design new circuits and prepare the circuits for implantation into silicon chips.
2. **Wafer fabrication.** Skilled technicians and manual workers make the chips holding the circuits.
3. **Assembly into components.** Unskilled workers assemble the chips into electronic components.

Many semiconductor firms split their operations into three parts. Research and development occurs in the Silicon Valley to exploit localization economies generated by the large concentration of semiconductor firms. The Silicon Valley is also considered a desirable location for engineers and scientists. Advanced manufacturing (wafer production) is typically located outside the Silicon Valley. For example, National Semiconductor has manufacturing facilities in Utah, Arizona, and Washington State; Intel has plants in Oregon, Arizona, and Texas; Advanced Micro Devices has a plant in Texas. These facilities are located in areas that provide (1) a plentiful supply of skilled manual laborers; (2) an environment attractive to engineers and technicians; and (3) easy access, by air transportation, to the Silicon Valley. The firms' assembly facilities are typically overseas, in locations such as Southeast Asia that have a plentiful supply of low-skilled workers.

Computer Manufacturers

The splitting of manufacturing operations also occurs among computer makers. Hekman (1985) has studied the location decisions of firms producing large mainframe computers. The five largest firms, which control over 95 percent of the U.S. market, have their main research and development facilities in large metropolitan areas, one each in Boston, New York, Philadelphia, and two in Minneapolis. Because of the frequent design changes in mainframe computers, there is a great deal of nonroutine communication between designers and manufacturers, so proximity between design and fabrication activities is important. Four of the five mainframe makers assemble their computers near their research and design facilities.

In contrast, peripheral equipment (terminals, tape drives, and printers) are produced in branch plants outside the home metropolitan area. Because peripherals are not subject to rapid design changes, they can be produced far from the design facilities, in Tennessee, Nebraska, South Dakota, Utah, North Carolina, Florida, and Michigan. Similarly, individual computer components are standardized inputs and are produced in Mexico, Brazil, Hong Kong, Taiwan, and Puerto Rico.

The Relative Importance of Local Inputs: Empirical Results

On a theoretical level, all local inputs (labor, energy, intermediate inputs) influence location choices. Which local inputs are the most important? A number of recent empirical studies of location decisions address this question.

Carlton (1979) examines the location choices of firms in three input-oriented industries: plastics products, electronic transmitting equipment, and electronic components. These industries have relatively low transport costs, so they are oriented toward local inputs, not output markets or natural resources. Table 3–4 shows Carlton's results for the electronic components industry, reported as the elasticities of the number of new firms ("births") with respect to the various location factors. The elasticity of the number of births with respect to the wage is −1.07; that is, a 10 percent increase in the SMSA wage decreases the number of births by

TABLE 3–4 **Relative Strengths of Location Factors**

Variable	Elasticity of Number of Births with Respect to Variable
Wage	−1.07
Energy cost	−0.38 to −0.95
Output of industry	0.43
Number of engineers	0.25
Taxes	Close to zero
Government incentives	Close to zero

SOURCE: Dennis W. Carlton, "The Location and Employment Choices of New Firms: An Econometric Model," in *Interregional Movements and Regional Growth,* ed. William C. Wheaton (Washington, D.C.: Urban Institute, 1979).

10.7 percent. The elasticity for energy cost is lower, from −0.38 for natural gas and −0.95 for electricity. The elasticity for industry output (0.43) suggests that agglomerative economies are important: the number of births increases as the size of the industry increases. The technical expertise of the SMSA (measured by the number of engineers) also affects the number of new firms.

Carlton's results suggest that tax policies do not affect the location decisions of firms producing electronic components. The elasticities for the tax and incentive variables are close to zero, implying that SMSAs with low taxes and lucrative incentive packages do not experience higher birth rates. These results are consistent with earlier studies of the influence of taxes on location decisions.

Carlton's results for the other two industries (plastics products and electronic transmitting equipment) were similar. The most important location factors were wages, energy costs (less important for electronic transmitting equipment), industry output, and technical expertise.

Taxes and Location Choices

Do taxes affect location decisions? Until recently, the common view among economists was that taxes didn't matter. More recent evidence casts some doubt on this conclusion.

In a review of recent studies of location decisions, Newman and Sullivan (1988) cite several studies that provide evidence of a strong connection between taxes and location choices. The results of Bartik (1985) suggest that corporate and property taxes affect location choices, with the corporate tax having a stronger effect. Helms (1985) examines the effects of taxes *and* expenditures on location decisions, showing that the effect of a tax depends on how the tax revenue is spent. An increase in taxes increases the relative attractiveness of a jurisdiction if the money is spent on local public services (e.g., highways, education, public health and safety), but it decreases the relative attractiveness of the jurisdiction if the money is spent on redistributional programs for the poor.

A Case Study: The Location of GM's Saturn Plant

In 1985, General Motors announced that its new Saturn plant would be located in Spring Hill, Tennessee, a crossroads community about 30 miles from Nashville. The plant cost several billions of dollars to build, employs about 3,000 workers and supports thousands of jobs in the Nashville area. Why did GM choose Nashville over the dozens of other cities that sought the plant?

A case study by Bartik et al. (1987) suggests that the most important factor in the site choice was labor costs. Transportation costs and taxes also influenced the decision. A labor contract between GM and its unionized workers stipulates that the Saturn workers will be paid the same wage regardless of the plant's location, so GM will not decrease its own wage bill by locating in Tennessee, a state with low wages. However, GM will purchase a large fraction of its inputs from nearby suppliers, who will pay low wages and pass on the savings to GM.

The first step in the case study addressed the issue of transportation costs and market access. The authors estimated the costs of shipping finished cars from hundreds of alternative production sites to GM's markets in the continental United States. Based on 1984 sales figures, the cost-minimizing location (the location offering the best market access) was Indianapolis, Indiana. Based on the distribution of projected sales in the year 2000, the location offering the best market access was Terre Haute, Indiana. The shift from Indianapolis to Terre Haute reflects the shift in population and car consumers to the southern and western areas of the United States.

The second part of the study incorporated labor costs and taxes into the analysis. The authors estimated labor costs and taxes for production sites that provided reasonable access to GM's markets (a total of 130 sites in seven different states). Table 3–5 shows the costs (expressed as costs per car) for one site in each of the seven states.

1. **Transportation costs.** The variation in transportation costs among the seven sites was relatively small. The gap between the lowest cost site (Terre Haute) and the most expensive site (Kalamazoo) was only $17 per car. Nashville was ranked fifth, with transport costs per car only $13 higher than Terre Haute.

2. **Labor costs for local suppliers.** The variation in labor costs was relatively large. The difference between the lowest cost site (Nashville) and the highest cost site (Kalamazoo) was $85 per car.

3. **State and local taxes.** The table shows the tax cost per car in the absence of special subsidies and exemptions. The difference between the

TABLE 3–5   Case Study of GM's Location of Saturn Plant

	Estimated Cost: Dollars per Car			
Location	Average Transport Costs (to markets)	Labor Costs for Local Suppliers	State and Local Taxes (excluding subsidies)	Total Measured Cost
Nashville, TN	426	159	118	703
Lexington, KY	423	186	106	715
St. Louis, MO	419	172	134	725
Bloomington, IL	417	202	162	781
Kalamazoo, MI	430	244	116	790
Terre Haute, IN	413	209	168	790
Marysville, OH	427	219	169	815

Source: Timothy J. Bartik, Charles Becker, Steve Lake, and John Bush, "Saturn and State Economic Development," *Forum for Applied Research and Public Policy* (Spring 1987), pp. 29–40.

highest tax site (Marysville) and the lowest tax site (Lexington) was $63 per car. Nashville was ranked third, with tax costs per car $12 higher than Lexington.

The case study suggests that in the absence of special tax treatment, Nashville was the lowest cost site. The sum of its transportation, local labor, and tax costs was $12 less per car than Lexington, the second-ranked site, and $87 less than Terre Haute, the site that minimizes transportation costs. Nashville's slight disadvantage in market access is offset by its lower labor costs.

Tennessee offered three types of inducements to GM. The first was a $30 million highway project that connected the plant with Interstate 65. The second was a subsidized job-training program for Saturn workers, worth about $4 per car. The third was a program of property tax subsidies, worth about $30 per car. Although these subsidies would not have been necessary in the absence of similar subsidies from other states, it appears that Tennessee offered them to stay competitive with other states bidding for the plant.

Summary

1. Cities develop around the concentrations of employment generated by firms, so the location choices of firms play a role in the location of cities.

2. Trading firms collect goods from suppliers and distribute them to consumers, and locate at transshipment points. The location of trading and transportation firms explains the development of port cities and junction cities.

3. A transfer-oriented firm spends a relatively large amount on transport costs and chooses the location that minimizes total transport costs.
   a. A resource-oriented firm has relatively high transport costs for its inputs, so it locates near its input source. The location choices of resource-oriented firms cause the development of resource-based cities and port cities.
   b. A market-oriented firm has relatively high transport costs for its output, so it locates near its market. The location choices of market-oriented firms cause the development of port cities and the growth of existing cities.

4. According to the principle of median location, a market-oriented firm locates at its median transport location, defined as the location that splits its customers into two halves.
   a. This principle explains why big cities grow. The median location is often in a large city, so many market-oriented firms locate in large cities.
   b. This principle explains why some resource-oriented firms locate at transshipment points (ports). The port is often the median location for the firm

because it provides a central collection point for inputs and a single distribution point for the output.

5. A *local input* is defined as an input that cannot be transported long distances. Examples are certain types of energy, labor, and intermediate goods.
   a. A firm is oriented toward a local input if (1) it uses a local input whose price varies across space, and (2) it spends a large fraction of its budget on the local input.
   b. The input-oriented firm will locate near inexpensive local inputs, causing the development of cities and regions near sources of inexpensive energy, labor, and intermediate goods.

6. Firms that employ people who are sensitive to amenities (good weather, high-quality local schools, a clean environment, cultural opportunities) are attracted to locations that offer these amenities. Instead of workers following firms, firms follow workers. Amenities are most important for firms that employ high-income workers.

7. One study of the location decisions of firms producing electronic components, plastics products, and electronic transmitting equipment suggests that the most important location factors were wages, energy costs, industry output (a measure of agglomerative economies), and technical expertise. Taxes and incentive programs do not seem to affect location decisions.

8. Until recently, most studies of location decisions suggested that taxes were not an important locational factor. Recent studies cast some doubt on this conclusion. One study suggests that the effect of a tax depends on how the tax revenue is spent: an increase in taxes increases the relative attractiveness of a jurisdiction if the money is spent on local public services (e.g., highways, education, public health and safety), but it decreases the relative attractiveness of the jurisdiction if the money is spent on redistributional programs.

9. In the last several decades, the relative importance of transport costs has decreased, a result of innovations in transportation (which decreased unit transport costs) and production (which decreased the physical weight of inputs).
   a. Many resource-oriented and market-oriented firms have been transformed into firms oriented toward local inputs.
   b. The change in locational orientation provides one reason for the shift in economic growth from resource-rich regions (e.g., the United States) to places with low labor costs (e.g., Asia).

Exercises and Discussion Questions

1. Comment on the following statement from the owner of a successful plywood mill: "Firms don't use location theory to make location decisions. I

chose this location for my plywood mill because it is close to my favorite fishing spot."

2. Depict graphically the effects of the following changes on the bat firm's cost curves (shown in Figure 3–1). Explain any changes in the optimum location.
   a. The cost of shipping bats increases from $1 per ton to $4 per ton, while the cost of shipping wood remains at $1 per ton.
   b. The forest at point F burns down, forcing the firm to use wood from point G, which is 10 miles west of point F (20 miles from the market).
   c. The firm starts producing bats with wood and cork, using three tons of wood and two tons of cork to produce three tons of bats. Cork is ubiquitous (available at all locations for the same price).

3. Why do breweries typically locate near their markets (far from their input sources), while wineries typically locate near their input sources (far from their markets)?

4. The building of wooden ships was a weight-losing activity, as evidenced by the piles of scrap wood generated by shipbuilders. Yet shipbuilders located in ports, far from their input sources (inland forests). Why?

5. Consider a firm that delivers video rentals to its customers. The spatial distribution of customers is as follows: 10 videos are delivered to location W, 10 miles due west of the city center; 50 videos are delivered to the city center; 25 units are delivered to point E, 1 mile due east of the city center; and 45 videos are delivered to point F, 2 miles east of the city center. Production costs are the same at all locations. Using a graph, show where the firm should locate. Explain your location choice.

6. Figure 3–4 shows the location choice of Ann's pizza firm. Discuss the effects of the following changes on Ann's location choice:
   a. A tripling of the distance between Y and Z (from 7 miles to 21 miles).
   b. A tripling of the number of customers at point W. Instead of two customers at W, there are six.

7. In Figure 3–5, the weight-losing firm is located at point P (the port). If the monetary weight of location B is $27 instead of $15, will the firm still locate at point P?

8. There is some evidence that people have become more sensitive to air pollution. In other words, people are willing to pay more for clean air. If this is true, what influence will it have on the location decisions of firms?

References and Additional Reading

Alonso, William. "Location Theory." In *Readings in Urban Economics*, ed. M. Edel and J. Rothenberg. New York: Macmillan, 1972. Outlines the theory of firm location, focusing on the role of transport costs. Contains a brief bibliography of the seminal works in location theory.

Bartik, Timothy J. "Business Decisions in the United States: Estimates of the Effects of Unionization, Taxes, and Other Characteristics of States." *Journal of Business and Economics Statistics* 3 (1985), pp. 14–22. Estimates the effects of corporate and property taxes on location decisions.

Bartik, Timothy J., Charles Becker, Steve Lake, and John Bush. "Saturn and State Economic Development." *Forum for Applied Research and Public Policy* (Spring 1987), pp. 29–40.

Carlton, Dennis W. "The Location and Employment Choices of New Firms: An Econometric Model." In *Interregional Movements and Regional Growth*, ed. William C. Wheaton. Washington, D.C.: Urban Institute, 1979. Estimates the effects of wages, energy costs, industry output, and taxes on location decisions.

Castells, Manuel. "The New Industrial Space: Information Technology Manufacturing and Spatial Structure in the United States." In *America's New Market Geography*, ed. George Sternlieb and James Hughes. New Brunswick, N.J.: Center for Urban Policy Research, 1988. Examines the location patterns of information-technology industries (semiconductors, computers, communication equipment, electronic automated machines, and genetic engineering).

Chinitz, Benjamin. "The Effect of Transportation Forms on Regional Economic Growth." *Traffic Quarterly* 14 (1960), pp. 129–42.

Glaab, Charles, and A. Theodore Brown. *A History of Urban America*, 3rd ed. New York: Macmillan, 1983. A textbook on American urban history; discusses the origins of many American cities.

Graves, Phillip E. "A Life-Cycle Empirical Analysis of Migration and Climate by Race." *Journal of Urban Economics* 6 (1979), pp. 135–47. Estimates the effect of climate variables on migration patterns in the 1960s.

Hekman, John S. "Branch Plant Location and the Product Cycle in Computer Manufacturing." *Journal of Economics and Business* 37 (1985), pp. 89–102. Examines the influence of product development on the location decisions of computer manufacturers.

Helms, L. Jay. "The Effect of State and Local Taxes on Economic Growth: A Times Series–Cross Section Approach." *Review of Economics and Statistics* 68 (1985), pp. 574–82. Estimates effects of taxes on location decisions and growth rates; concludes that the effect of a tax increase depends on how the tax revenue is spent.

Hoover, Edgar M. *Regional Economics*. New York: Alfred A. Knopf, 1975. Chapters 2, 3, and 4 provide a concise analysis of the location decisions of firms.

Levy, John M. *Economic Development Programs for Cities, Counties, and Towns*. New York: Praeger, 1981. Discusses the factors affecting the location choices of firms.

Meiszkowski, Peter. "Recent Trends in Urban and Regional Development." In *Current Issues in Urban Economics*, ed. Peter Meiszkowski and Mahlon Straszheim. Baltimore, Md.: Johns Hopkins, 1979, pp. 3–39. Describes the broad patterns of urban and regional development since World War II, focusing on interregional migration, shifts in employment, and changes in regional income differentials.

Newman, Robert J., and Dennis H. Sullivan. "Econometric Analysis of Business Tax Impacts on Industrial Location: What Do We Know, and How Do We Know It?" *Journal of Urban Economics* 23 (1988), pp. 215–34. Reviews empirical evidence of the effects of business taxes on location choices.

Porell, Frank W. "Intermetropolitan Migration and Quality of Life." *Journal of Regional Science* 22 (1982), pp. 137–58. Estimates the effects of economic and quality-of-life variables on migration patterns.

Schmenner, Roger W. *Making Business Location Decisions*. Englewood Cliffs, N.J.: Prentice Hall, 1982. Discusses how firms make location decisions.

———. "Energy and Location." In *Energy Costs, Urban Development, and Housing*, ed. Anthony Downs and Katherine Bradbury. Washington, D.C.: Brookings Institution, 1984. Discusses the role of energy costs in location decisions.

Market Areas and the Urban Hierarchy

This chapter examines urban development from the regional perspective. In contrast to earlier chapters, which explore the development of individual cities in isolation, this chapter explains how cities develop as integral parts of a larger regional economy. A region supports cities of different size and scope, causing the development of a **regional system of cities.**

Table 4–1 shows the size distribution of urbanized areas in the United States in 1986. There were only 3 urbanized areas with more than 6.4 million people, but 172 with between 50,000 and 100,000 people. Table 4–1 raises two questions about cities in a regional economy. First, what are the effects of market forces on the equilibrium number of cities? Second, why are some cities larger than others? The answers to these questions are provided by **central place theory.**

The chapter is divided into two sections. The first section shows how firms in a market-oriented industry carve a region into individual market areas, including a discussion of why some industries have larger market areas than others. The second section uses central-place theory to explain how the location patterns of different industries are merged to form a regional system of cities.

The Analysis of Market Areas

Market-area analysis was developed by Christaller (translated in 1966) and refined by Losch (translated in 1954). A firm's **market area** is defined as the area over which the firm can underprice its competitors. The firm's net price is the sum of the price charged by the firm and the travel costs incurred by consumers.

**TABLE 4-1   Size Distribution of U.S.
Urbanized Areas, 1990**

Population of Urbanized Area	Number of Areas
More than 12.8 million	1
6.4 million to 12.8 million	2
3.2 million to 6.4 million	4
1.6 million to 3.2 million	14
800,000 to 1.6 million	19
400,000 to 800,000	33
200,000 to 400,000	52
100,000 to 200,000	99
50,000 to 100,000	172

SOURCE: U.S. Bureau of Census, *Press Release,*
August 16, 1991.

To explain the notion of a market area, consider a region where consumers buy compact discs (CDs). The region has the following characteristics:

1. **Fixed store price.** All music stores have the same production technology and face the same input prices, so they charge the same price.
2. **Travel costs.** Every consumer buys one compact disc (CD) per trip to the music store. The travel cost (the monetary and time costs of travel) is 50 cents per round-trip mile.
3. **Shape.** The region is rectangular, 60 miles long and 20 miles wide.

Because music stores sell the same product at the same price, they differ only in location.

Pricing with a Monopolist

Suppose that there is a single music store (owned by Bob) at the center of the region described above. The net price per CD is the sum of the store price and the consumer's travel cost. Figure 4–1 shows the net price of CDs for consumers living in different parts of the region. If Bob charges $8 per CD, the net price rises from $8 for a household living next to the music store, to $13 for a household living 10 miles from the music store, to $23 for a household 30 miles from the store.

Suppose that at a price of $8, Bob the monopolist makes positive economic profit. Other entrepreneurs will enter the music-store business and set up rival stores and perhaps set a lower price. The entry process will continue until all music stores make zero economic profit (normal accounting profit). Figure 4–2, p. 70, shows the market areas for music stores under the assumption that there are three stores in equilibrium. Tammy and Dick set up music stores 20 miles from Bob, and all three charge the same price for CDs ($6). Tammy underprices Bob for the western third of the region, and Dick underprices Bob for the eastern third

---
FIGURE 4–1   Net Price of CDs under Monopoly

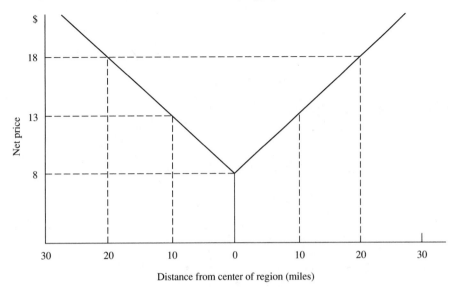

Distance from center of region (miles)

The net price of CDs is the sum of the store price ($8) and the cost of traveling to the music store (50 cents per round-trip mile per CD).

of the region. The three music stores split the region into three equal market areas, so every store has a circular market area with a 10-mile radius.

The market arrangement in Figure 4–2 has two implications for CD consumers. First, if the spaces between the circular market areas are ignored, the maximum net price is $11, the sum of the price charged by music stores ($6), and the maximum travel cost ($5). Second, every household patronizes the music store closest to its home. All stores charge the same price for the same product, so a household will patronize the store with the lowest travel costs.

Determinants of the Market Area: Fixed Demand

What factors determine the size of the market areas of market-oriented firms? The size of the market area depends on a number of factors, including travel costs, per capita demand, population density, and scale economies. This section uses a simple algebraic model to identify the determinants of market areas.

The Algebra of Market Areas.   An expression for the size of the market area can be derived with some simple algebra. The following symbols represent the market for CDs in a region:

d = monthly per capita demand (number of CDs)
e = population density (people per square mile)
A = land area of the region (in square miles)

FIGURE 4-2   Equilibrium Market Areas

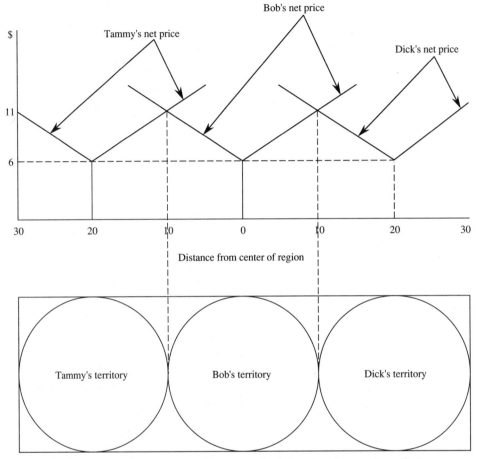

Each store's market area is the area over which its net price is less than the net prices of other stores. Each store has a circular territory with a 10-mile radius.

> q = output of the typical music store (CDs sold per month)
> Q = total (regionwide) demand for CDs

To simplify matters, per capita demand (d) is assumed to be independent of the net price of CDs: The individual consumer demands a fixed number of CDs regardless of the net price. In other words, the individual demand curve is perfectly inelastic. Later in the chapter, this assumption will be relaxed.

What is the equilibrium number of music stores? The total demand for CDs (Q) equals the product of per capita demand (d), population density (e), and the land area of the region (A):

$$Q = d \cdot e \cdot A \tag{4-1}$$

TABLE 4–2   Numerical Example of Number of Stores and Market Area

Variable	Symbol		Numerical Example
Per capita demand (number of CDs)	d		4
Population density (people per square mile)	e		50
Demand density (CDs per square mile)	$d \cdot e$		200
Land area (square miles)	A		300
Output per store (CDs sold per month)	q		1,000
Total demand	Q	$= d \cdot e \cdot A$	60,000
Number of stores	N	$= Q/q$	60
Market area (square miles)	M	$= q/(d \cdot e)$	5.0

Table 4–2 provides a numerical example that shows how to compute the equilibrium number of stores. Per capita demand is four CDs and population density is 50 people per square mile, so **demand density** (CD demand per square mile, equal to d times e) is 200. The region has an area of 300 square miles, so total demand is 60,000 CDs (200 times 300). The equilibrium number of music stores in the region is total demand divided by the output per firm:

$$N = \frac{Q}{q} \qquad (4–2)$$

Output per firm is 1,000 CDs, so there will be 60 music stores in the region (60,000 divided by 1,000).

How large is the market area of music stores? The size of the market area equals the land area of the region divided by the number of firms:

$$M = \frac{A}{N} \qquad (4–3)$$

If the region has a land area of 300 square miles and there are 60 stores, the market area of the typical store is 5 square miles. Using the expressions for N and Q, the expression for M can be rewritten as

$$M = \frac{q}{d \cdot e} \qquad (4–4)$$

In other words, the size of the market area is determined by output per store (q), per capita demand (d), and population density (e). In Table 4–2, $q = 1,000$, $d = 4$, and $e = 50$, so the market area is 5.0 square miles.

The algebraic model identifies three factors that determine the size of the firm's market area: per capita demand, population density, and output per store. Output per store is affected by both scale economies and transportation costs. How do changes in each of these variables affect market areas?

Changes in Market Areas.   An increase in scale economies increases the market area of the typical music store. An increase in scale economies increases the optimum output per store, so fewer stores are required to serve the region. Using the numbers in Table 4–2, if output per store increases from 1,000 to 1,200, the number of stores will decrease from 60 to 50 (60,000/1,200). The decrease in the number of stores increases the market area from 5 square miles to 6 square miles (300 divided by 50). Because an increase in scale economies increases output per store, every store needs a larger market area to exploit its scale economies. Note that this conclusion depends on the assumption that per capita demand is fixed, an assumption to be relaxed later in the chapter.

How does a decrease in travel cost affect output per store and the market area of the typical firm? Suppose that the development of a faster and cheaper travel mode decreases the monetary and time costs of travel. The decrease in travel costs increases the output per store; the lower the travel cost, the greater the ability of the store to exploit its scale economies in production. Using the numbers in Table 4–2, if output per store increases from 1,000 to 1,250, the number of stores will decrease from 60 to 48 (60,000/1,250). The decrease in the number of stores increases the market area per store from 5 square miles to 6.25 square miles (300 divided by 48). Again, this result depends on the assumption that per capita demand is fixed, an assumption to be relaxed later in the chapter.

How does an increase in per capita demand affect the size of the market area? An increase in per capita demand increases the demand density (the number of CDs sold per square mile, or d times e). If output per store is fixed, each store needs a smaller market area to exhaust its scale economies. For example, a doubling of per capita demand doubles total demand, so it doubles the number of stores. If there are twice as many stores in the region, the market area per store will be cut in half (from 5 square miles to 2.5 square miles).

How does an increase in population density affect the market area? Like an increase in per capita demand, an increase in population density increases demand density. If output per store is fixed, each store needs a smaller market area to exhaust its scale economies. For example, a quadrupling of population density quadruples total demand for CDs, so it quadruples the number of stores. If there are four times as many stores in the region, the market area per store decreases to one fourth its original size (from 5 square miles to 1.25 square miles).

Market Areas and the Law of Demand

Up to this point, the discussion of the market area has assumed that per capita demand is fixed. In other words, the individual demand curve is perfectly inelastic. What happens if consumers obey the law of demand, increasing the quantity of CDs demanded as the net price decreases?

Decrease in Travel Costs.   If consumers obey the law of demand, a decrease in travel costs has an ambiguous effect on the size of the market area. As explained earlier in the chapter, a decrease in travel costs increases output per store, which tends to increase market areas. This is the **output effect** of a decrease in travel cost. The decrease in travel cost also decreases the net price of CDs (the sum of the store price and travel cost). If consumers obey the law of demand, per capita demand will increase, so each firm will need a smaller territory to exploit its scale economies. This is the **demand effect** of a decrease in travel costs.

The net effect of a decrease in travel cost depends on the relative strengths of the output effect and the demand effect. The expression for the size of the market area is

$$M = \frac{q}{d \cdot e} \qquad (4\text{--}5)$$

Suppose that the output effect increases q from 1,000 to 1,250 and that population density (e) is 50. If the demand effect is relatively weak and d increases from four to five, the market area will grow from five square miles (1,000/200) to six square miles (1,250/250). Alternatively, if the demand effect is relatively strong and d increases from 4 to 10, the market area will shrink from 5 square miles to 2.5 square miles (1,250/500). The strength of the demand effect depends on the price elasticity of demand for CDs: the more elastic the demand for CDs, the stronger the demand effect. Therefore, a decrease in travel cost is more likely to decrease the market area if the price elasticity is large.

For an example of the effects of changes in travel costs on market areas, consider the effects of parcel post on farm communities. Before the introduction of parcel post in 1913, most farmers purchased most of their goods, including clothing and tools, in general stores in small farm communities. The introduction of parcel post decreased the cost of shipping goods from big-city merchants to farmers. Mail-order houses such as Sears, Roebuck, and Montgomery Ward underpriced the local general store, and farmers started buying clothing and tools from the mail-order houses. In the year following the introduction of parcel post, the sales of Sears and Montgomery Ward quintupled, and many general stores disappeared.

The introduction of parcel post decreased the cost of transporting clothes and tools, increasing the market area of the typical firm. The general store, with its small market area, was replaced by Sears and Montgomery Ward, with their large market areas. In this case, the output effect was stronger than the demand effect, so the market area grew. Although farmers consumed more trousers and shovels as the net prices fell, the increases in per capita demands were not large enough to offset the output effect.

Market Area and Scale Economies.   If consumers obey the law of demand, an increase in scale economies has an ambiguous effect on the size of the market area. As explained earlier in the chapter, an increase in scale economies increases the output per store, increasing the market area required to exhaust scale economies (the output effect). If the net price falls as a result of the increased scale economies, the per capita demand for CDs will increase, generating a demand effect that provides downward pressure on the market area: the firm needs a smaller territory to sell a given output. The net effect of an increase in scale economies depends on the relative strengths of the output effect and the demand effect. If the demand for the good is relatively inelastic, an increase in scale economies will increase the market area.

Market Areas of Different Industries

Market areas vary from industry to industry, reflecting differences in travel costs, per capita demand, and scale economies. If scale economies are large *relative* to per capita demand, the industry will have a small number of firms, each of which has a large market area. In contrast, if scale economies are small relative to per capita demand, there will be a large number of firms with small market areas.

Consider the market areas of pizza parlors and Tibetan restaurants. Suppose that both activities are subject to the same sort of scale economies, so the optimum output for both types of restaurants is 200 meals per day. If the total demand for pizza is 10,000 meals per day, the region will have 50 pizza parlors (10,000/200). If the total demand for Tibetan food is 200 meals per day, a single Tibetan restaurant will serve the entire region. The market area is not determined by scale economies per se, but by scale economies *relative* to per capita demand.

Central Place Theory

Central place theory, which was developed by Christaller (translated in 1966) and refined by Losch (translated in 1954), is used to predict the number, size, and scope of cities in a region. The theory is based on a simple extension of market-area analysis. Market areas vary from industry to industry, depending on scale economies and per capita demand, so every industry has a different location pattern. Central place theory shows how the location patterns of different industries are merged to form a regional system of cities. The theory answers two questions about cities in a regional economy:

1. How many cities will develop?
2. Why are some cities larger than others?

A Simple Central-Place Model

Consider a region with three consumer products: CDs, pizzas, and jewelry. The region has the following characteristics:

1. **Population density.** The initial distribution of population is uniform. The total population of the region is 80,000.
2. **Perfect substitutes.** For each product, the good provided by one store is a perfect substitute for the good provided by another store. There is no comparison shopping.

3. **Single-purpose shopping trips.** Each consumer purchases a single good on each shopping trip.

4. **Ubiquitous inputs.** All inputs are available at all locations at the same prices.

5. **Uniform demand.** For each product, per capita demand is the same throughout the region.

6. **Number of stores.** The three goods have different per capita demands and scale economies:

   a. **Jewelry:** Scale economies are large relative to per capita demand. Every jewelry store requires a population of 80,000, so a single jeweler will serve the entire region.

   b. **CDs:** Scale economies are moderate relative to per capita demand. Every music store requires a population of 20,000, so there will be four music stores in the region.

   c. **Pizza:** Scale economies are small relative to per capita demand. Every pizza parlor requires a population of 5,000, so there will be 16 pizza parlors in the region.

The central place model is a model of **market-oriented firms**, defined in Chapter 3 as firms that base their location decisions exclusively on access to their consumers. Because all inputs are ubiquitous, the firms ignore input costs in their location decisions.

The single jeweler will locate at the center of the region. Because production costs are the same at all locations (all inputs are ubiquitous), the jeweler will minimize its total costs by minimizing its travel costs. According to the principle of median location (discussed in Chapter 3), travel costs are minimized at the median location. Because population density is uniform, the median location is the center of the region. Therefore, the jeweler will locate at the center of the region.

A city will develop around the jewelry store. Jewelry workers will locate near the store to economize on commuting costs. The population density near the jeweler will increase, generating a city (a place of relatively high density) at the center of the region. In Figure 4–3, a city develops at point *L*.

The music stores will carve up the region into market areas, causing the development of additional cities. If the region's population density were uniform, music firms would carve out four equal market areas. However, because there is a city surrounding the jeweler in the center of the region, there will be enough demand to support more than one music store in city *L*. If city *L* has enough people to support two music stores, the two other music stores will split the rest of the region into two market areas. In Figure 4–3, two more cities develop at the locations marked with an *M*.

The pizza parlors will also carve up the region into market areas, causing the development of more cities. Because the population density is higher in the cities that develop around the jewelry store and the music stores, there will be more

FIGURE 4–3   The Central Place Hierarchy

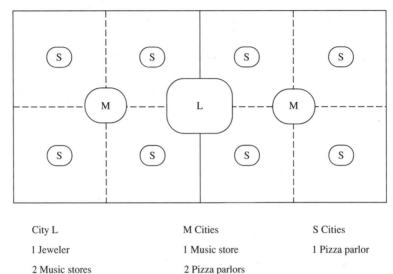

City L	M Cities	S Cities
1 Jeweler	1 Music store	1 Pizza parlor
2 Music stores	2 Pizza parlors	
4 Pizza parlors		

There are 11 cities in the region: 1 large city (*L*), 2 medium-sized cites (*M*), and 8 small cities (*S*). The larger the city, the greater the variety of goods sold.

than one pizza parlor in *L* and in the two *M* cities. Suppose that *L* will support four pizza parlors, and each of the *M* cities will support two pizza parlors. If so, a total of eight pizza parlors will locate in cities *L* and *M*. The remaining eight pizza parlors will divide the rest of the region into eight market areas, causing the development of eight additional cities (the places marked with an *S* in Figure 4–3).

The rectangular region has a total of 11 cities. The large city (*L*) at the center of the region sells jewelry, CDs, and pizza. City *L* has a population of 20,000, meaning that it is large enough to support four pizza parlors (5,000 people per pizza parlor). City *L* sells CDs to consumers from the four surrounding *S* cities, so the total number of CD consumers is 40,000 (20,000 from *L* and 5,000 each from four *S* cities), enough to support two music stores. The two medium-sized cities (*M*) sell CDs and pizza. Each of the *M* cities has a population of 10,000, meaning that each city is large enough to support two pizza parlors. Each city sells CDs to consumers from two nearby *S* cities, so the total number of CD consumers in each *M* city is 20,000 (10,000 from *M* and 5,000 each from two *S* cities), enough to support one music store per *M* city. The eight small cities (*S*) sell only pizza. Each of the *S* cities has a population of 5,000, meaning that each city can each support one pizza parlor.

Figure 4–4 shows the size distribution of cities in the region. The vertical axis measures city size (population), and the horizontal axis measures the rank of the city. The largest city (*L*) has a population of 20,000; the 2nd and 3rd largest

FIGURE 4–4   Size Distribution of Cities with a Simple Central Place Model

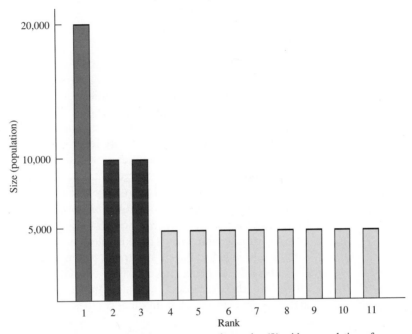

The simple central place model generates one large city (*L*) with a population of 20,000, two medium-sized cities (*M*) each of which has a population of 10,000, and eight small cities (*S*), each of which has a population of 5,000.

cities (*M* cities) have populations of 10,000; and the 4th through the 11th largest cities have populations of 5,000.

The simple central place model generates a **hierarchical system of cities**. There are three distinct types of cities: *L* (high order), *M* (medium order), and *S* (low order). The larger the city, the greater the variety of goods sold. Each city imports goods from higher-order cities and exports goods to lower-order cities. Cities of the same order do not interact. For example, an *M* city imports jewelry from *L* and exports CDs to *S* cities, but does not interact with the other *M* city. Similarly, an *S* city imports jewelry from *L* and CDs from either *L* or an *M* city, but does not trade with other *S* cities. The system of cities is hierarchical in the sense that there are distinct types of cities and distinct patterns of trade dominance.

Three lessons can be learned from the simple central place model:

1. **Diversity and scale economies.** The region's cities differ in size and scope. This diversity occurs because the three consumer products have different scale economies relative to per capita demand, so they have different market areas. To explain the importance of differences in relative scale economies, suppose that the three goods have the same scale

economies relative to per capita demand, so the region has 16 jewelers, 16 music stores, and 16 pizza parlors. The market areas of the three goods would coincide, so the region would have 16 identical cities, each of which provides all three goods. In other words, if there are no differences in scale economies relative to per capita demand, the region's cities will be identical.

2. **Large means few.** The region has a small number of large cities and a large number of small cities. Why isn't there a large number of large cities and a small number of small cities? A city is relatively large if it provides more goods than a smaller city. The extra goods provided by a large city are those goods that are subject to relatively large scale economies. Since there are relatively few stores selling the goods subject to relatively large scale economies, few cities can be large. In the simple central place model, L is larger than an M city because L sells CDs, pizza, *and* jewelry. Since there is only one jewelry store in the region, there is only one city larger than the M cities.

3. **Shopping paths.** Consumers travel to bigger cities, not to smaller cities or cities of the same size. For example, consumers from an M city travel to L to buy jewelry, but do not travel to the other M city or an S city to consume CDs or pizza. Instead, they buy CDs and pizza in their own city. Similarly, consumers in S cities travel to larger cities for jewelry and CDs, but do not shop in other S cities.

Relaxing the Assumptions

Several of the assumptions of the simple central place model are unrealistic. This section relaxes some of the assumptions, addressing two questions. First, does a more realistic model generate the same hierarchical pattern of cities? Second, does a more realistic model have more or fewer cities?

Shopping Externalities: Imperfect Substitutes.   Suppose that consumers buy used records instead of new CDs. Used records are imperfect substitutes: consumers engage in comparison shopping, comparing the used records from several stores before buying. Therefore, music stores will cluster to facilitate comparison shopping. If the optimum cluster is four music stores, the stores will cluster at the center of the region. The region will have only two types of cities, large ones (with jewelers, music stores, and pizza parlors) and small ones (with pizza parlors). The presence of imperfect substitutes reduces the equilibrium number of cities from 11 to 9 because music stores compromise on their "ideal" (central place) locations to exploit the shopping externalities. Although comparison shopping decreases the number of cities, it does not disrupt the hierarchical pattern of cities.

Shopping Externalities: Complements.   Suppose that pizza and CDs are complementary goods, so that the typical consumer purchases a CD and a pizza on the same shopping trip. If so, music stores and pizza parlors will pair up to facilitate one-stop shopping. If pizza parlors cannot survive without a companion music store, there will be only two types of cities in the region: large (with jewelry, CDs, and pizza) and medium (with CDs and pizza). Pizza parlors compromise on their ideal (central place) locations to exploit the shopping externalities associated with one-stop shopping, so the equilibrium number of cities decreases from 11 to 3. The presence of complementary goods does not, however, disrupt the urban hierarchy.

Other Types of Industry

Central place theory is applicable to market-oriented firms. The objective of a market-oriented firm is to minimize the travel costs of its consumers. The market-oriented firm is not concerned about (1) the cost of transporting its inputs or (2) the costs of local inputs. Central place theory predicts the pattern of cities that would result if all firms were market-oriented.

As explained in Chapter 3, there are two other types of firms, resource-oriented firms and input-oriented firms. For the resource-oriented firm (e.g., the producer of baseball bats), the cost of transporting raw materials is relatively high, so the firm locates near its input sources. For the input-oriented firm, the costs of local inputs vary across space, and the firm locates near sources of inexpensive labor, energy, or intermediate goods.

The location decisions of resource-oriented firms may disrupt the central place hierarchy. Suppose that a bat factory is located near the coastal forests of the region. Once the coastal city is established, it may attract some market-oriented firms (e.g., pizza parlors). In addition to the three types of cities described above—large (*L*), medium (*M*), and small (*S*)—there will be a coastal city, with a bat factory and pizza parlors. The urban hierarchy is disrupted because the coastal city has one activity (bat production) not available in the largest city.

It is possible that the bat factory will not disrupt the region's urban hierarchy. Suppose that the coastal city becomes large enough to become the median location for the jeweler. If so, the coastal city will have all four types of activities (jewelry, bats, CDs, and pizza). The medium-sized cities will have two activities (pizza and CDs), and the small cities will have only one activity (pizzas). In this case, the hierarchy is preserved because the coastal city takes the place of city *L*.

The same arguments apply to input-oriented activities such as textile firms (labor-oriented), aluminum producers (energy-oriented), corporate headquarters (oriented to intermediate inputs), and firms engaging in research and development (oriented to amenities valued by engineers and scientists). If the input-oriented firm locates near its input source, the resulting city will have some goods that are not available in the largest city. If, however, the resulting city becomes the median location in the region, it may replace city *L* as the largest city in the region.

Central Place Theory and the Real World

While central place theory is not literally true for many regions, it provides a useful way of thinking about a regional system of cities. The theory identifies the market forces that generate a hierarchical system of cities. It explains why some cities are larger than others and why the set of goods sold in a particular city is typically a subset of the goods sold in a larger city. Exceptions to the hierarchical pattern result from (1) systematic variation in per capita demand and (2) the location decisions of firms oriented toward raw materials and local inputs.

Empirical Studies of Central Place Systems.   Table 4–3 shows the results of an empirical study of central place theory. Berry and Garrison (1958) examined the economic activities of urban places in Snohomish County, Washington. They concluded that the dozens of communities could be divided into three distinct types of urban places: town (high order), village (medium order), and hamlet (low order). The largest urban place, a town, was about twice as large as a village, which was in turn about twice as large as a hamlet. There were about half as many towns as villages, and about half as many villages as hamlets. As one moves down the hierarchy, the number of establishments and the number of functions decrease, which is exactly what is predicted by central place theory. Berry and Garrison concluded that the system of urban places was indeed hierarchical, with individual communities exporting to lower-order places and importing from higher-order places.

Most of the empirical studies of central place theory examine systems of small towns in agricultural regions. Such regions have little industrial activity, so most firms are oriented toward the local market, not toward natural resources or local inputs. What about the national economy? As explained earlier, the central place hierarchy is disrupted by the location choices of resource-oriented firms and input-oriented firms. Since a large fraction of national employment comes from resource-oriented and input-oriented activities, it would be quite surprising if a study of the national economy provided much support for the simple central place model.

Size Distribution of Cities: The Rank-Size Rule.   Figure 4–5a shows the size distribution of the 25 largest urbanized areas in the United States in 1990. Population decreases from about 16 million in the largest urbanized area (New York) to 1.32 million in the 25th largest (Norfolk, Virginia). Figure 4–5b shows

TABLE 4–3   **The Urban Hierarchy in Snohomish County, Washington**

	Type of Place		
	Town	*Village*	*Hamlet*
Number of places	4	9	20
Average population	2,433	948	417
Average number of establishments per place	149	54.4	6.9
Average number of functions per place	59.8	32.1	5.9
Average number of establishments per function	2.5	1.7	1.2

Source: Brian J. L. Berry and William Garrison, "The Functional Bases of the Central Place Hierarchy," *Economic Geography* 34 (April 1958), pp. 145–54.

FIGURE 4–5a   Size Distribution of 25 Largest U.S. Urbanized Areas

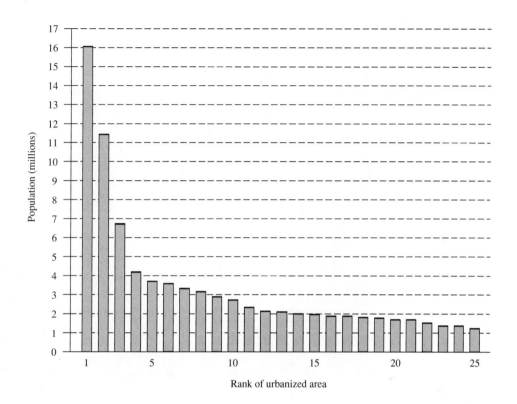

Rank of urbanized area

the size distribution for the 26th through the 396th largest urbanized areas. Note that the vertical scale is different from the scale in Figure 4–5a. Population decreases from 1.27 million in the 26th largest metropolitan area (Kansas City) to 50,066 in the smallest urbanized area (Brunswick, Georgia).

How does the U.S. size distribution of cities compare to the size distribution generated by the simple model of central place theory? To compare the two size distributions, compare Figure 4–4 to Figure 4–5. Both figures show a small number of large cities and a large number of small cities. In addition, as one moves down in the ranking (to smaller cities), the size difference between two successive cities decreases.

Geographers and economists have estimated the relationship between city size and rank. The relationship is approximated by the **rank-size rule:**

$$\text{Rank} \cdot \text{size} = \text{Constant} \qquad (4\text{--}6)$$

This rule suggests that the product of rank and size is the same in all cities in a region. For example, if the largest metropolitan area has a population of 16 million, the rank-size rule suggests that the 2nd largest city has a population of

FIGURE 4–5b   **Size Distribution of 26th through 396th Largest U.S. Urbanized Areas**

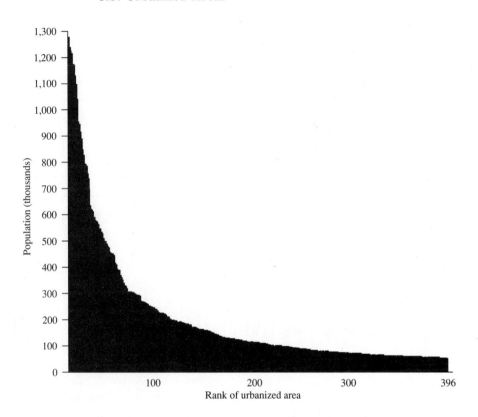

8 million, the 3rd largest city has a population of 5.33 million, and the 16th largest city has a population of 1 million.

Empirical evidence concerning the rank-size rule comes from statistical studies of the distribution of city sizes. Rosen and Resnick (1980) estimate the rank-size relationship for 44 countries. The evidence supports the rank-size rule for U.S. cities, but does not support the rule for cities in other countries. In most countries, population is more evenly distributed than would be predicted by the rank-size rule. Rosen and Resnick conclude that the rank-size rule is only a first approximation to the relationship between rank and size.

Summary

1. The net price of a retail product is the sum of its price and consumers' travel cost. The market area is the area over which the firm offers the lowest net price.

2. The size of a firm's market area depends on output per firm, per capita demand, and population density. The market area increases as
   a. Output per firm increases.
   b. Per capita demand decreases.
   c. Population density decreases.

3. Because an increase in scale economies increases output per firm (the output effect) and per capita demand (demand effect), it has an ambiguous effect on market area.

4. A decrease in transportation costs increases output per firm and per capita demand. The market area will grow if the price elasticity of demand is relatively small.

5. Central place theory, which is based on market-area analysis, predicts that the regional system of cities will be hierarchical, with a small number of large cities and a large number of small cities. The set of goods sold in smaller cities will be a subset of the goods sold in larger cities.

6. If the assumptions of the simple central place theory are relaxed to allow imperfect substitutes (comparison shopping) and complements (one-stop shopping), the equilibrium number of cities may decrease, but the urban hierarchy will not be disrupted.

7. If the assumptions of the simple central place theory are relaxed to allow variation in per capita demand, the equilibrium number of cities may change and the urban hierarchy may be disrupted.

8. Central place theory is not applicable to resource-oriented firms and firms oriented toward local inputs. The introduction of such firms into the central place model may disrupt the urban hierarchy.

9. The rank-size rule suggests that the product of rank and size is constant. It is an accurate predictor of city sizes in the United States, but does not perform so well elsewhere.

Exercises and Discussion Questions

1. The discussion of the market area of music stores assumed that Bob, Tammy, and Dick had the same production costs. As a result, each household patronized the store nearest its home. Suppose that Bob discovers a new way of marketing CDs that cuts his production costs (and store price) in half, from $6 to $3. Tammy and Dick continue to sell CDs for $6.
   a. How does the decrease in production cost affect Bob's market area?
   b. What is the net price at the border between Bob's and Tammy's market area?
   c. Will each household still patronize the firm closest to its residence?

2. Consider the market area of food stores in a region described by the following assumptions:

       i. The per capita demand for food is 30 units.

       ii. Population density is 40 people per square mile.

       iii. The land area of the region is 100 square miles.

       iv. The output of the typical food store is 6,000 units.

    a. How many food stores will there be in the region?

    b. How large is the market area of the typical food store?

3. Suppose that you intend to purchase the franchise rights for a pizza parlor. The franchiser has divided your region into two areas of equal size: *H* is a high-income area, and *L* is a low-income area. Suppose that the income elasticity of demand for pizza is zero; that is, the consumption of pizza is independent of income. The income elasticity of demand for land is 1.0. Your objective is to maximize the quantity of pizzas sold.

    a. Which of the two franchises will you choose?

    b. How would your response to (*a*) change if the income elasticity of demand for pizza is 1.5?

4. In 1930, most rural children walked to school. By 1980, most of them rode school buses. Would you expect the average "market area" of rural schools to increase or decrease as a result of the school bus?

5. The introduction of parcel post decreased transportation costs and increased the market area of the typical firm. Can you think of any good for which a decrease in transportation costs is likely to decrease the market area?

6. Consider a city with a uniform distribution of population where every household consumes the same number of video rentals. The city is two miles long and two miles wide. The mayor recently stated her policy for the location of video rental outlets: "Our four video outlets should be distributed uniformly throughout the city, with every outlet at the center of a one-square-mile market area." Comment on the mayor's policy. Will it lead to an efficient distribution of video outlets?

7. Explain why poor areas of cities typically are served by small grocery stores, not by large grocery-store chains.

8. Mr. Wizard, a regional planner, recently made the following statement: "If my assumptions are correct, all cities in this region will eventually be identical. They will be the same size and will sell the same set of goods."

    a. Assuming that Mr. Wizard's reasoning is correct, what are his assumptions?

    b. Are Mr. Wizard's assumptions realistic?

9. Some people claim that state capitals (e.g., Sacramento, California; Salem, Oregon; Olympia, Washington) are boring cities. Specifically, it is claimed that these cities have fewer goods than one finds in other cities of equal size. After checking a map to see where each of these capital cities is located, use central place theory to explain why they might be considered boring.

References and Additional Readings

Berry, Brian J. L. *Geography of Market Centers and Retail Distribution*. Englewood Cliffs, N.J.: Prentice Hall, 1967. Discusses central place theory, including a review of empirical tests of the theory.

Berry, Brian J. L., and William L. Garrison. "The Functional Bases of the Central Place Hierarchy." *Economic Geography* 34 (April 1958), pp. 145–54. An empirical analysis of central place theory.

Christaller, Walter. *Central Places in Southern Germany,* trans. C. W. Baskin. Englewood Cliffs, N.J.: Prentice Hall, 1966. The classic on central place theory.

Hoover, Edgar M. "Transport Costs and the Spacing of Central Places." *Papers of the Regional Science Association* 25 (1970), pp. 255–74. Discusses the effects of changes in transport costs on the size of the market area.

Losch, August. *The Economics of Location*. New Haven, Conn.: Yale University Press, translated in 1954. A refinement of central place theory.

Noyelle, Thierry, and Thomas Stanback. *The Economic Transformation of American Cities*. Totawa, N.J.: Rowman and Allalheld, 1984. Discusses exceptions to the central place framework.

Proudfoot, M. J. "The Outlying Business Centers of Chicago." *Journal of Land and Public Utility Economics* 13 (1937), pp. 57–70. Applies central place theory to the location of activities within cities.

Rosen, Kenneth T., and Mitchell Resnick. "The Size Distribution of Cities: An Examination of the Pareto Law and Primacy." *Journal of Urban Economics* 8 (1980), pp. 165–86. Estimates the rank-size relationship and concludes that the rank-size rule is a poor approximation to the true size distribution.

CHAPTER

5 Urban Economic Growth

Earlier chapters have shown why cities exist and where they develop. This chapter takes a closer look at the economy of a particular city, exploring the market forces that determine the size of the economy. The first part of the chapter uses a simple model of the urban labor market to describe the economic growth process. If **economic growth** is defined as an increase in total employment, growth results from an increase in the demand for labor (caused by an increase in the demand for the goods produced in the city) or an increase in labor supply (caused by migration to the city).

The second part of the chapter explores the effects of various public policies on urban economic growth. The public sector can influence both sides of the urban labor market. For example, the provision of local public services such as schools, parks, and public safety increases the relative attractiveness of the city, causing in-migration that increases the supply of labor. On the demand side, the provision of industrial infrastructure such as roads and sewer systems decreases production costs and attracts firms. A city's tax policy also affects the supply and demand for labor: an increase in residential taxes decreases labor supply, and an increase in business taxes decreases labor demand.

The third part of the chapter describes two techniques used to forecast urban economic growth. Both forecasting techniques (the economic base study and input-output analysis) suffer from a number of conceptual problems that limit their applicability and accuracy. Nonetheless, they are the most frequently used—and abused—forecasting techniques, and a clear understanding of their strengths and limitations is useful for both policymakers and firms. Local governments use these techniques to generate economic forecasts that are then used to project the demands for local public services, and firms use the same type of economic forecasts to project the demands for their products.

The fourth part of the chapter explores the effects of employment growth on other measures of economic welfare, including the city's unemployment rate, its labor-force participation rate, and per capita income. This part of the chapter addresses two questions. First, when a city grows, what fraction of the new jobs is filled by newcomers, and what fraction is filled by original residents who would otherwise not be employed? Second, how does employment growth affect real income per capita?

The fifth part of the chapter presents some facts on the composition of changes in total employment. The net change in total employment in a particular city can be divided into four components: jobs gained from the opening of new plants, jobs gained from the expansion of existing plants, jobs lost from plant closings, and jobs lost from the contraction of existing plants. This part of the chapter addresses the following question: Do cities that grow rapidly have relatively large employment gains (from openings and expansions) or relatively small losses (from closures and contractions)?

The Urban Labor Market and Economic Growth

This part of the chapter describes a model of the urban labor market for a city that is part of a larger regional economy. The model is a long-run model in the sense that it assumes that households and firms can move freely between cities in the region. In the long run, each household lives in the city that maximizes its utility, and each firm locates in the city that maximizes its economic profit. As explained later in the chapter, the long-run mobility of households has important implications for the effects of employment growth on the welfare of the original residents of the city.

Suppose that the size of an urban economy is defined in terms of total employment. Figure 5–1 shows the supply and demand curves for the city's labor market. The equilibrium wage is $1,000 per month, and equilibrium employment is 50,000 laborers. Economic growth, defined here as an increase in total employment, results from either an increase in demand (a rightward shift of the demand curve) or an increase in supply (a rightward shift of the supply curve).

The Demand for Labor

Labor demand comes from two types of activities. The **export,** or **basic, sector** sells its products to consumers outside the city. Examples of export firms are steel producers and computer manufacturers. In contrast, the **local,** or **nonbasic, sector** sells its products to consumers within the city. Examples of local producers are bakeries, bookstores, and local schools. Before discussing the city's labor-demand curve, it will be useful to explain the relationship between these two employment sectors.

The Multiplier Process.   Because export workers spend part of their income on local goods, an increase in export sales increases local sales. Table 5–1 shows

FIGURE 5-1   The Urban Labor Market

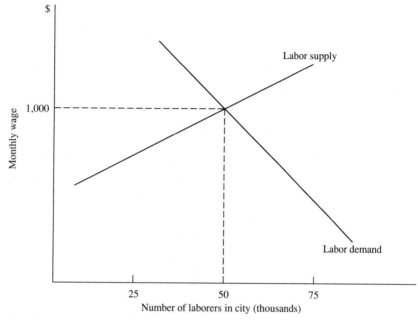

The labor market is in equilibrium if supply equals demand. The equilibrium wage is $1,000 per month, and the equilibrium number of laborers is 50,000.

TABLE 5-1   Increases in Local Spending from Increased Export Sales

Increase in	Round 1	Round 2	Round 3		Total
Local income	$100,000	$60,000	$36,000	$\cdots$	$250,000
Local consumption	60,000	36,000	21,600	$\cdots$	150,000
Imports	40,000	24,000	14,400	$\cdots$	100,000

the **multiplier effects** of a $100,000 increase in export sales. In Round 1, the increase in export sales is paid out to workers, capitalists, and landowners in the form of wages, interest, and land rent, so local income increases by $100,000. If 60 percent of the increased income is spent on local goods, local consumption increases by $60,000. The first-round increase in local consumption is the second-round increase in local income: local producers pay the $60,000 to their workers, capitalists, and landowners, who in turn spend 60 percent of the increased income on local goods. In other words, the second-round increase in local consumption is $36,000. The spending and respending of income continues forever, but every spending round is smaller than the previous one because 40 percent of income is spent on imports.

The increase in the city's total income exceeds the original increase in export income. The marginal propensity to consume locally (m) is the fraction of income spent locally (0.60 in Table 5–1). If the original change in export sales is ΔX, the increase in total income is the sum of the income changes from a series of spending rounds:

$$\Delta \text{Total income} = \Delta X + m \cdot \Delta X + m^2 \cdot \Delta X + m^3 \cdot \Delta X + m^4 \cdot \Delta X + \ldots \quad (5\text{--}1)$$

The change in total income is the sum of an infinite series, and can be rewritten as

$$\Delta \text{Total income} = \Delta X \cdot \frac{1}{1 - m} \quad (5\text{--}2)$$

The **income multiplier** is defined as the change in total income per unit change in export sales:

$$\frac{\Delta \text{Total income}}{\Delta X} = \frac{1}{1 - m} \quad (5\text{--}3)$$

For example, if the marginal propensity to consume locally (m) is 0.60, the multiplier is

$$\frac{\Delta \text{Total income}}{\Delta X} = \frac{1}{1 - 0.60} = 2.5 \quad (5\text{--}4)$$

For every additional dollar of export sales, total income increases by 2.5 dollars. In Table 5–1, export sales increase by $100,000, so local production increases by $150,000 and total income increases by $250,000.

The multiplier process also affects employment. The **employment multiplier** is the change in total employment per unit change in export employment. If there is one job per $1,000 of sales, an increase of $100,000 in export sales will increase export employment by 100 jobs. Similarly, the additional $150,000 in local sales will increase local employment by 150 jobs. Total employment in the city will increase by 250, meaning that the employment multiplier is 2.5.

The employment multiplier is the same as the income multiplier because the sales volume is assumed to be the same in both sectors. If sales volume per local jobs is less than sales volume per export jobs, the employment multiplier exceeds the income multiplier, because more local jobs will be supported by a given amount of sales. For example, if sales volume per local jobs is $500 instead of $1,000, local employment would increase by 300 instead of 150 and the employment multiplier would be 4.0 instead of 2.5. Conversely, if sales volume per local job exceeds $1,000, the employment multiplier would be less than the income multiplier.

A second method for computing the employment multiplier uses data on the composition of the work force. If B is the number of jobs in export industries and L is the number of jobs in local industries, total employment in the city is $B + L$, or T. The ratio (L/B) indicates how many local jobs are "supported" by each export job. For example, if $B = 20,000$ and $L = 30,000$, an economic "base" of 20,000 jobs supports 30,000 local jobs: each export job supports 1.5

local jobs. The employment multiplier, defined as the change in total employment per additional export job, is

$$\frac{\Delta T}{\Delta B} = \frac{T}{B} = 2.5 \tag{5-5}$$

Every additional export job increases total employment by 2.5 jobs: in addition to the export job, there are 1.5 new "support" jobs in local industry.

The Labor-Demand Curve.   The city's labor-demand curve is negatively sloped for two reasons. First, as the city's wage increases, both exporters and local producers substitute capital for the relatively expensive labor. This is the **substitution effect:** an increase in the wage causes factor substitution that decreases the quantity of labor demanded. In other words, an increase in the wage causes firms to substitute nonlabor inputs (capital, land, raw materials) for labor. Second, as the city's wage increases, production costs increase, increasing the prices charged by the city's firms. As the prices of exports increase, the quantity of exports demanded decreases, so exporters need fewer workers. As the price of local goods increase, city residents substitute imports for the relatively expensive local goods, so local firms need fewer laborers. This is the **output effect:** an increase in the city's wage increases prices and decreases output, decreasing the quantity of labor demanded. The demand curve is negatively sloped because an increase in the wage generates both a substitution effect and an output effect.

What causes the demand curve to shift to the right or the left? The following factors determine the position of the curve:

1. **Demand for exports.** An increase in the demand for the city's exports increases export production and shifts the demand curve to the right: at every wage, more workers will be demanded.

2. **Labor productivity.** An increase in labor productivity decreases production costs, allowing export firms to cut prices and increase output. Although firms need fewer workers to produce a given amount of output, the decrease in price means that firms produce more output. If the increase in output is relatively large (if the price elasticity of demand for the city's output is relatively large), the demand for export workers increases: the demand curve shifts to the right. Similarly, an increase in labor productivity allows local producers to underprice imports, increasing the demand for local workers. One way to increase productivity is to improve the quality of local public education.

3. **Business taxes.** An increase in business taxes (without a corresponding change in public services) increases production costs and decreases output, so the demand curve shifts to the left. The demand for labor decreases as export firms lose customers to exporters in other cities and local firms lose customers to importers. As discussed in Chapter 3, there is evidence that an increase in business taxes decreases business activity and thus decreases the demand for labor.

4. **Industrial public services.** An increase in the quality of industrial public services (without a corresponding increase in taxes) decreases production costs and increases output, so the demand curve shifts to the right. The demand for labor increases as export firms gain customers from exporters in other cities and local firms gain customers from importers. As discussed in Chapter 3, there is evidence that improvements in local infrastructure increase business activity and thus increases the demand for labor.

5. **Land-use policies.** Industrial firms require production sites that (*a*) are accessible to the intracity and intercity transportation networks and (*b*) have a full set of public services (water, sewage, electricity). By coordinating its land-use and infrastructure policies to ensure an adequate supply of industrial land, a city can accommodate (*a*) existing firms that want to expand their operations and (*b*) new firms that want to locate in the city.

Figure 5–2 shows the multiplier effect of an increase in export sales. Suppose that an increase in the demand for exports increases the demand for export workers by 10,000. The city's demand curve will shift to the right from D_1 to D_2: at a wage of $1,000 per month, an additional 10,000 export workers will be demanded. This is the **direct effect** of an increase in export demand. If the employment multiplier

FIGURE 5–2   Direct and Multiplier Effects of an Increase in Export Employment

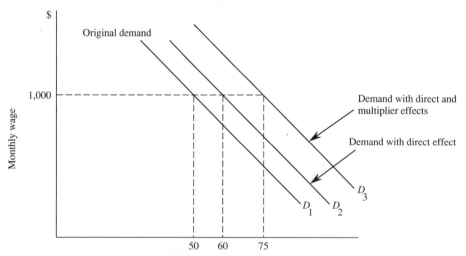

If export employment increases by 10,000 jobs, the demand curve shifts to the right in two steps. The shift from D_1 to D_2 is the direct effect of the increase in export employment: at a fixed wage, total employment rises from 50,000 to 60,000. The shift from D_2 to D_3 reflects the multiplier effect of the increase in export employment. If the employment multiplier is 2.5, local employment increases by 1.5 times the increase in export employment, increasing labor demand by an additional 15,000 jobs.

is 2.5, every export job supports 1.5 local jobs, so the demand curve shifts to the right by an additional 15,000 workers (from D_2 to D_3). This is the multiplier effect of an increase in export demand. Total labor demand increases by 25,000 (2.5 times the increase in the demand for export laborers).

The Supply Curve

Consider next the supply side of the urban labor market. The supply curve is positively sloped because of the **migration effect:** an increase in the wage increases the relative attractiveness of the city, causing the migration of workers from other cities in the region. One of the assumptions underlying the supply curve is that the number of work hours per laborer is fixed; changes in the wage do not affect the number of work hours per laborer. This assumption is consistent with empirical evidence concerning the elasticity of work hours with respect to the wage: in aggregate, this elasticity is close to zero. Another assumption underlying the supply curve is that the labor-force participation rate is unaffected by changes in the wage. In other words, an increase in the wage does not increase the fraction of the city's population in the work force. Given these two assumptions, an increase in the wage increases the supply of labor because more workers move to the city, not because existing workers work more hours or because more of the city's current residents join the work force.

Why is the supply curve positively sloped, and what determines the slope of the curve? An increase in total employment (and population) increases the total demand for most goods, causing increases in the prices of land, housing, and other goods. A growing city must offer a higher wage to compensate its workers for its higher cost of living. The results of Hamilton and Schwab (1985) and Bartik (1991) suggest that the elasticity of housing prices with respect to total employment is about 0.35: a 10 percent increase in total employment increases housing prices by about 3.5 percent. According to Bartik (1991), the elasticity of the cost of living with respect to city size (including all price changes) is about 0.20: a 10 percent increase in total employment increases the cost of living by about 2 percent. This means that to keep real wages constant, the city's nominal wage must rise by about 2 percent for every 10 percent increase in employment.

A number of empirical studies have estimated the responsiveness of wages to total employment. The results of Treyz and Stevens (1985), Robak (1982), and Bartik (1991) suggest that the wage for a given occupation increases at about the same rate as the cost of living. In other words, the elasticity of the nominal wage with respect to total employment is about 0.20: a 10 percent increase in total employment increases the wage by 2 percent. Alternatively, the elasticity of labor supply with respect to the wage is about 5.0: a 2 percent increase in the wage causes a 10 percent increase in labor supply. It's important to note that this is the labor-supply elasticity for an individual city. The elasticity is relatively large because workers migrate to cities that offer relatively high wages. The national supply elasticity is much lower than the local supply elasticity because there is less migration between nations than between cities.

What causes the supply curve to shift to the right or the left? The position of the supply curve is determined by the following factors:

1. **Environmental quality.**An increase in the quality of the environment (better air or water quality) increases the relative attractiveness of the city, causing migration to the city. The supply curve shifts to the right: at every wage, more workers are willing to work in the city.

2. **Residential taxes.** An increase in residential taxes (without a corresponding change in public services) decreases the relative attractiveness of the city, causing out-migration that shifts the supply curve to the left.

3. **Residential public services.** An increase in the quality of residential public services (without a corresponding increase in taxes) increases the relative attractiveness of the city, causing in-migration that shifts the supply curve to the right. The results of Eberts and Stone (1992) suggest that labor supply is responsive to changes in local infrastructure.

Equilibrium Effects of Demand and Supply Shifts

Figure 5–3 shows the effects of an increase in export sales on the urban labor market. The labor-demand curve shifts to the right by 25,000 workers, reflecting

---

FIGURE 5-3   Equilibrium Effects of an Increase in Export Employment

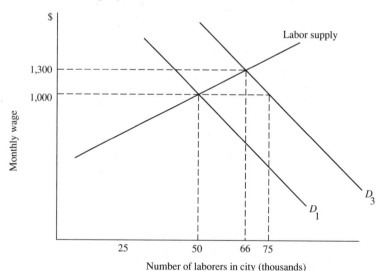

An increase in export shifts the demand curve to the right by 25,000. As the city grows, the prices of housing and land increase, requiring a higher wage to compensate workers for the higher cost of living. The equilibrium wage increases from $1,000 to $1,300, and the equilibrium number of laborers increases by only 16,000.

both the direct effect and the multiplier effect of an increase in 10,000 export jobs. As the population of the city increases, the prices of housing and land increase, requiring an increase in the wage to compensate workers for the higher cost of living. In other words, the city moves up its supply curve. The equilibrium wage rises from $1,000 per month to $1,300, and the equilibrium number of laborers increases from 50,000 to 66,000.

Figure 5–3 suggests that predicting the effects of an increase in export employment is tricky. The simple approach is to use the employment multiplier to predict the change in total employment from a projected change in export employment. In the numerical example, the predicted change in total employment from this method would be 25,000 (2.5 times 10,000). This approach provides an estimate of the horizontal shift of the demand curve, not the change in equilibrium employment. To accurately predict the change in total employment, one must also know the slopes of the supply and demand curves. The slope of the supply curve indicates how rapidly the wage increases with city size, and the slope of the demand curve indicates how rapidly the quantity of labor demanded decreases as the wage increases.

FIGURE 5–4   **Improvement in Public Services Shifts the Supply Curve and Increases Total Employment**

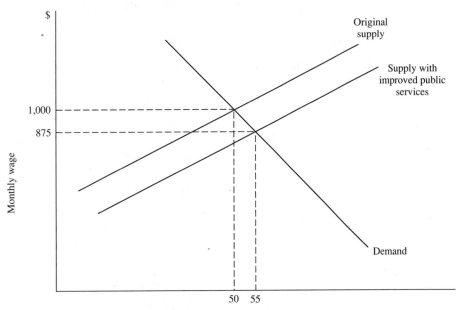

An improvement in local public goods increases the relative attractiveness of the city, shifting the supply curve to the right. The equilibrium number of laborers increases to 55,000, and the equilibrium wage falls to $875 per month. Workers accept a lower wage because the city provides a more efficient set of local public services.

Figure 5–4 shows the effects of a rightward shift of the supply curve. Suppose that the city improves its residential public services. For example, the city could improve its public-safety programs or alter its transportation system to decrease commuting costs. In Figure 5–4, the labor-supply curve shifts to the right: at each wage, more people are willing to work in the city. The shift of the supply curve increases equilibrium employment and decreases the equilibrium wage. Figure 5–4 is consistent with the empirical evidence provided by Eberts and Stone (1992) concerning the effects of improvements in local infrastructure on wages and total employment. Workers accept lower wages because the city provides a superior mix of local public goods.

Public Policy and Economic Growth

Public policy affects the equilibrium number of workers by shifting the city's supply and demand curves. As explained earlier in the chapter, local government can shift the demand curve to the right by improving the local education system, improving public services and business infrastructure, and cutting business taxes. Local government can shift the supply curve to the right by improving public services and residential infrastructure and cutting residential taxes. This part of the chapter explores the effects of two alternative policies: the subsidization of relocating firms and a tax on air pollution.

Subsidy Programs

Many cities try to attract export firms by offering special subsidies for new firms. Levy (1981) describes several types of subsidy programs, including the following:

1. **Tax abatement.** In some cities, new firms are exempt from local property taxes for some period of time, often up to 10 years. Some cities offer tax abatements to all new developments, while others offer abatements only to firms that are assumed to be particularly sensitive to tax differentials.

2. **Industrial bonds.** Some cities issue tax-free industrial bonds to finance property development. The local government uses the revenue from the bonds to purchase the land and then leases the property to a private firm. Because the interest income from industrial bonds is not subject to federal taxes, the bond buyer accepts a relatively low interest rate (for example, 8 percent instead of 12 percent). Therefore, the lessee pays less than the market interest rate on the money borrowed to finance the project. The use of industrial bonds was sharply curtailed by the Tax Reform Act of 1986.

3. **Government loans and loan guarantees.** Some cities loan money to developers, and others guarantee loans from private lenders to developers. In both cases, developers borrow money at a relatively low interest

rate: either the city charges an interest rate below the market rate, or the city decreases the risk associated with a private loan, allowing the developer to borrow private money at a relatively low interest rate.

4. **Site development.** Some cities subsidize the provision of land and public services for new development. The city purchases a site, clears the land, builds roads and sewers, and then sells the site to a developer at a fraction of the cost of acquiring and developing the site.

How do these subsidy programs affect the urban labor market? Any policy that decreases production costs will increase labor demand and increase equilibrium employment, everything else being equal. In the case of tax subsidies, not everything else is equal. Tax revenue supports local public services, so a community with low taxes is also likely to have inferior public services. The empirical evidence cited in Chapter 3 suggests that if a city cuts taxes and decreases its spending on public services (highways, education, public safety), the city is unlikely to grow and may in fact shrink. In contrast, if the city cuts taxes and decreases its spending on redistributional programs to the poor, the city is likely to grow. In other words, the effect of a tax cut depends on what types of services are cut along with taxes. If taxes are used to finance public services used by businesses, a tax cut is unlikely to stimulate economic growth.

What are the fiscal implications of these subsidy programs? Another objective of a subsidy program is to decrease the local tax burden. If a tax cut or a subsidy makes the city more attractive to firms, the city's tax base will increase, increasing total tax revenue. As the city grows, it will also spend more on local public services (roads, schools, police, fire protection). The subsidy program will be beneficial from the fiscal perspective if the increase in tax revenue exceeds the increase in the cost of public services.

Urban Growth and Environmental Quality

Is there a trade-off between environmental quality and economic growth? Suppose that a city adopts a pollution-abatement program. Will the abatement program increase or decrease the city's total employment?

Consider a city with two industries, a polluting steel industry and a relatively clean assembly plant. If the city imposes a pollution tax of $100, steel producers pay $100 for every ton of pollution they generate. The pollution tax affects both sides of the urban labor market.

1. **Shift of demand curve.** The tax increases the production costs of steel producers. In addition to paying for labor, capital, and land, a firm pays $100 for every ton of pollution. The increase in production costs increases the price of steel, which decreases steel production and the demand for labor. In Figure 5–5, the demand curve shifts to the left: at every wage, less labor is demanded.

2. **Decrease in pollution.** The tax decreases air pollution for two reasons. First, steel producers will install pollution-control equipment as a means

of decreasing their pollution taxes, so the amount of pollution generated per ton of steel will decrease. Second, the increase in the price of steel decreases total steel production.

3. **Shift of supply curve.** The improvement of the city's air quality increases the relative attractiveness of the city. People sensitive to air quality will move to the city, shifting the supply curve to the right.

Figure 5–5 shows one possible outcome of the abatement program. Since supply increases and demand decreases, the program decreases the equilibrium wage. Since the rightward shift of the supply curve is large relative to the leftward shift of the demand curve, equilibrium employment increases. The supply shift will be relatively large if households are relatively responsive to changes in environmental quality, meaning that a large number of households will migrate to the city as air quality improves.

How does the abatement program affect the distribution of employment between the polluting industry and the clean industry? As the wage falls, the production costs of both industries decrease. For the steel industry, the decrease in the wage

FIGURE 5-5   Pollution Tax Increases Total Employment

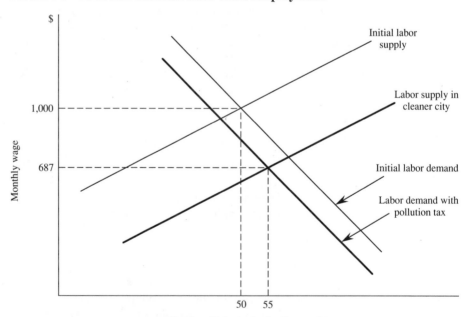

Number of laborers in city (thousands)

A pollution tax increases production costs, decreasing the demand for labor. It also improves environmental quality, increasing the supply of labor and decreasing the wage. The outward shift of the supply curve is large relative to the inward shift of the demand curve (people are relatively sensitive to air pollution), so total employment increases. The increase in employment in the clean industry more than offsets the decrease in employment in the polluting industry.

partly offsets the increase in pollution taxes. The abatement program is likely to generate a net increase in production costs, so the polluting industry is likely to decrease its total work force. In contrast, the clean industry will simply pay lower wages, so its production costs will decrease and its total employment will increase. In Figure 5–5, the increase in employment in the clean industry more than offsets the decrease in employment in the steel industry, so total employment increases. This occurs because households are relatively sensitive to pollution, so that migration to the cleaner city causes a large decrease in the wage.

Under what conditions will the abatement program decrease total employment? Suppose that households are not very sensitive to air pollution, so the supply curve shifts by a relatively small amount as a result of the abatement program. If the supply shift is smaller than the demand shift, the equilibrium number of laborers will decrease, not increase. Because the equilibrium wage decreases by a relatively small amount, the increase in employment in the clean industry will not be large enough to offset the decrease in employment in the steel industry.

The lesson from this discussion of the abatement program is that a pollution tax may either increase or decrease total employment. Total employment will increase if the supply response (migration that decreases wages) is large relative to the demand response (the decrease in labor demand from the polluting industry). Conversely, employment will decrease if the demand response is relatively large.

Predicting Economic Growth

This section discusses two techniques that are used to predict future growth patterns. The economic base study is a simple, low-cost method for projecting employment growth. An input-output study provides a more sophisticated approach to economic forecasting. Both techniques are designed to estimate the increase in labor demand from an increase in export sales.

The Economic Base Study

According to economic base theory, the export industries form the **economic base** of the urban economy. Like a household, a city earns its livelihood by producing goods for others. Exports bring money into the local economy, increasing local income and employment through the multiplier process. The ultimate purpose of an economic base study is to estimate the increase in total employment generated by an increase in export employment. In algebraic terms,

$$\Delta T = \text{multiplier} \cdot \Delta B = \frac{T}{B} \cdot \Delta B \qquad (5\text{--}6)$$

In other words, the predicted change in total employment (ΔT) equals the employment multiplier (T/B) times the change in export employment (ΔB). To predict the change in total employment, the economic forecaster needs both an estimate of the multiplier and a projection of the change in export employment.

To compute the employment multiplier, the economic forecaster estimates how much of the city's work force is involved in export production. The most precise method of estimating B is to collect information on the actual shipments of goods to other cities. This approach is costly, and most cities use less expensive and less precise methods to estimate export employment.

The simplest method is to classify each industry as either an export industry or a local industry. For example, if the mitten industry is assumed to be an export industry, all the employees of mitten producers would be counted as export workers. If restaurant meals are assumed to be local goods, all the employees of restaurants would be counted as local workers. The problem with this crude method is that some mittens may be consumed locally and some meals may be eaten by nonresidents. In other words, since few industries are exclusively exporters or local producers, it is inappropriate to classify them as such.

Location-Quotient Approach.   The location-quotient approach recognizes that each industry produces partly for export and partly for local consumption. The trick is to estimate what portion of each industry's output is exported. An industry's true **location quotient** is

$$L_1 = \frac{\text{Mitten production in the city}}{\text{Mitten consumption in the city}} \tag{5–7}$$

A quotient of 1.0 (the city's mitten production equals its mitten consumption) would indicate that all of the city's production is consumed within the city, so none of the mitten workers produce for export. If $L_1 = 5.0$, mitten production is five times local consumption, so only one fifth of mitten workers produce for the local market and four fifths produce for export.

Data limitations prevent the direct estimation of the true location quotient. Instead, a proxy for the true location quotient is

$$L_2 = \frac{\dfrac{\text{City's mitten employment}}{\text{City's total employment}}}{\dfrac{\text{Nation's mitten employment}}{\text{Nation's total employment}}} \tag{5–8}$$

The denominator (the share of national employment in mitten production) provides a measure of how much local production is needed to satisfy the local demand for mittens. For example, if 1 percent of national employment is in mitten production (the denominator is 0.01), the city is assumed to need 1 percent of its work force to satisfy its local mitten demand. If the city actually employs 6 percent of its workers in mitten production (if the numerator is 0.06), one sixth of the workers are assumed to produce for local consumption, and five sixths are assumed to produce for export.

There are three problems with the location-quotient approach. The first two are related to the choice of the national economy as the reference point:

1. **Uniform consumption patterns.** The approach assumes that every city in the nation has the same per capita demand for mittens. Of course, mitten consumption depends on weather, fashion, and the tastes for outdoor winter sports (skiing, ice fishing, snow shoveling). If a city's residents consume a relatively large amount of mittens, the location quotient L_2 will overestimate the number of export workers. Conversely, if city residents consume a relatively small amount of mittens, L_2 will underestimate the number of export workers.

2. **National self-sufficiency.** Another assumption of the location-quotient approach is that the nation neither imports nor exports mittens, so the share of national employment in mitten production is the share required for local self-sufficiency. If the nation exports mittens, the share of national employment in mitten production will overstate the share required for self-sufficiency, so the location quotient will underestimate the number of export workers. Conversely, if mittens are imported, the location quotient will overestimate the number of export workers.

3. **Industry grouping.** The location quotient is typically computed for a set of consumer goods, not for a particular product. For example, a city might compute a location quotient for the apparel industry, which includes mittens, pants, dresses, and children's clothes. Suppose that all the city's apparel workers produce mittens for export; no other apparel products are produced in the city. Suppose that the mitten industry is large enough that the city's location quotient for apparel is 1.0: the city uses the same share of its work force in mitten production as the nation uses in apparel production. The city's location quotient suggests that the city does not export apparel products, when in fact it exports mittens and imports other apparel. The grouping of goods into broad categories causes the location quotient to underestimate export employment.

The results of Tiebout (1962) suggest that location quotients systematically underestimate export employment. Tiebout compared estimates of export employment derived from location quotients to the estimates generated by direct surveys of manufacturers. Figure 5–6 shows his results for the city of Indianapolis. For example, the location quotient for the food industry suggests that 24 percent of food workers produce for export, while the direct survey suggests that 63 percent of food workers produce for export. For primary metals, the location quotient suggests that none of the workers in the industry produce for export, while the direct survey suggests that 99 percent of the workers produce for export. In general, Tiebout's results suggest that location quotients perform poorly in estimating export employment.

**FIGURE 5-6   Estimates of Export Employment from Surveys and
Location Quotients**

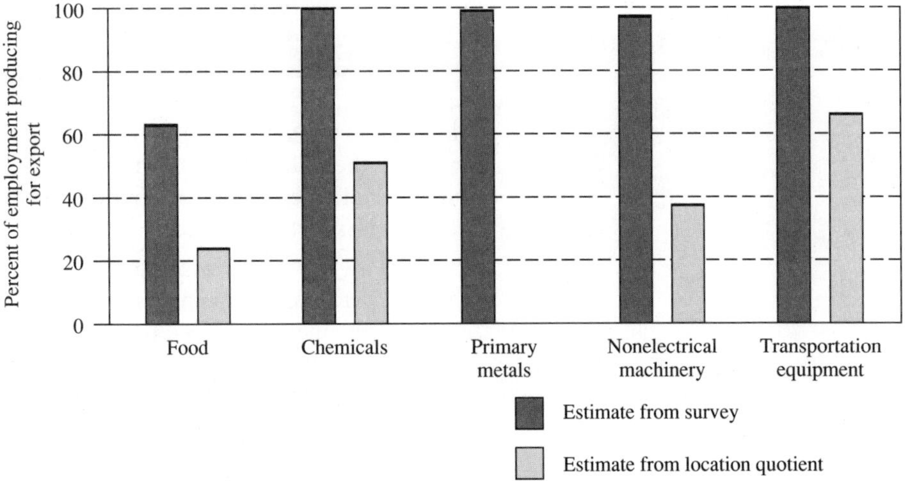

SOURCE: Charles M. Tiebout, *The Community Economic Base Study* (New York: Committee for Economic Development, 1962).

Estimating the Multiplier.   The second step in an economic base study is to compute the city's employment multiplier. For each industry, the location quotient generates an estimate of export employment. If T_i is total employment in industry i and L_i is the industry's location quotient, export employment in the industry is

$$B_i = \frac{L_i - 1}{L_i} \cdot T_i \qquad (5\text{--}9)$$

For example, if L_i is 4.0 and T_i is 800, B_i is 600: three fourths of the industry's workers produce for export. The city's total export employment is estimated by summing the export employment across individual industries. The employment multiplier is total employment divided by export employment.

Projecting Growth in Export Industries.   The third step in an economic-base study is to project the growth of the basic industry, that is, to estimate ΔB in equation (5–6). Given the uncertainties associated with predicting future events, export projection is more of an art than a science. One approach is to (*a*) estimate the national trend in the demand for a particular good, and (*b*) assess the city's relative attractiveness to the firms producing that good. The city's economic forecaster could estimate the national demand for mittens for the next decade, looking at the trends in weather, winter sports, and fashion. If the city's relative attractiveness is not expected to change, the city's mitten production should increase at the same rate as national mitten consumption: a doubling of mitten consumption should double the city's mitten production and employment. If the city's relative attractiveness increases over time, its mitten production and employment should increase at a relatively fast rate.

Using the Economic Base Study. Economic base studies are used to project population growth and the demand for public services. Suppose that a city projects that its mitten industry will grow by 1,000 jobs. If the employment multiplier is 2.5, the economic base approach suggests that total employment will increase by 2,500 jobs. If there are three residents per job, the population of the city will increase by 7,500 people, increasing the demand for all public services. For example, if there is one school-age child for every five residents, total enrollment in schools will increase by 1,500 students.

Local firms use the employment projections from the economic base study to predict the demands for their products. Suppose that the city's economic base study projects an increase in population of 7,500 people. If it takes 3,750 people to support a barber, there will be room for two more barbers in the city. If the city grows by 7,500 people per year and it takes 30,000 people to support a shopping center, there will be enough demand to support a new shopping center in four years.

Local governments also use economic base studies to guide their growth-management policies. If a local government can affect the sales and employment of its basic industry, it can control the city's population. Suppose that the city has a growth target of 15,000 additional people in the next 20 years. If there are three residents per job, the city will meet its population target if it allows an additional 5,000 jobs. If the employment multiplier is 2.5, the city will meet its employment and population targets if it allows 2,000 additional export jobs.

Input-Output Analysis

An alternative to an economic base study is an **input-output study**. Unlike the economic base study, the input-output study generates a complete accounting of the transactions between firms and households in the economy. This approach has two advantages over the economic base study. First, instead of assuming that every industry has the same multiplier, it derives a multiplier for each export industry. Second, instead of using the location-quotient approach to guess the volume of exports, it measures exports directly.

To explain the workings of an input-output study, consider a city that produces and consumes three goods: computers, electrical wire, and local consumer goods. Computers and wire products are produced for both export and local consumption. By definition, local merchants (restaurants, dry cleaners, grocery stores) produce goods for local consumption.

Transactions Table and Input Coefficients. Table 5–2 shows the transactions in the city's economy. The first column of numbers shows the input usage of firms

TABLE 5-2   **Transactions Table from Input-Output Study**

| | **Producers** | | | | | |
Inputs	Computer Firms	Wire Producer	Local Merchants	Households	Exports	Total
Computers	$ 0	$ 300	$ 150	$ 180	$1,570	$2,000
Wire	400	0	0	0	600	1,000
Local	0	0	0	2,500	—	2,500
Labor	1,000	600	2,000	0	0	3,600
Imports	600	100	350	920	—	2,170
Total	$2,000	$1,000	$2,500	$3,600	2,170	

in the computer industry. To produce computers, the firms buy $400 of electrical wire, $1,000 of labor from city residents, and $600 of imported inputs (raw materials and intermediate inputs). The sum of these input costs equals the total output of the computer industry ($2,000). The next column shows the input usage of wire producers, who use computers, labor, and imported inputs to produce $1,000 of wire. The third column shows the input usage local merchants, who use computers, labor, and imports to produce $2,500 of output. The household column shows how households divide their total income ($3,600) between computers ($180), local goods ($2,500), and imports ($920). The export column shows the exports of computers ($1,570) and wire ($600). The total column shows the sum of the items in each row. Note that the figures in the total column match the figures in the total row.

Table 5-3, which is derived from Table 5-2, provides a summary of the interactions between firms and households. The first column of numbers shows the **input coefficients** for the computer industry: for every dollar's worth of computer production, the computer industry uses 20 cents' worth of input from the wire industry, 50 cents' worth of labor, and 30 cents' worth of imported materials (e.g., silicon chips and plastic). The second and third columns show the input coefficients for wire producers and local merchants. The fourth column shows that households spend 5 percent of their income on home computers, 69 percent on local goods, and 26 percent on imports.

The Multiplier Process.   The information in Table 5-3 can be used to estimate the multiplier effects of an increase in computer exports. Suppose that computer exports increase by $100. The increase in computer sales will increase local spending, precipitating a series of spending rounds. The first three spending rounds are shown in Figure 5-7.

> **Round 1.** The increase in computer sales increases wire production by $20 (0.20 times $100) and wages by $50 (0.50 times $100).
>
> **Round 2.** The $20 increase in wire production increases computer sales by an additional $6 (0.30 times $20) and wages by an additional $12

TABLE 5–3   **Input Coefficients Table**

	Producers			
Inputs	*Computer Firms*	*Wire Producer*	*Local Merchants*	*Households*
Computers	0.00	0.30	0.06	0.05
Wire	0.20	0.00	0.00	0.00
Local	0.00	0.00	0.00	0.69
Labor	0.50	0.60	0.80	0.00
Imports	0.30	0.10	0.14	0.26
Total	1.00	1.00	1.00	1.00

FIGURE 5–7   **Multiplier Effects of a $100 Increase in Computer Exports**

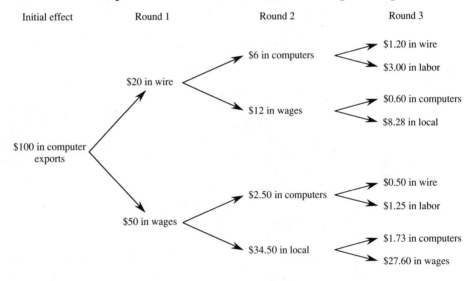

(0.60 times $20). The first-round increase in wages ($50) increases home-computer sales by $2.50 (0.05 times $50) and local consumption by $34.50 (0.69 times $50).

Round 3. The increases in computer sales, wages, and local sales cause additional increases in wire sales, wages, computer sales, and local consumption.

Because of the multiplier process, an increase in computer exports increases spending on all three goods.

The spending and respending of income continues forever, but every spending round is smaller than the previous one. The multiplier process eventually peters out

TABLE 5-4   **Spending Multipliers
from Input-Output Example**

	Added Sales per Dollar of Additional Export Sales of	
	Computer Industry	*Wire Industry*
Computers	1.23	0.52
Wire	0.25	1.10
Local	1.17	1.42
Total	2.65	3.04

because both producers and consumers spend some of their budgets on imports. As shown in the fifth row in Table 5–3 (Imports), there is a leakage of 30 percent in computer production, 10 percent in wire production, 14 percent in local goods production, and 26 percent from consumers. These leakages weaken the multiplier process, causing each spending round to be smaller than the previous round.

The input coefficients from Table 5–3 can be used to compute spending multipliers for the two export industries. For a description of the techniques used to derive the spending multipliers, see the readings listed at the end of this chapter. In Table 5–4, the first column shows the multiplier effects of a $1 increase in computer exports. Total computer sales increase by $1.23; wire production increases by 25 cents; and local sales increase by $1.17. The total multiplier effect is the sum of the effects on the three industries: a $1 increase in computer sales increases total sales by $2.65. Because the wire industry has a smaller import leakage (10 percent compared to 30 percent for the computer industry), it has a larger multiplier (3.04 versus 2.65).

Limitations of Economic Base and Input-Output Studies

This section discusses five defects that limit the applicability of the economic base and input-output approaches. There are two technical problems with the two approaches. First, the income and employment multipliers are assumed to be constant, regardless of city size. Second, the city's wage is assumed to be constant, regardless of city size. In addition, these approaches are misleading for three reasons. First, they suggest that the only way for a city to grow is by increasing its exports. Second, the approaches suggest that the only way to increase total employment is by increasing the demand for labor. Third, the approaches suggest that the city's fate is in the hands of outsiders.

Constant Multipliers.   The multipliers derived from both the input-output and economic base approaches are assumed to be constant. However, a city's multipliers can change for three reasons:

1. **City size and consumer products.** Multipliers increase with city size, reflecting the ability of a larger city to support a wider variety of firms. As explained in Chapter 4, a larger city has enough demand to support activities with scale economies that are large relative to per capita demand. For example, if a city grows to the point at which it can support its own Mexican restaurant, city residents will patronize the local restaurant instead of traveling to another city. A larger fraction of increases in income will be spent locally, so the income and employment multipliers will increase.

2. **City size and intermediate inputs.** As the city grows, the demand for intermediate inputs grows, and more of these inputs will be provided locally instead of being imported. For example, if the computer industry grows to the point at which the city can support its own silicon-chip maker, computer firms will spend less on imported inputs and more on locally produced inputs. Therefore, a given increase in computer exports will generate a larger increase in total income.

3. **Changes in input prices.** Changes in input prices cause factor substitution that changes the interactions among the economic sectors. Suppose that the city's wage increases, causing computer firms to substitute imported capital equipment for laborers. If the input coefficient for labor decreases from 0.50 to 0.40, only $40 of a $100 increase in computer exports will be paid to laborers. Because a smaller fraction of export income will be spent locally, the multiplier effect of an increase in exports will decrease.

Constant Wage.   The economic base and the input-output approaches assume that the city's wage is fixed regardless of city size. In other words, they estimate the horizontal shift of the city's labor-demand curve, not the equilibrium change in employment. Suppose that an economic base study computes a multiplier of 2.5 and projects an increase in export employment of 10,000 jobs. Based on these numbers, the economic base approach would predict that total employment in the city would increase by 25,000 jobs. This is incorrect because the city's labor-supply curve is positively sloped, so an increase in labor demand increases the city's wage. In Figure 5–3, total employment increases by only 16,000 jobs, not 25,000 jobs. Because the economic base and the input-output approaches assume a fixed wage, they overestimate the stimulative effect of increases in exports.

Focus on Exports as Source of Economic Growth.   The economic base and input-output approaches suggest that the only way for a city to grow is by increasing its exports. The notion that economic growth requires an increase in exports is incorrect. Growth may also occur as a result of (1) a decrease in imports, (2) an increase in labor productivity, or (3) an increase in trade within the metropolitan area.

A decrease in imports has the same stimulative effect as an increase in exports. While an increase in exports increases the flow of money into the urban economy, a decrease in imports decreases the flow of money out of the economy. The economy can be stimulated by either increasing the inflow of money (exports) or decreasing the outflow of money (imports). To explain the notion of **import substitution**, suppose that a city initially spends $10 million per year on imported chairs. If consumers switch to locally produced chairs, the $10 million that previously left the region will now be paid to local producers and will be spent and respent in the local economy. The spending and respending of the $10 million has the same effect as a $10 million increase in export sales: if the spending multiplier is 2.5, the change in total income resulting from import substitution is $25 million. The possibility of import substitution suggests that economic development policies should consider decreasing imports as well as increasing exports.

The most compelling counterexample to the export-oriented theories of urban economic growth is the world economy. The world's economy has grown, despite the absence of exports to other worlds. Economic growth has occurred for two reasons. First, technological advances have increased output per person, increasing real income per capita. Second, changes in production and transportation technologies have increased trade between regions. Trade increases real income because it allows each region to specialize in the production of goods for which it has a comparative advantage. The same phenomena occur at the urban level: increases in labor productivity or trade within a metropolitan area increase per capita income, so the city's economy can grow without increasing exports.

The Demand Side of the Urban Labor Market.   Both the economic base and the input-output approaches focus attention on the demand side of the urban labor market. The idea is that growth occurs when the demand for the city's labor increases. As explained earlier in the chapter, an increase in labor supply also increases equilibrium employment, so growth can occur as a result of increases in either demand or supply. There are a number of public policies that shift the supply curve and increase equilibrium employment, including environmental policy (see Figure 5–5) and infrastructure policy (see Figure 5–4).

Do Outsiders Determine the City's Economic Fate?   The economic base and input-output approaches incorrectly suggest that the city's economic fate is in the hands of outsiders. In fact, there are several local public policies that can be used to increase the city's equilibrium employment. On the demand side, the city can shift the demand curve to the right by (1) cutting its business taxes, (2) improving its industrial infrastructure, or (3) increasing labor productivity by improving its educational system. On the supply side, the city can shift the supply curve to the right by (1) cutting its residential taxes; (2) improving its residential infrastructure; (3) improving its residential services such as schools, recreation, and public safety; or (4) improving the local environment.

It's important to note that public policy need not focus exclusively on increasing the city's exports. As explained earlier, among the alternative strategies are import substitution and increased trade within the metropolitan area. To the extent that public policy encourages import substitution or intracity trade, it can increase employment and income without increasing the city's exports.

Benefits and Costs of Employment Growth

This section of the chapter explores the trade-offs associated with increases in city size, addressing two questions about the effects of employment growth on the welfare of a city's residents. First, how many of the new jobs generated by economic growth are filled by newcomers, and how many are filled by original residents of the city who would otherwise not be employed? Second, how does an increase in total employment affect real income per capita? As explained earlier in the chapter, changes in nominal wages and prices usually offset one another, so the real wage for a given occupation is unaffected by an increase in total employment. This section discusses three other factors that affect real income: the unemployment rate, the labor-force participation rate, and occupational rank.

Who Gets the New Jobs?

Bartik (1991) studied the effects of employment growth on unemployment rates, labor-force participation rates, and migration rates in 89 metropolitan areas. Table 5–5 uses his results to show the effects of employment growth on the characteristics of a hypothetical metropolitan area.

The first column of numbers shows the characteristics of the city's labor market in the initial equilibrium. In the sample of cities examined by Bartik, the average unemployment rate (the percentage of people who were unsuccessful in their search for work) was 5.40 percent, and the average labor-force participation rate (the percentage of working-age people who were actively involved in the labor market, either working or looking for work) was 87.50 percent. Suppose that the *employment rate* is defined as the percentage of working-age people who are employed. The employment rate is computed by multiplying the participation rate by 1 minus the unemployment rate. In Bartik's study, the average employment rate was 82.78 percent. The hypothetical city has a potential work force of 120,809 people. Given the participation rate (87.50 percent), 105,708 participate in the labor market; given the unemployment rate of 5.40 percent, 5,708 of the participants are unemployed, leaving 100,000 people who are employed.

The second column of numbers in Table 5–5 shows the predicted long-run effects of a 1 percent increase in total employment (1,000 jobs). According to Bartik (1991), the long run is about six years: it takes about six years for all the markets to fully adjust to the change in employment. Six years after the increase in total employment, the unemployment rate is 5.33 percent, the participation rate is 87.64 percent, and the employment rate is 82.97 percent. Migration to the city increases the city's potential work force by 928 people.

How many of the new jobs are filled by newcomers, and how many are filled by original residents who would otherwise not be employed? Since there are 1,000 new jobs and only 928 new potential workers, there are at least 72 new jobs for the original residents. If all the newcomers are employed (newcomers have a 100 percent participation rate and a zero unemployment rate), there will be only 72 new jobs for the original residents. If the newcomers have the same employment rate as the original residents, however, only 770 of the newcomers will be employed (82.97 percent of 928), so there will be 230 jobs left for the original residents. About one third of the 230 jobs will be filled by original residents who were previously unemployed, and the remaining two thirds will be filled by original residents who previously did not participate in the labor market. Figure 5–8 summarizes the results from Table 5–5: 77 percent of the new jobs are filled by newcomers, leaving 17 percent for original residents who were unemployed and 16 percent for original residents who did not participate in the labor market.

The simple lesson from Table 5–5 and Figure 5–8 is that employment growth causes in-migration and population growth. There are three implications from this lesson. First, if the city's work force is just as qualified for the new jobs as workers in other cities who have the option of migrating to the city, the original residents will get about a quarter of the new jobs. Second, if the city's workers are, on average, less qualified for the new jobs than workers in other cities, more of

---

TABLE 5–5   Long-Run Effects of Employment Growth on Employment Rate

Variable	Initial Equilibrium	Long-Run Equilibrium	Change
Unemployment rate (u)	5.40%	5.33%	–0.07%
Participation rate (p)	87.50%	87.64%	0.14%
Employment rate $(e = u \cdot p)$	82.78%	82.97%	0.19%
Potential work force	120,809	121,737	928
Participating	105,708	106,687	
Unemployed	5,708	5,687	
Working	100,000	101,000	1,000
Not working	20,809	20,737	
New jobs filled by newcomers		770	
New jobs filled by original residents		230	
Filled by unemployed		70	
Filled by nonparticipants		160	

SOURCE: Calculations based on Table 4.5 in Timothy J. Bartik, *Who Benefits from State and Local Economic Development Policies?* (Kalamazoo, Mich.: Upjohn Institute, 1991).

the jobs will be filled by workers migrating to the city. Third, employment growth increases population and thus increases the demands for housing, land, and public services. This suggests that local governments should coordinate their economic development policies with their policies concerning land use, transportation, and infrastructure investment.

Employment Growth and Real Income per Capita

How does employment growth affect a city's real income per capita? An increase in total employment could, in principle, increase per capita income in several ways:

1. **Increase in real wage for each occupation.** As explained earlier in this chapter, employment growth causes offsetting changes in nominal wages and living costs, so the real wage for a given occupation is unaffected by employment growth.

2. **Promotions.** Bartik (1991) shows that employment growth hastens workers' movement upward in the job hierarchy. It appears that an increase in the demand for labor causes firms to promote workers to higher-paying jobs more rapidly. Figure 5–9 shows, for different types of workers, the average percentage movement up the job hierarchy (and up the pay scale) that results from a 1 percent increase in total employment. The average worker is promoted to a job with a wage that is 0.16 percent higher than the wage for the old job. A less-educated worker (3 years less education than average) is promoted to a job that pays 0.196 percent more; a young worker (12 years younger than average) is promoted to a job that pays 0.188 percent more; a black worker is promoted to a job that pays 0.215 percent more.

FIGURE 5–8   Distribution of 1,000 New Jobs between Original Residents and Newcomers

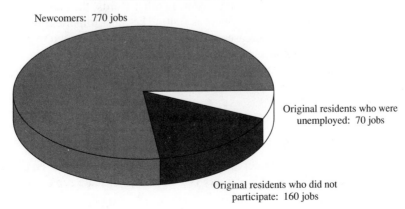

Newcomers: 770 jobs

Original residents who were unemployed: 70 jobs

Original residents who did not participate: 160 jobs

FIGURE 5–9   **Effect of Employment Growth on Occupational Rank
for Different Groups**

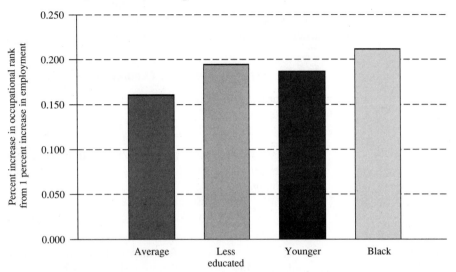

SOURCE: Timothy J. Bartik, *Who Benefits from State and Local Economic Development Policies?*
(Kalamazoo, Mich.: Upjohn Institute, 1991).

3. **Increase in employment rate.** As explained earlier, employment growth
   decreases the unemployment rate and increases the participation rate, so
   it increases the fraction of the working-age population that is employed.
   In Table 5–5, the 1 percent increase in employment increases the employment rate from 82.78 percent to 82.97 percent.

Figure 5–10 shows the combined effects of changes in real wages, occupational rank, unemployment rates, and participation rates on real income per capita.
For the average household, a 1 percent increase in employment increases real income per capita by 0.40 percent. In other words, the elasticity of real earnings with
respect to total employment is 0.40. The most important factors in the increase in
income are the increases in wages from being promoted to higher-paying jobs and
the increases in labor-force participation. The elasticity is larger for households
that are less educated, young, or black. The elasticities are larger because workers in these groups experience relatively large benefits from promotion to higher-
paying jobs.

Other Benefits and Costs of Employment Growth

There are a number of other benefits and costs from employment growth. On
the benefit side, a larger city is able to exploit scale economies in the production of

FIGURE 5-10   Effect of Employment Growth on Real Earnings per Capita for Different Groups

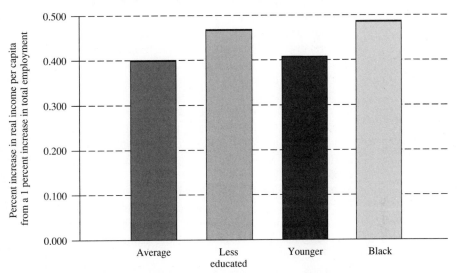

SOURCE: Timothy J. Bartik, *Who Benefits from State and Local Economic Development Policies?* (Kalamazoo, Mich.: Upjohn Institute, 1991).

consumer goods and some public services. As explained in Chapter 5, a large city can support activities that have relatively large scale economies, so a larger city has a wider variety of goods and services. In addition, there are scale economies in the provision of some local public goods, so an increase in population decreases the average costs of some public goods. On the cost side, a large city also has relatively high commuting costs: as the land area of the city increases, the average commuting distance increases, increasing the average commuting cost. In addition, larger cities often have greater problems with pollution and traffic congestion. Finally, large cities typically have higher crime rates.

It's important to note that the problems of congestion, pollution, and crime are not caused by city size per se. They are caused by market failures that become worse as the city grows. As explained later in the book, there are a number of policies that address these problems directly. Therefore, the problems can be solved (or decreased to their optimum levels) without decreasing city size.

Composition of Changes in Employment

This section of the chapter examines the composition of changes in total employment. A city experiences an increase in total employment when the number of jobs gained from the opening of new plants and from the expansion of existing plants exceeds the number of jobs lost from the closure and contraction of old plants. The question is whether cities that experience rapid employment growth have relatively large gains from plant openings and expansions or relatively small losses from plant closures and contractions. Conversely, do cities that grow slowly or shrink have relatively small gains from plant openings and expansions or relatively large losses from plant closures and contractions?

Eberts and Stone (1992) studied the composition of employment changes for 34 large metropolitan areas. In Table 5–6, the first column shows, for each city, the net change in employment as a percentage of total employment. For example, Pittsburgh lost 8.19 percent of its total employment over this period. The second and third columns show the gains from plant openings and expansions, and the sixth column shows the total gross gain (the sum of gains from openings and expansions). For example, Pittsburgh experienced an 11.46 percent gain from openings and a 5.82 percent gain from expansions, for a total gross gain of 17.28 percent. The fourth, fifth, and seventh columns show the losses from plant closures and contractions. For example, Pittsburgh experienced a 13.76 percent loss from closures and an 11.71 percent loss from contractions, for a total gross loss of 25.47 percent.

Three conclusions can be drawn from the data in Table 5–6. First, there is a large range of changes in net employment, from −8.19 percent for Pittsburgh to +19.36 percent for San Diego. Second, the gross changes in employment (gains and losses) are large relative to the net changes. The average change from openings and expansions is over 26 percent, and the average change from closures and contractions is over 20 percent, compared to an average net change of about 6 percent. The fact that a city has a relatively small net change in employment does not mean that its economy is stagnant, but simply that the employment gains are close to the losses. For example, the five cities that had positive net changes less than 1 percent (Akron, New York, Cleveland, New Orleans, and Detroit) had gross gains and losses between 20 and 23 percent.

The third conclusion that can be drawn from Table 5–6 is that rapidly growing cities have relatively large employment gains (from openings and expansions), not relatively small losses (from closures and contractions). Figure 5–11 shows the gross gains and gross losses for every third city in Table 5–6, arranged in ascending order of net employment changes. There is very little variation in the gross loss rates across cities. Except for Pittsburgh, all the cities have gross losses between 19 percent and 22.4 percent. In contrast, the gross gains vary considerably across cities, from about 17 percent to about 40 percent. The keys to rapid growth are openings and expansions: the three most rapidly growing cities (San Diego, Atlanta, and Seattle) have about the same gross losses as the three slowest growing cities (Pittsburgh, New York, and Detroit), but much larger gross gains.

TABLE 5-6 Employment Changes from Plant Openings, Expansions, Closings, and Contractions, 1984–1986

Metropolitan Area	Net Employment Change (%)	Percentage Employment Change Originating from				Percentage from Open + Expand	Percentage from Close + Contract
		Openings	Expansions	Closings	Contractions		
Pittsburgh	-8.19%	11.46%	5.82%	13.76%	11.71%	17.28%	-25.47%
Houston	-5.41	16.75	7.54	20.91	8.80	24.29	-29.71
Akron	0.46	16.20	6.43	13.99	8.18	22.63	-22.17
New York	0.61	12.64	8.33	15.38	4.98	20.97	-20.36
Cleveland	0.64	13.31	8.48	15.17	5.98	21.79	-21.15
New Orleans	0.86	15.41	6.03	13.94	6.65	21.44	-20.59
Detroit	0.97	13.20	8.96	15.40	5.80	22.16	-21.20
Miami	2.18	15.48	8.72	16.39	5.63	24.20	-22.02
San Francisco	2.26	13.48	8.81	14.27	5.76	22.29	-20.03
Buffalo	2.57	15.36	7.26	14.63	5.42	22.62	-20.05
Cincinnati	3.16	13.27	8.25	13.54	4.82	21.52	-18.36
Los Angeles	3.95	16.78	9.78	17.10	5.52	26.56	-22.62
Kansas City	4.28	16.26	8.24	14.76	5.46	24.50	-20.22
Milwaukee	4.36	13.57	7.96	11.71	5.45	21.53	-17.16
Portland	5.43	20.12	8.14	13.15	9.68	28.26	-22.83
Chicago	5.54	16.31	8.83	13.67	5.92	25.14	-19.59
Dallas	5.68	20.03	10.44	16.68	8.10	30.47	-24.78
Denver	6.16	20.18	8.87	15.16	7.72	29.05	-22.88
Philadelphia	6.16	15.54	10.01	13.87	5.52	25.55	-19.39
Anaheim	6.88	19.44	11.42	18.26	5.72	30.86	-23.98
Newark	7.18	16.36	8.88	12.61	5.45	25.24	-18.06
San Jose	7.50	19.19	10.74	16.21	6.21	29.93	-22.42
St. Louis	8.19	16.48	8.62	11.72	5.20	25.10	-16.92
Tampa	8.68	20.73	9.89	17.25	4.70	30.62	-21.95
Indianapolis	8.70	17.64	10.09	11.05	7.98	27.73	-19.03
Birmingham	8.73	21.12	10.25	15.51	7.13	31.37	-22.64
Baltimore	8.93	19.00	10.82	15.62	5.27	29.82	-20.89
Seattle	11.08	21.58	10.02	13.87	6.65	31.60	-20.52
Greensboro	13.24	17.21	9.34	8.73	4.57	26.55	-13.30
Minneapolis	15.29	19.42	11.22	9.82	5.53	30.64	-15.35
Atlanta	15.58	22.18	12.61	14.65	4.55	34.79	-19.20
Columbus	15.90	20.47	9.74	9.56	4.75	30.21	-14.31
Rochester	19.33	29.66	7.13	12.12	5.35	36.79	-17.47
San Diego	19.36	27.32	12.93	15.63	5.26	40.25	-20.89
Average	6.36	17.74	9.14	14.30	6.22	26.88	-20.52

Source: Table 2.3 in Randall W. Eberts and Joe A. Stone, *Wage and Adjustment in Local Labor Markets* (Kalamazoo, Mich.: Upjohn Institute, 1992).

FIGURE 5-11   **Gross Gains and Losses in Employment in Selected Cities, 1984–1986**

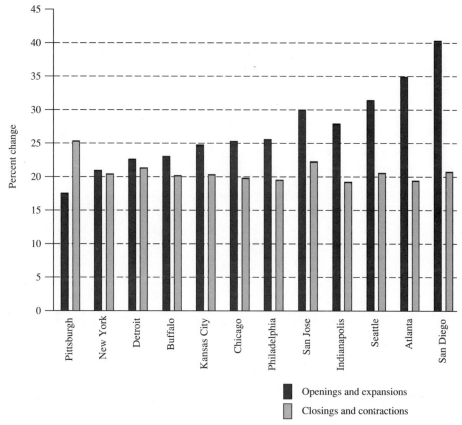

SOURCE: Table 2.3 in Randall W. Eberts and Joe A. Stone, *Wage and Adjustment in Local Labor Markets* (Kalamazoo, Mich.: Upjohn Institute, 1992).

Summary

1. Urban economic growth is represented by changes in the urban labor market.
   a. The demand for labor comes from exporters and local producers. An increase in export sales increases local sales through the multiplier process. The employment multiplier is the change in total employment per unit change in export employment.
   b. An increase in demand increases total employment and the city's wage. The demand curve shifts as a result of changes in the cost of producing exports and local goods.

    c. The supply of labor comes from city residents. The supply curve is positively sloped because an increase in city size increases housing and land prices, forcing firms to pay higher wages to compensate for the increased living costs. An increase in supply (caused by improvements in environmental quality or public services) increases total employment and decreases the wage.

2. Economic growth generates benefits and costs. The larger city can exploit scale economies in production, retailing, and public goods. On the cost side, the larger city has higher housing prices, longer commuting distances, and more pollution, congestion, and crime.

3. Public policy can stimulate economic growth by decreasing the production costs of exporters and local producers. Direct policies include public education and training programs (which increase labor productivity) and the efficient provision of public services and infrastructure. Indirect policies improve the quality of life of the city, attracting workers and decreasing wages.

4. Some cities try to attract firms by offering subsidies (tax abatement, industrial bonds, government loans, and subsidized site development).
       a. Because taxes support local public services, a tax cut may decrease spending on public services, making the city less attractive to firms.
       b. Subsidy programs that attract new firms often generate relatively small benefits for local workers because many of the new jobs are filled by newcomers.
       c. Subsidy programs often promote the growth of one city at the expense of another, causing inefficient location choices.

5. A pollution-abatement program may increase total employment. The abatement program decreases labor demand and increases labor supply. If people are relatively sensitive to pollution, the increase in supply will be large relative to the decrease in demand, and the city will grow.

6. An economic base study predicts trends in urban income and employment. It is based on the notion that a city must earn its livelihood by exporting. An economic base study has three steps:
       a. Estimate the amount of export employment. Location quotients provide inaccurate estimates of export employment.
       b. Compute the multiplier, equal to the ratio of total employment to export employment.
       c. Project growth in export sales or employment.

7. Economic base studies are used by local governments to predict the demands for local public goods (schools, sewage, fire protection) and by firms to predict the demands for private goods (groceries, shoes).

8. Input-output study is more sophisticated than the economic base study. It is based on a complete accounting of the economy's transactions, so it more accurately measures export and local activities. Input coefficients

summarize the interactions between different sectors and are used to derive income multipliers for each industry.

9. The economic base study and the input-output study share a number of defects that limit their applicability:
   a. The multipliers are assumed to be constant. The actual multiplier is likely to increase as the city grows and is likely to change with factor prices.
   b. The two approaches assume that the city's wage is fixed. They estimate the horizontal shift of the city's demand curve, not the change in equilibrium employment.
   c. Both approaches focus attention on the demand side of the economy, suggesting that the city's economic fate is determined by outsiders. In fact, local governments can stimulate growth through their provision of public services.

10. Employment growth increases real income per capita by (a) hastening the move up the job hierarchy and (b) increasing the labor-force participation rate. The elasticity of real earnings with respect to total employment is 0.40. The elasticity is larger for households that are less educated, young, or black, because such households experience relatively large benefits from being promoted to higher-paying jobs.

11. Rapidly growing cities have relatively large employment gains (from openings and expansions), not relatively small employment losses (from closures and contractions).

Exercises and Discussion Questions

1. Suppose that a consulting firm has generated the following information about the economy of Growville:
   i. The current employment in export industries is 50,000.
   ii. The current total employment in the city is 150,000.
   iii. Export employment is expected to grow by 10,000 jobs.

   a. Is there enough information to accurately predict the effect of the increase in export employment on total employment?
   b. If you have enough information, predict the employment effect and illustrate your answer with a graph.
   c. If there is insufficient information, proceed with the analysis as far as you can and list the additional information you need to complete the analysis. Illustrate your answer with a graph.

2. Consider a self-contained city, that is, a city in which everyone who works in the city also lives in the city. The initial equilibrium wage is W°, and the initial equilibrium employment is N°.

   a. Suppose that the demand for the city's exports increases. Use the conventional supply-demand graph to show the effects of the increase in export demand on the city's labor market. Label everything: the axes, the curves, the new equilibrium wage (W'), and the new equilibrium total employment (N').

   b. Suppose that the city institutes a growth-control program that holds the total housing stock (total square footage) at its initial level (before the increase in export demand). Use the same supply-demand graph to show the effects of the increase in export demand under the growth-control program. Label the equilibrium wage under the growth-control program W^* and the equilibrium total employment N^*.

   c. Explain the differences between the market equilibrium (*a*) and the growth-control equilibrium (*b*).

3. Consider a city that uses a business tax to finance the provision of industrial services (roads, water, sewers). If the city does not provide these services, the individual firms must supply their own roads, water, and sewers. Suppose that the city decides to cut business taxes and expenditures on industrial services by the same amount. Evaluate the effects of the new tax-expenditure policy on the city's labor market. Will total employment in the city increase or decrease?

4. The section on environmental quality suggests that a pollution tax may increase total employment. Suppose that instead of using a pollution tax to reduce citywide industrial pollution by a total of 25 percent, the city requires that *each* polluting firm decrease its pollution by 25 percent.

   a. Is the uniform-reduction policy more or less efficient than the pollution-tax program? In other words, will the total cost of abatement be larger or smaller under the uniform-reduction policy?

   b. Is the city more or less likely to grow under the uniform-reduction policy? Demonstrate, using a graph.

5. In a report issued in September 1989, a consulting firm estimated the economic impacts of moving the LA Raiders (a professional football team) to Sacramento. The economic-base study was based on the following assumptions:

   i. Total attendance at the Raider games will be 700,000 people per year.

   ii. The average ticket price will be $30.

   iii. The average fan will spend $10 on food, merchandise, and parking.

   iv. Based on *ii* and *iii*, the average fan will spend a total of $40.

   v. Total "direct" spending will be $28 million per year ($40 · 700, 000). Using a spending multiplier of 2.2, the consulting firm estimated the total economic impact of the Raiders to be $61.6 million per year. Critically appraise the methods used to compute the total economic impact of the Raiders.

6. Suppose that you have been given the following data on the transactions within a city's economy:

| | Producers | | | | | |
Inputs	Computer Firms	Wire Producer	Local Merchants	Households	Exports	Total
Computers	$ 0	$ 350	$	$ 300	$	$2,000
Wire	500	0	0	0	500	1,000
Local goods	0	0	0	2,500	0	
Labor	1,000	600	2,000	0	0	3,600
Imports			300			1,650
Total	$2,000	$	$	$3,600	$	$

    a. Fill in the transactions table.

    b. Will this city have a larger or a smaller export multiplier than the city with the transactions listed in Table 5–3? Explain.

  7. Suppose that wire production in the city with the input coefficients shown in Table 5–3 increases by $100.

    a. Compute the first, second, and third rounds of spending that result from the increase in wire sales, using the format of Figure 5–7 to report your results.

    b. By how much does spending on wire, computers, and local goods eventually increase?

    c. What is the ultimate increase in total sales?

References and Additional Readings

Bartik, Timothy J. *Who Benefits from State and Local Economic Development Policies?* Kalamazoo, Mich.: Upjohn Institute, 1991. Chapter 2 discusses the effects of various public policies on economic development. Chapters 4 and 7 discuss the effects of employment growth on employment rates and real income per capita. Chapters 5 and 6 explore the effects of employment growth on housing prices and real wages.

Birch, David. "Who Creates Jobs?" *Public Interest* (Fall 1981), pp. 3–14. Discusses the role of small business in economic development.

Chinitz, Benjamin. "Contrasts in Agglomeration: New York and Pittsburg." In *Readings in Urban Economics*, ed. Matthew Edel and Jerome Rothenberg. New York: Macmillan, 1972. A discussion of the supply side of the urban economy.

Eberts, Randall W., and Joe A. Stone. *Wage and Adjustment in Local Labor Markets.* Kalamazoo, Mich.: Upjohn Institute, 1992. Discusses how local labor markets adjust to shifts in supply and demand. Chapter 2 presents facts on employment changes from plant openings, expansions, closures, and contractions; Chapter 5 estimates the effect of changes in public infrastructure on the urban labor market.

Hamilton, Bruce, and Robert Schwab. "Expected Appreciation in Urban Housing Markets." *Journal of Urban Economics* 18 (1985), pp. 103–18. Estimates the relationship between city size and housing prices.

Harrison, Bennett, and Sandra Kanter. "The Political Economy of Job-Creation Business Incentives." *Journal of the American Institute of Planners* 44 (October 1978), pp. 424–35.

Levy, John M. *Economic Development Programs for Cities, Counties, and Towns*. New York: Praeger, 1981. Detailed discussion of economic-development policies.

Miernyk, William H. *The Elements of Input-Output Analysis*. New York: Random House, 1965. Describes the nuts and bolts of input-output analysis.

North, Douglass C. "Location Theory and Regional Economic Growth." In *Regional Policy: Readings in Theory and Application*, ed. John Friedmann and William Alonso. Cambridge, Mass.: MIT Press, 1975. States the case for the export-driven model of regional growth.

Robak, Jennifer. "Wages, Rents, and the Quality of Life." *Journal of Political Economy* 90 (1982), pp. 1257–78. Estimates the relationship between wages and city size.

Schmenner, Roger W. *Making Business Location Decisions*. Englewood Cliffs, N.J.: Prentice Hall, 1982. Discusses how firms make location decisions.

Tiebout, Charles M. *The Community Economic Base Study*. New York: Committee for Economic Development, 1962.

————. "Exports and Regional Economic Growth." In *Regional Policy: Readings in Theory and Application*, ed. John Friedmann and William Alonso. Cambridge, Mass.: MIT Press, 1975. Critiques the standard export-driven growth model.

Treyz, George, and Benjamin Stevens. "The TFS Regional Modeling Methodology." *Regional Studies* 19 (1985), pp. 547–62. Estimates the relationship between wages and city size.

U.S. Small Business Administration. *The State of Small Business: 1984*. Washington, D.C.: U.S. Government Printing Office, 1984. Chapters 1, 2, and 4 discuss the debate over David Birch's work.

Land Rent and Urban Land-Use Patterns

The first part of this book explained why cities exist and where they develop, but it did not explain how activities are arranged within the city. The second part examines the spatial structure of cities, taking a close look at land use within cities. It explores the market forces and government policies that determine the equilibrium land-use pattern.

Part II is divided into three chapters. Chapter 6 discusses land rent and land use in the monocentric city, explaining why commercial and industrial activity was concentrated in the central core areas of 19th-century cities. It also explains why the poor tend to locate in central cities. Chapter 7 explores the land-use patterns in modern cities, explaining why the traditional monocentric city was replaced with the modern multicentric city. Chapter 8 discusses the role of local government in the urban land market, exploring the market effects of zoning and other land-use controls.

Land Use in the Monocentric City

This chapter discusses the monocentric, or core-dominated, city, the dominant urban form until the early part of the 20th century. In the monocentric city, commercial and industrial activity is concentrated in the central core area. During the last 70 or 80 years, most large metropolitan areas have become multicentric, with suburban subcenters that complement and compete with the central core area. This chapter explains the market forces behind the development of the monocentric city, and Chapter 7 discusses the market forces behind the transformation of monocentric cities to multicentric ones.

Why study the monocentric city? Although few of today's large cities are monocentric, the analysis of the monocentric city is important for four reasons. First, the monocentric city was the dominant urban form until the early part of the 20th century, so urban history is largely a history of the monocentric city. Second, many of today's small- and medium-sized cities are still monocentric. Third, to understand the transition from the traditional monocentric city to the modern multicentric city, one must understand the forces behind the development of the monocentric city in the first place. Fourth, many of the lessons from the monocentric model can be extended to the modern multicentric city.

The remainder of this chapter is organized as follows. The first section provides definitions of land rent, market value, and the price of land. In addition, it describes the production and transportation technology of the traditional monocentric city. The second section discusses the location patterns of manufacturers and office firms. The third section examines the location choices of households. The fourth section explains why employment in the monocentric city is concentrated in the city center (why the city is monocentric). The final two sections deal with empirical issues, addressing three questions. First, why do poor households tend to locate in the central city, while wealthy households tend to locate in the suburbs? Second, how rapidly does land rent fall as distance to the city center increases? Third, what is the relationship between population density and distance to the city center?

Definitions: Land Rent, Market Value, and the Price of Land

It will be useful to define three terms: land rent, market value, and the price of land. Like other assets, land yields a stream of marketable services and thus a stream of income. For example, agricultural land yields a stream of agricultural output (bushels of corn), generating a stream of income for the farmer. Similarly, a parking lot in the city yields a stream of parking services, generating income for the parking firm. When a landowner grants the rights to use his land to another individual or firm, he charges **land rent**. If a corn farmer is granted the right to grow corn on a plot of land, the rent might be $1,000 per acre per year. If a parking firm is granted the right to operate a parking lot, the rent might be $5,000 per acre per year.

What determines the market value of land? The **market value of land** depends on the stream of rental income from the land. Suppose that the annual rental income from land (R) is constant and lasts forever. If i is the market interest rate, the market value (MV) of a plot of land that generates R of rental income per year is

$$MV = \frac{R}{i} \qquad (6\text{--}1)$$

For example, if the annual rent is $5,000 per acre and the market interest rate is 10 percent, the market value of land is $50,000 per acre. The market value of land makes an investor indifferent between buying the land (spending $50,000 to earn $5,000 per year in land rent forever) and putting the $50,000 in a bank account with a 10 percent interest rate. At a purchase price of $50,000, the annual income from the $50,000 investment in land is the same as the annual income from a bank account.

This book uses land rent—not market value—as the **price of land**. Most of the other relevant economic variables are defined as streams of revenue or costs. For example, a household earns an annual income, and a firm computes its annual profit as its annual revenue less its annual cost. To be consistent, the *price of land* will be defined as the annual payment in exchange for the right to use the land; the *price of land* is synonymous with *land rent*. Given the simple relationship between rent and value, it's easy to make the translation from land rent to market value: just divide the annual rent by the market interest rate.

The traditional monocentric city has the transportation technology of the 19th century. The monocentric model has four key assumptions:

1. **Central export node.** All manufacturing output is exported from the city through a railroad terminal at the city center (a central export node).
2. **Horse-drawn wagons.** Manufacturers transport their freight from their factories to the export node by horse-drawn wagons.

3. **Hub-and-spoke streetcar system.** Commuters and shoppers travel by streetcar from the residential areas to the central business district (CBD). The streetcar lines are laid in a radial pattern: the lines form spokes that lead into the CBD (the hub).

4. **Agglomerative economies.** The office industry is dependent on face-to-face contact: employees from different office firms meet in the city center to transact business.

Under these assumptions, the city center is the focal point of the entire metropolitan area: manufacturers are oriented toward the export node; office firms are oriented toward the central market area; retailers are oriented toward the hub of the streetcar system; and households are oriented toward employment and shopping opportunities in the central core area.

Commercial and Industrial Land Use

This section discusses land rent and land use in the central business district (CBD) of the monocentric city. Two types of firms occupy the central core area: manufacturers and office firms.

A Linear Bid-Rent Function for Manufacturers

Suppose that manufacturers in the monocentric city produce baseballs. Each firm uses labor, land, capital, and raw materials to produce six tons of baseballs per month. The prices of nonland inputs are assumed to be the same at all locations in the city. Baseballs are shipped by horse-drawn wagon from the factory to the central railroad terminal, where they are exported to other cities. The monthly freight cost increases by $900 for every additional mile from the factory to the city center: freight cost is $900 if the firm locates one mile from the center, $1,800 if the firm locates two miles from the center, and so on.

How much is the firm willing to pay for land at different locations in the city? The firm's **bid rent,** defined as the maximum amount the firm is willing to pay for land, equals the excess of total revenue over production costs and freight costs. Consider a firm that produces with fixed factor proportions: the firm uses the same input combination (land and other inputs) at all locations in the city. Specifically, suppose that the firm produces $6,000 worth of baseballs with one acre of land and $1,400 worth of nonland inputs. The bid-rent for a site adjacent to the city center (where freight cost is zero) is $4,600 ($6,000 minus $1,400). In other words, the firm is willing to pay up to $4,600 for land at the center.

Competition among prospective firms bids up the price of land to the point at which economic profit is zero (accounting profit is normal). Firms are willing to pay up to $4,600 for land near the railroad terminal and are forced by competition to do so: at any rent less than $4,600 per acre, the landowner will be able to find another firm willing to pay slightly more to use the land. In equilibrium, land rent equals the excess of total revenue over nonland costs (production costs plus freight costs). This is the **leftover principle:** because of competition among firms for land, the landowner gets the leftovers. If the firm were to pay less than the excess of total revenue over nonland costs, the landowner would evict the firm and replace it with another firm willing to pay its leftovers for the opportunity to earn normal accounting profit.

Figure 6–1 shows the firm's bid-rent function, defined as the maximum amount the firm is willing to pay for land at different distances from the city center. For a location one mile from the city center, nonland cost is $2,300 ($1,400 in production costs and $900 in freight cost), so the bid rent is $3,700 ($6,000 minus $2,300). For every additional mile from the city center, freight costs increase by $900, so the bid rent falls by $900. At three miles from the center, the bid rent is $1,900.

A Convex Bid-Rent Function for Manufacturers

The lower bid-rent function in Figure 6–1 is linear because the firm is inflexible. The firm produces its six tons of baseballs with one acre of land and $1,400 worth

FIGURE 6–1   Bid-Rent Function of Baseball Firms

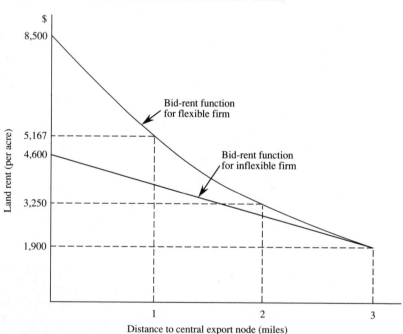

The bid-rent function of baseball firms is negatively sloped because freight costs increase as the distance to the city's central export node increases. It is convex if firms substitute nonland inputs for land as the price of land increases.

of nonland inputs, regardless of the relative price of land. Consider a flexible firm, defined as a firm that changes its input combinations as the relative price of land changes. If the firm moves to more expensive land, it substitutes nonland inputs (capital, labor, raw materials) for land, so it can produce six tons of baseballs on a smaller plot of land. To produce the same output on less land, however, the firm must spend more on other inputs (labor, machinery, buildings).

Table 6–1 shows how to compute the bid rent for a flexible firm. The different input combinations are shown in the second and fourth columns of the table. At a location three miles from the market, the flexible firm uses the same input combinations as the inflexible firm (one acre of land and $1,400 worth of nonland inputs) and is willing to pay the same amount in land rent ($1,900). As the firm moves toward the marketplace, the price of land increases, causing the firm to substitute nonland inputs for land. For example, at a site two miles from the city center, the firm uses 0.8 acres of land and $1,600 worth of nonland inputs. For each location, the pre-rent profit is total revenue less nonland costs and transport costs: at a distance of two miles, pre-rent profit is $2,600 ($6,000 − $1,600 − $1,800). The bid rent *per acre* equals the pre-rent profit divided by the size of the production site (in acres): at a distance of two miles, the bid rent is $3,250 (2,600 divided by 0.8). The bid rent increases as the firm approaches the city center, rising to $8,500 for a site adjacent to the railroad terminal.

In contrast to the linear bid-rent function of the inflexible firm, the bid-rent function of the flexible firm is convex: its slope increases as we approach the city center. Because the inflexible firm uses the same input combination at all locations, the bid-rent function simply reflects differences in transport costs: the bid-rent function is linear, with a slope equal to freight costs per mile. In contrast, because the flexible firm engages in factor substitution, the bid-rent function reflects the differences in both freight costs and input costs.

TABLE 6–1   The Bid-Rent Function of Baseball Manufacturers

Miles from City Center	Size of Site (acres)	Total Revenue	Nonland Costs	Travel Cost	Pre-Rent Profit	Rent per Acre
0	0.4	$6,000	$2,600	$ 0	$3,400	$8,500
1	0.6	6,000	2,000	900	3,100	5,167
2	0.8	6,000	1,600	1,800	2,600	3,250
3	1.0	6,000	1,400	2,700	1,900	1,900

Assumptions
  1. Output = 6 tons of baseballs
  2. Price = $1,000 per ton
  3. Transport cost = $900 per mile
  4. Pre-rent profit = Total revenue − Nonland costs − Freight cost
  5. Rent = $\dfrac{\text{Pre-rent profit}}{\text{Size of factory site}}$

The Bid-Rent Function of Office Firms

Although firms in the office sector provide a wide variety of goods and services, office firms share two important characteristics. First, they gather, process, and distribute information. Because information becomes obsolete quickly, office firms must be able to collect and distribute information quickly. Second, office firms rely on face-to-face contact in the collection, processing, and distribution of information. For example, accountants explain and interpret the information in accounting reports. The loan officers of banks meet with prospective borrowers to appraise their creditworthiness. The investment advisors of finance firms meet with clients to assess their attitudes toward risk and their investment inclinations. In general, office firms rely on speedy face-to-face contact in collecting and distributing information. In contrast to baseball manufacturers, who throw their baseballs into the back of a horse-drawn wagon, office firms transmit their output in the minds and the briefcases of their employees.

Suppose that office firms in the monocentric city provide financial services. The "output" of the firm is investment consultations, and each firm produces 200 consultations per month. Every finance firm is based in an office, and the manager of each firm travels from the office to the city center (the hub of the streetcar system) to consult with clients. The prices of nonland inputs are the same at all locations in the city. The travel cost of an office firm equals the opportunity cost of the manager's travel between the office and the clients in the city center. The monthly travel cost increases by $2,400 for every additional block from the office to the city center: travel cost is $2,400 if the firm locates one block from the center, $4,800 if the firm locates two blocks from the center, and so on.

The **office bid-rent function** indicates how much the typical office firm is willing to pay *per acre* for different office sites in the city. If markets are

---

TABLE 6-2   The Bid-Rent Function of Office Firms

Blocks from City Center	Size of Site (acres)	Total Revenue	Nonland Costs	Travel Cost	Pre-Rent Profit	Rent per Acre
0	0.40	$9,600	$3,600	$ 0	$6,000	$15,000
1	0.60	9,600	2,400	2,400	4,800	8,000
2	0.80	9,600	1,800	4,800	3,000	3,750
3	1.00	9,600	1,500	7,200	900	900

Assumptions
1. Output (A) = 200 consultations
2. Price = $48 per consultation
3. Travel time (t) = 3 minutes per block
4. Opportunity cost (W) = $4 per minute
5. Travel cost = $t \cdot A \cdot W$ = $2,400 per block
6. Pre-rent profit = Total revenue − Nonland costs − Travel cost
7. Rent = $\dfrac{\text{Pre-rent profit}}{\text{Size of office site}}$

FIGURE 6–2   The Bid-Rent Function of Office Firms

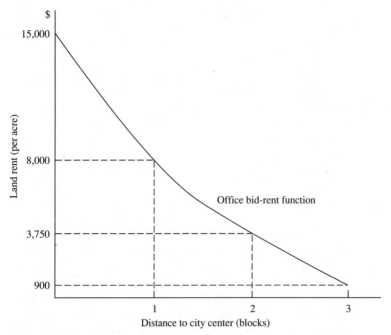

The office land-rent function is negatively sloped because travel costs increase as distance to the central marketplace increases. It is convex because firms substitute nonland inputs for land as the price of land increases.

perfectly competitive, the leftover principle is applicable: the firm is willing to pay its landowner the excess of total revenue over the cost of nonland inputs and travel cost. Table 6–2 (opposite page) shows how to compute the bid rent for different distances from the city center. The pre-rent profit equals total revenue ($9,600) less nonland costs and travel costs. The bid rent per acre is the pre-rent profit divided by the size of the office site. The bid-rent function, shown in Figure 6–2, is negatively sloped because travel costs increase as the firm moves away from the city center.

The bid-rent function is convex because firms engage in factor substitution. As the firm approaches the city center with its higher land cost, the firm substitutes nonland inputs (capital and labor) for land, producing the same number of consultations with less land and more of the other inputs. From Table 6–2, the firm uses one acre of land and $1,500 worth of other inputs for a location three blocks from the city center, and 0.40 acres and $3,600 worth of nonland inputs for a location near the city center. In other words, finance firms near the city center occupy taller buildings. The bid-rent function of the typical finance firm will be used to represent the bid-rent function of the entire office sector.

Land Use in the Central Business District

In the monocentric city, manufacturers and office firms are oriented toward the central business district. Manufacturers are attracted by the central export node, and office firms cluster around the city center to facilitate face-to-face contact. How is CBD land allocated between the two types of firms?

Figure 6–3 (opposite page) shows the bid-rent functions of manufacturers (R_m) and office firms (R_o). Figure 6–3 also shows the bid-rent function of city residents (R_h), which is derived later in this chapter. Because land is allocated to the highest bidder, office firms outbid manufacturers for land within u_o miles of the city center, generating an office district with a radius of u_o miles. Manufacturers outbid office firms and residents for land between u_o and u_m miles of the city center, generating a manufacturing district with a width of ($u_m - u_o$) miles. The central area of the city is occupied by the office industry because the office bid-rent function is steeper than the manufacturing bid-rent function.

The office bid-rent function is relatively steep because the office industry has relatively high transportation costs. Office firms rely on frequent face-to-face contact, using high-priced financial consultants to transport their output to clients in the city center. In contrast, the manufacturing industry ships its output by horse-drawn wagon, so its transport costs are relatively low. In the numerical examples shown in Tables 6–1 and 6–2, the baseball manufacturer has monthly freight costs of $900 per mile, while the office firm has monthly travel costs of $2,400 *per block*. The bid-rent functions are negatively sloped because of transportation costs, so the larger the transportation costs, the larger the slope.

Does the land market allocate land efficiently? In the terms used by land developers, is land allocated to its "highest and best use"? The office industry, with its higher transportation costs, occupies the land closest to the city center. This allocation is efficient because the office industry has the most to gain from proximity to the city center. To explain, suppose that a finance firm one block from the city center swaps locations with a manufacturer three blocks (one fifth of a mile) from the city center. The land swap will increase the finance firm's travel costs by $7,200 (three blocks times $2,400 per block) but will decrease the baseball firm's freight cost by only $180 (one fifth of a mile times $900 per mile). Office travel costs will increase by more than freight costs will decrease, so total transportation costs increase. The market allocation, which gives central land to the office industry, minimizes total transportation costs.

Residential Land Use

This section uses a simple model of the residential sector to explore residential land use in the monocentric city. According to the leftover principle, the bid rent for residential land equals the excess of total revenue over total cost. The first step in the analysis of residential land rent examines the revenue side of housing

FIGURE 6–3 **Bid-Rent Functions and Land Use in the Central Business District**

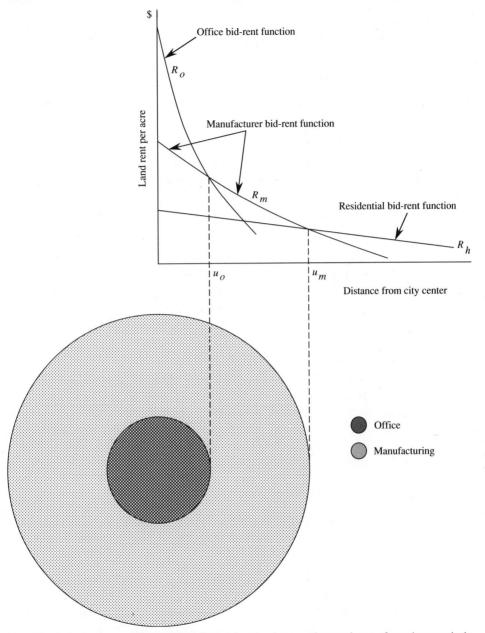

The office industry has a relatively steep bid-rent function because the travel cost of people exceeds the travel cost of freight. The office industry outbids manufacturers for land near the city center. Central land is occupied by the activity with the most to gain from proximity (lower transportation costs).

production. The housing-price function shows the relationship between housing prices and distance to the city center.

The simple model of the residential sector has a number of assumptions. Later in the chapter, each of these assumptions will be dropped.

1. One member of each household commutes to a job in the central business district (CBD).
2. Noncommuting travel is insignificant.
3. Public services and taxes are the same at all locations.
4. Air quality is the same at all locations.
5. All households have the same income and tastes for housing.
6. The opportunity cost of commuting time is zero.

The first four assumptions make the CBD the focal point of city residents. All jobs are in the CBD, while all the other things that people care about (public services, taxes, air quality) are distributed uniformly throughout the city. Given the fifth assumption, the choices of the "typical" household can be used to represent the choices of all households in the city. The sixth assumption means that the simple model ignores the time costs of commuting.

The Housing-Price Function

As explained in Chapter 11 (The Urban Housing Market), the price of housing is usually defined as the price per unit of housing service. For the purposes of this chapter, the **price of housing** will be defined as the price *per square foot* of housing per month. If a household rents a 1,000-square-foot house for $250 per month, the price of housing is 25 cents per square foot ($250 divided by 1,000 square feet). The **housing-price function** indicates how much a household is willing to pay for dwellings at different locations in the city. There are two types of housing-price functions, linear and convex.

Linear Housing-Price Function: No Consumer Substitution.   Figure 6–4 shows the housing-price function for a simple case described by the following set of assumptions.

1. **Identical dwellings.** Every dwelling in the city has 1,000 square feet of living space.
2. **Fixed budget.** The typical household has a fixed budget of $300 per month to spend on commuting and housing costs.
3. **Commuting cost.** The monthly cost of commuting is $20 per mile per month: the household pays $20 per month in commuting costs for a residence one mile from the city center, $40 per month for a residence two miles from the city center, and so on.

How much is the household willing to pay for dwellings at different locations in the city? At the city center, commuting costs are zero, so the household can spend its entire $300 budget on housing. For a 1,000-square-foot house, the price will be 30 cents per square foot. At a distance of six miles from the center, commuting cost is $120, so the household has $180 left to spend on housing (18 cents per square foot). In Figure 6–4, the slope of the function is 2 cents per mile.

The negatively sloped housing-price function is necessary for **locational equilibrium.** Locational equilibrium occurs when all households are satisfied with their location choices, that is, when no household wants to change its location.

To explain why the equilibrium housing-price function is negatively sloped, suppose that the function starts out as a horizontal line. If the price of housing is 15 cents per square foot throughout the city, the household can get a 1,000-square-foot dwelling anywhere in the city for $150 per month. Suppose that a household starts out in a house 10 miles from the city center. A move toward the city center will increase utility because the household will have lower commuting costs but will pay the same rent ($150). Therefore, the household will move closer to the city center. Other households have the same incentive to move closer to the center, so the demand for housing near the city center will increase (increasing

FIGURE 6–4   Housing-Price Function for City with Identical (1,000-Square-Foot) Dwellings

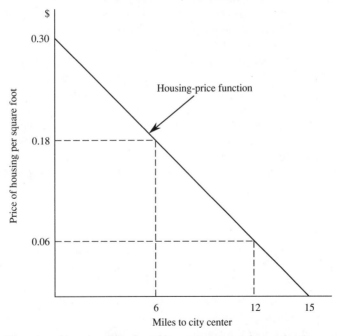

The price of housing drops from 30 cents per square foot at the city center to 6 cents per square foot 12 miles from the city center. The price increases as commuting cost decreases (as distance to the center decreases), making households indifferent among all locations within the city.

prices), and the demand for suburban housing will decrease (decreasing prices). In other words, the movement of households toward the city center will transform a horizontal housing-price function into a negatively sloped function.

The equilibrium housing-price function makes residents indifferent among all locations because differences in commuting costs are exactly offset by differences in housing costs. Consider a household that makes a one-mile move toward the city center. The good news from the move toward the center is that commuting costs decrease by $20 (commuting cost per mile). The bad news is that the price of housing increases by 2 cents per square foot, so housing costs (price times quantity) increase by $20. The household is indifferent between the two locations because the difference in commuting costs equals the difference in housing cost.

Convex Housing-Price Function: Consumer Substitution.   The housing-price function in Figure 6–4 is linear because the city's dwellings are identical: everyone lives in a 1,000-square-foot house, regardless of the price of housing. A more realistic assumption is that households obey the law of demand: an increase in price decreases the quantity demanded. As a household moves toward the city center, it will pay a higher price for housing, so it will occupy a smaller dwelling.

Figure 6–5 shows the effects of consumer substitution on the housing-price function. The assumed pattern of housing consumption is shown below the graph. Suppose that a household moves from a distance of 12 miles to the city center (where the price of housing is 6 cents per square foot) to 9 miles. If housing consumption is fixed at 1,000 square feet, the household would be willing to pay an additional $60 for housing (the decrease in commuting cost), or 6 cents more per square foot. Because its housing consumption drops from 1,000 square feet to 750 square feet, the household is willing to pay more than an additional 6 cents per square foot to offset the decrease in commuting costs. In general, as a household moves toward the high-priced city center, it occupies smaller dwellings, requiring progressively larger increases in the price *per square foot* of housing to offset the fixed $20 per mile decrease in commuting costs. The lesson from Figure 6–5 is that if consumers obey the law of demand, the housing-price function will be convex, not linear.

The Residential Bid-Rent Function

The **residential bid-rent function** indicates how much housing producers are willing to pay for land at different locations in the city. According to the leftover principle, housing producers are willing to pay land rent equal to the excess of total revenue over total cost. There are two types of bid-rent functions, one that occurs if housing is produced with fixed factor proportions, and one that occurs if housing firms engage in factor substitution.

The Bid-Rent Function with Fixed Factor Proportions.   Consider first the possibility that housing is produced with fixed factor proportions. Suppose that

---

FIGURE 6–5   Housing-Price Function with and without Consumer Substitution

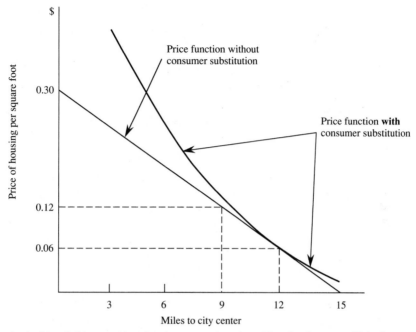

As the household approaches the city center, the price of housing increases. If the household substitutes other goods for housing, the housing-price function is convex, not linear.

Assumed consumption pattern

Distance to city center (miles)	3	6	9	12
Housing consumption (square feet)	400	600	750	1,000

each firm in the housing industry uses one acre of land and $1,000 worth of nonland inputs (capital and labor) to produce 10,000 square feet of housing. If markets are perfectly competitive, the leftover principle is applicable: the firm is willing to pay its landowner the excess of total revenue over the cost of nonland inputs. Table 6–3 shows how to compute the residential bid rent for different distances from the city center. For example, at a distance of three miles from the center, total revenue is $3,000 per month (10,000 square feet times a price of 30 cents per square foot), and nonland cost is $1,000, leaving $2,000 to be paid in rent. At a distance of 12 miles, revenue is less than nonland cost, so the bid rent is negative.

Figure 6–6 shows the residential bid-rent function. The horizontal line is nonland cost per firm, which is $1,000. Since the bid rent equals total revenue less nonland costs, the bid-rent function lies below the revenue function, with the distance between the two equal to the cost of nonland inputs. At u^*, total revenue equals nonland cost, so the bid rent for land is zero. The bid-rent function is convex because the housing-price function is convex.

TABLE 6-3 Residential Bid-Rent Function with Fixed Factor Proportions

Miles to Center	Price of Housing ($)	Quantity of Housing	Total Revenue	Nonland Cost	Rent per Acre
3	0.30	10,000	3,000	1,000	2,000
6	0.21	10,000	2,100	1,000	1,100
9	0.13	10,000	1,300	1,000	300
12	0.06	10,000	600	1,000	−400

FIGURE 6-6 Housing Prices and Bid-Rent Function

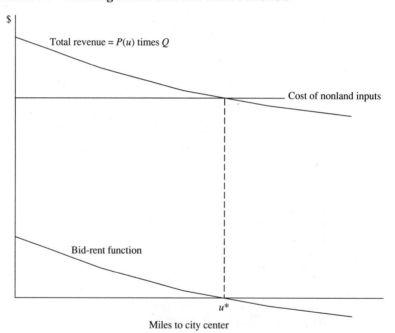

Miles to city center

The bid-rent of the housing firm equals total revenue per acre less the cost of nonland inputs. Total revenue (the price of housing times square footage produced) decreases as the distance to the city center increases because the housing-price function is negatively sloped. The cost of nonland inputs is the same at all locations. The bid-rent function is convex because the housing-price function (and the revenue function) is convex. At u^*, the cost of nonland inputs equals total revenue, so the bid rent equals zero.

The Bid-Rent Function with Factor Substitution.   The bid-rent function shown in Figure 6–6 is based on the assumption that housing is produced with fixed factor proportions. Housing firms use the same input combination at all locations, regardless of the price of land. What happens if firms substitute other inputs for land as the price of land increases?

Figure 6–7 shows the bid-rent functions for inflexible and flexible housing producers. The inflexible firm uses the same input combination throughout the city. In contrast, the flexible firm substitutes nonland inputs for land as the price of land increases, building progressively taller buildings as it approaches the city center. Because factor substitution decreases production costs, the flexible firm produces housing for a lower cost and thus outbids the inflexible firm.

Summary: The Convex Bid-Rent Function.   There are two lessons to be learned from the analysis of residential land rent. First, the bid-rent function is negatively sloped because the housing-price function is negatively sloped. Second, the bid-rent function is convex because of both consumer substitution (which makes the housing-price function convex) and factor substitution (which increases the convexity of the rent function).

FIGURE 6–7   **The Residential Bid-Rent Function with Factor Substitution**

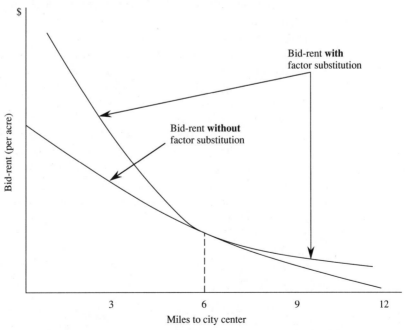

Factor substititution (substituting nonland inputs for land as the price of land increases) increases the convexity of the bid-rent function.

TABLE 6-4   **Population Density at Different Locations**

	Location	
	A	B
Distance to city center (miles)	0.2	4.0
Housing consumption (square feet)	1,404	3,000
Land per square foot of housing (square feet)	0.33	2.2
Lot size (square feet)	468	6,600
Lot size = Housing consumption · Land per unit of housing		

Residential Density

How does population density vary within the monocentric city? Table 6–4 shows how to compute lot sizes (land per household) at different locations in the city. Lot size increases as the distance to the city center increases for two reasons:

1. **Consumer substitution.** The price of housing decreases as the distance to the city center increases, and households respond to lower housing prices by consuming more housing. In Table 6–4, housing consumption rises from 1,404 square feet for a household 0.2 miles from the city center (location A) to 3,000 square feet for a household 4 miles from the center (location B).

2. **Factor substitution.** The price of land decreases as the distance to the city center increases, and housing firms respond to lower land prices by using more land per unit of housing. In Table 6–4, at a distance of 0.2 miles from the city center, every square foot of living space comes with 0.33 square feet of land. In other words, people live in three-story apartment buildings. At a distance of four miles from the center, the amount of land per square foot of housing is 2.2: households live in one-story houses with lot sizes 2.2 times the "footprint" of the house.

Lot size equals housing consumption (in square feet of living space) times the amount of land per unit of housing. Because of consumer substitution and factor substitution, the lot size increases as distance increases: a household located 0.2 miles from the center uses only 468 square feet of land (sharing the 1,404 square feet under the three-story apartment building with two other households), while a household located 4 miles from the center uses 6,600 square feet of land. Since density is the inverse of lot size, residential density decreases as one approaches the city's edge: the fact that the lot size increases means that there are fewer households per acre.

Land Use in the Monocentric City

Figure 6–8 shows the land-use pattern of the monocentric city. The office bid-rent function intersects the manufacturing function at a distance of u_o miles from the

FIGURE 6–8 **Bid-Rent Functions and Land Use in the Monocentric City**

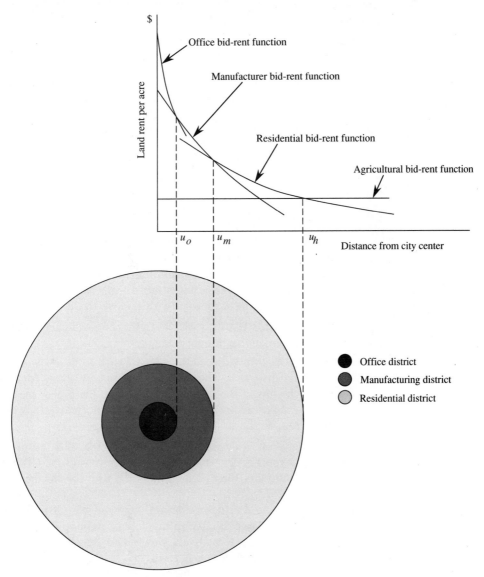

city center, so the office district is a circle with radius u_o miles. The manufacturing bid-rent function intersects the residential function at a distance of u_m miles from the city center, so the manufacturing district is a ring of width $(u_m - u_o)$ miles. The residential bid-rent function intersects the agricultural bid-rent function at a distance of u_h miles, so the residential district is a ring of width $(u_h - u_m)$ miles.

Activities are arranged according to their transportation costs: the higher the transportation cost, the closer to the city center. An activity with relatively high transport costs has a relatively steep bid-rent function and therefore locates closer to the marketplace. In the monocentric city, the market is the city center, where office workers meet with clients and manufacturers load their output onto ships or trains. The office sector, with the highest transport costs and thus the steepest bid-rent function, occupies land closest to the center. Manufacturing, with the next highest transport costs and thus the next steepest bid-rent function, occupies the next ring of land. The residential sector, with relatively low transport costs and thus a relatively flat bid-rent function, occupies the land farthest from the city center.

This spatial arrangement has two interesting features. First, office firms occupy the central area of the CBD. As explained earlier in this chapter, office firms have relatively high transport costs and thus a relatively steep bid-rent function because office output is transmitted by office workers, while manufacturing output is transported by horse-drawn wagon.

The second feature of the monocentric city is that employment is concentrated in the CBD, not distributed throughout the city. Why do all the manufacturers and office firms locate in the CBD? To explain this monocentric location pattern, consider a baseball firm that is considering a move from the CBD to a suburban location. What are the trade-offs associated with a move to the suburbs?

1. **Higher freight costs.** The firm will be farther from the central export node, so it will pay higher freight costs.
2. **Lower wages.** The firm will be closer to its work force, so workers will commute shorter distances. The wage compensates workers for commuting costs: the longer the commuting distance, the higher the wage. When the firm moves closer to its work force, it decreases its workers' commuting costs, so the firm can pay a lower wage.

The firm's location decision is determined by the outcome of a tug-of-war. On one side is the central export node, which pulls the firm toward the CBD. On the other side is its suburban work force, which pulls the firm toward the low-wage suburbs.

In the monocentric city, the tug-of-war was won by the CBD because the cost of moving freight was large relative to the cost of moving workers. Freight traveled by horse-drawn wagon, a relatively slow and expensive travel mode. In contrast, workers traveled by streetcar, a relatively fast and inexpensive travel mode. Although wages were lower in the suburbs, the wage differential was relatively small because commuting by streetcar was fast and efficient: workers demanded a relatively small premium to commute to CBD jobs. If a firm moved to the suburbs, the small savings in wages would be more than offset by an increase in the cost of shipping freight to the central export node. In the monocentric city, it was cheaper to bring the workers from the suburbs to the central-city factory than to bring the output from a suburban factory to the central export node.

The same analysis applies to office firms. Although a move from the CBD to the suburbs would decrease wages, it would also increase the costs of travel between the office and the central market area: managers would spend more time traveling between the office and clients in the city center. Given the frequency of travel to clients in the central market area, the increase in travel costs would outweigh the savings in wages. In the monocentric city, it was cheaper to bring the workers from the suburbs to a central-city office than to bring the output (in the minds and briefcases of managers) from a suburban office to clients in the city center.

Relaxing the Assumptions

The simple monocentric model has a number of unrealistic assumptions about residential land use. This section derives the residential bid-rent function under more realistic sets of assumptions. The assumption that the city is monocentric is maintained: all employment is assumed to be in the CBD.

Changes in Commuting Assumptions

The simple monocentric model is based on a number of simplifying assumptions about commuting. What happens if these assumptions are dropped?

1. **Time costs of commuting.** The simple model assumes that the only cost of commuting is a monetary cost, that is, money spent on cars (for gasoline and maintenance) or public transit (bus tickets). In fact, commuting time comes at the expense of work or leisure, so there is an opportunity cost associated with commuting. The unit cost of commuting (t) is actually the monetary *and* time costs per mile of travel. Studies of commuting behavior suggest that most people value commuting time at between one third and one half the wage rate. For a worker with a wage of $10, the time cost of commuting is between $3.33 and $5.00 per hour. Commuting costs are discussed in greater detail in the chapters on urban transportation.

2. **Noncommuting travel: uniform distribution of destinations.** The simple model assumes that non-commuting travel is insignificant. This assumption is unrealistic because households travel to different destinations within the city for shopping and entertainment. Suppose that shopping and entertainment destinations are distributed uniformly throughout the urban area. For example, the household commutes northward to a job in the city center and also travels north to a museum, south to a grocery store, west to a disco, and east to the shore. If the frequency and distance of travel to the four sites are about the same, any change in residence will cause a relatively small change in total noncommuting travel

time. If the household moves south, the cost of museum travel will increase, but the cost of the grocery travel will decrease. If the household travels in all directions for shopping and entertainment, noncommuting costs usually offset one another, and it is appropriate to focus on commuting as the primary factor in the location decision.

3. **Noncommuting travel: concentrated destinations.** Consider next the possibility that shopping and entertainment sites are concentrated rather than dispersed. Suppose that members of a household travel to the city center for work, shopping, and entertainment. As the household moves closer to the city center, it saves on travel costs for commuting, shopping, and entertainment, so the savings in travel cost will be relatively large and the housing-price function will be relatively steep. In general, the more frequent the travel to the city center, the steeper the housing-price function and the residential bid-rent function.

4. **Two-earner households.** The simple model assumes that a single person from each household commutes to the city center. Suppose that all the households in a city are suddenly transformed into two-earner households. What happens to the housing-price function? If two members of each household commute to the CBD, a household that moves closer to the city center will experience double the savings in commuting costs. In equilibrium, the housing-price function will be steeper in the two-earner city, reflecting the greater savings associated with living closer to central-city jobs. Therefore, the residential bid-rent function will be steeper.

Spatial Variation in Public Goods and Pollution

The simple monocentric model has a number of assumptions that make the city center the focal point of the city. Except for jobs in the CBD, all the things that people care about (public services, taxes, pollution, amenities) are distributed uniformly throughout the city. What happens if these things are not distributed uniformly?

Public Goods and Taxes.   Taxes and public services vary within a metropolitan area. Suppose that the quality of public schools varies within the city, but the costs of schools (tuition and taxes) are the same throughout the city. In equilibrium, the price of housing will be higher in the communities with better schools. Parents pay for better public schools indirectly: instead of paying higher taxes, they pay more for housing and residential land. Similarly, the prices of housing and land are higher in communities with lower crime rates. The same argument applies to variation in taxes. If two communities have the same level of public services but one community has higher taxes, the price of housing will be higher in the low-tax community.

Pollution and Amenities.   The simple model assumes that environmental quality is the same at all locations in the city. To explain the effects of pollution on housing and land prices, suppose that a polluting factory moves into the center of a previously clean city. If the smoke and smell from the factory are heaviest in the central area of the city, the factory will decrease the relative attractiveness of dwellings near the city center, decreasing the price of housing. In addition, the factory will increase the relative attractiveness of more remote dwellings, increasing the price of suburban housing.

Figure 6–9 shows the effects of the polluting factory on the housing-price function. P_c is the price function in the absence of pollution (the clean city), and P_s is the price function with a small amount of pollution. The pollution from the central-city factory decreases slope of the housing-price function. As a household moves toward the city center, there are costs (more pollution) as well as benefits (lower commuting costs), so the increase in the price of housing will be smaller in the polluted city. If the city has a high level of pollution, the housing-price function may be positively sloped, as shown by P_d. In this case, central-city pollution is so obnoxious that the advantages of a central-city dwelling (lower commuting costs)

FIGURE 6–9   **Pollution in the Central City and Housing Prices**

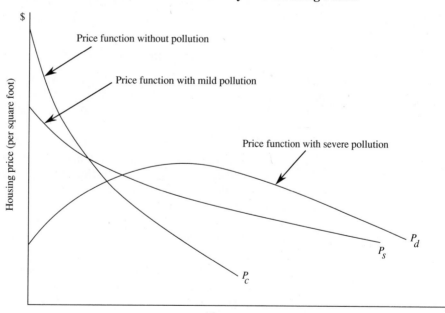

Air pollution from a central-city factory decreases housing prices near the city center and increases housing prices far from the city center. The more severe the pollution, the greater the change in housing prices.

are dominated by its disadvantages (greater exposure to pollution). As a result, people will live near the city center only if they are compensated in the form of lower housing prices.

Changes in the housing-price function cause similar changes in the residential bid-rent function. A relatively flat housing-price function (P_s) will generate a relatively flat bid-rent function. Similarly, a positively sloped housing-price function (P_d) will generate a positively sloped residential bid-rent function.

The same arguments apply to locations that have positive locational attributes (amenities) such as scenic views or access to parks. If people get utility from scenic views or park access, they will be willing to pay more for dwellings that provide such amenities.

Income and Location

In U.S. cities, the wealthy tend to locate in the suburbs and the poor tend to locate near the city center. In other words, average household income increases as one moves away from the city center. Because the most expensive land is near the city center, this location pattern is puzzling. Why should the poor occupy the most expensive housing and land? There are several theories of this observed pattern of income segregation. The first is based on the simple monocentric model, and the others are based on extensions of the monocentric model.

Trade-Off between Housing and Commuting Costs

According to the simple monocentric model, a household chooses the location that provides the best trade-off between housing costs and commuting costs. The location choice is determined by the outcome of a tug-of-war between two competing forces. The household is pulled toward the city center because commuting costs are lower for locations near jobs in the CBD. In addition, the household is pulled toward suburban locations because housing prices are lower in the suburbs. One theory of income segregation, developed by Alonso (1964) and Muth (1969), suggests that the poor choose central locations because the force pulling them toward the central city (lower commuting costs) dominates the force pulling them toward the suburbs (lower housing costs). In contrast, the wealthy choose suburban locations because the force pulling them toward the suburbs dominates the force pulling them toward the central city.

To explain how income segregation can occur, consider the location decisions of two households, a poor one and a wealthy one. Suppose that the poor household chooses a location near the city center, meaning that the force pulling toward the city center (lower commuting costs) dominates the force pulling toward the suburb (lower housing prices). Under what circumstances would the outcome of the tug-of-war be different for the wealthy household? In other words, under what circumstances will the wealthy household locate in the suburbs instead of the central city?

Compared to the poor household, the wealthy household experiences stronger pulls toward both the central city and the suburbs. The force pulling toward the central city is stronger because the wealthy household has a higher opportunity cost of commuting time: the household sacrifices more income per minute spent commuting instead of working. The force pulling the wealthy household toward the suburbs is stronger as well because the wealthy household consumes more housing and therefore has more to gain from lower housing prices in the suburbs. Suppose that the difference in housing consumption is large relative to the difference in commuting costs: the wealthy household consumes a lot more housing than the poor household does but doesn't have much higher commuting costs. In this case, the tug-of-war for the wealthy household is won by the forces pulling the household toward the low-price suburbs: the household lives in the suburbs because the savings in housing costs outweigh the higher commuting costs. In contrast, the tug-of-war for the poor household is won by the forces pulling the household toward the central city. Although the poor household would pay less for housing in the suburbs, its housing consumption is low enough that the savings in housing costs are outweighed by the increase in commuting costs.

Wheaton (1977) provides evidence that questions the validity of this theory of income segregation. His results suggest that the relative strengths of the competing forces are about the same for households of all income levels. In other words, the income-related differences in housing consumption (which pull toward the suburbs) are about the same as income-related differences in commuting costs (which pull toward the central city). Therefore, the observed pattern of income segregation cannot be explained by the competing forces described by the monocentric model. Wheaton's results suggest that we must look beyond the monocentric model to explain income segregation.

Other Explanations

Some alternative explanations of income segregation are based on factors excluded from the simple monocentric model:

1. **New suburban housing.** Suppose that the utility generated from a particular dwelling decreases over time as the dwelling deteriorates and becomes obsolete. In other words, people get less utility out of an older house because it is less fashionable, has higher maintenance costs, and is equipped with fewer modern gadgets. The wealthy, who demand high-quality housing, will occupy new housing instead of used housing. As an urban area grows, it expands outward, and developers build new housing for high-income households in the peripheral areas. The poor are left with old houses in the central city.

2. **Fleeing central city problems.** As explained later in the book, poverty contributes to three urban problems. First, crime rates are higher among the poor, in part because the poor face a relatively low opportunity cost of committing crime. Second, fiscal problems are more likely in a jurisdiction with a large fraction of low-income citizens. Third, students

from poor families have relatively low achievement levels and pull down the achievement levels of other students. To escape these problems, wealthy households flee to the suburbs, leaving large concentrations of poor households behind.

3. **Suburban zoning.** As explained in Chapter 8 (Land-Use Controls and Zoning), suburban governments use zoning to exclude low-income households. Therefore, only the wealthy have the opportunity to escape the problems of the central city.

Policy Implications

These alternative theories of income segregation suggest that public policy can affect the location choices of wealthy and poor households. A housing policy that encourages the renovation of the central-city housing stock may cause some high-income households to return to the central city. Policies that decrease poverty will decrease crime rates, reduce fiscal problems, and improve central-city schools, encouraging high-income households to live in the central city. Similarly, policies that address the crime and education problems directly will increase the relative attractiveness of central-city locations. Finally, policies that control exclusionary zoning will allow the poor to move to the suburbs.

FIGURE 6–10   Value of Land in Chicago in 1928

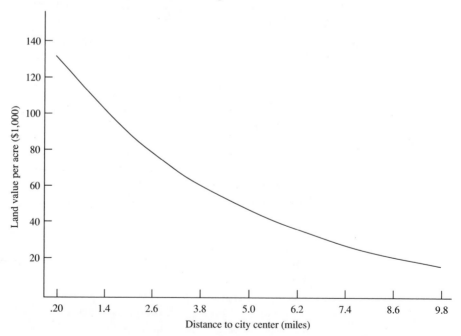

SOURCE: Edwin S. Mills, "The Value of Urban Land," in *The Quality of the Urban Environment*, ed. H. Perloff (Washington, D.C.: Resources for the Future, 1969).

Empirical Estimates of Rent and Density Functions

This section discusses empirical studies of land rent and land use in the monocentric city. The studies are based on data from the early 20th century, during the heyday of the monocentric city. Chapter 7 (Suburbanization and Modern Cities) discusses empirical work that is based on more recent data.

A number of researchers have estimated the relationship between land rent and distance to the city center. Mills (1969) used data collected by Homer Hoyt to estimate the relationship between land *value* and distance. As explained earlier in this chapter, land value is the present value of land rent, so it's easy to make the translation from value to rent. Figure 6–10 (opposite page) shows the estimated land-rent function for Chicago in 1928, a time when the city was monocentric. The value of land drops from about $140,000 per acre at the city center to about $114,000 per acre 1 mile from the city center, to about $17,000 per acre 10 miles from the city center.

How does population density vary within the monocentric city? The **density function** describes the relationship between population density and distance

FIGURE 6–11   Population Density in Baltimore in 1920

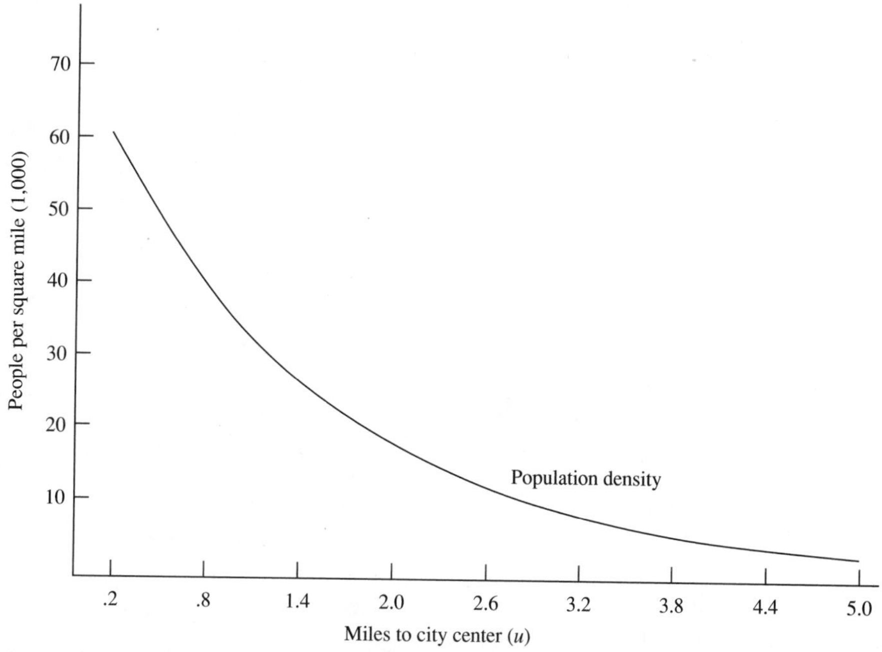

The density function is negatively sloped because (*a*) housing consumption increases with *u* (a result of declining housing prices), and (*b*) land per unit of housing increases with *u* (a result of declining land prices).

SOURCE: Edwin S. Mills, *Studies in the Structure of the Urban Economy* (Baltimore, Md.: Johns Hopkins, 1972).

to the city center. Mills (1972) estimated the density functions for 18 metropolitan areas for different years. Figure 6–11 shows the estimated density function for Baltimore in 1920, a time when the city was monocentric. Population density drops from about 60,000 people per square mile at a distance of 0.2 miles from the city center, to about 34,000 per square mile at a distance of 1 mile, to about 4,200 per square mile at a distance of 4 miles.

Summary

1. The monocentric city has the following characteristics:
   a. All manufacturers export their output through a central export node.
   b. Manufactured goods are transported within the city by horse-drawn wagon.
   c. Office workers travel by foot from offices to a central market area to exchange information.
   d. Commuters and shoppers travel on a hub-and-spoke streetcar system.
2. The manufacturing bid-rent function is negatively sloped because transport costs are lower near the export node. It is convex because of factor substitution.
3. The office bid-rent function is negatively sloped because travel costs are lower near the central market area, and it is convex because of factor substitution.
4. Transport costs in the monocentric city are relatively high for office firms, so the office bid-rent function is relatively steep and office firms occupy the central area of the city.
5. In the simple monocentric model, all employment is in the CBD and other things that residents care about (e.g., public services, taxes, pollution) are the same at all locations within the city.
6. The housing-price function shows the price of housing (per square foot of living space) for different locations in the city. The function is negatively sloped because commuting costs increase with the distance to the city center. It is convex because of consumer substitution: as the price of housing rises, consumers substitute other goods for housing.
7. The residential bid-rent function shows the amount housing producers are willing to pay for residential land at different locations in the city. It is negatively sloped because the housing-price function is negatively sloped. It is convex because of consumer substitution (which makes the housing-price function convex) and factor substitution.
8. The density function shows the number of people per acre for different locations in the city. It is negatively sloped for two reasons:
   a. Housing prices are higher near the city center, so housing consumption is lower (fewer square feet of living space per household).

   b. Land prices are higher near the city center, so the amount of land per square foot of housing is lower.

9. Activities in the monocentric city are arranged according to their transportation costs: the higher the transportation cost, the closer to the city center.

   a. The city center is occupied by the office sector rather than the manufacturing sector because office output is transmitted by high-cost office workers, while manufacturing output is transported by horse-drawn wagon.

   b. Employment is concentrated in the CBD because the cost of commuting (from the suburbs to the CBD factories and offices) is low relative to the cost of moving output (from the suburbs to the city center). Freight traveled by horse-drawn wagon, a relatively slow and expensive travel mode. In contrast, workers traveled by streetcar, a relatively fast and inexpensive travel mode.

10. If the assumptions of the simple monocentric model are dropped, the housing-price function and the residential bid-rent change.

   a. The opportunity cost of commuting is the value of forgone work or leisure time. The typical commuter values commuting time at between one third and one half of his or her wage. The unit cost of commuting is the sum of time and monetary costs.

   b. Noncommuting travel to the CBD increases the slopes of the housing-price and bid-rent functions because total travel costs increase more rapidly as the household moves away from the CBD.

   c. The two-earner household has a relatively steep housing-price function if both earners commute to the CBD.

   d. The prices of housing and land are higher in communities with superior local public goods and low taxes.

   e. The prices of housing and land are higher in communities with clean air, scenic views, and access to parks.

11. In U.S. cities, the wealthy tend to locate in the suburbs and the poor tend to locate near the city center. One theory of income segregation suggests that the wealthy and the poor make different location choices because they face different trade-offs between commuting and housing cost. This theory has been refuted by empirical evidence, suggesting that the observed pattern of segregation is caused by other factors, such as demand for new suburban housing, the desire to escape the central-city problems associated with poverty, and exclusionary zoning in the suburbs.

Exercises and Discussion Questions

1. In the city of Trekburg, manufacturers have two options for intracity freight. They can use a conventional transportation system (the truck) or a matter

transmitter. The transporter instantly transports the output from the factory to the central export node ("Beam it over, Scotty"). A transmitter can be rented for $C per year, and running the machine is costless. The transporter can transport output up to a distance of two miles. All manufacturing output goes through the export node.

a. Draw the bid-rent function for a firm that uses the matter transmitter, and label it M.

b. On the same graph, draw the bid-rent function for a firm that uses the truck, and label it T.

c. Will every manufacturer use the matter transmitter? If not, where will the firms using the truck be located?

2. Complete the following table, given the following assumptions:

   i. The office firm produces 100 consultations per month.

   ii. The consultation fee is $75.

   iii. Travel time is five minutes per block.

   iv. The opportunity cost of travel time is $3 per minute.

   v. Every consultation requires one trip to the city center.

Distance to City Center (miles)	Size of Site (acres)	Total Revenue	Nonland Cost	Travel Cost	Pre-Rent Profit	Rent per Acre
0	0.40		$3,600			
1	0.70		2,000			
2	0.90		1,200			
3	1.00		900			

3. Consider an office firm with the following characteristics: The wage of executives is $120 per hour, and the executive takes four minutes to walk one block (eight minutes to make a round trip). The price of output is $150, and the firm produces 50 consultations (requiring 50 trips to the city center). At a location four blocks from the city center, the firm occupies a one-acre site and spends $1,000 on nonland inputs.

a. What is the travel cost per block?

b. How much is the firm willing to pay for land four blocks from the city center?

c. Given the available information, is it possible to compute how much the firm is willing to pay for land one block from the city center? If not, what additional information do you need?

4. Depict graphically the effects of the following changes on the division of CBD land between office firms and manufacturers:

a. The unit freight cost decreases.

b. The price of office output increases.

c. The opportunity cost of executive travel decreases.

5. Consider a monocentric city in which the unit cost of commuting is $10 per mile per month. A household located eight miles from the city center occupies a dwelling with 1,200 square feet at a monthly rent of $600. Nonland cost per dwelling is $200, and there are four houses per acre.

   a. What is the price (per square foot) of housing at $u = 8$? What is the bid rent at $u = 8$?

   b. Assume that the demand for housing is perfectly inelastic. What is the price of housing at $u = 5$?

   c. Assume that housing firms do not engage in factor substitution. What is the bid rent at $u = 5$?

   d. How would your answers to (b) and (c) change if the demand for housing is price-elastic and firms engage in factor substitution? Would the prices of housing and land be larger or smaller?

6. Depict graphically the effects of the following changes on the equilibrium housing-price function:

   a. The workweek is shortened from five days per week to four days per week.

   b. The workers in two-earner households start riding to work together.

7. Suppose that a city restricts the heights of residential structures. The maximum height is four stories, the height that would normally occur at a distance of five miles from the city center. Draw two residential bid-rent functions, one for the city in the absence of height restrictions and one with height restrictions.

References and Additional Readings

Alcaly, Roger E. "Transportation and Urban Land Values: A Review of the Theoretical Literature." *Land Economics* 52 (1976), pp. 42–53. Discusses the effects of changes in transport costs on land rent.

Alonso, William. *Location and Land Use*. Cambridge, Mass.: Harvard University Press, 1964. Expands the Von Thunen model to the location decisions of households.

Downs, Anthony. *Urban Problems and Prospects*. Chicago: Markham, 1970. Suggests that the building of new housing on the peripheral area of the metropolitan area contributes to the suburbanization of high-income households.

Jackson, Jerry. "Intraurban Variation in the Price of Housing." *Journal of Urban Economics* 6 (1979), pp. 465–79. Estimates the housing-price function, finding that housing prices fall by about 2 percent per mile.

Kain, John F., and John M. Quigley. "Measuring the Value of Housing Quality." *Journal of the American Statistical Association* 65 (1970), pp. 532–38. Estimates the relationship between various housing characteristics (including location) and the price of housing.

Meyer, J.; John F. Kain; and M. Wohl. *The Urban Transportation Problem*. Cambridge, Mass.: Harvard University Press, 1965. Discusses the effects of the trend toward two-earner households and noncommuting travel on the residential rent function.

Mills, Edwin S. "The Value of Urban Land." In *The Quality of the Urban Environment,* ed. H. Perloff. Washington, D.C.: Resources for the Future, 1969. Estimates the land-rent function in Chicago from 1836 to 1959.

———. *Studies in the Structure of the Urban Economy.* Baltimore, Md.: Johns Hopkins, 1972. Chapter 3 estimates population and employment density functions for U.S. cities.

Muth, Richard. *Cities and Housing.* Chicago: University of Chicago Press, 1969. A classic study of residential location decisions in Chicago. Chapter 2 models the location decision. Chapter 7 estimates the density function for several U.S. cities. Chapter 10 provides empirical evidence that suggests that the tendency for higher-income households to locate farther from the city center is caused by differences in the trade-offs between housing and commuting costs.

Wasylenko, Michael J. "Disamenities, Local Taxation, and the Intrametropolitan Location of Households and Firms." In *Research in Urban Economics,* vol. 4, ed. Robert Ebel. Greenwich, Conn.: JAI Press, 1984. Reviews the empirical evidence concerning the effects of income on location; also reviews the evidence concerning the intrametropolitan location choices of firms.

Wheaton, William. "Income and Urban Residence: An Analysis of Consumer Demand for Location." *American Economic Review* 67 (1977), pp. 620–31. Suggests that the income elasticity of demand for land is close to the income elasticity of time costs, meaning that the tendency for the poor to locate near the city center cannot be explained by the simple monocentric model.

Suburbanization and Modern Cities

This chapter explains the decline of the traditional monocentric city and the rise of the modern multicentric city. In the traditional monocentric city, most economic activity was concentrated in the central core area. The entire metropolitan area was oriented toward the employment and shopping opportunities in the central city. In the modern multicentric city, a large fraction of employment is in suburban areas, with much of the suburban employment in subcenters. People who live in metropolitan areas are now less dependent on the central city for employment and shopping.

This chapter has seven parts. The first part discusses the facts on suburbanization, focusing on the changes in the spatial distributions of population and employment in the last several decades. The second through the fifth parts discuss the reasons for the suburbanization of manufacturers, population, retailers, and office firms. The sixth part discusses the development of suburban subcenters in Chicago, Los Angeles, and Houston. The final part of the chapter discusses land-use patterns in the modern multicentric city.

Suburbanization Facts

What are the facts on the suburbanization of employment and population? Figure 7–1 shows the distribution of population and employment between central cities and suburbs in 1948 and 1980. The percentage of the metropolitan population in central cities dropped from 64 percent in 1948 to 43 percent in 1980, and the percentage of manufacturing employment dropped from 67 percent to 46 percent. The losses in trade and service employment were even larger: the percentage of wholesaling employment in central cities dropped from 92 percent to 56 percent;

FIGURE 7-1   Percentage of Metropolitan Population and Employment in Central Cities, 1948 and 1980

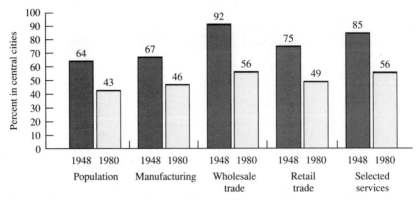

SOURCES: 1948 data from John F. Kain, "The Distribution and Movement of Jobs and Industry," in *The Metropolitan Enigma,* ed. James Q. Wilson (Cambridge, Mass.: Harvard University Press, 1968); 1980 data from U.S. Bureau of the Census, *Journey to Work.*

the percentage of retail employment dropped from 75 percent to 49 percent; and the percentage of service employment dropped from 85 percent to 56 percent. It's important to note that part of the measured increase in the share of activity in the suburbs results from urban growth with fixed central-city boundaries. As an urban area grows, most growth occurs on the periphery. As the metropolitan area expands outward, an increasing share of its population lives outside the fixed boundaries of the central city. If the suburban population is assumed to be the population outside the central-city border, growth causes suburbanization.

Table 7–1 provides a closer look at the distribution of employment between central cities and suburbs in 1980. The employment sectors are listed in declining order of importance. Three sectors had more than three fifths of metropolitan employment in central cities: public administration (62 percent); transportation, communications, and utilities (61 percent); and finance, insurance, and real estate (63 percent). The three service sectors (professional and related services, business and repair services, and personal services) had between 53 percent and 57 percent of their employment in central cities. The other sector that had a majority of employment in the central city is wholesale trade (56 percent).

What happened to the distribution of employment between central cities and suburbs during the 1980s? Unfortunately, the relevant data from the 1990 census will not be available until 1994. Figure 7–2 shows the spatial distributions of population and employment of the 60 largest metropolitan areas in 1986. The figure shows the percentages of population and employment in central cities (the political city), central business districts (the core area of the central city), the rest of the central cities, and outside central cities. Employment is more centralized than

TABLE 7–1 **Distribution of Employment between Central Cities and Suburbs by Type of Employment, 1980**

	Employment Total (000)	Employment in Central Cities (000)	Percent in Central Cities	Percent in Suburbs
Total	67,728	35,698	53%	47%
Manufacturing	15,190	7,060	46	54
Professional and related services	14,067	7,966	57	43
Retail trade	10,905	5,330	49	51
Transportation, communication, utilities	5,083	3,095	61	39
Finance, insurance, real estate	4,634	2,926	63	37
Public administration	3,780	2,343	62	38
Construction	3,673	1,716	47	53
Business and repair services	3,124	1,700	54	46
Wholesale trade	3,069	1,706	56	44
Other industries	2,173	779	36	64
Personal services	2,031	1,077	53	47

SOURCE: U.S. Bureau of the Census, *1980 Census of Population, Journey to Work,* PC80-2-6D (Washington, D.C.: U.S. Government Printing Office, 1984), Table 1.

FIGURE 7–2 **Distribution of Population and Employment for 60 Largest Metropolitan Areas, 1986**

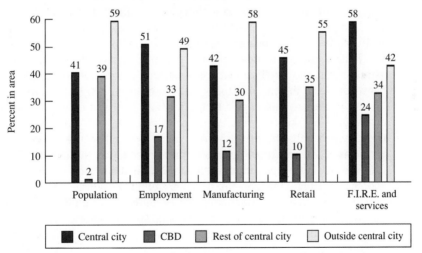

SOURCE: Author's calculations based on data from the Wharton Urban Decentralization Project.

population: central cities contain 51 percent of metropolitan employment but only 41 percent of metropolitan population; CBDs contain 17 percent of metropolitan employment but only 2 percent of metropolitan population. Manufacturing is the most suburbanized of the three types of employment: 58 percent of manufacturing jobs are located outside central cities. The jobs grouped under FIRE (finance, insurance, and real estate) and services are the most centralized: 58 Percent of these jobs are in central cities (24 percent in CBDs and another 34 percent in other parts of central cities), leaving 42 percent for suburban areas.

Suburbanization of Manufacturing

As shown in Figure 7–1, the share of metropolitan manufacturing employment in central cities decreased from about two thirds in 1948 to less than half in 1980. Mills (1972) provides evidence that the suburbanization of manufacturing started long before 1948. What caused the suburbanization of manufacturing employment?

The Intracity Truck

Moses and Williamson (1972) explain how the intracity truck encouraged the suburbanization of manufacturing. In the monocentric city of the 19th and early 20th centuries, freight was shipped within cities by horse-drawn wagons. Starting about 1910, manufacturers switched from the horse-drawn wagon to the truck. The truck was both faster and cheaper than the horse-drawn wagon: around 1920, the truck was half as costly (15 cents per ton per mile versus 33 cents), and at least twice as fast. Once the intracity truck was introduced, its use spread rapidly. The number of trucks in the city of Chicago increased from 800 in 1910 to 23,000 in 1920.

As explained in Chapter 6, the location decision of a manufacturing firm is determined by the outcome of a tug-of-war. On one side is the central export node, which pulls the firm toward the city center because freight costs are lower for firms near the export node. On the other side is the suburb, which pulls the firm toward low-wage suburban locations. In the era of the horse-drawn wagon and the streetcar, the cost of moving freight was large relative to the cost of moving people, so manufacturers located in the city center. It was cheaper to ship the workers from the suburbs to the central-city factory than to ship the output from a suburban factory to the export node. The intracity truck decreased freight costs, weakening the pull toward the central export node, so the tug-of-war was more frequently won by the suburb. Although a suburban location was inefficient with the horse-drawn wagon, it was efficient with the truck.

The Intercity Truck

Two decades after the truck was first introduced, manufacturers started using the truck for intercity transport. Improvements in the truck made long-distance travel feasible, and the expansion of the intercity highway system facilitated intercity truck traffic. Eventually, the truck became competitive with the train and the ship for intercity freight. As manufacturers switched from trains and ships to trucks, they were freed from their dependence on the railheads and ports in city centers, and moved to sites accessible to the intercity highways. The freight costs associated with suburban sites decreased, allowing manufacturers to move closer to their suburban workers.

In 1956, the interstate highway system was authorized by Congress, and the bulk of the system was in place by the late 1970s. The highway system decreased the relative cost of shipping by truck, causing more manufacturers to switch their freight operations from ships and trains to trucks. More recently, cities have built circumferential highways (beltways) that are connected to the interstate highway system. Manufacturers locate close to the suburban beltways because they provide easy access to the interstate system.

Figure 7–3 shows the bid rent for manufacturing land at different locations in a beltway city. The figure is drawn under the assumption that the beltway circles the city at a distance of 2.5 miles. In the beltway city, manufacturers can transport their output to the beltway or to a central export node (a railhead or a port at the

FIGURE 7–3   Manufacturing Bid Rent in a Beltway City

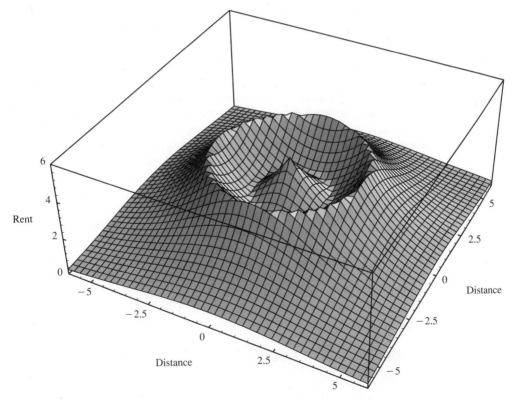

city center). The bid-rent function forms a peak at the central export node (as in the monocentric city) and a circular ridge centered on the beltway. Manufacturers are likely to outbid other land users for land near the suburban beltway.

The Automobile

The automobile contributed to the suburbanization of manufacturers. To explain the effects of the automobile, consider a firm with a highly skilled work force: only 1 in 1,000 people has the skills required to work for the firm. Suppose that the firm employs 100 people and is located in a streetcar city of 100,000. Where in the city will the firm locate? Because the firm draws laborers from the entire metropolitan area, it will locate at a point that is accessible to the entire urban area. In the hub-and-spoke streetcar city, the city center (the hub) is the most accessible location.

Where will the firm locate in a modern automobile city? In the auto city, employees can drive their cars from their homes to any location in the urban area. While the firm might still locate in the city center, it could also locate along an urban highway or a suburban beltway because such sites are accessible to residents throughout the metropolitan area. In general, the automobile loosened the ties to the streetcar nodes in the core area, allowing the suburbanization of firms with specialized labor forces.

Single-Story Plants

Another factor in the suburbanization of manufacturing was the switch from the traditional multistory plants of the 19th century to single-story plants. To exploit new production technologies (assembly-line production and materials-handling techniques such as the forklift truck), manufacturers built single-level facilities. As land consumption increased, the forces pulling the firms toward the suburbs (low-cost land and low wages) dominated the forces pulling the firms toward the central city (lower freight costs), and many manufacturers moved to the suburbs.

Suburban Airports

The increased importance of air freight is another reason for the suburbanization of manufacturing. A firm that transports a relatively large fraction of its output by air experiences a relatively strong pull toward an airport. For some types of firms, the suburban airport has replaced the old central export node (railhead or port facility) as the point of orientation. As explained later in this chapter, many modern cities have clusters of employment near suburban airports.

The Suburbanization of Population

As shown in Figure 7–1, the share of metropolitan population living in central cities dropped from about two thirds in 1948 to just over two fifths in 1980. Mills

TABLE 7–2   **Average Density Gradients for Four Metropolitan Areas, 1880–1963****

Year	Average Gradient	Percentage of Population within 3 Miles of City Center
1880	1.22	88%
1890	1.06	83
1900	0.96	78
1910	0.80	69
1920	0.69	61
1930	0.63	56
1940	0.59	53
1948	0.50	44
1954	0.40	34
1958	0.35	28
1963	0.31	24

*The metropolitan areas are Baltimore, Milwaukee, Philadelphia, and Rochester.
SOURCE: Edwin S. Mills, *Studies in the Structure of the Urban Economy* (Baltimore, Md.: Johns Hopkins University Press, 1972).

(1972) provides evidence of suburbanization as far back as 1880. As explained in Chapter 6, the **density function** describes the relationship between population density and distance to the city center. Mills estimated the density functions for four metropolitan areas (Baltimore, Milwaukee, Philadelphia, and Rochester) between 1880 and 1963. Table 7–2 shows the average density gradient (defined as the percentage change in population density per mile) for the four cities between 1880 and 1963. The gradient decreases over time, indicating that the population density function flattened out over time. The third column of the table uses the estimated density gradients to compute the percentage of the metropolitan population living within three miles of the city center. Between 1880 and 1963, the percentage dropped from 88 percent to 24 percent.

This section discusses five possible reasons for the suburbanization of population:

1. Increase in real income.
2. Decrease in commuting cost.
3. Central city problems: race, crime, taxes, and education.
4. Following the firms to the suburbs.
5. Public policy.

Increase in Real Income

Did income growth contribute to the suburbanization of population? As explained in Chapter 6 (Land Use in the Monocentric City), an increase in income has an ambiguous effect on the relative attractiveness of the suburbs because it has two conflicting effects on the relative costs of a suburban location:

1. **Increase in commuting cost.** An increase in real income increases the amount of income sacrificed per minute of travel time; that is, it increases the opportunity cost of commuting. Therefore, an increase in income increases the relative attractiveness of dwellings close to the workplace. For someone who works in the CBD, an increase in income increases the relative attractiveness of central-city housing. This is the **opportunity-cost effect:** an increase in income increases the opportunity cost of commuting, pulling households toward the central city.

2. **Increase in housing consumption.** Because housing is a normal good, an increase in income increases housing consumption. Income growth increases the relative attractiveness of locations with low-priced housing, that is, the suburbs. A household that occupies a large house is willing to commute long distances to rent a dwelling with a relatively low price *per square foot*. This is the **consumption effect:** an increase in income increases housing consumption, pulling households toward inexpensive suburban housing.

Given these conflicting effects, it is not possible to predict, on theoretical grounds, whether income growth will contribute to suburbanization. Income growth will cause suburbanization if the consumption effect dominates the opportunity-cost effect. This will occur if the demand for housing increases with income at a faster rate than commuting costs increase with income. As explained in Chapter 6, the evidence suggests that housing demand and commuting costs increase at about the same rate, so it does not appear that income growth contributed very much to suburbanization.

Decrease in Commuting Costs

Over the last 140 years, technological innovations have decreased the monetary and time costs of commuting. In the 1800s, the development of new transit systems decreased the cost of commuting from the suburbs to the central core. The most important innovations were the horse streetcar (developed in the 1850s) and the conventional streetcar (developed in the 1890s). In the last 60 years, improvements in the automobile and the intracity highway network have decreased the costs of personal commuting. The automobile increased travel speeds, decreasing the time cost of commuting. The decrease in commuting costs increased the relative attractiveness of suburban locations.

In the late 1800s and early 1900s, many landowners profited from the introduction of streetcars. In a number of cities, speculators bought large tracts of undeveloped land just outside the city's borders and patiently awaited the extension of streetcar service to their land. Other investors took a more active role. In Cleveland, the Von Sweringen brothers bought a large parcel of undeveloped land from the local society of Shakers. When the Cleveland State Railways refused to extend its streetcar service to the undeveloped area, the Von Sweringen brothers built their own streetcar line to the area, which became known as Shaker Heights. The brothers' land, which was appraised at $240,000 in 1900, increased in value to $80 million by 1930.

Central-City Problems

Other theories of suburbanization focus on the negative locational attributes (disamenities) of central cities. The following factors will encourage households to move from the central city to the suburbs:

1. **Old housing.** The deterioration of the central-city housing stock encourages households to move to the suburbs, where newer housing is available.

2. **Race and income.** Some households move to the suburbs to escape racial conflict; others move to avoid living near low-income households.

3. **Central-city fiscal problems.** Many central cities have relatively high taxes, encouraging households to move to low-tax suburbs. The causality goes both ways: fiscal problems cause suburbanization, and suburbanization contributes to central-city fiscal problems.

4. **Crime.** Most central cities have relatively high crime rates, encouraging households to move to the suburbs. The reasons for the relatively high central-city crime rates will be discussed in Chapter 18 (Crime and Punishment).

5. **Education.** Suburban schools are typically superior to central-city schools, encouraging households to relocate in suburban school districts. The reasons for the inferiority of central-city schools will be explained in Chapter 17 (Education).

Empirical studies of the suburbanization process provide support for the theory that central city problems encourage suburbanization. The empirical literature is reviewed by Wasylenko (1984). Bradbury, Downs, and Small (1982) tested various theories of suburbanization, using a sample of 121 SMSAs for the period 1970 to 1975. They found that a metropolitan area experienced relatively rapid suburbanization if its central city had (1) a relatively old housing stock, (2) relatively high taxes, and (3) a relatively large black population. Another factor in suburbanization was the number of suburban local governments: the larger the number of suburban governments to choose from, the more rapid the suburbanization. Frey (1979) found that metropolitan areas with high taxes, high crime rates, and low educational expenditures experienced relatively rapid suburbanization.

Following Firms to the Suburbs

As explained earlier in this chapter, the development of the truck and the building of circumferential highways shifted manufacturing employment from the central

TABLE 7-3   Commuting Patterns within Metropolitan Areas for Different Regions, 1980

Region	Percentage of Total Work Trips within Metropolitan Areas			
	Central City to Central City	*Central City to Suburb*	*Suburb to Central City*	*Suburb to Suburb*
Total United States	33.1%	6.7%	20.1%	40.1%
Northeast	32.2	4.7	15.3	47.8
North central	30.7	7.0	20.3	42.0
South	36.1	6.1	23.7	34.1
West	32.4	9.3	19.9	38.4

SOURCE: U.S. Bureau of the Census, "Metropolitan Commuting Flows," *1980 Census of Population, Journey to Work* (Washington, D.C.: U.S. Government Printing Office, 1984).

city to the suburbs. As explained later in this chapter, retailers and office firms have also moved to the suburbs, forming suburban subcenters. The suburbanization of employment contributed to the suburbanization of population because some workers followed their employers to the suburbs.

In the multicentric city, workers commute to jobs in suburban subcenters. Table 7–3 shows commuting patterns within metropolitan areas in 1980. In the United States, around 40 percent of workers commute within suburban areas, about twice the percentage of those who commute from the suburbs to the central city. In the Northeast, the number of workers commuting within the suburbs is over three times the number commuting from the suburbs to the central city.

How does the suburbanization of employment affect the residential bid-rent function? Workers are willing to pay more for housing near suburban subcenters because such locations have relatively low commuting costs. In the modern multicentric city, the housing-price function has several peaks, one at the city center, and one for each suburban subcenter. The residential bid-rent function will look like the housing-price function, with a series of peaks, one at the city center and one for each subcenter.

Public Policy and Suburbanization

A number of public policies affect the intraurban location choices of households, encouraging households to live in the suburbs. Among the public policies to be discussed later in the book are the following:

1. **Tax subsidy for home ownership.** The federal tax code allows the deduction of interest paid on home loans, providing an implicit subsidy for home ownership. As explained in Chapter 12 (Housing Policies), the favorable treatment of home ownership encourages suburbanization.

2. **Commuting externalities.** Because commuting generates congestion externalities and pollution externalities, the marginal private cost of com-

muting is less than the marginal social cost. As explained in Chapter 15 (Autos and Highways), the internalization of these externalities would increase the relative cost of suburban living, encouraging commuters to live closer to their workplaces.

3. **Fragmented system of local government.** Some households move to the suburbs to flee central-city fiscal problems. The fragmented system of local government encourages suburbanization because it provides alternatives to the central-city government. Chapter 13 (Overview of Local Government) explores the role of metropolitan consolidation (a switch to a metropolitan government) on the location decisions of households. The issue is whether consolidation would discourage suburbanization.

4. **Highway construction.** The building of the highway system decreased commuting costs, increasing the relative attractiveness of the suburbs.

Gentrification: Return to the City?

In the 1970s and 1980s, the popular press publicized the renovation of central-city housing by wealthy households. To many people, the efforts of these households signaled a change in residential location patterns: it appeared that many high-income households were abandoning the suburban lifestyle to embrace an urban one. The process is labeled *gentrification* because poor households are replaced by relatively wealthy ones.

The most important fact about renovation and gentrification is that the number of renovations is relatively small. In most cities, the number of renovations is a small fraction of the number of dwellings abandoned. In the late 1970s, renovation and gentrification in the 30 largest cities were concentrated in about 100 neighborhoods and involved less than one half of 1 percent of the housing stock in these cities (Frieden and Sagalyn, 1991). Kern (1984) describes the characteristics of renovators. The typical renovator is wealthy, young, highly educated, and either single or married with fewer than two children. Such households are attracted to central-city locations because they (1) patronize cultural establishments in the central city, (2) have relatively high commuting costs, and (3) have relatively low demands for housing and land. Most of the renovators moved from one part of the central city to the area being renovated, not from the suburbs back to the central city. These facts suggest that gentrification involves a relatively small number of households and does not signal a fundamental change in residential location patterns.

Suburbanization of Retailers

As shown in Figure 7–1, the suburban share of retail employment increased from one fourth in 1948 to over one half in 1980. There are three principal reasons for the suburbanization of retailing.

Following the Consumers

The suburbanization of population caused some retail activity to move to the suburbs. According to the simple version of central place theory (Chapter 4: Market Areas and the Urban Hierarchy), a retailer locates at the center of its market area. If scale economies are small relative to per capita demand, market areas will be small. A retailer with a relatively small market area is likely to follow its consumers to the suburbs. In contrast, a retailer with relatively large scale economies would not necessarily follow its customers to the suburbs: if there will be a single store for the entire metropolitan area, the most accessible location might still be in the city center.

The more sophisticated version of central place theory considers the effect of shopping externalities on location choices. If there are benefits from one-stop shopping and comparison shopping, retailers may compromise on their ideal (central place) locations to exploit the externalities associated with comparison shopping and one-stop shopping. The more sophisticated theory predicts that some retailers will not follow their consumers to the suburbs, but will stay in the city center to exploit shopping externalities.

The Automobile

The automobile, which replaced the hub-and-spoke streetcar system, loosened the retailer's ties to the city center. Before the development of the automobile, a retailer with relatively large-scale economies was tied to the CBD because that's where the streetcar delivered all the consumers. If shoppers use the auto instead of the streetcar, they can easily travel from their homes to any point in the metropolitan area, so even a suburban store can draw consumers from the entire metropolitan area. Retailers no longer had to be in the city center to be accessible to consumers throughout the metropolitan area, and many moved to the suburbs.

What about a retailer with moderate scale economies? In the hub-and-spoke streetcar city, travel from the suburb to the city center (along the spokes) was fast and inexpensive, while travel within the residential areas (between the spokes) was costly. A suburban store could not survive because intrasuburban travel costs were high: if it located at the geographical center of its suburban market area, few consumers would show up. If shoppers use the auto instead of the streetcar, travel costs within the residential area will decrease, allowing the store to locate at the center of its suburban market area.

Population Growth

The third reason for retail suburbanization is population growth. As the population of a metropolitan area increases, the total demand for retail goods increases. As total demand increases, the equilibrium number of retail stores increases. Some of the new stores will locate in the suburban areas.

To explain this idea, consider the demand for wigs. Suppose that scale economies in wig retailing are exhausted with an output of 500 wigs per store per month and that the per capita demand for wigs is 0.01 wigs per person per month. A city with a population of 50,000 has a total demand of 500 wigs per month and can support a single wig store in the city center. If the city grows to 500,000 and the demand for wigs *per capita* remains constant, the city will support 10 wig stores. If wig shopping is not subject to shopping externalities (comparison shopping and one-stop shopping), the wig stores will divide the metropolitan area into 10 market areas, and each wig store will locate in the center of a market area. Because some of the market areas will be centered in the suburbs, some wig stores will locate in the suburbs. If there are shopping externalities, wig stores may compromise on their ideal (central place) locations, but some wig stores are still likely to locate in the suburbs.

Suburbanization of Office Employment

Before the early 1970s, most office firms were still located in the city center because they were dependent on face-to-face contact with other firms, and the CBD provided a central meeting place for workers from different firms. Although some office activities had moved to the suburbs by the early 1970s, these were typically the "back-office" operations of insurance firms and banks, operations involving paper processing rather than face-to-face contact. For such activities, a CBD location was unnecessary. For most office activities, the advantages of the CBD (opportunities for timely contact with other firms) outweighed the disadvantages (high wages and rents).

During the 1970s and 1980s, suburban office space grew at a rapid rate. Nationwide, suburban office employment grew over seven times faster than central-city office employment during the 1970s (116 percent versus 15 percent). According to Cervero (1986), the most rapid growth in suburban office employment occurred in medium-sized metropolitan areas (with population between 250,000 and 1 million). The suburban office boom continued into the 1980s. For example, suburban office space in the Chicago metropolitan area more than doubled between 1980 and 1987, increasing the suburban share of total office space from 29 percent to 38 percent.

Suburbanization and Clustering of Offices

Pivo (1990) discusses the suburbanization of office space in six metropolitan areas: Denver, Houston, Los Angeles, San Francisco, Seattle, and Toronto. Some of his results are shown in Table 7–4. The first column of numbers shows, for each metropolitan area, the percentage of office space contained in the central business district. In five of the six metropolitan areas, the CBD contained less than half of the total office space; in four of six, the CBD contained less than 32 percent

TABLE 7–4   **Characteristics of Suburban Office Clusters**

Metropolitan Area	Percentage of Space in CBD	Number of Clusters	Percentage of Suburban Cluster Space Close to		
			Freeway	Interchange	Rail Transit
Denver	27	63	73	36	—
Houston	20	160	70	29	—
Los Angeles	12	270	66	30	—
San Francisco	31	102	93	52	10
Seattle	45	30	93	69	—
Toronto	54	52	79	27	25

SOURCE: Gary Pivo, "The Net of Mixed Beads: Suburban Office Development in Six Metropolitan Regions," *Journal of the American Planning Association* (Autumn 1990), pp. 457–69.

of the total office space. At the national level, central business districts contain about 47 percent of metropolitan office space.

The second column of numbers in Table 7–4 shows the number of suburban office clusters. Pivo defines a cluster as two or more office buildings within a quarter-mile area. Under this relatively permissive definition of a cluster, about 88 percent of the suburban office space in the six metropolitan areas is clustered. The number of clusters varies across metropolitan areas, reflecting differences in total suburban office space: the larger the total office space in a metropolitan area, the larger the number of suburban clusters. The size distribution of clusters was consistent across metropolitan areas: the largest 10 percent of clusters contained about $1/2$ of the total office space; the largest 25 percent contained about $2/3$ of the total space; and the largest 50 percent of clusters contained about $9/10$ of the total space.

The third, fourth, and fifth columns of numbers in Table 7–4 demonstrate the importance of access in the location of the clusters. The third column of numbers shows the percentage of suburban (clustered) office space within half a mile of a freeway: the percentages range from 66 percent (Los Angeles) to 93 percent (San Francisco and Seattle). The fourth column of numbers shows the percentage of office space within a mile of a freeway interchange: the percentages range from 29 percent (Houston) to 69 percent (Seattle). The fifth column of numbers shows, for the two cities with rail transit systems, the percentage of office space within walking distance of a rail transit station (a quarter mile): 10 percent for San Francisco and 25 percent for Toronto.

Communications Technology and Office Suburbanization

One factor in the suburbanization of office employment is the advances in communications technology (satellites, fiber optics, and solid-state electronics) that have decreased the cost of transmitting data, voices, and pictures. The new technology has generated two new methods of communications electronic mail and teleconferencing. These new communication methods have made some types of office activities less dependent on face-to-face contact. As an activity becomes less dependent on face-to-face contact, the relative attractiveness of a CBD location decreases.

Electronic Mail.   Office firms use electronic mail to send messages, documents, and data over computer lines. Electronic mail decreases the need for face-to-face contact because information can be sent over computer lines instead of being delivered by employees. Electronic mail allows the suburbanization of firms involved in the rapid turnaround of documents and reports.

To explain the effects of electronic mail, consider Abby, who runs an accounting firm. Abby gets 50 pages of data from her client (another firm) and condenses the information into an income statement. The client demands that the income statement be ready within 24 hours. In the absence of electronic mail, Abby would locate near her CBD customers to ensure the timely pickup of her client's data and the timely delivery of her income statement. The development of electronic mail allows Abby to move to the suburbs. Her inputs (the client data) and her output (the income statement) can be sent over telephone lines, so she can do her accounting in the suburbs, far from her CBD clients. Because Abby is not dependent on face-to-face contact, but on report-to-face contact, electronic mail allows her to escape the high wages and high rents of the CBD.

Electronic mail has caused the **decoupling** of some CBD firms. Many firms split their operations into suburban activities and CBD activities. Suppose that a firm has a large number of accountants, whose only task is to condense information into reports; that is, they compute bottom lines. The accountants do not interact with people outside the firm, but simply provide condensed information to the firm's executives, who then use the information in their interactions with other firms.

In the absence of electronic mail, the firm's accountants and executives must be in the same location to facilitate the rapid turnaround of information. Given the need for face-to-face interactions among the executives of different firms, the firm locates in the CBD. If the accounting information can be transmitted electronically, however, the accounting division can move to the suburbs, and the firm can send information between the suburban accountants and the CBD executives over telephone lines. Because electronic mail facilitates intrafirm communication, it allows the firm to decouple its operations, moving its support staff to the suburbs while keeping its executives in the CBD.

Teleconferencing.   The second new communication method, the teleconference, is essentially a video meeting. The teleconference is superior to the telephone conference because it allows both visual and verbal communication. The teleconference decreases the need for face-to-face contact within and between firms: instead of sending employees across town to another office, the firm can send them down the hall to the video room.

Because the video camera does not transmit as much information as a face-to-face encounter, the teleconference is not a perfect substitute for face-to-face contact. While the video camera focuses on one or two people in a meeting, a person who is physically present can watch everyone in the room, picking up verbal and nonverbal cues from a large number of people. In addition, the video camera cannot transmit tactile information. The tactile information provided by face-to-face encounters is sometimes useful: a firm, enthusiastic handshake sends a message that cannot be easily conveyed through a video camera.

Because the teleconference is not a perfect substitute for face-to-face contact, it is unlikely to cause substantial suburbanization of office firms. Most of the face-to-face contact that occurs in the CBD is between employees of different firms. The subtle interactions between firms often require face-to-face contact. When people from different firms meet, one of the purposes of the meeting is to establish trust. Because it is easier to establish trust in a face-to-face encounter, a video meeting is inappropriate for some types of interactions.

The teleconference approach is inefficient for firms whose interactions are infrequent and unpredictable. If two firms contact each other only once or twice a year, it may be inefficient for each of them to incur the fixed costs of establishing a video link. If a firm has a small number of encounters with a large number of firms, it may be more efficient to locate near the other firms in the CBD and rely on face-to-face contact.

In most urban areas, office employment occurs in both the CBD and suburban areas. The CBD contains activities for which face-to-face contact is still important (negotiation, design, marketing, and research). In contrast, suburban areas contain activities for which electronic communication is a good substitute for face-to-face contact.

Suburban Subcenters and Modern Cities

Many of the firms that moved to the suburbs located close to other firms. The clustering of firms in a few suburban locations caused the development of suburban subcenters. This part of the chapter discusses the rationale for suburban subcenters and presents some facts on subcenters in three metropolitan areas: Chicago, Los Angeles, and Houston.

The clustering of firms in suburban subcenters results from agglomerative economies in production. In a cluster of manufacturers or office firms, the total demand for some intermediate inputs is large enough to support external suppliers, who can exploit scale economies and thus produce the intermediate inputs at a lower cost. For example, manufacturers in a cluster may save money by purchasing business services (repair, maintenance, accounting) from a common supplier. Alternatively, if there are scale economies in printing glossy brochures and reports, a large cluster of office firms can support a printing firm, allowing each firm to save on printing costs. The same principle applies to restaurants and hotels. One rule of thumb is that a cluster of office firms with total office space of 2.5 million square feet can support a 250-room hotel.

Subcenters in Chicago

McDonald and McMillen (1990) show that there were four employment subcenters in the Chicago metropolitan area in 1970. They define a *subcenter* as an area with a relatively high employment density (workers per acre) and a relatively large employment ratio (total employment divided by the number of residents). In other words, a subcenter has more workers per acre and more jobs per resident than the area surrounding the subcenter. The authors identified three manufacturing subcenters, which contained 13.9 percent of the metropolitan area's manufacturing employment. The rest of the area's manufacturing employment was divided between the CBD (15.2 percent) and locations outside the CBD and subcenters (70.9 percent). Together, the four subcenters contained 14.4 percent of the metropolitan area's total employment. The rest of the area's employment was divided between the CBD (23 percent) and locations outside the CBD and subcenters (62.6 percent).

McDonald and McMillen (1990) note four changes in Chicago's subcenters since 1970. First, the O'Hare Airport has emerged as a major employment subcenter. Second, the older manufacturing subcenters have declined in importance, a result of a shift in the metropolitan economy away from its heavy reliance on manufacturing. Third, DuPage County has developed a subcenter that is based on research and development, communications, corporate headquarters, and light manufacturing. Fourth, like other cities, Chicago has experienced rapid growth in suburban offices, and some of the new offices are located in subcenters. Between 1980 and 1987, the amount of office space in the suburbs more than doubled, increasing the percentage of the metropolitan area's office space outside the CBD from 29 percent to 38 percent.

Subcenters in Los Angeles

Giuliano and Small (1991) use data on the spatial distribution of activity in the Los Angeles metropolitan area to show that there were 28 subcenters in Los Angeles County and Orange County in 1980. They define a *subcenter* as a zone where the employment density is at least 10 workers per acre and total employment is at least 10,000 workers. In contrast, employment density in the CBD (downtown Los Angeles) is 36 workers per acre and total employment is 469,000. Figure 7–4 shows the shares of employment and population in the CBD (downtown LA), the subcenters, and other locations. Total employment in the subcenters was about twice the employment in the CBD (23 percent versus 11 percent). Two thirds of the metropolitan area's employment was outside the center and the subcenters. In terms of population, 1 in 10 people lived in either the CBD or a subcenter.

Table 7–5 shows the characteristics of the CBD and the 28 subcenters. The subcenters are listed after the CBD in descending order with respect to total

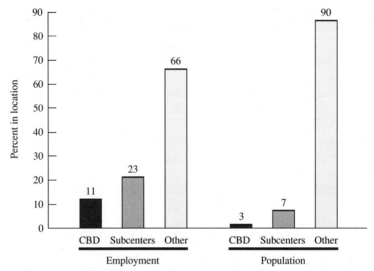

SOURCE: Genevieve Giuliano and Kenneth Small, "Subcenters in the Los Angeles Region," *Regional Science and Urban Economics* 21 (1991).

employment. The subcenters vary in employment density (workers per acre). The average employment density of the subcenters is 17.7 workers per acre, compared to 36.0 in the CBD. Giuliano and Small (1991) examined the relationship between employment density and distance to the CBD, and found a negative relationship between density and distance. This result is consistent with the predictions of the model of the monocentric city. In the case of Los Angeles, there is a negative relationship despite the fact that a relatively small fraction of total employment is in the CBD.

The subcenters vary with respect to employment ratios (jobs per resident). The average employment ratio of the subcenters is 1.58 jobs per resident, compared to 1.47 in the CBD and 0.43 for the entire metropolitan area. Except for the airport subcenters, which have few residents and thus large employment ratios, the employment ratios of the subcenters are relatively small. This suggests that the subcenters are not isolated employment centers, but instead provide a healthy mixture of jobs and dwellings.

Giuliano and Small (1991) suggest that the subcenters can be divided into five types: mixed industrial, mixed service, specialized entertainment, specialized manufacturing, and specialized service. Most of the mixed industrial subcenters started out as low-density manufacturing areas near transport nodes (airport, port, or marina) and grew as they attracted other activities. Most of the mixed service

TABLE 7–5   Characteristics of the CBD and Subcenters in the Los Angeles Metropolitan Area

Rank	Location	Employment (000)	Workers per Acre	Jobs per Resident	Distance to CBD (miles)
1	Downtown Los Angeles (CBD)	469	36.0	1.47	0.1
2	Los Angeles West	176	25.5	1.37	15.8
3	Santa Monica	65	16.9	1.11	16.7
4	Hollywood	64	21.4	0.73	7.3
5	Los Angeles Airport	59	16.7	4.32	18.8
6	Orange County Airport	48	16.1	1,589.87	40.7
7	Glendale	43	15.5	1.07	12.3
8	Commerce	42	17.0	4.05	9.8
9	Vernon/Huntington Park	39	33.2	2.42	4.9
10	San Pedro	38	15.7	2.74	23.3
11	Santa Ana	38	17.3	1.51	32.9
12	Inglewood	37	14.6	1.24	14.7
13	Pasadena	36	25.3	1.73	12.1
14	Long Beach Airport	33	15.5	3,684.78	23.3
15	Marina Del Rey	32	11.4	1.28	14.0
16	Long Beach	30	18.0	0.84	25.3
17	Van Nuys Airport	28	12.6	2.04	22.1
18	Burbank Airport	26	28.4	10.86	16.5
19	Hawthorne	18	12.4	0.74	13.5
20	Conoga Park/Warner Center	17	11.2	1.21	27.4
21	Lawndale	17	17.1	1.36	20.5
22	Los Angeles East	16	37.3	2.30	6.8
23	Fullerton	16	11.4	4.97	27.3
24	Downey	15	17.3	2.38	14.8
25	Santa Ana South	14	12.2	1.76	37.4
26	Sherman Oaks	13	11.9	1.04	18.6
27	Burbank SW	13	18.0	1.92	14.1
28	Anaheim/Orange/Garden Grove	11	11.3	1.06	30.2
29	Garden Grove/Stanton	10	12.9	5.60	26.6
	All subcenters	994 (total)	17.7 (average)	1.58 (average)	—

SOURCE: Genevieve Giuliano and Kenneth Small, "Subcenters in the Los Angeles Region," *Regional Science and Urban Economics* 21 (1991).

subcenters are like traditional downtowns: they provide a wide range of services. Many of these subcenters functioned as independent centers before they were absorbed into the metropolitan economy. The specialized manufacturing subcenters include areas near airports that produce aerospace equipment and older manufacturing areas. In the service-oriented subcenters, 90 percent of employment is in service activities such as medical care, entertainment, and education.

There are four basic conclusions that can be drawn from this study of the Los Angeles area. First, the subcenters differ in the mixes of goods and services they provide, suggesting that the subcenters play diverse roles within the metropolitan economy. Second, many of the subcenters are highly specialized, suggesting that there are large agglomerative economies (clustering of firms in the same industry to share input suppliers, save on labor costs, and share information). Third, employment in the metropolitan area is relatively dispersed: two thirds of total employment is outside the CBD and the subcenters. Fourth, employment density decreases as distance from the center increases, despite the fact that the center contains a relatively small fraction of total employment.

Subcenters in Houston

Mieszkowski and Smith (1991) explore the land-use patterns in the Houston metropolitan area and identify 10 subcenters. In 1985, total employment in the individual subcenters was between 16,000 and 86,000, compared to total employment in the CBD of 156,000. In 1985, the CBD contained about 10 percent of the metropolitan area's total employment, leaving 23 percent for the subcenters and 67 percent for areas outside the CBD and subcenters. The corresponding figures for 1970 were 14 percent for the CBD, 11 percent for the subcenters, and 75 percent for areas outside the CBD and subcenters.

FIGURE 7–5   **Percentages of Houston's Office Employment in the CBD, Subcenters, and Other Areas, 1969 and 1989**

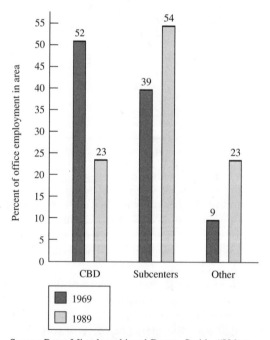

SOURCE: Peter Mieszkowski and Barton Smith, "Urban Decentralization in the Sunbelt: The Case of Houston," *Regional Science and Urban Economics* 21 (1991).

Like many other cities, Houston has experienced rapid growth in its office space. Between 1969 and 1989, total office space increased more than sevenfold, from 25 million square feet to 182 million square feet. The most rapid increases occurred in the suburbs, both inside and outside subcenters, so the suburban share of office space increased. Figure 7–5 shows the shares of office space in the CBD, the subcenters, and other areas for 1969 and 1989. By 1989, over three fourths of office space was outside the CBD, and over half of the office space was in suburban subcenters.

Land Use in the Modern City: Urban Villages?

The monocentric, core-dominated city has been gradually replaced with the multicentric, suburbanized city. Figure 7–6 shows land rent at different locations in a metropolitan area that has a beltway (located 2.5 miles from the city center) and two employment subcenters along the beltway. The land-rent surface has local peaks at the city center and the subcenters, and forms a circular ridge centered on the beltway. Because the key factor in determining employment density and

FIGURE 7–6   Bid Rents in a Modern City

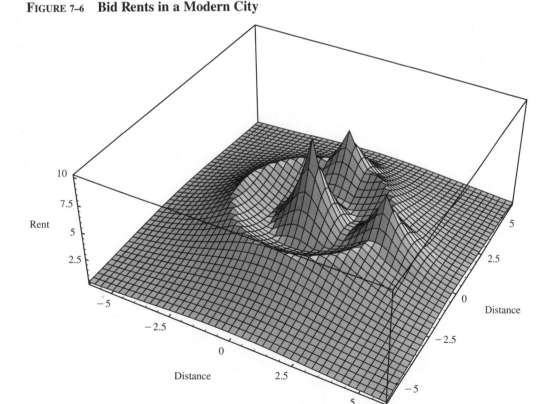

population density is the price of land, Figure 7–6 could also be used to show density at different locations in the metropolitan area.

The modern city, with its suburban subcenters, has been called a system of **urban villages**. In many metropolitan areas, suburban subcenters contain midrise office buildings, hotels, shopping malls, and entertainment facilities. Therefore, people in the area surrounding an employment subcenter have the option of traveling to the subcenter for work, shopping, and play. In other words, the subcenter is the core of an urban village. The urban village idea was recently incorporated into the planning process in Phoenix. For planning purposes, there are nine urban villages, with an average population of 100,000. By the year 2000, planners expect to have a total of 12 urban villages, with an average population of 125,000.

Most cities in the United States are experiencing the urban village phenomenon. Subcenters are developing in the rapidly growing Sunbelt cities (Atlanta, Phoenix, Dallas, Houston, and San Francisco) as well as in cities with less rapid growth (St. Louis, Detroit, and Kansas City). Subcenters are also developing in the nation's oldest and most traditional cities (New York, Boston, Chicago, Baltimore). In most urban areas, the fraction of office and retail employment in suburban subcenters is increasing.

The development of urban villages results from the suburbanization and clustering of retailers and office firms. Retailers moved to the suburbs to be closer to their suburban customers, and many retailers clustered in malls and subcenters to exploit shopping externalities. Office firms moved to the suburbs to get better access to their suburban work forces and clustered in subcenters to exploit agglomerative economies in the provision of business services, restaurants, and hotels.

Summary

1. The truck contributed to the suburbanization of manufacturing employment for two reasons:
   a. The intracity truck replaced the horse-drawn wagon, decreasing freight costs relative to commuting costs and pulling firms toward the low-wage suburbs.
   b. The intercity truck replaced the boat and train for intercity freight, freeing manufacturers from central export nodes. Firms moved closer to their suburban workers.

2. The growing importance of air freight has caused some manufacturers to locate close to suburban airports.

3. The automobile replaced the streetcar as the principal means of commuting, making locations throughout the urban area accessible to workers. Firms with specialized labor forces were able to move to the suburbs.

4. Because the demand for housing and commuting costs increase at about the same rate as income increases, it appears that income growth did not contribute to suburbanization.

5. The suburbanization of population occurred for five reasons:
   a. Decreases in commuting costs (from the streetcar and the auto) increased the accessibility of suburban locations.
   b. Central-city problems (racial tensions, deteriorating housing, high taxes, high crime rates, inferior schools) encouraged some households to flee to the suburbs.
   c. The suburbanization of employment opportunities contributed to the suburbanization of population as households followed the firms to the suburbs.
   d. The underpricing of commuting (commuting and pollution externalities) decreases the relative costs of suburban locations.
   e. The fragmented system of local government allows households to escape central-city housing problems.

6. In the modern multicentric city, workers commute to jobs in both the CBD and suburban subcenters. Workers are willing to pay more for housing near employment centers (everything else being equal), so the housing-price function has several peaks, one near the CBD and one near every subcenter. Similarly, the residential bid-rent function has several peaks, one for the city center and one for each subcenter.

7. Retailers moved to the suburbs for three reasons:
   a. Some retailers followed consumers to the suburbs.
   b. The replacement of the streetcar with the automobile increased the accessibility of noncentral locations.
   c. Population growth increased the equilibrium number of retailers. Some of the new retailers located in the suburban areas.

8. During the 1970s and 1980s, suburban office space grew at a rapid rate. Nationwide, suburban office employment grew over seven times faster than central-city office employment during the 1970s (116 percent versus 15 percent).

9. Advances in communication technology decreased the need for face-to-face contact among office workers, allowing some firms to move to the low-wage suburbs and allowing others to decouple their operations into CBD activities and suburban activities.

10. The clustering of firms in suburban subcenters results from agglomerative economies in production. Firms in the subcenters share input suppliers, a labor force, and information.

11. The 28 subcenters in the Los Angeles metropolitan area contain about 23 percent of the area's employment and 9 percent of its population. The subcenters are specialized: they differ in the mixes of goods and services they provide.

12. The monocentric, core-dominated city has been gradually replaced with the multicentric, suburbanized city. The land-rent surface has local peaks at the city center and the subcenters, and forms a ridge centered on the beltway.

13. The development of suburban subcenters (urban villages) is explained by the suburbanization and clustering of retailers and office firms. Retailers

moved to the suburbs to be closer to their customers, and clustered in sub-centers to exploit shopping externalities. Manufacturing and office firms moved to the suburbs to be closer to their work forces and clustered to exploit agglomerative economies in production.

Exercises and Discussion Questions

1. Consider a manufacturing firm that exports some of its output by train (through a central export node) and the rest by truck (the truck exits the metropolitan area using a suburban beltway). Suppose that production costs (including labor costs) are the same at all locations. Under what conditions will the firm's bid-rent function be positively sloped?

2. Consider a metropolitan area with a 10-mile radius. Two members of the Dink household work: Mr. Dink commutes to the city center ($u = 0$), and Ms. Dink commutes to a suburban subcenter four miles due east of the city center. Depict the household's housing-price functions for three cases:
    a. Travel time per mile is the same in both directions (toward the city center and away from the city center), and Mr. and Ms. Dink have the same opportunity cost of travel time.
    b. Because the bulk of workers commute to the city center, the travel time per mile of inward commuting (toward the city center in the morning rush hour and away from the center in the evening rush hour) exceeds the travel time of outward commuting (away from the city center during the morning rush hour and toward the center during the evening rush hour). Mr. and Ms. Dink have the same opportunity cost of travel time.
    c. Travel time per mile is the same in both directions, but Ms. Dink has a higher opportunity cost of travel time.

3. Comment on the following statement: "Instead of investing money in traditional radial mass-transit systems (hub-and-spoke systems), we should be investing in circumferential transit systems. We should build a circular transit system along the urban beltways."

4. The development of the internal-combustion engine caused fundamental changes in urban land-use patterns. The transformation from the core-dominated city to the modern suburbanized city took only about 50 years. Given the rapid pace of technological change, it seems likely that some future innovation will cause another transformation of cities. Given your knowledge of science fiction and fact, describe an innovation that would cause fundamental changes in the spatial structure of cities.

5. *Telecommuting* refers to a system under which employees work at home for one or more days per week and use personal computers and telephone lines to interact with people in the office. Consider an office firm that must decide whether to locate in the CBD or along a suburban beltway (to be closer to

its suburban work force). Discuss the effects of telecommuting on the relative attractiveness of the CBD.

6. Consider a modern city in which office employment has been steadily shifting from the city center to suburban locations along beltways. Suppose that the city improves its mass-transit system, decreasing the monetary and time costs of radial travel. Assume that the improvement of the transit system does not affect residential location choices. Will the improvement in the transit system speed up or slow down the movement of office firms to the suburbs?

7. Consider two metropolitan areas, Anville and Diamondburg. The names indicate the type of industry in each metropolitan area: export workers in Anville produce anvils; export workers in Diamondburg cut diamonds. Suppose that all output is exported through an export node at the center of the city. Would you expect the two cities to have the same spatial distributions of employment? If not, what differences would you expect?

References and Additional Readings

Anas, Alex, and Leon Moses. "Transportation and Land Use in the Mature Metropolis." In *The Mature Metropolis,* ed. Charles L. Leven. Lexington, Mass.: D. C. Heath, 1978.

Bradbury, Katharine L.; Anthony Downs; and Kenneth A. Small. *Urban Decline and the Future of American Cities.* Washington, D.C.: Brookings Institution, 1982. Discusses the reasons behind the decline of central cities.

Bureau of Population and Economic Research. *The Socio-Economic Impact of the Capital Beltway on Northern Virginia.* Charlottesville, Va.: Bureau of Population and Economic Research, University of Virginia, 1968. Discusses the effect of the beltway in the Washington, D.C., metropolitan area.

Cervero, Robert. *Suburban Gridlock.* New Brunswick, N.J.: Center for Urban Policy Research, 1986. Discusses the recent growth in office employment and its implications for transportation planning.

Chinitz, Benjamin. *City and Suburb.* Englewood Cliffs, N.J.: Prentice Hall, 1965. A collection of essays on the causes and effects of suburbanization.

———. "The Influence of Communication and Data Processing Technology on Urban Form." In *Research in Urban Economics*, vol. 4, ed. Robert Ebel. Greenwich, Conn.: JAI Press, 1984, pp. 67–77. Discusses the effects of new communications technology on the location decisions of office firms.

Frey, W. H. "Central City White Flight: Racial and Non-Racial Causes." *American Sociological Review* 44 (1979), pp. 425–88. Tests various theories of suburbanization, focusing on the effects of central-city problems on suburbanization.

Frieden, Bernard J., and Lynne B. Sagalyn. *Downtown, Inc.: How America Rebuilds Cities.* Cambridge, Mass.: MIT Press, 1991. Discusses efforts to rebuild downtown areas.

Giuliano, Genevieve, and Kenneth Small. "Subcenters in the Los Angeles Region." *Regional Science and Urban Economics* 21 (1991). Discusses the characteristics of the CBD and 28 subcenters in the Los Angeles metropolitan area.

Hoover, Edgar M., and Raymond Vernon. *Anatomy of a Metropolis.* Cambridge, Mass.: Harvard University Press, 1959. Discusses the suburbanization of manufacturers in the New York area.

Hughes, James W., and George Sternlieb. "The Suburban Growth Corridor." In *America's New Market Geography,* ed. George Sternlieb and James W. Hughes. New Brunswick, N.J.: Center for Urban Policy Research, 1988. Discusses the market forces behind the recent office construction boom in suburbs.

Kern, Clifford R. "Upper Income Residential Revival in the City." In *Research in Urban Economics*, vol. 4, ed. Robert Ebel. Greenwich, Conn.: JAI Press, 1984. Discusses the facts on gentrification, including the characteristics of renovators.

Levitan, Don. "Massachusetts Route 128: A Nonemulative Enigma." *Transportation Research Record* 583 (1976), pp. 45–54. Discusses the effects of Boston's beltway.

Macrae, Norman. "Tomorrow's Agglomeration Economies." In *The Mature Metropolis,* ed. Charles L. Leven. Lexington, Mass.: D. C. Heath, 1978. Predicts future development patterns based on predictions about agglomeration economies.

McDonald, John F., and Daniel McMillen. "Employment Subcenters and Land Values in a Polycentric Urban Area: The Case of Chicago." *Environment and Planning,* A–22 (1990), pp. 1561–74. Identifies four employment subcenters in the Chicago metropolitan area and discusses the effects of subcenters on residential land values.

Mieszkowski, Peter, and Barton Smith. "Urban Decentralization in the Sunbelt: The Case of Houston." *Regional Science and Urban Economics* 21 (1991). Discusses the characteristics of the CBD and 10 subcenters in the Houston metropolitan area.

Mills, Edwin S. *Studies in the Structure of the Urban Economy.* Baltimore, Md.: Johns Hopkins University Press, 1972. Documents the suburbanization of employment and population between 1880 and 1963.

————. "Service Sector Suburbanization." In *America's New Market Geography,* ed. George Sternlieb and James W. Hughes. New Brunswick, N.J.: Center for Urban Policy Research, 1988. Discusses the recent trends in the suburbanization of services and compares the spatial distributions of workplaces and residences.

Mills, Florence. "Effects of Beltways on the Location of Residences and Selected Workplaces." *Transportation Research Record*, no. 812 (1981), pp. 26–33. Compares changes in population and employment in metropolitan areas with and without beltways.

Moses, Leon, and Williamson, Harold. "The Location of Economic Activity in Cities." In *Readings in Urban Economics,* ed. Matthew Edel and Jerome Rothenberg. New York: Macmillan, 1972. Discusses the role of the intraurban and interurban truck on the suburbanization of manufacturing.

Pivo, Gary. "The Net of Mixed Beads: Suburban Office Development in Six Metropolitan Regions." *Journal of the American Planning Association* (Autumn 1990), pp. 457–69. Discusses the suburbanization and clustering of office space between 1960 and the late 1980s.

Stanback, Thomas, and Richard Knight. *Suburbanization and the City.* Montclair, N.J.: Allanheld, Osmun and Company, 1976. Documents suburbanization trends and the implications for the metropolitan economy.

Wasylenko, Michael J. "Disamenities, Local Taxation, and the Intrametropolitan Location of Households and Firms." In *Research in Urban Economics*, vol. 4, ed. Robert Ebel. Greenwich, Conn.: JAI Press, 1984. Reviews the empirical evidence concerning the effects of income on location.

Land-Use Controls and Zoning

This chapter discusses the government's role in the urban land market. The analysis in Chapters 6 and 7 assumes that land is allocated to the highest bidder, that is, that the government is not involved in the urban land market. In fact, local governments use a number of policies to control land use. Most cities have zoning plans that limit the location choices of firms and households. Some cities use zoning and other land-use controls to limit population growth. This chapter discusses various types of land-use controls, addressing three basic questions. First, why do cities control land use? Second, what are the market effects of land-use controls? Third, what are the legal foundations for zoning and other land-use controls?

Controlling Population Growth

Some local governments use land-use policies to limit population growth. The purpose of a growth-control policy is to control the undesirable side effects of growth (e.g., pollution, congestion, crime, the loss of a small-town atmosphere). This section discusses two growth-control policies: urban service boundaries and limits on the number of building permits issued.

Urban Service Boundary

One way to control population growth is to limit the land area of the city. If a city refuses to extend urban services (e.g., sewers, roads, schools, parks) beyond an **urban service boundary,** it limits growth to the area within the boundary.

Figure 8–1 shows the equilibrium land-use pattern in a monocentric city. The residential bid-rent function intersects the agricultural bid-rent function at a

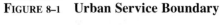

FIGURE 8-1   Urban Service Boundary

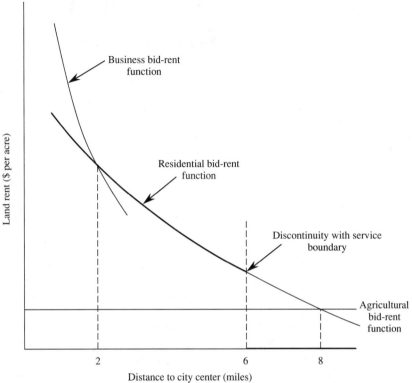

In the market equilibrium, the city radius is 8 miles. An urban service boundary prevents residential development beyond 6 miles, so the residential bid rent drops to zero between 6 and 8 miles from the city center.

distance of eight miles from the city center, so the city radius is eight miles. An implicit assumption of this model is that the city government provides urban services out to a distance of eight miles from the city center. The business bid-rent function intersects the residential bid-rent function at a distance of two miles from the city center, so the equilibrium CBD radius is two miles.

Suppose that the city refuses to extend urban services beyond six miles from the city center. Unless residents can provide their own roads, sewage systems, and schools, residential development outside the boundary will be impossible. Therefore, the residential bid rent will fall to zero at a distance of six miles from the city center. This is shown in Figure 8–1 as a discontinuity in the residential bid-rent function at a distance of six miles. The urban service boundary makes land beyond six miles from the city center uninhabitable, so the market rent on land outside the boundary drops to the agricultural bid rent.

How does the urban service boundary affect the price of land within the boundary? The boundary policy decreases the supply of developable land, so the price of land within the boundary increases: households that would otherwise live between six and eight miles from the city center bid up the price of land within the boundary. Therefore, the urban service boundary produces winners and losers. People who own land outside the service boundary lose: the market rent drops to the agricultural bid rent, decreasing the market value of land. People who own residential land within the service boundary win: the increase in land rent generated by the decrease in the supply of developable land increases the market value of land.

The urban service boundary affects both the total population of the city and the distribution of population within the city. The increase in the price of developable land discourages some firms and households from moving to the city, so the city's total population is lower than it would be without the urban service boundary. In addition, the city is more compact: all growth occurs within the service boundary, and the increase in the price of developable land increases residential density because households economize on the relatively expensive land by occupying smaller lots.

Building Permits

Some cities control residential growth by limiting the number of building permits issued. By limiting the number of new dwellings built per year, a city can control its growth rate.

Consider a city that initially has no limit on the number of building permits issued. Figure 8–2 shows the city's market for new housing: the supply curve *AG* intersects the demand curve at point *F,* generating an equilibrium quantity of 100 houses per year and an equilibrium price of $50,000 per house. The city will issue 100 free permits per year, which will be used to build houses with a market value of $50,000. Developers make zero economic profits (normal accounting profits), meaning that the cost of producing each house (the sum of land, labor, and capital cost) will be $50,000.

Suppose that the city limits the number of building permits to 60 per year. The new supply curve for housing is *ACE:* the maximum number of new houses is 60, so the supply curve becomes vertical at 60 dwellings. The new supply curve intersects the demand curve at an equilibrium price of $70,000. In other words, the permit policy increases the equilibrium price of housing by $20,000.

The permit policy also decreases the cost of producing housing. The permit policy decreases the number of houses built, so it decreases the demand for land. For example, if houses are built on quarter-acre lots, the permit policy will decrease the demand for land from 25 acres per year (100 times 0.25) to 15 acres per year. The decrease in the demand for land will decrease the market price of land, decreasing the cost of producing housing. This is shown by the housing supply curve: if 100 houses are built, the production cost is $50,000 per house;

FIGURE 8-2   Market Effects of Building Permits

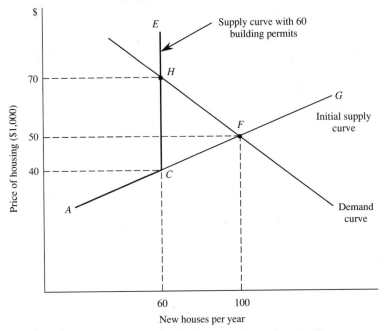

If the city decreases the supply of building permits from 100 to 60, the supply curve for housing shifts from *AG* to *ACE*. The new equilibrium is point *H*
(price of housing = $70,000). Point *C* shows the cost of producing 60 houses
($40,000). The difference between the price and the cost is the equilibrium price
of the building permit ($30,000).

if only 60 houses are built, the cost drops to $40,000 per house. Because the
permit policy decreases the number of houses built, it decreases the price of land,
allowing developers to build houses at a lower cost.

The city must decide how to allocate the 60 building permits among its
developers. One option is to auction the permits to the highest bidders. What
is the monetary value of a building permit? A person with a building permit
can make a profit equal to the difference between the market price of a house
($70,000) and the cost of producing the house ($40,000), so the monetary value
of a permit is $30,000. If the city auctions the permits, the market price would
be $30,000.

Some cities allocate their building permits to development projects that promote their development objectives. If the city is interested in high-density housing,
it could allocate the permits to a high-density housing project. Alternatively, the
city could allocate the permits to a project in an area targeted for development.
Many cities use sophisticated point systems to rate and rank alternative devel-

opment proposals. Among the criteria for which points are assigned are various design features (the exterior appearance of the dwellings, the amount of open space within the project), density, and the proximity of the project to existing public infrastructure (roads, schools, sewer lines).

Land-Use Zoning: Types and Market Effects

A zoning plan designates a set of admissible land uses for each plot of land in a city. In theory, the purpose of zoning is to promote public health, safety, and welfare. The principal means of promoting health, safety, and welfare is the separation of incompatible land uses. The first zoning ordinances were used by the wealthy to exclude the poor. In the 1880s, the city of San Francisco passed laws to segregate its Chinese population. When explicit segregation was declared unconstitutional, the city passed a zoning law that banned laundries from certain neighborhoods. The zoning law did not violate the constitution because it promoted public welfare by keeping an undesirable land use (laundries) out of some residential areas. Because the Chinese operated most of the city's laundries, the zoning law provided a legal means of segregation. In New York City in 1916, the rapid growth of employment in offices and garment factories increased the number of low-wage women on the streets of midtown Manhattan. The owners of exclusive Fifth Avenue stores feared that the increased traffic of poor women would be bad for business and therefore proposed zoning laws that limited building sizes and building heights. The law limited the growth of office buildings and garment factories, decreasing the number of clerical and garment workers walking along Fifth Avenue. The zoning law was declared constitutional because it promoted public welfare by controlling the nuisances created by tall buildings (shadows, blocked light, disruption of views).

There are many types of zoning, each of which has at least one purpose. This section divides zoning into three types. The purpose of **nuisance zoning** is to separate incompatible land uses. Cities use **fiscal zoning** to exclude households that would not pay their share of the costs of local government. **Design zoning** is a sort of macro-architecture: planners arrange activities within the city to promote the efficient use of the city's infrastructure.

Nuisance Zoning

Nuisance zoning (or externality zoning) is the practice of separating land uses that are considered incompatible. The classic example is the glue factory: one way of dealing with the air pollution generated by the glue factory is to move the factory into an industrial zone, far from residential areas. Similarly, the externalities generated by retailers (traffic congestion and noise) can be controlled by establishing a retail zone. There are also externalities generated by high-density housing: apartment buildings cause traffic and parking problems, and also block views and light. These externalities can be controlled by establishing a zone for high-density housing.

Industrial Nuisances.   Industrial firms generate all types of externalities, including noise, glare, dust, odor, vibration, and smoke. Zoning separates residential and industrial land uses, reducing the exposure to air and noise pollution. Zoning is appealing as an environmental policy because of its simplicity: the easiest way to limit exposure to pollution is to separate polluters from their potential victims. The problem with zoning as an environmental policy is that zoning does not reduce the total amount of pollution, it just moves it around. If one municipality's industrial zone is far from its own residents but close to the residents of a nearby municipality, industrial zoning may actually increase the total exposure to pollution. Because zoning does not provide firms with the incentive to decrease pollution, it is less effective than other environmental policies.

Alternative to Industrial Zoning: Effluent Fees.   When economists hear the word *pollution,* their knee-jerk response is "effluent fees." An effluent fee is a tax on pollution. For efficiency purposes, the fee should be set equal to the marginal external cost of pollution, that is, the cost to society of an additional unit of pollution. For example, if one ton of sulfur dioxide generates a social cost of $2, the effluent fee should be $2 per ton. The effluent fee "internalizes" the pollution externality, forcing polluters to pay for pollution in the same way that they pay for labor, capital, and raw materials. The firm has an incentive to decrease pollution because abatement decreases the firm's effluent bill. If the effluent fee equals the marginal external cost of pollution, pollution will decrease to the socially optimum level.

Why do cities use zoning instead of effluent fees to control industrial pollution? There are two principal reasons. First, industrial zoning is simple compared to a system of effluent fees. To set the effluent fees, the city would have to estimate the marginal external cost of pollution for different locations in the city, and to collect the fees, the city would have to monitor the polluting firms. It would certainly be easier to put all the polluters in an industrial zone. Second, a switch from zoning to effluent fees may increase pollution in some neighborhoods. Although the factory will produce less pollution under the effluent-fee policy, it may locate closer to the residential district. Therefore, some neighborhoods may become more polluted. The fact that pollution is at its optimum level is small consolation to those who breathe the dirty air. The switch to effluent fees would improve efficiency and generate a net gain for society, so it would be possible, in principle, to compensate those who breathe dirtier air. In fact, compensation is rarely attempted, so local opposition to effluent fees remains.

Performance Zoning.   Traditional zoning is based on a zoning map and a land-use list. The zoning map shows the zoning classification for each plot of land in the city, and the list shows the admissible land uses for each zoning classification. If an activity is designated *heavy industry,* every firm involved in this activity must locate in the heavy-industry zone, regardless of how much noise, odor, or smoke the individual firms actually generate. The alternative to traditional zoning is **performance zoning,** under which the city sets performance standards for each zone. For industrial uses, performance standards typically set upper limits for the amount of noise, glare, odor, vibration, gas, and smoke emitted by the firms. Performance zoning is a sort of compromise between traditional zoning and effluent fees: although performance zoning does not force firms to pay for pollution, it does encourage abatement because it gives cleaner firms more location options.

Retail Nuisances.   Retailers generate a number of externalities that affect nearby residents. The traffic generated by retailers causes congestion, noise, and parking problems. The establishment of retail zones decreases the exposure to these externalities. For example, zoning prevents the invasion of quiet residential neighborhoods by shoppers and delivery trucks.

Under performance zoning, the city allows retailers in a particular zone as long as they satisfy performance standards for parking, traffic, and noise. For each area, the city may specify a minimum number of parking places, a minimum rate of traffic flow, and a maximum noise level. These performance standards force commercial developments to provide off-street parking to control parking problems, signalization and street improvements to control traffic problems, and berms and landscaping to control noise problems. Performance zoning allows the mixing of commercial and residential land uses because retailers take steps that shield residents from the undesirable effects of commercial development.

Residential Nuisances.   Most residential externalities are generated by high-density housing. Suppose that a developer builds a four-story apartment complex in a neighborhood with single-family homes. The apartment complex will increase traffic volume, increasing congestion and noise, and increase the demand for on-street parking, causing a shortage of parking spaces. In addition, the tall apartment building is likely to deprive neighbors of scenic views and sunlight.

Under conventional zoning, the apartment building would be excluded from the low-density neighborhood. Conventional zoning shields the residents of single-family homes from externalities by excluding high-density housing.

The alternative to conventional zoning is performance zoning. Under a performance-based zoning policy, the apartment complex would be allowed if the developer took the following steps:

1. **Off-street parking.** The developer provides enough off-street parking to prevent parking problems.
2. **Street improvements.** The developer pays for street improvements that prevent congestion problems.
3. **Building design.** The building is designed to prevent loss of views and sunlight. The developer uses landscaping to establish a buffer between the apartment building and the single-family homes.

The idea behind performance zoning is that the apartment building should be judged on the basis of its actual effects on the neighborhood, not on the simple fact that it is high-density housing. If a high-density project does not generate externalities, it would be allowed in the neighborhood.

Income-Related Residential Externalities.   Three types of residential externalities encourage wealthy households to exclude poor ones.

1. **Education.** As explained in Chapter 17 (Education), the students from poor families have relatively low average achievement levels and pull down the achievement levels of other students. By excluding poor households, wealthy households may improve the quality of their neighborhood schools.

2. **Crime.** As explained in Chapter 18 (Crime and Punishment), crime is more prevalent among the poor. By excluding poor households, wealthy households may decrease the neighborhood crime rate.

3. **Housing externalities.** Housing is a normal good, so the poor consume less housing than the wealthy. In addition to consuming fewer square feet of living space, they also tend to spend less on upkeep and the external appearance of their houses and lots. Because the market value of a particular house depends on the external appearance of neighboring houses, property values are typically lower in neighborhoods with a large number of poor households. By excluding poor households, wealthy households may keep their property values high.

Fiscal Zoning

The second type of zoning occurs because local governments finance public services with the property tax. Under **fiscal zoning,** a city excludes households that would impose fiscal burdens on local government. Suppose that a household consumes $3,000 worth of local services but pays only $2,000 in local property taxes. Such a household generates a fiscal burden because its tax contribution is less than the cost of its local public services. Fiscal burdens may be generated by (1) households living in high-density housing, (2) households living in the fringe areas of the city, and (3) new commercial and industrial development.

High-Density Housing.   As explained in Chapter 14 (Local Taxes and Intergovernmental Grants), the most important source of local revenue is the property tax. Because a household's tax liability increases with its housing consumption, a household in a small house or apartment pays a relatively small amount in taxes and is therefore more likely to impose a fiscal burden on local government. Local governments exclude households by zoning for low-density (high-value) housing.

Large-lot zoning establishes a minimum lot size for residential development. Land and housing are complementary goods, so the city can use restrictions on lots size to indirectly establish a minimum house value. Suppose that a city breaks even on a house worth $125,000: the tax liability of such a house equals the cost of supplying public services to the household living in the house. According to one rule of thumb, the market value of land is about 20 percent of the total property value (the value of the structure and the land). If the price of land is $50,000 per acre, a half-acre lot ($25,000 worth of land) will produce a house worth $125,000 (five times $25,000). A minimum lot size of one half of an acre will ensure that the government breaks even on all new houses.

Exclusionary and Inclusionary Zoning.   Large-lot zoning is often labeled **exclusionary zoning** because it excludes low-income households. The exclusion is both direct and indirect. Suppose that a large-lot zoning policy prevents the construction of 20 acres of apartments. Because low-income households are more likely to occupy apartments, the decrease in the number of apartment buildings decreases the number of low-income residents. In addition, the zoning policy increases the price of apartments, excluding low-income households indirectly: the apartments that are built will be too expensive for many poor households.

In response to the exclusion problem, many cities have developed **inclusionary zoning** policies. Under an inclusionary housing program, the local government forces local developers to build dwellings for low-income households. The dwellings are typically sold to low-income households for less than the cost of construction. By providing subsidized dwellings for low-income residents, the local community partly offsets the exclusionary effects of fiscal zoning. Most dwellings built for inclusionary purposes are not typical low-income dwellings, but are medium-income dwellings provided to the poor at the price of low-income dwellings.

Who pays for inclusionary zoning? The requirement of subsidized housing has the same effect as a development tax. Suppose that a developer builds five inclusionary units and loses $10,000 per unit, generating a total loss of $50,000. If the developer is allowed to build 50 houses for the open market, the effective tax per market dwelling is $1,000 ($50,000 divided by 50). The developer will make zero economic profit (normal accounting profit) with or without inclusionary zoning, so the implicit tax is passed on to consumers (housing prices increase) and landowners (the price of vacant land decreases). In other words, housing consumers and landowners pay for inclusionary zoning.

Fringe Land Use.   New housing is usually built on the fringe of the metropolitan area. If the costs of supplying public services are higher in fringe areas, the tax contribution of new housing may be less than the cost of public services. Therefore, new housing may impose a fiscal burden on the city.

To explain the fiscal burden of fringe housing, consider a city with the following characteristics:

1. The current average cost of public services is $500 per household per year.

2. The typical household owns a house worth $50,000 and pays a property tax of $500 per year (1 percent of market value).

3. A developer has proposed a new residential development on fringe land. The market value of the new houses is the same as existing houses ($50,000).

4. The new development would require the expansion of the city's public services (widening of streets, expansion of the sewage system, extension of bus routes). The full cost of serving the new houses would be $600 per house per year.

Given these assumptions, every new house generates a fiscal burden of $100 per year ($600 − $500). A simple way to prevent the new development and the associated fiscal burden is to zone the vacant land for agricultural use. If the city sets a minimum lot size of 20 acres, no additional houses will be built on the land, so the expansion of city services will be unnecessary.

An alternative to low-density zoning is a tax surcharge for new development. Suppose that the city imposes an annual surcharge of $100 per new house. The annual tax liability of new housing would be $600 ($500 in property tax plus the $100 surcharge), and the occupants of new housing would pay the full costs of the new public services. The surcharge would eliminate the fiscal burden of new housing, so the city would be more likely to approve the development project.

An alternative to an annual tax surcharge is a one-time **impact fee,** or **development tax**. By paying an impact fee, the developer compensates the local government for the fiscal burden of new housing. If the city collects a $1,000 impact fee from the developer and invests the money in the bank at a 10 percent interest rate, it can use the annual interest earnings ($100) to cover the difference between the tax contribution and the public-service costs of new housing. Who pays the impact fee? Because the developer makes zero economic profits, the fee is passed on to consumers (housing prices increase) and landowners (land prices decrease).

Lillydahl and her coauthors (1988) describe impact-fee policies in four states: California, Florida, Oregon, and Colorado. In California, local communities are allowed to impose fees for transportation facilities (bridges, major thoroughfares, and freeways); drainage facilities; sewers; parks; and schools. In 1985, the average impact charge was $3,527 per dwelling in the San Francisco Bay area and $9,500 in San Diego. In Florida, the most common impact fees are for water and sewers; in 1985, the average impact fee was about $3,000 per dwelling. In Oregon, impact fees are called *systems development charges* and are typically used to support water, sewer, street, and park facilities. During the 1980s, impact fees averaged about $2,500 per dwelling in the Portland metropolitan area. In Colorado, cities along the Front Range (from Colorado Springs to Fort Collins and including the Denver area) impose impact fees most frequently for water, sewer, parks and recreation, drainage, and street facilities.

Commercial and Industrial Development.   In some cities, commercial and industrial development generates fiscal burdens. If the city cannot pass on the cost of new infrastructure to new firms and employees, it may restrict development by (1) limiting the supply of commercial and industrial land and (2) restricting building heights.

The city of San Francisco recently adopted a zoning plan that restricts building heights in its downtown area. The objective of the policy is to limit the number of people working downtown. By limiting the number of downtown workers, city officials hope to control the volume of traffic on the bridges into the city, all of which are already congested. An alternative to the zoning policy would be to increase the carrying capacity of the bridges, with the cost of the capacity expansion imposed on new employers. Since this is impractical, the city has decided to use its zoning policy to limit total employment.

Some cities impose impact fees on commercial and industrial developers, using the revenue from the fees to expand local transportation networks. For example, in the Westchester area of western Los Angeles, developers pay a one-time fee of $2,010 for each additional rush-hour trip generated by new office buildings. The revenue from the impact fee is used to widen the roads used by the employees of the new office buildings. Impact fees can reduce the fiscal burden of new development, decreasing the opposition to development.

Design Zoning

The third type of zoning is a form of macro-architecture. Just as an architect designs an individual house, the planner designs a city, arranging activities to promote the efficient use of the city's infrastructure (streets, sewage systems, water systems). Residential and employment growth is directed to areas where infrastructure can be efficiently provided. Design zoning is also used to preserve open space.

Directed Development.   Some cities use zoning to direct residential development to particular areas. To explain the effect of such zoning, consider a metropolitan area with the following characteristics:

1. There are 50 acres of vacant land: 25 acres to the north of the city, and 25 acres to the south.
2. The city wants to accommodate 500 new households on its vacant land.
3. Under the initial zoning ordinance, both areas are zoned for 10 dwellings per acre: 250 households would live in the north, and 250 would live in the south.

Suppose that the city changes its zoning policy. It decides to preserve the north area and accommodate all 500 households in the south area. It could do so by zoning the north area for low-density use and the south area for 20 dwellings per acre. What are the effects of the rezoning on land prices? The rezoning will decrease the market price of northern land because the landowner has fewer land-use options. In contrast, the southern landowner has more options, so the price of southern land will increase. The change in zoning policy is clearly inequitable: southern landowners gain at the expense of northern landowners.

An alternative to rezoning is a system of **transferable development rights (TDRs)**. Under a TDR policy, the city establishes a **preservation zone** (the north area) and a **development zone** (the south area). The south area is zoned for 10 dwellings per acre, giving Mr. South (the southern landowner) the right to build a total of 250 dwellings. Ms. North (the northern landowner) is not allowed to develop her land, but is instead issued 250 development coupons. These development coupons can be used to override zoning restrictions in the development zone. If South wants to build 20 dwellings on one acre of land, he must purchase 10 development coupons from North. The TDR policy gives each landowner development rights (the right to build 250 houses) and allows the owners of preserved land to transfer their development rights to other areas of the city. When the southern landowner sells her coupons, she is at least partially compensated for the losses in property value caused by the rezoning of her land.

Open-Space Zoning.   Some cities zone parcels of land as "open space," "green belts," or "agricultural preserves." This type of zoning provides city dwellers with open space by denying landowners the full use of their land.

Is open-space zoning efficient? The alternative to zoning is the outright purchase of land for open space. If the city were to purchase land instead of zoning it for open space, the city would preserve land only if the marginal benefit of open space exceeds the marginal cost. In other words, the city will choose the optimum amount of open space. In contrast, if the city simply zones the land for open space, the city is likely to consume too much open space.

A City Without Zoning?

What would an unzoned city look like? Would glue factories and pizza parlors invade quiet residential neighborhoods? Would land use be disorderly and ugly?

Some tentative answers to these questions come from Siegen's (1972) analysis of Houston, the only metropolitan area in the United States without zoning. Land use in the city is controlled by **restrictive covenants,** voluntary agreements among landowners that limit land uses and structures. The covenants governing residential subdivisions (over 7,000 in number) are typically more strict than conventional zoning. There have detailed restrictions on architectural design, external appearance, and lot maintenance. The covenants for industrial parks limit the activities that can locate in the park.

How does Houston compare to zoned cities? Although a rigorous comparison of land-use patterns may be impossible, some tentative observations can be made:

1. **Dispersion of industry.** The spatial distribution of Houston's industrial firms is similar to those of zoned cities. As in other cities, Houston's industrial firms locate close to the transportation network (near railroads and highways) and tend to cluster to exploit localization economies.

2. **Retailers.** Like retailers in most cities, most retailers in Houston locate along major thoroughfares in strip developments and shopping centers. Few retailers locate in quiet residential neighborhoods. This is the same pattern observed in zoned cities. Retailers locate along major thoroughfares because such locations provide large volumes of foot and auto traffic. Many retailers are subject to shopping externalities (from the benefits of one-stop shopping and comparison shopping), so they cluster in shopping centers, malls, and downtown areas.

3. **Strip development.** Houston appears to have more strip development (retail and commercial establishments along arterial routes) than zoned cities.

4. **Apartments.** Low-income housing in Houston is more plentiful and less expensive than in other cities. There is a wide range of densities in apartment projects: the projects occupied by the wealthy have more open space and lower density, while the projects occupied by the poor have higher density.

5. **Single-family homes.** In some areas, Houston homes have relatively small backyards; in other areas, lot sizes are similar to those in zoned cities.

There are two lessons from Houston's experience without zoning. First, in the absence of zoning, landowners have the incentive to negotiate restrictions on land use. It seems that neighborhood externalities are large enough to justify the costs of developing and enforcing restrictive covenants. This is the **Coase solution** to externalities (named after R. H. Coase): the parties affected by externalities negotiate a contract to solve the externality problem. Second, in the absence of zoning, most industrial firms cluster in locations accessible to the transportation network, and most retailers cluster in shopping centers and retail strips. If a city were to drop its zoning plan, it is unlikely that glue factories and pizza parlors would invade quiet residential neighborhoods.

The Legal Environment of Land-Use Controls

Local governments, which are creatures of state governments, derive their power to control land use from the states. In most states, enabling legislation for zoning is patterned after the Standard State Zoning Enabling Act, which was developed by the U.S. Department of Commerce in 1926. Section 1 of the Enabling Act states:

Grant of Power. For the purpose of promoting health, safety, morals, or the general welfare of the community, the legislative body of cities and incorporated villages is hereby empowered to regulate and restrict the height, number of stories, and size of buildings and other structures, the percentage of the lot that may be occupied, the size of yards, courts, and other open spaces, the density of population, and the location and use of buildings, structures, and land for trade, industry, residence, or other purposes.

The model legislation grants local governments broad powers in the regulation of land use. Zoning is considered a legitimate exercise of the **police power** of local government if it promotes the public health, safety, and welfare.

Current zoning laws are the result of over 60 years of legal decisions. In the last six decades, individuals affected by specific zoning laws have sued local governments, forcing state and federal courts to rule on the constitutionality of zoning ordinances. If a particular type of zoning is declared unconstitutional, all cities get the message from the courts; they rewrite their zoning ordinances to drop the illegal practices. On the other hand, if a zoning practice is upheld as constitutional, the practice spreads to other local governments. In other words, zoning law is evolutionary. Early court decisions established three criteria for the constitutionality of zoning: substantive due process, equal protection, and just compensation.

Substantive Due Process

The case of *Euclid* v. *Ambler* (1924) established the standards for **substantive due process**. According to the due-process criterion, zoning must be executed for a legitimate public purpose using reasonable means. In the early 1920s, the city of Euclid, Ohio, enacted a zoning ordinance that restricted the location, size, and height of various types of buildings. Ambler Realty had purchased some property between the railroad tracks and a major thoroughfare, and expected to sell the land to an industrial developer. When the city zoned its land for residential use, Ambler sued, claiming that the separation of industrial and residential land uses did not serve a legitimate public purpose. The Supreme Court ruled against Ambler, concluding that the zoning ordinance satisfied the standards for substantive due process because it had some "reasonable relation" to the promotion of "health, safety, morals, and general welfare." In other words, nuisance zoning (the separation of different land uses) is a legitimate use of the city's police power because it promotes public health and safety.

One interpretation of the *Euclid* decision is that a zoning ordinance is constitutional as long as it generates some benefit for the local community. The court did not say that the benefits of zoning must exceed its costs, but that the benefits of zoning must be positive. Fischel (1985) calls this "benefit" analysis, as opposed to "benefit-cost" analysis. The court defined the possible social benefits from zoning in broad terms, to include monetary, physical, spiritual, and aesthetic benefits.

Equal Protection

The second criterion for the constitutionality of zoning is **equal protection**. The equal-protection clause of the Fourteenth Amendment requires that all laws be applied in an impersonal (nondiscriminatory) fashion.

Recent court cases have tested whether fiscal zoning violates the principle of equal protection. Fiscal zoning excludes households who do not pay their share of the costs of local public services. Local governments have been sued by people outside the city, who claim that fiscal zoning systematically excludes some types of people from the city. The plaintiffs argue that zoning laws are not applied in an impersonal manner, but instead treat some people differently than others: rich and poor are treated differently, as are whites and blacks.

The federal courts have upheld the constitutionality of exclusionary zoning. In the *Euclid* decision, the Supreme Court suggested that although a zoning ordinance must generate some benefit for insiders (citizens of the community), the effects of zoning on outsiders are unimportant. In *Warth* v. *Selden* (1975), the court dismissed the claims of outsiders because they did not prove that the zoning ordinance caused specific personal damage. In *Village of Arlington Heights* v. *Metropolitan Housing Corporation* (1977), the court dismissed the claims of outsiders because they did not prove discriminatory intent on the part of zoning officials. In *Ybarra* v. *Town of Los Altos Hills*, the court ruled that although zoning laws that discriminate on the basis of race are unconstitutional, zoning laws that discriminate on the basis of income are legal. In general, the federal courts have adopted a noninterventionist approach to exclusionary zoning.

Some state courts have adopted a more activist role. In *Southern Burlington County NAACP* v. *Mount Laurel* (1975), the New Jersey Supreme Court ruled that Mount Laurel's exclusionary zoning harmed low-income outsiders. The court directed the city to develop a new zoning plan under which the city would accommodate its "fair share" of low-income residents. The implication from *Associated Home Builders Inc.* v. *City of Livermore* (California Supreme Court) is that the courts will judge zoning on the basis of its effects on both insiders and outsiders. If a zoning ordinance does not represent a reasonable accommodation of the competing interests of insiders and outsiders, it may be declared unconstitutional. In Oregon, state law requires municipalities to plan and zone land for a diversity of housing types and income levels. According to Fischel (1985), few state courts have followed the lead of the New Jersey court, so the Mount Laurel decision has not affected exclusionary zoning practices in many states. Given the decisions from federal courts, exclusionary zoning is still considered legal.

Just Compensation

The third criterion for the constitutionality of zoning is **just compensation**. The Fifth Amendment states "... nor shall private property be taken for public use, without just compensation." This is the **taking clause:** if the government converts land from private to public use, the landlord must be compensated.

How is the taking clause applied to zoning? Most zoning ordinances do not actually convert land to public use, but merely restrict private use. For example, nuisance zoning prevents a landowner from building a factory in a residential area, and large-lot zoning prevents a landowner from building high-density housing. By restricting the private use of land use, zoning decreases the market value of the property. The policy issue is whether landowners should be compensated for the loss of property value caused by zoning. For example, if large-lot zoning decreases a landowner's property value by $5,000, should the local government pay $5,000 in compensation?

According to Fischel (1985), the courts have provided mixed and confusing signals to local zoning authorities. The courts have routinely upheld zoning laws that cause large losses in property values, suggesting that as long as the landowner is left with some profitable use of his land, compensation is not required. The courts have developed four rules to determine whether compensation is required:

1. **Physical invasion.** Compensation is required if the government physically occupies the land. The invasion rule is applicable only when the government actually occupies the land. It does not apply to most zoning actions, in which the government merely restricts private land use.

2. **Diminution of value and reasonable beneficial use.** The origin of this rule is *Pennsylvania Coal* v. *Mahon*, in which Justice Holmes states, "... while property may be regulated to a certain extent, if regulation goes too far it will be recognized as a taking." In other words, compensation is required if zoning decreases the property value by a sufficiently large amount. Unfortunately, the courts have not indicated how far zoning must go before compensation is required. A related rule is **reasonable beneficial use:** if zoning leaves the landowner with options that provide a "reasonable" rate of return, no compensation is required.

3. **Balancing means (benefit-cost).** According to this rule, compensation is required if the cost of a zoning ordinance (the loss in property value) exceeds the benefit to the local community. Because this rule requires compensation for inefficient zoning ordinances, it discourages inefficient zoning practices. For example, suppose that a zoning ordinance decreases property values by $50 and generates a $30 benefit to the community. According to the balancing-means rule, compensation must be paid. Taxpayers will oppose the ordinance because the cost of compensating landowners exceeds the benefit generated by the ordinance. If the balancing-means rule were used, voters would approve only efficient zoning ordinances.

4. **Harm prevention.** According to this rule, compensation is not required if the zoning ordinance prevents a "harmful" use of the land. In other words, zoning is not a "taking" if it prevents the landowner from using land in ways that are detrimental to the general public. The harm-prevention rule suggests that a landowner, like a car owner, has limited property rights. The car owner has the right to drive his car, but he must stop at red lights. Should the driver be compensated for the opportunity cost of time spent waiting for the light to turn green? Since the traffic light prevents a harmful use of the car, compensation is not required. Similarly, landowners have limited property rights: if zoning prevents the

landlord from building a polluting factory in a residential district, compensation is unnecessary because nuisance zoning prevents a harmful use of the land.

Most zoning ordinances are judged under a broad interpretation of the harm-prevention rule: if an ordinance promotes public health, safety, or welfare, compensation is usually not required.

Summary

1. Some cities use land-use regulations to control population growth.
   a. An urban service boundary controls population growth by decreasing the supply of land available for development. Land prices within the boundary increase, and prices outside the boundary decrease.
   b. A limit on building permits decreases the number of houses that can be built, increasing housing prices and decreasing land prices.
2. A zoning plan designates a set of admissible land uses for each plot of land in the city. There are three types of zoning: nuisance zoning, fiscal zoning, and design zoning.
3. Nuisance zoning decreases the exposure to pollution, noise, and congestion externalities.
   a. An alternative to industrial zoning is a system of effluent fees.
   b. An alternative to industrial and commercial zoning is a performance zoning, under which the city develops performance standards for noise, odor, smoke, parking, and traffic.
   c. High-density housing produces congestion, noise, and parking problems, and sometimes blocks light and views. Performance zoning can be used to shield low-density housing from these effects, allowing high-density housing to locate near single-family homes.
4. Fiscal zoning excludes households who impose a fiscal burden on the city. Fiscal burdens may be generated by high-density housing, fringe housing, and new commercial and industrial development.
5. Local governments use large-lot zoning to exclude high-density (low-income) housing.
   a. Zoning decreases the supply of high-density housing, excluding the poor in two ways: there are fewer low-income dwellings, and the available dwellings are more expensive.
   b. The price of land zoned for high-density housing increases, and the price of land zoned for low-density housing decreases.
6. Under an inclusionary zoning policy, developers provide subsidized new dwellings to low-income residents. The costs of inclusionary housing are borne by housing consumers (higher housing prices) and landowners (lower land prices).

7. Fringe development often imposes a fiscal burden on the city: the taxes from new development fall short of the costs of extending public services to the urban fringe.
   a. Cities prevent fringe development by zoning vacant land for low density use (e.g., agriculture).
   b. The alternative to fiscal zoning is a system of impact fees or development taxes.

8. Commercial development sometimes generates fiscal burdens. If the city cannot pass the cost of new infrastructure on to new firms and employees, it may limit the supply of land and restrict building heights. Some cities use impact fees to pay for new infrastructure.

9. Design zoning is a form of macro-architecture: zoning promotes the efficient use of infrastructure and provides open space.
   a. Some cities use zoning to direct development to particular areas and use transferable development rights to prevent horizontal inequities.
   b. Open-space zoning is likely to produce more than the socially efficient amount of open space.

10. The zoning authority of local governments comes from state governments. There are three criteria for the constitutionality of zoning: due process, equal protection, and just compensation.
    a. Zoning satisfies the due-process criterion if it promotes public health, safety and welfare.
    b. Federal courts have rejected the claims that fiscal (exclusionary) zoning violates the equal-protection clause of the U.S. Constitution. In contrast, some state courts have declared fiscal zoning unconstitutional.
    c. Zoning is one of the police powers of local government, so compensation is generally not required.

Exercises and Discussion Questions

1. In Figure 8–2, the equilibrium price of building permits is $30,000. Suppose that the demand curve shifts down and intersects the supply curve at a quantity of 50 dwellings per year. What is the equilibrium price of permits?

2. Consider the building-permit policy depicted in Figure 8–2, with an equilibrium price of permits equal to $30,000. Suppose that the city announces on January 1 that 300 days later (October 28) it will give the 60 permits to the first 60 licensed building contractors through the planning office door. Because the police department expects a line to form outside the planning office, the police chief announces that the following queuing rules will be enforced:
   i. No cuts: when a person joins the queue, he or she goes to the end of the queue.
   ii. No substitutions: no one can reserve a place in line for anyone else.

To receive a permit, a licensed contractor must be one of the first 60 people in line and must remain in the line until October 28. Therefore, instead of an equilibrium price for the permits, there is an equilibrium waiting time (time spent in line). Suppose that 25 of the city's 100 licensed contractors have an opportunity cost of $150 per day; 25 have an opportunity cost of $300 per day; 25 have an opportunity cost of $600 per day; and 25 have an opportunity cost of $1,000 per day.

a. What is the equilibrium waiting time?

b. Suppose that the city eliminates the no-substitution rule. Would you expect the equilibrium waiting time to increase, decrease, or not change?

3. Consider a city where a polluting industry is separated from the residential area by a five-mile-buffer. The table below lists the wages and effluent fees for different locations within the buffer zone: the closer the firm to the residential district, the lower the wage and the higher the effluent fee. Suppose that the firm uses 450 hours of labor per week and generates 20 units of pollution per week.

Commute Distance	Effluent Fee	Wage
5	1.0	10.0
4	2.5	9.9
3	4.5	9.8
2	7.0	9.7
1	10.0	9.6

a. Assume that the quantities of output and inputs are constant. What is the optimum location for the firm?

b. What is the social cost of the segregation zoning policy? In other words, if the city prevents the firm from locating at its optimum location, what is the cost to society?

4. Suppose that a city eliminates all zoning. What types of retailers would you expect to move from the retail zones to the residential zones?

5. Suppose that all local taxes are eliminated and all funding for local public services comes from state governments. Would you expect any changes in local zoning practices?

6. Consider the following quote: "Depending on the variable one controls, a zoning policy may either increase or decrease the price of undeveloped land within and around the zoned city." Explain this statement, using examples of the various variables that are controlled by the various zoning policies.

7. Consider two of the compensation rules developed by the courts: the *diminution of value* rule and the *balancing means* rule. Will these rules promote horizontal equity (the equal treatment of equals)?

8. Comment on the following statement: "The courts should not be involved in overseeing local zoning practice. Such matters are the responsibility of the legislative branch of government. Let democracy work."

References and Additional Readings

Babcock, Richard R., and Charles Siemon. *The Zoning Game Revisited.* Boston: Oelgeschlager, Gunn, and Hain, 1985. Accounts of 11 zoning conflicts.

Davidoff, P., and L. Davidoff. "Opening the Suburbs: Toward Inclusionary Controls." *Management and Control of Growth* 1 (1975), pp. 540–50.

Dowall, David E. "Reducing the Cost Effects of Local Land Use Controls." *Journal of the American Planning Association* 47 (1981), pp. 145–53. Discusses the effects of land-use controls on the prices of housing and land, and proposes a monitoring system to control the inflationary effects of land-use controls.

————. "The Suburban Squeeze: Land-Use Policies in the San Francisco Bay Area." *Cato Journal* 2 (1982), pp. 709–33. Discusses local land-use policies and their effects on the regional economy.

————. "The Effects of Tax and Expenditure Limitations on Local Land Use Policies." *Perspectives on Local Public Finance and Public Policy* 1 (1983), pp. 69–87. Suggests that fiscal limitations (e.g., Proposition 13) will make fiscal zoning more prevalent, and discusses the implications of fiscal zoning for housing costs and the imbalance between jobs and residents.

Fischel, William. *The Economics of Zoning Laws.* Baltimore, Md.: Johns Hopkins University Press, 1985. A comprehensive economic analysis of land-use zoning, including discussions of the legal foundations of zoning and the effects of zoning on housing prices and location patterns.

Lillydahl, Jane H.; Arthur C. Nelson; Timothy V. Ramis; Antero Rivasplata; and Steven R. Schell. "The Need for a Standard State Impact Fee Enabling Act." *Journal of the American Planning Association* 54 (Winter 1988), pp. 7–17. Describes impact-fee policies in four states (California, Florida, Oregon, and Colorado) and argues for a national standard for impact fees.

Mills, Edwin S. "Economic Analysis of Urban Land-Use Controls." In *Current Issues in Urban Economics,* ed. Peter Mieszkowski and Mahlon Straszheim. Baltimore, Md.: Johns Hopkins University Press, 1979. A discussion of the use of zoning as a means of controlling externalities. Includes a historical sketch of land-use controls.

Moore, Terry. "Why Allow Planners to Do What They Do?" *American Institute of Planners Journal* (October 1978) pp. 387–98. Describes the reasons for planning and zoning in terms of market failure.

Patterson, T. *Land Use Planning: Techniques of Implementation.* New York: Van Nostrand Reinhold, 1977. Chapter 2 describes the basic features of zoning policies.

Porter, Douglas R.; Patrick L. Phillips; and Terry J. Lassar. *Flexible Zoning: How It Works.* Washington, D.C.: Urban Land Institute, 1988. Contrasts traditional zoning with more flexible approaches developed in recent years, and discusses the effects of flexible zoning in seven communities.

Roddewig, Richard J., and Cheryl A. Inghram. *Transferable Development Rights Programs: TDRs and the Real Estate Marketplace.* Chicago: American Society of Planning Officials, Report 401, 1987. Case studies of TDR programs in four cities (New

York, Denver, Seattle, and San Francisco) and two counties. Also explores the legal foundations of TDRs.

Siegan, Bernard. *Land Use without Zoning*. Lexington, Mass.: D. C. Heath, 1972. A discussion of land use in Houston, a city without zoning.

White, Michelle. "Self-Interest in the Suburbs: The Trend toward No-Growth Zoning." *Policy Analysis* 4 (1978), pp. 185–204. Discusses the reasons for no-growth zoning, and suggests public policies that might reverse the no-growth trend.

Urban Problems and the Federal Response

Part III discusses two urban problems that are addressed by the federal government: poverty and housing. The federal government uses a number of policies to combat poverty, including cash assistance, education and training programs, and payments in kind (food stamps, medical care, housing assistance). The problem of inadequate housing is related to the poverty problem in the sense that an increase in income would allow an ill-housed family to move to a better dwelling. Most housing policies, like antipoverty policies, are redistributional in nature.

The federal government is responsible for income redistribution because local redistributional efforts will be weakened by the mobility of taxpayers and transfer recipients. Suppose that a city imposes a tax on its wealthy citizens to finance transfer payments to the poor. Some wealthy households would leave the city to escape the tax, and some poor households would enter the city to get the transfer payment. In combination, the fleeing of the wealthy and the migration of the poor would weaken the city's redistribution program: there would be less money to transfer to more poor households. A national redistribution program will be more successful because there is less mobility between nations than between cities.

There are four chapters in this section, two chapters on poverty and two chapters on housing. Chapter 9 discusses the causes of poverty, including slow economic growth, racial segregation and discrimination, and the increase in the number of female-headed households. Chapter 10 explores the effects of various types of antipoverty policies and discusses several proposals to reform the current welfare system. Chapter 11 explains why housing is different from other goods. Chapter 12 takes a detailed look at several types of housing policies, including public housing, housing vouchers, and community development programs.

What Causes Poverty?

Although there are poor people in every segment of society, the incidence of poverty is greatest among women, children, racial minorities, and central-city residents. This chapter explores the various causes of poverty, including slow macroeconomic growth, racial segregation and discrimination, inferior education, and the increase in the number of female-headed households. In the passionate debates over poverty, the facts on poverty are often overlooked, misunderstood, or manipulated to support a particular position. In the words of Mark Twain, some people "use the facts like a drunk uses a lamp post—for support, not illumination." An informed discussion of poverty and its policy implications must be preceded by a careful discussion of the facts. The first section of the chapter discusses the facts on poverty, many of which are in conflict with the popular images of poverty and the facts used in public debates.

Poverty Facts

What is poverty? The U.S. government defines a poor household as one whose total income is less than the amount required to satisfy the "minimum needs" of the household. The government estimates a minimum food budget for each type of household and multiplies the food budget by three to get the official **poverty budget**. A household with income less than the official poverty budget is considered poor. In 1989, the poverty budget was $6,250 for a single person, $12,560 for a four-person household, and $21,100 for an eight-person household.

Who and Where Are the Poor?

Table 9–1 shows the composition of the poor population in 1990. For each type of household, the poverty rate equals the percentage of households with incomes less than the official poverty budget. Several facts stand out from the table:

TABLE 9-1   The Poverty Population in 1990

Group	Persons in Poverty (000)	Poverty Rate (percent)
All persons	33,585	13.50
Race		
White	22,326	10.70
Black	9,837	31.90
Hispanic	6,006	28.10
Location		
In metropolitan areas	24,510	12.70
In central cities	14,254	19.00
Outside central cities	10,255	8.70
Outside metropolitan areas	9,075	16.30
Household Head		
Married-couple families	2,981	5.70
Male householder	349	12.00
Female householder	3,768	33.40
Age		
Aged persons (over 65)	3,658	12.20
Children (under 15 years)	11,802	21.40
Education of Household Head		
Did not complete high school	8,092	23.60
Completed high school, no college	5,457	8.90
Some college education	1,679	5.80
Completed college	961	2.80

SOURCE: U.S. Bureau of the Census, "Poverty in United States: 1990," *Current Population Reports,* Series P-60, no. 175, Tables 1, 11.

1. **Race.** The number of poor whites is over twice the number of poor blacks and about four times the number of poor Hispanics. Nonetheless, the poverty rates for blacks and Hispanics are about three times the white rate. Figure 9–1 shows the poverty rates for different races. For Hispanics, poverty rates vary between groups with different cultural backgrounds: poverty rates are highest among those of Puerto Rican and Mexican heritage (38 percent and 26 percent, respectively) and lowest among those of Cuban heritage (14 percent). The poverty rate among Asians and Pacific Islanders is about 14 percent, close to the national average.

2. **Location.** The poverty rate of central cities is more than twice the suburban rate. The poverty rate outside metropolitan areas is about one third higher than the metropolitan rate. Figure 9–1 shows the poverty rates for different locations.

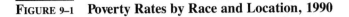

FIGURE 9-1   **Poverty Rates by Race and Location, 1990**

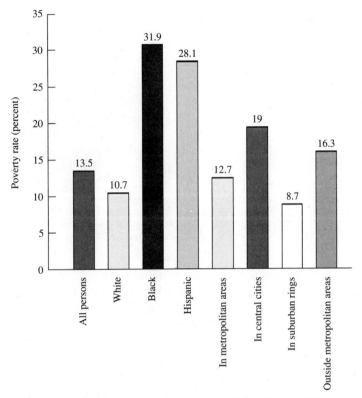

Source: U.S. Bureau of the Census, "Poverty in United States: 1990," *Current Population Reports,* Series P-60, no. 175, Tables 1, 11.

3. **Male versus female.** The poverty rate for female-headed households is almost six times the rate for households headed by a married couple. The table does not show the poverty rate for households headed by a black female, which is over 50 percent.

4. **The aged.** One of the successes in the war on poverty has been the decrease in poverty among the aged: their poverty rate dropped from 35 percent in 1959 to 12.2 percent in 1990, largely as a result of increased Social Security benefits.

5. **Children.** Over one fifth of all U.S. children lived in poverty in 1990. Figure 9–2 provides a closer look at poverty among black and white children. Over half of black children spend more than 4 of their first 10 years in poverty, compared to only 8 percent of white children. Only about a quarter of black children escape poverty altogether, compared to about three quarters of white children.

FIGURE 9–2   **Years of Pretransfer Poverty from Birth to Age 10 for White and Black Children**

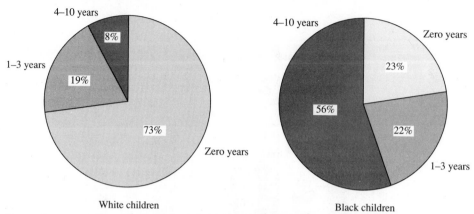

White children   Black children

Pretransfer poverty: income below the poverty line *before* counting government transfer payments.
SOURCE: David T. Ellwood, *Poor Support* (New York: Basic Books, 1988), Figure 6.2.

6. **Education.** Poverty rates are negatively related to the level of education. The poverty rate of high-school dropouts is over twice the rate for high-school graduates, and about four times the rate of those who attend at least one year of college.

Where Do the Poor Get Their Money?

Table 9–2 shows the distribution of work effort of poor household heads in 1987. Over half of the poor household heads worked at least part-time for part of the year, and over 1 million worked full-time for the entire year. Because the typical poor household has four members, this means that over 4 million poor people were in households with a full-time worker. If one assumes that part-time workers averaged 20 hours per week, over 2 million household heads worked at least the equivalent of 20 full-time weeks (800 hours for the year). In other words, about a quarter of the poor (8 million of 32 million) were in households where the household head worked the equivalent of 20 weeks per year. The implication is clear: half-time employment is not enough to escape poverty.

The working poor receive relatively low wages. Among poor household heads who work full-time, the typical wage is between $3.50 and $4.00. The annual income from a $4 wage is $8,320, which falls short of the poverty level for a three-person household by $1,480. For the poor who work part-time, the gap between market income and the poverty level is even larger.

Table 9–3 provides a closer look at the income sources of poor households. Male-headed households receive a large part of their income from earnings

TABLE 9–2   **Work Effort of Poor Nonaged Household Heads, 1987**

Weeks Worked	Full-Time Workers (000)	Part-Time Workers (000)	Total (000)
50–52	1,024	309	1,333
40–49	254	110	364
27–39	236	128	391
14–26	361	212	573
1 to 13	371	278	649
Total 1–52	2,273	1,037	3,310
Did not work	—	—	2,961
Total			6,271

SOURCE: Bradley Schiller, *The Economics of Poverty and Discrimination,* 5th ed. (Englewood Cliffs, N.J.: Prentice Hall, 1989).

(63 percent) and a small share from welfare programs (23 percent). For female-headed households, the percentages are reversed (26 percent from earnings and 60 percent from welfare). The differences are explained in large part by the greater child-care responsibilities of women, which limit their working time.

Tables 9–2 and 9–3 suggest two principal reasons for poverty. The first is the lack of employment: a large fraction of poor households lack a full-time worker. The second is low wages: a full-time job at a wage of $4 per hour does not generate enough income to lift a household out of poverty. To escape poverty, the household head must earn more than the minimum wage. The remainder of the chapter explores the reasons why some types of workers have low employment rates and low wages.

Economic Growth and Stagnation

Perhaps the most important reason for poverty is slow macroeconomic growth. Stated another way, the most powerful means of decreasing poverty is through economic growth. According to the **queuing theory** of unemployment, prospective workers form an employment line (a queue) outside the factory or office building. A worker's position in the line is determined by his productivity: the lower his productivity, the further down the line he is positioned. Because employers draw workers from the front of the line, the lowest productivity workers are the last to be hired. They are more likely to be hired when economic growth increases the demand for labor: firms hire workers further down the employment

TABLE 9–3   Income Sources for Poor Households

	Male-Headed		Female-Headed	
	Amount ($)	*Percent of Total*	*Amount ($)*	*Percent of Total*
Earnings	$5,136	62.63%	$1,722	25.70%
Welfare programs	1,909	23.28	4,049	60.43
Cash benefits	1,110	13.54	2,398	35.79
Food stamps	666	8.12	1,106	16.51
Housing assistance	133	1.62	545	8.13
Social Security	562	6.85	414	6.18
Unemployment	340	4.15	91	1.36
Other	253	3.09	424	6.33
Total	8,200	100.00	6,700	100.00

SOURCE: Bradley Schiller, *The Economics of Poverty and Discrimination,* 5th ed. (Englewood Cliffs, N.J.: Prentice Hall, 1989).

queue, employing low-productivity workers who would normally be unemployed. Because economic growth generates jobs for marginal (low productivity) workers, it decreases poverty. In contrast, a recession decreases the demand for labor, and the least productive workers are the first fired.

There is conclusive evidence that economic growth decreases poverty. Ellwood (1987) predicts poverty rates for different years using two macroeconomic variables (the unemployment rate and median earnings) and compares the predicted rates with the actual poverty rates. His results for male-headed households are shown in Figure 9–3. The predicted rates are very close to the actual poverty rates, suggesting that the state of the economy has a strong influence on the poverty rates of male-headed households: an increase in the unemployment rate increases the poverty rate, and vice versa. In contrast, economic growth plays a less important role in the poverty of female-headed households. Because fewer female household heads work, they are less affected by changes in the demand for labor.

A number of studies have estimated the effects of recessions on poor households. Gramlich and Laren (1984) estimated the effects of changes in unemployment rates on the earnings of different types of households. The earnings of both poor- and middle-income households decrease as the unemployment rate rises, but the relative loss of poor households was about three times the loss of middle-income households. In terms of racial differences, a one-point increase in the unemployment rate decreased the income of white males by 1.2 percent, but decreased the earnings of nonwhite males by 2.0 percent. The implications are clear: since recessions impose relatively large costs on the poor, policies that promote macroeconomic growth reduce poverty.

Blank and Blinder (1986) examined the effects of changes in unemployment and inflation on poverty rates. They conclude that the rising unemployment

FIGURE 9–3   **Expected versus Actual Poverty**

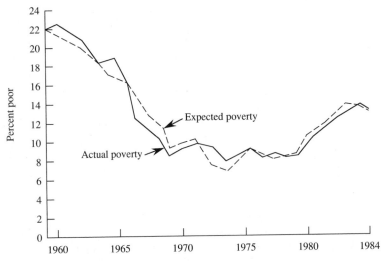

Expected poverty is based solely on the median earnings of full year, full-time
male workers, and the unemployment rate.
SOURCE: David Ellwood, *Divide and Conquer* (New York: Ford Foundation, 1987),
p. 16.

between 1973 and 1983 added over five percentage points to the poverty rate:
if the 1983 unemployment had been equal to the 1973 rate, the 1983 poverty
rate would have been 10.1 percent instead of 15.2 percent. Stated another way, a
one-point increase in the prime-age male unemployment rate increases the poverty
rate by 0.70 percentage points. Although the poverty rate also increases with the
inflation rate, the relationship is weak relative to the relationship between poverty
and unemployment. In other words, the poor are harmed more by unemployment
than by inflation.

The results of Bartik's (1991) study of urban employment growth are consistent with the notion that poor households experience relatively large benefits
from economic growth. When a city's economy grows by 1,000 jobs, 770 of
the new jobs are filled by newcomers, leaving 230 jobs for the original residents
of the city. About one third of the 230 jobs are filled by original residents who
were previously unemployed, and the remaining two thirds are filled by original
residents who previously did not participate in the labor market. The increase in
employment increases real income per capita because it increases the labor-force
participation rate and speeds up the promotion of city residents to higher-paying
jobs. Bartik predicts that a 1 percent increase in total employment increases real
per capita income by 0.40 percent for the population as a whole, 0.43 percent for
less educated workers, and 0.44 percent for black workers.

Residential Segregation

As shown in Table 9–1, the black poverty rate is over three times the white poverty rate. One reason for the greater poverty among black households is residential segregation. In most metropolitan areas, blacks are concentrated in central cities: in 1980, about 74 percent of metropolitan blacks lived in central cities, compared to only 35 percent of whites (Kain, 1985). In other words, only 26 percent of blacks lived in the suburbs, compared to 65 percent of whites.

How does racial segregation affect poverty rates? As discussed in earlier chapters, almost half of the jobs in manufacturing, retailing, and offices are now in suburban areas. Because only about a quarter of blacks live in the suburbs, blacks have limited access to suburban employment opportunities. According to the **spatial mismatch theory,** the segregation of blacks in the central city, far from suburban employment opportunities, contributes to black poverty. The suburban-ization of employment in recent decades has increased poverty because blacks have not followed jobs to the suburbs.

Residential segregation can decrease real income and increase poverty in three ways. First, if blacks are forced to commute relatively long distances to suburban jobs, they have a lower net hourly wage (the gross wage less commuting costs) and less time for work or leisure. Therefore, central-city blacks who work in the suburbs have lower net incomes. Second, to the extent that higher commuting costs discourage work efforts, segregation decreases employment rates. Third, much of the information about job opportunities comes through informal channels: workers find out about job openings from neighbors and friends. The segregation of blacks in the center city decreases their access to this informal information network, increases search costs, and thus decreases employment rates.

Why don't central-city blacks commute to suburban jobs? Commuting is costly for central-city residents because (1) most transit systems are designed to deliver suburban residents to the city center and are ill-suited for bringing central-city residents to suburban jobs, and (2) relatively few central-city households own cars. Even if commuting were feasible, finding a suburban job would be difficult be-cause blacks in the center city have limited access to the informal job-information network.

Why Segregation?

Why are blacks concentrated in central cities? Kain (1985), discusses several possible reasons for segregation:

1. **Voluntary segregation.** Perhaps blacks prefer to live in segregated neighborhoods. However, the evidence from attitudinal surveys sug-gests the opposite: most blacks would in fact prefer to live in integrated neighborhoods (Kain, 1985). To a black household, an "integrated" neighborhood is one that is equally divided between whites and blacks (Clark, 1991).

2. **Lower incomes.** Perhaps blacks cannot afford suburban housing and are forced to live in low-cost housing in the central city. A recent study by Gabriel and Rosenthal (1989) suggests that a black household with the same income and other characteristics as the average white suburban household is much less likely to live in the suburbs. Kain (1985) poses the following question: If location decisions were based strictly on non-racial characteristics (income, family type, age of household head), how many black households would live in the suburbs? His answer is that 3.6 million black households would live in the suburbs, about twice the actual number of black suburban households. The results of Gabriel and Rosenthal and Kain suggest that the low rate of black suburbanization is caused by factors other than income.

3. **Racial prejudice.** It appears that many whites prefer to live in segregated neighborhoods. Among whites who prefer integrated neighborhoods, an "integrated" neighborhood is one in which 80 percent of the residents are white and only 20 percent are black (Clark, 1991). In contrast, blacks prefer neighborhoods that are split equally between whites and blacks.

4. **Discrimination by real estate agents.** The actions of real estate agents promote racial segregation. A 1979 study by the Department of Housing and Urban Development estimated that 27 percent of rental agents and 15 percent of house sellers discriminated against blacks. Discrimination was defined as "failing to provide important, necessary information to rent or purchase a home" to a person of a particular race. Black home buyers who inquired about four different advertised homes had a 48 percent chance of encountering discriminatory treatment for at least one home, and renters had an 85 percent chance of encountering discriminatory treatment for at least one of four rental properties.

5. **Exclusionary zoning.** As explained in the chapter on land-use controls, suburban governments use zoning to exclude low-income households from their jurisdictions. Exclusionary zoning is motivated in part by fiscal concerns: if low-income households do not pay their "fair share" of the costs of local public services, they are excluded by suburban governments. Since the average income of blacks is lower than the white average, exclusionary zoning has a larger effect on black households. Exclusionary zoning is also motivated by concerns over crime and education: the wealthy exclude the poor to keep crime rates low and educational achievement high.

There is some evidence that racial segregation decreased during the 1970s. According to Kain (1985), the fraction of black households living outside central cities increased from 18.1 percent in 1970 to 25.8 percent in 1980. Most of the increase in the number of black suburbanites was caused by (*a*) the expansion of central-city ghettos across central-city lines and (*b*) the growth of suburban concentrations of blacks. There was, however, a small movement of blacks into previously white suburban neighborhoods. In the San Francisco Bay area, the number of suburban communities with between 50 and 1,000 black households increased from 22 in 1970 to 40 in 1980. In Chicago, the number of such neighborhoods increased from 11 to 39. Although these changes are relatively small, they may suggest that the forces that inhibit black suburbanization are weakening.

Evidence on the Spatial Mismatch Theory

The spatial mismatch theory suggests that racial segregation in central cities increases black poverty. The first evidence in support of this theory is from Kain (1968), who estimated that racial segregation in Chicago decreased employment opportunities for blacks by over 20,000 jobs. Two recent studies of the spatial mismatch theory have generated conflicting results.

Using data from Chicago, Ellwood (1986) suggests that the spatial mismatch is a relatively small factor in black youth unemployment. Although jobs are moving to the suburbs faster than black teenagers are, most teenagers (both black and white) do not work in their own neighborhoods anyway, so the location of jobs is relatively unimportant. The unemployment rates of blacks seem to be unrelated to their proximity to jobs. For example, the West Side of Chicago, where jobs are plentiful, has about the same black teenage unemployment rate as the South Side, where jobs are scarce. Ellwood concludes that the high unemployment rates and low participation rates of black teenagers are caused by racial factors, not by a spatial mismatch between residence and workplaces. As pointed out by Leonard (1986) and Ihlanfeldt and Sjoquist (1990), there are a number of problems with the data used by Ellwood, so his results must be interpreted with caution.

Using data from the Philadelphia metropolitan area, Ihlanfeldt and Sjoquist (1990) suggest that the spatial mismatch is an important factor in black youth unemployment. For all youths, black and white, the likelihood of being employed drops as commuting distance (the distance between the residence and employment opportunities) increases. One reason for the lower employment rate for black youths (27 percent versus 49 percent for white youths) is that the average commute time for blacks is 26 minutes, compared to 18.5 minutes for whites. The authors conclude that between a third and a half of the gap in employment rates was explained by the fact that black youths lived further from jobs.

In another study, Ihlanfeldt (1991) tests for the mismatch hypothesis in 50 metropolitan areas. His principal conclusions are as follows:

1. Overall, inferior access to employment opportunities explains between 24 percent and 27 percent of the gap between black and white employment rates and between 29 percent and 34 percent of the gap between Hispanic and white employment rates.

2. The spatial mismatch is more important in larger metropolitan areas. In small cities, only 3 percent of the gap between black and white employment rates is explained by inferior access; in medium-sized cities,

inferior access is responsible for 14 percent of the gap; in large cities, inferior access is responsible for about a quarter of the gap.

What conclusions can be drawn from the conflicting evidence concerning the spatial mismatch theory? The three recent studies suggest that there is still some uncertainty about the relative importance of the spatial mismatch effect. Nonetheless, there is a consensus that even if the spatial mismatch theory is correct, the other factors in black poverty are probably more important. A reasonable conclusion from the studies by Ihlanfeldt and Sjoquist is that the mismatch is responsible for about a quarter of the gap between black and white employment rates, leaving three quarters to be explained by labor-market discrimination, differences in education, and other factors.

The Policy Response

The government can promote the suburbanization of blacks in three ways. First, if the federal government enforces its fair-housing laws, it could reduce the discriminatory treatment of blacks in the suburban housing market. Second, local governments could change their zoning laws to allow the suburbanization of blacks and other minorities. Third, if state governments provided more support for local-government services, the incentives for exclusionary zoning would decrease.

Education and Poverty

As shown in Table 9–1, the poverty rate depends on the education level of the household head: the lower the education level, the greater the poverty rate. Table 9–4 provides a closer look at the effects of education on employment and earnings, showing the relationship between education and unemployment rates, labor-force participation rates, work time, and average earnings. The unemployment rate of high school dropouts is over six times the rate for college graduates, and almost twice the rate for high school graduates. The lower labor-force participation rate among less educated people is evidence of "discouraged workers." Because these people have a more difficult time finding jobs, they are less likely to continue looking.

How does education affect employment and earnings? The theory of human capital stresses the effects of increased education on worker productivity. The idea is that schools teach skills that (1) can be directly applied to tasks on the job and (2) allow workers to learn more quickly on the job. Education is also a signaling device: a diploma shows a prospective employer that the person is sufficiently smart and dedicated to survive a rigorous educational program and is thus likely to be a good worker.

Education and Changes in Central-City Employment

The employment problems of central-city blacks have been exacerbated by changes in the structure of the central-city economy. Table 9–5 shows the changes

TABLE 9–4   Education and Success in the Labor Market

	High School Dropouts	High School Graduates	College Graduates
Unemployment rate	15.4%	8.6%	2.5%
Labor force participation rate	61%	81%	88%
Full-time workers	57%	76%	84%
Average earnings	$15,266	$18,370	$28,519

SOURCE: Bradley Schiller, *The Economics of Poverty and Discrimination,* 5th ed. (Englewood Cliffs, N.J.: Prentice Hall, 1989).

in central-city employment between 1953 and 1985 for five cities (New York, Philadelphia, Boston, Baltimore, and St. Louis). Total employment in jobs requiring relatively low skills and education has decreased: in 1985, manufacturing employment was 40 percent of its 1953 level, and retail and wholesale employment was 70 percent of its 1953 level. In contrast, employment in jobs requiring higher skills and education has increased: total employment in white-collar services more than tripled between 1953 and 1985.

Kasarda (1988) provides further evidence of the increased educational requirements of central-city employment. Figure 9–4 shows employment changes between 1970 and 1985 in two groups of cities. In the five northern and eastern cities, the number of jobs requiring less than a high school education dropped by over 900,000, while the number of jobs requiring some college education increased by 428,000. In the four growing southern and western cities, employment growth was more rapid in jobs requiring some college education.

Because the average education level of blacks is relatively low, blacks are unable to take full advantage of the new employment opportunities in white-collar industries. Most of the new white-collar service jobs in central cities require at least some college education. Nationwide, the high school completion rates for blacks and Hispanics is much lower than the completion rate for whites. In the high school class of 1982, 22 percent of the black students and 28 percent of the Hispanic students failed to graduate with their class, compared to 15 percent of whites and 8 percent of Asians (O'Hare et al., 1991). Only about 27 percent of central-city blacks complete at least one year of college, compared to 40 percent of central-city whites (Kasarda, 1988).

Evidence on the Effects of Education on Poverty

The National Bureau of Economic Research (NBER) completed a comprehensive study of black youths in the inner-city areas of Boston, Chicago, and Philadelphia (Freeman and Holzer, 1986). The study explored the various factors that contribute to the inner-city unemployment problem, including inadequate education. Some of the conclusions of the study are as follows:

TABLE 9-5   **Employment in Five Central Cities by Sector, 1953 and 1985***

	1953		1985	
Employment Sector	*Number (000)*	*% of Total*	*Number (000)*	*% of Total*
Total employment	4,940	100%	4,662	100%
Manufacturing	1,867	38	743	16
Retail and wholesale	1,335	27	954	20
White-collar services	925	19	2,218	48
Blue-collar services	577	12	561	12
Other	236	5	186	4

Definitions
1. Total employment: total classified employment excluding government employment and sole proprietors.
2. White-collar services: service industries (excluding government, retail, wholesale) in which more than half of employees hold executive, managerial, professional, or clerical positions.
3. Blue-collar services: service industries (excluding government, retail, wholesale) in which less than half of employees hold executive, managerial, professional, or clerical positions.

*Central cities: New York, Philadelphia, Boston, Baltimore, and St. Louis.
SOURCE: Computed from Table 9 in John Kasarda, "Jobs, Migration, and Emerging Urban Mismatches," in *Urban Change and Poverty,* ed. by Michael McGeary and Laurence Lynn (Washington, D.C.: National Academy Press, 1988).

1. Graduation from high school increased earnings in two ways: it increased wages by 15 percent and increased hours worked by 6 percent.
2. An increase in the number of years in school increased wages, decreased participation in crime, and decreased the amount of time spent in nonproductive activities (activities other than schooling and employment, including hanging out, watching TV, and getting high).
3. An increase in school performance (measured by grades) increased wages, decreased the likelihood of dropping out, and improved work habits.

The general conclusion of the study is that education has a strong effect on the employment prospects of inner-city youths.

The Title I programs of the federal government are special programs for disadvantaged youths. In 1984, the federal government spent $3.4 billion on Title I programs. A total of 5 million children were served by the programs, with an average cost per child of about $700 (Glazer, 1986). What are the effects of these programs?

A study of the Perry Preschool Program in Ypsilanti, Michigan, suggests that the program is a resounding success (Berrueta-Clement et al., 1984). The study

**FIGURE 9–4   Change in Number of Jobs with Different Education
Requirements, 1970–1985**

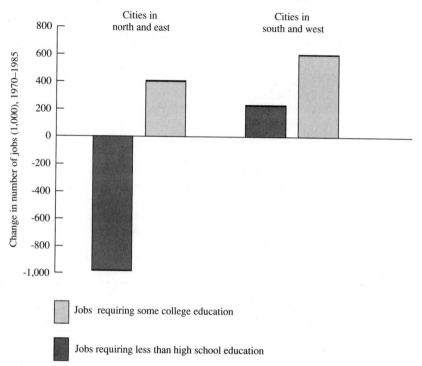

Cities in north and east: New York, Philadelphia, Boston, Baltimore, St. Louis. Cities in
south and west: Atlanta, Houston, Denver, San Francisco.
SOURCE: Computed from Table 9 in John Kasarda, "Jobs, Migration, and Emerging Urban
Mismatches," in *Urban Change and Poverty,* ed. by Michael McGeary and Laurence
Lynn (Washington, D.C.: National Academy Press, 1988).

compares teenagers who participated in the preschool program to those who did
not. Compared to the control group, program participants had higher high school
completion rates (67 percent versus 49 percent), lower arrest rates (by a margin of
40 percent), and half the teenage pregnancy rate. The estimated benefit-cost ratio
of the program was 7.0. This study shows that preschool programs may generate
substantial long-term benefits.

Glazer (1986) summarizes the results of several other studies of Title I programs. One comprehensive study suggests that Title I programs have increased
achievement in mathematics and reading, with the largest gains in the early grades.
Other studies by the National Assessment of Educational Progress (NAEP) show
that Title I programs have narrowed the achievement gaps between black and
white students, with the largest relative gains at the elementary level (NAEP,
1981; National Center for Education Statistics, 1982).

Labor Market Discrimination

Discrimination in the labor market takes two forms, employment discrimination and wage discrimination. Employment discrimination refers to the practice of systematically hiring one racial group over the other, despite the fact that both groups are equally productive and are paid the same wage. Wage discrimination is defined as paying different wages to equally productive workers. Both types of discrimination have the potential to increase poverty among racial minorities because minority workers either are not hired or are hired at a lower wage.

Differences in Earnings

Table 9–6 shows the median earnings for white, black, and Hispanic men. For all workers, the gap between white and black earnings is $7,776, and the gap between white and Hispanic earnings is $9,119. Part of this gap is caused by differences in education. The gaps for workers of particular educational levels are slightly smaller: the black-white gap for high school graduates is $6,895, and the black-white gap for college graduates is $5,544. Because blacks typically receive inferior education, a simple comparison based on years of schooling is deceptive. According to Schiller (1989), the typical black high school graduate has the same educational preparation as the typical white high school dropout, so the gap for a black high school graduate and a white person with the same educational preparation is $1,918. Schiller concludes that a black worker earns about 90 percent of what a white worker with an equivalent educational background earns.

The earnings gap is decreased further if one controls for other factors such as age, labor skills, and location. Research on race differences in earnings suggest that about three fourths of the earnings gap can be explained by differences in

TABLE 9–6   Median Annual Earnings by Race and Education, Men Aged 16 and Over, 1986

Education Level	White Workers	Black Workers	Hispanic Workers
All workers	$25,890	$18,114	$16,711
High school dropout	18,547	14,681	13,816
High school graduate	23,524	16,629	17,984
Some college time	26,206	21,182	22,254
College graduate	32,789	27,245	28,332

SOURCE: Bradley Schiller, *The Economics of Poverty and Discrimination,* 5th ed. (Englewood Cliffs, N.J.: Prentice Hall, 1989).

education, age, skills, and location, leaving one quarter of the gap unexplained. The unexplained portion is caused by racial discrimination.

Theories of Discrimination

There are two theories of labor market discrimination. The first theory, developed by Becker (1957), explains the competitive forces that limit discrimination. The second theory, developed by Phelps (1972) and Arrow (1973), explains why discrimination may persist.

Becker's theory suggests that market forces limit the extent of wage discrimination. Consider a city with two types of workers, black and white. Suppose that they have the same **value of marginal product (VMP)**, defined as the marginal physical product of labor times the market price of the product produced. Suppose that white workers are paid their VMP ($6) but blacks are paid only $5. If you were a profit-maximizing firm, what would you do? If you hire black workers, you will have lower production costs than your all-white competitors, so your sales and profits will increase. What's good for you is good for other capitalists, so other firms will hire the undervalued black workers. As the demand for blacks increases and the demand for whites decreases, the gap between black and white wages decreases. In equilibrium, whites and blacks have the same wage.

Under what conditions does wage discrimination persist? If a white firm can keep other firms from entering the its industry, it can protect itself from the competition of color-blind firms. Bigotry is not costless, however. The white monopolist pays relatively high wages to its white workers, and its higher production costs force its consumers to pay a relatively high price. In addition, profits are lower, so stockholders pay for bigotry in the form of lower dividends and stock prices. Job discrimination may persist if (*a*) bigoted firms are protected from competition and (*b*) consumers and stockholders are willing to pay for their bigotry.

The same arguments apply to sex discrimination. If the female wage is less than the male wage, and men and women are equally productive, profit-seeking firms will hire women and fire men, narrowing the wage gap. In equilibrium, one would expect equally productive men and women to earn the same wage. Job discrimination may persist if (*a*) sexist firms are protected from competition, and (*b*) consumers and stockholders are willing to pay for their sexism.

As explained earlier, the empirical evidence does not support this simple theory of discrimination. After controlling for all nondiscriminatory factors, there is still a large gap between the wages of whites and blacks. Obviously, there is something wrong with the simple model.

The theory of **statistical discrimination** shows that the black-white wage differential persists if there is imperfect information about worker productivity. Suppose that an employer must hire one of two workers, a black or a white. If the firm knew which worker had the higher VMP, it would obviously hire the more productive worker. Such information is not available, however, so the employer must guess which worker has the higher VMP. Suppose that because of differences in education and work experience, the average black is less productive than the average white, although some blacks are more productive than some whites. If the employer has no other information on the productivities of the applicants, the best choice, in a statistical sense, is the white worker. White workers are chosen over equally productive (or more productive) black workers because black workers are less productive *on average*. In this case, discrimination occurs because of imperfect information, not bigotry.

Demographic Change: Female-Headed Households

As shown in Table 9–1, the poverty rate of female-headed households is over three times the poverty rate of male-headed households. Female-headed households are more likely to be poor for three reasons. First, most of these households are single-parent households, so the woman must juggle employment and child-care responsibilities. For many women, especially those with preschool children, full-time work is not feasible. Second, women earn lower wages than men, so a given amount of work generates less income. Third, only one third of female-headed households receive child-support payments from absent fathers.

Facts on Family Structure

The number of female-headed households has increased rapidly in the last few decades. Between 1970 and 1985, the percentage of white households headed by a female increased from 9.6 percent to 13.4 percent (U.S. Bureau of the Census, 1986). For blacks, the percentage of households headed by a female increased from 31.8 percent to 43.9 percent. According to Sawhill (1988), the increase in the number of female-headed households between 1967 and 1985 added between one and two percentage points to the overall poverty rate.

An increase in the number of female-headed households means that fewer children are raised in two-parent households. Figure 9–5 shows, for both white and black households, the percentage of children living with married couples. Between 1960 and 1988, the percentage of black children living in two-parent households dropped from 67 percent to 39 percent. For whites over the same period, the percentage of children in two-parent households dropped from 91 percent to 79 percent.

Another part of the increase in the number of female-headed households is the increase in the number of births to single mothers. Figure 9–5 shows, for both white and black households, the percentages of births to unmarried women. By 1988, well over half of black births were to single mothers, compared to a figure of 23 percent in 1960. Between 1960 and 1988, the share of white births to single women increased almost sevenfold, from 2.3 percent to 15.7 percent.

FIGURE 9–5   **Living Arrangements of White and Black Children**

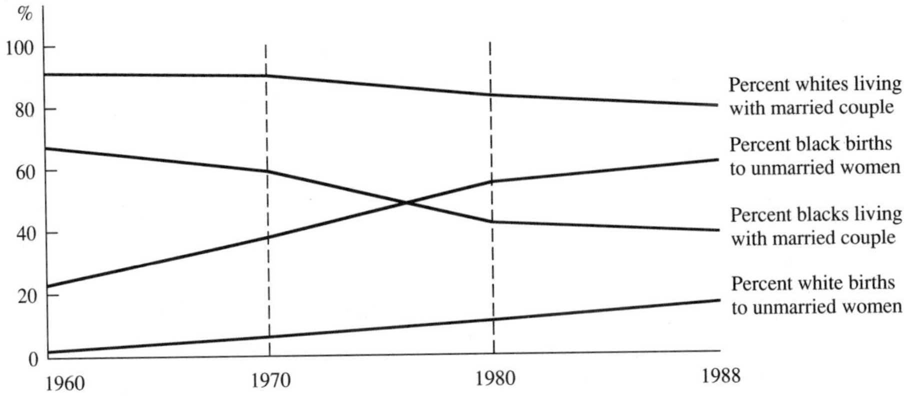

SOURCE: David T. Ellwood and Jonathan Crane, "Family Change Among Black Americans: What Do We Know?" *Journal of Economic Perspectives* 4 (1990), pp. 65–84.

Family Structure and Welfare Payments

What caused the changes in family structure shown in Figure 9–5? What changes over the last few decades caused the increases in (1) the number of female-headed households, (2) the percentage of children in single-parent households, and (3) the percentage of births to single mothers?

One theory of the changing family structure, popularized by Murray (1984) is that the welfare system is responsible for the increases in female-headed households. Murray argues that generous welfare payments make it possible for women to raise children outside of marriage: because single women can rely on the welfare system for support, they have less need for a husband. According to this theory, the growth in female-headed households (and the associated increases in the percentage of children in single-parent households) result from increases in the real value of welfare payments.

This theory is easily refuted by looking at the facts on welfare payments and single-parent households. Figure 9–6 shows the time trends of welfare payments per household (Aid to Families with Dependent Children [AFDC] and food stamps, in 1988 dollars) and the percentage of black children living in single-parent households. Although there was a positive relationship between welfare payments and the percentage of children in single-parent households during the 1960s, the relationship has been negative since 1970. Between 1970 and 1988, the real value of welfare payments per household decreased by about 22 percent, while the percentage of children in single-parent households increased, from 42 percent to 61 percent.

Figure 9–6 also shows the time trend in the percentage of black children residing in households receiving AFDC. If AFDC were responsible for the in-

FIGURE 9-6   Welfare Benefits and Living Arrangements of Black Children

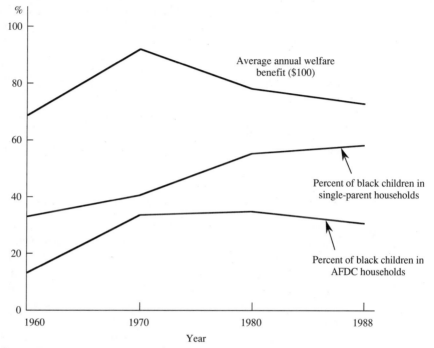

SOURCE: David T. Ellwood and Jonathan Crane, "Family Change Among Black Americans: What Do We Know?" *Journal of Economic Perspectives* 4 (1990), pp. 65–84.

creases in the number of children in single-parent households, we would expect the percentage of children in AFDC households to increase more rapidly than the percentage in single-parent households. In fact, between 1970 and 1988, while the percentage of children in single-parent households increased, the percentage of children in AFDC households decreased.

There have been a number of rigorous statistical studies of the effects of welfare payments on family structure. On a theoretical level, the idea that an increase in support for single mothers increases the number of single mothers is a sensible one: if we decrease the cost of single parenthood, we expect that, at the margin, some women will choose single motherhood over the alternatives. The issue is really an empirical one: by how much does AFDC increase the number of single parents?

Wilson and Neckerman (1986) review the literature on the connection between welfare payments and family structure. They come to the following conclusions:

1. There is no evidence that welfare payments affect the number of out-of-wedlock births. States with relatively generous welfare programs did not have higher birth rates among unmarried women.

2. There is some evidence that welfare encourages divorce and separation. States with relatively generous welfare programs have higher rates of marital dissolution. Ellwood and Bane (1985) estimate that a $100 increase in monthly AFDC benefits would cause a 10 percent increase in the number of divorced or separated mothers.

In general, it appears that AFDC encourages women to set up independent households, but does not encourage them to bear more children. Garfinkel and McLanahan (1986) suggests that rising AFDC benefits between 1960 and 1975 increased the number of female-headed households by between 9 percent and 14 percent. Because the actual number of female-headed households increased by over 100 percent, it is clear that AFDC played a small role in the growth of female-headed households.

Family Structure and the Status of Black Men

Wilson and Neckerman (1986) propose an alternative theory for the increase in female-headed households. They compute a "marriageability index" for black men, which is defined as the number of employed black men per 100 black women. The idea behind this theory is that a decrease in the employment rate of black men discourages marriage and the formation of two-parent households.

Figure 9–7 shows the time trends in the marriageability index and marriage rates for young black men (20 to 24 years old). Between 1960 and 1988, the index dropped from 68 (68 employed men per 100 women) to 55, while the marriage rate dropped from 35 percent to 11 percent. Between 1960 and 1980, the two curves move in the same direction, providing some support for the theory. Between 1980 and 1988, however, the marriageability index rose while the marriage rate fell. Over this period, eligible men became more plentiful, but the marriage rates among employed men dropped. In fact, marriage rates among employed men have been dropping since 1970, suggesting that eligibility is not the primary factor in declining marriage rates.

There have been a number of rigorous studies of the relationship between employment rates and marriage rates. According to Ellwood and Crane (1990), these studies suggest that although there is a positive relationship between employment and marriage rates, the relationship is weak. In other words, there is evidence that changes in black male employment rates have a relatively small effect on marriage rates and family structure.

Summary: What Causes Changes in Family Structure?

The reasons for the recent changes in family structure are still unknown, at least to economists. Ellwood and Crane (1990) suggest that changes in family structure result from complex interactions of social, cultural, legal, and economic factors, and that it will be difficult to disentangle these factors to determine which factors are the most important and thus worthy of attention by the public sector. Since

FIGURE 9-7   **Black Males Marriageability Index and**
              Percentage Married, 1960–1988

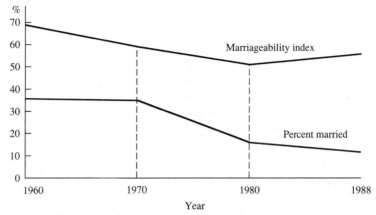

SOURCE: David T. Ellwood and Jonathan Crane, "Family Change Among Black
Americans: What Do We Know?" *Journal of Economic Perspectives* 4 (1990),
pp. 65–84.

poverty rates are the greatest among single-parent households, our ignorance about
the reasons for changes in family structure is troublesome.

Poverty in the Central City

One of the most difficult problems in the urban economy is the concentration of
poverty in the central city. Particularly disturbing is the continued concentration of
poor blacks in certain areas of central cities. In 1983, under half of the inner-city
blacks in Boston, Philadelphia, and Chicago were employed (Freeman and Holzer,
1986). In contrast, 61 percent of U.S. blacks and 76 percent of U.S. whites were
employed. Along with low employment rates, central cities have high crime rates
and widespread drug abuse.

The reasons for central city poverty are discussed earlier in this chapter.
Although the majority of jobs are now in the suburbs, the vast majority of blacks
continue to live in central cities. Moreover, an increasing share of central-city jobs
requires a college education, so most blacks are unable to take advantage of new
job opportunities in the central city. Racial discrimination contributes to the black
poverty problem: segregation inhibits the movement of blacks to the suburbs,
and job discrimination limits their employment options. Education problems also
contribute to poverty: central cities have inferior schools, so the average black
teenager emerges from the education system with lower skills than his white
counterpart.

As mentioned earlier, the National Bureau of Economic Research (NBER) completed a comprehensive study of the black youth unemployment problem. Freeman and Holzer (1986) summarize the findings of the study. Some of their conclusions are as follows:

1. **Local labor market.** Cities with relatively strong labor markets had relatively low black teenage unemployment rates. For example, the employment rate in Boston (a city with a relatively healthy economy) was 10 percentage points above the employment rates in Chicago and Philadelphia. This finding is consistent with the notion that the most effective way to reduce poverty is through macroeconomic growth.

2. **Spatial mismatch.** Blacks who lived relatively close to jobs did not have lower unemployment rates, that is, physical proximity to jobs did not decrease unemployment rates. This conclusion is based on Ellwood's (1986) study of Chicago (discussed earlier in this chapter). Blacks on the West Side, where jobs are plentiful, did not have lower unemployment rates than blacks on the South Side, where jobs are scarce. In addition, whites hold most of the jobs in the border areas between white and black neighborhoods.

3. **Competition with women.** Cities with the highest proportion of women in the labor market had the worst labor market for black teenagers (the lowest wages and participation rates). It seems that increases in female participation rates have decreased employment opportunities for young blacks.

4. **Discrimination.** Prospective employers treated black applicants differently than white ones. In general, employers were less courteous to black applicants.

5. **Family experience.** Black youths were more likely to be employed if other members of the family were employed. This suggests that adult joblessness increases youth unemployment, that is, that employment problems are passed from generation to generation.

6. **Reservation wage.** Black and white youths had comparable reservation wages (defined as the lowest acceptable wage). Because employers perceived that blacks were less productive, the relatively high black reservation wage increased black unemployment.

7. **Illegal opportunities.** Crime rates were higher in cities with fewer legal opportunities. Crime rates were also affected by the perceived risks and returns of crime: teenagers who perceived that the risks were low and returns were high were more likely to commit crime.

8. **Welfare involvement.** Teenagers from welfare families had more trouble in the labor market, even after controlling for differences in income and family structure. Youths living in public housing did worse than their peers who lived in private housing.

9. **Education.** Employment and wages were affected by the amount of schooling and school performance. Youths with more years of school-

ing and higher grades had higher wages, more work hours, and lower crime rates.

The NBER study suggests that the problems of black inner-city teenagers are caused by many factors, including weak labor markets, competition with women, discrimination, opportunities for crime, and inadequate education. It suggests that a comprehensive approach is required to decrease youth unemployment.

Summary

1. A poor household is defined as one whose total income is less than three times the minimum food budget. Poverty rates are greatest among racial minorities, women, and central-city residents.
2. Economic growth decreases poverty because the poor are the last hired and the first fired.
3. One theory of black poverty is that blacks have been confined to the central city while employment has shifted to the suburbs. There is conflicting evidence about the effects of residential segregation (and limited access to jobs) on black poverty rates.
4. The poverty rate depends on the education level of the household head: the unemployment rate of high school dropouts is over six times the rate for college graduates, and about twice the rate for high school graduates. A study of inner-city youths suggests that increased education increases wages and earnings, and decreases crime rates.
5. Studies of education programs suggest that some of them increase achievement.
    a. The Perry Preschool Program increased high school completion rates and decreased arrest rates.
    b. Studies of Title I programs suggest that they have increased achievement, with the largest gains at the elementary level.
6. Job discrimination contributes to poverty: in some circumstances, blacks are paid less than whites, and women are paid less than men. Although market forces limit the extent of job discrimination, wage differences persist because of statistical discrimination.
7. Economic growth is a necessary—but not sufficient—condition for reducing poverty: because the poor are the last hired, it is necessary; because the poor must have the skills for the new jobs and must live near the new jobs, it is not sufficient.
8. The number of female-headed households has increased rapidly in the last few decades, increasing poverty rates.
    a. It appears that AFDC has increased the number of female-headed households by a small amount.

    b. The increase in male joblessness played a minor role in the increase in female-headed households.

9. One of the most difficult problems in the urban economy is the concentration of poverty among blacks in the central city. A study of the black youth unemployment problem suggests that low employment rates are caused by weak labor markets, competition with women, discrimination, opportunities for crime, and inadequate education.

Exercises and Discussion Questions

1. The section on job discrimination suggests that the market penalizes racist and sexist firms because such firms are underpriced by color-blind and sex-blind firms. As a result, there are limits on the extent of wage discrimination.

   a. What if all firms (capitalists and managers) are color-blind, but white laborers refuse to work with black laborers? Will wage discrimination (lower wages for blacks) persist?

   b. What if firms and employees are color-blind, but white consumers refuse to purchase goods produced by blacks? Who bears the cost of bigotry? Will wage discrimination persist?

2. Consider a city with 10,000 jobs in the central city and 20,000 jobs in a suburban jurisdiction. Suppose that black workers are confined to the central city, but whites can live in either jurisdiction. Suppose further that travel costs are so high that workers live and work in the same jurisdiction.

   a. Under what circumstances will racial segregation not affect the wages of white and black workers?

   b. Suppose that the circumstances you identify in (*a*) occur in 1950. Would you still expect them to occur in 1990?

3. Comment on the following statement: "Black central-city residents are poor because they do not have access to suburban employment opportunities. I propose that we supply each central-city household with a car. Such a plan will reduce poverty at a relatively low cost."

4. The proportion of households headed by females increased rapidly during the 1960s and 1970s. Comment on the following statement: "The most important factor in the increase in female-headed households were increases in AFDC payments (Aid to Families with Dependent Children)."

References and Additional Readings

Aaron, Henry J. *Politics and the Professors—The Great Society in Perspective*. Washington, D.C.: Brookings Institution, 1978. Discusses the uncertainty about the relationship between education and poverty.

Arrow, Kenneth. "The Theory of Discrimination." In *Discrimination in Labor Markets*, ed. Orley Ashenfelter and Albert Rees. Princeton, N.J.: Princeton University Press, 1973. Describes the phenomenon of statistical discrimination, which explains the persistence of wage differentials.

Bane, Mary Jo. "Household Composition and Poverty." In *Fighting Poverty: What Works and What Doesn't*, ed. Sheldon H. Danziger and Daniel H. Weinberg. Cambridge, Mass.: Harvard University Press, 1986. Discusses the effects of changes in family structure on poverty rates, suggesting that such changes between 1959 and 1979 increased the 1979 poverty rate by two percentage points.

Bartik, Timothy J. *Who Benefits from State and Local Economic Development Policies?* Kalamazoo, Mich.: Upjohn Institute, 1991. Chapter 2 discusses the effects of various public policies on economic development. Chapters 4 and 7 discuss the effects of employment growth on employment rates and real income per capita. Chapters 5 and 6 explore the effects of employment growth on housing prices and real wages.

Becker, Gary S. *The Economics of Discrimination.* Chicago: University of Chicago Press, 1957. Describes the market theory of discrimination, which suggests that competition limits the extent of wage discrimination.

Berrueta-Clement, John R., et al. *Changed Lives: The Effects of the Perry Preschool Programs on Youths Through Age 19.* Ypsilanti, Mich.: High-Scope Press, 1984. Reports the results of a successful preschool program.

Blank, Rebecca M., and Alan S. Blinder. "Macroeconomics, Income Distribution, and Poverty." In *Fighting Poverty: What Works and What Doesn't*, ed. Sheldon H. Danziger and Daniel H. Weinberg. Cambridge, Mass.: Harvard University Press, 1986. Explores the relationship between macroeconomic conditions (unemployment and inflation) and poverty; concludes that the poor suffer more from unemployment than inflation.

Clark, William A. "Residential Preferences and Neighborhood Racial Segregation: A Test of the Schelling Segregation Model." *Demography* 28 (1991), pp. 1–19. Describes the differences in preferences for integrated neighborhoods between whites and blacks.

Ellwood, David T. "The Spatial Mismatch Hypothesis: Are There Teenage Jobs Missing in the Ghetto?" In *The Black Youth Employment Crisis*, ed. Richard B. Freeman and Harry J. Holzer. Chicago: University of Chicago Press, 1986, pp. 147–85. Provides evidence from Chicago that questions the validity of the spatial mismatch hypothesis.

————. *Divide and Conquer.* New York: Ford Foundation, 1987.

————. *Poor Support.* New York: Basic Books, 1988. A detailed description and analysis of poverty among two-parent families, single-parent families, and residents of inner-city neighborhoods.

Ellwood, David T., and Mary Jo Bane. "The Impact of AFDC on Family Structure and Living Arrangements." *Research in Labor Economics*, 1985. Explores the relationship between welfare benefit levels and family structure.

Ellwood, David T., and Jonathan Crane. "Family Change among Black Americans: What Do We Know?" *Journal of Economic Perspectives* 4 (1990), pp. 65–84.

Freeman, Richard B., and Harry J. Holzer. "The Black Youth Employment Crisis: Summary of Findings." In *The Black Youth Employment Crisis*, ed. Richard B. Freeman and Harry J. Holzer. Chicago: University of Chicago Press, 1986. Summarizes the results of a series of studies that explore the reasons for the high unemployment among black youths.

Gabriel, Stuart A., and Stuart S. Rosenthal. "Household Location and Race: Estimates of a Multinomial Logit Model." *Review of Economics and Statistics* (1989), pp. 240–49.

Shows that the location choices of black households are relatively insensitive to changes in income and other socioeconomic characteristics.

Garfinkel, Irwin, and Sara S. McLanahan. *Single Mothers and Their Children: A New American Dilemma*. Washington, D.C.: Urban Institute Press, 1986.

Glazer, Nathan. "Education and Training Programs and Poverty." In *Fighting Poverty: What Works and What Doesn't*, ed. Sheldon H. Danziger and Daniel H. Weinberg. Cambridge, Mass.: Harvard University Press, 1986. Discusses the effects of compensatory education on poverty, suggesting that preschool and elementary-school programs are most effective.

Gramlich, Edward, and Deborah Laren. "How Widespread Are Income Losses in a Recession?" In *The Social Contract Revisited*, ed. D. Lee Bauden. Washington, D.C.: Urban Institute, 1984. Estimates the distributional effects of recessions.

Ihlanfeldt, Keith R. *Intra-Urban Job Accessibility and Youth Employment Rates*. Atlanta: Georgia State University, Policy Research Center Paper no. 18, 1991. Provides evidence from 50 metropolitan areas that relatively low employment rates for black and Hispanic youths are caused, in part, by inferior access to employment opportunities.

Ihlanfeldt, Keith R., and David L. Sjoquist. "Job Accessibility and Racial Differences in Youth Employment Rates." *American Economic Review* 8 (1990), pp. 267–76. Provides evidence from Philadelphia that inferior access is responsible for between a third and a half of the gap between black and white employment rates.

Kain, John F. "Housing Segregation, Negro Employment, and Metropolitan Decentralization." *Quarterly Journal of Economics* 82 (1968), pp. 175–97.

———. "Housing Segregation, Negro Employment, and Metropolitan Decentralization: A Retrospective View." In *Patterns of Racial Discrimination. Volume I: Housing*, ed. George Von Furstenburg, Bennett Harrison, and Ann R. Horowitz (Lexington, Mass.: D. C. Heath, 1974). Kain's response to Mooney.

———. "Black Suburbanization in the Eighties: A New Beginning or a False Hope?" In *American Domestic Priorities*, ed. John Quigley and Daniel Rubinfeld. University of California, 1985. Describes recent trends in the suburbanization of blacks.

Kasarda, John. "Urban Change and Minority Opportunities." In *The New Urban Reality*, ed. Paul Peterson. Washington, D.C.: Brookings Institution, 1985. Discusses the effects of changes in the spatial distribution of employment on central-city blacks. Also discusses the mismatch between central-city employment opportunities and the labor skills of central-city residents.

———. "Jobs, Migration, and Emerging Urban Mismatches." In *Urban Change and Poverty*, ed. Michael McGeary and Laurence Lynn. Washington, D.C.: National Academy Press, 1988.

Lemann, Nicholas. "The Origins of the Underclass." *Atlantic Monthly* (June–July, 1986). Discusses the development of a black underclass in central cities.

Leonard, Jonathan. "Comment." In *The Black Youth Employment Crisis*, ed. Richard B. Freeman and Harry Holzer. Chicago: University of Chicago Press, 1986, pp. 185–90. Critiques the Ellwood (1986) paper.

Murray, Charles. *Losing Ground: American Social Policy, 1950–1980*. New York: Basic Books, 1984. Argues that welfare policy was a large factor in the growth of female-headed households.

National Assessment of Educational Progress. *Has Title I Improved Education for Disadvantaged Students? Evidence from Three National Assessments on Reading*. Washington, D.C.: U.S. Department of Education, 1981. Reports the results of NAEP tests showing increasing relative scores for minority students participating in Title I programs.

National Center for Education Statistics. *The Condition of Education: A Statistical Report.* Washington, D.C.: U.S. Department of Education, 1982. Reports the results of NAEP tests showing increasing relative scores for minority students participating in Title I programs.

O'Hare, William P.; Kelvin J. Pollard; Taynia L. Mann; and Mary M. Kent. "African Americans in the 1990s." *Population Bulletin* 46 (July 1991).

Phelps, Edmund. "The Statistical Theory of Racism and Sexism." *American Economic Review* 62 (1972), pp. 659–61. Explains the theory of statistical discrimination.

Ricketts, Erol R., and Isabel V. Sawhill. "Defining and Measuring the Underclass." *Journal of Policy Analysis and Management* 7 (1988), pp. 316–25.

Sawhill, Isabel V. "Poverty in the U.S.: Why Is It So Persistent?" *Journal of Economic Literature* 26 (1988), pp. 1073–119. Explores the reasons for the persistence of poverty between the mid-1960s and 1988. Examines the influence of five factors: demographic changes (increased number of female-headed households), sluggish macroeconomic growth, inadequate investment in human capital, work disincentives of the welfare system, and the growing underclass. Concludes that the most important factors were demographic changes and rising unemployment.

Schiller, Bradley. *The Economics of Poverty and Discrimination*, 5th ed. Englewood Cliffs, N.J.: Prentice Hall, 1989).

U.S. Bureau of the Census. *Current Population Reports*, Series P-60. Washington, D.C.: U.S. Government Printing Office, 1986. Estimates poverty rates by status of household head and place of residence. Reports unemployment rates for different races and education levels.

U.S. Commission on Civil Rights. *Unemployment and Underemployment Among Blacks, Hispanics, and Women.* Washington D.C.: U.S. Government Printing Office, 1982. Discusses labor-market discrimination against minority groups.

Wilson, William Julius. "The Urban Underclass in Advanced Industrial Society." In *The New Urban Reality*, ed. Paul Peterson. Washington, D.C.: Brookings Institution, 1985. Discusses the special problems of the urban underclass.

Wilson, William Julius, and Kathryn Neckerman. "Poverty and Family Structure: The Widening Gap between Evidence and Public Policy Issues." In *Fighting Poverty: What Works and What Doesn't*, ed. Sheldon H. Danziger and Daniel H. Weinberg. Cambridge, Mass.: Harvard University Press, 1986. Examines changes in fertility rates and family structure and the effects of welfare policy on the number of female-headed households. Concludes that male joblessness is the most important factor in the increase in female-headed households.

Yinger, John. "Prejudice and Discrimination in the Urban Housing Market." In *Current Issues in Urban Economics*, ed. Peter Meiszkowski and Mahlon Straszheim. Baltimore, Md.: Johns Hopkins University Press, 1979.

10 Poverty and Public Policy

This chapter discusses several programs designed to reduce poverty, including education and training programs, cash assistance, and in-kind transfers (food stamps and medical care). The principal question is, How effective are these policies in decreasing poverty and welfare dependence? The chapter also evaluates various welfare-reform proposals, including the negative income tax, workfare, and a recent proposal that would combine child support from absent fathers with tax credits for poor working mothers. A final issue concerns the special problems of the central city. The question is, What can be done to increase the incomes and decrease the welfare dependence of central-city residents?

Employment and Job-Training Programs

As explained in Chapter 9, the federal government can use macroeconomic policies to stimulate economic growth and decrease poverty. Since the early 1960s, the federal government has supplemented its macroeconomic policies with employment and job-training programs. Employment programs operate on the demand side of the market, providing direct employment for the poor. These programs are sometimes used when the government fears that the stimulation of the national economy will increase the inflation rate. Job-training programs operate on the supply side of the labor market: they increase the labor skills of the poor, making them more attractive to private industry. Spending on employment and training programs increased during the 1960s and 1970s, and then fell during the 1980s: real spending per capita (in 1972 dollars) rose from 2.9 cents in 1965 to 29 cents in 1979, and then fell to 6.4 cents in 1984 (Bassi and Ashenfelter, 1986).

Since the early 1960s, there have been dozens of employment and training programs. Bassi and Ashenfelter (1986) and Schiller (1989) outline the history of the various programs and summarize the results of many of the benefit-cost studies of the programs. Some of the most important programs are the following:

1. **Manpower Development and Training Act (1962).** Although the original purpose of this program was to provide training to experienced workers displaced by changes in the labor market (typically male heads of households), it evolved into a program to assist the hard-core unemployed. The program increased the earnings of male participants by about $200 per year and increased the earnings of women by about $500 per year.

2. **Job Corps (1965).** The Job Corps program is an intensive training and counseling program for disadvantaged youths (low-income and minority youths between age 6 and 12). In 1980, the cost per participant was $13,000. The program increases employment rates and earnings, and decreases welfare dependence, out-of-wedlock births, and criminal activity. The estimated benefit-cost ratio of the program is about 1.45.

3. **Work Incentive Program (WIN) (1965).** The purpose of WIN was to encourage AFDC recipients to get jobs. The program provided day care, transportation, counseling, and job-placement services to welfare mothers. Funding for this program decreased sharply during the 1980s, and the program was eventually dropped in 1987.

4. **Public Employment Program (PEP) (1971).** Under PEP, the federal government subsidized employment in state and local governments. A small amount of money was also provided for training. After they left the program, women and minorities earned significantly more than they did before entering the program. In contrast, the program did not increase the earnings of men.

5. **Comprehensive Employment and Training Act (CETA) (1974).** The CETA program was a mixture of employment and training programs. The federal government gave money to local "prime sponsors" to run employment and training programs. Between 1974 and 1982, CETA served a total of 30 million people, with most of the participants coming from low-income and minority households: in 1983, about 95 percent of the participants came from disadvantaged households. Researchers have examined the effects of CETA on the earnings of participants who have left the program. There are four basic results:
   a. The earnings of women increased, but the earnings of men did not. Three years after participation, women were earning between $600 and $1,200 more as a result of the program, a substantial increase relative to their preprogram earnings ($2,700).
   b. The earnings of women increased as a result of increases in hours worked, not increases in wages.
   c. The largest gains were experienced by the most disadvantaged workers.

    d. The most effective components of CETA were classroom training, on-the-job training, and public service employment. The least effective component was a program that acclimated participants to the work environment without much training or actual work.

6. **National Supported Work Demonstration (NSWD) (1975).** This experimental program enrolled several "problem" groups (long-term AFDC recipients, reformed drug addicts, ex-offenders, and high school dropouts) in a highly structured program with counseling and work experience. For AFDC recipients, the program increased both wages and the hours worked. For ex-addicts, the program generated a large decrease in crime rates but only a small increase in earnings. The estimated benefit-cost ratio was over 2.0 for AFDC recipients and about 1.9 for ex-addicts. The program had relatively small effects on youths and ex-offenders, so the benefit-cost ratios for these groups were less than 1.0.

7. **Youth Employment Demonstration Projects Act (YEDPA) (1977).** This program was similar to the Job Corps program, and it generated similar results. The most effective parts of the YEDPA program were remedial education, job training, and training in job-search skills.

8. **Job Training Partnership Act (JTPA) (1982).** JTPA replaced CETA, bringing two basic changes in employment and training policies. First, JTPA does not provide any public employment, but instead focuses on job training. Second, JTPA enrolls disadvantaged people *and* dislocated workers (people who have lost jobs because of plant closures and permanent layoffs). In 1988, about 1 million people participated in JTPA job-training and job-search programs (Schiller, 1989).

There are four general conclusions from the benefit-cost studies of employment and job-training programs. First, programs that focus on youths (e.g., Job Corps and YEDPA) are successful. Second, programs that stress classroom teaching and on-the-job training often increase the earnings of women, particularly those with little prior work experience. Third, the successful job-training programs increase earnings by increasing the number of hours worked, not by increasing wages. Fourth, training programs have relatively small effects on the earnings of adult men.

Direct Income Transfers: AFDC and SSI

Table 10–1 shows federal spending on various antipoverty programs in 1987. Total spending was over $100 billion. About one quarter of this sum was spent on direct income transfers: Aid to Families with Dependent Children (AFDC), Supplemental Security Income (SSI), and General Assistance. The bulk of AFDC money went to female-headed households. SSI is a special program for the aged,

TABLE 10-1   **Spending on Transfer Programs in 1987**

Program	Number of Recipients (millions)	Average Monthly Benefit ($)	Annual Cost ($ billion)
Income Transfers			
Supplemental Security Income (SSI)	4	$252	$9.9
Aid to Families with Dependent Children (AFDC)	11	123	16.3
General Assistance (GA)	1	144	1.4
In-Kind Transfers			
Food stamps	21	46	12.5
Medicaid	23	179	49.3
Housing assistance	4	57	11.2
School lunch program	24	11	3.2
Total			$103.8

SOURCE: Bradley Schiller, *The Economics of Poverty and Discrimination,* 5th ed. (Englewood Cliffs, N.J.: Prentice Hall, 1989).

the blind, and the permanently disabled. General Assistance is a program for the poor who do not qualify for AFDC or SSI.

Total spending on AFDC was $16 billion in 1987. AFDC payments went to a total of 11 million people, with an average payment of $123 per recipient per month. The federal government provides about half the funds for AFDC, with state and local governments contributing the other half. State governments set the eligibility requirements and the benefit levels. In most states, eligibility for AFDC is limited to families in which one parent is either absent or disabled. In 1987, the average monthly payment for a three-person household ranged from $114 in Alabama to $553 in California. Nationwide, the average monthly payment for a three-person household was $359.

AFDC and SSI are "means-tested" programs in the sense that the payment to a household depends on its earnings (market income). Under AFDC, the first $30 of monthly market income does not affect the AFDC payment, but every additional dollar decreases the AFDC payment by $1. Under SSI, the recipient can earn $65 of market income per month without affecting the SSI grant, and every additional dollar decreases the SSI payment by 50 cents.

How does AFDC affect the labor supply of recipients? Consider the incentives for Judy, who is eligible for AFDC. Suppose that she could work half-time and earn $400 per month. If the AFDC payment is $500 per month, AFDC generates more income and leaves more time for child care and other activities, so Judy's choice is easy: she will quit her job and receive AFDC. If the AFDC payment is only $300, Judy will choose AFDC if the sacrifice of income is dominated by the increase in time for child care and other activities. In general, AFDC is attractive to single mothers with low wages and/or small children. If the wage is low, the income sacrificed by accepting AFDC (and quitting the job) will be relatively small. The presence of preschool children encourages participation in AFDC because (*a*) many mothers want to participate in their child's development and (*b*) child-care expenses decrease the net wage.

What are the actual effects of AFDC on labor supply? A number of studies have shown that AFDC decreases the labor supply of recipients (see Blank, 1985). The reasons are rather simple. First, recipients have relatively low wages, so their market incomes either exceed the AFDC payment by a small amount or are less than the AFDC payment. AFDC is a good deal because it (*a*) increases the opportunities for nonwork activities and (*b*) either increases total income or decreases it by a small amount. Second, for income above $30 per month, the net wage of an AFDC recipient is zero (AFDC falls by $1 for every dollar of market income), so there is little incentive to work more than a few hours per week. Given the combination of low market earnings, child-care responsibilities, and a 100 percent tax rate, it is not surprising that few AFDC recipients work.

The Negative Income Tax

An alternative to the conventional welfare program is a **negative income tax**. Figure 10–1 shows labor-income trade-offs under a negative income tax. The wage of the household's worker is $4 per hour. The negative income tax has a **basic grant** of $100 and a **marginal tax rate** of 50 percent. A household with zero market income receives the basic grant ($100). For every additional dollar of market income (every quarter hour of work), the grant decreases by 50 cents. For example, if the household works 10 hours per week and earns $40, the grant decreases by $20, from $100 to $80, so the household's total income would be $120. The grant is exhausted at a market income of $200 (50 hours of work).

The negative income tax differs from the traditional AFDC program in two ways. First, under the negative income tax, recipients keep a relatively large share of their market earnings: if the marginal tax rate is 50 percent, the recipient keeps 50 cents per dollar. Second, the negative income tax would be available to all households, while eligibility for AFDC is restricted to families with dependent children. The idea behind switching from AFDC to the negative income tax is that the lower marginal tax rate would encourage current AFDC recipients to work more hours. At the same time, the negative income tax discourages work effort among households currently ineligible for AFDC but eligible for the negative income tax. The net effect on work effort cannot be predicted on theoretical grounds.

What are the facts on the labor-supply effects of the negative income tax? The federal government ran a series of experiments in the 1960s and 1970s to test the effects of a negative income tax. Poor households were divided into two groups: one group was eligible for a negative income tax program, and the other group continued to receive conventional welfare payments. The negative income tax program was more generous than existing programs, with basic grants between 95 percent and 140 percent of the official poverty level. The marginal tax rates

FIGURE 10–1   Labor-Income Choice under a Negative Income Tax

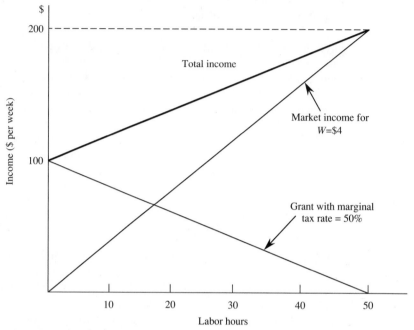

The wage is $4 per hour, the basic grant under the negative income tax is $100, and the marginal tax rate is 50 percent. The grant is exhausted when labor equals 50 hours per week (market income is $200). Total income is the sum of market income and the grant.

were all above 50 percent. The negative income tax decreased labor supply of men, women, and youths: the average reduction in hours worked was 10 percent for men, 14 percent for female household heads, and 24 percent for youths. These supply responses were large enough to disturb most policymakers. As a result, the negative income tax dropped from the welfare-reform agenda.

The basic problem with the negative income tax is that it enrolls two different types of households in a single program. For a household in which no one is capable of working, the basic grant should be high enough to provide adequate support. In contrast, for a household with people capable of working, the marginal tax rate should be low enough to encourage work effort. The government is unlikely to adopt a program with both a large basic grant and a low marginal tax rate because such a program would be extremely expensive. If the government chooses a large basic grant and a high marginal tax rate, it would provide adequate support for workerless households but would also discourage work effort. If it chooses a small basic grant and a low tax rate, work effort would be encouraged, but workerless households would receive inadequate support. One response to this problem is to have one redistributional program for workerless households and another program for households with people capable of working.

In-Kind Transfers

As shown in Table 10–1, federal spending on in-kind programs exceeded $76 billion in 1987, about three times the total spending on direct transfers. The three largest in-kind programs are medicaid ($49.3 billion), food stamps ($12.5 billion), and housing ($11.2 billion). This section discusses medicaid and food stamps. Housing programs are discussed in Chapter 12.

Medicaid provides free medical care to the recipients of AFDC and SSI. It is essentially a free medical insurance policy: the government agrees to cover all the recipient's medical expenses, just as a private insurer would. The difference is that medicaid is free. In 1987, two thirds of medicaid funds went to aged and disabled households (SSI recipients). In a comprehensive evaluation of the medicaid program, Starr (1986) suggests that the program was responsible for increases in life expectancy and decreases in infant mortality among the poor.

Under the food-stamp program, poor households are given coupons that can be exchanged for food. The food-stamp allotment depends on household income. Every additional dollar of market income decreases the food-stamp allotment by 30 cents, so the effective marginal tax rate is 30 percent.

Effects of Cash and In-Kind Transfers on Poverty

This section addresses two questions about the effects of government transfer programs. First, how do the transfer programs affect the typical poor household? Second, to what extent do the programs decrease poverty?

Effects of Transfers on the Typical Poor Household

Table 10–2 shows an example of the options faced by the typical poor household, a female-headed household with two children. It shows annual disposable income for different amounts of work and wages, taking into account the effects of market income on income transfers and in-kind transfers. If the household head does not work, her disposable income equals the sum of AFDC and food stamps ($6,284). As her income increases, her benefits from transfer programs decrease.

If the woman accepts a minimum-wage job, there is bad news and good news. The bad news is that she spends money on day care and receives less from AFDC and food stamps. The good news is that she earns income and also gets an earned income tax credit. Poor households receive a 14 percent tax credit on earned income, with a maximum credit of $868. The net result of these changes in day-care costs, welfare payments, wages, and tax credits is an increase in disposable income of $872 for part-time work and $532 for full-time work.

Working is slightly more lucrative at higher wages. Although a higher wage generates more earnings, it also increases taxes (the earned income tax credit is eventually dominated by income and payroll taxes) and decreases the AFDC

TABLE 10–2   **Earnings, Benefits, and Income for a Single Parent with Two Children**

Work and Wages	Earnings	Day Care	Taxes and EIC	AFDC and Food Stamps	Disposable Income	Medicaid
No work	$ 0	$ 0	$ 0	$6,284	$6,284	Yes
Half-time at minimum wage	3,350	−1,000	229	4,577	7,156	Yes
Full-time at minimum wage	3,700	−3,000	373	2,744	6,816	Yes
Full-time at $4.00/hour	8,000	−3,000	171	1,624	6,795	Yes
Full-time at $5.00/hour	10,000	−3,000	−172	970	7,798	No
Full-time at $6.00/hour	12,000	−3,000	−515	538	9,023	No

Taxes and EIC include:
1. Social Security tax of 7.15 percent.
2. EIC: refundable credit of 14 percent of earned income to maximum of $868.

SOURCE: David T. Ellwood, *Poor Support* (New York: Basic Books, 1988).

payment and the food-stamp allotment. Even if the woman worked a full-time job at a wage of $6, her income would still be below the poverty line ($9,800). An added problem is that she eventually loses her medicaid coverage. For a low-wage single mother, the benefits of working are relatively small.

Effects of Transfer Programs on Poverty

Table 10–3 shows the effects of various transfer programs on poverty rates. In the absence of transfer payments, the overall poverty would have been over 20 percent, and the poverty rate for aged persons would have been over 55 percent. Social security and other nonwelfare transfers cut the poverty rate for the aged to 15 percent and decrease the poverty rate for families by about two percentage points. Cash transfers decrease the poverty rates of nonaged households by an additional percentage point. Finally, food stamps and housing programs cut poverty rates of aged persons and families by an additional two percentage points.

TABLE 10–3   **Effects of Transfer Programs on Poverty, 1988**

Group	Percentage of Group in Poverty			
	Before Transfers	After Social Security and Nonwelfare Transfers	After Cash Welfare Transfers	After Cash, Food Stamps, Housing
All persons	20.8%	14.5%	13.6%	12.2%
Families with children	19.5	17.4	16.5	14.6
Aged persons	55.8	15.3	13.9	11.8

SOURCE: U.S. Congress, Committee on Ways and Means, *Background Material and Data on Programs within the Jurisdiction of the Committee on Ways and Means* (Washington, D.C.: U.S. Government Printing Office, 1988).

Welfare Reform

The Family Support Act of 1988 is the most recent attempt to reform the U.S. welfare system. The legislation is designed to move people off the welfare rolls and into productive employment. States are directed to enroll their welfare recipients in programs offering remedial education, job training, work experience, and assistance with job search. By 1995, 20 percent of welfare recipients are supposed to be enrolled in these self-help programs. Parents with small children (under three years old) are not required to participate in the training and search programs. The legislation also directed the states to require 16 hours of community service per month from two-parent welfare households.

Workfare

Workfare is defined as a program under which welfare recipients are forced to participate in various employment and training programs. Wiseman (1987) describes workfare as a process, a series of steps that a potential welfare recipient must go through to qualify for support. Figure 10–2 shows Wiseman's version of the workfare process.

1. **Preliminary assessment.** A social worker gathers information about the applicant's skills and employment record, and finds out what kind of assistance will be needed (e.g., child care, transportation) to get the person back to work.
2. **Job search.** After developing a job-search strategy, the applicant searches for a job under the close supervision of a search supervisor. If the applicant finds a job, she drops out of the workfare process; if the job pays enough, she also drops out of the welfare system.
3. **Counseling.** If the applicant does not find a job after several weeks, she moves into a counseling program. The counselor determines the reasons for the unsuccessful job search and designs a program to enhance the applicant's employability.
4. **Skill enhancement program.** Some of the enhancement options are unpaid work experience (community service), on-the-job training (public or private), or classroom training for specific skills.
5. **Job search.** When the enhancement program is completed, the applicant searches again, and hopefully finds a job and drops out of the workfare process. If not, she is recycled, that is, sent back to counseling.

This model of workfare differs from the popular vision of workfare in one important respect. The "work" in workfare is often assumed to be mandatory community service for no pay. In fact, community service is but one of the options under the skill enhancement step of the program. Participants can also "work" in the classroom or earn money while acquiring on-the-job training.

FIGURE 10-2   The Workfare Process

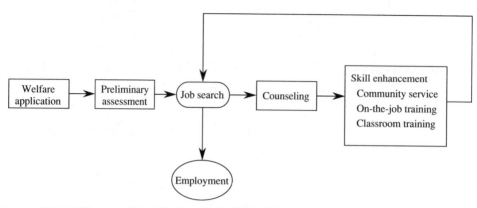

SOURCE: Michael Wiseman, "How Workfare Really Works," *Public Interest* 89 (Fall 1987).

What happens if the applicant refuses to go through the workfare process? A mild form of punishment is to remove some of the applicant's discretion in spending her welfare check. For example, the agency might pay her landlord and deduct the rent from her welfare check. A more severe punishment is to cut the welfare payment.

The experiments with workfare suggest that it can move a small number of people off the welfare rolls. In a widely cited experimental program in San Diego, 47.3 percent of workfare participants were receiving public assistance nine months after enrolling in the program, compared to 53 percent of a control group that did not go through the workfare process. In other words, workfare decreased the welfare caseload by a relatively small amount.

Reform Proposal: Child Support and the Earned Income Credit

Garfinkel and Uhr (1984) and Ellwood (1988) have proposed several changes in welfare policy. Their reform proposals have four features:

1. **Child support requirements.** Absent fathers would be required to pay child support. For example, an absent father of two children would be required to pay one quarter of his income for child support. Under the current system, only about one third of female-headed households receives child support.

2. **Minimum child support.** The federal government would guarantee a minimum level of child support (for example, $1,750 per child per year). The federal government would make up the difference between

the father's contribution and the minimum support level. The minimum child-support program would replace AFDC.

3. **Increased earned income tax credit.** The current EIC, which is 14 percent of earned income with a maximum credit of $868, would be increased to 25 percent of earned income with a maximum credit of $2,000.

4. **Child-care tax credit.** Poor families would receive a 30 percent tax credit for child care.

Table 10–4 shows the effects of such a scheme on the typical poor female-headed household. The figures are based on the assumption that the mother receives only the minimum level of child support. Many poor female-headed households would in fact receive greater child-support payments from the absent father. The proposed scheme allows a single working mother to keep more of her earned income because (*a*) the earned income tax credit is more generous, (*b*) the cost of day care is reduced by the child-care credit, and (*c*) the child-support payment does not decrease as her income increases.

The proposal has several desirable features. First, if the absent father earns enough income, the 25 percent support payment will lift many female-headed households out of poverty. For example, if the father's income is $22,000, the child-support payment would be $5,500. If the mother works a half-time job at the minimum wage, her disposable income would be $9,985, just above the poverty line. Second, because the working woman keeps more of her earnings, it encourages work effort. Finally, it may actually save money. According to Garfinkel and Uhr (1984), if the collection rate from absent fathers is 80 percent and the minimum child-support benefit is $2,000 per child, the program would

---

TABLE 10–4   Earnings, Benefits, and Income for a Single Parent with Two Children under Higher Earned Income Tax Credit and Guaranteed Child Support

Level of Work and Wages	Earnings	Day Care	Taxes and EIC	Child Support	Disposable Income
No work	$ 0	$ 0	$ 0	$3,500	$ 3,500
Half-time at minimum wage	3,350	−1,000	+1,085	3,500	7,985
Full-time at minimum wage	3,700	−3,000	+1,511	3,500	10,811
Full-time at $5.00 per hour	10,000	−3,000	+1,185	3,500	11,685
Full-time at $6.00 per hour	12,000	−3,000	+642	3,500	13,142

Taxes and EIC include:
1. 30 percent child-care tax credit.
2. Social Security tax of 7.15 percent.
3. EIC of 25 percent up to $8,000; reduced by 20 cents per dollar above $8,000.

Source: David T. Ellwood, *Poor Support* (New York: Basic Books, 1988).

cost less than the current welfare system. The program is so attractive that it is being tried in the state of Wisconsin.

The Problems of the Central-City Economy

One of the most difficult problems in the urban economy is the concentration of poverty in the central city. Among the reasons for central-city poverty (discussed in Chapter 9) are (1) the segregation of blacks in central cities, far from suburban employment opportunities (the spatial mismatch problem); (2) increases in the education and skill requirements of central-city jobs; (3) labor-market discrimination; and (4) inadequate education. The NBER study of black teenage unemployment (cited in Chapter 9) suggests that the problems of black inner-city teenagers are caused by weak labor markets, competition with women, discrimination, opportunities for crime, and inadequate education.

One approach to solving the inner-city poverty problem is based on the spatial mismatch theory. The idea is that poverty is caused by spatial considerations and can be solved by one of two spatial policies: dispersal of the central-city population or economic development of the inner-city economy.

Dispersal Policies

Under a dispersal policy, central-city blacks would be moved to suburban communities. The idea behind dispersal is that blacks should live near suburban employment centers. As discussed earlier in Chapter 9, the government could promote black suburbanization with fair-housing laws, less restrictive zoning, and state support of local governments.

The critics of the dispersal option raise four questions:

1. **Integration.** Will dispersal cause real integration or the development of smaller, more numerous concentrations of racial minorities (minighettos)?

2. **Black underclass.** Will dispersal allow the most mobile and wealthy blacks to move to the suburbs, leaving immobile and poor blacks in the central city? When middle-income blacks (e.g., clerical workers and midlevel managers) leave the central city, it becomes a less attractive location for employers, so employment opportunities for poor blacks (e.g., janitors) decrease. In addition, the departure of middle-income blacks decreases the demand for retail goods, decreasing the employment opportunities for low-skilled retail workers. Some people fear that the departure of middle-income blacks will cause more poor blacks to slip into the underclass, a group of people dependent on crime, drugs, and welfare.

3. **Cultural disruption.** Will the dispersal of blacks disrupt black culture and society?

4. **Spatial mismatch.** If the spatial mismatch theory is incorrect and geo-graphical access to jobs is not the source of the black unemployment problem, simply moving blacks to the suburbs will not solve the prob-lem. If poverty is caused by job discrimination, inferior education, and low skills, these other problems must be addressed.

The Development Option

The alternative to dispersal is the development of the central-city economy. In contrast to the dispersal policy, which brings workers to suburban jobs, the de-velopment policy brings jobs to central-city residents.

There are three approaches to development policy. First, under the **black capi-talism** approach, the government encourages the development of black businesses. The experiences with black capitalism have not been encouraging (see Bates and Bradford, 1979). Second, **community development corporations (CDCs)** assist black businesses, oversee large development projects, and run various community projects (housing assistance, job training). Third, the government can establish **enterprise zones,** areas of the city where firms (*a*) pay lower taxes, (*b*) receive subsidies for worker training, and (*c*) are exempted from many local regulations. Given the limited experience with enterprise zones, it is too early to say whether they will be effective.

The critics of the development option raise five questions:

1. **Viable location.** Is the central city a viable location for firms? The sub-urbanization of jobs was caused by fundamental changes in the economy (e.g., the development of the auto and the truck, innovations in infor-mation technology). Given the advantages of a suburban location, a firm in the central city may be unable to compete with its suburban counter-part.
2. **Zero-sum employment changes.** Will the gain in central-city employ-ment come at the expense of employment elsewhere in the city?
3. **Low skills.** Do central-city residents have the education and skills to work in new stores, factories, and offices?
4. **Migration.** How many of new central-city jobs are filled by current res-idents of the central city? How many are filled by newcomers? As ex-plained in Chapter 5, at the metropolitan level, about three fourths of new jobs are usually filled by newcomers. Since intracity mobility is greater than intercity mobility, an even larger fraction of new central-city jobs are likely to be filled by newcomers.
5. **Spatial mismatch.** Is the spatial mismatch theory correct? If the spatial mismatch theory is incorrect and geographical access to jobs is not the source of the black unemployment problem, bringing jobs to the central city will not solve the problem. Other reasons for poverty (job discrimi-nation, inferior education, and low skills) must be addressed.

The debate over dispersal versus development has continued for decades. The issues are complex, and the questions raised by each side are not easily answered. In recent years, several states have experimented with enterprise zones. The results of these experiments will provide valuable information for the debate over the merits of the development option.

Conclusion: What Can Be Done about Poverty?

There is no single policy that will eliminate poverty. Nonetheless, there are many policies that could be used to whittle the problem down to a more manageable size. Title I education programs have increased the achievement level of disadvantaged students, increasing their earnings potential. Job-training programs have increased the earnings of the most disadvantaged workers. The reform of child-support laws would increase support from absent fathers, decreasing poverty among female-headed households. An increase in the earned income tax credit would decrease poverty and increase the incentives for welfare recipients to work. Finally, workfare may increase the employment opportunities of welfare recipients. Each of these policies may have a small effect on the poverty problem, but together they could decrease poverty significantly.

Summary

1. Some government job-training programs have been successful for some participants.
   a. Youth programs (Job Corps and YEPTA) have increased earnings and decreased crime rates.
   b. Programs that stress classroom teaching and on-the-job training have increased the earnings of women, particularly those with little prior work experience.
2. Because AFDC recipients have low wages, AFDC increases the opportunities for nonwork activities (e.g., child care) and either increases income or decreases it by a small amount. AFDC discourages work effort because the marginal tax rate is close to 100 percent.
3. The alternative to AFDC is a negative income tax, under which recipients would keep a large fraction of their market income. The problem with such a program is that some households (those not eligible for AFDC) would decrease their labor supply.
4. The two largest in-kind transfer programs are medicaid and food stamps.
   a. Medicaid is equivalent to a private medical insurance policy. Medicaid has improved the health of the poor.
   b. Food-stamp allotments typically fall short of the food consumption of recipients, so food stamps are equivalent to cash payments.

5. Federal transfer programs decreased the overall poverty rate from 20.8 percent to 12.2 percent.

6. Under workfare, welfare recipients participate in various employment and training programs. The Family Support Act of 1988 has a workfare component that is designed to move people off the welfare rolls and into productive employment.

7. One reform proposal combines required child-support payments from the absent father, a minimum child-support payment from the government, a tax credit for day care, and an increase in the earned income tax credit. Such a program would eliminate the need for AFDC and would encourage work effort.

8. Under a dispersal policy, blacks would be moved closer to suburban employment centers. The critics of the dispersal approach suggest that the suburbanization of employable blacks will contribute to the development of a permanent underclass in the central city.

9. Under a development policy, jobs would be moved closer to central-city blacks. Development strategies include black capitalism, community development corporations, and enterprise zones. The critics of the development approach suggest that the central city is not a viable location for most firms and that any central-city employment gains come at the expense of other areas of the city. If central-city residents do not have the skills for the new jobs, the new jobs will be filled by newcomers.

Exercises and Discussion Questions

1. Predict the effects of the following changes in the AFDC program:
   a. Instead of increasing with the number of dependent children, the monthly payment is independent of the number of children beyond two: the payment increases with the arrival of the second dependent child, but not for the third, fourth, and so on.
   b. The monthly payment decreases if the dependent children do not regularly attend school.

2. One of the proposed reforms of the AFDC program is to decrease the marginal tax rate from 100 percent to 50 percent. In other words, AFDC recipients would keep half of their earnings. Discuss the merits of this proposal.

References and Additional Readings

Aaron, Henry J. "Six Welfare Questions Still Searching for Answers." *Brookings Review* (1984). Summarizes the results of the negative income tax experiment and discusses the political feasibility of converting from in-kind to cash programs.

Bane, Mary Jo, and David T. Ellwood. "Slipping into and out of Poverty: The Dynamics of Spells." *Journal of Human Resources* (1986). Discusses the fact that many families stay on welfare for long periods of time.

Banfield, Edward C. "Why Government Cannot Solve the Urban Problem." In *The Urban Economy*, ed. Harold M. Hochman. New York: W. W. Norton, 1976, pp. 257–72.

Bassi, Laurie, and Orley Ashenfelter. "The Effect of Direct Job Creation and Training Programs on Low-Skilled Workers." In *Fighting Poverty: What Works and What Doesn't*, ed. Sheldon H. Danziger and Daniel H. Weinberg. Cambridge, Mass.: Harvard University Press, 1986. Discusses the history of employment and job-training programs and summarizes the conclusions from several studies of these programs.

Bateman, Worth, and Harold M. Hochman. "Social Problems and the Urban Crisis: Can Public Policy Make a Difference?" In *The Urban Economy*, ed. Harold M. Hochman. New York: W. W. Norton, 1976, pp. 283–93.

Bates, Timothy, and William Bradford. *Financing Black Economic Development*. New York: Academic Press, 1979. Describes experiences with subsidized loans for black capitalism.

Blanchard, Lois; J. S. Butler; T. Doyle; R. Jackson; J. Ohls; and Barbara Posner. *Final Report, Food Stamp SSI/Elderly Cash-Out Demonstration Evaluation*. Princeton, N.J.: Mathematica Policy Research, 1982. When food-stamp recipients were given cash instead of food stamps, expenditures on food did not change. This suggests that food stamps are equivalent to cash payments.

Blank, Rebecca M. "The Impact of State Economic Differentials on Household Welfare and Labor Force Behavior." *Journal of Public Economics* 28 (1985), pp. 20–30.

Blank, Rebecca M., and Alan S. Blinder. "Macroeconomics, Income Distribution, and Poverty." In *Fighting Poverty: What Works and What Doesn't*, ed. Sheldon H. Danziger and Daniel H. Weinberg. Cambridge, Mass.: Harvard University Press, 1986. Explores the relationship between macroeconomic conditions and poverty. Concludes that the poor suffer more from unemployment than from inflation.

Brimmer, Andrew F., and Henry S. Terrell. "The Economic Potential of Black Capitalism." In *The Urban Economy*, ed. Harold M. Hochman. New York: W. W. Norton, 1976, pp. 239–56. Discusses the problems confronting the black-capitalism approach. Concludes that the approach is unlikely to substantially improve the economic position of blacks.

Danziger, Sheldon H.; Robert H. Haveman; and Robert D. Plotnick. "Anti-Poverty Policy: Effects on the Poor and the Non-Poor." In *Fighting Poverty: What Works and What Doesn't*, ed. Sheldon H. Danziger and Daniel H. Weinberg. Cambridge, Mass.: Harvard University Press, 1986. Estimates the combined effects of cash and in-kind transfers on poverty; concludes that these programs decreased the number of people in poverty by about 46 percent.

Edel, Matthew. "Development versus Dispersal: Approaches to Ghetto Poverty." In *Readings in Urban Economics*, ed. Matthew Edel and Jerome Rothenberg. New York: Macmillan, 1972, pp. 307–25.

Ellwood, David T. *Poor Support*. New York: Basic Books, 1988. A detailed description and analysis of poverty among two-parent families, single-parent families, and residents of inner-city neighborhoods. Chapter 5 discusses poverty among female-headed households and describes a reform proposal centered on requirements for child support by absent fathers.

Frielander, Daniel; Barbara Goldman; Judith Gueron; and David Wong. "Initial Findings from the Demonstration of State Work-Welfare Initiatives." *American Economic Re-*

view, Papers and Proceedings 76, no. 2 (1986), pp. 224–29. Discusses the effects of a program under which AFDC recipients receive work experience and job training; concludes that workfare may decrease the number of welfare recipients.

Garfinkel, Irwin, and Elizabeth Uhr. "A New Approach to Child Support." *Public Interest* (Spring 1984). Proposes a scheme under which absent parents would pay a child-support tax.

Gideonse, Sarah K., and William R. Meyers. "Why Workfare Fails." *Challenge* 31 January–February 1988. Argues that the poor will not escape poverty unless they receive basic education and job skills. Discusses some of the reasons for the failure of the Work Incentives Program (WIN) and the implications for workfare.

Gueron, Judith M. "Work and Welfare: Lessons from Employment Programs." *Journal of Economic Perspectives* 4 (1990), pp. 79–98. Discusses the design of work/welfare programs and their effects on employment, earnings, and the costs of the welfare system.

Harrison, Bennett. "Ghetto Economic Development." *Journal of Economic Literature* (1974), pp. 1–37.

Kain, John F., and Joseph J. Persky. "Alternatives to the Guilded Ghetto." *Public Interest* (Winter 1969), pp. 74–87. Reprinted In *The Urban Economy*, ed. Harold M. Hochman. New York: W. W. Norton, 1976, pp. 211–25.

Orfield, Gary. "Ghettoization and Its Alternatives." In *The New Urban Reality,* ed. Paul Peterson. Washington, D.C.: Brookings Institution, 1985.

Schiller, Bradley. *The Economics of Poverty and Discrimination*, 5th ed. Englewood Cliffs, N.J.: Prentice Hall, 1989. Chapter 12 provides a historical sketch of employment and training programs.

Smeeding, Timothy M. "Alternative Methods for Evaluating Selected In-Kind Transfer Benefits and Measuring Their Effect on Poverty." Washington, D.C.: U.S. Bureau of the Census, Technical Paper no. 50, U.S. Government Printing Office, 1982. Estimates the value of in-kind transfers to the recipients. Estimates that $1 of food stamps is worth 97 cents to the typical recipient, $1 of medicaid is worth 44 cents, and $1 of public housing is worth 80 cents.

Starr, Paul. "Health Care for the Poor: The Past 20 Years." In *Fighting Poverty: What Works and What Doesn't*, ed. Sheldon H. Danziger and Daniel H. Weinberg. Cambridge, Mass.: Harvard University Press, 1986. Discusses the effects of medicaid on the health of the poor.

U.S. Office of Management and Budget. *Budget of the United States Government, Fiscal Year 1987*. Washington, D.C.: U.S. Government Printing Office, 1986. Projects spending on antipoverty programs.

Wiseman, Michael. "How Workfare Really Works." *Public Interest* 89 (Fall 1987), pp. 36–47. Describes the features of the typical workfare system, and discusses the key questions to be asked in the evaluation of a workfare program.

11 The Urban Housing Market

This is the first of two chapters on urban housing. This chapter explains why housing is a unique commodity, focusing on four features that make housing different from other goods. First, the stock of housing is heterogeneous: dwellings differ in size, location, age, floor plan, interior features, and utilities. Second, housing is immobile: it is impractical to move dwellings from one location to another. Third, housing is durable: if properly maintained, a dwelling can be used for several decades. Finally, some people care about the racial and ethnic background of their neighbors, leading to racial discrimination and segregation. This chapter explains how these four characteristics affect the urban housing market.

Heterogeneity and Immobility

The housing stock is heterogeneous in the sense that each dwelling offers a different set of features, or a different *bundle* of housing services. There are two types of housing features: dwelling characteristics and site characteristics.

Consider first the features of the dwelling itself. Dwellings differ in size (square footage of living space) and layout (the arrangement of rooms within the dwelling). They also differ in the quality and efficiency of kitchen equipment and utility systems (heating, air conditioning, plumbing, electrical). Other differences occur in the interior design (type of flooring, windows, cabinets) and structural integrity (the durability of the foundation and the roof). To summarize, each dwelling offers a different combination of size, layout, utilities, interior design, and structural integrity.

Because housing is immobile, one component of the housing bundle is the residential location. A house buyer purchases both a dwelling and a set of site characteristics. One site characteristic is accessibility: sites differ in their access to jobs, shopping, and entertainment. Another characteristic is the provision of local public services: metropolitan areas have dozens of local governments, each of which provides a different combination of taxes and public services (schools, fire protection, police services). A third characteristic is environmental quality: sites differ in the quality of air and the amount of noise (from cars, trucks, airplanes, and factories). A final site characteristic is the appearance of the neighborhood (the exterior features of neighboring houses and lots). To summarize, housing is consumed along with a residential site, so the housing bundle includes several site attributes, including access to different facilities, tax liabilities, public services, environmental quality, and neighborhood characteristics.

The Price of Housing: The Hedonic Approach

What determines the equilibrium price of a dwelling? The **hedonic approach** is based on the notion that a dwelling is composed of a bundle of individual components, each of which has an implicit price. The market price of a dwelling is the sum of the prices of the individual components.

To explain the hedonic approach, consider a housing market in which dwellings differ in only six ways. The dwellings differ in access to jobs in the city center, the number of bedrooms, the age of the roof, air pollution, and the quality of local schools. A hedonic study of the market might generate the following information:

1. **Base price.** The average house has three bedrooms, is five miles from the city center, and has a six-year-old roof. The price of the average house is $70,000.
2. **Access price.** The price of housing drops by $1,000 for every additional mile from the city center: more accessible dwellings have higher prices.
3. **Bedroom price.** The price of housing increases by $10,000 for every additional bedroom: larger dwellings have higher prices.
4. **Roof price.** The price of housing decreases by $100 for every additional year of roof age: an older roof means that the roof must be replaced sooner, so the market price of the dwelling is lower.
5. **Air quality price.** The price of housing decreases by $500 for every additional unit of air pollution: dwellings in areas with relatively clean air have higher prices.
6. **School price.** The price of housing increases by $600 for a one-unit increase in the quality of the local elementary school (measured by the average test score): dwellings in areas with better schools have higher prices.

To predict the price of a particular dwelling, one needs information on location, the number of bedrooms, and the age of the roof. For example, consider a four-bedroom house that is located three miles from the city center and has a two-year-old roof. The pollution level is three units below the average, and the average test score of the local school is two points above the average. Such a house sells for $85,100, the base price of $70,000 plus $10,000 for the extra bedroom, $2,000 for the shorter commute, $400 for the four extra years of roof life, $1,500 for the relatively low pollution level, and $1,200 for the relatively high average test score.

Kain and Quigley (1975) used data from the St. Louis housing market in the 1960s to estimate the dollar values of different housing attributes. Table 11–1 shows some of their results. There are three types of housing characteristics: the quality of the dwelling itself, the size of the dwelling, and the characteristics of the site. The numbers in the table show the increases in monthly rent (for rental housing) and market value (for owner-occupied housing) resulting from one-unit increases in the various housing attributes. For example, a one-unit increase in interior quality (a measure of the quality of floors, windows, walls, ceilings, stairways) increases monthly rent by $1.31 (about 2.1 percent of the average monthly rent of $61.54) and increases market value by $818 (about 5.6 percent of the average market value of $14,596). Rental units with central heating rent for $4.44 more per month, and older dwellings have lower rent and market value. The price of housing is also affected by dwelling size: a second bathroom adds $9.07 to monthly rent and $769 to market value. The exterior quality of nearby dwellings was measured on a scale of 1 (bad) to 5 (excellent). A one-unit increase in the quality of adjacent dwellings increased rent by $1.86 and market value by $777, while a one-unit increase in the quality of dwellings on the block increased rent by $3.71 and market value by $419. The final variable is distance to the central business district: a one-mile increase in distance to the employment center decreased rent by $0.30 and value by $354.

Neighborhood Effects

The quantity of housing services produced by a particular dwelling depends not only on the characteristics of the dwelling but also on the characteristics of its neighborhood. When one homeowner improves the appearance of his house by painting it or repairing its broken windows, the neighborhood becomes a more desirable place to live, so the market values of surrounding houses increase. This is the **neighborhood effect:** changes in the exterior appearance of one house cause spillover benefits (increases in market value) for surrounding houses. Although there is no doubt that neighborhood effects exist, there is some question as to their magnitude and geographical extent.

Economists use the hedonic approach to estimate the magnitude of neighborhood effects (see Crecine, Davis, and Jackson, 1967; Kain and Quigley, 1975). In Table 11–1, a one-unit increase in the quality of adjacent dwellings increased monthly rent by $1.86 and increased market value by $777. Similarly, improvements to other dwellings on the block increased rent and market value. The evidence from hedonic studies suggests that neighborhood effects are highly

TABLE 11–1   **Change in Housing Prices from One-Unit Increases in Housing Attributes: A Hedonic Study of the St. Louis Housing Market**

Attribute	Rental Market: Increase in Monthly Rent ($)	Owner-Occupied Market: Increase in Market Value ($)
Dwelling Quality		
Interior	1.31	818
Central heating	4.44	—
Age	−0.29	−100
Size of Dwelling		
Number of rooms	22.63	1,453
Number of baths	9.07	769
Site Characteristics		
Exterior quality of adjacent dwellings	1.86	777
Exterior quality of dwellings on block	3.71	419
Miles from CBD	−0.30	−354
Average monthly rent = $61.34		
Average market value = $14,596		

SOURCE: John F. Kain and John M. Quigley, *Housing Markets and Racial Discrimination: A Microeconomic Analysis* (New York: National Bureau of Economic Research, 1975), Table 8.3.

localized: the spillover benefits from changes in the exterior appearance of one house are confined to dwellings within a few hundred feet of the house.

Durability of Housing

Housing is more durable than most goods. If a dwelling is maintained properly, it can last a hundred years or more. Although dwellings deteriorate over time, they do so at a relatively slow rate. The durability of housing has three implications for the housing market. First, the landlord can control the rate of physical deterioration by spending money on repair and maintenance. Second, there is a large supply of used housing on the market every year. The general rule of thumb is that new construction in a given year is between 2 percent and 3 percent of the total housing stock. Over the course of a decade, new dwellings provide about 20 percent to 30 percent of the housing stock, so between 70 percent and 80 percent of households live in dwellings that are at least 10 years old. The final implication is that the supply of housing is relatively inelastic: the market is dominated by the stock of used housing, so changes in price cause relatively small changes in the quantity supplied.

Maintenance, Retirement, and Abandonment

A property owner can control the rate of physical deterioration by spending time and money on repair and maintenance. The benefit of maintenance is that it increases the attractiveness of the dwelling, allowing an increase in rent and market value. The general rule for maintenance is that the landlord should increase spending on maintenance as long as the marginal benefit of maintenance (the increase in rent or market value) exceeds the marginal cost.

For some dwellings, the profit from rental housing is negative. If rental housing is unprofitable, the landlord has three options: conversion, boarding up, and abandonment.

1. **Conversion.** A dwelling can be converted to nonresidential use, such as an office, a store, or a parking lot. Conversion will be profitable if the alternative activity generates enough profit to offset the costs of conversion to the nonresidential use. If conversion would require the demolition of the dwelling and the construction of a new building, conversion costs will be relatively high.

2. **Boarding up.** A dwelling can be boarded up and taken off the market temporarily. The board-up option will be profitable if two conditions are met. First, if the landlord expects the market rent to increase sometime in the future, expected future profits will be positive. Second, if the landlord's carrying costs (the opportunity cost of keeping his or her money in housing instead of a bank account) are relatively low, there will be relatively low costs associated with waiting for the market rent to increase. This type of temporary retirement was common during the Great Depression.

3. **Abandonment.** The owner can disown the dwelling, walking away from the property. Abandonment will be profitable if the alternative uses (retail, commercial, industrial) do not generate enough profit to cover the cost of converting the property from residential to nonresidential use. If conversion costs are high, the market value of the property will be zero, so there will be no reason to keep title to the land.

Retirement results from three types of changes that decrease the profitability of rental housing. On the demand side of the market, a decrease in average income or a decrease in population will decrease the demand for housing in certain areas. On the supply side, an increase in the supply of rental housing will decrease market rents and profits. Finally, as the dwelling ages, increases in maintenance costs will decrease profits, increasing the likelihood of conversion or abandonment.

There is some evidence that local property-tax systems encourage abandonment. Consider an area in which market rents and property values are falling. If tax liabilities do not fall with market rents, profits from rental housing will eventually become negative and landlords will have the incentive to abandon their properties to avoid paying property taxes. White (1986) explores the effects of various factors on abandonment in New York City and concludes that the property tax is by far the most important factor. She estimates that a 10 percent increase in the property tax increases the frequency of abandonment by 16.5 percent. For example, if the average assessed value of properties in the Brownsville section of Brooklyn was cut by $1,000 (a 6 percent reduction) the resulting decreases in property taxes would cut the abandonment rate from 17 percent per year to 14.8 percent. Given this large response, a tax cut would generate a fiscal surplus for the city: although the tax liability per property would decrease, the direct revenue loss would be offset by (1) an increase in the number of properties on the tax rolls and (2) a decrease in the number of properties that the city must either take over or demolish.

Because abandonment is the ultimate neighborhood externality, it contributes to the problems of central-city neighborhoods. Abandoned buildings provide targets for vandals and graffiti artists, and quickly become eyesores. Even worse, they often become temporary homes for transients and retail outlets for drug dealers, so they contribute to crime. For these reasons, abandonment decreases the relative attractiveness of the neighborhood, decreasing the rent that other landlords can charge for their properties. Abandonment feeds on itself, transforming livable neighborhoods into unlivable ones.

Durability and Supply Elasticity

The durability of housing also has important implications for the market supply curve. Consider the response to an increase in the demand for housing. In the short run, the supply of housing is fixed, so the increase in demand will increase the equilibrium price. In the long run, suppliers will respond to the increase in market price by increasing the quantity of housing supplied. The question is, By how much will supply increase, and how soon will it increase?

There are three types of supply responses to an increase in price:

1. **Build new dwellings.** As the price rises, new housing will become more profitable, so more dwellings will be built. Most of the new dwellings will be built on vacant land in the suburbs.
2. **Maintain used dwellings.** As the price of housing increases, the benefit of maintaining dwellings will increase. Landlords will spend more on maintenance and repair, slowing the deterioration rate and decreasing the number of dwellings retired from the housing stock.
3. **Remodel used dwellings.** Some landlords will upgrade their dwellings, increasing the quantity of housing services generated.

Because the bulk of housing is used housing, the supply response will be relatively large only if the second and third responses (the used-housing responses) are relatively large.

How elastic is the supply of used housing? Because dwellings deteriorate slowly over time, a decrease in the deterioration rate has only a small effect on the housing market. Although an increase in price slows down the deterioration process, the process is slow in the first place. In addition, remodeling is extremely expensive, so it takes a very large price hike to make modifications worthwhile. For these two reasons, housing supply will be relatively inelastic for relatively long periods of time. In other words, the supply side of the housing market is sluggish: it takes suppliers a long time to respond to an increase in the demand for housing. In the meantime, the price of housing will remain relatively high.

The same argument applies to a decrease in housing demand and the resulting decrease in the market price. A decrease in price decreases the incentives for maintenance, so dwellings will deteriorate at a faster rate, and more dwellings will be retired. Even the fastest deterioration rate is relatively slow, so the decrease in the quantity supplied will be relatively small for relatively long periods of time. Although dwellings can be converted to other uses, the high cost of conversion inhibits this response. Because a decrease in price causes relatively small changes in a large part of the market, supply will be relatively inelastic for a long period of time. Therefore, the lower price of housing will prevail for a long period of time.

What is the price elasticity of demand for housing? Unfortunately, economists have been unable to answer this question. It is difficult to estimate the supply elasticity because it is difficult to measure the quantity of housing services. The existing studies of housing supply suffer from a number of statistical problems (see Olsen, 1987, and Quigley, 1979), so their results must be interpreted with caution. Ozanne and Struyk (1978) estimate that the supply elasticity of used housing is between 0.20 and 0.30. In other words, a 10 percent increase in the market price increases the quantity of used housing on the market by between 2 percent and 3 percent. Over a 10-year period, new construction provides only about 30 percent of the housing stock, so Ozanne and Struyk's estimate applies to 70 percent of the housing stock for a 10-year period. De Leeuw and Ekanem (1971) estimate that the long-run supply elasticity for rental housing is between 0.30 to 0.70. In other words, the available evidence suggests that the supply of housing is relatively inelastic over relatively long periods of time.

The Filtering Model of the Housing Market

The filtering model captures some of the essential features of the market for used housing. It describes the interactions between different housing submarkets and the process through which a dwelling passes from one use to another. The filtering process has two basic features:

1. **Decrease in housing service.** The quantity of housing service produced by a particular dwelling decreases over time. The decrease in quantity results from physical deterioration, technological obsolescence, and changes in housing fashion.
2. **Decrease in occupant income.** The dwelling is occupied by households with progressively lower incomes. As quantity decreases, the dwelling

is occupied by households that demand progressively lower quantities of housing service, typically households with lower incomes.

The filtering model can be used to address two questions. First, why do the poor occupy used housing instead of new housing? Second, do the poor benefit from policies that subsidize the construction of new housing for the wealthy?

Why Do the Poor Occupy Used Housing?   To explain the rationale for housing poor households in used housing, consider a city with two income groups, poor and wealthy. Suppose that real income is rising over time, causing each household to demand more housing over time. Assume that it is costly to upgrade used housing, so it is cheaper to build new housing than to improve old housing. Suppose that 10 percent of the city's dwellings are retired each year and replaced with new dwellings.

Should new housing be built for the wealthy or for the poor? If the wealthy did not occupy new housing, they could be accommodated by upgrading used houses to meet the demand for higher-quality housing (given rising incomes). Rooms could be added, the roofs and plumbing could be upgraded, and the houses could be remodeled to accommodate changes in housing tastes. Since these modifications would be costly, it is usually more efficient to build new housing for the wealthy.

If new housing is built for the wealthy, there will be a plentiful supply of used housing for poor households. When the wealthy vacate the used dwellings, the market values of the leftover houses decrease. The market value of a used dwelling is likely to be less than the cost of building an equivalent new low-cost dwelling, so poor households are better off in used housing than in new housing. Since there is a plentiful supply of used housing (with unfashionable design and old pipes), it is efficient to accommodate poor households in used housing.

Subsidies for New Housing and Growth Controls.   Consider next the issue of who benefits from subsidies that encourage the building of new dwellings for high-income households. The subsidies for new housing cause wealthy households to move from used housing to new housing, so the supply of used housing increases. The increase in the supply of used housing decreases the equilibrium price of used housing, providing benefits for poor households who occupy the used housing. In other words, the filtering process transmits some of the benefits of subsidies to the occupants of used housing.

Because the filtering process cuts both ways, the poor bear some of the costs of policies that restrict the supply of new housing. Suppose that growth controls restrict the supply of new, high-quality houses. The decrease in supply of new housing will slow the filtering process because fewer wealthy households will move from used dwellings into new ones. Because fewer dwellings filter down to poor households, the growth-control policy increases the price of low-quality used housing. Consequently, some of the costs of growth control are borne by poor households.

Demand Elasticities

What is the income elasticity of demand? There have been dozens of studies of housing demand, and there is consensus on three points. First, the overall income elasticity is about 0.75 (Ellwood and Polinski, 1979): a 10 percent increase in income will increase housing consumption by about 7.5 percent. Second, the income elasticity for renters is less than the income elasticity for owner-occupants. Third, the income elasticity increases with income. According to Ihlanfedlt (1982), the elasticity for low-income households is between 0.14 and 0.62, and the elasticity for high-income households is between 0.72 and 1.10.

The results of hedonic studies can be used to estimate the income elasticities of demand for individual components of the housing bundle. Follain and Jimenez (1985) summarize the results from several hedonic studies and come to three conclusions:

1. The demand for living space is inelastic with respect to income: in seven of nine cases, the elasticity is below 0.46.
2. The demand for structural quality is highly elastic with respect to income: in four of five cases, the elasticity exceeds 1.64.
3. The demand for neighborhood amenities such as public safety is highly elastic with respect to income.

The hedonic studies suggest that, compared to the demand for housing in general, the demand for living space is less income-elastic and the demands for structural quality and neighborhood amenities are more income-elastic.

What is the price elasticity of demand for housing? Most estimates of the price elasticity fall between −0.75 and −1.20 (Ellwood and Polinski, 1979). The consensus is that demand is slightly price-inelastic (an elasticity slightly less than 1.0 in absolute value). This means that an increase in price will increase total expenditures on housing by a small amount: an increase in price decreases the quantity demanded by a slightly smaller percentage amount, so total expenditure (price times quantity) increases by a small amount.

Racial Discrimination and Segregation

This section explores the issues of racial discrimination and segregation in the urban housing market. After reviewing facts on discrimination and segregation, the section discusses the effects of discrimination on (1) housing prices paid by blacks and whites, and (2) the transformation of white neighborhoods into mixed or black neighborhoods.

Yinger (1979) provides a useful set of definitions of prejudice, discrimination, and segregation. **Prejudice** is defined as a negative *attitude* toward members of a particular racial group. For the purposes of this chapter, prejudice is reflected in an aversion to living near members of another race. **Racial discrimination** is defined as *behavior* that results in differential treatment based on race: members of a group subject to racial discrimination are denied rights or opportunities because of their race, not because they lack the formal qualifications for those rights or opportunities. The degree of **residential segregation** indicates the racial mixture of a city's neighborhoods. A city is completely segregated when racial groups are divided into homogeneous neighborhoods, so that no neighborhood contains members of more than one racial group. A city is completely integrated when each neighborhood is heterogeneous, with proportional representation of each racial group in each neighborhood.

Segregation Facts

The most popular measure of the segregation of two racial groups is the **index of dissimilarity.** The index shows the percentage of either racial group that would have to relocate to achieve complete integration. A value of zero implies that the city is completely integrated: each neighborhood has the same racial mixture as the metropolitan area, so there is no need to relocate people to achieve proportional representation. In contrast, a value of 100 implies that the city is completely segregated, so that all the members of one race would have to relocate to achieve complete integration.

Figure 11–1 shows the index of dissimilarity for eight central cities and their suburbs (in 1980). Among the central cities, the most segregated is Chicago: to achieve complete integration, 92 percent of minority households would have to relocate. The least segregated of the central cities is Denver, with a value of 70. The suburbs are less segregated than the central cities: the average index value for the suburbs is 57, compared to 82 for the central cities. Between 1970 and 1980, the index values dropped in seven of the eight central cities and in three of the eight suburban areas. During this period, the average central-city index value dropped from 86 to 82 and the average suburban index value dropped from 57 to 56.

Blacks are the most segregated of all the racial minorities. Using data from Chicago, Woolbright and Hartmann (1987) show that the black-white index of dissimilarity is 24 points higher than the Hispanic-white index and 40 points higher than the Asian-white index. Using data from Kansas City, Darden (1987) shows that blacks are highly segregated regardless of education, income, and occupational status. Although segregation is less severe among more educated households, even college graduates are highly segregated: the index value for college graduates is 74, compared to 82 for high school graduates and 83 for those who have not attended high school. The index varies slightly with household income without an obvious pattern: the index value is 83 for households with income of $5,000; 84 for those with an income of $10,000; 83 for those with an income of $20,000; 82 for those with an income of $30,000; and 88 for those with an income of $50,000.

FIGURE 11–1   Index of Dissimiliarity for Selected Central Cities and Their Suburbs, 1980

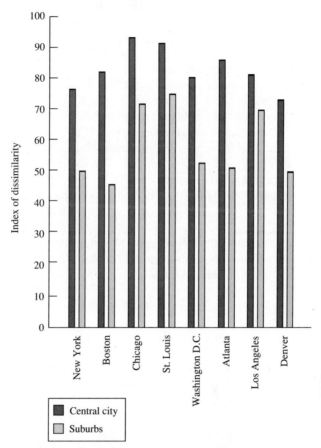

SOURCE: Thomas A. Clark, "The Suburbanization Process and Residential Segregation," in *Divided Neighborhoods,* ed. Gary A. Tobin (Sage Publications, 1987).

What Causes Segregation?

Racial segregation is caused, in part, by segregation with respect to income. To explain, consider a city in which neighborhoods are homogeneous with respect to income: there is a poor neighborhood and a wealthy neighborhood. If blacks are poorer than whites, income segregation contributes to racial segregation. As an extreme example, suppose that all the poor are black and that all the blacks are poor. In this case, the city is completely segregated even if there is no racial prejudice: the poor neighborhood is 100 percent black, and the wealthy neighborhood is 100 percent white. As a more realistic example, suppose that black households have a lower average income, but there are some wealthy black households. In this case, income segregation causes partial racial segregation: the poor neighborhood has a relatively large number of black households.

How important is income segregation in explaining racial segregation? There is conclusive evidence that differences in income play a relatively small role in racial segregation. According to Farley (1983), differences in income and other socioeconomic characteristics are responsible for about 25 percent of the segregation in central cities and about 15 percent of the segregation in suburban areas. The studies by Gabriel and Rosenthal (1989) and Kain (1985) discussed in Chapter 9 suggest that the low rate of black suburbanization is caused by factors other than income.

A common misconception is that all racial groups (whites, blacks, and Hispanics) prefer segregated neighborhoods. If this were true, it would suggest that racial segregation is voluntary. The evidence from household surveys suggests that blacks and Hispanics prefer integrated neighborhoods, not segregated ones. Figure 11–2 shows the neighborhood preferences of black, Hispanic, and white

**FIGURE 11–2   Preferences for Mixed and Segregated
Neighborhoods: Blacks, Hispanics,
and Whites**

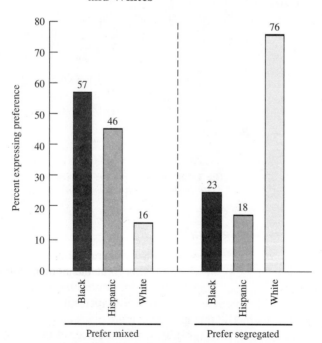

SOURCE: U.S. Department of Housing and Urban Development, *The 1978 HUD Survey of the Quality of Community Life: A Data Book* (Washington, D.C.: U.S. Government Printing Office, 1979).

households. About one sixth of white households prefer to live in mixed neighborhoods (50 percent white), compared to 57 percent of blacks and 46 percent of Hispanics. In contrast, about three fourths of white households prefer highly segregated neighborhoods (few or no households of other races), compared to 23 percent of blacks and 16 percent of Hispanics. These results suggest that there is a basic conflict between whites, who generally prefer segregation, and blacks and Hispanics, who generally prefer integration.

Housing Prices with Fixed Populations

This section explores the effects of racial prejudice and discrimination on housing prices. The principal question is, How does the price of housing vary within a segregated city? The answer is that in a city with a fixed black population, blacks pay less than whites for identical dwellings.

To explain effects of prejudice and discrimination on the price of housing, consider a mixed-race city with the following characteristics:

1. There is a fixed number of households of each race.
2. All households have the same income.
3. All dwellings in the city are identical.
4. All dwellings are equally accessible to employment opportunities.
5. Blacks have a moderate preference for living near white households.
6. Whites have a strong aversion to living near black households.

Suppose that the city starts with a segregated housing market: blacks live close to the city center, and whites live in a suburban ring. The question is, What housing-price function is consistent with racial segregation? In other words, what set of housing prices will sustain the segregated housing pattern?

Figure 11–3 shows a housing-price function that is consistent with racial segregation. The border between the black and white areas is u^*. The solid line shows the price function under which households have no incentive to relocate. In the black area ($u < u^*$), the price function is positively sloped, reflecting blacks' preferences for proximity to whites. Black households are willing to pay $48,000 for a dwelling in the city center, compared to $60,000 for a dwelling at the border between the two areas. In the white area ($u > u^*$), the positively sloped price function reflects whites' aversion to living close to blacks. White households are willing to pay $60,000 for a dwelling at the border, compared to $84,000 for a dwelling at the location most distant from the black area. The white price function is steeper than the black price function because blacks have relatively weak preferences for living near whites.

Figure 11–3 suggests that blacks pay less than whites for identical dwellings. All dwellings are assumed to be identical in terms of their physical characteristics and accessibility, yet the equilibrium price increases with the distance from the city center. The average black household (located in the center of the black area)

FIGURE 11-3   Equilibrium Housing-Price Function in a Segregated City

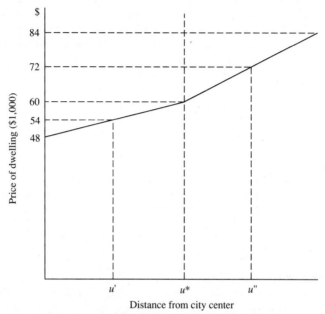

In a segregated city where both blacks and whites prefer to live near whites, the housing price function is positively sloped. Blacks living at $u < u^*$ are willing to pay more for dwelling closer to the white area, and whites living beyond $u*$ are willing to pay less for dwellings close to the black area.

pays $54,000, compared to $72,000 for the average white household (located in the center of the white area). In this case, whites pay for their aversion to living near blacks in the form of higher housing prices.

As pointed out by Yinger (1979), there are two key assumptions underlying the result that blacks and whites are completely segregated. First, the preference of blacks for white neighbors is weaker than the preference of whites for white neighbors (assumptions 5 and 6). This means that whites outbid blacks for all dwellings beyond u^*. In contrast, if some blacks had relatively strong preferences for white neighbors, they could outbid whites for dwellings beyond u^* and thus disrupt the segregated pattern. In this case, complete segregation is not a market equilibrium. The second key assumption is that all households have the same income (assumption 2). In combination with the assumption that blacks have relatively weak preferences for living close to whites, the assumption of equal incomes means that whites outbid blacks for all dwellings beyond u^*. If this assumption were dropped, wealthy black households could outbid whites for some dwellings beyond u^*, so complete segregation would not be a market equilibrium.

Population Growth and Broker Discrimination

Figure 11–3 predicts that blacks pay less than whites for identical dwellings. This prediction is inconsistent with empirical studies from the 1970s, which suggest that blacks paid more—not less—than whites. The apparent inconsistency can be explained by the rapid growth of urban black populations during the 1960s and 1970s. In other words, assumption 1 was not satisfied during this period.

Consider a city that experiences rapid growth in its black population. In the absence of restrictions on the size of the black area, we would expect the black area to expand outward to accommodate the larger black population. As the black population increases, competition for housing increases the amount blacks are willing to pay for housing near the old border (u^*). If black households are allowed to compete with white households for housing near u^*, blacks will outbid whites, causing the black area to expand outward.

If whites are averse to living near blacks, they have an incentive to prevent the expansion of the black area. White households can turn their prejudicial attitudes into discriminatory behavior by refusing to deal with real estate brokers who sell dwellings to blacks. A broker who sells to blacks will have fewer white customers and may make less money. If the penalty for selling to blacks (fewer white customers) is large enough, brokers will engage in discriminatory behavior that promotes segregation and prevents the expansion of the black area.

Brokers use a number of techniques to discourage black buyers. The first technique is called racial steering: the broker directs individual buyers to neighborhoods full of households of the same race. In other words, black buyers are not given information about dwellings in predominantly white neighborhoods. Second, brokers provide inferior service to black households by (1) misrepresenting the housing market, (2) delaying transactions, and (3) giving less help in arranging financing.

A **fair housing audit** provides information on the extent of racial discrimination. The auditor sends two individuals who are identical except for race (they have the same income, education, household size) to real estate brokers to inquire about housing. According to Yinger (1987), there is conclusive evidence that blacks are treated differently from otherwise identical whites: blacks are shown fewer dwellings, steered into certain neighborhoods, and given less advice and assistance on financing options.

Figure 11–4 shows effects of the black population growth when the border between the black and white areas is fixed. Population growth shifts the black portion of the housing-price function upward. If racial discrimination on the part of brokers prevents the expansion of the black area, the typical black household (at the midpoint u') pays $78,000 for a dwelling, compared to $72,000 for the typical white (at u''). These figures are roughly consistent with empirical results from the 1970s that showed blacks paying higher housing prices. Unfortunately, there have been no careful studies of the black-white price differential since the late 1970s, so it's unclear whether blacks continue to pay more for housing.

FIGURE 11-4   Black and White Housing Prices with Black Population Growth

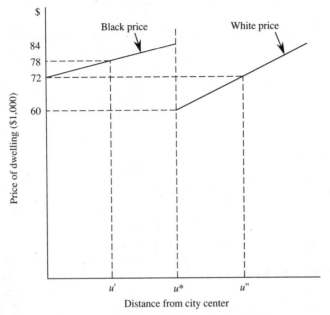

In a city with a growing black population and a fixed black area, the typical black (at u') pays more than the typical white (at u'') for housing.

Neighborhood Transition

Consider a neighborhood that is changing from a segregated white neighborhood to a mixed-race neighborhood. This section discusses the factors that determine how rapidly the neighborhood changes.

An important factor in speed of neighborhood transition is the attitude toward integration. A white household that prefers a segregated neighborhood is likely to leave the neighborhood as its minority population grows. According to household surveys, the number of departing whites increases with the minority's share of the neighborhood population. According to one survey, the percentage of whites who say that they will leave increases from 7 percent in a neighborhood with 7 percent minorities, to 24 percent in a neighborhood with 20 percent minorities, to 41 percent in a neighborhood with 33 percent minorities, to 64 percent in a neighborhood with 60 percent minorities. These numbers explain why many neighborhoods change rapidly from highly segregated white neighborhoods to highly segregated minority neighborhoods. An increase in the share of minority households decreases the attractiveness of the neighborhood to many white households, causing white flight and further increases in the minority share.

Galster (1990) studied the racial transformation of neighborhoods in the Cleveland metropolitan area during the 1970s. He explored the factors that determine the rate at which the black share of a neighborhood's population increases over time. The most important factors are (1) the initial black share of population, (2) white attitudes toward segregation, and (3) the proximity of the neighborhood to other neighborhoods where blacks are in the majority.

Figure 11–5 shows Galster's results for three types of neighborhoods. The curves show the gains in the black share of population (in percentage points) over the 1970–80 decade for different initial black shares. Curve *A* shows this relationship for a neighborhood that (1) is not adjacent to a black-majority neighborhood and (2) has "average" white preferences for segregation. For example, a neighborhood that starts the decade as 10 percent black gains 5.5 percentage points over the decade, so the neighborhood is 15.5 percent black at the end of the decade. Along the positively sloped portion of the curve, the gain in the black share increases with the initial black share. For example, if the initial share is 20 percent, the gain is 19.5 percentage points, so the 1980 share is 39.5 percent. For the type of neighborhood shown by curve *A*, there is a black majority by the end of the decade if the initial black share exceeds about 37 percent (point *X*).

FIGURE 11-5   Change in the Racial Composition of Cleveland Neighborhoods: 1970–1980

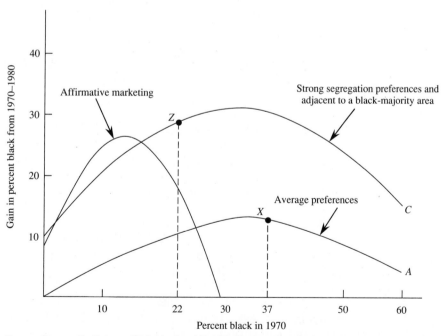

SOURCE: George C. Galster, "Neighborhood Racial Change, Segregationist Sentiments, and Affirmative Marketing Policies," *Journal of Urban Economics* 27 (1990), pp. 344–61.

Curve *C* in Figure 11–5 shows the changes in the black share of population for a neighborhood that (1) is adjacent to a black-majority neighborhood and (2) has relatively strong white preferences for segregation. For a given initial share, this neighborhood experiences more white flight than the average neighborhood, so the gain in the black share is relatively large. For example, for an initial share of 10 percent, the gain is 20 percentage points, so the black share at the end of the decade is 30 percent. This type of neighborhood is more likely to have a black majority by the end of the decade than the average neighborhood: for any initial share greater than 22 percent (point *Z*), the black gain is large enough to generate a black majority.

During the 1970s, two municipalities in the Cleveland area (Shaker Heights and Cleveland Heights) used public policy to encourage racially balanced neighborhoods. The idea was to encourage blacks to move into white neighborhoods, but to prevent the development of black-majority neighborhoods. There were a number of features of this "affirmative marketing" policy, including (1) information and persuasion campaigns to attract blacks, (2) policies to maintain the quality of housing and public services (especially education) to discourage the departure of households that placed a high value on the quality of housing and public services, and (3) special broker services for members of the "under-represented" racial group, typically whites. To prevent the white flight that might drop the number of white households below 50 percent, the municipalities catered to white households.

The third curve in Figure 11–5 shows the gain in the black share for a neighborhood that (1) has engaged in affirmative marketing and (2) is not adjacent to a black-majority neighborhood. For a neighborhood with a small initial black share, the black gain in this type of neighborhood exceeds the gain experienced by the average neighborhood (shown by curve *A*). For example, for an initial share of 10 percent, the black gain in the affirmative-marketing neighborhood is 24.5 percentage points, compared to 5.5 points in the average neighborhood. In contrast, for a large initial black share, the affirmative-marketing neighborhood experiences a relatively small gain. For example, for an initial share of 28 percent, the black gain is 3 percentage points, compared to 12 percentage points in the average neighborhood. In the neighborhood with affirmative marketing, the black share of the population is stable if the initial share is about 30 percent.

The success of affirmative marketing depends on whether the neighborhood is adjacent to a black-majority neighborhood. For a neighborhood that is not adjacent to a black-majority neighborhood, the black share of population by the end of the decade never exceeds 30 percent, so the policy achieves its objective of a racially balanced neighborhood. In contrast, the policy is ineffective in neighborhoods that are adjacent to black-majority neighborhoods: if such a neighborhood starts the decade with a black share of at least 12 percent, it will have a black majority by the end of the decade.

Figure 11–6 summarizes Galster's (1990) results for neighborhoods that did not adopt affirmative-marketing policies. For each type of neighborhood, the figure

FIGURE 11–6   Threshold of Black Shares for Different Types of Neighborhoods

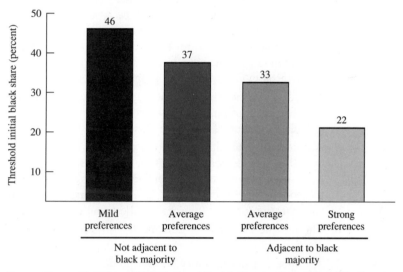

SOURCE: George C. Galster, "Neighborhood Racial Change, Segregationist Sentiments, and Affirmative Marketing Policies," *Journal of Urban Economics* 27 (1990), pp. 344–61.

shows the minimum initial black share that generates a black majority by the end of the decade. The threshold share is larger for neighborhoods that are distant from black-majority neighborhoods and have relatively weak white preferences for segregation. The smallest threshold (22 percent) is for a neighborhood that is adjacent to a black-majority area and has strong white preferences for segregation.

Summary

1. Housing is different from other commodities because it is heterogeneous, immobile, and durable.
2. Housing is heterogeneous in the sense that every dwelling provides a different bundle of features. Dwellings differ in size, layout, the quality of utility systems, and interior design. Sites differ in access, tax liabilities, local public goods, environmental quality, and neighborhood appearance.
   a. The hedonic approach is based on the notion that a dwelling is composed of a bundle of individual components, each of which has an implicit price.
   b. Changes in the exterior appearance of one house cause spillover benefits (increases in market value) for surrounding houses (the neighborhood effect).

3. Housing is durable, and the landlord can control the rate of physical deterioration by spending money on repair and maintenance.
    a. When the profits from housing are negative, dwellings are retired from the housing stock. There are three types of retirement: conversion to another use, boarding up, and abandonment.
    b. Retirement results from a decrease in market price (from a decrease in demand or an increase in supply) or an increase in maintenance costs.
    c. There is evidence that the property tax encourages abandonment.
4. The supply of housing is relatively inelastic for relatively long periods of time because the bulk of the housing stock is used housing. There are no reliable estimates of the price elasticity of supply.
5. According to the filtering model, the quantity of housing services generated by a dwelling decreases over time, so the dwelling is occupied by households with progressively lower incomes. The filtering model explains why the poor occupy used housing and shows that the poor benefit from the subsidization of new housing for the wealthy.
6. The income elasticity of demand for housing is about 0.75, and the price elasticity is between -0.75 and -1.20.
7. The index of dissimilarity shows the percentage of one racial group that would have to relocate to achieve complete integration.
    a. In eight selected metropolitan areas between 1970 and 1980, the average central-city index value dropped from 86 to 82 and the average suburban index value dropped from 57 to 56.
    b. Blacks are the most segregated of all the racial minorities and are highly segregated regardless of education, income, or occupational status.
    c. Differences in income and other socioeconomic characteristics are responsible for about 25 percent of segregation in central cities and about 15 percent of segregation in suburban areas.
    d. About one sixth of white households prefers to live in mixed neighborhoods, compared to 57 percent of blacks and 46 percent of Hispanics.
8. Racial prejudice and discrimination affect the prices of housing paid by blacks and whites.
    a. In a city with a fixed black population, blacks pay less than whites for identical dwellings.
    b. If discrimination prevents the expansion of the black area when the black population grows, blacks pay more—not less—than whites for identical dwellings. A number of empirical results from the 1970s showed that blacks paid higher housing prices.
9. A study of the racial transformation of neighborhoods in the Cleveland metropolitan area during the 1970s suggests that the most rapid transformation occurs in neighborhoods that (a) start with a relatively large black share of population, (b) have white households with strong preferences for living with other whites, and (c) are close to neighborhoods where blacks are in the majority.

10. An affirmative-marketing program is more likely to result in a racially balanced neighborhood if the neighborhood is not close to a black-majority neighborhood.

Exercises and Discussion Questions

1. Suppose that you own an apartment building that does not generate enough rental revenue to cover your costs. You have two options: first, you could demolish the building and set up a parking lot; second, you could abandon the building. Suppose that the cost of demolition is $20,000, and the annual profit from the parking lot would be $1,500. Should you demolish or abandon? If you don't have enough information to answer this question, list the information you need and explain how you would use it.

2. In city E, all households have the same income and real income is constant over time. Will there be filtering in the city?

3. Consider city B, which has a fixed population. In an attempt to decrease total residential energy consumption, the city has adopted the following policy, Policy E: All new housing in the city must be equipped with an energy-saving device that decreases the dwelling's energy consumption by 10 percent.

    a. Evaluate the effects of Policy E on the city's new and used housing markets. What happens to the prices of new and used housing?

    b. What happens to the quantities of new and used housing?

    c. Under what circumstances will total energy consumption in the city increase?

    d. Describe and analyze a more effective conservation policy.

4. The real estate brokers in city F are baffled. Although dwellings are subject to the normal physical and fashion deterioration over time, there is little filtering. In contrast to most cities, in which the typical house changes hands every 7 years (usually going to a household with a lower income than that of the previous owner), the typical house in the city changes hands every 50 years. Explain this phenomenon.

5. In city D, landlords charge a "security deposit" of $900 and do not refund the money when the tenant leaves. Suppose that a new deposit law is passed. The law requires that all landlords refund 100 percent of the security deposit unless the landlord can prove that the tenant damaged or dirtied the dwelling. Comment on the following statement: "The new law will save the typical tenant $900."

6. Comment on the following statement: "I live in an apartment complex built in a year when interest rates were relatively low. My rent is lower than the rent on other apartments because the cost of financing the complex is relatively low."

7. In Figure 11–3, the housing-price function for whites is steeper than the housing-price function for blacks. Why?

8. One of the assumptions lurking behind Figure 11–3 is that all dwellings are equally accessible to employment opportunities. Draw a new housing-price function under the assumption that all workers commute to the city center, so commuting costs increase with u (distance to the center).

References and Additional Readings

Arnott, Richard. "Economic Theory and Housing." In *Handbook of Regional and Urban Economics,* vol. 2, ed. Edwin S. Mills. New York: Elsevier, North Holland Publishing, 1987, Chapter 24. Reviews various models of the urban housing market and suggests future directions for research.

Crecine, John; Otto Davis; and John Jackson. "Urban Property Markets: Some Empirical Results and Their Implications for Municipal Zoning." *Journal of Law and Economics* 10 (1967), pp. 79–100.

Darden, Joe T. "Choosing Neighbors and Neighborhoods: The Role of Race in Housing Preference." In *Divided Neighborhoods,* ed. Gary A. Tobin. Beverly Hills, Calif.: Sage Publications, 1987, Chapter 1. Shows that racial segregation is caused largely by racial discrimination, not by income segregation or voluntary segregation.

De Leeuw, Frank, and Nkanta Ekanem. "The Supply of Rental Housing." *American Economic Review* 61 (1971), pp. 806–17.

Ellwood, David, and Mitchell Polinski. "An Empirical Reconciliation of Micro and Grouped Estimates of the Demand for Housing." *Review of Economics and Statistics* 61 (1979), pp. 199–205.

Farley, John E. *Segregated City, Segregated Suburbs: Are They Products of Black-White Socioeconomic Differentials?* Edwardsville, Ill.: Southern Illinois University, 1983. Concludes that differences in income and other socioeconomic characteristics play a small role in racial segregation.

Follain, James R. "The Price Elasticity of the Long-Run Supply of New Housing Construction." *Land Economics* (1979), pp. 190–99.

Follain, James R., and Emmanuel Jimenez. "Estimating the Demand for Housing Characteristics." *Regional Science and Urban Economics* 15 (1985), pp. 77–107. A survey and critique of hedonic studies of the housing market.

Gabriel, Stuart A., and Stuart S. Rosenthal. "Household Location and Race: Estimates of a Multinomial Logit Model." *Review of Economics and Statistics* (1989), pp. 240–49. Shows that the location choices of black households are relatively insensitive to changes in income and other socioeconomic characteristics.

Galster, George C. "Neighborhood Racial Change, Segregationist Sentiments, and Affirmative Marketing Policies." *Journal of Urban Economics* 27 (1990), pp. 344–61. Explores the factors that determine the rate at which the racial composition of a neighborhood changes.

Ihlanfeldt, Keith R. "Property Tax Incidence on Owner-Occupied Housing: Evidence from the Annual Housing Survey." *National Tax Journal* 35 (1982), pp. 89–97.

Kain, John F., and John M. Quigley. *Housing Markets and Racial Discrimination: A Microeconomic Analysis*. New York: National Bureau of Economic Research, 1975. Chapter 9 is a hedonic study of the St. Louis housing market.

Ohls, James C. "Public Policy Toward Low Income Housing and Filtering in Housing Markets." *Journal of Urban Economics* Vol. 2 (1975), pp. 144–71. Uses a computer model to simulate the effects of public housing on the filtering process.

Olsen, Edgar O. "The Demand and Supply of Housing Service: A Critical Survey of the Empirical Literature." Chapter 25. In *Handbook of Regional and Urban Economics*, vol. 2, ed. Edwin S. Mills. New York: North Holland, 1987. Reviews empirical studies of housing supply and demand.

Ozanne, L., and Raymond Struyk. "The Price Elasticity of Supply of Housing Services." In *Urban Housing Markets: Recent Directions in Research and Policy,* ed. L. S. Bourne and J. R. Hitchcock. Toronto: University of Toronto Press, 1978. Estimates the supply elasticity of used housing.

Polinski, Mitchell. "The Demand for Housing: A Study in Specification and Grouping." *Econometrica* 45 (1977), pp. 447–62.

Quigley, John M. "What Have We Learned about Housing Markets?" In *Current Issues in Urban Economics*, ed. Peter Meiszkowski and Mahlon Straszheim. Baltimore, Md.: Johns Hopkins University Press, 1979. A review of theoretical and empirical research in housing.

Sterlieb, George, and Robert Burchell. *Residential Abandonment: The Tenement Landlord Revisited*. New Brunswick, N.J.: Rutgers University Press, 1973.

White, Michelle. "Property Taxes and Urban Housing Abandonment." *Journal of Urban Economics* 20 (1986), pp. 312–30. Explores the effects of inflexible property taxation on the frequency of abandonment, and concludes that the property tax encourages abandonment.

Woolbright, Louie Albert, and David J. Hartmann. "The New Segregation: Asians and Hispanics." In *Divided Neighborhoods,* ed. Gary A. Tobin. Beverly Hills, Calif.: Sage Publications, 1987, Chapter 6.

Yinger, John. "Prejudice and Discrimination in the Urban Housing Market." In *Current Issues in Urban Economics,* ed. P. Meiszkowski and M. Straszheim. Baltimore, Md.: Johns Hopkins University Press, 1979, pp. 430–68. Discusses the causes and consequences of racial prejudice and discrimination. Summarizes the empirical evidence that blacks paid more than whites for housing.

————. "The Racial Dimension of Urban Housing Markets in the 1980s." In *Divided Neighborhoods,* ed. Gary A. Tobin. Beverly Hills, Calif.: Sage Publications, 1987, Chapter 2. Discusses recent evidence of discriminatory treatment of black house buyers and the policy implications.

12 Housing Policies

This is the second of two chapters on the urban housing market. This chapter discusses three types of housing policies. The first is housing assistance: the federal government uses various policies to improve the housing conditions and decrease the housing costs of poor households. Second, the federal government uses a number of community development programs to support local efforts to improve housing conditions and revitalize neighborhoods. Third, under a rent-control policy, the local government sets a maximum price for rental housing.

There are two distinct types of housing-assistance programs. The first type operates on the supply side of the housing market: the government either builds new housing for the poor (public housing) or subsidizes private developers to build and manage low-income housing. The second type of assistance policy operates on the demand side of the market: the government hands out coupons that can be used to rent existing housing.

Since 1980, the focus of federal housing policies has shifted back and forth between supply-side and demand-side policies. In 1980, about 188,000 households were added to housing-assistance programs, with about 130,000 households placed in new dwellings and 58,000 given housing coupons. In 1986, 99,000 households were added, with only 13,000 housed in new dwellings. The National Housing Affordability Act of 1992 represents a shift back to supply-side policies. The legislation provides funds to build an additional 360,000 low-income housing units over a two-year period.

Conditions of Housing and Neighborhoods

The original goal of federal housing policy was to provide "a decent home and a suitable environment for every U.S. family." Have these objectives been met? Are most citizens living in decent houses in suitable neighborhoods?

Housing Conditions and Rent Burdens

Table 12–1 shows the number and percentage of households that experienced housing problems in 1987. The definitions of housing problems come from the U.S. Department of Housing and Urban Development (HUD). A dwelling is considered inadequate if it has incomplete plumbing or kitchen facilities; structural problems (e.g., cracked walls, leaking roof, broken plaster); deficiencies in common areas (stairwells, hallways); or unsafe heating or electrical systems. A dwelling is considered crowded if there is more than one person per room. A household is considered cost burdened if it spends more than 30 percent of its gross income on housing.

There are three conclusions that can be drawn from Table 12–1. First, overcrowding is a relatively small problem: only 2.7 percent of all households live in overcrowded housing, and only 7.5 percent of poor households (income less than half the median area income) are overcrowded. Second, the most prevalent

TABLE 12–1   The Condition of the Housing Stock and Housing Cost Burdens

	Number	Percentage of Households
All Households		
Inadequate	6,408	7.1%
Crowded	2,434	2.7
Cost burdened	25,918	28.5
Total with problems	34,760	38.2
Poor Households		
Inadequate	2,175	18.2
Crowded	898	7.5
Cost burdened	8,412	70.3
Total with problems	11,485	96
Metropolitan Residents		
Inadequate	4,631	6.5
Crowded	1,991	2.8
Cost burdened	21,043	29.7
Total with problems	27,665	39.1
Black Households		
Inadequate	1,898	18.5
Crowded	565	5.5
Cost burdened	4,116	40.2
Total with problems	6,579	64.2

Source: U.S. Bureau of the Census, *Annual Housing Survey* (1987).

problem is affordability. The number of cost burdened households is over four times the number of households in inadequate housing. The affordability problem is most extensive among black and poor households: 4 in 10 black households and 7 in 10 poor households are cost burdened. Third, the most severe problems are experienced by poor households and black households. Almost all (96 percent) of poor households have some sort of housing problem, and 7 in 10 are cost burdened. Almost two thirds of black households experience problems: about 1 in 4 black households lives in inadequate or overcrowded housing, and an additional 4 in 10 are cost burdened.

In the last several decades, there has been considerable progress in improving the condition of the housing stock. The percentage of urban households in overcrowded housing dropped from 13.5 percent in 1950 to 2.7 percent in 1987. The percentage of urban households living in "substandard" housing (defined differently from "inadequate" housing) dropped from 21.9 percent in 1950 to 1 percent in 1983. Despite this progress, many urban households continue to live in inadequate housing.

In the last two decades, the fraction of income spent on housing has increased for most households. Between 1970 and 1983, the median rent-income ratio rose from 0.20 (the median renter household spent 20 percent of its income on housing) to 0.29. Over the same period, the median rent-income ratio in central cities increased from 0.21 to 0.31; the ratio for female-headed households increased from 0.27 to 0.44; and the ratio for the poor rose from 0.35 to 0.40. The rent-income ratios increased over this period because real income declined while housing rents rose. Between 1983 and 1987, the percentage of households that were cost burdened rose from 17 percent to 28.5 percent.

Neighborhood Conditions

Table 12–2 provides evidence concerning the level of neighborhood dissatisfaction for various types of households. The first column of numbers shows the percentage of households of each type that gave their neighborhood a score of 3 or less on a 10-point scale. The greatest dissatisfaction is among households living in multifamily dwellings in central cities. For example, 16.8 percent of the low-income black households living in multifamily housing in the central city said that their neighborhood was of "poor" quality, and 36.1 percent of these households said that the neighborhood was so bad that they wanted to move. Among similar households living in single-family housing in the suburbs, only 3.3 percent considered their neighborhood to be of poor quality and only 13.6 percent said that they wanted to move. The figures for low-income white households are 11.2 percent (poor quality) and 22.3 percent (want to move) for multifamily housing in the central city, and 3.4 percent (poor quality) and 10.0 percent (want to move) for single-family housing in the suburbs. Neighborhood dissatisfaction varies with race and income: blacks are generally more dissatisfied than whites, and low-income households are more dissatisfied than high-income households.

TABLE 12–2   **Opinion of Neighborhood by Race, Income, Structure Type, and Location**

Household Type	*Neighborhood Quality Is Poor*	*Want to Move*
Black, low, multi, city	16.8%	36.1%
Black, high, multi, city	9.7	32.2
White, low, multi, city	11.2	22.3
Black, low, multi, subs	10.5	25.6
White, high, multi, city	5.7	21.8
Black, high, multi, subs	6.3	25.7
Black, low, single, city	10.3	19.7
Black, high, single, city	5.4	17.4
White, low, single, city	6.5	15.9
White, high, multi, subs	3.9	16.3
White, low, multi, subs	5.2	14.1
White, high, single, city	3.3	15.4
Black, high, single, city	3.3	14.9
Black, low, single, subs	3.3	13.6
White, low, single, subs	3.4	10.0
White, high, single, subs	1.8	10.4

Definitions
Poor quality:	score of 3 or less on a 10-point scale.
Low:	income in bottom third of income distribution.
High:	income in top two thirds of income distribution.
Multi:	live in multifamily housing.
Single:	live in single-family dwelling.
City:	live in central city.
Subs:	live in suburban area.

SOURCE: Thomas P. Boehm and Keith R. Ihlanfeldt, "The Revelation of Neighborhood Preferences: An N-Chotomous Multivariate Probit Approach," *Journal of Housing Economics* 1(1991), pp. 33–59.

Boehm and Ihlanfeldt (1991) explore the effects of various neighborhood characteristics on the perceived quality of the neighborhood. Their results suggest that dissatisfaction is most prevalent in neighborhoods with high crime rates, high noise levels, rundown and abandoned buildings, and large quantities of trash, litter, and junk.

One of the implications of Table 12–2 is that the incidence of neighborhood dissatisfaction is higher among black households. Boehm and Ihlanfeldt (1991) show that the most important factors in explaining the difference in satisfaction are differences in (1) crime rates; (2) the amount of litter, trash, and junk; (3) the quality of buildings; and (4) the number of abandoned buildings. Figure 12–1 shows the results of the following thought experiment. Suppose that the crime rate in the typical black neighborhood changes to the crime rate that prevails in the typical white neighborhood. By how much would the gap between black

FIGURE 12–1 **Reasons for the Gap between White and Black Neighborhood Dissatisfaction**

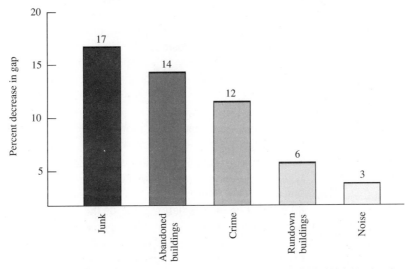

SOURCE: Thomas P. Boehm and Keith R. Ihlanfeldt, "The Revelation of Neighborhood Preferences: An N-Chotomous Multivariate Probit Approach," *Journal of Housing Economics* 1 (1991), pp. 33–59.

and white dissatisfaction decrease? The answer is that the gap would decrease by 12 percent. Figure 12–1 shows the results of repeating this thought experiment for the other factors that contribute to neighborhood dissatisfaction: abandoned buildings are responsible for 14 percent of the gap, and litter, trash, and junk is responsible for another 17 percent.

Supply-Side Policy: Public Housing

In 1987, about 1.3 million households lived in public housing. The number of public housing units increased from 478,000 in 1960 to 1.2 million in 1980. Since then, the number of occupied units has increased slowly, reflecting the shift in funding toward demand-side policies. Public housing is built and managed by local public housing authorities. The federal government is involved in four ways:

1. **Capital subsidies.** Public housing is built with tax-exempt bonds. After the federal government pays off the bonds, the project becomes the property of the local housing authority.

2. **Operating subsidies.** Originally, the public housing program was based on the notion that the local housing authority would charge enough rent to cover the project's operating costs. During the 1960s, operating costs

rose rapidly while the average income level of tenants decreased. As a result, the rent-income ratios of public housing tenants increased to relatively high levels. The federal government intervened, setting a maximum rent-income ratio of 0.25. To cover the difference between the tenant contribution and the project's operating costs, the federal government provided operating subsidies. In 1981, the maximum rent-income ratio was raised to 0.30. By 1984, operating subsidies covered about 40 percent of operating costs and cost the federal government a total of $1.6 billion per year.

3. **Modernization subsidies.** The federal government also provides subsidies for the repair and renovation of old housing projects. In 1984, the total budget for modernization was $1.4 billion.

4. **Tenant selection.** The federal government places restrictions on what type of households qualify for public housing. One rule specifies that houses are eligible for public housing only if their income is less than 80 percent of the median income of the area. In 1974, Congress directed local housing authorities to admit households from every income group within the eligible range. The idea was to integrate the projects with respect to income, thus preventing large concentrations of the poorest households. In 1981, Congress reversed itself, directing the housing authorities to allocate the bulk of units (75 percent of units built before 1981 and 95 percent of units built after 1981) to households with "very low" income (less than half the median area income).

Public Housing and the Recipient

To explain the trade-offs associated with public housing, consider a city with the following characteristics:

1. The quantity of housing services generated by a dwelling is measured by its square footage of living space.

2. The equilibrium price of housing is 25 cents per square foot.

3. The typical public-housing unit is an 800-square foot apartment and is provided to eligible households for $100 per month.

Consider the incentives for an eligible household that initially occupies a 600-square-foot apartment at a cost of $150 per month. For this household, the choice is easy: public housing provides more living space at a lower cost, so the household will accept the offer of subsidized public housing. Consider next the incentives for a household that initially occupies a 900-square-foot apartment at a cost of $225 per month. By moving into public housing, the household is forced into a smaller dwelling (800 square feet instead of 900 square feet) but also saves $125 per month. The household will move into public housing if the additional $125 worth of nonhousing goods is worth the sacrifice of 100 square feet of living space.

Would the household be better off with cash instead of subsidized public housing? Consider first the possibility that the cost of public housing is the same as the cost of private housing (25 cents per unit). It will cost the government $200 to build and maintain the 800-unit apartment, so the subsidy per dwelling is $100 ($200 less the $100 rent charged to tenants), and the alternative to public housing is a $100 cash payment to the household. Suppose that the household's market income is $1,000 per month and it initially spends $150 on housing (occupying a 600-square-foot apartment). The public housing program gives the household the option to consume 800 square feet of public housing and spend $900 on other goods. A cash payment of $100 gives the household this same option: the household could spend $200 of its total income ($1,100) on housing (renting an 800-square-foot private dwelling for 25 cents per square foot), leaving $900 to spend on other goods. The difference between public housing and cash is that cash gives the household more spending options: the money can be spent on any combination of housing and other goods. For example, the household may spend only $175 on housing (consuming 700 square feet), leaving $925 for other goods. Because the cash gives recipients more options, they will prefer the cash to subsidized public housing.

How much is public housing worth to the tenant? The value of public housing can be measured by answering the following question: What cash payment would make the household indifferent between the cash and a $100 housing subsidy? A study by Smeeding (1982) suggests that tenants receive a benefit of about 80 cents per dollar spent on public housing.

How does the cost of new public housing compare to the cost of private housing? Public housing is more expensive for two reasons. First, the private sector can build *new* low-income housing more efficiently than can the public sector: Weicher (1979) cites a number of studies showing that new public housing costs more than new private housing. Second, there is a plentiful supply of used low-quality housing, so even the least costly new housing costs more than used housing. According to the National Housing Review (1974), the cost of new public housing is about 33 percent higher than the cost of used private housing.

Living Conditions in Public Housing

Public housing projects suffer from a number of problems, including high rates of drug abuse and crime. Figure 12–2 shows the incidence of violent crime in three public housing projects in the city of Chicago. The crime rates in the projects were between 1.86 and 3.81 times the crime rate for the central city as a whole.

The crime rates in housing projects are relatively high for three reasons. First, the residents of the projects are relatively poor (in Chicago, the median household income of project residents is $5,000, compared to $22,000 for the central city as a whole), and crime rates are higher among the poor. Second, many of the units in the projects have been abandoned by the city and have been taken over by drug abusers and gangs. Third, the physical layout of the typical project—a

FIGURE 12-2   **Crime Rates in Chicago Housing Projects**

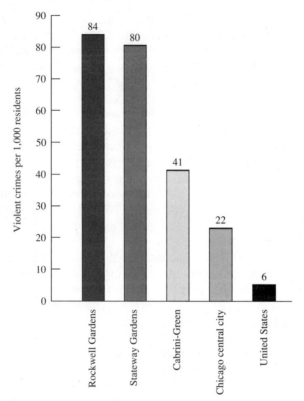

SOURCE: *Newsweek*, January 2, 1989, p. 25.

cluster of high-rise buildings—may contribute to crime. If crime rates are higher in high-density clusters of poor households, one option for decreasing crime is to replace the high-rise clusters with low-rise buildings dispersed throughout the metropolitan area.

The Market Effects of Public Housing

The provision of public housing affects the market for private housing. Figure 12–3 shows the short-run and intermediate-run effects of public housing on the market for private housing. In the short run, the supply of housing from the private sector is perfectly inelastic: 500 dwellings are provided, regardless of price. At the initial equilibrium (point *B*), the price is $250 per dwelling per month. If the local housing authority builds 200 new public housing dwellings, the 200 households that move to public housing leave the private housing market, so the

FIGURE 12–3   Short-Run and Long-Run Effects of Public Housing

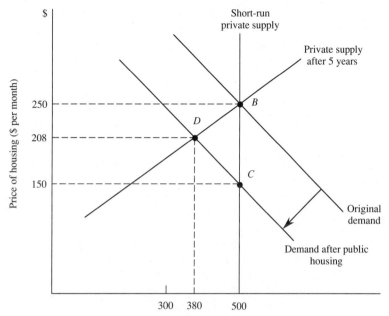

Public housing decreases the demand for private low-income housing by 200 households. In the short run, the supply of private housing is fixed, so the price of private dwellings drops from $250 to $150. Over a five-year period, the decrease in the price of private housing decreases the quantity of housing supplied from 500 to 380, so the price rises to $208. The longer the period of time, the greater the displacement of private housing and the smaller the net decrease in price.

demand curve for private housing shifts to the left by 200 dwellings. The decrease in demand decreases the equilibrium price of housing from $250 to $150 (point *C*). In the short run, all housing consumers gain from the public housing program: some households occupy subsidized public housing, and others pay lower prices for private housing.

What happens to the private market over time? In Figure 12–3, the intermediate-run supply curve (the supply curve over a five-year period) is positively sloped: the higher the price of housing, the larger the number of dwellings supplied. At a price of $150, some private dwellings are unprofitable, so they are withdrawn from the housing market. As the number of dwellings decreases, the market price rises. The exit process continues until the price is high enough to restore zero economic profits ("normal" accounting profit). In Figure 12–3, a total of 120 private dwellings are withdrawn from the market, and the price rises from $150 to $208. Because public housing displaces some private housing, the provision of 200 public housing units generates a net increase in supply of only 80 dwellings.

Supply-Side Policy: Subsidies for Private Housing

An alternative to public housing is the subsidization of private housing. There are two subsidy programs for new low-income rental housing, Section 236 and Section 8. Under both rental programs, the federal government subsidizes landlords who build new housing and rent to poor households. A third program, Section 235, provides interest subsidies to poor homeowners.

Section 236

Under the Section 236 program (started in 1968), the government contracts with a private developer to build low-income housing. The government pays the landlord an annual subsidy to cover the difference between the rental payments of tenants and the cost of building and operating the property.

The tenant's monthly rent is determined by the household's income. The **basic rent** is defined as the rent that would have prevailed if the project had been financed with money borrowed at a 1 percent interest rate. The tenant's rent is either the basic rent or 30 percent of household income, whichever is greater: if the basic rent is more than 30 percent of income, the household pays the basic rent; if the basic rent is less than 30 percent of household income, the household pays 30 percent of its income. The government pays the landlord the difference between the tenant contribution and **market rent,** which is defined as the rent required to cover all of the developer's costs.

To explain, suppose that the market rent is $300 and the basic rent is $200. For a household with a monthly income of $500, the basic rent is more than 30 percent of income ($150), so the household will pay the basic rent. The federal government will pay the difference between the market rent and basic rent, or $100. For a household with income of $800, the basic rent is less than 30 percent of income, so the household will pay $240 (30 percent of its income) to the landlord, and the government will pay the remaining $60.

Section 8–New Housing

Under the Section 8–New Housing program (started in 1974), private developers and local housing authorities submitted plans for low-income housing to the Department of Housing and Urban Development (HUD). If HUD approved a particular project, it signed a 20-year contract to provide annual payments to cover the difference between tenants' rental payments and the landlord's costs. The subsidy per eligible tenant equals the difference between the **fair market rent** and the rent actually paid by low-income tenants. Under the contract, the developer was guaranteed the fair market rent on all units occupied by eligible households.

The tenant's rental payment depends on the tenant's income. To qualify for assistance, the household must live in a new dwelling that satisfies minimum physical standards and rents for no more than the *fair market rent*, defined by HUD as the rent that would be charged for a standard low-income dwelling. The eligible household pays 30 percent of its income toward housing. The subsidy to the landlord equals the gap between the tenant's payment and the fair market rent:

$$\text{Fair market rent} = \text{Subsidy} + 0.30 \cdot \text{Income}$$

For example, if the fair market rent is $400 and household income is $600, the household pays $180 in rent (30 percent of $600), and the subsidy is $220 ($400 − $180).

The Section 8–New Housing program was eliminated in 1983. The program was ended in large part because it was so expensive: in 1982, the average annual subsidy for a new Section 8 unit was over $6,000.

Demand-Side Policy: Consumer Subsidies

The supply-side housing policies help the poor by building more low-income housing. An alternative approach is to give subsidies directly to the poor and let them choose their own housing. Under a demand-side policy, low-income households are given housing coupons that can be redeemed for housing. Like the food-stamp program, the housing-coupon program allows the poor to make their own consumption choices. Coupons have two advantages over public housing. First, under some circumstances, the coupons are equivalent to cash. As shown earlier in this chapter, a cash payment generates a larger increase in utility than an equal expenditure on public housing. Second, the coupons can be spent on used dwellings, which are typically less expensive than new dwellings. There are two types of housing coupon programs: rent certificates and housing vouchers.

Rent Certificates: Section 8–Existing Housing

Under the Section 8–Existing Housing program (started in 1975), poor households are issued rent certificates that can be used to rent existing housing. To qualify for Section 8 assistance, household income must be less than 80 percent of the area's median family income. Under legislation passed in 1981, the bulk of funds is allocated to households with "very low" income (less than half the median area income). In 1988, about 780,000 households received rent certificates. There are two restrictions on the housing choices of recipients. First, the rental dwelling must meet minimum physical standards for size and quality. Second, the household cannot spend more than the fair market rent. The eligible household pays 30 percent of its income toward housing and receives a rent certificate to cover the difference between its contribution and the actual rent:

$$\text{Subsidy} = \text{Actual rent} - 0.30 \cdot \text{Income}$$

For example, suppose that the fair market rent is $400 and the household's income is $600. The household's contribution will be $180, and the subsidy equals the difference between the actual rent (up to a maximum of $400) and $180.

The subsidy to the household depends on the actual rent paid. For example, if the fair market rent is $400 and the household rents an apartment for $181, it receives a subsidy of $1; if it rents an apartment for $400, it receives a subsidy of $220. Because the government pays the difference between actual rent and $180, the net cost of an apartment renting for $181 is the same as the net cost of an apartment renting for $400. Therefore, it is reasonable to expect recipients to occupy apartments that have a market rent close to the fair market rent.

One of the surprising results of the rent-certificate program was that relatively few households moved to dwellings that rented for the fair market rent. This occurred despite the fact that the entire increase in rent would have been covered by the subsidy. Most households stayed in their existing dwellings and used the subsidy to cut their housing costs. This result suggests that moving costs are relatively large: for most households, the benefits from moving from a $300 apartment to a $400 apartment were smaller than the costs of moving.

Housing Vouchers

The housing voucher program was started on an experimental basis in 1983. The eligibility requirements for housing vouchers are similar to those for rent certificates: the bulk of payments goes to the very poor. To qualify for a voucher, the household must occupy a dwelling that meets the minimum quality standards. A voucher differs from a rent certificate in one important respect: the recipient can use the certificate to rent any dwelling that meets minimum physical standards. In 1988, about 156,000 households received vouchers.

The face value of the voucher is based on household income and the fair market rent. The formula is

$$\text{Face value} = \text{Fair market rent} - 0.30 \cdot \text{Income}$$

The voucher program gives the household more options than the rent-certificate program because the voucher is equivalent to a cash transfer: the voucher household has the option of spending more than the fair market rent for housing.

In 1988, the budgetary cost of housing vouchers exceeded the cost of rent certificates by about $23 per recipient (Mariano, 1989). The reason is simple: under the voucher program, the voucher covers the gap between the fair market rent and 30 percent of income, while the rent certificate covers the gap between the household's *actual rent* and 30 percent of income. As long as the actual rent is less than the fair market rent, the subsidy will be larger under the voucher.

Market Effects of Consumer Subsidies

What are the market effects of rent certificates and housing vouchers? Figure 12–4 shows the short-run and intermediate-run effects of the coupon program on the housing market. The voucher program increases the income of recipients, so it shifts the demand curve outward. Given the perfectly inelastic supply, the equilibrium price increases from $250 (point *B*) to $350 (point *E*). Because the supply of housing is fixed in the short run, the vouchers simply bid up the price of housing. Who gains and who loses in the short run? Although voucher recipients pay more for housing, they also have more money to spend on housing. In contrast, nonrecipients (middle-income households) pay higher housing prices without the benefit of the housing voucher.

What happens to the private market over time? In Figure 12–4, the intermediate-run supply curve (the supply curve over a five-year period) is positively sloped: the higher the price of housing, the larger the number of dwellings supplied. At a price of $350, housing is profitable, so firms produce more housing. As the number of dwellings increases, the market price drops. The entry process continues until the price is low enough to restore zero economic profits ("normal" accounting profit). In Figure 12–4, the number of dwellings increases to 620 and the price of housing drops to $292 (point *F*).

FIGURE 12–4   **Short-Run and Long-Run Effects of Housing Vouchers**

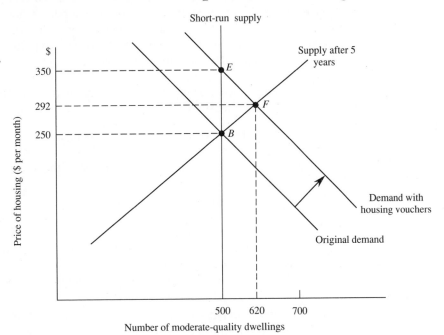

The housing voucher program increases the demand for moderate-quality dwellings. In the short run, the supply of moderate-quality housing is fixed, so the price increases from $250 to $350. Over a five-year period, the increase in the price of housing increases the quantity supplied from 500 to 620, and the price drops to $292. The longer the period of time, the greater the increase in the quantity supplied and the smaller the net increase in price.

The Experimental Housing Allowance Program

An alternative to a housing voucher is a housing allowance. A housing allowance is a cash payment, the size of which equals the gap between a given fraction of household income (e.g., 30 percent) and the fair market rent. To qualify for a housing allowance, the household must occupy a dwelling that meets minimum quality standards. A housing allowance will be equivalent to a housing voucher if (*a*) the two programs have the same quality standards, (*b*) the face value of the voucher equals the allowance payment, and (*c*) the household's rent exceeds the face value of the voucher. If the household spends more than the voucher value on housing, the household can substitute the voucher for its own spending on housing, freeing up an amount of cash equal to the face value of the voucher.

Under the Experimental Housing Allowance Program (EHAP), the federal government conducted a number of experiments with housing allowances. The demand experiment offered housing allowances to a small sample of poor renter households in two cities (Phoenix and Pittsburgh). The purpose of the experiment was to examine the effects of the program on eligible households. The most important policy issues concerned participation rates (how many would participate), the mobility of participants (how many would move to higher quality dwellings), and housing consumption (how much would housing consumption increase). The supply experiments offered allowances to all poor households in two counties (Brown County, Wisconsin, and St. Joseph County, Indiana). The purpose of the supply experiment was to examine the effects of housing allowances on the market price of housing. The principal question was whether a citywide assistance program would increase housing prices.

The housing-allowance experiments generated three conclusions about the responses of eligible households:

1. **Low participation rates.** Between 40 percent and 45 percent of the eligible households participated in the allowance programs. Participation rates were sensitive to the quality standards: the stricter the standards, the lower the participation rate.

2. **Small changes in housing consumption.** Between one quarter and one third of the allowance payment was used to increase housing consumption, and the remainder was spent on other goods. In other words, most of the allowance money was used to decrease rent burdens. The measured income elasticity of demand of allowance recipients was relatively low: between 0.20 and 0.44 for renters, and about 0.45 for owner-occupiers.

3. **Mobility.** Relatively few households changed dwellings. In Pittsburgh, 40 percent of allowance recipients moved over a two-year period, compared to 35 percent of households in a control group. In Phoenix, 63 percent of recipients moved, compared to 53 percent of the control households. The allowance program did not encourage integration with respect to race or income.

The general conclusion is that the housing allowances caused relatively small changes in housing choices. Recipients spent most of the money on nonhousing goods, and few moved from their original dwellings.

The allowance program did not cause any measurable price increases in the two cities involved in the supply experiment. Because participation rates were relatively low and recipients spent a relatively small fraction of their allowances on housing, the rightward shift of the demand curve was relatively small. To the extent that the demand for housing increased, the supply of housing was sufficiently elastic to accommodate the increased demand without any measurable price effects.

What are the lessons from the supply experiment? As pointed out by Kain (1981), the supply experiment tested the effects of one type of allowance program, one with minimal housing quality standards and relatively low participation rates. Because the allowance program increased the housing consumption of a small number of households by relatively small amounts, it is not surprising that housing prices did not rise. If a national housing allowance program had higher participation rates, larger allowance payments, and more stringent housing standards, it would shift the housing demand curve by a larger amount and would probably increase housing prices. Kain cites studies by the National Bureau of Economic Research and the Urban Institute that suggest such an allowance program would increase prices in some housing submarkets.

Supply versus Demand Policies

What are the trade-offs associated with supply-side policies (public housing) and demand-side policies (housing vouchers)? From the perspective of the recipient, the voucher program has two advantages over subsidized public housing. First, the voucher is equivalent to an income transfer, so it generates a larger increase in utility per dollar spent on housing programs. Second, the voucher allows tenants to occupy relatively inexpensive used housing, so a fixed budget will provide more housing per budget dollar.

The disadvantage of the voucher program is that it increases the price of housing. The recipient will be better off under the voucher program if the program causes a relatively small increase in the price of housing. This will occur if the elasticity of supply is relatively large. As explained earlier in this chapter, little is known about the intermediate-run and long-run elasticities of supply of housing. Unless one knows something about the individual housing submarkets in a city, it will be difficult to predict the effects of a voucher program on the price of housing.

What about taxpayers and nonrecipients? Two factors contribute to public support of public housing over housing vouchers. First, taxpayers seem to care about the housing consumption of recipients, not necessarily their utility levels. If public housing generates a larger increase in housing consumption, it is considered a superior policy. Second, nonrecipients pay a higher price of housing under a demand-side policy and a lower price under a supply-side policy. For these two reasons, taxpayers and nonrecipients may prefer public housing over housing vouchers even if recipients would be better off under the voucher program.

Community Development and Urban Renewal

There are dozens of programs and polices that fit under the term *community development*. The legislated mandate for federally supported community development calls for

> systematic and sustained action by the federal, state, and local governments to elimi-
> nate blight, to conserve and renew older areas, to improve the living environment of
> low- and moderate-income families, and to develop new centers of population growth
> and economic activity.

The two principal purposes of community development policies are to (*a*) revitalize declining areas of the city and (*b*) improve the housing of poor households. Community development policies are neighborhood-oriented in the sense that they concentrate spending in relatively small geographical areas.

Urban Renewal

Urban Renewal, the first community development program in the United States, was established under the Housing Act of 1949 and was eventually dropped in 1973. The national government provided local governments with the power and the money to demolish and rebuild parts of their cities. Local agencies acquired property under the right of eminent domain, cleared the site of "undesirable" uses (like low-income housing and small businesses), and then either built a public facility or sold the site to a private developer. The local agencies charged the developer less than the cost of acquiring and clearing the site, and the federal government covered two thirds of the local government losses. The private developer built housing (usually for middle-income and high-income households), government buildings, or commercial establishments.

According to the Congressional Research Service, Urban Renewal had the following effects:

1. **Demolition.** A total of 600,000 dwellings were demolished, displacing about two million people, most of whom were poor.
2. **New housing.** A total of 250,000 new dwellings were built, most of which were occupied by middle-income and high-income households.
3. **Public facilities.** The total floor space of new public facilities was 120 million square feet.
4. **Commercial facilities.** The total floor space of new commercial facilities was 224 million square feet.

5. **Property assessments.** The assessed value of property on renewed sites increased by 360 percent.

In sum, urban renewal generated both costs and benefits. It displaced poor households but also provided housing for middle-income and rich households, allowed the construction of commercial and public facilities, and increased tax revenue.

Was urban renewal worthwhile? The critics of the program focus on the demolition aspects of the program, pointing out that 2 million poor people were displaced. The defenders of the program focus on the rebuilding aspects of the program, pointing out that the new commercial developments provided jobs for the poor residents of the central city.

Recent Community Development Programs

More recent federal community development programs have avoided many of the problems of the Urban Renewal program. The newer programs are executed on a smaller scale, so they displace fewer households, and they place a greater emphasis on providing housing for the poor.

Table 12–3 shows the 1987 budget for community development. The total budget was over $3.5 billion, with about $2 billion used for Community Development Block Grants (CDBGs). The CDBG program is an entitlement program, with funds allocated to cities and states on the basis of population and other factors. The allocation formula gives relatively large grants to cities with relatively old and overcrowded housing, high poverty rates, and slow growth rates. The second largest program is the State and Small Cities Program, which gives money to states that is then distributed to small cities ineligible for CDBG funds. The third largest allocation goes to Urban Development Action Grants (UDAGs), which are used to leverage private investments in community development. Under the UDAG program, the federal government provides small subsidies to transform slightly unprofitable private development projects into profitable ones. The fourth largest allocation is for rental rehabilitation: these grants subsidize the renovation of low-income rental housing. The fifth largest allocation is for emergency shelter: these grants subsidize shelters for the homeless.

Cities can spend their community development grants on a wide variety of projects. Under the Carter administration, cities were required to spend a large fraction of the grants on projects that directly benefited poor households and low-income neighborhoods. Under the Reagan administration, many of these restrictions were dropped. The projects funded by the various funding programs can be divided into into four types:

1. **Improved housing.** Some programs support local projects that renovate buildings, enforce building codes, and build new low-income housing.

   • The Boston Housing Partnership used $8.5 million in CDBG funds to acquire and rehabilitate 700 rental units.

TABLE 12–3   **Community Development Budget of Department of Housing and Urban Development, 1987**

Program	Funding ($ million)
Community Development Block Grants (GDBGs)	
Housing rehabilitation	$ 876
Jobs programs	254
Public works	536
Public services	242
Assistance to homeless	46
Total	$1,954
State and Small Cities Program	$ 883
Urban Development Action Grants (UDAGs)	325
Rental rehabilitation	200
Emergency shelter grants	60
Other	133
Total	$3,555

SOURCE: U.S. Department of Housing and Urban Development, *1988 Community Development Programs: State Reports* (Washington, D.C.: U.S. Government Printing Office), pp. 1–4.

- The city of Cleveland joined with a nonprofit organization and a private developer to build a 183-unit rental housing project, using $4.4 million in federal funds ($1.7 million from a CBDG and $2.7 million from a UDAG) to leverage $9.9 million from private and other sources.

2. **Renewed infrastructure.** Some programs support projects that improve streets, roads, and water and sewage facilities.

   - In Fort Worth, Texas, the Main Street Project used $2.6 million in UDAG funds to improve the street's infrastructure (new curbs, gutters, sidewalks, and street lighting). As part of the renovation program, private developers agreed to build a $48 million hotel.
   - The city of Oshkosh, Wisconsin, used $600,000 in CDBG and UDAG funds to expand its airport to accommodate increased traffic.

3. **Job development.** Some programs support projects that encourage economic development and job creation.

   - In St. Louis, the Union Station was renovated with $10.2 million in CBDG and UDAG money and $126 million in other public and private funds. The station was developed into a hotel-retail-entertainment complex that produced 2,000 new jobs, over 50 percent of which were filled by minorities. The project rejuvenated a part of the city that had been dormant for 15 years.

- Salt Lake City is using a $1.1 million UDAG to support the construction of a downtown auto mall, using the grant to leverage $4.7 million in private financing.

- Baltimore used $10 million in UDAG funds to support the revitalization of its Inner Harbor. Private investment in office space, retail space, and a hotel totaled $73.4 million and produced 1,600 jobs.

4. **Responsive public services.** Some programs support public services for the elderly, the homeless, and children.

   - Orange County, California, used $892,000 in CDBG funds to support the construction of a $7.5 million facility to provide emergency services for abused, abandoned, or neglected children.

   - Phoenix used $361 in CDBG funds to build a recreation center for the handicapped.

   - Fort Worth, Texas, used $106,000 in CDBG funds to start a neighborhood youth project designed to curtail gang activity.

These examples show that community development funds are spent on a wide variety of projects.

What are the effects of community development programs? The programs that support housing projects supplement federal housing programs (public housing, subsidized new construction, housing vouchers). The difference is that the city has more control over the spending of community development funds. Other community development programs support economic development projects and can be evaluated as alternative means of promoting local economic growth. The costs and benefits of economic development programs are discussed in Chapter 5.

Rent Control

During World War II, the federal government instituted a national system of rent controls. Following the war, New York City was the only city to retain rent controls. During the 1970s, rent control returned to dozens of cities, including Boston; Cambridge; Los Angeles; Washington, D.C.; Albany; Berkeley; and Santa Monica.

Market Effects of Rent Control

What are the market effects of rent control? To answer this question, consider a city with the following characteristics:

1. All households live in identical apartments.
2. The equilibrium rent is $600 per month.

3. The equilibrium number of apartments is 90.
4. The apartments are made of stone and do not deteriorate over time.
5. The city sets a maximum rent of $400.

Figure 12–5 shows the short-run effects of rent control. The *short run* is defined as the period of time over which the supply of housing is fixed at 90 dwellings. In the short run, rent control does not affect the supply of housing, but simply transfers $200 per month from the landlord to the tenant.

In the long run, the supply of apartments depends on the price of rental housing. As rent decreases, some landlords convert their property to more lucrative uses: some apartment buildings are converted to condominiums, and other buildings are demolished to make way for commercial land uses. In Figure 12–5, rent control decreases the number of apartments from 90 to 50. As the price of rental housing decreases, the market moves downward along the long-run supply curve. The supply response to rent control depends on the long-run elasticity of supply. The more elastic the supply, the larger the decrease in the quantity of housing supplied.

FIGURE 12–5   Short-Run and Long-Run Effects of Rent Control

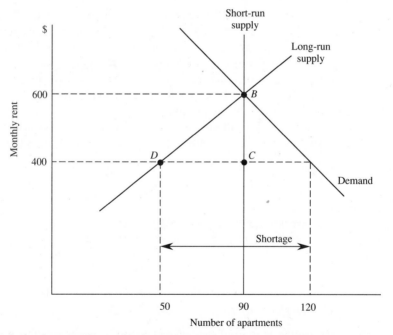

In the short run, the supply of apartments is fixed, so rent control (maximum rent $400) simply transfers income from landlords to tenants: the market moves from point *B* to point *C*. In the long run, the decrease in price decreases the quantity supplied: the market moves from point *C* to point *D*. The shortage (the gap between demand and supply) is 70 apartments.

Rent control causes a shortage of housing. At the controlled price of $400, the quantity of apartments demanded is 120, compared to a supply of only 50 apartments. There are too many tenants chasing too few apartments. In such a market, tenants spend relatively large amounts of time and money searching for apartments. For tenants, rent control brings good news and bad news: although rent control decreases the rent, it also increases search costs.

Rent control produces winners and losers. The city's population can be divided into four groups:

1. **Nonmovers.** Some households live in the city when rent control is implemented and occupy the same apartment forever. These households are winners in the rent-control game: they pay a lower price for the same apartment.

2. **Successful searchers.** Some people move to the city after rent control is implemented. They spend several months searching for an apartment and eventually find one. The full cost of a rent-controlled apartment is the sum of the rent ($400 per month) and the opportunity cost of search time. The full cost of a rent-controlled apartment may exceed the full cost of an uncontrolled apartment ($600 per month and small search costs). In general, if search costs are relatively large, the benefit of rent control (decreased rent) is smaller than the cost (increased search costs), so successful searchers are losers in the rent-control game.

3. **Displaced households.** Some tenants are displaced when apartments are converted or demolished, and are unsuccessful in their search for a new apartment. In Figure 12–5, the number of dwellings decreases by 40 (from 90 to 50), so 40 households are displaced. The displaced households are obviously losers.

4. **Landlords.** Rent control decreases the annual rental income per apartment from $7,200 ($600 times 12 months) to $4,800. Because the market value of an apartment building reflects its income-earning potential, the announcement of the rent-control program decreases the market value of the city's apartment buildings. If Barney owns an apartment building when rent control is announced, he pays for rent control in the form of a decreased market value. He cannot escape the effects of rent control by selling the building to someone else: once prospective owners hear about rent control, they are willing to pay less for the building. According to Smith and Tomlinson (1981), Toronto's rent-control program decreased the market value of apartment buildings by about 40 percent over a five-year period (1975–1980).

Olsen (1972) estimated the effects of New York City's rent-control program on tenants and landlords. Ignoring search costs, he estimated that the occupants of controlled units experienced a 3.4 percent increase in real income. On the other hand, landlords experienced losses in real income about twice as large as the total gain of tenants.

Distributional Effects of Rent Control

Gyourko and Linneman (1989) use data from 1968 to estimate the distributional effects of New York City's rent-control program. They estimate the decrease in rents experienced by different types of households. Their results provide insights into the distribution of benefits from rent control across income groups. The principal policy question is, Do most of the benefits from rent control go to poor households?

Figure 12–6 shows the relationship between the benefit from rent control (the decrease in annual rental payments) and household income. All the figures are in 1984 dollars. The top line shows the benefit-income relationship for households that occupy controlled units. The average benefit among occupants of controlled dwellings was $2,440 per year, and the average savings as a percentage of income was 27 percent. The benefit per household increases slowly with income. At each income level, there is a wide variation in the benefits experienced by individual households. For example, the average gain for households with income of $20,000 was $2,440, but many households had much larger benefits and many had much smaller benefits.

The middle line in Figure 12–6 shows the benefit/income relationship for all renting households. The average benefit among renting households was about $1,311 per year. The average benefit among renting households is smaller than the average benefits among the occupants of controlled units because the benefits are spread over more households: only 57 percent of renting households occupy controlled units. The benefit per household decreases as income increases, reflecting the fact that the average income of households in controlled units is lower than the average income of renting households: poor households are overrepresented in controlled dwellings, so poor households, on average, experience larger benefits from rent control.

The lower line in Figure 12–6 shows the benefit/income relationship for all households, including both renters and homeowners. The average benefit among all households was about $856 per year. The average benefit among all households is relatively small because less than one third of the households occupy controlled units. The benefit decreases as income increases, reflecting the relatively low income of households in controlled units.

Figure 12–6 suggests that the benefits of rent control are mildly progressive in the sense that the average benefit per household decreases as income increases. It's important to note, however, that the benefits experienced by households within an income group vary widely across households. The variation in benefits across households within an income group occurs for two reasons. First, only some of the households of a given income level occupy controlled dwellings (and receive benefits from rent control). The other households (renters of uncontrolled units and homeowners) receive no benefits from rent control. Second, among households that occupy controlled dwellings, there is a large variation in the benefits from rent control. Given the large variation in the benefits within each income group, rent control is a very blunt tool for income redistribution.

FIGURE 12–6   Benefits from Rent Control for Different Income Levels in New York City

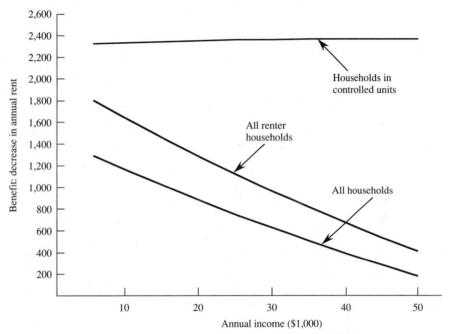

SOURCE: Joseph Gyourko and Peter Linneman, "Equity and Efficiency Aspects of Rent Control: An Empirical Study of New York City," *Journal of Urban Economics 26* (1989), pp. 54–74.

Deterioration and Maintenance

One of the assumptions of the simple model of the rent-control city is that apartments are made of stone, so dwellings do not deteriorate over time. This is clearly unrealistic. Suppose that housing is subject to physical deterioration: to maintain a dwelling at a given service level, the landlord must spend money on routine maintenance and repair. Suppose that in the initial equilibrium, the typical $600 apartment generates 1,000 units of housing service ($Q = 1,000$).

Rent control discourages routine maintenance, so apartments deteriorate more rapidly. In an uncontrolled city, landlords spend money to keep their apartments at a service level high enough to justify a $600 rent. If the apartment deteriorates to $Q = 900$, tenants are unwilling to pay $600 rent for the dwelling. In the rent-control city, there is no incentive to keep the apartment at $Q = 1,000$ because the landlord cannot charge $600 for the dwelling. Landlords decrease their spending on repair and maintenance, thus allowing apartments to deteriorate to a service level consistent with the $400 rent. Under a rent-control program, tenants may eventually get what they pay for.

Studies of rent-control cities show that landlords do indeed cut back on maintenance and repair. The Rand Corporation (1970) studied the effects of rent controls in New York City and concluded that rent control decreased the quality and quantity of rental housing. Between 1960 and 1967, the inventory of "sound" housing increased by 2.4 percent, the inventory of "dilapidated" housing increased by 44 percent, and the inventory of "deteriorating" housing increased by 37 percent. Between 1965 and 1967, 114,000 dwellings were retired from the housing stock. A study of Cambridge, Massachusetts, found that maintenance cost per apartment decreased by $50 per year (Navarro, 1987).

Gyourko and Linneman (1990) examined the effects of rent controls on the quality of rental housing in New York City in 1968. They show that rent-controlled buildings are less likely than uncontrolled buildings to be in sound condition, meaning that rent-controlled buildings are more likely to be deteriorating or dilapidated. One measure of the effect of rent control is the decrease in the probability that a building is sound, given that the building is subject to rent control. For example, if the probability of being sound is 0.90 for uncontrolled buildings (90 percent of uncontrolled buildings are sound) but only 0.85 for controlled buildings, rent control decreased the probability of being sound by 0.05.

Figure 12–7 shows the decrease in the probability that a building is sound for several types of low-rise buildings (less than seven stories). For buildings in Manhattan built before 1947, rent control decreased the probability by about 0.09 (from 0.63 to 0.54). Newer buildings, which are more likely to be sound, experience smaller decreases in the probability of being sound. For buildings in Manhattan built between 1947 and 1959, rent control decreased the probability of being sound by about 0.04 (from 0.89 to 0.85); for buildings built between 1960 and 1968, rent control decreased the probability of being sound by 0.01 (from 0.98 to 0.97). The effects of rent control are smaller in the two other boroughs.

Housing Submarkets

One of the assumptions of the rent-control model is that all households live in identical apartments. If there are housing submarkets, the analysis changes in two ways.

Consider first the possibility that there are two controlled submarkets. There are large apartments (equilibrium rent of $600 and controlled rent of $400) and small apartments (equilibrium rent of $300 and controlled rent of $200). Rent control inhibits movement between the two markets because search costs are large. Suppose that a household would like to move from a large apartment to a small one. In the rent-control city, there are two options. First, the household can stay in the large apartment, paying $400 per month. Second, it can spend time and money searching for a small apartment (which rents for $200). If search costs are relatively high, the household is better off staying in the original apartment.

Consider next the possibility that some of the dwellings in the city are not subject to rent control. Rent control decreases the supply of housing in the controlled sector. The displaced households move into the uncontrolled submarket,

**FIGURE 12–7   The Effect of Rent Control on the Probability
that a Building Is Sound**

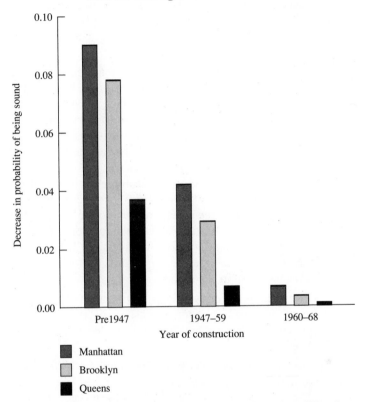

Year of construction

■ Manhattan
□ Brooklyn
■ Queens

SOURCE: Joseph Gyourko and Peter Linneman, "Rent Controls and Rental
Housing Quality: A Note on the Effects of New York City's Old Controls,"
Journal of Urban Economics 27 (1990), pp. 398–409.

bidding up the price of housing. Therefore, part of the costs of rent control are
borne by households living in uncontrolled dwellings.

Controlling the Supply Response to Rent Control

Rent control decreases the quantity and quality of rental housing. Cities have
developed a number of policies to diminish this supply response.

1. **Rent adjustments.** Most rent-control laws allow periodic increases in
   rent, with the allowable increase tied to some price index, for example,
   the consumer price index (CPI). Rent adjustments weaken rent controls
   and diminish the negative supply effects of the controls. In most rent-
   control cities that use rent adjustments, controlled rents rise slower than

the costs of building and maintaining rental housing. In New York City, controlled rents rose by 110 percent between 1943 and 1968, while the operating costs of rental housing increased by 285 percent (de Salvo 1971). In Toronto, controlled rents increased by 39 percent between 1975 and 1980, while operating costs of rental housing increased by 75 percent (Smith and Tomlinson, 1981).

2. **Exemption of new housing.** Most rent-control laws exempt new construction from controls. If new housing is exempt from controls, it may be unaffected by rent control. In fact, tenants displaced from the controlled market increase the demand for new rental housing, stimulating the supply of new rental housing. It is possible that new housing offsets the loss in housing stock caused by rent control. But there are two reasons to suspect that new housing will not offset the effects of rent control. First, new housing is typically a small part of the housing market, so it would take a relatively large increase in the supply of new housing to counteract the effects of rent control. Second, builders and owners are likely to be skeptical about the city's promise never to impose rent control on this year's new rental housing. If builders suspect that today's new housing will become tomorrow's rent-control housing, they may be reluctant to supply new housing.

3. **Restrictions on conversions.** Many cities restrict the conversion of rental housing to condominiums. If successful, these restrictions limit the conversion of rental housing to other uses, diminishing the supply effects of rent control.

4. **Subsidies for new construction.** Public policies encourage the building of new dwellings to replace the dwellings lost as a result of rent control. The city of Toronto offered low-interest construction loans to housing firms. In the United States, one of the purposes of public housing is to replace the dwellings lost because of rent control.

5. **Vacancy decontrol.** In some cities, rent is fixed during a tenancy but can be changed when a new tenant moves into the dwelling. This provision increases the landlord's rental income, weakening rent control. It increases the incentive for long-term occupancy.

Another way to decrease the supply effect of rent control is to cheat. Tenants and landlords often find ways to violate the spirit of rent-control laws. Landlords charge tenants "key money" (e.g., $5,000 for a key to the apartment) or nonrefundable security deposits. To the extent that landlords use indirect payments to increase the net price of housing, the negative supply responses to rent control are reduced. Tenants also collect bribes for rent-controlled apartments: when a tenant vacates a controlled apartment, he or she can charge the new tenant a "finder's fee." The fee is often implicit: in California, old tenants reportedly sold beanbag chairs to new tenants, charging hundreds of dollars for chairs that sold for just a few dollars in thrift stores. Tenant bribery does not increase the supply of housing but simply transfers income from the existing tenant to the new one.

Alternatives to Rent Control

In many cities, rent control is viewed as an indirect form of income redistribution. The idea is to take money from wealthy landlords and give it to poor tenants. At best, rent control is a blunt instrument for redistribution. Rent control helps all of the occupants of controlled dwellings, rich and poor alike. Moreover, a poor person who occupies a controlled dwelling is worse off under rent control if the search costs are larger than the savings in rent.

Suppose that a city wants to redistribute income from the wealthy to the poor. What are the alternatives to rent control? The first option is to finance income redistribution with a land tax. Because the supply of land is perfectly inelastic, the land tax will not affect the supply of land or the supply of housing. Therefore, the land tax will not cause the same supply problems as rent control. The second approach is to leave income redistribution to the federal government. Local attempts at income redistribution are likely to be frustrated by the movement of households into and out of the city. If the city gives the proceeds of a land tax to its poor residents, poor people from other cities may migrate to the city, diluting the effects of the redistribution program. Because international mobility is less than intercity mobility, a national redistribution program does not suffer from this problem.

Summary

1. The condition of the U.S. housing stock has improved considerably over the last several decades. Nonetheless, about two thirds of poor households experience some sort of housing problem, usually inadequate housing or high housing costs. Over half of black households experience housing problems.

2. The rent-income ratio is a measure of the affordability of housing. For the population as a whole, the median ratio increased from 0.20 in 1970 to 0.31 in 1983; for poor households, the median ratio rose from 0.35 to 0.40.

3. In 1987, about 1.3 million households lived in public housing. Public housing is built and managed by local housing authorities. The federal government provides subsidies for capital costs, operating costs, and modernization, and specifies who is eligible for public housing.

    a. Public housing may increase or decrease housing consumption, depending on the recipient's willingness to trade off consumption of housing and other goods.

    b. Public housing produces a relatively small increase in recipient welfare per dollar because (*i*) the monetary value of public housing is about 75 percent of its market value and (*ii*) public housing costs more than used private housing.

c. In the short run, the supply of private housing is fixed, so public housing decreases the market price of housing by a large amount.

d. Over time, the decrease in the price of housing decreases the quantity of private dwellings supplied as more dwellings are retired and fewer dwellings filter down to the low-quality submarket. The more elastic the supply, the greater the displacement of private housing and the smaller the net decrease in market price.

4. There are two subsidy programs for new low-income rental housing, Section 236 and Section 8. Both programs have the same market effects of public housing: they decrease the price of private housing and decrease the quantity supplied.

   a. Under the Section 236 program, the tenant pays 30 percent of his or her income or the basic rent, whichever is larger, and the government pays the landlord the difference between the tenant contribution and the market rent.

   b. Under the Section 8 program, the tenant pays 30 percent of his or her income, and the government pays the difference between the tenant contribution and the fair market rent.

5. There are two types of consumer subsidies: Section 8 rent certificates and housing vouchers.

   a. The rent certificates cover the difference between the actual rent and 30 percent of household income, and can be used on dwellings that rent for less than the fair market rent.

   b. The face value of a housing voucher equals the gap between fair market rent and 30 percent of household income, and can be used on any dwelling satisfying minimum physical standards.

   c. Both subsidy programs shift the demand curve outward, increasing the market price in the short run. Over time, the quantity of housing increases as (*i*) fewer dwellings are retired, and (*ii*) more dwellings filter down from higher-quality submarkets. The larger the supply elasticity, the smaller the net increase in price.

6. The Experimental Housing Allowance Program (EHAP) tested a program of housing allowances (cash payments to poor households). The demand for housing increased by a relatively small amount because (*a*) participation rates were relatively low, (*b*) few households changed dwellings, and (*c*) only a small fraction of the allowance payment was spent on housing. The small shift of the demand curve caused no measurable increases in housing prices.

7. There are dozens of policies and programs that fit under the term *community development*. The two principal purposes of such policies are to (*a*) revitalize declining areas of the city and (*b*) improve the housing of poor households.

8. Under the Urban Renewal program, the federal government subsidized the replacement of low-income housing with middle-income and high-income housing, public facilities, and commercial establishments.

9. More recent community development programs support local projects that improve low-income housing and local infrastructure; stimulate economic development, and develop new public services for handicapped, elderly, and disadvantaged citizens.

10. Rent control has the following effects on the housing market:
    a. The supply of dwellings decreases, causing a housing shortage that increases search costs.
    b. Spending on maintenance and repair decreases, so individual dwellings produce lower quantities of housing services.
    c. Consumer mobility decreases, and consumers make inefficient housing choices.

11. Rent-control cities use a number of policies to control the decrease in supply caused by rent control, including rent adjustments, exemption of new housing, restrictions on conversion, subsidies for new construction, and vacancy decontrol.

Exercises and Discussion Questions

1. Comment on the following statement by Mr. Taxpayer: "I support public housing rather than cash transfers because I want to be sure that the recipients of public assistance increase their housing consumption. If we give them cash, they will spend the money on something else."

2. According to Mr. Wizard, a realtor in Modville, "If my assumptions are correct, the long-run market effects of public housing are nil. The building of 200 public housing dwellings will affect neither the equilibrium price of housing nor the quantity of housing."
    a. What are Mr. Wizard's assumptions?
    b. Use Mr. Wizard's assumptions to predict the long-run market effects of housing vouchers.

3. Suppose that the poor households of city H are enrolled in a federal housing-allowance program. You are a middle-income renter in the city.
    a. Will you be helped or harmed by the allowance program?
    b. If you will be harmed, what variables determine how much you will be harmed? In other words, what are the relevant elasticities, and how does the cost you incur vary with the elasticities?
    c. How would your answer to (a) change if you owned your home?

4. Contrast the effects of rent control in two cities. In city R, the price elasticity of supply of housing is 5.0 (i.e., a 10 percent increase in the price of housing

increases the quantity of housing by 50 percent). In city S, the supply of housing is less elastic: the supply elasticity is 0.40.

5. Figure 12–7 suggests that the effects of rent control increase with the age of the building. Provide an explanation for this result.

6. Discuss the trade-offs associated with demolishing the high-rise clusters of public housing and replacing them with dispersed low-rise buildings.

References and Additional Readings

Aaron, Henry J. "Policy Implications: A Policy Report." In *Do Housing Allowances Work?* ed. Katherine Bradbury and Anthony Downs. Washington, D.C.: Brookings Institution, 1981. Compares the effect of allowances to cash transfers and construction subsidies. Discusses the value of social experiments such as EHAP.

————. "Rationale for a Housing Policy." In *Federal Housing Policies and Programs*, ed. J. Paul Mitchell. New Brunswick, N.J.: Center for Urban Policy Research, 1985. Discusses the frequently cited justifications for federal housing policies.

Aaron, Henry, and George M. von Furstenberg. "The Inefficiency of Transfers in Kind: The Case of Housing Assistance." *Western Economic Journal* 9 (1971), pp. 184–91. Estimates a welfare loss from public housing of between 10 percent and 18 percent.

Anderson, Martin. *The Federal Bulldozer*. Cambridge, Mass.: MIT Press, 1964. Argues that Urban Renewal destroyed low-income housing, displacing poor households.

Boehm, Thomas P., and Keith R. Ihlanfeldt. "The Revelation of Neighborhood Preferences: An N-Chotomous Multivariate Probit Approach." *Journal of Housing Economics* 1 (1991), pp. 33–59.

Davis, Otto, and Whinston, Andrew B. "The Economics of Urban Renewal." In *Urban Renewal: The Record and the Controversy*, ed. James Q. Wilson. Cambridge, Mass.: MIT Press, 1966, pp. 50–67.

de Salvo, J. S. "Reforming Rent Controls in New York City." *Regional Science Association Papers* 2 (1971), pp. 195–227.

Grisby, William. *Housing Markets and Public Policy*. Philadelphia: University of Pennsylvania Press, 1963. Discusses the filtering process.

Gyourko, Joseph, and Peter Linneman. "Equity and Efficiency Aspects of Rent Control: An Empirical Study of New York City." *Journal of Urban Economics* 26 (1989), pp. 54–74.

————. "Rent Controls and Rental Housing Quality: A Note on the Effects of New York City's Old Controls." *Journal of Urban Economics* 27 (1990), pp. 398–409.

Heilbrun, James. "On the Theory and Policy of Neighborhood Consolidation." *Journal of the American Planning Association* (1979), pp. 417–27. Advocates a resettlement program for central cities, under which households would be moved to certain neighborhoods. The remaining neighborhoods would be cleared for new development.

Irby, Iredia. *Attaining the Housing Goal*. Washington, D.C.: U.S. Department of Housing and Urban Development, Division of Housing and Demographic Analysis, July 1986. Describes the condition of the housing stock in 1983.

Jacobs, Barry G.; Kenneth R. Harney; Charles L. Edson; and Bruce S. Lane. *Guide to Federal Housing Programs*, 2nd ed. Washington, D.C.: Bureau of National Affairs,

1986. A detailed description of federal housing policies (public housing, housing subsidies, consumer subsidies, and community development).

Kain, John F. "A Universal Housing Allowance Program." In *Do Housing Allowances Work?* ed. Katherine Bradbury and Anthony Downs. Washington, D.C.: Brookings Institution, 1981. Discusses the implications of EHAP for a national housing-allowance program. Suggests that EHAP was not a true test of a national program because participation rates housing-quality standards were relatively low.

Mariano, Ann. "The Voucher Controversy Drags On." *Washington Post*, February 18, 1989. Discusses the budgetary costs of vouchers and rent certificates.

National Housing Review. *Housing in the Seventies*. Washington, D.C.: U.S. Government Printing Office, 1974. Discusses the equity and efficiency effects of housing programs.

Navarro, Peter. "Rent Control in Cambridge, Massachusetts." *The Public Interest* (1987), pp. 83–100.

Ohls, James C. "Public Policy toward Low-Income Housing and Filtering in Housing Markets." *Journal of Urban Economics* 2 (1975), pp. 144–71. Uses a computer model to simulate the effects of public housing on the filtering process.

Olsen, Edgar. "An Econometric Analysis of Rent Control." *Journal of Political Economy* 80 (1972), pp. 1081–1100.

————. "Housing Programs and the Forgotten Taxpayer." *The Public Interest* 66 (1982), pp. 97–109. Discusses alternative housing policies from the perspective of taxpayers.

Rand Corporation. "The Effects of Rent Control on Housing in New York City." In *Rental Housing in New York City: Confronting the Crisis,* RM-6190-NYC, 1970.

Rothenberg, Jerome. *Economic Evaluation of Urban Renewal*. Washington, D.C.: Brookings Institution, 1967.

Smeeding, Timothy M. *Alternative Methods for Evaluating Selected In-Kind Transfer Benefits and Measuring Their Effect on Poverty*. Washington, D.C.: U.S. Bureau of the Census, Technical Paper no. 50, U.S. Government Printing Office, 1982. Estimates the value of in-kind transfers to the recipients. Estimates that $1 of public housing is worth 80 cents to the typical recipient.

Smith, Lawrence B., and Peter Tomlinson. "Rent Control in Ontario: Roofs or Ceilings?" *American Real Estate and Urban Economics Journal* 9 (1981), pp. 93–114.

U.S. Department of Housing and Urban Development. *1988 Community Development Programs: State Reports*. Washington, D.C.: U.S. Government Printing Office, 1989, pp. 1–4. Shows HUD's community development budget, and describes how cities and states have used federal community development funds.

Weicher, John. "Urban Housing Policy." In *Current Issues in Urban Economics,* ed. Peter Meiszkowski and Mahlon Straszheim. Baltimore, Md.: Johns Hopkins University Press, 1979.

Urban Problems and Local Government

In contrast to the federal government, whose urban policies are primarily redistributional in nature, local governments are involved in resource allocation. Local governments build the streets, provide mass transit, run the public school system, and manage the criminal justice system. Local spending programs are supported by taxes on property, income, and retail sales. This section discusses the efficiency and distributional effects of local spending and tax policies. Chapter 13 provides an overview of local government spending and taxing policies, and Chapter 14 deals with local revenue sources, examining the incidence of local taxes and the local responses to intergovernmental grants.

Chapters 15 through 18 examine individual spending programs of local governments. Chapters 15 and 16 discuss urban transportation. Chapter 15 explores two problems caused by automobiles, congestion and pollution, and Chapter 16 deals with mass transit, showing how commuters choose a travel mode and how planners choose a transit system. Chapter 17 considers the spatial aspects of education, showing how the fragmented system of local government causes inequalities in educational spending and achievement. It also discusses various policies to offset spending and achievement inequalities, including intergovernmental grants and desegregation plans. Chapter 18 presents the economic approach to crime and crime fighting, discussing the optimum amount of crime and the alternative means of controlling crime.

CHAPTER 13 Overview of Local Government

This chapter provides an overview of the taxing and spending policies of the local public sector. The first part of this chapter presents the facts on local government, including information on spending programs and revenue sources. The second and third parts of this chapter discuss the economic rationale for local government, explaining why goods such as public schooling, public safety services, parks, and transit systems are produced by local governments rather than private firms or higher levels of government. The fourth part explores the reasons for our fragmented system of local government, and the fifth part explores the trade-offs associated with metropolitan consolidation. The sixth part discusses the reasons for—and responses to—the rising costs of local public services. The final part of this chapter explores the reasons for the fiscal distress experienced by many central cities in the last few decades.

Local Government Facts

Local governments are creatures of state governments in the sense that localities derive their taxing and spending powers from the states. There is considerable variation across states in the amount of power delegated to local governments. One measure of the relative importance of a local government in a particular state is the ratio of local spending to state spending: the larger the ratio, the greater the spending power of localities. In 1985, the average ratio was 0.75: local spending was about 75 percent of state spending (Advisory Commission on Intergovernmental Relations, 1987). Some of the states with relatively low spending ratios were Alaska (0.05), Hawaii (0.25), New Mexico (0.29), Delaware (0.37), Massachusetts (0.43), and Kentucky (0.43). Some of the states with relatively high spending ratios were New York (1.27), New Hampshire (1.12), Texas (1.04), and Colorado (1.04).

As shown in Table 13–1, there are over 82,000 local governments in the United States. In terms of total expenditures, the most important types of local government are municipalities (35 percent of local government expenditures) and school districts (30 percent of local expenditures).

Local Government Spending

Table 13–2 shows the spending of local governments and municipalities on various goods and services. The largest spending category is education, with spending of $684 per capita, about 42 percent of total spending. The spending of municipalities is more evenly divided, with the largest expenditures on police protection ($99 per capita), education ($89), highways ($68), sewerage ($61), and fire protection ($99).

In the postwar period, there have been two distinct trends in local spending. Between 1950 and 1976, local spending rose from about 5 percent to 9.2 percent of GNP. Three factors contributed to the steady growth in the postwar period. First, increases in real income increased the demand for many of the services provided by local governments. Second, the postwar baby boom increased the number of children attending local public schools. Third, for reasons described later in this chapter, the costs of providing local public services increased. The second trend

---

TABLE 13–1   **Types of Local Government**

Type of Government	Number of Units (1987)	Total Expenditures (1985–86) (millions)	Percent of Total Local Expenditure
County	3,042	$ 92,660	21%
Municipal	19,200	152,181	35
Township	16,691	13,619	3
School district	14,721	128,396	30
Special district	29,532	47,333	11
Total	83,186	$434,189	100%

Definitions
1. **Municipality:** municipal corporation provides general local government for a specific concentration of population.
2. **Township:** serves the inhabitants of an area defined without regard to population concentrations.
3. **Special district:** independent, special-purpose governmental unit.

SOURCES: U.S. Bureau of the Census, *Statistical Abstract of the United States, 1990* (Washington, D.C.: U.S. Government Printing Office, 1990); *Government Finances in 1986* (Washington, D.C.: U.S. Government Printing Office, 1987).

TABLE 13-2   Per Capita Expenditures of Local Government

Expenditure Category	Annual Spending per Capita, 1986–87	
	All Local Governments	*Municipalities*
Education Services		
Education	$684	$ 89
Libraries	12	11
Social Services		
Public welfare	79	43
Hospitals	92	37
Health	32	13
Transportation		
Highways	87	68
Other	27	31
Public Safety		
Police protection	88	99
Fire protection	43	53
Other	31	17
Environment and Housing		
Natural resources	11	1
Parks and recreation	38	40
Housing and community development	43	37
Sewerage	61	61
Solid-waste management	27	30
Administration and finance	186	122
General expenditure	85	83

SOURCES: Column one: U.S. Bureau of the Census, *Government Finances,* vol. 4; *Compendium of Government Finances,* no. 5 (April 1990). Column two: U.S. Bureau of the Census, *Government Finances,* vol. 4; *Finances of Municipal & Township Government,* no. 4 (March 1990), Series GF-89-4 U.S.

in local spending is the decrease in the relative importance of local government in the last fifteen years: between 1976 and 1986, local spending dropped from 9.2 percent to around 8 percent of GNP. Since the middle 1970s, real income has increased at a relatively slow rate and the number of school children has increased slowly. As a result, the relative size of the local sector has decreased.

Revenue Sources

Table 13–3 shows the distribution of revenue for different types of local governments. For local governments as a whole, 40 percent of total revenue comes from intergovernmental grants, 37 percent comes from local taxes, and the

TABLE 13–3   **Revenue Source of Local Governments, 1985–1986**

Type of Government	Percentage of General Revenue from		
	International Grants	*Local Taxes*	*Charges and General Revenue*
County	37%	37%	26%
Municipal	30	42	28
Township	29	56	15
School district	55	37	8
Special district	29	15	57
All local government	40	37	23

SOURCE: U.S. Bureau of the Census, *Government Finances in 1986* (Washington, D.C.: U.S. Government Printing Office, 1987).

remaining 23 percent comes from charges and general revenue. School districts are heavily dependent on intergovernmental grants, receiving about 55 percent of their revenue from the federal and state governments. For municipal governments, 30 percent of revenue comes from grants, 42 percent comes from local taxes, and 28 percent comes from user charges and general revenue. In contrast, special districts are heavily dependent on user charges, receiving about 57 percent of their revenue from charges and general revenue.

Figure 13–1 shows the distribution of tax revenue for municipalities and all local governments. In 1984, the property tax generated about three fourths of all local tax revenue. Municipalities are less dependent on the property tax: for municipalities as a whole, the property tax generated about half of tax revenue; for large municipalities (population greater than 300,000), the property tax generated only about 41 percent of tax revenue. The second largest revenue source is the sales tax: it generated 16 percent of total tax revenue and 29 percent of municipal tax revenue. The third largest source is the local income tax, which generated 6 percent of local taxes and 14 percent of municipal taxes.

Figure 13–2, p. 314, shows the time trends for intergovernmental grants from the federal and state governments. The relative importance of state grants increased steadily between 1965 and 1975, reaching a peak of almost 40 percent of the amount generated by local governments. Since then, the relative importance of state grants has fallen to about 24 percent of locally generated revenue. Federal grants have followed a similar path: the relative importance rose steadily between 1965 and 1978, and has fallen since then.

Intergovernmental grants support dozens of local programs. The programs receiving the largest amount of grants are education (about 18 percent of all intergovernmental grants), public welfare (14 percent), housing and community devel-

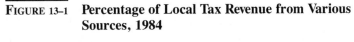

FIGURE 13–1   **Percentage of Local Tax Revenue from Various Sources, 1984**

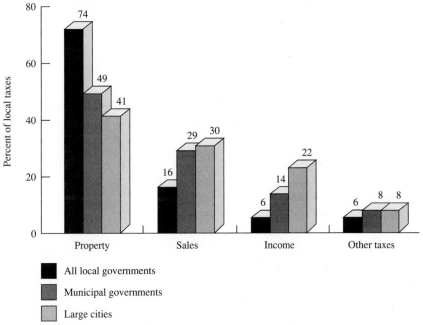

SOURCE: U.S. Bureau of the Census, *Census of Governments* and *City Government Finances in 1984–1985* (Washington, D.C.: U.S. Government Printing Office, 1987).

opment (10 percent), highways (8 percent), and health and hospitals (2 percent). The municipal spending programs that are most heavily dependent on intergovernmental grants are education (52 percent of spending from grants), welfare (76 percent), and housing and community development (62 percent) (U.S. Bureau of the Census, 1987).

The Role of Local Government

What is the role of local government in the market economy? This question can be answered by first asking two separate questions. First, what is the role of government in the market economy? Second, how does local government fit into the general scheme of government involvement?

Musgrave and Musgrave (1979) distinguish between three types of government policies. The first is stabilization policy: the government uses monetary and fiscal policy to control unemployment and inflation. Under the second type of

FIGURE 13-2   Federal and State Grants to Cities as Percentages of Locally Generated Revenue, 1965–1988

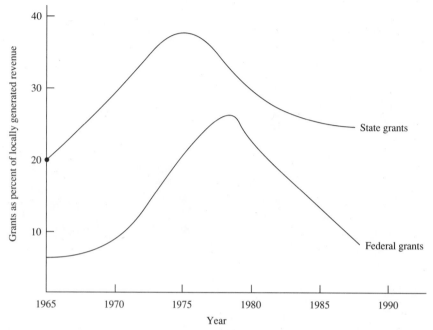

SOURCE: Helen Ladd and John Yinger, *America's Ailing Cities: Fiscal Health and the Design of Urban Policy* (Baltimore, Md.: Johns Hopkins University Press, 1989).

policy, income redistribution, the government uses taxes and transfers to alter the distributions of income and wealth. The third policy is resource allocation: the government makes decisions about what to produce and how to produce it. When the government actually produces a particular good or service, it makes these resource-allocation decisions directly. When the government subsidizes or taxes private activities, it influences the resource-allocation decisions of the private sector.

How do local governments fit into this three-part scheme of governmental activity? The responsibility for stabilization policy has been assumed by the national government for two reasons. First, although each local government could print its own money and execute its own monetary policy, such a system would be chaotic. Instead, the national government prints the money and manages a national monetary policy. Second, because a large fraction of local income is spent on goods produced outside the local area, local monetary and fiscal policies would be relatively weak and ineffective. Consider a city that wants to stimulate the local economy and tries to do so by cutting its taxes without changing its spending on local public goods. This deficit-spending policy will be ineffective because a large fraction of the tax cut will be spent on imports, so the tax cut will have a relatively small local multiplier effect. Fiscal policy is more effective at the national level because a relatively small fraction of national income is spent on imports, so a national tax cut has a relatively large multiplier effect.

Consider next the distribution role of government. Local attempts to redistribute income will be frustrated by the mobility of taxpayers and transfer recipients. Suppose that a city imposes a tax on its wealthy citizens and uses the tax revenue to finance transfer payments to the poor. To escape the tax, some wealthy households will leave the city, causing a decrease in total tax revenue. At the same time, some poor households will migrate to the relatively generous city, causing a decrease in the transfer payment per recipient. In combination, the fleeing of the wealthy and the in-migration of the poor weakens the city's redistribution program: there is less money to transfer to more poor households. A national redistribution program is more effective because there is less mobility between nations than between cities.

The third role of government is resource allocation. As shown in Table 13–2, local governments are responsible for the provision of several goods and services, including education, highways, police and fire protection, parks, and sewers. Under what conditions can government provision of these goods be justified on efficiency grounds? There are three possibilities. First, the good may be produced under conditions that generate a natural monopoly. Second, the good may generate positive externalities. Finally, the good may have the characteristics of a local public good.

Natural Monopoly

A natural monopoly occurs if the production of a particular good is subject to scale economies large enough that it is efficient to have a single producer serve the entire market. For example, there are large scale economies in the provision of sewage services, so a single sewage operation could serve the city more efficiently than a system with several operations. Similarly, if there are large scale economies in the provision of mass transit, a single transit system could produce at a relatively low average cost. As explained in Chapter 16 (Mass Transit), some policymakers have questioned the conventional wisdom that mass transit is a natural monopoly.

The government has several options for dealing with a natural monopoly. First, the government can provide the service itself and make all the decisions concerning its provision. Second, the government can get a private firm to provide the service subject to regulations concerning price and quantity.

What level of government should operate or regulate a natural monopoly? Should sewage and transit services be run by local, metropolitan, regional, state, or national governments? The appropriate level of government depends in part on the extent of scale economies: the greater the scale economies, the larger the political jurisdiction required to realize the scale economies associated with providing the service. As explained later in this chapter, the optimum level of government depends on other factors as well. In general, local governments are responsible for the provision and regulation of services for which scale economies are exhausted at the local level.

Externalities

One of the roles of government is to internalize externalities. An externality occurs if one person's consumption of a good generates benefits or costs for other people. The basic efficiency rule is that an activity should be increased to the point at which the marginal social benefit equals the marginal social cost. An externality causes a divergence between private and social benefits or private and social costs. Individual consumers, who base their decisions on private benefits and costs, will make choices that are inefficient from the social perspective. When this occurs, government intervention may promote efficiency.

Education Externalities.   To explain the role of local government in addressing externalities, consider education. In addition to the private benefits that go to the student, education generates external benefits for the student's fellow workers and fellow citizens. As a person becomes more educated, he becomes a better team worker: he understands instructions more readily and is more likely to suggest ways to improve production. In addition, a more educated citizen is more likely to make wise choices on election day, generating external benefits for his fellow citizens. Because education generates workplace and civic externalities, the marginal social benefit of education exceeds the marginal private benefit. In the absence of government intervention, the worker-citizen will ignore these external benefits and is likely to choose less than the optimum level of education.

The government has two options to solve the externality problem. The first is to assume responsibility for providing the good. A system of free compulsory education could encourage citizens to consume more education. Alternatively, the government could subsidize education, encouraging citizens to consume more education while allowing them to choose their own schools. As discussed in Chapter 17 (Education), there is heated debate over whether the government should supplement the public school system with subsidies for private education (tuition tax credits and education vouchers).

What level of government should control externalities? Should the school system (or education subsidies) be managed by local, metropolitan, regional, state, or national governments? One factor in determining the optimum level of government is the geographical extent of the externalities. If people throughout the country benefit from the education of its children, national participation in education decisions (e.g., national schools or a national subsidy) may promote efficiency. On the other hand, if the benefits are confined to a particular city or municipality, local decision making may be efficient. As explained later in this chapter, there are other factors that affect the optimum level of government.

Public Safety Externalities.   Spending on police protection generates positive and negative externalities. Both types of externalities occur because criminals can move from one jurisdiction to another. The positive externality occurs when one municipality uses its police force to capture a criminal: by doing so, the municipality generates benefits for the surrounding municipalities, so the marginal social benefit of police spending exceeds the marginal local (municipal) benefit. The negative externality occurs when one municipality's crime-fighting activities cause criminals to victimize people in the surrounding localities. In other words, the police sometimes chase criminals from one municipality to another. In this case, the police just move crime around, so the marginal local benefit of police spending exceeds the marginal social benefit.

What is the optimum level of government for police protection? One factor in determining the appropriate level of government is the geographical extent of the positive and negative externalities. The greater the mobility of criminals, the larger the jurisdiction required to contain all the people affected by crime-fighting activities. As explained later in this chapter, there are other factors that affect the optimum level of government. In most metropolitan areas, police services are provided by the municipal government.

Characteristics of a Local Public Good

A local public good has three characteristics. First, it is **nonrivalrous** in consumption: several people can consume the same good at the same time. Second, it is **nonexcludable:** it is impossible or impractical to exclude some people (e.g., those who do not pay for the good) from consuming the good. Third, the benefits of the good are confined to a relatively small geographical area.

Nonrivalrous Consumption (Joint Consumption).   Consider first the issue of rivalry in consumption. A private good (a hot dog) can be consumed by only one person. In contrast, a public good can be consumed by many people at the same time. For example, hundreds of people can watch a parade without interfering with each other's enjoyment of the parade. In other words, a parade is subject to **joint consumption:** everyone can consume the same good. The parade is a **pure local public good** if the marginal cost of an additional parade viewer is zero. This occurs if an additional viewer does not decrease the enjoyment of other parade viewers.

Many of the goods provided by local governments are semirivalrous. If the number of consumers becomes large enough, an individual consumer's benefit decreases. For example, if the city does not set up bleachers for parade viewers, tall people block the views of short people. This is a problem only if the number of parade viewers is so large that short citizens do not get a front-row view. In this case, the parade is an **impure,** or **congestable, public good**. Other examples of impure public goods are city streets and highways: during the peak travel periods, travel speeds decrease as traffic volume increases, so the benefit of using the highway decreases as the number of consumers increases.

What about police and fire services? Although two citizens cannot use a police officer or a fire truck at the same time, public safety systems are designed to respond quickly to emergencies. Most cities have enough police officers and fire trucks to simultaneously handle a reasonable number of calls for help. If everyone called at once, consumption would, of course, be rivalrous, but not everyone needs safety services at the same time.

Nonexcludability.   The second characteristic of a local public good is that it would be impractical to exclude some people from consuming the good. In other words, the good is nonexcludable. Consider the parade example. Although it may be possible to charge everyone for watching the parade and exclude those who don't pay, it would be very costly to do so. The government would have to first empty the streets and buildings along the parade route, and then admit people who paid a parade-viewing fee. If some people promised not to watch the parade, they might be permitted to enter a building along the route, but the government would have to find a way to prevent them from sneaking a look. Such a scheme would obviously be impractical.

What about streets and public parks? One way to charge people for using city streets would be to set up a system of toll booths, one on each corner. Such a system would be costly: the city would have to hire a large number of toll collectors, and road users would incur substantial time costs in stopping at every corner to pay the tolls. Chapter 15 (Autos and Highways) describes a low-cost system for charging drivers for using streets and highways. There is little political support for such a system, so streets are likely to remain nonexcludable. The same argument applies to parks. Although it might be possible to install fences and turnstiles in city parks, such a system would be relatively costly.

What about public safety services? For some safety activities, it would be easy to identify the beneficiaries and send them a bill for the safety services rendered. For example, the fire department could charge a fee for putting out fires, and the police could charge a fee for responding to burglaries and robberies. Under such a system, the fire and police departments would not provide services to people who could not afford the service fees. This system of user charges is politically infeasible because it would violate most people's notions of equity and fairness. For other types of safety activities, it would be more difficult to identify the beneficiaries and charge for the safety services. For example, when a city captures, prosecutes, and imprisons a criminal, every potential crime victim benefits. Other examples are crowd and traffic control. For these services, it would be impractical to exclude people who do not pay.

Localized Benefits.   The third characteristic of a local public good is that its benefits are confined to a relatively small geographical area. Unlike national defense, which generates benefits for the entire nation, most of the benefits of the local police force and local fire department go to local citizens. Similarly, local citizens get most of the benefits from local streets and highways. The appropriate size of the jurisdiction is determined by the "localness" of the public good (the geographical extent of the benefits from the public good): the more extensive the benefits, the larger the jurisdiction required to contain all the beneficiaries.

The Tiebout Model of Community Formation

Most metropolitan areas in the United States have dozens of municipalities, school districts, and other local governments. A model developed by Tiebout (1956) shows the role of consumer choice in the development of our fragmented system of local governments. The idea is that people vote with their feet, choosing the local government that provides the best combination of taxes and local public goods. One of the implications of the Tiebout model is that interjurisdictional mobility (voting with feet) may promote efficiency in the provision of local public goods.

The Simple Model

There are five assumptions in the simple version of the Tiebout model:

1. **Jurisdictional choice.** A household "shops" for a local government and chooses the jurisdiction that provides the ideal level of local public goods. There are enough jurisdictions to ensure that every household finds the perfect jurisdiction.
2. **Information and mobility.** All citizens have access to all relevant information about the alternative jurisdictions, and moving is costless.
3. **No interjurisdictional spillovers.** There are no spillovers (externalities) associated with local public goods: all the benefits from local public goods accrue to citizens within the local jurisdiction.
4. **No scale economies.** The average cost of production is independent of output.
5. **Head taxes.** Local governments impose head taxes to pay for public goods: if you have a head, you pay the head tax.

Citizens in the Tiebout world sort themselves into municipalities and school districts according to their demands for local public goods. For example, a household with a relatively low demand for parks chooses a municipality with a relatively small park budget (and a relatively low head tax). Other households with similar preferences choose the same municipality. Similarly, households with relatively large demands for parks collect in a municipality with a relatively large park budget. In equilibrium, there is a large number of local jurisdictions, each of which provides a different level of public services to its homogeneous population. Citizens vote with their feet and sort themselves into jurisdictions that are homogeneous with respect to the demand for public services.

The simple model suggests that shopping and sorting increase the efficiency of local governments. If there were no shopping and sorting, local jurisdictions would be heterogeneous, with different households demanding different levels of public services. There is no reason to expect the citizens in a diverse municipality to agree on the efficient level of public services. Under the Tiebout process, households sort themselves into homogeneous communities, so citizens in each community agree on how much to spend. In the absence of externalities, they choose the efficient level of public services.

Tiebout Model with Property Taxes

Hamilton (1975) made the Tiebout model more realistic by introducing property taxes into the model. His model assumes that local governments finance their spending programs with a property tax, not a head tax. To explain the effects of the property tax, consider a municipality with the following characteristics:

1. Every household demands $500 worth of spending on parks.
2. There are two income groups: the wealthy live in $75,000 houses, and the poor live in $25,000 houses.
3. Under a head tax, every household pays $500 in local taxes to support the local park system.

Suppose that the municipality switches from a $500 head tax to a 1 percent property tax. Under the property tax, each wealthy household will pay $750 in taxes (up from $500), and each poor household will pay $250 (down from $500).

How does the property tax affect location choices? The wealthy, who now pay $750 for $500 worth of parks, will try to decrease their tax liabilities. One option is to set up a new municipality for wealthy households. If every household in the new wealthy municipality owns a house worth $75,000, a property tax of 0.667 percent will generate a tax bill of $500 per household. In other words, if the wealthy households form an exclusive municipality, they will again pay $500 in taxes for $500 worth of parks.

How do the wealthy establish their exclusive suburb? If it were legal, they might simply outlaw houses worth less than $75,000, thus guaranteeing that every household would pay at least $500 in taxes. Because this is illegal, they use **large-lot zoning:** the municipality establishes a minimum lot size for every dwelling. Since land and housing are complementary goods, the municipality can control housing consumption by controlling land consumption. One rule of thumb is that the market value of land is about one fifth of the total property value (the value of the structure and the land). If the price of land is $30,000 per acre, a half-acre lot ($15,000 worth of land) will generate a property value of $75,000 (five times $15,000). Therefore, a minimum lot size of half an acre will meet the target property value.

What about the poor people who remain in the original municipality? The wealthy households will eventually be replaced by poor households in less expensive housing. The average property value in the original municipality will decrease, requiring an increase in the tax rate to generate $500 of taxes per household. If the average property value falls to $25,000, the property tax rate will rise to 2 percent.

The switch from the head tax to the property tax causes households to sort themselves with respect to housing consumption. There is one community for households with a large demand for housing and one for households with a small demand for housing. This sorting occurs because tax liabilities are based on housing consumption. If the municipalities were to tax Spam instead of housing, citizens would sort themselves into two communities, one where people consume large quantities of Spam and one where people consume small quantities.

The switch from a head tax to a property tax increases the equilibrium number of municipalities. Citizens sort themselves with respect to two characteristics: the demand for local public goods and the demand for housing. The equilibrium number of municipalities depends on the number of housing types and the number of public-good types. Suppose that there are three income groups (rich, middle-income, and poor) and three types of houses—large (occupied by the wealthy), medium (middle-income), and small (poor). Suppose further that for each income group, there are two different levels of demand for public goods: some households in each income group have relatively high demands for local public goods, and others have relatively low demands. Given these assumptions, there will be six communities: three high-spending municipalities (one with large houses, one with medium houses, and one with small houses), and three low-spending municipalities. If local governments used a head tax instead of a property tax, there would be only two municipalities, a high-spending one and a low-spending one.

Evidence of Shopping and Sorting

There is a good deal of evidence that citizens shop for municipalities and school districts. Using data for the New York metropolitan area, Oates (1969) estimated the relationship between housing values, taxes, and school expenditures. He found that communities with relatively low tax rates had higher property values. This result suggests that people shop for school districts, bidding up the price of housing in areas with favorable combinations of taxes and local public goods. In other words, differences in taxes and expenditures are capitalized into housing values.

There is also evidence that citizens sort themselves with respect to their demands for local public goods. Gramlich and Rubinfeld (1982) examined the tastes for local public goods in different metropolitan areas. In a metropolitan area with a single large municipality, households have no opportunity for shopping, so the single municipality will contain households with a wide variety of demands for local public services. In contrast, if the metropolitan area has a large number of jurisdictions, each household can pick a municipality that provides the preferred level of public services, so households will sort themselves into homogeneous communities. Using data from questionnaires, Gramlich and Rubinfeld concluded that the greater the number of municipalities to choose from, the more homogeneous the demand for local public goods within each municipality.

The Tiebout process is primarily a suburban phenomenon. In the suburbs, households can choose from dozens of municipalities and school districts. In the central city, there is typically a single large jurisdiction. One reason for the suburbanization of population is that the only option for central-city foot voters is to move to a suburban municipality. If large central-city governments were broken up into smaller municipalities, central-city residents would be able to vote with their feet without moving to the suburbs.

Critique of the Tiebout Model

Like any simple model, the Tiebout model can be criticized on a number of grounds. Some of the model's assumptions are unrealistic. For example, the model assumes that households are perfectly informed and perfectly mobile, so they can easily change jurisdictions if they become dissatisfied with their local government. This is clearly unrealistic: information about alternative locations is costly to acquire, and moving costs are large. As discussed in Chapter 12 (Housing Policies), most households tolerate some dissatisfaction with their dwelling because moving is costly. In the context of the Tiebout model, a household that is unhappy with its local government will change jurisdictions only if the benefits from moving to a different jurisdiction are large enough to offset the associated moving costs. Although the shopping and sorting predicted by the Tiebout model certainly occurs, the matching of households and jurisdictions is by no means perfect.

Another assumption of the Tiebout model is that there are enough local governments to allow every household to pick the ideal jurisdiction. In the Tiebout world, every household finds a local government that spends exactly the right amount on every public good. This is clearly unrealistic: there are simply not enough local jurisdictions to provide every household with the ideal level of every public good. This problem is complicated by the use of the property tax: if local governments use the property tax instead of a head tax, households must also sort themselves with respect to house value. If there are not enough jurisdictions to allow every household to choose the ideal jurisdiction, citizens will compromise on their ideal tax-spending package, choosing a jurisdiction that comes closest to their ideal package. Households will then express their preferences for local public goods in local budget elections: after the household votes with its feet, it starts voting with ballots.

A final criticism of the Tiebout model concerns its efficiency implications. The model suggests that the fragmented system of local government is efficient because the sorting of households allows each household to consume its ideal level of local public goods. A key assumption of the model is that local public goods do not generate interjurisdictional externalities: all the benefits and costs of local public goods are confined within the local jurisdiction, regardless of the size of the jurisdiction. In the Tiebout world, even a one-person jurisdiction is efficient: the model assumes that all the benefits of spending on police, fire protection, sewage, and education would be confined to the single person in the jurisdiction. Under this assumption, there is no real difference between local public goods and private goods. Therefore, the household's choice of a jurisdiction, however small it might be, is just as efficient as its choice of private goods.

The goods provided by local governments are indeed different from private goods. Some of the goods are nonrivalrous in consumption. When a small municipality uses its police force to capture a criminal, people outside the municipality benefit. The municipality will ignore these external benefits and will therefore spend too little on police services. Some goods provided by local governments generate externalities for people in surrounding areas. If a child educated in one city moves to another city as an adult, workers and citizens in the second city benefit from the education program of the first. An individual city will ignore the benefits of its education program on outsiders and will therefore spend too little on eduction. In general, the goods provided by local governments are nonrivalrous and generate externalities, so the fragmented system of local governments generated by the Tiebout process may be inefficient.

Federalism and the Optimum Level of Government

Under the federal system of government, the responsibility for providing public goods is divided between the federal, state, and local governments. Some goods, such as defense and space exploration, are provided at the national level. Others, such as education and police protection, are provided at the local level. Why are some public goods provided by local governments rather than state or federal governments?

Oates (1972) discusses the advantages and disadvantages of the local provision of public goods:

1. **Diversity in demand.** A system of small local governments allows communities to choose different levels of spending on public goods (parks, public safety, education, libraries). Because local governments can accommodate the diverse demands for public goods, they promote efficiency.

2. **Externalities.** If the local jurisdiction is not large enough to contain all the people affected by its spending programs, there are externalities (benefit spillovers). Under a system of small local governments, local voters ignore the benefits that accrue to people outside the jurisdiction and therefore make inefficient choices.

3. **Scale economies.** If there are scale economies in the provision of public goods, a system of small local governments has relatively high production costs.

The local provision of a public good is efficient if the advantages outweigh the disadvantages. In other words, local provision is efficient if (a) diversity in demand is relatively large, (b) externalities are relatively small, and (c) scale economies are relatively small.

Metropolitan Consolidation

Should local governments be consolidated into metropolitan governments? Four arguments have been advanced in support of metropolitan consolidation: suburban exploitation could be prevented, scale economies could be exploited, tax rates could be equalized, and spending could be equalized.

Prevention of Suburban Exploitation

According to the suburban exploitation hypothesis, suburban commuters do not pay their "fair share" of the costs of central-city public services. Consider a worker who commutes from her suburban home to the city. Although she uses city services (streets, water, fire protection, police protection), she pays her property taxes to a suburban government. Does the commuter "exploit" central-city residents by using city services without paying for them?

The exploitation hypothesis ignores the fact that commuters pay taxes to the city. As shown in Chapter 14 (Local Taxes and Intergovernmental Grants), over two fifths of municipal tax revenue comes from sales and income taxes, meaning that suburbanites who work and shop in the city center pay taxes to city governments. For large cities (population greater than 300,000), sales and income tax generate over half of the municipal tax revenue. In addition, most cities have user fees for public services (tolls, admission prices for zoos and museums), so suburbanites pay directly for some city services. Most studies of the exploitation hypothesis suggest that suburbanites pay close to their share of the costs of city services (see Bradford and Oates, 1974, for a review of these studies).

Exploitation of Scale Economies

Another argument advanced in favor of consolidation is that a metropolitan government can exploit scale economies in the provision of public services and thus provide public services at a lower cost. The scale-economy argument is incomplete. The switch to metropolitan government requires communities to compromise on their ideal levels of public goods, so the cost savings from scale economies must be compared to the welfare losses resulting from the uniform provision of public goods. Metropolitan consolidation will be efficient if scale economies are large relative to the diversity in demand.

Equalization of Tax Rates

Under a system of fragmented local government, municipalities with large tax bases often have relatively low tax rates. Under a metropolitan government, there would be a single property-tax base and thus a single tax rate. Therefore, the switch from a municipal system to a metropolitan government would increase tax rates in relatively wealthy communities and would decrease tax rates in relatively poor communities.

To what extent does the equalization of tax rates redistribute income from the wealthy to the poor? Consider a metropolitan area with two municipalities, one with middle-income households and one with poor households. Everyone in the poor municipality lives in rental housing, and every household in the middle-income municipality owns the home it occupies. The poor community has a low tax base and a high tax rate, and the middle-income community has a large tax base and a low tax rate. Therefore, metropolitan consolidation increases property taxes in the middle-income community and decreases taxes in the poor community.

The changes in tax liabilities affect housing prices and property values in the two communities. In the poor community, the tax cut increases the profitability of housing, so the supply of housing increases and the price of housing (monthly rent) falls. Therefore, tenants benefit from the tax cut. Property owners also benefit: the decrease in the tax on rental housing increases the net income from rental property, increasing market values. This is the **capitalization** process: changes in tax liabilities are capitalized into property values. In the middle-income community, homeowners face higher tax liabilities, so their property values fall.

Who gains and who loses as a result of the equalization of taxes? Tenants and landlords in the poor community gain: the tenants pay lower rent, and the landlords have higher property values. Homeowners in the middle-income community lose because their property values fall. To predict the distributional effect of the equalization of tax rates, one needs information on the income levels of tenants, landlords, and homeowners. If landlords in the poor community are relatively wealthy, the equalization of tax rates could actually increase income inequality.

Equalization of Spending

Under the fragmented system of local government, spending varies within the metropolitan area, reflecting variation in the demands for public services. The consolidation of local government would equalize spending on local public goods. Because spending on public services typically increases with income, metropolitan consolidation would narrow the spending gap between wealthy and poor communities.

Bradford and Oates (1974) explored the effects of metropolitan consolidation in northeastern New Jersey. They predicted the effects of consolidating 58 local jurisdictions (5 central cities and 53 suburban governments) into a single metropolitan government.

Bradford and Oates evaluated the trade-offs associated with the equalization of educational spending. To explain their results, suppose that there are only two school districts, a wealthy one and a poor one. Before consolidation, the wealthy community spends $3,000 per pupil on education, and the poor one spends $2,600. Suppose that under the consolidated government, spending is equalized at $2,800 per pupil: spending increases by $200 in the poor district and decreases by the same amount in the wealthy district. According to Bradford and Oates, the extra $200 of education spending is worth only about $130 to the typical poor household: the household would be indifferent between receiving $200 in educational spending and $130 in cash. In contrast, the typical wealthy household would be indifferent between losing $200 in educational spending and giving up $230 in cash. Therefore, the equalization program produces a $130 benefit (to poor households) at a cost of $230 (to wealthy households).

Using the Bradford-Oates numbers, the equalization program seems to be foolish. Both the poor and the wealthy would be better off if the government used cash transfers—not education spending—to redistribute income. For example, if the government took just $130 from the wealthy and gave it to the poor, the poor would be just as well off, but the wealthy would be better off by $100.

This simplistic analysis is deceptive. As pointed out by Bradford and Oates, these calculations ignore the external benefits of education. As explained earlier in this chapter, education generates externalities, so individual households spend less than the optimum amount on education. The question is whether the external benefits of the equalization program are large enough to offset the private costs. Suppose that the equalization program increases the educational achievement of the poor by a relatively large amount. The net external benefit is defined as the external benefit of extra education for the poor less the external cost of less education for the wealthy. If the net external benefit is relatively large, the apparent inefficiency of the equalization program disappears: the equalization program would not be foolish, but would promote efficiency.

Another possible justification for the equalization program is that education may be a **merit good**, defined as a good that is assumed to be systematically undervalued by consumers. If individuals do not make rational choices concerning education, their willingness to pay for education understates the private value of education. In the example above, perhaps the poor don't realize that they would actually receive a benefit of $190 from the increase in education spending. If so, it wouldn't take much of an external benefit to make the equalization program socially efficient. The notion of a merit good can also be stated in terms of the willingness to donate: if the donors (the people in the wealthy school district) are allowed to make choices for the recipients (in the poor district), they are willing to donate more. They may be willing to give only $50 in cash, but $200 in extra education. If so, everyone is better off under the equalization program than they would be under the cash transfer program.

Alternatives to Metropolitan Consolidation

An alternative to metropolitan consolidation is a **metropolitan federation.** Under a federated government, a metropolitan government would be responsible for the provision of goods with large scale economies (e.g., water and sewage systems, sanitation, highways, transit). Municipalities would continue to provide goods with relatively small scale economies (e.g., schools, police and fire protection, parks). The Toronto area established a federated government in 1954.

Another alternative to metropolitan consolidation is to contract with another level of government to provide public services. According to a recent survey conducted by the Advisory Commission on Intergovernmental Relations (ACIR, 1983), over half of all U.S. cities provided some public services under intergovernmental contracts (under which one unit of government arranges with another to provide a public service), and over half used joint-service contracts (under which two or more governmental units join to produce a public service). Both types of arrangements allow a relatively small jurisdiction to realize scale economies in the provision of public services.

The Growth in Local Spending

As mentioned earlier in this chapter, local spending rose from 5 percent of GNP in 1950 to around 8 percent in the 1980s. This section explores some of the reasons for this growth in local public spending. Because total spending equals the quantity of output times unit cost, an increase in spending could be caused by an increase in unit cost, an increase in the quantity produced, or increases in both cost and quantity.

Increases in Labor Cost: The Baumol Model

Baumol (1967) argues that rising labor costs have contributed to increases in local spending. To explain the Baumol model, consider an economy that produces manufactured goods (watches) and personal services (haircuts, public education). The labor market has the following characteristics:

1. **Manufacturing productivity.** The productivity of manufacturing workers increases over time, a result of innovations that allow the substitution of capital for labor.
2. **Service productivity.** The productivity of service workers (barbers and teachers) is constant. A haircut is a nonstandardized good: every head has a different shape, and every customer wants a unique haircut. Since a barber cannot be replaced by a machine, productivity is constant. Like the barber, the teacher provides a nonstandardized output: every child enters the classroom with a different set of skills and educational needs, and requires personal attention. In addition, every child requires a different educational output. Given the difficulty of capital substitution, teacher productivity is constant.
3. **Worker mobility and wages.** Workers move costlessly between manufacturing and service jobs. In equilibrium, all workers earn the same daily wage.
4. **Fixed labor supply.** The total supply of workers is fixed.

Figure 13–3 shows the market for labor in the two-sector economy. The demand curves for both manufacturing and services are negatively sloped. In the initial equilibrium (points *B* and *C*), the wage is $13.

Suppose that the productivity of manufacturing workers increases. An increase in productivity shifts the demand curve for manufacturing workers to the right: at every wage, more workers are demanded. In the short run, the supply of manufacturing workers is fixed, so the manufacturing wage rises to $17 (point *F*).

In the long run, the increase in the manufacturing wage causes some service workers to switch to manufacturing jobs. As the quantity of manufacturing workers increases, the manufacturing wage drops: the market moves downward along the new demand curve from point *F* toward point *D*. In addition, the decrease in the number of service workers causes a shortage of service workers, so the service wage increases: the market moves up the service demand curve, from point *C* toward point *E*. Equilibrium is restored when two conditions are satisfied. First, total employment in the two sectors equals the fixed supply of labor ($M° + S°$). Second, workers are indifferent between the two types of jobs. Workers will be indifferent if the two sectors pay the same wage. These two conditions are satisfied at points *D* and *E*.

What are the implications for the prices of manufacturing goods and services? Because the productivity of manufacturing workers increases over time, the increase in the wage is offset by increases in labor productivity, so production costs and market prices do not change. In contrast, the wages of service work-

FIGURE 13–3   Effects of Increased Manufacturing Productivity on Wages in the Service Sector

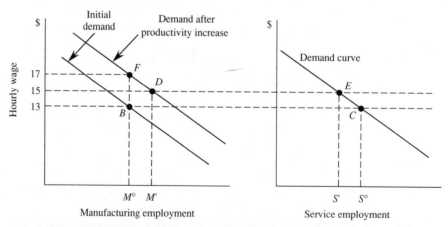

In the initial equilibrium (points *B* and *C*), the wage is $13. An increase in manufacturing productivity shifts the demand curve for manufacturing workers upward, causing excess demand for labor. As the manufacturing wage rises, service workers move to the manufacturing sector, causing a labor shortage in the service sector that increases the wage. In the new equilibrium (points *D* and *E*), the wage is $15.

ers increase while their productivity is constant, so production costs and market prices increase over time. In other words, the price of haircuts and the unit cost of education increase over time.

Other local public goods share the personal-service features of haircuts and education. Consider the costs of police protection. Police officers interview witnesses and look for clues at the scene of the crime. Neither of these tasks can be performed by a machine, so the growth in police productivity is relatively slow. The same is true for fire fighting: every fire presents a different set of circumstances, preventing the sort of capital substitution that occurs in the manufacturing sector. If the productivities of police and fire fighters are constant, an increase in wages (caused by an increase in the wage of manufacturers) increases the costs of police and fire protection.

Other Reasons for Rising Labor Cost

The Baumol model suggests that the labor costs of government increase because the government provides personal-service goods, not because public servants are lazy or greedy. There are two other possible reasons for increases in labor costs:

1. **Competition and innovation.** The nature of the public sector discourages innovation. Unlike a firm in a competitive market, the local government is shielded from competition, so there is less incentive to develop new labor-saving techniques. If this view is correct, the monopoly status of local government prevents innovations that would increase labor productivity.

2. **Union power.** Most government workers are represented by powerful labor unions. If unions use their power to increase the wages of government workers, public servants will be overpaid relative to their private-sector counterparts, increasing the costs of government. Freeman (1985) examined the wages of private and government employees. He compared the wages of public and private workers with similar qualifications (education, work experience, personal characteristics). He found that state and local administrators earn about 5 percent more than equally qualified private-sector workers, and public school teachers earn about 6 percent less than equally qualified private workers. On balance, it appears that the differences between private and government wages are relatively small. Freeman did not include pension plans in his analysis. Since public pension plans are generally more generous than private plans, the inclusion of pension benefits would increase public-sector wages relative to private-sector wages.

Increases in Quantity

An increase in local spending may be caused, in part, by an increase in the quantity of local services demanded. The Baumol model provides a useful framework for analyzing changes in the quantity of local public goods.

Under what circumstances does the quantity of education demanded increase over time? The demand for education changes over time for two reasons. The first is the **income effect.** The increase in manufacturing productivity increases the real income of the economy: the total output of the economy increases, increasing the purchasing power of its citizens. As real income increases, the citizens spend more on all normal goods, including education. In Figure 13–4, the demand curve for education shifts to the right: at every price, more education is demanded. At P', the quantity of education increases from $E°$ to E'.

The **substitution effect** causes movement upward along the new demand curve. Because the productivity of manufacturing workers increases while the productivity of teachers is constant, the price of education increases relative to the price of other goods. As a result, consumers substitute manufactured goods for education (and other personal-service goods), decreasing the quantity of education demanded. In Figure 13–4, the price of education increases from P' to P'', and the substitution effect causes movement upward along the new demand curve from point C to D.

FIGURE 13–4   Changes in Quantity of Education Demanded

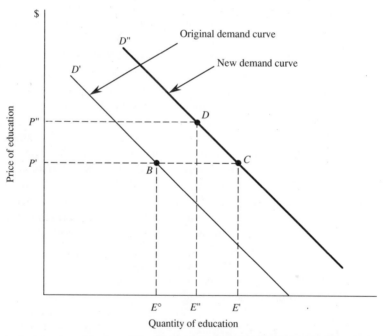

An increase in real income shifts the demand curve for education outward and increases the quantity demanded (the income effect: B to C). If the unit cost (price) of education increases from P' to P'', the quantity demanded decreases (the substitution effect: C to D). In this case, the income effect is large relative to the substitution effect, so the quantity demanded increases (B to D).

Figure 13–4 shows a net increase in the quantity of education demanded from E° to E''. The income effect (the outward shift of the demand curve) dominates the substitution effect (the upward movement along the new demand curve), so the equilibrium quantity of education increases. This occurs under the assumption that the income elasticity of demand for education is large relative to the price elasticity of demand. Total spending on education increases: the community consumes more education (E'' instead of E°) at a higher unit cost (P'' instead of P').

Another possibility is that the quantity of education demanded decreases over time. If the income effect is small relative to the substitution effect (if the income elasticity is small relative to the price elasticity), the outward shift of the demand curve would be small relative to the movement up the new demand curve, and the quantity of education demanded would decrease. If this happens, total expenditures on education may either increase or decrease. If the decrease in the quantity demanded is large enough to offset the increase in unit cost, total expenditures would decrease. But if the decrease in quantity demanded is relatively small, total expenditures would increase.

Taxpayer Revolt: Expenditure Limits

The share of GNP spent on local government has decreased since 1976. The decrease in the relative importance of local spending was caused in part by new restrictions on local taxes and spending. By 1981, a total of 30 states had tightened restrictions on local tax rates, tax revenue, and spending. According to Aronson and Hilley (1986), there is evidence that tax and expenditure limits have decreased local spending in Arizona, California, Colorado, Indiana, Iowa, and New Jersey.

Aronson and Hilley discuss the responses of local governments to the tax and expenditure limitations. Local governments have mitigated the effects of the limitations in four ways:

1. Local governments have shifted to user fees and taxes that are not subject to restrictions (income, sales, and business taxes).
2. Some spending programs have been transferred to special districts to evade the spending limits.
3. Intergovernmental grants from state governments have increased.
4. In cases where limits apply to specific spending categories, programs have been moved from restricted categories to unrestricted ones.

The debate over tax and spending limitations has been spirited. The supporters of limitations view local governments as inefficient monopolies. According to this view, the limitations force local governments to "cut out the fat" by increasing productivity and decreasing wages. According to Courant, Gramlich, and Rubinfeld (1987), many of the people who vote for tax and spending limitations hold this view.

The critics of tax and spending limitations believe that the Baumol model is applicable to the local public sector. They believe that the cost of local services has increased because of rising productivity in the private sector, not because public workers are lazy and wasteful. According to this view, there is little "fat" in the local public budget, so the spending limitations decrease the quantity of local public services. Another concern is that local tax limitations may increase the state involvement in local budget choices, decreasing local control of tax money.

Fiscal Health of Central Cities

Since the early 1970s, many cities have experienced serious fiscal problems. The most sensational episode was the near default of New York City in 1975. In many other cities, tax revenues have fallen short of the amount required to provide the typical or average level of public services, requiring either tax hikes or service cuts to prevent budget deficits. This part of the chapter explores some of reasons for the fiscal problems experienced by central cities in the last few decades.

The most severe fiscal problems have been experienced by large, older cities in the northeastern and north-central states. There are several reasons for the fiscal problems of these cities:

1. **Suburbanization and the tax base.** The suburbanization of employment and population has decreased the cities' tax bases (income, property, sales), decreasing tax revenue.

2. **Increase in production costs.** As the population of a city falls, the costs of urban services do not necessarily fall at the same rate. The reason is simple: if a city invests in plant and equipment for a city of 5 million, it pays the same capital costs for its streets, transit systems, schools, and fire stations even if its population drops to 4 million. A decrease in population increases per capita costs because there are fewer "capitas" to pay the costs.

3. **Inflexible labor force.** In some cities, labor unions are powerful enough to prevent layoffs when the city's population decreases. If a city maintains a constant work force as it shrinks, a fiscal squeeze is inevitable.

Peterson (1976) examined the sources of fiscal distress in declining cities during the 1970s. Compared to growing cities, declining cities had (a) larger public expenditures per capita, (b) more municipal employees per capita, (c) higher municipal wages, and (d) declining real tax bases. Why did declining cities have higher wages? According to Peterson, cities used the large federal grants of the 1960s and 1970s to increase the wages of municipal workers.

Ladd and Yinger (1989) developed an index of fiscal health and estimated the index for dozens of the nation's central cities. Figure 13–5 shows the values of the index for 19 of the cities. In the average city, the value of the index is zero. A city with a negative value is in worse shape than the average city; a city with a positive value is in better shape. The values of the index range from −87 in New Orleans to 49 in Greensboro, North Carolina. In the figure, cities are arranged, top to bottom, in decreasing order of total population. It's clear that the largest cities (at the top of the figure) are in the worst fiscal shape.

The Ladd-Yinger index is based on two assumptions. First, in each city, the tax system imposes the same burden on residents: residents of each city are assumed to pay 3 percent of their income in municipal taxes. Second, each city is assumed to provide the same level of public services. Under the assumption of a standardized package of taxes and services, this index shows the fiscal health of cities in the absence of intercity differences in taxes and spending.

The value of the fiscal health index indicates the fiscal deficit or surplus associated with the standard packages of taxes and services. If the value is negative,

FIGURE 13–5   **Standardized Fiscal Health of Selected Central Cities in 1988**

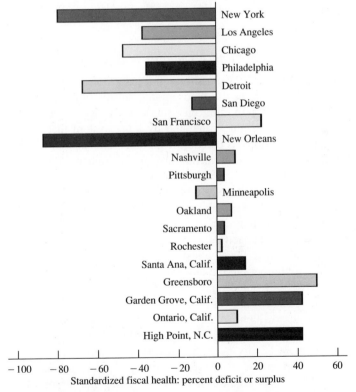

SOURCE: Helen Ladd and John Yinger, *America's Ailing Cities: Fiscal Health and the Design of Urban Policy* (Baltimore, Md.: Johns Hopkins University Press, 1989), Table E.1.

it indicates the percentage deficit resulting from the standard tax/service package. Alternatively, if the deficit is to be eliminated by intergovernmental grants, the index indicates the size of the transfer (as percent of local revenue) required to fill the gap between local tax revenue and the costs of providing the standard service level. For example, New York's value is −83: to provide the standard level of public services with the standard tax system, the city would need a transfer equal to 83 percent of its tax revenue. If the value of the index is positive, it indicates the percentage surplus resulting from the standard tax/spending package. For example, High Point's value is 41: if the city were to provide the standard service package, the standard tax system would generate a surplus of 41 percent.

The Ladd-Yinger index shows the effects of the economic environment on urban fiscal health. Since each city is assumed to provide the same services with the same tax system, fiscal problems are caused by either a relatively low tax base or a relatively high cost of providing the standard services. This approach ignores other possible sources of fiscal problems, including relatively low tax rates, relatively high service levels, or mismanagement. In the words of Ladd and Yinger, "We determine the fiscal cards each city is dealt; other approaches are needed to see how well each city plays its hand."

Revenue Capacity and Expenditure Needs

Ladd and Yinger (1989) examine both sides of the budget equation. The index of standardized fiscal health incorporates information about revenue-raising capacity and the costs of providing city services. A city's revenue-raising capacity is the amount of tax revenue generated by a tax system that imposes a burden on city residents equal to of 3 percent of income. The standard tax system includes taxes on property, sales, and earnings. A city's standardized expenditure need is determined by the cost of providing the standard set of city services. To be considered healthy in a fiscal sense, a city must have either a relatively large revenue-raising capacity or a relatively low standardized expenditure need, or both.

Table 13–4 shows the characteristics of cities with small, medium, and large revenue-raising capacities. Compared to the five cities with the highest capacities, the five cities with the smallest capacities have about half the capacity. The second column of numbers in the table shows that, in general, there is a positive relationship between revenue-raising capacity and per capita income. The third column of numbers shows the employment ratios, defined as the number of private-sector jobs per city resident. A large employment ratio means that a large fraction of the city's work force lives outside the city but pays city taxes on sales and earnings. The payment of city taxes by outsiders increases the revenue raised by the standard tax system, so the revenue-raising capacity increases with the employment ratio. The fourth column of numbers shows that larger cities tend to have lower revenue-raising capacities. The larger the central city, the smaller the fraction of city taxes paid by outsiders, so the smaller the revenue raised by the standard tax system.

TABLE 13-4   **Revenue-Raising Capacity and City Characteristics, 1982**

	Revenue-Raising Capacity	*Per Capita Income*	*Employment Ratio*	*Population (000)*
Small Capacity				
Memphis, Tennessee	$282	$ 7,542	0.41	645
Jacksonville, Florida	283	8,217	0.37	556
Philadelphia, Pennsylvania	292	7,109	0.36	1,665
Portsmouth, Virginia	306	7,382	0.22	105
Newark, New Jersey	309	5,292	0.41	320
Medium Capacity				
Cleveland, Ohio	409	6,799	0.58	588
Akron, Ohio	409	8,106	0.46	231
Ontario, Canada	409	7,967	0.21	96
Tampa, Florida	427	7,855	0.63	276
High Point, North Carolina	429	7,893	0.64	63
Large Capacity				
Rochester, New York	527	8,072	0.73	243
Albany, New York	565	8,305	0.60	100
Anaheim, California	590	10,149	0.61	226
Salt Lake City, Utah	591	8,765	0.92	163
Ft. Lauderdale, Florida	639	12,099	0.71	153
Average for small	294	7,108	0.35	658
Average for medium	417	7,724	0.50	245
Average for large	582	9,478	0.71	177

SOURCE: Helen F. Ladd and John Yinger, *America's Ailing Cities: Fiscal Health and the Design of the Urban Policy* (Baltimore, Md.: Johns Hopkins University Press, 1989).

Consider next the standardized expenditure need. Table 13–5 shows the characteristics of cities with large, medium, and small expenditure needs. For the five cities with the largest expenditure needs, the average need is 2.4 times the average expenditure need of the five cities with the smallest needs. This index is derived from cost indices for three types of services: general services, police services, and fire services. The cost index shows the cost of providing the standard level of service relative to the cost incurred by the average city, with a value of 100 for the average city. For example, Newark's cost of general services was 2 percent above average, while its cost of police services was over seven times the average and its cost of fire services was over three times the average. Newark's value for standard expenditure need (170) suggests that its total costs were 70 percent above the average. In contrast, in Virginia Beach the cost of the standard service package is about half the average cost.

TABLE 13-5 **Standard Expenditure Need and City Characteristics, 1982**

	Standard Expenditure Need	General Cost	Police Cost	Fire Cost	Population (000)	Poverty Rate	Old Housing	Metro Share	Employment Ratio
Large Need									
Newark, New Jersey	170	102	710	344	320	44%	83%	17%	0.41
Cleveland, Ohio	145	151	300	218	558	29	89	29	0.58
Atlanta, Georgia	143	130	387	224	428	35	64	20	0.74
Detroit, Michigan	143	155	288	158	1,138	29	92	25	0.31
New York, New York	141	124	474	113	7,086	26	79	86	0.41
Medium Need									
Milwaukee, Wisconsin	101	122	132	118	631	18	78	45	0.44
Sacramento, California	100	121	123	125	288	19	57	26	0.41
Providence, Rhode Island	99	99	193	207	155	25	86	17	0.66
Indianapolis, Indiana	98	127	89	100	202	15	56	60	0.45
San Bernadino, California	98	121	110	121	124	20	61	08	0.37
Small Need									
Pawtucket, Rhode Island	67	79	73	118	71	15	84	08	0.40
San Jose, California	66	86	60	66	659	10	28	52	0.29
Garden Grove, California	63	81	59	72	126	11	49	06	0.27
Hollywood, Florida	58	74	51	70	122	09	35	10	0.43
Virginia Beach, Virginia	52	70	38	43	282	11	21	37	0.19
Average small	148	132	432	211	1,906	33	81	35	0.49
Average medium	99	118	129	134	280	19	68	31	0.47
Average large	61	78	56	74	252	11	43	23	0.31

SOURCE: Helen F. Ladd and John Yinger, *America's Ailing Cities: Fiscal Health and the Design of Urban Policy* (Baltimore, Md.: Johns Hopkins University Press, 1989).

Figure 13–6 shows effects of various city characteristics on the costs of providing the standard service package. The cost elasticities provide a measure of the independent effects of the various characteristics on service costs. For example, the wage elasticity for general services is about 1.0, meaning that if two cities differ only in private-sector wages, a 10 percent difference in wages generates a 10 percent difference in the cost of providing general services. The elasticities of costs with respect to population are 0.14 for general services and 0.21 for police services. This means that a 10 percent difference in population between two cities causes a 1.4 percent difference in general costs and a 2.1 percent difference in police costs. These numbers suggest that in the cities studied by Ladd and Yinger, there are diseconomies of scale in providing general services and police services.

The costs of public services increase with the poverty rate and the fraction of the housing stock that is relatively old. In Figure 13–6, the elasticity of police costs with respect to the poverty rate is 1.1, meaning that a 10 percent difference in poverty rates between cities causes an 11 percent difference in the costs of police services. This occurs because crime rates and victimization rates are generally higher among the poor, so crime control is more costly. The elasticity of general costs with respect to the quantity of old housing (the fraction of housing stock that is older than 20 years) is 0.40: a 10 percent difference in the amount of old housing causes a 4 percent difference in general service costs. This occurs because cities with relatively old houses typically have relatively old public infrastructure as well, and old infrastructure has relatively high maintenance and repair costs. The elasticities for fire services (not shown in the figure) are 0.84 for the poverty rate and 0.40 for the amount of old housing. These elasticities reflect the fact that it is more costly to protect older, low-quality housing (typically occupied by the poor) from fire.

The cost of providing the standard service package also depends on the role of the central city in the metropolitan economy. A central city that has a relatively small share of metropolitan population has higher costs because it provides services for its own residents as well as a relatively large number of commuters. The elasticity of general costs and police costs with respect to the metropolitan share of population are 0.14 and 0.19, respectively. The same phenomenon is reflected in the elasticities with respect to the employment ratio (jobs per city resident): a city with a large employment ratio provides services to more commuters and thus has higher costs. The cost elasticities are 0.29 for general services and 0.40 for police and fire services.

The cost elasticities shown in Figure 13–6 are reflected in the data on standardized expenditure need in Table 13–5. Larger cities tend to have greater expenditure needs because of diseconomies of scale in providing public services. Cities with high poverty rates and relatively old housing have greater expenditure needs because they have higher police and fire costs. Finally, expenditure needs are higher in cities with relatively large numbers of commuters (cities with a small fraction of metropolitan population or large employment ratios).

FIGURE 13-6   Elasticities of Service Costs with Respect to Various City Characteristics

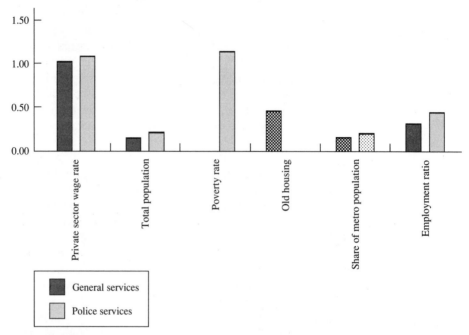

SOURCE: Helen Ladd and John Yinger, *America's Ailing Cities: Fiscal Health and the Design of Urban Policy* (Baltimore, Md.: Johns Hopkins University Press, 1989), Table 4.1.

Standard versus Actual Fiscal Health

Table 13–6 shows the characteristics of cities with low, medium, and high scores for standardized fiscal health. Larger cities and cities with relatively large numbers of poor people have relatively small revenue-raising capacities and relatively large expenditure needs, so they have low scores for standardized fiscal health. Similarly, cities with relatively low per capita income and relatively high poverty rates have problems on both sides of the budget equation, so they have low scores for fiscal health. Ladd and Yinger (1989) estimate that 68 percent of the variation across cities in fiscal health scores results from differences in population, per capita income, and poverty rates. Other characteristics that affect fiscal health are (1) the fraction of the city's housing stock that is over 20 years old and (2) the central city's share of metropolitan population. In contrast, the employment ratio has a very weak effect on fiscal health: the presence of commuters is a mixed blessing. Although commuters pay taxes (and increase the city's revenue-raising capacity), they also require services (and increase the standard expenditure need).

TABLE 13-6   Standard Fiscal Health and City Characteristics, 1982

	Standard Economic Health	Population (000)	Per Capita Income	Poverty Rate	Old Housing	Employment Ratio
Low Score						
Newark, New Jersey	−110	320	$5,292	44%	83%	0.41
New York, New York	−105	7,086	8,736	26	79	0.41
Detroit, Michigan	−92	1,138	7,090	29	92	0.31
New Orleans, Louisiana	−73	564	8,017	33	73	0.39
Philadelphia, Pennsylvania	−60	1,665	7,109	27	85	0.36
Medium Score						
Norfolk, Virginia	−8	266	7,408	23	69	0.36
Pittsburgh, Pennsylvania	−8	414	8,277	21	88	0.68
Omaha, Nebraska	−6	328	9,194	14	64	0.51
Long Beach, California	−5	371	9,978	18	74	0.36
St. Paul, Minnesota	−3	275	9,173	14	75	0.55
High Score						
Warwick, Rhode Island	33	86	9,084	09	64	0.34
Anaheim, California	33	226	10,149	10	36	0.61
Garden Grove, California	44	126	9,668	11	49	0.27
Ft. Lauderdale, Florida	45	153	12,099	18	43	0.71
Hollywood, Florida	47	122	10,752	09	35	0.43
Average low	−88	2,155	7,249	32	82	0.38
Average medium	−6	331	8,806	18	74	0.49
Average high	40	143	10,350	11	45	0.47

SOURCE: Helen Ladd and John Yinger, *America's Ailing Cities: Fiscal Health and the Design of Urban Policy* (Baltimore, Md.: Johns Hopkins University Press, 1989).

According to Ladd and Yinger, these two effects cancel each other out so that, everything else being equal, an increase in the employment ratio does not have much of an effect on standardized fiscal health.

How do state and federal policies affect the fiscal health of cities? The policies of higher levels of government affect the fiscal circumstances of cities in three ways:

1. **Grants.** Cities receive grants from the states and the national government.
2. **Service responsibilities.** The states specify which public services will be provided by cities. For example, in some states, cities are responsible for providing education.
3. **Tax restrictions.** The states impose restrictions on city taxes. For example, some states prohibit city taxes on earnings (payroll taxes).

To estimate a city's actual fiscal health, Ladd and Yinger (1989) adjusted the scores for standardized fiscal health to incorporate the effects of these state and federal policies.

Figure 13–7 shows the effect of state and federal policies on the fiscal health of cities with low, medium, and high scores for standardized health. The computations are based on data from 1982, before the large decreases in state and federal grants. For the five cities with the lowest scores for standardized health, the average health score drops from −88 to −42. In other words, the gap between total revenue and the cost of providing the standard service package is cut in half. For cities with medium and high values of standardized health, the involvement of state and local governments decreases fiscal health: the positive effect of grants is more than offset by the negative effects of greater service responsibilities and tax restrictions. In general, it is clear that state and federal policies decreased the intercity differences in fiscal health.

Between 1982 and 1988, two trends had conflicting effects on the fiscal health of cities. First, the national economy grew steadily and per capita income increased. In most cities, the increase in income increased the tax base and de-

FIGURE 13–7   Effects of State and Federal Governments on the Fiscal Health of Cities

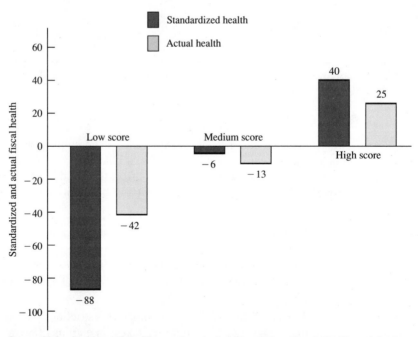

SOURCE: Helen Ladd and John Yinger, *America's Ailing Cities: Fiscal Health and the Design of Urban Policy* (Baltimore, Md.: Johns Hopkins University Press, 1989).

creased service costs. Second, state and federal assistance from intergovernmental grants decreased. According to Ladd and Yinger (1989), the positive effect of rising income was almost completely offset by the negative effect of less grant money, so there was little change in the average fiscal health of cities between 1982 and 1988.

Summary

1. There are over 82,000 local governments in the United States, including municipalities, school districts, counties, and special districts. Municipalities are responsible for about 35 percent of local government spending, and school districts are responsible for about 29 percent. The largest spending program is education (42 percent of local government spending).

2. In 1984, 37 percent of local revenue came from taxes on property, income, and sales, and 40 percent came from intergovernmental grants. The rest of local money comes from user fees and charges. The fraction of local funds from intergovernmental grants has decreased steadily since the late 1970s.

3. The national government is responsible for stabilization and redistribution policies.

4. Local governments are involved in resource allocation for three types of goods:
   a. Natural monopoly. Local governments either produce or regulate the private production of goods produced by natural monopolies (water, sewage, transit).
   b. Externalities. One option is for the government to provide goods that generate externalities. Another option is to internalize the externality with a subsidy.
   c. Local public goods. A local public good is nonrivalrous and nonexcludable, and its benefits are confined to a relatively small geographical area.

5. There are advantages and disadvantages associated with the local provision of public goods.
   a. Local governments promote efficiency if there is diversity in demand for public goods.
   b. Local governments inhibit efficiency if the benefits or costs of public goods spill over into other jurisdictions (externalities).
   c. Local governments inhibit efficiency if there are scale economies in the production of public goods.

6. Local provision of a public good is efficient if the diversity in demand for local public goods is large relative to externalities and scale economies.

7. Metropolitan consolidation has been advocated as a way to prevent suburban exploitation, exploit scale economies, equalize tax rates, and equalize spending.

8. The Baumol model suggests that increases in the labor cost of personal services (haircuts and education) result from rising productivity in manufacturing, which pulls up the wages of all workers.
   a. Other theories of rising labor costs focus on the monopoly power of local governments and labor unions.
   b. The quantity of public services demanded will increase if the income effect (from rising productivity) is large relative to the substitution effect (from rising unit costs).

9. Between the late 1970s and 1981, a total of 30 states tightened restrictions on local tax rates, tax revenue, and spending.

10. Since the early 1970s, many cities have experienced serious fiscal problems. The most severe fiscal problems have been experienced by large, older cities with declining population and employment.

11. The index of standardized fiscal health shows the fiscal health of cities in the absence of intercity differences in taxes and spending.

12. The costs of providing city services depend on the characteristics of the city.
    a. The elasticity of general costs with respect to population is 0.14, meaning there are diseconomies of scale in providing general services.
    b. The elasticity of police costs with respect to the poverty rate is 1.1: a 10 percent difference in poverty rates between cities causes an 11 percent difference in the costs of police services.
    c. The cost of providing the standard service package increases with the number of commuters working in the city.

13. Larger cities and cities with relatively large numbers of poor people have relatively small revenue-raising capacities and relatively large expenditure needs, so they have low scores for standardized fiscal health. About 68 percent of the variation across cities in fiscal health scores result from differences in population, per capita income, and poverty rates.

14. State and federal policies (grants, mandates, and tax restrictions) decrease the differences across cities in fiscal health.

Exercises and Discussion Questions

1. Why do we have public libraries? Why don't people rent books from firms, just as they rent trucks, rototillers, and videos? If we have U-Haul, why not U-Read; if we have Captain Video, why not Captain Book?

2. Consider Metro, a metropolitan area with two municipalities, each of which has a small police force. The only activity of the police is chasing criminals; the police never capture criminals.
   a. Suppose that the provision of police services is subject to scale economies. If the two municipal police forces are consolidated into a single metropoli-

tan force, will total expenditures on police services increase, decrease, or stay the same?

    b. If you don't have enough information to answer the question, describe the information you need and explain how you would use it.

3. The conventional head tax is a fixed amount per head: if you have a head, you pay a $500 tax. Suppose that the head tax is based on head weight: the heavier your head, the larger your tax. Would you expect the switch from the conventional property tax to the head-weight tax to increase or decrease the equilibrium number of municipalities?

4. In Metro, there are three types of houses: E (expensive), M (medium), and C (cheap). A recent survey suggests that there are three types of preferences for fire protection: H (high), I (intermediate), and L (low). Mr. Wizard, an economic consultant to the city, recently made the following statement: "If my assumptions are correct, the shopping and sorting from the Tiebout process will generate three municipalities."

    a. Assume that Mr. Wizard's reasoning is correct. What are his assumptions?

    b. Suppose that the equilibrium number of municipalities turns out to be nine, not three. Where did Mr. Wizard go wrong? What set of assumptions would have given him the correct prediction?

5. In the example of the Tiebout model with a property tax, wealthy households established an exclusive suburb with a property tax rate of 0.667 percent, spending of $500, and a minimum lot size of 0.50 acres. Discuss the effects of the following changes on the property tax rate and the minimum lot size:

    a. The market value of houses is $100,000 instead of $75,000.

    b. The market value of land is $50,000 instead of $30,000 (and the market value of houses is $100,000).

6. In the city of Crewville, everyone gets crew cuts: the output of the barber is standardized. The output of the teacher is also standardized: the only objective is to teach children how to add and subtract. Will the costs of haircuts and education increase over time relative to the costs of manufactured goods?

References and Additional Readings

Advisory Commission on Intergovernmental Relations. *Intergovernmental Service Arrangements for Delivering Local Public Services: Update 1983*. Washington, D.C.: U.S. Government Printing Office, 1985. A survey of the use of intergovernmental and joint-service contracts in the provision of local public services.

———. *Significant Features of Fiscal Federalism*. Washington, D.C., U.S. Government Printing Office, 1987.

Aronson, J. Richard, and John L. Hilley. *Financing State and Local Governments*. Washington, D.C.: Brookings Institution, 1986.

Baumol, William. "The Macroeconomics of Unbalanced Growth: The Anatomy of Urban Crisis." *American Economic Review* 65 (1967), pp. 414–26.

Bradbury, Katharine L.; Anthony Downs; and Kenneth A. Small. *Urban Decline and the Future of American Cities.* Washington, D.C.: Brookings Institution, 1982. Discusses the reasons for the economic problems of cities.

Bradford, David, and Wallace E. Oates. "Suburban Exploitation of Central Cities and Government Structure." In *Redistribution through Public Choice,* ed. Harold Hochman and George Peterson. New York: Columbia University Press, 1974. Discusses the suburban exploitation hypothesis and predicts the effects of metropolitan consolidation on tax rates, expenditure levels, and income segregation.

Courant, Paul; Edward Gramlich; and Daniel Rubinfeld. "Why Voters Support Tax Limitation Amendments: The Michigan Case." Chapter 3. In *Tax and Expenditure Limitations,* ed. Helen Ladd and Nicholas Tideman. Washington, D.C.: Urban Institute, 1987, pp. 37–72.

Freeman, Richard B. *How Do Public Sector Waste and Employment Respond to Economic Conditions?* Cambridge, Mass.: National Bureau of Economic Research, Working Paper no. 1653, 1985.

Gramlich, Edward M., and Daniel L. Rubinfeld. "Microestimates of Public Spending Demand Functions and Test of the Tiebout and Median-Voter Hypothesis." *Journal of Political Economy* 90 (1982), pp. 536–60. Found relatively small differences in the demands for local public goods in metropolitan areas where there are many local jurisdictions.

Hamilton, Bruce W. "Zoning and Property Taxation in a System of Local Governments." *Urban Studies* 12 (1975), pp. 205–11. Discusses the role of zoning in maintaining the Tiebout equilibrium under property-tax finance.

————. "Capitalization of Interjurisdictional Differences in Local Tax Prices." *American Economic Review* 66 (1976), pp. 743–53. Explores the roles of zoning and capitalization in attaining a Tiebout equilibrium in a community whose citizens have different demands for housing.

Hirsch, Werner. "Expenditure Implications of Metropolitan Growth and Consolidation." *Review of Economics and Statistics* 41 (1959). Estimates the degree of scale economies for police, fire protection, and public schools. Did not detect scale economies for police services or public schools, but found scale economies for fire protection up to a population of about 100,000.

Inman, Robert P. "The Fiscal Performance of Local Governments: An Interpretive Review." In *Current Issues in Urban Economics,* ed. Peter Meiszkowski and Mahlon Straszheim. Baltimore, Md.: Johns Hopkins University Press, 1979, pp. 270–321. Discusses various models of decision making in the local public sector, including the median-voter model and the dominant-party model. Summarizes studies of the price and income elasticities of demand for local public goods, and the elasticity of local expenditures with respect to intergovernmental aid.

Ladd, Helen F., and Julie Boatwright Wilson. "Why Voters Support Tax Limitations: Evidence from Massachusetts' Proposition 2½." *National Tax Journal* (1982), pp. 137–40.

Ladd, Helen F., and John Yinger. *America's Ailing Cities: Fiscal Health and the Design of Urban Policy.* Baltimore, Md.: Johns Hopkins University Press, 1989. A comprehensive study of the factors that determine a city's fiscal health.

Musgrave, Richard A., and Peggy B. Musgrave. *Public Finance in Theory and Practice.* New York: McGraw-Hill, 1980.

Oakland, William H. "Central Cities: Fiscal Plight and Prospects for Reform." In *Current Issues in Urban Economics,* ed. Peter Meiszkowski and Mahlon Straszheim. Baltimore, Md.: Johns Hopkins University Press, 1979, pp. 322–58. Discusses the sources of central-city fiscal distress, suggesting that fiscal distress is caused in large part by the attempt of local governments to redistribute income. Suggests that intergovernmental grants should be designed to compensate local governments for the money spent on high-cost, low-revenue citizens.

Oates, Wallace E. "The Effects of Property Taxes and Local Public Spending on Property Values: An Empirical Study of Tax Capitalization and the Tiebout Hypothesis." *Journal of Political Economy* 77 (1969), pp. 957–70. Estimates the effects of local taxes and expenditures on property values. Provides evidence that households shop for local jurisdictions.

————. *Fiscal Federalism.* New York: Harcourt Brace Jovanovich, 1972. Analyzes the division of responsibilities between different levels of government, focusing on spillovers, scale economies, and diversity in demand.

Peterson, George E. "Finance." In *The Urban Predicament,* ed. William Gorham and Nathan Glazer. Washington, D.C.: Urban Institute, 1976. Provides a comprehensive analysis of the reasons for the fiscal crises of large cities and suggests ways to avoid future problems.

Tiebout, Charles. "A Pure Theory of Local Expenditures." *Journal of Political Economy* 64 (1956), pp. 416–24. The original statement of the Tiebout model.

U.S. Bureau of the Census. *Census of Governments.* Washington, D.C.: Department of Commerce, 1987.

14 Local Taxes and Intergovernmental Grants

The revenue for local government comes from local taxes and grants from higher levels of government. The first part of this chapter examines the economic effects of local taxes. When a government imposes a tax, the people who pay the tax in a legal sense have the incentive to change their behavior to avoid the tax. By doing so, they shift the tax to someone else. The policy question is, After taxpayers have fully adjusted to the new tax, who actually pays the tax? The second part of this chapter explores the role of intergovernmental grants. The principal question is, How do local governments respond to state and federal grants? Do they spend all of the grant on additional local public goods, or do they use the grant to cut local taxes?

Who Pays the Residential Property Tax?

The property tax is a tax on residential, commercial, and industrial property. This section considers the effect of the residential property tax, using a model of a residential city to explore the market effects of the tax. The analysis focuses on two principal questions about the residential property tax. First, How do property owners respond to the tax? Second, To what extent do property owners pass on the tax to consumers, landowners, and other property owners?

It will be useful to divide rental housing into two components: the dwelling itself (the structure) and the land that comes with the dwelling. The annual rent on the residential property is the sum of dwelling rent and land rent. For example, an annual rent of $5,000 can be broken down into $4,000 of dwelling rent and $1,000 of land rent. Similarly, the market value of residential property is the sum

347

of the market values of the dwelling and the land. As explained in Chapter 6 (Land Use in the Monocentric City), the market value of property equals the **present value** of the rental income from the property. If the market interest rate is 10 percent, the market value of the dwelling is $40,000 ($4,000/0.10); the market value of the land is $10,000 ($1,000/0.10); and the market value of the residential property (both dwelling and land) is $50,000.

The residential property tax is an annual tax based on the market value of the property. For example, under a 2 percent property tax, the owner of a $50,000 property would pay $1,000 per year in taxes. This can be broken down into an $800 tax on the dwelling itself (2 percent of a market value of $40,000) and a $200 tax on the land (2 percent of a market value of $10,000).

To explain the market effects of the property tax, consider the city of Taxville, where all land is used for rental housing. The city has the following characteristics:

1. **Identical dwellings.** The city has 900 identical rental housing units.
2. **Housing inputs.** There are two inputs to housing: land and improvements (the dwelling). Every dwelling occupies a quarter-acre lot.
3. **Capital mobility.** Dwellings are immobile in the short run but can be moved from one city to another in the long run.
4. **Unit property tax.** The annual property tax is paid in legal terms by the landlord (property owner). The tax is $200 per quarter-acre lot and $800 per dwelling, regardless of the market values of land and improvements.

The fourth assumption means that the property tax is not based on market value, but is a fixed-unit tax. This assumption simplifies the exposition without changing the analysis in any substantive way.

The Land Portion of the Property Tax

Consider first the effect of the land portion of the property tax. Figure 14–1 shows the city's land market. The supply of land is perfectly inelastic, with a fixed supply of 900 quarter-acre lots. The demand curve intersects the supply curve at point *B*, generating an annual rent of $1,000 per lot. If the market interest rate is 10 percent, the market value of land is $10,000 per lot.

Will landowners be able to shift the land tax onto land consumers? The $200 property tax increases the landlord's tax liability by $200 per year. Suppose that the landlord increased land rent from $1,000 per year (point *B*) to $1,200 (point *C*). At point *C*, the quantity of land demanded (450 lots) is less than the fixed supply (900 lots), so some land will be vacant. The excess supply of land will cause landowners to cut prices to attract consumers. The price cutting will continue until the gap between supply and demand is eliminated. In equilibrium, land rent falls to $1,000, and the net return to landlords drops to $800 ($1,000 less the $200 tax). Because the supply of land is fixed, the land tax is ultimately borne by landowners. The decrease in net rental income decreases the market value of land from $10,000 to $8,000 ($800/0.10).

FIGURE 14-1   Land Market and Land Tax

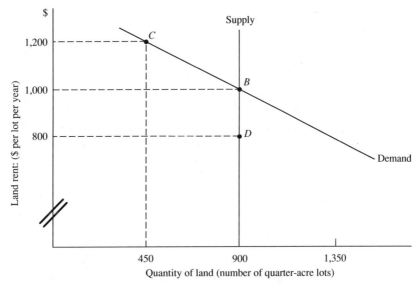

In the initial equilibrium, land rent is $1,000 per lot per year. Since the supply of land is fixed, annual land rent decreases by the amount of the tax. If the landowner tried to pass on the $200 annual tax to consumers, the net cost of land would rise to $1,200 (point *C*), and the quantity supplied (900) would exceed the quantity demanded (450). The surplus of land would cause rent to fall to $800.

The Improvement Tax: The Traditional View

The traditional analysis of the property tax examines the effects of the property tax on the city that imposes the tax. The traditional view is based on **partial-equilibrium analysis.** The analysis is "partial" in the sense that it ignores the effect of the tax on other cities.

Figure 14–2 shows the market for improvements (dwellings) in the taxing city. In the long run, the supply of dwellings is assumed to be perfectly elastic: the city is assumed to be a small part of a national market for dwellings, so the market price is unaffected by events in the city. Given the supply and demand curves, the initial equilibrium (point *B*) generates a dwelling rent of $4,000 per year and 900 dwellings. If the market interest rate is 10 percent, the market value of the rental dwelling is $40,000.

Why is the long-run supply curve perfectly elastic? One way to picture the long run is to imagine that landlords can put wheels on their dwellings and roll them to other cities. Although landlords do not literally move their dwellings from place to place, they can decrease the supply of housing in other ways. As explained in Chapter 11 (The Urban Housing Market), landlords can (1) decrease their investment

FIGURE 14-2   **Partial-Equilibrium Effects of Improvement Tax**

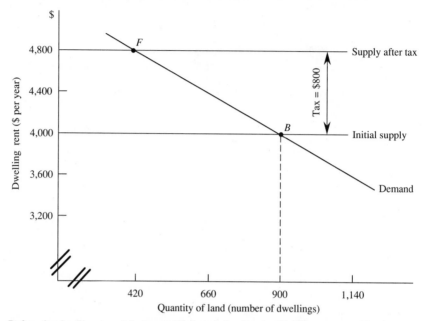

Before the dwelling tax, *B* is the equilibrium point (rent = $4,000 per year). The $800 tax on improvements shifts the supply curve up by $800. Dwelling rent increases to $4,800 per year and the number of dwellings drops to 420.

in repair and maintenance, (2) abandon dwellings, (3) convert property to other uses, and (4) not respond to increased demand for housing. In these four cases, landlords can decrease the effective supply of housing without actually moving their dwellings to another location. The house-on-wheels metaphor captures the idea that landlords can decrease the supply of housing in the long run.

The improvement portion of the property tax is $800 per dwelling. Because the landlord pays the improvement tax (in legal terms), it shifts the long-run supply curve up by the amount of the tax: the supply curve is a marginal cost curve, and the tax increases the marginal cost of rental property by $800 per dwelling per year. The market moves from point *B* to point *F*: the equilibrium rent rises by the full amount of the tax (from $4,000 to $4,800), and the quantity of dwellings drops from 900 to 420. Net rental income remains at $4,000: the landlord collects $4,800 in rent and pays $800 in taxes, leaving $4,000 in net income. The tenant pays the entire tax: the annual cost of rental housing rises by $800.

The improvement tax is borne by consumers because the supply of dwellings is perfectly elastic. The city is a small part of the national market for dwellings, so it takes the national rent of $4,000 as given: if the city's landlords were to receive anything less than $4,000 in net rental income, they would roll their dwellings out of town. In fact, the decrease in the supply of dwellings (from 900 to 420) increases dwelling rent to restore the original net rental income of $4,000.

The Residential Property Tax: The New View

The partial equilibrium analysis explores the effects of the property tax on the markets for land and improvements in the taxing city. **General equilibrium analysis** explores the effects of the property tax on markets outside the city, providing a new view of the property tax.

A Simple General Equilibrium Model.   Suppose that Taxville shares a region with Notax, a residential city without a property tax. The region has the following characteristics:

1. **Fixed supply of dwellings.** The total number of dwellings in the region is fixed at 1,800.
2. **Capital mobility.** In the short run, dwellings cannot be moved between cities. In the long run, dwellings can be moved between cities at zero cost.
3. **Household mobility.** Households are immobile in the sense that they cannot move from one city to another.
4. **Equilibrium price.** Landlords move their dwellings to the city with the highest return (the highest annual rent). In equilibrium, the market rent on dwellings is the same in the two cities.

The regional dwelling market is shown in Figure 14–3. Each city has a negatively sloped demand curve, and the initial equilibrium occurs with points *B* (in Taxville) and *K* (in Notax). The equilibrium price of dwellings is $4,000, and each city has 900 dwellings.

The Effects of the Improvement Tax.   In the short run, the supply of dwellings in each city is fixed. The $800 tax decreases the net rental income in Taxville from $4,000 (point *B*) to $3,200 (point *T*). The property tax is borne by landlords because the supply of dwellings is perfectly inelastic. In the nontaxing city, rent stays at $4,000.

In the long run, landlords will move their dwellings to the more lucrative market in Notax. Suppose that landlords move 120 dwellings from Taxville to Notax. In Figure 14–3, the Taxville market moves from point *B* (900 dwellings) to point *C* (780 dwellings), causing the rent on Taxville dwellings to rise from $4,000 to $4,200. The net income of Taxville's landlords increases from $3,200 ($4,000 rent less $800 tax) to $3,400 ($4,200 less $800). Taxville's loss is Notax's gain: the Notax market moves from point *K* to point *L* (an increase of 120 dwellings, from 900 to 1,020), and rent drops from $4,000 to $3,800.

Is the dwelling market in equilibrium with points *C* and *L?* Equilibrium occurs when two conditions are satisfied. First, the total number of dwellings in the two

FIGURE 14-3 General-Equilibrium Effects of Improvement Tax

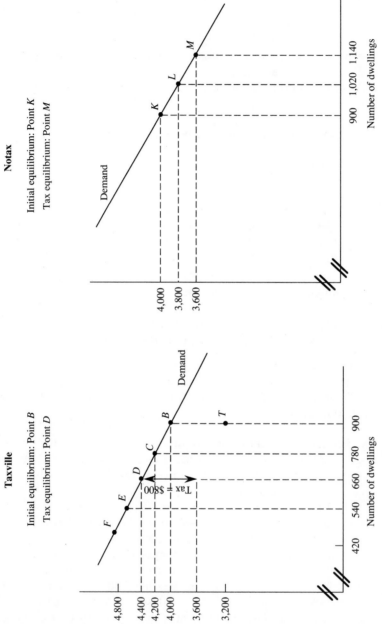

Taxville

Initial equilibrium: Point B

Tax equilibrium: Point D

Notax

Initial equilibrium: Point K

Tax equilibrium: Point M

The initial (pretax) equilibrium consists of points B and K. A 2 percent improvement tax increases the landlord's tax liability by $800 per dwelling per year. In the short run, dwellings are immobile, so dwelling rent is fixed at $4,000 and landlords pay the tax. In the long run, landlords move their dwellings to the nontaxing city, increasing dwelling rent in the taxing city (movement upward along the demand curve) and decreasing rent in the nontaxing city (moving down the demand curve). In long-run equilibrium, landlords receive the same net (posttax) return, so Taxville rent exceeds Notax rent by the amount of the tax: with points D and M, Taxville's rent is $4,400 (net landlord return = $3,600) and Notax's rent is $3,600. The tax is shifted to property owners in the nontaxing city.

cities must equal 1,800 (the fixed supply). Second, landlords have no incentive to move their dwellings from one city to another: the net rental income must be the same in the two cities. For points *C* and *L,* the first condition is satisfied (720 + 1,020 = 1,800), but the second condition is violated: the net income in Taxville ($3,400) is still less than net income in Notax ($3,800). Therefore, there will be additional movement up the Taxville demand curve and down the Notax demand curve. The movements along the demand curves will continue until both equilibrium conditions are satisfied. Equilibrium occurs with points *D* and *M:* there are 660 dwellings in Taxville and 1,140 in Notax, and the net income is $3,600 per rental dwelling.

There are two lessons to be learned from the general equilibrium analysis:

1. **Landlords pay the tax.** The tax decreases net rental income in both cities to $3,600. The movement of dwellings to the untaxed city decreases rent in the untaxed city (to $3,600) and increases rent in the taxing city (to $4,400). The tax is paid by landlords throughout the region, not just landlords in the taxing city.
2. **Consumer effects.** Consumers in Taxville lose (they pay $4,400 instead of $4,000), and consumers in Notax gain (they pay $3,600). The changes in housing costs offset one another, so the tax does not change the average rent.

The general equilibrium analysis suggests that the improvement tax is paid by landlords (the owners of dwellings). Because the total (regional) supply of dwellings is perfectly inelastic, landlords are unable to escape the tax. On the other side of the market, housing consumers as a class escape the tax: the losses of Taxville households are offset by the gains of Notax households. The improvement tax causes zero-sum changes in rent, so housing consumers are no worse off as a result of the tax.

Summary: Who Pays the Residential Property Tax?

The different views and models of the property tax are cleverly designed to baffle students. Who actually pays the property tax? The incidence of the land tax is straightforward: given the perfectly inelastic supply of land, the tax is paid by landowners. The incidence of the improvement tax is not so easily summarized. The incidence of the tax depends on one's perspective.

The Local Effects of a Local Tax

Tom is the mayor of a small city in a nation of 100 cities. To predict the effects of his city's improvement tax, he should use the partial-equilibrium model. Because his city is small, the tax will not affect the national market for dwellings, so the assumption of a perfectly elastic supply of dwellings is a good approximation of reality. Using the partial-equilibrium model, Tom would predict that a 2 percent improvement tax will increase dwelling rent by the full amount of the tax ($800): the tax will be borne entirely by housing consumers.

Table 14–1 shows the distribution of the property tax burden from the local perspective (the traditional view). In computing the numbers, Pechman (1985) assumes that (*a*) the land tax is borne entirely by landowners, and (*b*) the improvement tax is borne entirely by housing consumers. In other words, the computational results are based on partial-equilibrium analysis. Since the income elasticity of demand for housing (or improvements) is slightly less than 1.0, the improvement tax is regressive: the ratio of tax to income decreases as income increases. In contrast, land ownership rises rapidly with income, so the land portion of the property tax is progressive. In combination, the two components of the tax cause the property tax to be highly regressive for incomes less than $20,000 and roughly proportional for incomes above $20,000.

The National Effects of a Local Tax

Bertha, the president of a nation of 100 cities, wants to estimate the national effects of a property tax in a single city. She should use the general-equilibrium model. Under the assumption of a fixed national supply of dwellings, the improvement tax will be paid by capitalists in the form of a lower return on capital (lower net income

TABLE 14–1   Property Tax Incidence, Local and National Perspective

Income ($)	Property Tax as Percentage of Income	
	Local Perspective *(partial equilibrium)*	National Perspective *(general equilibrium)*
0–5,000	7.9%	1.0%
5,000–10,000	3.0	0.6
10,000–15,000	2.4	0.9
15,000–20,000	2.1	0.9
20,000–25,000	2.1	1.0
25,000–30,000	2.1	1.2
30,000–50,000	2.2	1.4
50,000–100,000	2.3	2.2
100,000–500,000	2.2	3.9
500,000–1 million	2.2	5.2
Over 1 million	2.3	5.8

SOURCE: Joseph A. Pechman, *Who Paid the Taxes, 1966–85?* (Washington, D.C.: Brookings Institution, 1985), Table 3–1.

from rental property). The tax will cause zero-sum changes in housing costs: consumers outside the taxing city gain at the expense of consumers in the taxing city.

Table 14–1 shows the distribution of the property tax burden from the national perspective (the new view). In computing the numbers, Pechman (1985) assumes that (*a*) the land tax is borne entirely by landowners, and (*b*) the improvement tax is borne entirely by capitalists. In other words, the computational results are based on general-equilibrium analysis. Because capital and land ownership increase rapidly with income, the property tax is progressive: the tax burden as a fraction of income increases with income.

The Effects of a National Tax

Sam is the president of a nation in which all 100 cities have the same property tax. He wants to estimate the effect of the improvement tax. Because all cities impose the tax, the improvement tax does not cause any movement of capital between cities. Under the assumption of a fixed national supply of capital, the tax is borne entirely by capitalists. The tax does not affect the cost of housing because there is nowhere for the dwellings to flee.

The Tax on Commercial and Industrial Property

Because Taxville has only residential property, the property tax is effectively a tax on residential property. This section discusses the effects of the general property tax (a tax on residential, commercial, and industrial property) in cities with all three types of property.

The General Property Tax

The analysis of the land portion of the general property tax is straightforward. Because the supply of land is perfectly inelastic, the tax is paid entirely by landowners. The land tax does not affect land rent, but simply decreases the annual rental income by the annual tax. The decrease in net rental income decreases the market value of the land.

What about the tax on improvements? Suppose that a city imposes a 2 percent tax on residential, commercial, and industrial structures. In the short run, the supply of structures is fixed, so the tax decreases the net income of the city's landlords. In the long run, landlords will move their structures to Notax, the other city in the region. The movement of capital will increase the rent on structures in the taxing city and decrease it elsewhere. For example, rent might rise from $4,000 to $4,400 in the taxing city and decrease to $3,600 elsewhere. The changes in structure rents will change the prices of consumer goods: the price of consumer goods will increase in the taxing city and decrease elsewhere. The changes in structure rents will also equalize net property income at $3,600.

Differential Tax Rates

Most jurisdictions impose the same nominal tax rate on residential and business property. Because assessment ratios differ across property types, however, effective tax rates often differ. Consider a city with the following characteristics:

1. There are two types of structures: houses and pizza parlors.
2. The city starts with the same effective tax rates on pizza parlors and houses.
3. The total capital in the city (the total number of structures) is fixed.
4. Structures can be used for either houses or pizza parlors.
5. In the initial equilibrium, the structure rent is $4,000.

Suppose that the city cuts the property tax rate on pizza parlors and increases the tax rate on housing. The change in tax policy is revenue-neutral: the loss of revenue from pizza parlors equals the gain in tax revenue from residences. The new tax policy causes the following changes in the city:

1. **Transfer of capital.** Landlords will move capital from the residential sector to the more lucrative pizza sector.
2. **Increased dwelling rent.** The movement of capital out of the housing sector will increase dwelling rent.
3. **Decreased pizza prices.** The movement of capital into the pizza sector will decrease the price of pizza.

Who gains and who loses? The change in tax policy is revenue-neutral, so landlords are not affected by the change in tax policy. Housing consumers lose because the price of housing increases, and pizza consumers gain because the price of pizza decreases. This general equilibrium analysis suggests that differences in effective tax rates are reflected in differences in consumer prices. If a city taxes residential property at a higher rate than business property, its citizens pay more for housing, but less for other goods.

The Tiebout Model and the Property Tax

The Tiebout model, introduced in Chapter 13, suggests that citizens shop for municipalities and school districts. In equilibrium, households sort themselves with respect to (a) the demand for public goods and (b) housing consumption. This section discusses the implications of the Tiebout process for the incidence of the property tax.

To explain the effects of the property tax in the Tiebout world, consider Metro, a metropolitan area with the following characteristics:

1. **Local public good.** Municipalities provide a single public good (parks).
2. **Income and house value.** Half the households are wealthy and have $100,000 houses. Half are poor and have $50,000 houses.
3. **Park demands.** Half the households in each income group want a large park budget ($2,000), and half want a small park budget ($200).
4. **Municipalities and zoning.** Households can set up new municipalities, using large-lot zoning to establish minimum house values.

As shown in Table 14–2, households will sort themselves with respect to park demands and property values, forming four municipalities. There are two wealthy communities, one with a large park budget (tax rate = 2.0 percent) and one with a small park budget (tax rate = 0.20 percent). Similarly, there are two poor municipalities.

Because the households in Metro sort themselves into homogeneous communities, the property tax is a user fee, not a conventional tax. The tax liability of a particular household depends on its park consumption, not on its housing consumption (property value). Every household pays a tax equal to its desired park budgets, regardless of its property values: the poor pay a higher tax rate to generate the same park budget as their counterparts in the wealthy community; the low spenders pay a lower tax rate than their counterparts in the high-spending municipalities. In the Tiebout world, there is no link between property value and property tax liability. Instead, the tax liability depends strictly on park consumption.

In the Tiebout world, an increase in housing consumption will not affect property taxes. Suppose that a few of the wealthy, high-spending households decide to buy $200,000 homes. They will form a new community of high-spending households with $200,000 houses and will finance their $2,000 park program with a 1 percent property tax. The doubling of housing consumption cuts the property tax in half, so property taxes remain at $2,000. In general, a change in housing consumption will cause the household to move to a community where other households have (*a*) the same demand for public goods and (*b*) the same housing consumption.

In the Tiebout world, the discussion of the incidence of the property tax is meaningless. If households are sorted into homogeneous communities, the property tax is a user fee, and every household gets exactly what it pays for. The "incidence" of a $200 tax liability is the same as the "incidence" of a $1 hot

TABLE 14–2   Tiebout Sorting and the Property Tax

Municipality	*Property Value ($)*	*Park Budget ($)*	*Tax Rate (%)*
Wealthy—large budget	$100,000	$2,000	2.0%
Wealthy—small budget	100,000	200	0.2
Poor—large budget	50,000	2,000	4.0
Poor—small budget	50,000	200	0.4

dog: you pay the $1 to get the hot dog; you pay the $200 to get $200 worth of parks. Since the consumer's tax liability is independent of his housing choice, the property tax is a user fee, not a conventional tax.

How realistic is the Tiebout model? The conditions required for Tiebout equilibrium are unlikely to be satisfied. There are simply not enough local governments to allow households to sort themselves into perfectly homogeneous communities. The Tiebout model is clearly inapplicable to central cities, where a single municipality serves a large and diverse population. Therefore, the central-city property tax is not a user fee, but a conventional tax. In the suburbs, where there is more sorting of households with respect to demands for public services and housing consumption, the property tax is closer to a user fee.

Other Taxes

Property taxes generate less than half of municipal tax revenue. As shown in Figure 13–1, the sales tax raises about $3/10$ of municipal tax revenue, and the income tax raises about $1/6$ of municipal revenue. Larger cities rely to a greater extent on the municipal income tax: the income tax generates about one fifth of tax revenue in cities with populations greater than 300,000. This section discusses the incidence of the municipal sales tax and income tax.

Municipal Sales Tax

Who pays the municipal sales tax? According to the theory of tax incidence, the distribution of the tax burden depends on the elasticities of supply and demand: the relatively inelastic side of the market will pay a relatively large share of the tax.

Figure 14–4 shows the effects of a 25 percent general sales tax. The market starts at point *B*, with an equilibrium price of $8 and an equilibrium quantity of 30 units. The tax is paid, in legal terms, by the city's merchants: their costs increase by 25 percent, shifting the supply curve upward. The equilibrium net price (the price charged by the merchant plus the tax) will rise to $9.00, and total sales will decrease to 25 units (point *C*). Merchants charge consumers $9.00 and pay the government $1.80 in taxes, leaving them with $7.20. In this example, consumers pay about 55 percent of the tax (the $1 increase in price divided by the $1.80 tax).

How does a change in the elasticity of demand affect the distribution of the tax burden? Suppose that the demand curve in Figure 14–4 becomes more elastic: its slope decreases, and it pivots around point *B*. The flatter demand curve (shown by the dashed line) intersects the posttax supply curve at a lower net price, so consumers pay a smaller fraction of the tax. A relatively elastic demand means that consumers can more easily change their behavior, so they are better able to escape the tax.

How does a change in supply elasticity affect the distribution of the tax burden? For example, suppose the initial supply curve in Figure 14–4 is horizontal

FIGURE 14–4   Effects of Municipal Sales Tax

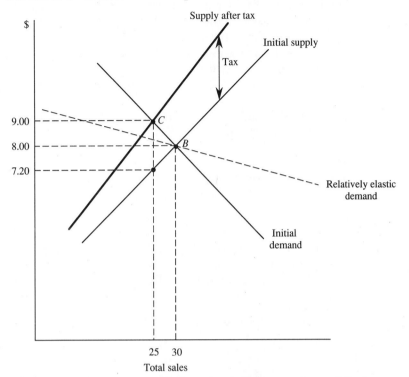

Before the sales tax, *B* is the equilibrium point. A 25 percent sales tax shifts the supply curve upward by 25 percent, generating a new equilibrium at point *C*. The consumer price rises from $8 to $9, and the net revenue of the merchant (price less tax) drops from $8.00 to $7.20.

(perfectly elastic). The sales tax will shift the supply curve up by the amount of the tax, and the posttax supply curve will intersect the demand curve at a price equal to the original price plus the tax. In other words, if supply is perfectly elastic, the consumer bears the entire tax. In general, the more elastic the supply curve (the flatter the curve), the smaller the supplier burden and the larger the consumer burden.

The sales tax also affects the urban land market. As the city's sales volume decreases, the demands for all inputs (labor, land, capital) decrease: merchants need fewer laborers, machines, buildings, and land. In the short run, the prices of these inputs will fall. In the long run, inputs that are mobile (e.g., labor and capital) will leave the taxing city, and the prices of the mobile inputs will recover. In contrast, land is immobile, so the tax-induced decrease in the demand for land will cause a long-term decrease in the price of land. Therefore, part of the sales tax will be borne by landowners. Although merchants receive a lower net price

($7.20 instead of $8), they can still make zero economic profit (normal accounting profit) because they pay less for immobile inputs (e.g., land).

This discussion of the city's input markets shows the link between tax policy and economic development. The sales tax increases the net price of the city's products, so the city will produce less output and use less capital, labor, and land. In other words, the tax decreases output and employment. The local economy is particularly sensitive to changes in taxes because firms and households can easily move between jurisdictions. Because of the high degree of intercity mobility, relatively small differences in tax rates can cause relatively large changes in the level of economic activity.

Municipal Income Tax

As shown in Chapter 13, the income tax generates about one sixth of municipal tax revenue. It will be useful to compare the municipal income tax to a national income tax. Figure 14–5 shows the effect of a national income tax. In the initial equilibrium (point B), the wage is $8 and the quantity of labor is N_o. Suppose that the federal government imposes an income tax of $2 per hour, which is paid in legal terms by the employer. The tax shifts the demand curve down by $2,

FIGURE 14-5   Effects of a National Income Tax

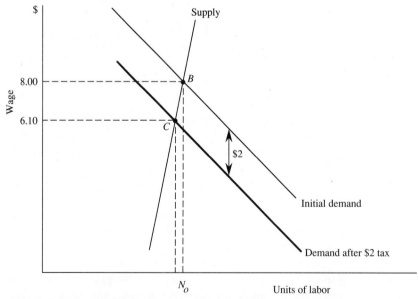

The initial equilibrium is point B. A $2 labor tax (paid by the employer) shifts the demand curve down by the amount of the tax, generating a new equilibrium at point C. The equilibrium wage (paid to laborers) drops from $8 to $6.10, meaning that workers pay about 95 percent of the $2 tax.

decreasing the market wage (paid to employees) from $8 to $6.10. The net cost of labor (the wage plus the employer's tax liability) rises from $8 to $8.10. Workers pay almost the entire tax because the supply of labor is relatively inelastic.

Figure 14–6 shows the effect of a municipal income tax. Since laborers can move easily from one municipality to another, the municipal supply curve is more elastic than the national supply curve. When the municipality imposes a $2 income tax, the demand curve shifts down by $2, decreasing the market wage from $8 to $7. Compared to the national income tax, the municipal tax causes a smaller decrease in the market wage ($1 instead of $1.90) because it is easier to escape the municipal tax. Because intercity migration is less costly than international migration, laborers bear a smaller fraction of the municipal tax.

The municipal income tax increases the net cost of labor from $8 to $9. In other words, the demander's share of the tax is $1. If all firms make zero profits, who actually pays this part of the tax? The tax is paid by the owners of immobile resources, that is, inputs that cannot be moved to other cities with the fleeing laborers. As the level of economic activity in the taxing city decreases (the number of laborers decreases from M' to M''), the demand for land decreases, decreasing the price of land. Although firms pay a higher net wage ($9 instead of $8), they also pay less for land, so they can still make zero economic profit.

FIGURE 14–6   **Effects of a Municipal Income Tax**

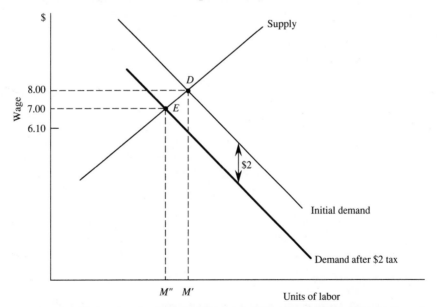

The initial equilibrium is point D. A $2 labor tax (paid by the employer) shifts the demand curve down by the amount of the tax, generating a new equilibrium at point E. The equilibrium wage (paid to laborers) drops from $8 to $7, meaning that suppliers pay only about half of the $2 tax. Workers pay a smaller portion of the municipal tax because the municipal supply of labor is more elastic than the national supply.

Intergovernmental Grants

As shown in Chapter 13, intergovernmental grants provide about two fifths of local government revenue. The spending programs receiving the largest amount of grant money are education, public welfare, housing and community development, highways, and health and hospitals.

Types of Grants

There are four types of grants to local governments:

1. **Unconditional grant.** An unconditional grant is a lump-sum grant with no strings attached. An example of an unconditional grant is general revenue sharing, under which the federal government provides unrestricted grants to localities.

2. **Conditional, or categorical, grant.** The money from conditional, or categorical, grants must be spent on a specific program. Conditional grants are provided for education, public welfare, health and hospitals, highways, housing, and community development. There are program-specific grants within each expenditure group. For example, there are education grants for remedial reading, school libraries, special education, and other programs.

3. **Matching grant.** Under a matching grant, the government contributes $m for every $1 of local spending on a program. One possibility is a one-for-one matching grant: every $1 of local spending generates $1 in grant money, so $1 of local spending buys $2 worth of local public goods. There are two types of matching grants, closed-ended and open-ended. Under a closed-ended matching grant, the government specifies a maximum grant amount. In contrast, there are no limits on the amount of money available under an open-ended grant.

4. **Block grant.** Under a block grant program, dozens of conditional grants are consolidated into a single general grant. For example, all grants for education (for special education, remedial reading, kindergartens, libraries, etc.) could be consolidated into a single block grant for education. The block grant is a compromise between unconditional and conditional grants. Although the city is forced to spend the entire education block grant on education, it can choose how to allocate the money between special education, remedial reading, kindergartens, and libraries. This greater flexibility is welcomed by local officials but is often opposed by state and federal officials, who lose some control over grant money.

Using Intergovernmental Grants

How will a local government use the money from an intergovernmental grant? Suppose that the state gives a city an unconditional grant of $2 million. The city makes the following announcement to its citizens: "The state has just given us a $2 million grant. Tell us how much to spend on public services, and we'll cut taxes to distribute the rest of the grant to you." If the city adheres to the preferences of its voters, it is likely to spend only a part of the grant on public service and use the rest of the grant to cut taxes. The empirical question is, What fraction of grant money is used for additional local spending, and how much is used to cut taxes? Inman (1979) summarizes the results of several studies of the local response to grants. He concludes local government spending increases by about 30 cents per dollar of grant money, leaving 70 cents per dollar for tax relief.

Summary

1. The property tax is a tax on land and improvements (capital). Since the supply of land is fixed, the land tax is borne by landowners.

2. There are two perspectives on the incidence of the improvement portion of the property tax:
   a. The traditional view takes a partial-equilibrium approach, focusing on the effect of the improvement tax on the taxing jurisdiction. The supply of dwellings is perfectly elastic, so the tax is paid by housing consumers.
   b. The new view takes a general-equilibrium approach, focusing on the effect of the tax on people inside *and* outside the taxing jurisdiction. Landlords throughout the region bear the tax, and consumers outside the taxing city gain at the expense of consumers in the taxing city.

3. The incidence of the improvement tax depends on one's perspective.
   a. A mayor should use the partial-equilibrium model (the traditional view) to estimate the effects of the city's property tax. From the local perspective, the tax is paid by local housing consumers.
   b. The president of the nation should use the general-equilibrium model to estimate the national effect of one city's tax. Because the tax causes zero-sum changes in housing rent, the president can ignore the effects on housing consumers. The tax is paid by the nation's capitalists.
   c. If all cities in the nation have the same property tax rate, the tax is paid by capitalists. There are no housing-price effects because there is nowhere for capitalists to move their capital.

4. In the Tiebout world, a household's property tax bill is independent of its housing consumption: households sort themselves into homogeneous communities, so a household's tax bill depends only on its consumption of public goods.

5. Taxes on sales and income are paid in part by landowners.

a. The municipal sales tax is paid by consumers, who pay higher prices, and landowners, who receive less rent.

b. The municipal income tax is paid by laborers, who receive lower wages, and landowners. Because labor is more mobile between municipalities than between nations, labor's share of a municipal income tax is smaller than its share of a national income tax.

6. The states provide the bulk of grants to local governments (86 percent of all grants). Grants are used to internalize externalities and to solve the mismatch problem (desired spending rising faster than tax revenue).

7. Under a block grant program, dozens of conditional grants are consolidated into a single general grant.

Exercises and Discussion Questions

1. Consider the new view of the property tax. Compute the long-run effects of Taxville's property tax on the following individuals. How much do they gain or lose?
   a. Ms. Partial rents a house in Taxville.
   b. Mr. Wash is a traveling salesman who rents one dwelling in Taxville and one in Notax.
   c. Ms. Capitalist owns five dwellings in Taxville.
   d. Mr. Capitalist owns five dwellings in Notax.

2. Mr. Javelin is the economic forecaster for the city of Drip, Oregon. You are his research assistant and do all of his computations. The city is considering a tax of $2 per raincoat. In estimating the revenue from the raincoat tax, you make the following assumptions:
   i. The supply of raincoats to the city is perfectly elastic.
   ii. The current price of raincoats is $20, and the current quantity of raincoats demanded is 1,000 per week.
   iii. The price elasticity of demand for raincoats is -2.0.
   a. Estimate the tax revenue from the raincoat tax.
   b. When Mr. Javelin sees your computations, he says, "Those revenue projections look pretty low. You know, the state imposed a $2 raincoat tax several years ago, and it raised $39,000 per week. Since about 5 percent of the state's raincoats are bought in Drip, I would expect that we would raise about 5 percent of the revenue raised by the state tax. If your revenue projection is less than $1,950, it's wrong." Is Mr. Javelin correct? If so, what is your mistake? If not, what is wrong with his analysis?

3. Suppose that Collegetown eliminates its tax on pizza parlors and increases its tax on residential property. Under what conditions will the change in tax policy decrease the tax liability of Joe College?

References and Additional Readings

Aaron, Henry J. *Who Pays the Property Tax? A New View*. Washington, D.C.: Brookings Institution, 1975. Discusses the traditional and new views of the property tax.

Aronson, J. Richard, and John L. Hilley. *Financing State and Local Governments*. Washington, D.C.: Brookings Institution, 1986.

Bradbury, Katharine L.; Anthony Downs; and Kenneth A. Small. *Urban Decline and the Future of American Cities*. Washington, D.C.: Brookings Institution, 1982. Discusses the reasons for the economic problems of cities.

Humphrey, Nance; George Peterson; and Peter Wilson. *The Future of Cleveland's Capital Plant*. Washington, D.C.: Urban Institute, 1979. Discusses the fiscal problems of Cleveland.

Inman, Robert P. "The Fiscal Performance of Local Governments: An Interpretive Review." In *Current Issues in Urban Economics,* ed. Peter Meiszkowski and Mahlon Straszheim. Baltimore, Md.: Johns Hopkins University Press, 1979, pp. 270–321. Summarizes studies of the price and income elasticities of demand for local public goods, and the elasticity of local expenditures with respect to intergovernmental aid.

Meiszkowski, Peter. "The Property Tax: An Excise Tax or a Profits Tax?" *Journal of Public Economics* 1 (1972), pp. 73–96. Discusses the new view of the property tax.

Pechman, Joseph A. *Who Paid the Taxes, 1966–85?* Washington, D.C.: Brookings Institution, 1985.

CHAPTER

15 Autos and Highways

This is the first of two chapters on urban transportation. This chapter discusses the most popular travel mode, the automobile, which is used by about 83 percent of U.S. commuters. It examines two transportation problems caused by the automobile: congestion and air pollution. Congestion during rush hours is inevitable, and a certain level of congestion is actually efficient. Just as it would be inefficient to eliminate all air pollution, it would be inefficient to eliminate all congestion. The question is whether congestion is at the optimum level. If not, there are a number of policies that could decrease congestion, including various taxes on auto travel, subsidies for mass transit, and highway construction. The second problem is air pollution, which is controlled by the federal government through its auto emissions policies. The question is whether other pollution-control policies such as pollution taxes or gas taxes might be more efficient in controlling pollution.

Table 15–1 shows commuting patterns and auto usage in U.S. cities in 1980. About one third of workers commute within the central city, and about one fifth commute from a suburban residence to a central-city job. The most frequent commuting trip is from a suburban residence to a suburban job, a trip made by about 40 percent of commuters. Over four fifths of commuters travel to work by car, truck, or van, and about three fourths of these commuters drive to work alone. The private vehicle is most popular among suburbanites: it is used by over 90 percent of the workers who commute from the suburbs to the city center and by over 87 percent of the workers who commute from one suburb to another.

Congestion: Equilibrium versus Optimum Traffic Volume

Most cities suffer from traffic congestion during the morning and evening rush hours. To explain the congestion phenomenon, consider a city with the following characteristics:

TABLE 15–1   **Commuting Patterns and Auto Use, 1980**

Type of Commute Trip	Percentage of All Trips	Percentage Using Car, Truck, or Van	Percentage Driving Alone	Percentage in Car Pools
Central city to central city	33.1%	72.4	56.1	16.3
Central city to suburb	6.8	91.3	69.2	22.1
Suburb to central city	20.1	90.3	68.1	22.2
Suburb to suburb	40.1	87.5	69.7	17.8
Total	100	83.3	64.9	18.5

SOURCE: U.S. Bureau of the Census, *1980 Census of Population: Journey to Work—Metropolitan Commuting Flows* (Washington, D.C.: U.S. Government Printing Office, 1984).

1. **Radial highway.** There is a two-lane highway from the suburbs to the city center (a distance of 10 miles).
2. **Monetary travel cost.** The monetary cost of auto travel is 20 cents per mile.
3. **Time cost.** The opportunity cost of travel time is ten cents per minute.

The total cost of a commuting trip is the sum of the monetary and time costs of the 10-mile trip. The monetary cost is $2 (10 miles times 20 cents per mile). The time cost depends on travel time: a trip that takes 30 minutes has a time cost of $3 (30 minutes times 10 cents per minute); a 20-minute trip has a time cost of only $2. Therefore, the total cost of a 30-minute trip is $5.00 ($2 plus $3), and the total cost of a 20-minute trip is $4.

The Demand for Urban Travel

Consider first the demand side of the urban travel market. Figure 15–1 shows the demand curve for travel along the radial highway. The horizontal axis measures the number of vehicles per lane per hour. The vertical axis measures the cost of the commuting trip, the sum of the monetary and time costs of the 10-mile trip. The demand curve shows, for each trip cost, how many travelers will use the highway. For example, if the trip cost is $12.80, there will be 1,200 people for whom the benefit of the trip exceeds the cost, so there will be 1,200 vehicles per lane per hour. As the cost of the trip decreases, there are more people for whom the benefit exceeds the cost, so the city moves downward along the travel demand curve: there are 1,400 vehicles at a cost of $9.14, and 1,600 vehicles at a cost of $5.48.

The demand curve is a **marginal benefit curve.** For each traffic volume, it shows how much the marginal traveler is willing to pay for the highway trip. Suppose that the city starts with a trip cost of $9.15 and a traffic volume of 1,399. If the trip cost decreases to $9.14, traffic volume increases to 1,400, meaning that the 1,400th driver is willing to pay $9.14 to make the trip: at any cost above $9.14, the trip would not be worthwhile. The demand curve shows

FIGURE 15–1   Congestion Externalities and the Congestion Tax

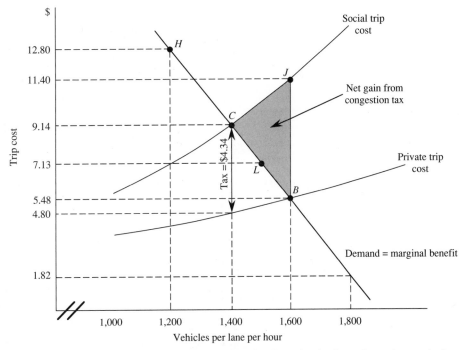

Drivers use the highway as long as the marignal benefit (shown by the demand curve) exceeds the private trip cost, so the equilibrium traffic volume is 1,600 vehicles per lane per hour. At the optimum, the marginal benefit equals the marginal social cost (the social trip cost). The equilibrium volume (1,600) exceeds the optimum volume (1,400) because drivers ignore the external costs of their trips. A congestion tax of $4.34 will "internalize" the congestion externality, generating the optimum traffic volume.

that the marginal benefit of the 10-mile trip decreases from $12.80 for the 1,200th driver to $1.82 for the 1,800th driver.

The Private and Social Costs of Travel

Table 15–2 shows the relationships between traffic volume and travel time. Column *B* lists the trip time (the travel time per driver) for different traffic volumes. For traffic volumes up to 400 vehicles per lane per hour, there is no congestion: everyone travels at the legal speed limit of 50 miles per hour, and the 10-mile trip takes 12 minutes. For traffic volume above 400 vehicles, the computations are based on the following formula:

$$\text{Trip time} = 12.0 + 0.001 \cdot (\text{Volume} - 400) + 0.000015 \cdot (\text{Volume} - 400)^2$$

TABLE 15–2 Traffic Volume, Travel Time, Travel Costs, and Congestion Externalities

A Traffic Volume (vehicles)	B Trip Time (minutes)	C Increase in Travel Time per Driver (minutes)	D Increase in Total Travel Time (minutes)	E External Trip Cost ($)	F Private Trip Cost ($)	G Social Trip Cost ($)	H Marginal Benefit (demand)
200	12.00	0	0	0	3.20	3.20	31.10
400	12.00	0	0	0	3.20	3.20	27.44
600	12.80	0.007	4.19	0.42	3.28	3.70	23.78
800	14.80	0.013	10.39	1.04	3.48	4.52	20.12
1,000	18.00	0.019	18.98	1.90	3.80	5.70	16.46
1,200	22.40	0.025	29.98	3.00	4.24	7.24	12.80
1,400	28.00	0.031	43.37	4.34	4.80	9.14	9.14
1,600	34.80	0.037	59.16	5.92	5.48	11.40	5.48
1,800	42.80	0.034	77.36	7.74	6.28	14.02	1.82
2,000	52.00	0.049	97.95	9.80	7.20	17.00	

When the 401st driver enters the highway, the congestion threshold is crossed. As the highway becomes crowded, the space between vehicles decreases, and drivers slow down to maintain safe distances between cars. As more and more drivers enter the highway, travel speeds decrease and travel times increase: the trip takes 12.8 minutes if there are 600 vehicles, 22.4 minutes for 1,200 vehicles, and 52.0 minutes for 2,000 vehicles.

Columns *C* and *D* show the effects of the marginal driver on the travel times of other drivers. For low traffic volumes (below 400 vehicles), an additional driver does not affect speeds or travel times. For volumes above 400 vehicles, however, an additional driver slows traffic and increases travel times. For example, the 600th driver increases the travel time *per driver* by 0.007 minutes (column *C*): when the driver enters the highway, the trip time increases from 12.793 to 12.80. The increase in total travel time is simply the extra time per driver (0.007) times the number of other drivers (599), or 4.19 minutes (column *D*). This is the **congestion externality:** the marginal driver slows traffic and increases travel time, forcing other drivers to spend more time on the road. The congestion externality increases with traffic volume: the 1,200th driver increases travel time by 29.98 minutes (0.025 minutes times 1,199), and the 1,600th driver increases travel time by 59.16 minutes (0.037 times 1,599).

The **external trip cost** equals the monetary value of the congestion externality. The figures in column *E* are based on the assumption that the opportunity cost of travel time is 10 cents per minute. For the 600th driver, the external trip cost equals the increase in total travel time (4.2 minutes) times 10 cents per minute, or 42 cents (rounded to two decimal points). The external trip cost increases with traffic volume, rising to $3.00 for the 1,200th driver; $5.92 for the 1,600th driver; and $9.80 for the 2,000th driver.

Columns *F* and *G* show the private and social costs of travel. The **private trip cost** is the travel cost incurred by the individual commuter, defined as the sum of the monetary cost ($2.00) and the private time cost. To compute the private time cost, multiply the trip time by the opportunity cost of travel time: the opportunity cost is 10 cents per minute, so the private time cost is $1.20 for a volume of 200 vehicles, $1.28 for 600 vehicles, and so on. Therefore, the private trip cost is $3.20 for 200 vehicles, $3.28 for 600 vehicles, and so on. The **social trip cost** is the sum of the private trip cost (column *G*) and the external trip cost (column *E*). Figure 15–1 shows the cost curves for private trip cost and social trip cost. The social-cost curve lies above the private-cost curve, with the gap between the two curves equal to the external trip cost.

There are some alternative labels for private and social trip costs. An alternative label for private trip cost is **average travel cost,** defined as total travel cost divided by the number of drivers. Since each driver travels at the same speed and thus has the same travel cost, the average travel cost equals the private trip cost. An alternative label for social trip cost is **marginal travel cost,** defined as the increase in the total costs of travel resulting from adding one more traveler. Since the social trip cost equals the trip cost incurred by the marginal driver plus the external costs he imposed on other drivers, the social trip cost is the same as the marginal travel cost.

Equilibrium versus Optimum Traffic Volume

What is the equilibrium number of drivers? A driver will use the highway if the marginal benefit of the trip (from the demand curve) exceeds the private trip cost. In Figure 15–1, the demand curve intersects the private-trip-cost curve at 1,600, so the equilibrium number of vehicles is 1,600 and the equilibrium private trip cost is $5.48. The 1,601st driver does not use the highway because the marginal benefit of using the highways is less than the trip cost.

What is the optimum number of drivers? The basic efficiency rule is that an activity should be increased as long as the marginal social benefit exceeds the marginal social cost; at the optimum level, the marginal benefit equals the marginal cost. In Figure 15–1, the marginal social benefit is shown by the demand curve and the marginal social cost is shown by the social-trip-cost curve. The demand curve intersects the social-trip-cost curve at a volume of 1,400, so the optimum traffic volume is 1,400 vehicles. For the first 1,400 drivers, the social benefit of travel exceeds the social cost, so their use of the highways is efficient. For the 1,401st driver, the social cost exceeds the benefit, so his use of the highway is inefficient.

The equilibrium volume exceeds the optimum volume because drivers ignore the costs they impose on other drivers. An additional driver slows traffic, forcing other drivers to spend more time on the road. Suppose that Carla, the 1,599th driver, has a private benefit of $5.49. From column F in Table 15–2, the private trip cost for 1,599 vehicles is about $5.48, so Carla will use the highway. Her use of the highway is inefficient because the benefit of the trip ($5.49) is less than the social cost of the trip ($11.40, equal to the sum of Carla's private cost of $5.48 and the external trip cost of $5.92). Because Carla ignores the $5.92 worth of external cost, she makes an inefficient choice.

The Policy Response: Congestion Tax

The government could use a congestion tax to generate the optimum traffic volume. A tax equal to the external trip cost would internalize the congestion externality, generating the optimum number of drivers. In Figure 15–1, a congestion tax of $4.34 per trip would shift the private-trip-cost curve upward by $4.34, decreasing the equilibrium number of drivers from 1,600 to 1,400. The 1,401st driver would not use the road because the benefit of the trip ($9.14) would be less than the full cost of the trip ($9.14, the sum of the $4.80 private cost and the $4.34 congestion tax). Because the congestion tax closes the gap between private and social costs, the individual driver bases his travel decision on the social cost of travel. Therefore, the highway will be used efficiently.

From the perspective of the individual traveler, the imposition of congestion taxes generates good news and bad news. Suppose that Helen is one of the 1,400 travelers who continues to use the highway after the congestion tax is imposed. For Helen, the bad news is that she must pay a congestion tax of $4.34. One bit of goods news is that because traffic volume falls, her commuting trip takes less time: from column *F* of Table 15–2, the decrease in traffic volume decreases the private trip cost from $5.48 to $4.80, a savings of 68 cents. The second bit of good news is that she will pay lower taxes on other goods: the government will use the revenue from the congestion tax to decrease other local taxes. For example, the government could substitute congestion taxes for the gasoline tax, which is currently used to finance highways. If Helen's tax cut is at least $3.66, she will be better off after the imposition of the congestion tax.

Peak versus Off-Peak Travel

To be efficient, the congestion tax must vary across time and space. The tax will be higher on relatively congested highways. The most congested highways are the ones leading to and from employment centers. Most congestion occurs during the morning rush hours and the evening rush hours. According to Straszheim (1979), about a quarter of all trips are made during the morning and evening rush hours. McConnell-Fay (1986) reports that 64 percent of the trips from homes to workplaces in the San Francisco Bay area occur between 6:30 and 8:30 A.M., and 57 percent of the workplace-home trips occur between 4:30 and 6:30 P.M.. Figure 15–2 shows the demand curves and congestion tolls for the peak period and the off-peak period. Given the high volume of traffic during the peak period (V_p, compared to V_o during the off-peak period), the peak-period congestion toll is higher.

Estimates of Congestion Taxes

What is the optimum congestion tax? In a study of the San Francisco Bay area, Keeler and Small (1977) estimated congestion taxes for different locations and times. Pozdena (1988) has recently updated the Keeler and Small estimates. He estimates that during the peak travel periods, the congestion tax would be 65 cents per mile on central urban highways, 21 cents per mile on suburban highways, and 17 cents per mile on fringe highways. During the off-peak periods, the taxes would be between 3 and 5 cents per mile at all locations. Because the San Francisco Bay area is more congested than most metropolitan areas, the optimum congestion taxes would be lower in most other metropolitan areas.

Suppose the San Francisco Bay area implemented such a system of congestion tolls. How much would different types of commuters pay for travel during the peak periods? Consider first a suburban commuter who travels to a job in the central city, traveling seven miles on suburban highways and three miles on central urban highways. The commuter's one-way congestion bill would be $3.42 (seven times 21 cents plus three miles times 65 cents), so the daily congestion tax would be

FIGURE 15-2   Congestion Tax during Peak and Off-Peak Periods

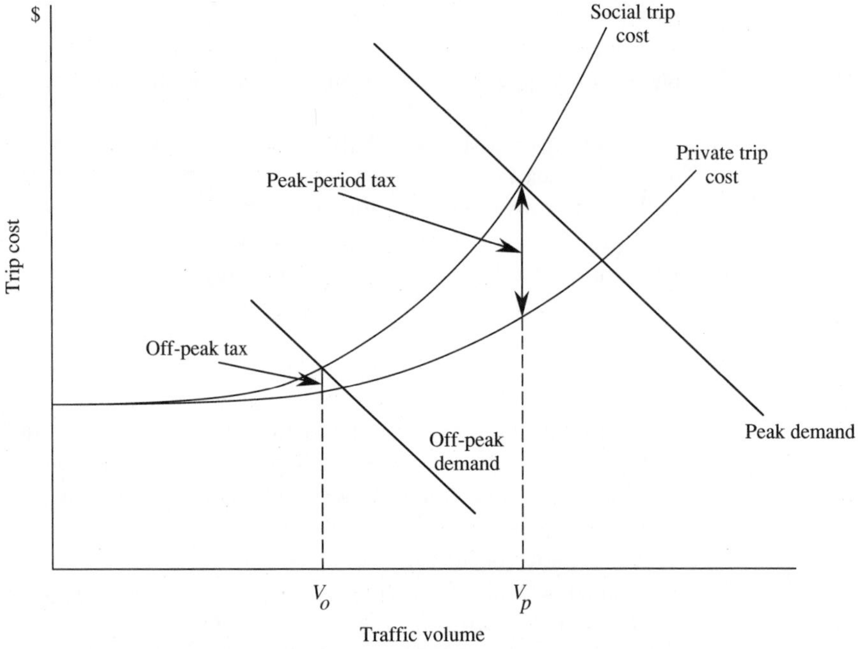

During the off-peak period, the demand for travel is relatively low, generating a low traffic volume (V_o, compared to V_p during the peak period), so the optimum congestion tax is relatively low.

$6.84. Consider next a suburban commuter who travels eight miles to a job in another suburb. The commuter's one-way congestion tax would be $1.68 (eight miles times 21 cents per mile).

Implementing the Congestion Tax

How would the government collect the congestion tax? One possibility is to install toll booths on every road and collect the tax directly from drivers. This option is impractical because the collection process will slow traffic, causing more congestion. The high-technology version of toll booths is a vehicle identification system (VIS). Under a VIS, every car is equipped with an electronic device that allows sensors along the road to identify the car as it passes. The system records the number of times a vehicle uses the congested highway and sends a congestion bill to the driver at the end of the month. For example, a driver who travels 10 miles along a congested highway 20 times per month would pay a monthly congestion bill of $86.80 (20 times $4.34).

Why haven't cities used the VIS to impose congestion taxes? The systems are relatively inexpensive, so the opposition is not based on the costs of installing and running the system. Some people oppose the VIS because they oppose congestion taxes of any form. A common complaint is that congestion taxes would be "regressive" (the poor would pay a larger fraction of their income for taxes). There is no evidence to support this view. Even if congestion taxes were regressive, the government could presumably adjust other taxes to offset the undesirable distributional effects of tolls. Other people oppose the VIS because they are troubled by the potential threat to civil liberties: the information gathered from the VIS might be used by an inquisitive government to spy on its citizens.

Alternatives to a Congestion Tax: Taxes on Auto Use

Given the practical difficulties in imposing a congestion tax, a number of alternative policies have been proposed. One set of policies discourages auto use by increasing the cost of auto travel. Three of the pricing options are gasoline taxes, parking taxes, and congestion-zone taxes. How effective are these policies compared to the congestion tax?

To evaluate the efficacy of the alternative policies, it will be useful to list the four ways that the congestion tax decreases traffic volume:

1. **Modal substitution.** The congestion tax increases the cost of auto travel relative to carpooling and mass transit (buses, subways, light rail), causing some travelers to switch to these other travel modes.
2. **Time of travel.** The congestion tax will be highest during the peak travel periods, causing some travelers to travel at different times. Because work and study schedules are relatively inflexible, commuters and students would be less likely than other travelers (e.g., shoppers) to change their travel times. Nonetheless, firms would have a greater incentive to change work schedules to allow their workers to avoid costly travel during the peak period. The institution of "flextime" and the rearrangement of shift times would cause some workers to change their travel times.
3. **Travel route.** The congestion tax will be highest on the most congested routes, causing some travelers to switch to alternative routes.
4. **Location choices.** The congestion tax increases the unit cost of travel (travel cost per mile), causing some commuters to decrease their commuting distances. Some workers may move closer to their jobs, and others may switch to a job closer to their residence.

These four changes cause the city to move up the travel demand curve as the cost of travel increases. In Figure 15–1, the congestion tax decreases traffic volume from 1,600 to 1,400 because it changes travel modes, times, routes, and distances.

Gasoline Tax

One alternative to the congestion tax is a gasoline tax. The idea is that if travel is more expensive, traffic volume will decrease. The problem is that the gas tax increases the costs of all automobile travel, not just travel along congested routes during peak periods. In contrast to the congestion tax, which changes travel times and routes, the gas tax does not encourage drivers to switch to other travel times or routes.

Suppose the government wants to use the gasoline tax to decrease the peak-period traffic volume to its optimum level. What is the required gasoline tax? To have the same effect as the congestion tax in Figure 15–1, the gas tax must increase the cost of travel by 43.4 cents per mile ($4.34 per 10-mile trip). If the typical car gets 25 miles per gallon of gasoline, the required gas tax will be $10.85 per gallon (43.4 cents times 25). Such a gasoline tax is obviously infeasible. Even if it were feasible, it would be inefficient because it also increases the cost of off-peak travel by 43.4 cents per mile.

Parking Tax

A number of cities use parking taxes to discourage driving to CBD jobs. In an experiment in Madison, Wisconsin, a tax surcharge of $1 was imposed on drivers who arrived at parking garages during the peak travel period (7:00 A.M. to 9:00 A.M.) and left their cars for more than three hours. As explained by Parody (1984), the surcharge decreased traffic volume because (*a*) some commuters switched to car pools and mass transit, and (*b*) some travelers changed their travel times. In Washington, D.C., the government increased parking costs for its employees, causing some workers to switch to car pools and mass transit (Miller and Everett, 1982). In Ottowa, Canada, the government increased parking rates for government employees from 0 to 70 percent of the commercial rate, causing (*a*) a 23 percent decrease in the number of workers driving to work, (*b*) a 6 percent increase in the auto occupancy rate (from 1.33 to 1.41), and (*c*) a 16 percent increase in bus ridership (DiRenzo, Cima, and Barber, 1981). In a series of experiments in Los Angeles, the elimination of free parking decreased the number of solo drivers by 18 percent to 83 percent. When one Los Angeles firm increased its parking fee from 0 to $28.75 per month, the number of solo drivers dropped by 44 percent; when the firm increased the monthly fee to $57.50, solo driving decreased 81 percent (Small, 1992).

There are three potential problems with using parking taxes to decrease congestion. The first is that the taxes must be imposed only on peak-period commuters; drivers who travel during the off-peak period should be exempt from the tax. As shown by the Madison experiment, this problem can be solved by imposing a surcharge for drivers who arrive at parking garages during the peak travel period. Second, in contrast with the congestion tax, which increases the unit cost of travel and decreases travel distances, the parking tax does not depend on the distance traveled. Therefore, there will be less incentive for commuters to economize on travel costs by living closer to their workplaces. Third, because much of the congestion problem is caused by cars that do not park in congested areas, the tax will not force all peak-period travelers to pay for their congestion.

Shoup (1982) suggests that the subsidization of parking by private employers contributes to the congestion problem. Using data from the 1970s, he shows that over 90 percent of commuters parked for free. Shoup estimates that if private parking subsidies were eliminated, about 20 percent of drive-alone commuters would switch to some sort of ride sharing or mass transit. A recent study of Los Angeles (Willson, 1988) suggests that subsidies are widespread and large. Only 14 percent of employers in the city did not offer any subsidies, and the median subsidy was $3.71 per day (compared to a median parking cost of $5 per day). If employers replaced the parking subsides with cash payments, the increase in parking costs would encourage some workers to carpool or use mass transit.

Congestion Zones and Permits

A third congestion policy involves the establishment of congestion zones, areas where access would be limited to drivers who paid a special fee. Under a scheme proposed for London in 1974, all vehicles using the inner streets between 8:00 A.M. and 6:00 P.M. were to pay a flat fee (Altshuler, 1979). The scheme generated heated debate and was never implemented. Singapore implemented a congestion-zone scheme in 1975. To drive in the central area of the city between 7:30 and 10:15 A.M., auto drivers must buy a permit costing about $1.30 per day. Travel within the control area is free to buses, motorcycles, and car pools.

Singapore's zone policy generated some interesting results. During the morning hours, auto traffic in the control zone decreased by 74 percent and travel speeds increased by 22 percent (Altshuler, 1979). Many commuters drove their cars to the edge of the control area and then rode buses to their downtown workplaces. During the afternoon rush hours (when driving permits were not required), the changes in traffic volume and travel speeds were relatively small. Some commuters took public transit to central-city workplaces in the morning but were picked up at the end of the day by family members. Through traffic, which used circumferential routes during the morning control period, resumed its radial travel pattern in the afternoon.

Alternatives to Auto Taxes

The congestion policies discussed so far decrease congestion by increasing the cost of driving. There are several alternative approaches. One option is to increase the carrying capacity of the highway, and another is to subsidize transit ridership.

Capacity Expansion and Traffic Design

One response to the congestion problem is to widen the highway to increase its carrying capacity. Figure 15–3 shows the effects of such a policy on travel times and traffic volume. The wider road reaches the congestion threshold at a

FIGURE 15–3   **Effects of Widening the Highway**

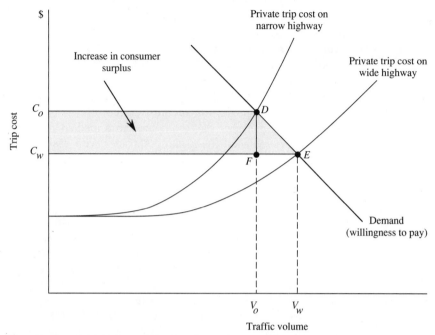

The widening of the highway shifts the private trip cost to the right: the congestion threshold increases, and trip cost is lower at every traffic volume above the original threshold volume. The decrease in trip cost increases traffic volume from V_o to V_w.

higher traffic volume and has a lower private trip cost at all volumes above the original congestion threshold ($V = 400$). The decrease in trip costs increases traffic volume as the city moves down the demand curve from point D to point E.

The city could also improve the flow of traffic on the existing highway. Street lights can be synchronized to keep traffic flowing at a steady speed. The use of one-way streets and restrictions of on-street parking increase the carrying capacity of streets. Some cities have placed stoplights on expressway on-ramps, thus smoothing the flow of vehicles onto expressways. In the language of transportation engineers, the ramp lights decrease the "turbulence" caused by entering vehicles, increasing travel speeds. In Los Angeles, the installation of such a system on the Harbor Freeway increased average travel speeds from 15 miles per hour to 40 miles per hour. A similar system in Dallas increased travel speeds from 14 miles per hour to 30 miles per hour.

Subsidies for Transit

Another alternative to the taxation of auto travel is the subsidization of mass transit (buses, subways, commuter trains, light rail). Transit and autos are substitute travel modes, so a decrease in the cost of transit will cause some consumers to switch from autos to transit. In other words, a transit subsidy will decrease the auto volume, narrowing the gap between the equilibrium and optimum traffic volumes.

The fundamental problem with a transit subsidy is that it underprices transit, increasing ridership above its optimum level. In the absence of congestion taxes, a transit subsidy may improve the efficiency of the transportation system, but the subsidy will never be as efficient as a system of congestion taxes.

Autos and Air Pollution

Another urban transportation problem is air pollution. Autos and trucks contribute to air pollution in a number of ways:

1. **Photochemical smog.** Smog results from the combination of hydrocarbons, nitrogen oxides, sunlight, and heat. In the typical city, autos and trucks generate about 40 percent of hydrocarbons and about 40 percent of nitrogen oxides. For healthy people, smog causes physical discomfort, coughing, and nausea. For people who suffer from respiratory disease, smog causes more serious health problems.

2. **Carbon monoxide.** About 83 percent of carbon monoxide is generated by motor vehicles. In high concentrations, carbon monoxide decreases the breathing capacity and alertness of healthy individuals, and causes pain and discomfort for people who suffer from cardiovascular disease.

3. **Lead.** About 88 percent of lead comes from motor vehicles. If lead is absorbed into the blood at high concentrations, it can cause serious health problems.

4. **Suspended particulates.** About 9 percent of particulate matter comes from motor vehicles. Some particulates cause respiratory problems, and others are suspected of causing cancer.

5. **Nitrogen oxides.** Autos and trucks generate about two fifths of nitrogen oxides. The experts disagree about the health effects of nitrogen oxides.

Although everyone agrees that automobiles and trucks are significant sources of air pollution, there is disagreement about what should be done about the problem.

The Economic Approach: Effluent Fees

The economic approach to air pollution starts with a description of the externality problem. Drivers base their travel decisions on the marginal private cost of driving, which is less than the marginal social cost because autos and trucks cause air pollution. The pollution externality causes people (*a*) to drive cars that generate a relatively large amount of pollution per mile driven and (*b*) to drive too many miles. To an economist, the obvious response is to force people to pay for pollution, that is, to internalize the externality.

One approach would be to install a monitoring device in every car. Such a device would measure the car's emissions, allowing the government to tax the car owner for the air pollution caused by the car. For example, if the estimated pollution cost per unit of carbon monoxide is 1 cent, the monthly bill would be $2 for a vehicle that emits 200 units per month and $3 for a vehicle that emits 300 units. Such a scheme is obviously impractical, but it illustrates the basic objective of policy: drivers should pay for the pollution their cars generate. The trick is to estimate how much pollution each car generates.

An alternative approach is to impose a one-time pollution tax on automobiles. The government could estimate (*a*) the lifetime emissions of a particular car model and (*b*) the cost per unit of pollution. The pollution tax for a particular model would be set equal to the product of total emissions and the unit cost. For example, if model B is expected to emit 5,000 units of carbon monoxide (CO) over its lifetime and the unit cost of CO is 1 cent, its CO tax would be $50. If the same car is expected to emit 400 units of lead and the unit cost of lead pollution is 50 cents, its lead tax would be $200. The car's total pollution tax would equal the sum of the taxes for CO, lead, nitrogen oxides, hydrocarbons, and particulates. Under this scheme, car buyers would pay more for cars that generate more pollution, so consumers would have the incentive to buy cleaner cars.

Another approach is to use a gasoline tax to increase the private cost of auto travel. The tax would increase the cost per mile driven, so it would decrease the total miles driven, decreasing air pollution. The problem with the gas tax is that every driver would pay the same tax, regardless of how much pollution his or her car generates. In other words, there would be no practical way to impose a higher tax on cars that generate more pollution. Such a tax would decrease pollution by decreasing miles driven, not by persuading people to drive cleaner cars.

What is the marginal external cost of auto driving? Straszheim (1979) summarizes the results of a number of studies of auto-related air pollution. In the 1970s, the cost of auto pollution was between 0.5 and 0.8 cents per mile driven. Since then, auto emissions rates have decreased as a result of federal emissions policy, pulling down the cost per mile driven. Between 1970 and 1983, hydrocarbon emissions per mile dropped by two thirds, carbon monoxide dropped by three fifths, and nitrogen oxides dropped by one third (Crandall, Gruenspecht, Keeler, and Lave, 1986). During this same period, the price level rose, pulling up the pollution cost per mile. The net effect of inflation and falling emission rates is a moderate increase in the cost per mile driven. If the cost per mile is 1 cent and the typical car gets 25 miles per gallon, the appropriate gasoline tax would be about 25 cents per gallon.

Regulatory Policy

The Environmental Protection Agency (EPA) has adopted a two-part strategy for controlling air pollution. First, the EPA has established emissions standards for autos and trucks. The standards control four pollutants: nitrogen oxides (NO_x), carbon monoxide (CO), hydrocarbons (HC), and lead. Second, the EPA has established standards for ambient air quality, specifying maximum concentration (parts per million) for NO_x, lead, CO, sulfur oxides (SO_x), and particulate matter.

Emissions Policy.   The national emissions policy started with the Motor Vehicle Pollution Control Act of 1965. In 1963, the state of California set maximum emission levels for CO, HC, and NO_x. The emissions standards were first applied to the 1966 model year. In 1965, the federal government extended the California standards to the rest of the nation, with the standards applied to the 1968 model year. In 1970, the amendments to the Clean Air Act mandated 90 percent reductions in CO, HC, and NO_x by 1975. Automakers were unable to meet the deadlines for the emissions standards, so the EPA relaxed the standards and extended the deadlines. By 1980, new-car emissions of HC and CO had been reduced to the target levels. The NO_x emissions proved more difficult to control: by 1980, they had been reduced by half.

The emissions program has decreased auto emissions considerably. Although the total miles driven increased between 1970 and 1983, total emissions decreased. In 1983, the volume of hydrocarbons generated per mile was only 33 percent of the corresponding figure for 1970 (Crandall, Gruenspecht, Keeler, and Lave, 1986). The 1983 figure for carbon monoxide was 40 percent of the 1970 figure, and the 1983 figure for nitrogen oxides was 65 percent of the 1970 figure.

Costs and Benefits of the Emissions Policy.   What are the benefits of the emissions policy? Freeman (1982) estimated the benefits that would occur if all auto-related pollution were eliminated. He divides the benefits of cleaner air into health benefits (e.g., decreased risk for cardiac patients); the reduction of damage to vegetation (e.g., increased crop and forest yields); and aesthetic benefits (e.g., increased visibility). He estimated that the total benefit from eliminating air pollution from autos would be about $8.3 billion per year (in 1984 dollars).

What are the costs of the emissions policy? Crandall, Gruenspecht, Keeler, and Lave (1986) estimated that the national emissions standards added $1,601 to the cost of a 1984 car, including $592 in additional equipment and $1,009 in additional fuel and maintenance costs. Based on this figure, they estimate that the total cost of emissions standards was about $16.8 billion per year. In other words, the total cost of the 1984 emissions policy, which decreased but did not eliminate auto pollution, is about twice the estimated benefit that would occur if all auto-related pollution were eliminated ($8.3 billion).

It's important to note that there is a great deal of uncertainty about the health effects of air pollution. Therefore, it is difficult to estimate the benefits of pollution abatement, and Freeman's estimates should be used with caution. In addition, the estimates do not take into account the greenhouse effect or the depletion of the ozone, two phenomena that scientists are only beginning to explore. Nonetheless, the available evidence suggests that the costs of the current emissions program far outweigh the benefits we know about and can quantify. There is heated debate in policy circles about some subtle health effects of air pollution that are not included in benefit-cost studies.

Ambient Air Quality Standards.   As part of the 1970 amendments to the Clean Air Act, the EPA established standards for ambient air quality. The individual states were made responsible for meeting the standards. In response, most states issued permits for stationary sources of pollution but did little to control mobile sources (autos and trucks).

In the early 1970s, it became clear that many cities would not satisfy the EPA air-quality standards by 1975. To prevent widespread violations of the standards, the EPA granted two-year extensions to the 1975 deadline. In addition, the EPA drafted plans to regulate auto traffic in cities that were expected to continue to violate the standards. The EPA plan for Los Angeles, for example, would have decreased auto traffic by 84 percent. The plans for three other cities called for reductions of at least 50 percent. The EPA planned to decrease traffic by imposing parking taxes and decreasing the supply of parking slots. The resulting public outcry forced the EPA to abandon these plans.

The 1977 amendments to the Clean Air Act were weak and ineffective. The deadline for meeting the EPA standards was extended 10 years, to 1987. Some cities did not satisfy the standards by the end of 1982. The EPA directed these cities to develop plans to implement inspection and maintenance programs for auto emissions. Many cities developed plans but did not implement them and were therefore subject to trivial penalties. The EPA got the cities to do the paperwork, but it was less successful in getting the cities to meet its criteria for pollution control.

The 1977 amendments did include one innovative feature for the control of stationary pollution sources. In cities where the EPA standards were exceeded, new pollution sources were allowed if two conditions were satisfied. First, the new sources had to adopt the most effective abatement technology. Second, existing sources had to decrease their emissions to ensure that there was a net improvement in air quality. This policy set the stage for the development of a market for pollution rights, in which new firms purchase pollution rights from existing firms. Because this "offset" policy mimics a system of effluent fees, it will generate efficient abatement activity.

Summary

1. The three most popular commuting trips are between suburbs (40 percent of commuters), within the central city (33 percent), and from a suburb to the central city (20 percent). About four in five workers (and 9 in 10 suburbanites) commute by auto, truck, or van.
2. The demand for travel depends on the private cost of travel, the sum of the monetary and time costs of the trip: the larger the trip cost, the fewer the drivers.

3. Auto travel is subject to congestion externalities.
   a. The external cost of travel is the time cost imposed on other drivers: the marginal driver slows down traffic, forcing other drivers to spend more time on the highway.
   b. The social trip cost is the sum of the private and external trip costs.
   c. Drivers base their travel decisions on private—not social—costs, so the equilibrium volume exceeds the optimum volume.
   d. A congestion tax internalizes the congestion externality, generating the optimum traffic volume.
   e. The congestion tax would be higher during peak travel periods and along more congested routes.
   f. Estimates for the San Francisco Bay area suggest that the congestion tax for travel during the peak period would be 65 cents on central highways, 21 cents per mile on suburban highways, and 17 cents per mile on fringe highways.

4. One way to implement congestion taxes is with a vehicle identification system, under which every car is equipped with an electronic device that allows sensors along the road to identify the car as it passes.

5. There are several alternatives to the congestion tax:
   a. The gas tax is inappropriate because it would be the same on all routes at all times.
   b. Experiences with parking taxes suggest that they decrease traffic volume by encouraging auto drivers to carpool and take mass transit. One problem is that the tax is not based on distance traveled.
   c. The supply response to congestion is to increase highway capacity.
   d. A transit subsidy would cause some auto drivers to switch to transit, decreasing the congestion problem.

6. Autos and trucks generate several types of air pollution, including smog, carbon monoxide, lead, suspended particulates, and nitrogen oxides.
   a. One response to the auto pollution problem is to impose pollution taxes on new cars.
   b. Another option is to impose a gasoline tax equal to the average external cost.
   c. A third option is to subsidize transit, a policy that decreases pollution but also increases transit ridership above its optimum level.
   d. The EPA sets emission standards for carbon monoxide, hydrocarbons, and nitrogen oxides. Emissions controls have decreased total emissions despite an increase in total miles driven. The estimated cost of the current emissions policy, which decreases but does not eliminate auto pollution, is about twice the estimated benefit of eliminating all auto pollution.

Exercises and Discussion Questions

1. Suppose that the relationship between traffic volume and travel time is as follows:

   $$\text{Trip time} = 12.0 + 0.001(\text{Volume} - 400) + 0.00001(\text{Volume} - 400)^2$$

   The marginal benefit (demand) is \$22.12 for a volume of 200, and drops by \$2.48 for every additional 200 drivers.
   a. Use this equation to derive a table like Table 15–2.
   b. What is the equilibrium traffic volume? What is the optimum volume?
   c. What is the appropriate congestion tax?

2. You have been assigned the task of estimating the external trip cost at a traffic volume of 1,600 vehicles per lane per hour for a one-mile section of an urban freeway between two exits. You have traffic data for the relevant stretch of highway for the last year. Outline your strategy for computing the external trip cost. What information would you collect and how would you use it?

3. Consider the following quote from Peabody and Associates, a transportation consulting firm: "According to the Peabody Principle, an increase in highway capacity increases traffic volume by an amount sufficient to leave the private trip cost unchanged."
   a. Use a graph to depict a situation in which the Peabody Principle is correct.
   b. Choose the word in the parentheses that makes the following statement correct, and then explain your choice: "As the price elasticity of demand for highway travel (*increases, decreases*) in absolute value, the Peabody Principle becomes a more accurate prediction of reality."

4. Sinead commutes from her suburban residence to the city center. When asked her opinion of a proposed congestion tax of \$5.00 per trip, she says, "Of course I oppose the congestion tax. It would make me worse off by \$5.00 per trip. What do you think I am, stupid?" Critically appraise Sinead's statement.

5. Consider a city that has both a congestion problem (it does not have a congestion tax) and an auto pollution problem (drivers do not pay for the pollution they generate).
   a. Draw the private-trip-cost curve and the social-trip-cost curve. How do your cost curves differ from those in Figure 15–1?
   b. Label the optimum volume V^* and the equilibrium volume V'.

6. Chopperville is evaluating the merits of using helicopters to clear up highway accidents. Suppose that an accident simply stops traffic from the time the accident occurs to the time the disabled vehicles are

removed from the highway. During rush hours, the typical accident stops traffic for 7,000 cars. The opportunity cost of travel time is 10 cents per minute. Under the current tow-truck system, the typical rush-hour accident stops traffic for 20 minutes; under a helicopter system, the typical rush-hour accident would stop traffic for only 8 minutes. Suppose that the cost of operating the tow-truck system (including the costs of labor, fuel, and equipment) is $200 per accident and the cost of operating the helicopter system (including the costs of labor, fuel, and equipment) would be $3,000 per accident. Your task is to determine whether the helicopter system is superior to the tow-truck system.

a. Is the helicopter system superior to the tow-truck system for rush-hour traffic?

b. Would you expect the helicopter system to be superior to the tow-truck system for non-rush-hour traffic?

References and Additional Readings

Altshuler, Alan A. *The Urban Transportation System*. Cambridge, Mass.: Joint Center for Urban Studies of MIT and Harvard, 1979, Chapter 9, pp. 317–73.

Crandall, Robert W.; Howard K. Gruenspecht; Theodore E. Keeler; and Lester B. Lave. *Regulating the Automobile*. Washington, D.C.: Brookings Institution, 1986. Chapter 5 discusses the effects of emissions policy on air pollution. Chapter 3 explores the costs of emissions controls. Chapter 7 discusses the conflicting goals of regulations on auto safety, auto emissions, and fuel economy.

DiRenzo, J.; B. Cima; and E. Barber. *Parking Management Tactics, Vol. 3: Reference Guide*. Washington, D.C.: U.S. Department of Transportation, 1981. Reports the results of the increase in parking costs in Ottowa, Canada.

Downs, Anthony. "The Law of Peak-Hour Expressway Congestion." *Traffic Quarterly* (July 1962), pp. 393–409. Reprinted in Anthony Downs, *Urban Problems and Prospects*, 2nd ed. (Chicago: Rand McNally, 1976), pp. 185–99.

Freeman, A. Myrick. *Air and Water Pollution Control: A Benefit-Cost Assessment*. New York: John Wiley & Sons, 1982. Estimates the benefits and costs of air pollution programs.

Gómez-Ibáñez, José A., and Gary R. Fauth. "Downtown Auto Restraint Policies: The Costs and Benefits for Boston." *Journal of Transport Economics and Policy* (1980), pp. 133–53.

Keeler, Theodore E., and Kenneth A. Small. "Optimal Peak-Load Pricing, Investment and Service Levels on Urban Expressways." *Journal of Political Economy* (1977). Develops a long-run model of highway pricing and investment, and uses the model to estimate optimum congestion taxes.

Kraft, Gerald, and Thomas A. Domencich. "Free Transit." In *Readings in Urban Economics*, ed. Matthew Edel and Jerome Rothenberg. New York: Macmillan, 1972, pp. 459–80. Reports estimates of the elasticities of demand for auto travel.

McConnell-Fay, Natalie. "Tackling Traffic Congestion in the San Francisco Bay Area." *Transportation Quarterly* 40 (1986), pp. 159–70. A planner's view of the congestion problem and alternative policy responses.

Meyer, John R., and José A. Gómez-Ibáñez. *Autos, Transit and Cities.* Cambridge, Mass.: Harvard University Press, 1981.

Miller, Gerald K., and Carol T. Everett. "Raising Commuter Parking Prices: An Empirical Study." *Transportation* 11 (1982), pp. 105–29. Examines the result of an increase in parking costs for government employees in Washington, D.C.

Parody, Thomas E. "Implementation of a Peak-Period Pricing Strategy for CBD Parking." *Transportation Quarterly* 38 (1984), pp. 153–69. Describes the results of an experiment with peak-period parking taxes in Madison, Wisconsin.

Pozdena, Randall J. "Unlocking Gridlock." *Federal Reserve Bank of San Francisco Weekly Letter* (December 1988), pp. 1–4. Updates the Keeler et al. estimates of congestion tolls.

Shoup, Donald C. "Cashing Out Free Parking." *Transportation Quarterly* 36 (1982), pp. 351–64.

Small, Kenneth A. *Urban Transportation Economics.* Philiadelphia: Harwood, 1992. A comprehensive survey of the economics of urban transportation.

Straszheim, Mahlon R. "Assessing the Social Costs of Urban Transportation Technologies." In *Current Issues in Urban Economics,* ed. Peter Meiszkowski and Mahlon Straszheim. Baltimore, Md.: Johns Hopkins University Press, 1979. Reviews the literature on the externalities associated with automobiles and highways.

Vickrey, William S. "Pricing in Urban and Suburban Transport." *American Economic Review* 53 (1963), pp. 452–65. Reprinted in *Urban Economics: Readings and Analysis,* ed. by Ronald E. Grieson. Boston: Little, Brown, 1973, pp. 106–18.

Walters, A. A. *The Economics of Road User Charges.* Baltimore, Md.: Johns Hopkins University Press, 1968, Chapters 2 and 3.

Williams, Stephen R. "Getting Downtown: Relief of Highway Congestion through Pricing." In *Urban Economic Issues,* ed. Stephan Mehay and Geoffrey Nunn. Glenview, Ill.: Scott, Foresman, 1984. Discusses the efficiency and equity effects of congestion tolls, and describes Singapore's congestion policy.

Willson, Richard W. *Parking Subsidies and the Drive-Alone Commuter: New Evidence and Implications.* Paper presented at the Transportation Research Board Annual Meeting, 1988. Reports the results of a survey of parking subsidies in Los Angeles.

Wohl, Martin. "Congestion Toll Pricing for Public Transport Facilities." In *Public Prices for Public Products,* ed. Selma Mushkin. Washington, D.C.: Urban Institute, 1972, pp. 245–46.

CHAPTER

16 Mass Transit

This is the second of two chapters on urban transportation. This chapter discusses three forms of mass transit: buses, heavy rail (subways, commuter railroads), and light rail (streetcars and trolleys). The chapter addresses four questions. First, how do individual commuters choose a travel mode, and why do so few commuters use mass transit? Second, under what circumstances would a bus system be more efficient than the alternative systems (e.g., an auto-based system, a light-rail system, or a heavy-rail system)? Third, why do most transit systems generate large operating deficits? Fourth, should the private sector play a greater role in the provision of mass transit?

Mass Transit Facts

Table 16–1 shows the commuting patterns and transit ridership in U.S. metropolitan areas. Mass transit includes buses, streetcars, subways, elevated trains, and railroads. Mass transit is most popular among workers who commute within the central city, being used by 15.8 percent of city commuters. Mass transit is less popular among workers who commute from a suburban residence to a central-city job: only 8 percent of these commuters use mass transit. For the most frequent commuting trip (from suburb to suburb), only 1.5 percent of commuters use mass transit.

Table 16–2 shows the trends in transit ridership. Between 1950 and 1980, the total number of transit trips decreased by 50 percent. Transit ridership reached its low point in the early 1970s and has recovered since then. The trolley coach (a bus powered by overhead electric wires) reached its peak in 1950 and has declined since then. The use of light-rail systems (streetcars) decreased steadily between 1940 and 1980, but has recently staged a recovery: systems have recently been

387

TABLE 16-1   **Commuting Patterns and Public Transit Use**

		Percentage Using		
Commute Pattern	*Percentage of Trips*	*Public Transit*	*Bus or Streetcar*	*Heavy Rail*
Central City Residents				
Job in central city	33.1%	15.8%	10.0%	5.8%
Job in suburb	6.8	5.5	4.9	0.6
Suburban Residents				
Job in central city	20.1	8.0	5.0	3.0
Job in suburb	40.1	1.5	1.4	0.1
Total	100.0	7.8	5.2	2.6

Definitions
1. **Public transit:** buses, streetcars, subways, elevated trains, and railroad.
2. **Heavy rail:** subways, elevated trains, and railroad.

SOURCE: U.S. Bureau of the Census, *1980 Census of Population. Journey to Work. Characteristics of Workers* (Washington, D.C.: U.S. Government Printing Office, 1984), Table 1.

TABLE 16-2   **Public Transit Ridership, 1940–1980 (numbers in thousands)**

Year	*Total Rides*	*Heavy Rail*	*Light Rail*	*Trolley Coach*	*Motor Bus*
1940	13,098	2,382	5,943	534	4,239
1950	17,246	2,264	3,904	1,658	9,420
1960	9,395	1,850	463	657	6,425
1970	7,332	1,881	235	182	5,034
1980	8,228	2,290	107	45	5,731

SOURCE: American Public Transit Association, *Transit Fact Book* (Washington, D.C., 1981).

built or restored in Portland, San Jose, Sacramento, Buffalo, San Diego, and Pittsburgh. In Canada, there are new light-rail systems in Edmonton and Calgary.

There is substantial variation in transit ridership between metropolitan areas. In 1980, the percentage of workers riding transit was 45 percent in New York, but no more than 18 percent in any other metropolitan area. In the 25 largest metropolitan areas, there were 4 areas with transit ridership between 15 and 18 percent (Chicago; San Francisco–Oakland; Washington, D.C.; and Boston) and 5 with transit ridership between 10 and 15 percent (Philadelphia, Baltimore, Pittsburgh, Cleveland, and New Orleans). In the remaining 16 metropolitan areas, less than 10 percent of commuters took mass transit. Among the areas with the lowest transit ridership were Detroit (3.7 percent), Dallas (3.4 percent), Houston (3 percent), and San Diego (3.3 percent).

What are the elasticities of demand for mass transit? By how much would transit ridership increase when transit fares decrease or transit service improves? There are four general conclusions from empirical studies of transit ridership:

1. **Price elasticity.** The demand for transit is price-inelastic, with a price elasticity between −0.20 and −0.50 (Beesley and Kemp, 1986). A common rule of thumb is that a 10 percent increase in fares will decrease ridership by about 3.3 percent, meaning that the price elasticity is −0.33.

2. **Time elasticities.** The demand for transit is more responsive to changes in travel time. For the line-haul portion of the trip (time spent in the vehicle), Domencich, Kraft, and Valette (1968) estimate an elasticity of −0.39: a 10 percent increase in line-haul time will decrease ridership by about 3.9 percent. For access time (time spent getting to the bus stop or transit station), they estimate an elasticity of −0.71.

3. **Value of travel time.** According to Small (1992), the average commuter values the time spent in transit vehicles at about half the wage: the typical commuter would be willing to pay a half of his hourly wage to avoid an hour on the bus or train. The value of time spent walking and waiting is two to three times larger: the typical commuter would be willing to pay between 1.0 and 1.5 times his hourly wage to avoid an hour of walking or waiting time. The value of travel time increases less than proportionately with income: a 50 percent difference in income generates less than a 50 percent difference in the value of travel time.

4. **Noncommuting trips.** The elasticities of demand for noncommuting travel are higher than the elasticities for commuting trips.

There are three principal implications from these empirical results. First, an increase in transit fares will increase total fare revenue. A fare increase will decrease ridership by a relatively small amount, so total revenue (fare times ridership) will increase. Second, a simultaneous improvement in service and fares may increase ridership. Suppose that a transit authority increases the frequency and speed of buses, and finances the improved service with increased fares. Because people are more sensitive to changes in time costs than changes in fares, ridership may increase. Third, service improvements that decrease walking and waiting time (more frequent service, shorter distances between stops) will generate larger increases in ridership than improvements that decrease line-haul time.

Choosing a Travel Mode: The Commuter

This section discusses modal choice from the perspective of the commuter. The commuter chooses the mode that minimizes the total cost of travel (the sum of time and monetary costs). Suppose that a commuter has three travel options: the automobile, the bus, and a fixed-rail transit system such as San Francisco's Bay Area Rapid Transit (BART) or Washington, D.C.'s Metro.

The commuting trip can be divided into three parts. The **collection phase** involves travel from the home to the main travel vehicle. The auto mode has no collection cost because the driver uses his own vehicle. The bus mode has a moderate collection cost because the rider must walk from his home to the bus stop. The fixed-rail system has the highest collection cost because there is a relatively long average distance between transit stations, so riders must either walk a long distance or take another mode (e.g., auto or bus) from the home to the transit station. The **line-haul phase** is the part of the trip spent on the main travel vehicle. The heavy-rail mode has the shortest line-haul time because it has an exclusive right-of-way, so it avoids rush-hour congestion. Although the bus and the auto both travel on congested streets and highways, the auto is faster because the bus must stop to pick up passengers along the way. The **distribution phase** involves travel from the end of the vehicular trip (at the downtown transit station, parking garage, bus stop) to the workplace. If parking is available near the workplace, the auto will have the shortest distribution time, followed by the bus and the fixed-rail system.

An Example of Modal Choice

Table 16–3 lists the monetary and time costs of the three travel modes for Carla, a commuter who travels 10 miles from her suburban home to a job in the central city. The computations are based on the assumption that Carla values the time spent on the transit vehicle at half her wage rate and values time spent walking and waiting at 1.5 times her wage rate. If her wage is $12 per hour, she is willing to pay $6 to avoid one hour of in-vehicle time, and $18 to avoid one hour of walking and waiting time. Therefore, the cost of walking and waiting time is 30 cents per minute, and the cost of in-vehicle time is 10 cents per minute.

1. **Collection time cost.** Carla walks to the bus stop or the BART station. Since the bus stop is closer to her home, the bus has lower collection costs.

2. **Line-haul time cost.** BART is the fastest mode (it operates on an exclusive right-of-way), followed by autos (which travel on congested streets) and buses (which travel on congested streets and stop to pick up passengers).

3. **Distribution cost.** Carla parks her auto in a company parking lot under her office building, so the distribution cost of the auto trip is zero. The bus stop is relatively close to the office, so the bus has lower distribution costs than BART.

4. **Monetary cost.** The monetary cost of the auto trip is 20 cents per mile, or $2.00. The bus fare is $1, and the BART fare is $1.50. Half of the $6.00 parking cost is allocated to the morning commute.

The cost of driving is less than the cost of the bus or BART. Although the monetary cost of driving exceeds the monetary cost of the bus by $4, the lower

---

TABLE 16–3   Costs of Travel Modes and Modal Choice

	Auto	Bus	BART
Collection Time Cost			
Collection time (minutes)	0	10	15
Cost per minute ($)	0.30	0.30	0.30
Collection time cost ($)	0.00	3.00	4.50
Line-Haul Time Cost			
Line-haul time (minutes)	40	50	30
Cost per minute ($)	0.10	0.10	0.10
Line-haul time costs ($)	4.00	5.00	3.00
Distribution Time Cost			
Distribution time (minutes)	0	5	9
Cost per minute ($)	0.30	0.30	0.30
Distribution time cost ($)	0.00	1.50	2.70
Monetary Cost			
Operating cost or fare ($)	2.00	1.00	1.50
Parking cost ($)	3.00	0.00	0.00
Total monetary cost ($)	5.00	1.00	1.50
Total time cost ($)	4.00	9.50	10.20
Total Cost ($)	9.00	10.50	11.70

time cost of the auto more than offsets its higher monetary cost. Similarly, the auto is more expensive but faster than BART. The largest difference in time cost is for collection and distribution costs, where the auto has a cost advantage of $4.50 over the bus ($3.00 for collection + $1.50 for distribution), and $7.20 over BART ($4.50 + $2.70). Since the auto has a lower cost than either the bus or BART, Carla will drive to work.

What would it take to persuade Carla to switch from her auto to mass transit? There are several possibilities:

1. **Subsidized transit.** If the bus and BART were free, Carla would still drive. To get her to switch to the bus, she would have to be paid a bribe of 50 cents per bus ride. A bribe of $1.20 would cause her to switch to BART. Transit fares must decrease by relatively large amounts to offset the time-cost advantages of the automobile.

2. **Line-haul time.** If the line-haul time of the bus decreased from 50 minutes to less than 35 minutes, Carla would ride the bus; she would take BART if its line-haul time decreased to less than 3 minutes.

3. **Collection and distribution time.** Carla would ride the bus if the collection and distribution time of the bus decreased from 15 minutes to

less than 10 minutes, and she would switch to BART if its collection and distribution time decreased from 24 minutes to less than 15 minutes.

4. **Auto monetary cost.** Carla would ride the bus if the unit cost of the auto increased from 20 cents to 36 cents per mile. As reported in Chapter 15, estimates of the congestion tax are in the range of 21 to 65 cents per mile for rush-hour traffic, so the imposition of a congestion tax would cause her switch to the bus. Similarly, if the city imposed a pollution tax of at least 16 cents per mile, Carla would stop driving.

5. **Parking cost.** Carla would ride the bus if the parking cost rose to at least $4.50 ($9 per day).

6. **Wage.** As the wage decreases, the opportunity cost of travel time decreases, increasing the relative attractiveness of the modes with relatively low monetary costs and high time costs.

To summarize, to get Carla to switch to transit, the changes in either monetary costs or line-haul time costs would have to be relatively large. On the other hand, she would switch to transit with relatively small changes in collection and distribution time costs. These conclusions are consistent with the transit elasticities discussed earlier in this chapter.

What would cause commuters to take mass transit instead of driving? There are five possibilities:

1. **Proximity to stops and stations.** A person who lives near a bus stop or a rail station has relatively low collection costs for transit and is more likely to take the bus or BART.

2. **Low opportunity cost.** For a person who has a low opportunity cost of travel time (a worker with a low wage, a student, a retired person), the time costs of travel are relatively low. As a result, the advantages of transit (lower monetary cost) dominate the disadvantages (longer commuting time). Such a person is more likely to choose transit.

3. **Low walking cost.** A person who enjoys walking will have relatively low collection and distribution costs, and is more likely to choose transit.

4. **Disutility of driving.** A person who dislikes the hassle and anxiety of driving is more likely to choose transit. In terms of the numerical example, such a person will have a relatively high cost for in-vehicle auto time and is more likely to take the bus or BART. In contrast, a person who considers driving a form of athletics will buy a pair of gloves and drive to work.

5. **No automobile.** Many of the poor do not have access to an auto, so their only option is to use public transit.

Transit Service and Modal Choice

How do changes in transit design and scheduling affect ridership? Transit ridership will increase when service improvements decrease the time costs of the transit.

As explained earlier, commuters are most responsive to changes in collection and distribution time (walking and waiting time).

Designing the Bus System.   Consider first the bus system. The bus company affects time costs in two ways. First, it chooses the bus headway, the period of time between buses on the bus route. As the headway decreases, riders spend less time waiting at the bus stop, so their time costs decrease. Second, the bus company chooses the frequency of stops in the residential collection area. An increase in the frequency of stops decreases walking distances and collection costs. Similarly, the more frequent the stops in the downtown distribution area, the lower the distribution costs. An increase in the frequency of stops also increases line-haul (in-vehicle) time: more time is spent picking up and dropping off passengers, so the trip takes a longer time.

Designing the Fixed-Rail System.   Consider next the design of a fixed-rail system. San Francisco's BART provides a nice illustration of the trade-offs associated with the design of a rail transit system. There are two basic design trade-offs:

1. **Mainline versus integrated system.** BART is considered a mainline system because it relies on other transit systems to collect its riders from residential neighborhoods. Riders must either walk, drive, or ride a bus to the BART station. The alternative to the mainline system is an integrated system, under which commuters make the entire commute trip on a single transit mode.

2. **Spacing between stations.** BART has widely spaced stations (about 2.5 miles apart), so there are few stops on the way to the city center. As a result, travel time from the suburban station to the downtown station (line-haul time) is relatively short, and in-vehicle time costs are relatively low. On the other hand, the average commuter must travel a relatively long distance from his home to one of the widely spaced transit stations, so collection costs (by foot, bus, or car) are relatively high.

BART was designed to compete with the line-haul portion of the automobile trip. It achieves this objective, providing comfortable, speedy service from the suburban stations to the city center. There is a trade-off, however: collection costs are relatively high because BART is a mainline system with widely spaced stations. Because walking and waiting time is more costly than in-vehicle time, the negative attribute (high collection costs) dominates the positive one (comfortable, speedy line-haul travel), so the full cost of a BART trip is relatively high and BART has diverted a relatively small number of auto commuters.

Bus and Car Pool Lanes.   Another design issue concerns the treatment of high-occupancy vehicles (HOV) such as car pools and buses. If a city establishes a "diamond" lane for the exclusive use of buses and car pools, the line-haul times of buses and car pools will decrease. Under the diamond-lane approach, buses and car pools have the advantages of the fixed-rail system (faster line-haul times) without the disadvantages (high collection and distribution costs). As a result, some drivers will switch to a bus or a car pool. Because the elasticity of transit demand with respect to line-haul time is moderate (−0.39), there will be a moderate diversion of auto traffic.

What are the effects of diamond lanes on commuters who continue to drive? There is good news and bad news. The good news is that some auto drivers will be diverted to buses and car pools, so there will be less auto traffic: in Figure 16–1, the diamond lane shifts the demand curve to the left, decreasing trip costs for the original trip-cost curve. The bad news is that there are fewer lanes for the remaining autos: the diamond lane decreases the amount of road space, so the congestion threshold decreases and the trip-cost curve shifts to the left. In this example, the shift of the demand curve is small relative to the shift of the cost curve, so the trip cost increases from $5 to $6. If shift of the demand curve were relatively large, the trip cost would decrease.

Figure 16–1 accurately depicts recent experiences with diamond lanes. The first experiment with diamond lanes occurred along the Santa Monica Freeway in

FIGURE 16–1   Diamond Lanes and Auto Trip Costs

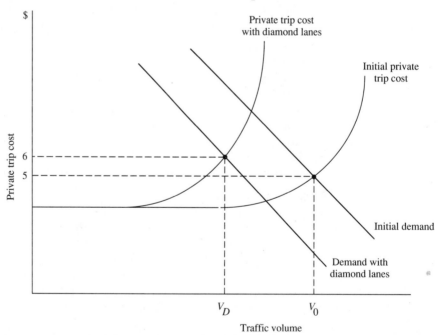

The addition of diamond lanes (reserved for buses and car pools) affects travel in nondiamond lanes in two ways. There are fewer vehicles in nondiamond lanes, so the demand curve shifts to the left. In addition, there are fewer lanes, so the trip cost curve shifts to the left. If a relatively small number of vehicles are diverted to the diamond lanes, the net cost of travel in nondiamond lanes will increase. In this example, the cost increases from $5 to $6.

Los Angeles. The diamond lanes increased the average trip costs of a vociferous group of auto commuters, and the experiment was short-lived. The city of Boston experienced similar problems when it set up diamond lanes along the Southeast Expressway.

Some cities have built new lanes for buses and car pools. Among the cities that have built new diamond lanes are Miami (along Interstate 95); Washington, D.C. (along the Shirley Expressway); and Los Angeles (along the San Bernardino Freeway). By building new lanes instead of taking away auto lanes, these cities did not impose any explicit costs on auto drivers, so there was little opposition to the diamond lanes. The new diamond lanes do, however, impose an implicit cost on drivers: if the new lanes were opened to auto traffic, the trip cost curve would shift to the right, decreasing travel times for auto commuters.

Choosing a System: The Planner's Problem

This section discusses modal choice from the perspective of a transportation planner. The planner must decide what type of transportation system to build. There are three options: an auto-based highway system, an integrated bus system, and a fixed-rail system like BART or Metro. Estimates of the costs of these alternative systems are provided by a study of transportation options in the San Francisco Bay area (by Keeler, Merewitz, Fisher, and Small, 1975).

Keeler and his associates estimated the costs of three different commuting systems: an auto-based system, an integrated bus system, and BART. The principal conclusions of their study are shown in Figure 16–2. The horizontal axis measures the number of commuters traveling through a transportation corridor during the one-hour peak period. The vertical axis measures the long-run average cost of a "typical" commuting trip (a six-mile line haul and additional time spent in residential collection and downtown distribution). The cost curves show that the bus system is more efficient than the auto system for volumes above 1,100 passengers per hour and is more efficient than BART for all traffic volumes. The auto system is more efficient than BART for volumes up to about 22,000 passengers per hour.

Costs of the Auto System

The cost of the auto system is the sum of the driver's time and operating costs and the public costs of auto traffic. The public cost includes the cost of building the optimum road system. As explained in Chapter 15, congestion taxes can be used both to internalize congestion externalities and to pay for the roads. Also included in the public cost are the costs of air and noise pollution.

The average-cost curve is horizontal for two reasons. First, Keeler et al. (1975) assume that the average operating cost and the average pollution cost (cost per mile) do not depend on traffic volume. Second, the trip time (and private trip cost)

FIGURE 16–2   **Costs of Alternative Transit Systems**

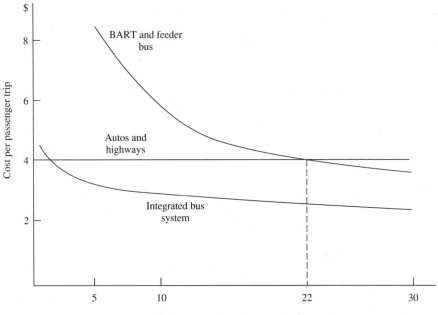

The average cost of auto traffic is independent of auto volume, but the average costs of an integrated bus system and BART decrease as volume increases. The bus system is more efficient than BART for all volumes studied and more efficient than an auto-based system for volumes exceeding 1,100.

does not depend on traffic volume: as volume increases, the road is widened to accommodate the increased traffic without any reduction of travel speeds. Given constant returns to scale in highways, a doubling of highway capacity doubles traffic volume without changing the trip time. Using data for 1972, Keeler et al. estimate that the full cost of an auto trip with a six-mile line haul is $4.15.

Costs of the Bus System

The cost of the integrated bus system is the sum of time costs, agency costs, and the public costs of the bus system. The agency costs include both operating costs and capital costs. Included in the public costs are (*a*) the costs of modifying the roadway to accommodate buses, and (*b*) pollution costs.

    The average-cost curve is decreasing for two reasons. First, as ridership increases, the fixed costs of administering the bus system are spread over more riders. Second, as ridership increases, collection and distribution times decrease. An increase in ridership decreases headways (the time between buses) and decreases the space between bus stops, so riders spend less time walking to and waiting for the bus. In addition, an increase in ridership allows a bus to fill up with a shorter collection route. Less time is spent picking up passengers, so in-vehicle time decreases. According to Keeler et al. (1975), if the traffic volume along the corridor exceeds 1,100 passengers, the express bus system is less costly than the auto system.

Costs of BART

The BART option involves the mainline heavy-rail system and feeder buses to bring commuters to the BART stations. The time cost of the BART option is the sum of walking and waiting time costs and in-vehicle time costs. The agency cost is the sum of the operating and capital costs of the feeder buses and BART. Given the substantial investment in tracks and right-of-ways, the capital costs of the BART option are large.

The cost curve is negatively sloped for three reasons. First, the system has substantial fixed costs, which are spread over more riders as ridership increases. Second, as ridership increases, BART headways decrease, decreasing waiting time. Third, an increase in bus ridership decreases the time and monetary cost of feeder-bus service.

BART is more costly than the bus system for three reasons. First, given its design as a mainline system with widely spaced stations, the collection and distribution costs are relatively high. Second, its capital costs are very large: the fixed cost of the system was $1.6 billion. According to Webber (1976), BART could buy enough buses to carry its passengers for only $40 million ($\frac{1}{40}$ of BART's capital costs). Third, BART has surprisingly high operating costs: in 1975, the operating cost was 15.7 cents per passenger mile, compared to 13.6 cents for a bus. Most planners were surprised to discover that the large investment in capital equipment did not generate much savings in operating costs.

System Choice

The Keeler et al. (1975) study provides important information for transit planners. For all corridor volumes studied (up to 30,000 passengers per hour), BART was more costly than an integrated bus system. At a peak volume of 30,000 passengers per hour, BART is 50 percent more costly than the bus system. In 1984, BART's peak ridership through the transbay tube was 15,300 passengers per hour. The lesson for planners is clear: with the possible exceptions of New York City and Chicago, which have corridor volumes exceeding 30,000 passengers per hour, an integrated bus system is likely to be more efficient than a modern fixed-rail system like BART.

Experiences with new heavy-rail systems in other metropolitan areas are similar to the BART experience. To cover its operating and capital costs the Metro system in Washington, D.C. would have to charge a one-way fare of $8 (Gordon and Richardson, 1989). Ridership on the new systems in Atlanta, Miami, and Baltimore has fallen well short of the projected levels. The problems with heavy-rail systems should not be surprising, given Keeler et al.'s conclusion that corridor volumes must exceed 30,000 to make heavy rail competitive with a bus system.

Light Rail

In recent years, many medium-sized cities have built light-rail transit systems. Light rail is the modern version of the trolley and streetcar systems that were built in the late 1800s and early 1900s. The first modern light-rail system opened in Edmonton, Alberta, Canada, in 1978. Since then, new systems have opened in San Diego, Calgary (Canada), Buffalo, Portland, Vancouver (Canada), Sacramento, and San Jose. Many other cities are planning to build new systems or extend old streetcar and trolley systems.

How does light rail compare to buses and heavy rail? Gómez-Ibáñez (1985) studied the costs and performance of new light-rail systems in San Diego, Edmonton, and Calgary, and came to the following conclusions:

1. **Capital costs.** The capital costs of light rail include the costs of the vehicles, the track, and the power distribution system. These costs make a light-rail system more costly than a bus system, which uses less expensive vehicles and travels along regular streets and highways. Light rail is much less costly than heavy rail: the cost per mile is $7 million to $20 million per mile, compared to $50 million to $200 million per mile for heavy rail. Light rail is less expensive than heavy rail because it typically uses surface streets (instead of requiring subways or elevated guideways) and is designed for lower speeds.

2. **Operating costs.** Compared to a bus system, light rail has lower labor costs because it needs fewer operators: a three-car train can be operated by one person and can carry about 10 times as many riders as a standard bus. Because light rail has higher maintenance costs on its vehicles and its right-of-way, however, its total operating costs are equal to or greater than the operating costs of buses.

3. **Performance.** Most light-rail systems consist of one or two radial rail lines, with feeder buses for the collection and distribution phases of the transit trip. Like the heavy-rail systems, the light-rail systems have higher collection and distribution costs than the bus. Light rail also has shorter line-haul times and provides a more comfortable ride than the bus.

Table 16–4 compares the costs of the San Diego light-rail system to those of the bus routes it replaced. The total cost per light-rail passenger was $3.11, compared to $1.16 for the bus system. Light rail has moderately higher operating costs and much higher capital costs. The light-rail system seems to have increased transit ridership: ridership in the area served by the system increased from about 3.4 million to about 4.8 million per year. According to Gómez-Ibáñez (1985), much of the increased ridership was caused by population growth in the corridor

TABLE 16–4   **Comparison of San Diego's Light-Rail and Bus Systems**

	Light-Rail System	Bus System
Costs per Passenger		
Operating costs	0.82	1.02
Capital costs	0.34	2.09
Total costs	1.16	3.11
Ridership (thousands per year)	3,398	4,845
Cost per new light-rail passenger ($)		5.74

SOURCE: José A. Gómez-Ibáñez, "A Dark Side to Light Rail?" *Journal of the American Planning Association* (1985), pp. 337-51.

served by light rail. If one assumes that the entire increase in ridership was caused by the introduction of the light-rail system, the cost per additional driver was $5.47. The San Diego experience suggests that although light rail may increase ridership, it does so at a relatively high cost.

Subsidies for Mass Transit

In 1985, passenger fares covered only about 39 percent of the operating costs of mass transit. As shown in Figure 16–3, the remaining operating costs were covered by local governments (providing 22 percent of revenue), state governments (13 percent), and the federal government (12 percent).

Reasons for Transit Deficits

Table 16–5 shows recent trends in transit revenues and costs. (All dollar figures are in 1980 dollars.) In 1965, the fare-box ratio (the ratio of fare revenue to operating cost) was 0.99, meaning that transit riders covered most of the operating costs of transit. By 1980, the fare-box ratio decreased to 0.42, meaning that transit riders paid only 42 percent of operating costs.

One reason for the growth in the transit deficit is that operating revenue decreased over time. Between 1965 and 1980, operating revenue per vehicle mile decreased from $1.72 to $1.23 (in 1980 dollars). Three factors contributed to the decline in revenue. First, the average passenger fare decreased from 47 cents in 1965 to 40 cents in 1980. Second, total ridership decreased slightly, from 8.25 billion to 8.23 billion. Third, the total vehicle miles increased, from 2.01 billion miles to 2.09 billion miles. The number of riders decreased while vehicle miles increased, so the number of riders per vehicle mile decreased. Since there were fewer riders paying lower fares, revenue per vehicle mile decreased.

FIGURE 16–3   Transit Revenue Sources

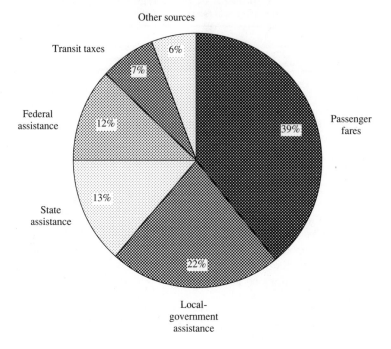

TABLE 16–5   Transit Revenue, Costs, and Deficits, 1960–1980

	1960	*1965*	*1970*	*1975*	*1980*
Fare-box ratio	1.02	0.99	0.86	0.54	0.42
Revenue					
Operating revenue per vehicle mile ($)	1.71	1.72	1.77	1.33	1.23
Fare per passenger ($)	0.46	0.47	0.54	0.47	0.4
Passengers (millions)	9,345	8,253	7,332	6,972	8,325
Cost					
Operating cost per vehicle mile ($)	1.65	1.72	2.06	2.67	2.98
Vehicle miles (millions)	2,143	2,008	1,883	1,990	2,093
Employees (thousands)	156	145	138	160	187
Vehicle miles per employee	13,737	13,848	13,645	12,438	11,193
Passengers per employee	59,904	56,917	53,130	43,575	44,519
Federal funds ($ millions)	0	27	299	1,608	3,367

SOURCE: Gordon Fielding, *Managing Transit Strategically* (San Francisco: Jossey-Bass, 1987), Tables 2 and 3.

The primary reason for the growth of the deficit is rising costs. Between 1965 and 1980, the operating cost per vehicle mile increased from \$1.72 to \$2.98 (in 1980 dollars). Operating costs increased because of rising wages, increased energy costs, and decreased labor productivity. One of the reasons for rising wages is explained in Chapter 13 (Overview of Local Government): the Baumol model shows that the wages of service workers will rise despite constant productivity because of rising productivity (and wages) in manufacturing.

The simple facts on labor productivity are startling. Between 1965 and 1980, total transit employment increased from 145,000 to 187,000. Since the number of vehicle miles increased by a smaller amount, the number of vehicle miles per employee decreased from 13,848 to 11,193. While the number of transit workers increased, the number of transit riders decreased, so the number of passenger rides per transit worker decreased from 56,917 to 44,519. Why did the number of passengers per employee decrease? According to Fielding (1987), an important factor was an increase in the fraction of transit trips taken during peak periods. To explain the peaking problem, consider a city where transit ridership is uniform throughout the day: the city can serve its transit riders with a single bus running all day. Suppose that all the riders suddenly decide to travel during two rush hours: traffic volume during the two rush hours quadruples. The city will no longer be able to serve its transit riders with a single bus and a single bus driver but will be forced to buy three more buses and hire more drivers.

What are the effects of the shift to peak ridership on the city's labor productivity and labor costs? Consider first the possibility that the city hires part-time drivers. If the city hires drivers by the hour, productivity does not change: the city hires four part-time drivers instead of one full-time driver. On the other hand, if the city must hire four full-time drivers (who will be idle for six hours per day), its labor productivity will decrease and its labor costs will rise. In other words, if the shift to peak-period travel is combined with restrictive work rules that prevent part-time workers and split shifts, labor productivity decreases and labor costs increase.

Pickrell (1983) examined the relative importance of five factors that contributed to the growth of the transit deficit between 1970 and 1980. The factors, and their contributions to the growing deficit, are as follows:

1. Decrease in fares: responsible for 28 percent of the growth in deficit.
2. Increase in wages: 25 percent.
3. Decrease in labor productivity: 18 percent.
4. Increase in transit mileage: 16 percent.
5. Increase in energy costs: 12 percent.

Pickrell's results suggest that many factors contributed to the growing deficit. It's important to note that two of the contributing factors (the decrease in fares and the increase in mileage) were integral parts of transportation policy: in an attempt to divert commuters from polluting autos on congested highways, the government has improved transit service while keeping fares relatively low. As explained earlier, an alternative policy would be to force auto drivers to pay the full cost of travel, including the costs of congestion and air pollution.

History of Federal Assistance

Federal assistance to mass transit grew from only $27 million in 1965 to $2.84 billion in 1985 (Fielding, 1987). The Urban Mass Transit Act of 1964 established a program of capital subsidies for transit. For the first several years, most of the federal money was used to purchase unprofitable bus companies. Later, the money was used to invest in new capital equipment (buses, rail vehicles, tracks, and right-of-ways). Before 1973, the federal government paid two thirds of the cost of new transit projects. In 1974, the federal contribution increased to four fifths of the project cost.

Federal assistance for operating costs started with the National Mass Transportation Act of 1974. By 1984, a total of $5.3 billion of operating assistance was provided by all levels of government, with about half of the money coming from local governments, one third from state governments, and one sixth from the federal government. Federal operating subsidies were originally allocated to cities on the basis of total population. This allocation scheme caused large cities to receive relatively small subsidies per transit rider. Suppose that every city receives a 1-cent subsidy per citizen. A large city (e.g., New York), in which 25 percent of the population uses public transit, would receive a subsidy of 4 cents per transit rider. A small city (e.g., Santa Barbara), in which 2 percent of the population uses transit, would receive a subsidy of 50 cents per rider. To solve this problem, allocations are now based primarily on transit ridership.

Since 1983, a portion of the revenue from the federal gasoline tax has been funneled to mass transit. When the gas tax was increased by 5 cents per gallon, 1 cent of the increase was earmarked for a mass-transit fund. In 1984, a total of $1.2 billion was generated by the gas tax. The money was used to support bus systems ($300 million), existing rail systems ($500 million), and new transit systems ($400 million). A city receiving money from the transit fund must either use the money for mass transit or lose it. This creates the incentive to undertake transit projects when other projects (e.g., highway improvements) might be more efficient.

Deregulation: The Private Provision of Transit

In most cities, mass transit is provided by the public sector. To shield the public transit system from competition, private transit activity (e.g., taxis and private bus service) is heavily regulated. Given the large deficits generated by public transit authorities, an obvious question is whether private industry could provide transit services more efficiently. There are two possible strategies for transit deregulation: (1) the private provision of transit services through service contracts and (2) free entry into the mass-transit market.

Contracting for Transit Services

Under the first type of deregulation, the local transit monopoly would be granted to a private firm instead of a government agency. Under a contracting arrangement, the local government specifies the service characteristics of the transit system (e.g., headways, travel times, location of bus stops, fares) and then accepts bids from private firms for the transit service. The transit monopoly is granted to the firm that provides the service at the lowest cost.

The experiences with contracting arrangements are discussed by Lave (1985), Echols (1985), and Rosenbloom (1985). The city of Tidewater, Virginia, contracted for bus service to low-density areas. The private transit company provided the same transit service at a fraction of the cost of public bus service. Along one route, the deficit per passenger decreased from $4.75 to $1.63. Other cities using transit contracts have had similar experiences: the typical private bus company provides transit service for about half the cost of the public bus system. Contracts are also used for subsidized dial-a-ride services: in 1983, the city of Phoenix paid a local taxi company $104,425 to provide dial-a-ride services on Sundays, about one sixth the cost of using city buses for Sunday service.

Private firms provide transit services for lower costs for three reasons. First, they pay lower wages. Second, they have more flexible work rules; they have split shifts and use part-time workers, so they don't pay idle workers during the off-peak periods. Third, they use minibuses on low-density routes. In Phoenix, the private bus company uses minibuses with operating costs of $1.22 per mile, compared to $2.86 per mile for the standard bus.

Entry and Competition

Most cities grant monopoly power to the local transit authority and protect the transit authority from competition. There are two rationales for restricting entry:

1. **Cross subsidization.** The city sets a single transit fare and then forces the transit authority to cover all routes, including some unprofitable ones. For some routes, fares exceed costs, providing a surplus that is used to subsidize service along unprofitable routes. If entry were allowed, a new firm would provide service along the lucrative routes, underpricing the public transit and capturing its riders. The transit authority would make less money along the profitable routes, destroying the cross-subsidization scheme.

2. **Scale economies.** As explained earlier, there are substantial fixed costs in providing mass transit, so transit service is a natural monopoly. Although fixed-rail systems are certainly natural monopolies, the case is not so clear for bus systems. Walters (1982) and Morlok and Viton (1985b) suggest that scale economies in bus transit are exhausted at a ridership level well below the volume of the typical medium-sized city.

Some cities allow private bus companies to compete with the public bus authority. The experiences with private bus companies are discussed by Johnson and Pilarsky (1985) and Walder (1985). In the city of Chicago, commuter bus clubs provide subscription bus service. In 1981, the full cost (including vehicle cost) of a private bus trip was $1.15, compared to a partial cost (excluding vehicle cost) of $1.44 for a public bus trip. In New York City, private commuter vans travel from Staten Island to Manhattan. The private vans charge the same fare as the public bus but cover all of their costs and take less time to make the trip.

Would deregulation increase fares along some routes? Under deregulation, a route would not be served unless its total revenue exceeds its total cost. Therefore, transit fares along low-volume routes are likely to increase. If policymakers are concerned about poor households along low-volume routes, they could give money to the poor to compensate for the higher fares. The problem with cross-subsidization is that the transit subsidies go to rich and poor alike. Another option is to provide explicit subsidies for service along low-volume routes, a strategy adopted by Phoenix and other cities.

A second proposal for deregulation is to allow taxis to serve as transit vehicles. Under current regulations, a taxi cannot serve as a common carrier: the taxi can carry an individual or a small group of people traveling together, but it cannot give rides to strangers in transit. If taxis were deregulated, they could pick up customers along routes of their own choice, serving as flexible transit vehicles.

The proposals for taxi deregulation have revived the jitney concept. Between 1915 and 1920, private cars were used as transit vehicles. The fare was 5 cents and the slang word for a nickel was "jitney," so the private vehicles were called *jitneys*. Most jitneys operated during rush hours, allowing the driver to work at another job during the off-peak hours. Some jitneys operated as carpools: the driver posted his workplace on his windshield and picked up riders along his way to work. Other jitney drivers started driving without a specific destination and then modified their routes as they picked up passengers. If taxis were deregulated to serve as common carriers, they would operate much like the jitneys of the early 1900s.

British Experience with Deregulation

In Great Britain, the transit industry was deregulated under the British Transport Act of 1985. As explained by Gómez-Ibáñez and Meyer (1990), the act relaxed controls on entry into the transit industry, reorganized most public transit authorities as for-profit organizations, and introduced competitive bidding for certain transit services. Local governments can continue to subsidize transit services as long as the subsidized service is provided by the low bidder in a competitive auction. Although Greater London was not covered under the Transport Act, contracting out is used extensively in the metropolitan area, and full deregulation is expected some time in the 1990s.

Britain's new transit policy combined deregulation with substantial cuts in transit subsidies. For example, transit subsidies were cut by about 23 percent in the metropolitan counties and about 6 percent in other counties. The decrease in transit subsidies generated pressure to increase fares and cut services. Gómez-Ibáñez and Meyer (1990) and Small (1992) summarize some of the results of the new transit policy:

1. **Service.** In the first full year following deregulation, total mileage was up by 3.3 percent in the metropolitan counties and 16.5 percent in other counties. The use of minibuses (with 12 to 25 seats) increased dramatically. Some unprofitable services were curtailed: for example, some off-peak and low-density routes were abandoned.

2. **Fares.** Transit fares increased by about 35 percent in real terms over a two-year period.

3. **Ridership.** Ridership decreased by about 14 percent.

4. **Production costs.** Production costs fell as a result of labor concessions (relaxed work rules and lower compensation), the introduction of minibuses, and the elimination of excess capacity. According to Heseltine and Silcock (1990), unit costs fell by between 15 percent and 30 percent.

Gómez-Ibáñez and Meyer (1990) discuss three lessons from the British experience with the deregulation of transit. First, it is possible to have both competition in the local bus industry and subsidies for unprofitable services. By using competitive bidding to pick a firm to provide the subsidized services, the public sector can provide the services at the lowest possible cost. Second, in addition to cutting costs and increasing productivity, deregulation generates service innovations: the private bus companies introduced minibuses, and local governments improved the services along unprofitable routes. Third, because most of the benefits from deregulation come from competition among transit firms, the public sector must develop policies to ensure competition.

Transportation and Land-Use Patterns

Part II of this book discusses the effects of changes in transportation technology on urban land-use patterns. The development of the internal-combustion engine allowed the development of new travel modes (the car and the truck) that were more flexible and less costly than streetcars and horse-drawn wagons. The new modes decreased the reliance of firms and households on the central area of the city, allowing the decentralization of employment and residents. This section discusses two types of changes in transportation: an increase in gasoline costs and the construction of fixed-rail transit systems.

Gasoline Prices

Suppose that the real cost of gasoline increases. How will the increased cost of auto travel affect housing and land prices? As explained in Part II of this book, an increase in transportation costs will increase the slopes of the housing-price function and the residential bid-rent function. Studies by Small (1986) and Coulson and Engle (1987) confirm these theoretical predictions: an increase in the price of gasoline increases the relative attractiveness of locations near employment centers, increasing the prices of housing and land.

How will an increase in the cost of gasoline affect the distributions of employment and population? The changes are likely to be relatively small for three reasons. First, the cost of gasoline is a relatively small part of the cost of travel. Second, other responses to an increase in gasoline prices (buying more fuel-efficient cars, carpooling, switching to transit) allow drivers to decrease travel costs without changing residences or workplaces. For these two reasons, the change in the prices of housing and land will be relatively small. Even if the changes in price were relatively large, it would be a long time before we would see large changes in population density near employment centers, because structures last a long time and are costly to demolish. Small (1986) estimated that a $1 per gallon increase in the price of gasoline would cause a relatively small number of suburban households to move to the central city.

Fixed-Rail Systems and Land Use

How do fixed-rail systems affect land rent and land use? Dewees (1976) examined the effect of Toronto's subway on housing prices near the new transit stations and concluded that the subway increased the price of housing within one third of a mile of the stations. The largest increases in prices occurred for the locations closest to the stations.

Do fixed-rail systems affect land-use patterns? Webber (1976) studied the effects of BART on land-use patterns in the San Francisco Bay area. His conclusions are as follows:

1. There was a boom in downtown office construction during the construction of BART. The office boom was caused by several factors, and it is impossible to identify BART's contribution.
2. There is no evidence that downtown office development would have been any slower if transit authorities had expanded bus service instead of building BART.
3. There has been little development of activities around the suburban train stations. In a different study, Dyett and Escudero (1977) concluded that BART caused some clustering of activities within the central city.

In summarizing the results from several studies of the effects of rail systems on land-use patterns, Altshuler (1979) makes two observations:

1. In a growing economy, rail transit contributes to the clustering of activities near downtown stations. These clustering effects are usually negligible outside the CBD.

2. Investment in rail transit is sensible only if it is used in concert with more powerful land-use instruments such as zoning and property taxation. If the government uses its zoning and tax policies to generate high-density development, rail transit provides an efficient means of delivering a large number of workers to the dense central area.

In general, there is evidence that fixed-rail systems cause small changes in the spatial distribution of employment. The primary effect of transit is an increase in downtown employment.

Summary

1. Mass transit is most popular among workers who commute within the central city (used by 15.8 percent of commuters) and least popular among workers who travel from one suburb to another (used by 1.5 percent).

2. Transit ridership is relatively unresponsive to changes in monetary costs (fares) but is responsive to changes in time costs, especially waiting and walking costs. Commuters value in-vehicle time at about one third the wage rate, and collection and distribution time at about the wage rate.

3. The time cost of a trip is the sum of collection costs, in-vehicle costs, and distribution costs. Commuters choose the mode that minimizes the sum of monetary and time costs. Mass transit has lower monetary costs than autos, but higher collection and distribution and time costs.

4. There are trade-offs associated with bus service: a decrease in the headway or an increase in the frequency of stops decreases collection and distribution costs, but increases line-haul costs.

5. There are two basic trade-offs in the design of a fixed-rail system:
   a. A mainline system forces commuters to use other travel modes in the collection and distribution phases of the trip. An alternative is an integrated system, which allows commuters to take the entire trip on a single mode.
   b. A system with widely spaced systems has shorter line-haul times but higher collection and distribution costs.

6. BART is a mainline system with widely spaced stations. Because its collection and distribution costs are relatively high, it caused a relatively small number of commuters to switch from autos to transit.

7. Diamond lanes cause a moderate number of commuters to switch from autos to buses. The decrease in the number of auto lanes increases congestion, increasing the time cost of auto commuters.

8. A study of alternative transport systems for the San Francisco Bay area generated the following conclusions:
   a. For all corridor volumes studied, BART was more costly than an integrated bus system.

b. For corridor volumes exceeding 1,100 vehicles per hour, an integrated bus system was less costly than an auto-based system.

9. In 1985, passenger fares covered only about 39 percent of the operating costs of transit. Transit deficits have increased over the last few decades, a result of decreases in fares and productivity, and increases in wages, energy costs, and transit mileage.

10. Deregulation of transit could take two forms: (*a*) the private provision of transit through service contracts and (*b*) free entry into the transit market. Contracting arrangements have decreased the costs of providing transit services in a number of cities. Free entry could involve private buses or taxis serving as common carriers.

11. Increases in gasoline prices change housing and land prices, but do not cause large changes in location patterns.

12. Fixed-rail systems increase land rent for locations near the stations but cause relatively small changes in location patterns. If the government uses its zoning and tax policies to generate high-density development, rail transit can provide an efficient means of delivering workers to the high-density areas.

Exercises and Discussion Questions

1. Fill in the blanks in the following table.

	Auto	*Bus*	*BART*
Collection Time Cost			
Collection time (minutes)	0	12	16
Cost per minute ($)	0.20	0.20	0.20
Collection time cost ($)	____	____	____
Line-Haul Time Cost			
Line-haul time (minutes)	30	40	20
Cost per minute ($)	0.15	0.15	0.15
Line-haul time costs ($)	____	____	____
Distribution Time Cost			
Distribution time (minutes)	0	4	11
Cost per minute ($)	0.20	0.20	0.20
Distribution time cost ($)	____	____	____
Monetary Cost			
Operating cost or fare ($)	3	1.5	2
Parking cost ($)	4	0	0
Total monetary cost ($)	____	____	____
Total time cost ($)	____	____	____
Total Cost ($)	____	____	____

2. Buster has proposed that the distance between bus stops along a certain route be shortened to decrease the walking distance for the typical rider from 10 blocks to 8 blocks. The decrease in bus-stop distance will increase line-haul time from 50 to 55 minutes and increase the total operating costs of the route by 10 percent.

   a. Given the available evidence concerning the size of the relevant elasticities, is ridership likely to increase or decrease?

   b. Suppose that the transit authority passes on the higher operating costs in the form of an increased fare. Given the available evidence concerning the relevant elasticities, is ridership likely to increase or decrease?

3. Figure 16–2 shows average-cost curves for three types of travel systems: an auto system, an integrated bus system, and a heavy-rail system.

   a. Contrast the auto curve in Figure 16–2 to the cost curves in Figure 15–1. Why is the cost curve in Figure 16–2 flat while the cost curves in Figure 15–1 are positively sloped?

   b. Suppose that public opposition prevents the expansion of the highway network. Draw a new pair of cost curves for Figure 16–2, one for the auto system and one for the BART system. Explain any differences between the new curves and the old ones.

4. In drawing the cost curves in Figure 16–2, Keeler et al. (1975) assumed that the disutility of time spent riding a bus is the same as the disutility of time driving a car.

   a. Based on your own preferences, is this a realistic assumption?

   b. Draw a new set of cost curves consistent with your preferences.

5. Zirconium City just converted one of the four lanes on its freeways to "diamond" lanes. The conversion shortened the line-haul time of buses by 10 minutes and increased the line-haul time of autos by 3 minutes. Consider the responses of two commuters: Maeve switched from driving to taking the bus, but Cormac continues to drive. Explain these different responses to the changes in travel times caused by the diamond lanes. How does Maeve differ from Cormac?

6. The city of Congestville is examining alternative policies to deal with its congestion problem. One of the options is free rush-hour bus service. Depict graphically the effects of free bus service on auto congestion and auto trip costs.

7. Consider the effects of dropping a planner's bomb on the San Francisco Bay area. A planner's bomb doesn't hurt any people, but destroys everything except BART infrastructure (tracks, vehicles, and station). Most important, it destroys all buildings, so the metropolitan area must be completely rebuilt. Design a set of public policies that will ensure that in the rebuilt San Francisco Bay area, BART ridership will be high enough so that BART is as efficient as an integrated bus system.

8. In the city of Phoenix, private companies provide bus service on low-volume routes at a fraction of the cost of the public bus agency. In New

York City and Chicago, private companies provide bus service on high-volume (peak-period) routes at a fraction of the cost of the public bus agency. If private firms can underprice the public sector on high-volume and low-volume routes, what, if anything, should be the role of the public sector in the provision of transit services?

References and Additional Readings

Altshuler, Alan A. *The Urban Transportation System*. Cambridge, Mass.: Joint Center for Urban Studies of MIT and Harvard, 1979.

American Public Transit Association. *Transit Fact Book*. Washington, D.C., 1981.

Anas, Alex, and Leon N. Moses. "Transportation and Land Use in the Mature Metropolis." In *The Mature Metropolis*, ed. C. L. Leven. Lexington, Mass.: D. C. Heath, 1978, p. 161.

Beesley, Michael E., and Michael A. Kemp. "Urban Transportation." In *Handbook of Regional and Urban Economics*. Vol. 2 of *Urban Economics*, ed. Edwin S. Mills. Amsterdam: North Holland, 1986, Chapter 26.

Coulson, N. Ed, and Robert F. Engle. "Transportation Costs and the Rent Gradient." *Journal of Urban Economics* 21 (1987), pp. 287–97.

Dewees, D. N. "The Effect of a Subway on Residential Property Values in Toronto." *Journal of Urban Economics* 3 (1976), pp. 357–69.

Domencich, T.; G. Kraft; and J. Valette. "Estimation of Urban Passenger Travel Behavior." *Highway Research Record* no. 238 (1968).

Dyett, Michael V., and Emilio Escudero. *Effects of BART on Urban Development*. 1977. Mimeo.

Echols, James C. "Use of Private Companies to Provide Public Transportation Services in Tidewater, Virginia." Chapter 4. In *Urban Transit: The Private Challenge to Public Transportation,* ed. Charles Lave. Cambridge, Mass.: Ballinger, 1985.

Fielding, Gordon J. *Managing Public Transit Strategically: A Comprehensive Approach to Strengthening Service and Monitoring Performance*. San Francisco: Jossey-Bass, 1987.

Gómez-Ibáñez, José A. "A Dark Side to Light Rail?" *Journal of the American Planning Association* 51 (1985), pp. 337–51. Compares the costs of new light-rail systems to the costs of conventional bus systems.

Gómez-Ibáñez, José A., and John R. Meyer. "Privatizing and Deregulating Local Public Services: Lessons from Britain's Buses." *Journal of the American Planning Association* (Winter 1990), pp. 9–21. Discusses Britain's experience with the deregulation of the bus industry, focusing on the effects of deregulation on service, fares, ridership, and production costs.

Gordon, Peter, and Harry Richardson. "Notes from Underground: The Failure of Urban Mass Transits." *The Public Interest* 94 (1989), pp. 77–86.

Heseltine, P. M., and D. T. Silcock. "The Effects of Bus Deregulation on Costs." *Journal of Transportation Economics and Policy* 24 (1990), pp. 239–54. Discusses the effects of the deregulation of the British bus industry on production costs.

Johnson, Christine M., and Milton Pilarsky. "Toward Fragmentation: Transportation in Chicago." Chapter 3. In *Urban Transit: The Private Challenge to Public Transportation*, ed. Charles Lave. Cambridge, Mass.: Ballinger, 1985.

Kain, John F. "How to Improve Urban Transportation at Practically No Cost." *Public Policy* 20 (Summer 1972), pp. 335–58.

Keeler, Theodore E.; L. Merewitz; P. Fisher; and K. Small. *The Full Costs of Urban Transport.* Berkeley, Calif.: University of California, Institute of Urban and Regional Development, Monograph no. 21, part 3, 1975. Estimates the costs of alternative travel modes.

Kraft, Gerald, and Thomas A. Domencich. "Free Transit." In *Readings in Urban Economics,* ed. Matthew Edel and Jerome Rothenberg. New York: Macmillan, 1972, pp. 459–80.

Lave, Charles A. "Transportation and Energy: Some Current Myths." *Policy Analysis* 4 (Summer 1978), pp. 297–315.

————. "The Private Challenge to Public Transportation: An Overview." Chapter 1. In *Urban Transit: The Private Challenge to Public Transportation*, ed. Charles Lave. Cambridge, Mass.: Ballinger, 1985.

Meyer, John R., and José A. Gómez-Ibáñez. *Improving Urban Mass Transportation Productivity.* Washington, D.C.: U.S. Department of Transportation, Urban Mass Transportation Administration, 1977.

————. *Autos, Transit and Cities.* Cambridge, Mass.: Harvard University Press, 1981.

Meyer, John R.; John F. Kain; and Martin Wohl. *The Urban Transportation Problem.* Cambridge, Mass.: Harvard University Press, 1965.

Mohring, Herbert. "Minibuses in Urban Transportation." *Journal of Urban Economics* (1983), pp. 293–317.

Morlok, Edward K., and Philip A. Viton. "The Comparative Costs of Public and Private Providers of Mass Transit." In *Urban Transit: The Private Challenge to Public Transportation,* ed. Charles Lave. Cambridge, Mass.: Ballinger, 1985a, pp. 233–50.

————. "Recent Experience with Successful Private Transit in Large U.S. Cities." In *Urban Transit: The Private Challenge to Public Transportation,* ed. Charles Lave. Cambridge, Mass.: Ballinger, 1985b, pp. 121–48.

————. "The Comparative Costs of Public and Private Providers of Mass Transit." Chapter 10. In *Urban Transit: The Private Challenge to Public Transportation,* ed. Charles Lave. Cambridge, Mass.: Ballinger, 1985c.

Pickrell, Don H. "The Causes of Rising Transit Operating Deficits." *Transportation Research Record* no. 915 (1983), pp. 18–24.

Rosenbloom, Sandra. "The Taxi in the Urban Transport System." Chapter 8. In *Urban Transit: The Private Challenge to Public Transportation,* ed. Charles Lave. Cambridge, Mass.: Ballinger, 1985.

Small, Kenneth. "The Effect of the 1979 Gasoline Shortages on Philadelphia Housing Prices." *Journal of Urban Economics* 19 (1986), pp. 371–81.

————. *Urban Transportation Economics.* Philadelphia: Harwood, 1992. A comprehensive summary and review of the economics of urban transportation.

Walder, Jay H. "Private Commuter Vans in New York." In *Urban Transit: The Private Challenge to Public Transportation,* ed. Charles Lave. Cambridge, Mass.: Ballinger, 1985, pp. 101–18.

Walters, A. A. "Externalities in Urban Buses." *Journal of Urban Economics* 11 (1982). Discusses the advantages of small buses.

Warner, Samuel B., Jr. *Streetcar Suburbs: The Process of Growth in Boston, 1870–1900.* Cambridge, Mass.: Harvard University Press, 1932.

Webber, Melvin W. "The BART Experience—What Have We Learned?" *The Public Interest* (Fall 1976), pp. 79–108.

17 Education

This chapter explores some of the spatial aspects of elementary and secondary education. Given the large number of school districts in most metropolitan areas, households can choose from a wide variety of schools, each of which provides a different combination of teaching philosophies, educational quality, and tax costs. As explained in Chapter 13 (Overview of Local Government), the Tiebout process causes households to sort themselves geographically with respect to desired spending on local public goods, property values, and income. This chapter explains how the sorting process contributes to inequalities in educational spending and achievement, and discusses the effects of public policies designed to equalize spending and achievement.

What's special about education? Spending inequalities occur for other local public goods: poor municipalities spend less than rich municipalities on parks, recreation, and fire protection. Education is special because a good education is necessary for economic survival. A person with an inferior education is unlikely to find a high-wage job and is therefore more likely to be poor. Moreover, such a person is more likely to turn to crime. One approach to solving the problems of poverty and crime is to improve the educational opportunities for poor children in the central city.

The remainder of this chapter is organized as follows. The first section discusses the education production function, which is used to estimate the relative importance of various inputs to the education process. The most important factors in educational achievement are the home environment of the student and the intelligence and motivation of his fellow students. The second section explains the effects of the Tiebout sorting process on the educational system, showing how the sorting process causes inequalities in educational spending, racial and income segregation, and inequalities in educational achievement. The third and fourth sections discuss two policy responses to these inequalities: grants can be used to equalize educational spending, and desegregation can be used to integrate students with respect to race and income. The question is whether these policies actually decrease spending inequalities and segregation. The final section explores the effects of education vouchers on the educational system.

The Education Production Function

The production function summarizes the relationship between the inputs to the educational process and the output (achievement). The production-function approach can be used to estimate the relative importance of the various inputs to the education process.

Inputs and Outputs of the School

What is the output of a school? The purpose of education is to develop cognitive, social, and physical skills. The basic cognitive skills (reading, writing, mathematics, logic) are necessary for employment and participation in a democracy. Cognitive skills also increase the enjoyment of leisure activities: they allow people to read books, understand jokes, and compute bowling scores. Schools also develop social skills: they teach children how to exchange ideas and make group decisions. Finally, schools develop physical skills: they teach children how to exercise and play games.

Education is different from other production activities because the output (educational achievement) is difficult to measure. While tests have been developed to measure basic cognitive skills, it is virtually impossible to accurately measure social and physical skills. Consequently, any empirical study of schools can, at best, measure only one component of the output of schools. Because empirical studies ignore social and physical skills, they provide an incomplete picture of the education process and must be interpreted with caution.

The production-function approach explores the contributions of different inputs to the cognitive achievement of students. Cognitive achievement is measured by scores on standardized achievement tests. Suppose that achievement is defined as the change in the test score of a particular child over a one-year period. Achievement depends on five inputs: the school's curriculum and educational equipment, the classroom teacher, the home environment, and the achievement level of the child's classmates.

The five inputs to the production function can be divided into three groups:

1. **School resources.** The school has control over three inputs: curriculum, instructional equipment, and classroom teachers. Under the supervision of the local school district, the school designs a curriculum; purchases

instructional equipment (building, books, science labs, computers); and hires teachers. An increase in the number of teachers decreases class size, increasing the teacher input per student.

2. **Home environment.** Educational achievement is influenced by the home environment of the child in three ways. First, parents set the rules of the household, establishing an environment that is either favorable or unfavorable to education. For example, an unfavorable environment is one in which children watch television instead of reading books or doing their homework. Second, parents can motivate their children by encouraging reading, helping with homework, and rewarding success. Third, parents can provide instructional materials such as books and home computers, encouraging independent learning. The quality of the home environment depends in part on the income and education level of the parents. The children of wealthy and educated parents learn more because they receive more encouragement and assistance at home, and also pick up verbal and quantitative skills in everyday interactions with their parents. In contrast, children from poor and less educated families learn less because there is often less encouragement of achievement and less learning from parents. In addition, children living in poverty are often malnourished, inhibiting their ability to learn.

3. **Peer group effects.** The final input to the production process is the peer group of the child. A child learns more if he or she is surrounded by smart and motivated children. Smart peers promote achievement because of cooperation (children learn from one another) and competition (children compete with one other). Motivated peers promote achievement because the teacher can spend less time disciplining and motivating students, and more time teaching them. In addition, an unmotivated student provides an undesirable role model for other students.

The Coleman Report

Which inputs to the production process are the most important? Using the production-function approach, educators and economists have estimated the contributions of the various inputs to the education process. The Coleman report (Coleman et al., 1966) was the first attempt to estimate the education production function. The conclusions of the report are as follows:

1. The most important inputs are the home environment of the student and the characteristics of the peer group.

2. High-income families have more favorable home environments, so children from wealthy families learn more than children from poor families.

3. Children from wealthy families provide a more favorable peer group, so children with wealthy classmates learn more than children with poor classmates.

4. School inputs (curriculum, instructional equipment, teachers, and class size) do not affect achievement.

The Coleman report shocked the education community. The report was disturbing and perplexing for three reasons. First, it implies that schools don't matter, that educational achievement is determined by factors beyond the control of educators. This was a surprise to teachers and educators, who had assumed that they contributed to the education process. Second, the report suggests that education cannot be used to lift children out of poverty. If achievement depends exclusively on the child's home environment and peer group, children in poor areas are trapped: they receive inferior education precisely because they come from poor families (with inferior home environments) and live in poor neighborhoods (with inferior peer groups). If school resources do not affect achievement, the government cannot compensate for inferior home and peer environments by spending more money on the schools of poor students. Third, the report suggests that teachers do not matter, that all teachers are equally effective, regardless of education, experience, innate intelligence, and motivation. In other words, a teacher is a standardized input like a blackboard: put one in the classroom and it works just as well as any other teacher.

To put the conclusions of the Coleman report in perspective, suppose that you are a parent choosing a school for your child. What questions would you ask about a prospective school? According to the Coleman report, you need to ask only one question: What is the average income level of students in the school? It would be senseless to ask questions about curriculum, instructional equipment, and teachers because, according to the Coleman report, these inputs do not affect achievement.

The Coleman report precipitated a flood of criticism. As several researchers pointed out, the statistical methods of the report were flawed. There are two basic problems with the statistical methods:

1. **Unit of observation.** Coleman chose the school, not the individual student, as the unit of observation. The report explored the relationship between the average achievement level of a school and the average school inputs (e.g., average class size, average level of teacher experience, average income), and found that schools with different inputs did not have different achievement levels. The alternative approach is to examine the relationship between the achievement level of an individual child and the quantities of inputs experienced by that child (e.g., the size of the child's class, the teacher's experience and education level, the family income). Because Coleman used schoolwide data, his approach obscures important differences between students in a given school and may have generated inaccurate assessments of the relative importance of education inputs.

2. **Robustness of results.** The second problem is that Coleman's results are not robust; that is, they change with small changes in the statistical

methodology. His results are sensitive to the order in which the various inputs (home environment, peer environment, and school resources) are incorporated into the statistical analysis. If the home variables enter the analysis before the school variables, it appears that school inputs don't matter. If, however, the school variables are entered first, it appears that school inputs affect achievement. Since Coleman's results are sensitive to the order in which inputs are included in the study, his results are of questionable validity.

Other Studies of the Production Function

Researchers did more than criticize the statistical methods of the Coleman report. Using superior data and more sophisticated statistical methods, they generated new estimates of the education production function. The new results cast doubts on some of the conclusions of the Coleman report. The results of these new studies are by no means definitive, so many issues remain unresolved. There is a consensus emerging, however, on the influences of the home environment, the peer group, and teachers.

Home Environment and Peer-Group Effects.   Most researchers agree that the home environment has an extraordinary effect on achievement. Wealthy and well-educated parents provide a more favorable home environment. Researchers also agree about the effects of the peer group on achievement: a student learns more if she is surrounded by smart and motivated students. There is some evidence that the largest peer-group effects are experienced by low achievers: the students at the bottom of the class have the most to gain from adding smart and motivated students to the class. There is also evidence that these peer effects are most important in the middle and upper grades (grades 5 through 12).

The Effectiveness of Teachers.   There is also agreement that teachers matter. Contrary to the conclusions of the Coleman report, teachers are not like blackboards, but in fact vary in effectiveness. The most effective teachers are the ones who are smart, motivated, innovative, and flexible.

While researchers agree that some teachers are more effective than others, they do not agree on what makes a good teacher. In looking for teacher characteristics that explain differences in effectiveness, researchers have focused on education level (years of postgraduate study), communication skills (verbal ability), and experience (years of teaching). The results of the studies are as follows:

1. **Education level.** There is no evidence that teachers increase their teaching skills by going to graduate school. It appears that students do not learn more from teachers with advanced degrees.
2. **Verbal skills.** The most effective teachers have superior communication skills. Students learn more from teachers who score high on standard tests of verbal ability.

3. **Experience.** There is some disagreement about the effects of experience on teaching skills. Murnane (1975, 1983, 1985) suggests that teaching effectiveness increases for the first few years of teaching and then levels off. In contrast, Hanushek (1971, 1981) suggests that teaching skills are independent of teaching experience. Summers and Wolfe (1977) found that low achievers learn more from inexperienced—but enthusiastic—teachers, while high achievers learn more from experienced teachers. Given these conflicting results, the link between teacher experience and effectiveness is still an open question.

Curriculum and Instructional Equipment.   There is evidence that curriculum matters. One of the most important factors in the highly publicized decline in Scholastic Aptitude Test (SAT) scores during the 1970s and 1980s was the relaxation of graduation requirements: under the "smorgasbord" approach to education, students were allowed to choose from a wide variety of courses, many of which were not academic in nature. The typical student took fewer rigorous academic courses, and academic achievement declined. This is the "Twinkie" effect: students skipped the meat and vegetable courses (academic courses), and filled up on the Twinkie courses.

Researchers agree that differences in achievement are not caused by differences in instructional equipment. In other words, students do not learn more in schools that spend a relatively large amount on books, projectors, and buildings. This does not mean that achievement would be unaffected if society returned to the days of log schoolhouses and shared books. It means that, given the current levels of spending on books and buildings, small changes in spending do not affect achievement.

Class Size.   There is some disagreement about the effects of class size on achievement. As Hanushek (1981) points out, there have been 112 studies of the relationship between class size and achievement, with 9 studies finding a negative relationship, 14 studies finding a positive relationship, and 89 studies finding no significant relationship. Summers and Wolfe (1977) suggest that low achievers learn more in small classes and that high achievers learn more in large classes. Given these conflicting results, the link between class size and achievement is still an open question. The issue is not whether class size matters at all, but whether small changes from the current class size affect achievement. No one doubts that achievement would decline if the average class size increased from 20 to 60 students.

The Tiebout Process and Inequalities in Achievement

How does the Tiebout sorting process affect educational spending and achievement? Under the Tiebout process, households sort themselves with respect to three characteristics: desired spending on schools, property values, and peer-group characteristics. Consider first the sorting with respect to educational spending. The desired spending on education varies across households, reflecting differences in income and preferences for education, so households sort themselves into high-spending and low-spending school districts. In this case, spending inequalities result from the simple fact that the wealthy spend more on education, just as they spend more on clothes, cars, and housing. The spending inequalities cause inequalities in educational opportunity: the low-spending school districts have less money for teachers, so they have lower achievement levels.

Because local schools are financed with the property tax, households also sort themselves with respect to property values. Because housing is a normal good (positive income elasticity), the sorting with respect to house value causes sorting with respect to income. Suppose that all the households in a city, wealthy and poor, have the same desired spending on education. Under the property tax, the city has two school districts, one for the wealthy (who live in large houses) and one for the poor (small houses). Although the two school districts have the same per pupil spending, achievement is higher in the wealthy school district for two reasons. First, the average income level is higher in the wealthy district, so the average achievement level is higher. Second, the wealthy district has a better peer environment and thus a higher achievement level for a given student. Income segregation deprives poor students of the possible benefits of being surrounded by smart and motivated students.

Consider finally the effects of student peer groups on location choices. Parents care about educational achievement, not simply educational spending. Given the importance of the peer group in achievement, households look for a school with smart and motivated students. In practical terms, this means that the household looks for a neighborhood full of high-income, well-educated parents who provide a favorable home environment. The shopping for a good peer group reinforces income segregation. Suppose that a poor household has the same desired spending on education as middle-income households and occupies a house with the same market value (same tax liability). In the absence of peer-group effects, middle-income households would welcome the poor household into their school district. However, because the poor student is likely to have a below-average achievement level, middle-income households have an incentive to exclude the child from their school. In general, the peer-group effect adds another item to the household's shopping list, increasing the pressures for segregation with respect to income, race, and social status. As a result, it widens the spatial inequalities in educational achievement. Poor households are denied access to schools that provide a favorable peer environment.

Spending Inequalities

By how much does educational spending vary across school districts in a particular state? Figure 17–1 shows the spending inequalities in four states where the courts

FIGURE 17-1   Inequalities in Spending per Pupil in Selected States, 1986–1987

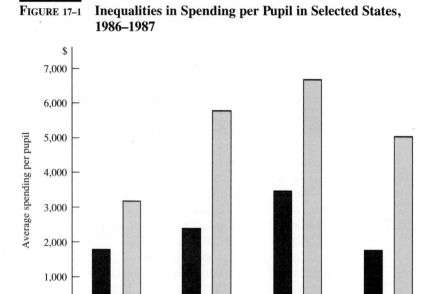

SOURCE: Jeffrey Katz, "The Search for Equity in School Funding," *Governing* (August 1991), pp. 20–22.

have recently declared school-finance systems unconstitutional. For each state, the figure shows the average spending per pupil in the 10 highest spending districts and in the 10 lowest spending districts. In three of the four states, the high-spending districts spend more than twice as much as the low-spending districts. As shown by Katz (1991), spending ratios above 1.5 are common among other states as well.

Segregation and Achievement Inequalities

How segregated is the U.S. school system? Figure 17–2 shows the percentages of minority students (blacks, Hispanics, and other minorities) in schools with different degrees of segregation. Almost half of minority students (46 percent) attended highly segregated schools (where over 80 percent of the students were minorities). About one quarter (24 percent) of minority students attended schools that were moderately segregated (50 percent and 80 percent of the students were minorities). Only 30 percent of minority students attended schools where they were a minority of the student body.

FIGURE 17–2   **Percentage of Minority Students in Schools
with Different Degrees of Segregation, 1986**

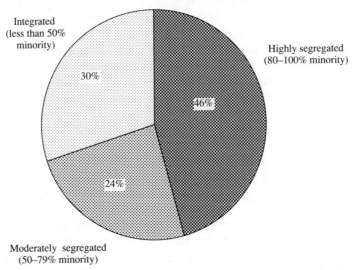

SOURCE: Bradley Schiller, *The Economics of Poverty and Discrimination*, 5th
ed. (Englewood Cliffs, N.J.: Prentice Hall, 1989).

According to a recent report from the U.S. Department of Education (1987), classrooms are even more segregated than schools. Under the **ability tracking system,** students are segregated with respect to ability and achievement: the high achievers are put in one class, and the low achievers are put in another class. Because minority students quickly fall behind white students in the early grades, ability tracking in the later grades contributes to racial segregation within the schools.

How does the educational achievement of blacks and Hispanics compare to that of whites? At age 9, black and Hispanic students are, on average, 25 percent behind their white counterparts in reading, science, and math; by age 17, the achievement gap grows to 30 percent (National Center for Education Statistics, 1982). Although there has been some progress in the last 20 years in decreasing these achievement gaps, the gaps continue to be rather large.

Two other measures of educational achievement are the completion rates for high school and college. According to the U.S. Department of Education (1986), in 1985, only 63 percent of blacks had completed high school by age 19 (up from 56 percent in 1974), compared to 77 percent of whites (up from 76 percent in 1974). Although the gap in high school completion rates has narrowed, it is still large. In 1986, only 11 percent of Hispanics and 12 percent of blacks between ages 24 and 29 had completed at least four years of college, compared to 23 percent of whites (Schiller, 1989).

Programs to Decrease Spending Inequalities

Under the traditional system of education finance, school districts finance their education programs with the local property tax. Therefore, spending per pupil depends on local property values, which of course vary across school districts. In response to spending inequalities, states have developed a number of programs that redistribute money to school districts with relatively low tax bases. Figure 17–3 shows the contributions of the three levels of government to local education. In 1985, state governments provided about half of the funds for education.

Flat Grants

At the turn of the century, 38 states distributed funds to local school districts in the form of flat grants. Under a system of flat grants, the state gives each school district a fixed amount per student, thus guaranteeing a minimum level of spending.

Will a system of flat grants narrow the gap between the spending of wealthy and poor communities? Since every school district receives the same per pupil grant, spending on education increases in every district. As explained in Chapter 14 (Local Taxes and Intergovernmental Grants) the school district

FIGURE 17-3   Sources of Education Funding, 1930–1985

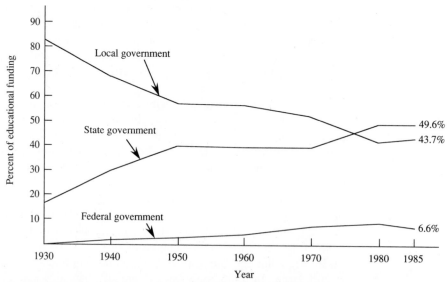

SOURCE: Advisory Commission on Intergovernmental Relations, *State Aid to Local Governments* (Washington, D.C.: U.S. Government Printing Office, 1969); *Statistical Abstract of the United States* (Washington, D.C.: U.S. Government Printing Office, 1987).

is likely to spend only a part of the grant on education and use the rest to cut taxes. One rule of thumb is that local government spending increases by about 30 cents per dollar of grant money, leaving 70 cents per dollar for tax relief. Unless poor school districts spend a larger fraction of the grant on education, a system of flat grants will not decrease spending disparities.

Foundation Grants

In the 1920s, some states switched from flat grants to foundation grants. Under the foundation program, the education grant is inversely related to the property wealth of the school district. The grant for a particular school district is calculated as follows:

Grant = Transfer rate · (Threshold property value − Property value per student)

If the district's property value per student is less than the threshold property value, the district is eligible for a foundation grant. The grant is computed as the transfer rate times the gap between the threshold property value and the actual property value. For example, suppose that the threshold property value is $80,000 and the transfer rate is 0.01. A school district with a property value per student of $30,000 has a property-value gap of $50,000 ($80,000 − $30,000) and receives $500 per pupil (0.01 times $50,000). A school district with a property value per student of $60,000 receives $200 per pupil.

The only difference between the foundation grant and the flat grant is that the foundation grant is a decreasing function of the local tax base. In contrast with the flat grant, which is the same for all school districts, the foundation grant decreases as the local tax base increases.

Most states that use foundation plans have experienced relatively small changes in spending inequalities. The foundation plans have failed to significantly narrow spending inequalities for two reasons. First, most foundation programs provide relatively small grants. Second, school districts spend a small fraction of their grants on education, using the rest of the grant to increase spending on other goods. Because foundation plans do not stimulate education spending by very much, they have not narrowed spending inequalities very much.

The Legal Mandate to Equalize Expenditures

State courts became involved in the financing of education in the 1970s. In response to persistent inequalities in education spending, parents from poor school districts sued state governments, claiming that the spending inequalities violated state constitutions. In a number of states, the courts ruled in favor of the parents, finding that inequalities in educational spending violated the equal-protection clauses of state constitutions. Education is considered a fundamental right of citizens of the state, meaning that all citizens are to receive the same quality of education. The courts developed the **principle of fiscal neutrality:** The quality of education may *not* be a function of the wealth of the local community. In other words, children from poor school districts must receive the same quality of education as children from wealthy school districts. The courts directed state governments to equalize spending on primary and secondary education.

Serrano v. Priest.   The most frequently cited court case is *Serrano v. Priest*, decided in 1974 by the California Supreme Court. When John Serrano complained about the low quality of the local high school's education program, the school's principal suggested that Mr. Serrano move his family to a school district where per pupil spending was higher. Instead of moving, Mr. Serrano sued the state of California, arguing that spending inequalities were unconstitutional.

To illustrate the spending disparities, Serrano cited the differences between two school districts in the Los Angeles area, Beverly Hills and Baldwin Park. As shown in Table 17–1, Beverly Hills used its larger property-tax base to spend more per student while charging a lower tax rate. Ruling in favor of Serrano, the court ruled that the property-tax system violated the equal-protection clause of the state's constitution. The Court ordered the state legislature to develop a financing system under which per pupil spending would vary by no more than $100.

Courts in other states have produced similar decisions. Between 1971 and 1973, there were 51 court actions in a total of 31 states. By 1985, 36 states had been ordered to reform their school-finance systems.

Limits on Reform.   Two court cases established the limits on education reform. In *McInnis* v. *Ogilvie*, the plaintiffs argued that the U.S. Constitution guarantees the right to equal educational *outcomes* rather than equal educational *spending*. They argued that government should eliminate inequalities in educational achievement, spending more on low-achieving students to bring them up to the level of high achievers. The Court ruled against the plaintiffs, arguing that there was no practical way to enforce an equal-achievement standard. Given this decision, the objective of reform efforts is to equalize spending, not achievement.

Another case, *San Antonio Independent School District* v. *Rodriguez*, established the limits for federal involvement in school finance. The Court ruled that education is not a fundamental right guaranteed to U.S. citizens. This ruling is

---

TABLE 17–1   **Taxes and Spending in Baldwin Park and Beverly Hills**

	Baldwin Park	Beverly Hills
Property value per student	$4,169	$49,501
Property tax rate	3.34%	2.55%
Educational spending per student	$272	$1,535

SOURCE: James Guthrie, "United States School Finance Policy 1955–1980," in *School Finance Policies and Practices*, ed. James Guthrie (Cambridge, Mass.: Ballinger, 1980), p. 14.

based on the fact that education is not mentioned in the U.S. Constitution. Consequently, the equal-protection clause of the U.S. Constitution does not apply to education, and variation in per pupil spending is not proscribed by the U.S. Constitution. There are two implications from the *San Antonio* decision. First, any reform of the school-finance system must come from state governments, not the federal government. Second, although the court system may promote equalization of spending within individual states, the courts will do nothing to promote equalization of spending across states.

The Guaranteed Tax Base (GTB) Plan

The court cases of the 1970s demonstrated that the conventional grant programs had failed to reduce spending inequalities to tolerable levels. In response to court orders, states adopted new programs to decrease spending inequalities. Under the **guaranteed tax base (GTB) plan** (also called **district power equalizing**), every school district has access to the same *effective* tax base. If the guaranteed tax base is $50,000 per student, every school district would receive $500 for every 1 percent of the local tax rate: $500 for a 1 percent tax rate, $1,000 for a 2 percent tax rate, and so on. Every school district has the same taxing power, regardless of its local tax base.

The GTB Plan and the Poor School District.   Figure 17–4 shows the effect of a guaranteed tax base on the tax and spending options of a poor school district. The horizontal axis measures the local property tax rate, and the vertical axis measures spending per pupil. The lower line is local tax revenue. Given a local tax base of $30,000 per student, local tax revenue increases by $300 for every 1 percent of property tax. The upper line is the guaranteed tax revenue for different local tax rates, given a guaranteed tax base of $50,000 per student. The state grant is the difference between the guaranteed tax revenue and local tax revenue. For a 1 percent local tax, the school district is guaranteed a total of $500. The local district raises $300 locally, and the state provides the $200 difference between the guaranteed revenue and local revenue. For a 3 percent tax, the district receives a total of $1,500 ($900 from local taxes and $600 from the state).

The GTB plan decreases the opportunity cost of spending on education. Before the grant program, there is a dollar-for-dollar trade-off between spending on education and other goods: every dollar spent on education requires $1 of local taxes, so every dollar of education decreases spending on other goods by $1. Under the GTB plan, the trade-off is $1 for 60 cents. In Figure 17–4, the district can increase spending on education from $0 to $500 by imposing a 1 percent tax. A 1 percent tax generates $300 of local tax revenue and a $200 grant, so the district gives up only $300 worth of other goods to get $500 worth of education. On average, the school district can get $1 of education by sacrificing only 60 cents' worth of other goods. The GTB program is equivalent to a matching grant with a matching rate of two thirds ($300 of local taxes generates a $200 grant).

FIGURE 17-4   Guaranteed Tax Base: Poor School District

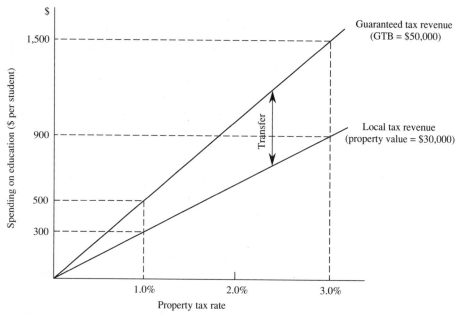

Under a GTB plan, all districts have access to the same effective tax base. If the GTB is $50,000 per student, the guaranteed tax revenue is $500 for every 1 percent of local tax rate. If the local tax rate is 3 percent, the guaranteed revenue is $1,500 per pupil, so the state supplements the $900 of local revenue with a $600 grant. In this case, the GTB plan decreases the opportunity cost of education spending from $1 to 60 cents.

The GTB Plan and the Wealthy School District.   How would the GTB plan affect the tax-spending options of a wealthy school district? Suppose that the wealthy district has $60,000 of property value per student, compared to a guaranteed tax base of $50,000. The local tax revenue exceeds the guaranteed tax revenue: the surplus tax revenue is $100 for a 1 percent tax, $200 for a 2 percent tax, and so on. Under a "pure" GTB plan, the state collects this surplus tax revenue.

The GTB plan increases the opportunity cost of education spending in the wealthy district. If the district imposes a 1 percent tax, it raises $600 of local tax revenue, decreasing spending on other goods by $600. Since $100 of the $600 tax revenue is collected by the state, only $500 is left for local education. On average, the district must give up $1.20 worth of other goods to get $1 worth of education, so the GTB plan increases the opportunity cost of education from $1 to $1.20.

The GTB Plan as an Equalization Tool.   Compared to the foundation plan, the pure GTB plan is a more powerful equalization tool. The GTB plan is more powerful for two reasons. First, the GTB plan has a Robin Hood feature: it takes from wealthy school districts and gives to poor ones. The resulting income effects decrease spending in wealthy districts and increase spending in poor ones. Second, the GTB plan increases the opportunity cost of education in wealthy districts and decreases the opportunity cost in poor districts. The resulting substitution effects reinforce the income effects, narrowing the spending gaps.

Most states with GTB plans have adopted an "impure" version of GTB. School districts are allowed to raise and spend more than the guaranteed tax revenue. In the language of local government, states do not "recapture" or "recycle" the surplus tax revenue of wealthy school districts. Because the impure GTB plan does not recapture surplus tax revenue, it is a relatively weak equalization tool: the plan increases spending in poor school districts, but does not decrease spending in wealthy school districts. According to Carroll (1979), GTB plans have had relatively small effects on spending inequalities.

Michigan's Equalization Plan

Michigan adopted an equalization plan that combined the features of a foundation plan and a GTB plan. The state's 531 school districts were divided into three groups, according to local tax rates and tax bases:

1. **GTB districts.** About one third of the school districts were included in a GTB plan. The GTB districts had tax rates less than 2.2 percent and tax bases less than $38,000 per student. The guaranteed tax base was $38,000.

2. **Foundation districts.** About three fifths of the school districts were included in a foundation plan. The foundation districts had tax rates greater than 2.2 percent and property value less than $38,000 per student. The transfer rate was 2.2 percent, and the threshold property value was $38,000.

3. **Ineligible districts.** The remaining school districts had tax bases greater than $38,000 per student and therefore received no state aid.

The Michigan program had a relatively small effect on spending inequalities. Three factors contributed to its limited effect. First, only about one third of the school districts—those eligible for the GTB plan—experienced significant changes in state support. The districts eligible for foundation grants continued to receive about the same level of state support. Second, the state did not recapture the surplus tax revenue of the relatively wealthy school districts, so the plan did not decrease the spending of wealthy districts. Third, the GTB school districts increased their spending on education by relatively small amounts. The Michigan program failed to equalize spending because it caused relatively small effects in only about one third of the state's school districts.

The California Equalization Program

Under the California equalization plan, the state has equalized expenditures by assuming complete control of education finance. The state of California responded to the *Serrano* decision by establishing spending limits for local school districts. The state limited the rate at which each district could increase its per pupil spending. Because the state allowed low-spending districts to increase their spending more rapidly than high-spending districts, the spending limits narrowed the spending gaps over time. Until 1979, a school district could override its spending limit if it received the approval of two thirds of its voters. Starting in 1979, the spending limits could not be exceeded under any circumstances.

The state's equalization plan received a boost from the tax revolt. In 1978, California voters approved Proposition 13, which imposed strict limits on local property tax rates. The state made the following offer to every school district: if the district imposed a property tax of 1 percent (the maximum allowable under Proposition 13), the state would make up the difference between local tax revenue and the district's state-imposed spending limit. If the school district agreed to the deal, its actual spending would equal its maximum spending. Since every school district accepted the state's offer, the state is now in full control of education spending: every school district spends the maximum amount allowed by the state.

The California equalization plan has sharply reduced spending inequalities. The *Serrano* decision directed the state to decrease spending inequalities to no more than $100 per student. The court would be satisfied, for example, if all school districts spent between $4,000 and $4,100 per student. Since 1974, the percentage of students within the $100 interval increased from 50 percent to more than 90 percent. The equalization program increased state support of education: the state's share of education spending increased from about two fifths in 1974 to about two thirds in 1984.

Desegregation Policy

What causes racial segregation in the schools? One reason for segregation is racial prejudice. Some white parents are unwilling to let their children be educated with racial minorities, regardless of the achievement level of the minority children (and their peer-group effects). Others use race as a signal about the likely achievement level of students: if minority children have, on average, a lower achievement level, a simple way to produce a more favorable peer group is to exclude all racial minorities.

Racial segregation can be accomplished in a number of ways. The first approach is to use explicit segregation, a method used in many southern cities until the early 1970s. A more subtle approach, used by many northern cities, is to manipulate attendance boundaries to send most black children to predominantly black schools. The third approach is to set up neighborhood schools and let households sort themselves with respect to race: households interested in sending their children to white schools can move to wealthy suburban school districts that exclude blacks. A final approach to segregation is to send children to private schools, which are typically too expensive for blacks.

Court-Ordered Desegregation

The courts have outlawed the first two methods of segregation. In *Brown* v. *Board of Education of Topeka* (1954), the Supreme Court declared that explicit racial segregation is unconstitutional. The *Brown* case reversed *Plessy* v. *Ferguson* (1896), which established the constitutionality of "separate but equal" schools. The *Brown* decision required the desegregation of schools only in areas where local governments pursued a policy of explicit segregation. Most of the cities forced to desegregate their schools under the Brown decision were in the South. As pointed out by Clotfelter (1979), the mandate for desegregation was extended in the 1970s to northern cities that used attendance boundaries and other subtle techniques to promote segregation. The Court ordered several large northern and western cities to desegregate their schools. The objective was to integrate the schools to the extent that would have occurred in the absence of earlier government policies that had encouraged segregation. In other words, the Court did not require the cities to develop a truly integrated school system, only one in which government policy had a neutral effect. The segregation that results from the individual location choices of households (the Tiebout shopping process) is considered constitutional.

How did white households respond to forced desegregation? One of the lessons from the history of desegregation policy is that it often increases rather than decreases segregation. There are powerful forces behind segregation that are not neutralized by court-ordered desegregation, and households can take a number of actions to counteract desegregation plans. There are two responses that weaken or reverse the effects of desegregation: households can move from the integrating school district to an all-white school district, or parents can enroll their children in a private school.

Moving to Another School District

Consider first the possibility of moving to another school district. In the South, many central cities had marblelike spatial distributions of households: black areas were interspersed within white areas. The cities used explicit segregation to send whites and blacks living in the same area to different schools. When the courts outlawed explicit segregation, many central-city white families moved to the predominantly white suburbs to keep their children in all-white schools.

Clotfelter (1979) examined the various responses to desegregation in Baltimore and Atlanta, and came to the following conclusions:

1. The fleeing of whites to the suburbs decreased the demand for central-city housing and decreased housing prices. In stable neighborhoods, the price of central-city housing decreased by about 4.7 percent, which led to a 10 percent increase in the proportion of blacks in local public schools.
2. Families with school-age children were the most likely to move to the suburbs when central-city schools were integrated.

The same phenomenon occurred in other cities that used busing to integrate their schools: some white households moved from desegregating school districts to predominantly white school districts.

Switching to Private Schools

Another option for parents in a desegregating school district is to enroll their children in a private school. In choosing between public and private schools, parents face a trade-off between the consumption of education and other goods. Private schools charge tuition, but they also provide a better education, on average, than a public school. A parent sends a child to a private school only if the increase in educational achievement is worth the private-school tuition.

Why do students in private schools learn more than their counterparts in public schools? According to Murnane (1986), private schools are superior in part because they have more favorable peer-group effects. As discussed earlier in this chapter, a particular student learns more if he is surrounded by smart and motivated classmates, and the smartest and most motivated students come from high-income families. Since a large fraction of private-school children come from high-income families, the peer groups in private schools are superior to the peer groups in public schools. According to Murnane, the favorable peer-group effects explain over half of the difference between the achievement levels of public and private students.

Murnane quantifies the peer-group effect by predicting student test scores under different circumstances. The first question he poses is "How would the test score of the typical public-school student change if the student transferred from the public school to a private school?" The answer is that the student's score would increase from 24.4 to 26.1. By transferring to a private school, the typical student would experience a 7 percent increase in achievement. The second question posed by Murnane is "How would the test score of the typical public-school student change if the student, along with his public-school classmates, transferred from the public school to a private school?" The answer is that the student's score would increase from 24.4 to 25.1, an increase of about 2.9 percent. If the student brings his public-school peers along with him to the private school, he experiences less than half the achievement gain that occurs if he leaves his public-school peers behind.

Murnane's results suggest that a large part of the difference between public and private schools is caused by peer-group effects. A student in a private school is surrounded by smarter and more motivated students, and therefore learns more. The other half of the achievement difference is presumably caused by differences in curriculum, teachers, educational methods, and discipline. An important advantage of private schools is that they have more flexibility in expelling troublemakers.

Desegregation and Private Schools

How does desegregation affect the household's choice between private and public schools? Suppose that desegregation enrolls more poor children in the public schools and decreases the average achievement level of public schools. Consider a household that initially (before desegregation) chose the public school because the difference in achievement was not large enough to justify paying the private-school tuition. If desegregation decreases the achievement level of public schools, the difference in achievement between public and private schools may be large enough to justify paying the private-school tuition. If so, desegregation causes the household to move its children to a private school.

There is conclusive evidence that desegregation causes "white flight" to private schools. Using data from Mississippi, Clotfelter (1976) showed that white enrollment in private schools increases with the number of blacks in public schools. The relationship is especially strong when black enrollment in public schools exceeds 50 percent. If the percentage of public students who are black is less than 50 percent, a one-unit increase in the black percentage increased the proportion of whites in private schools by 0.4 percentage point; for black percentages greater than 50 percent, a one-unit increase in the black percentage increased the proportion of whites in private schools by 2.8 percentage points. In other words, the **tipping point** (where the relationship between black and white enrollment suddenly becomes much stronger) is about 50 percent.

Tiebout-Based Segregation

The segregation that results from the individual location choices of households (the Tiebout shopping process) is considered constitutional. What sort of government actions would diminish this type of segregation? In other words, what policies would diminish the incentives for households to sort themselves with respect to income and race?

One approach would be to consolidate local school districts into a metropolitan school district or a statewide school authority. Such a policy would generate a uniform spending level and a single tax base, so there would be less incentive for households to sort themselves with respect to desired school spending and property values. As explained in Chapter 13 (Overview of Local Government), there are some trade-offs with this policy: to the extent there is diversity in demand for education, the large jurisdiction—with its uniform provision of education—is less efficient than the system of smaller jurisdictions. Moreover, as pointed out by Bradford and Oates (1974), such a policy would not eliminate segregation because parents still seek a school that provides a favorable peer group for their children. Middle-income households still have an incentive to exclude poor children from their neighborhoods and schools because the poor have lower average achievement levels.

A less drastic approach would be to use intergovernmental grants to equalize spending. This policy has an advantage over the consolidation approach because it gives the local school district greater control over how to spend its fixed budget. Such a policy would eliminate the incentive for fiscally based sorting (sorting with respect to desired spending levels and property values), but would not affect the sorting motivated by peer-group effects. As explained earlier in this chapter, state governments have tried a number of grant programs, none of which narrowed spending gaps significantly. The only equalization policy that worked was the California program, under which the state assumed complete control of education funding.

Is there any way to diminish the sorting motivated by peer-group effects? Suppose that state grants were tied to students (they traveled with the student to his school) and were inversely related to the income level of the student. By admitting a low-income student, a school would increase its grant revenue, and the school could use the extra money to improve its education program (e.g., decrease class sizes, hire better teachers). Such a scheme would decrease the incentive for middle-income and wealthy households to exclude poor students, so it would promote integration. Even if this plan fails to integrate the schools, a school full of poor (highly subsidized) students could at least use the extra money to provide a better education program.

Public Subsidies for Private Education: Education Vouchers

Should the government subsidize students who attend private as well as those who attend public schools? The advocates of private-school subsidies view the public school system as an inflexible and inefficient monopoly. They argue that a subsidy for private education would force public schools to compete with private schools for students, so public schools would be more concerned about efficiency and more responsive to parental concerns. Would the public support of private schools lead to greater inequalities in educational achievement?

Under a voucher system, every child is issued a coupon that can be used to pay for either public or private education. The typical voucher plan has the following features:

1. The state gives each child an educational voucher with a face value equal to the current per pupil spending in public schools (e.g., $2,500).

2. The family uses the voucher to pay for tuition at a qualifying school, public or private. The school redeems the voucher with the state government.

3. Public schools charge tuition equal to $2,500, making public education effectively free.

4. To qualify for the voucher program, a school must teach basic cognitive skills and civics, and must admit students without regard for race, sex, or religion.

5. The family is free to supplement the voucher with its own funds, so the child is free to attend a school charging more than $2,500 in tuition.

6. The government collects and disseminates information on the teaching methods, curriculum, and test scores of qualifying schools.

The voucher program involves a mixture of subsidies and regulations. The subsidies place private and public schools on equal footing with respect to governmental support. The regulations prevent explicit racism and sexism, and force private schools to teach basic cognitive skills and civics. The government's information program helps parents choose among the alternative schools.

The debate over education vouchers has been spirited. Like most policy proposals, the voucher plan has some good points and some bad points. Because a true voucher plan has never been tried, there is a great deal of uncertainty about the possible effects of a voucher plan. The obvious response is to experiment with voucher systems in one or more school districts. The advocates of education vouchers stress two points:

1. **Competition.** The voucher plan would allow private schools to compete more effectively for students. Competition would presumably improve the efficiency of the educational system, increasing educational achievement per dollar spent.

2. **Diversity.** The voucher plan would encourage diversity in educational philosophy and methods, providing parents with more options.

Voucher advocates argue that vouchers would break up the public-school monopoly, leading to greater efficiency and wider consumer choice.

The opponents of education vouchers stress four points:

1. **Unequal educational opportunities.** Under a voucher system, wealthy families may supplement the voucher with their own money, sending their children to expensive (and high-quality) schools. The children from poor families would receive inferior education.

2. **Income segregation.** Under the voucher system, there would be low-cost schools (patronized by poor families) and high-cost schools (patronized by wealthy families). The educational system would presumably be stratified with respect to income.

3. **Pluralist decision making.** Children educated in a stratified educational system would be less aware and tolerant of other viewpoints and lifestyles, so decision making in today's pluralist society would become more difficult.

4. **Occupational choices.** Children educated in a stratified system would be more likely to choose the same occupation and social status as their parents. The educational system would inhibit occupational and social mobility between generations.

The opponents of vouchers consider the public school system a necessary component of a pluralist democratic society. Education in public schools forces children from different social classes to interact, resulting in citizens who are more tolerant and flexible. If the voucher system generates a more stratified educational system, children from different social classes would not have the opportunity to interact, so children would not develop the traits necessary for managing a pluralist democracy.

There are clearly trade-offs associated with the voucher scheme. A system of vouchers would improve the efficiency of the school system by fostering competition between schools and providing more choice. The plan may also increase inequalities in educational spending, causing greater inequalities in educational achievement. In addition, it may increase income segregation, causing the school system to produce citizens who are less tolerant of alternative viewpoints and lifestyles. Given the lack of experience with voucher plans, these trade-offs cannot be quantified, so it is difficult to make an informed policy decision.

Summary

1. The production function summarizes the relationship between education inputs and achievement.
   a. There are five inputs to education: curriculum, educational equipment, teachers, the home environment, and the peer group.
   b. The home environment has an extraordinary effect on achievement.
   c. A child learns more when he is surrounded by smart and motivated peers.
   d. Teachers vary in effectiveness. Teacher productivity increases with communication skills but is not affected by graduate education. Some researchers suggest that productivity increases for the first few years of teaching, while others suggest that productivity is independent of teaching experience.
   e. The link between class size and achievement is still an open question. If there is a negative relationship, it seems to be a weak one.
2. Under the Tiebout process, households sort themselves with respect to three characteristics: desired spending on schools, property values, and peer-group characteristics.

3. Education spending varies considerably across school districts, a result of differences in desired spending and differences in property tax bases.

4. U.S. schools are highly segregated: in 1986, almost half of minority students attended schools in which over 80 percent of the students were minorities. Under the ability-tracking system, classrooms are even more segregated than the schools.

5. Blacks and Hispanics have relatively low achievement levels: at age 17, they are 30 percent behind white students. In the last few decades, the test scores of blacks and Hispanics have increased relative to those of whites. In 1985, the high school completion rate was 63 percent for blacks, compared to 77 percent for whites.

6. The traditional education grants (flat grants and foundation grants) are lump-sum grants. Under a flat-grant program, the state gives the same per pupil grant to every school district. Under a foundation plan, the grant is inversely related to the district's tax base per pupil.

   a. The grant increases spending on education and also decreases taxes, so households can spend part of the grant on other goods.

   b. Foundation plans have had small effects on spending inequalities because the grants are small and school districts spend a relatively small fraction of the grant on education.

7. In the 1970s, state courts declared that intrastate spending inequalities were unconstitutional. The states responded by developing new grant programs.

   a. Under the guaranteed tax base (GTB) plan, every school district has access to the same *effective* tax base.

   b. The pure version of the GTB plan would decrease spending inequalities by a relatively large amount because it (1) decreases the tax base of wealthy districts and increases the tax base of poor districts, and (2) increases the opportunity cost of education in the wealthy district and decreases the opportunity cost in the poor district.

   c. Most states have adopted an impure version of the GTB plan, under which wealthy districts keep the excess of local taxes over the guaranteed tax revenue.

8. In California, the state government has assumed complete control for education finance and has almost eliminated spending inequalities.

9. The Supreme Court outlawed segregation based on explicit and implicit government actions, and ordered many cities to desegregate their school systems.

   a. Many white households moved from central-city school districts to all-white school districts in the suburbs.

   b. Other white households switched to private schools.

10. In choosing between public and private schools, parents face a trade-off between the consumption of education and other goods.

   a. Achievement is higher in private schools, a result of more favorable peer groups and other factors.
   b. Desegregation causes some households to switch to private schools if the integration of public schools decreases achievement.
11. Under a voucher system, every child is issued a coupon to pay for either public or private education. The voucher plan has advantages and disadvantages:
   a. Competition among schools would increase, improving efficiency and increasing consumer choice.
   b. Spending inequalities may increase, violating the principle of equal educational opportunity.
   c. Income segregation may increase, causing the school system to produce citizens who are less tolerant of alternative viewpoints and lifestyles.

Exercises and Discussion Questions

1. According to Summers and Wolfe (1977), low achievers learn more in small classes and with inexperienced teachers, while high achievers learn more in large classes with experienced teachers. Why?
2. The objective of the state of Egalitaria is to equalize educational opportunity (defined as the same average achievement level in every school). Comment on the following: "To achieve its objective, the state must equalize educational spending, spending the same amount per student in every school."
3. Suppose that a school district has a tax base per student of $40,000 and per pupil spending of $600.
   a. Draw the district's tax-spending line, and label its chosen point *A*.
   b. Suppose that the state offers the school district a GTB plan under which the guaranteed tax base is $80,000. Map the new tax-expenditure line.
   c. What is the new opportunity cost of spending on education?
4. One of the criticisms of a voucher program for education is that it would increase spending inequalities and achievement inequalities. Design a new voucher plan that would narrow—rather than widen—spending and achievement differences across schools. How would you change the conventional voucher proposal to decrease spending and achievement inequalities?
5. Consider Creditland, a state that recently implemented a system of income tax credits for private school. The characteristics of the state and the program are as follows:

    i. Each family has one child in school.

    ii. The government spends $4,000 on each child in the public school system.

    iii. Tuition in private schools is $3,500.

    iv. The tuition tax credit is 50 percent of private-school tuition.

    v. The price elasticity of demand for private education is -0.50.

    vi. The initial enrollment in private schools is 100, and the initial enrollment in public schools is 500.

Compute the fiscal effects of the tax-credit program. By how much does the program decrease total spending on public schools? By how much does the program decrease tax revenue?

References and Additional Readings

Advisory Panel on the Scholastic Test Score Decline. *On Further Examination*. New York: College Entrance Examination Board, 1977. Discusses some of the reasons for the decline in SAT scores.

Bradford, David, and Wallace E. Oates. "Suburban Exploitation of Central Cities and Government Structure." In *Redistribution through Public Choice*, ed. Harold Hochman and George Peterson. New York: Columbia University Press, 1974.

California Department of Education. *Selected Financial and Related Data for California Public Schools, K–12, 1984*. Sacramento: State of California, 1985.

Carroll, Stephen J. *The Search for Equity in School Finance: Summary and Conclusions*. Santa Monica: Rand Corporation, 1979. Discusses the reasons why GTB plans have not had a significant effect on spending inequalities.

Clotfelter, Charles T. "The Effect of School Desegregation on Housing Prices." *Review of Economics and Statistics* 57 (1975), pp. 446–51. Shows that desegregation in the South decreased the demand for central-city housing, decreasing housing prices.

————. "School Desegregation, Tipping, and Private School Enrollment." *Journal of Human Resources* 11 (1976), pp. 28–50. Shows that an increase in black enrollment increases the proportion of whites enrolled in private schools.

————. "School Desegregation as Urban Public Policy." In *Current Issues in Urban Economics*, ed. Peter Meiszkowski and Mahion Straszheim. Baltimore, Md.: Johns Hopkins University Press, 1979, pp. 359–88. Describes the evolution of desegregation policy, explores the "white flight" phenomenon, and discusses the effects of desegregation on achievement.

Coleman, James S.; Thomas Hoffer; and Sally Kilgore. *Achievement in High School: Public and Private Schools Compared*. New York: Basic Books, 1981. Shows that students in private schools have higher test scores than students in public schools, and suggests that achievement depends on the number of academic courses completed.

Coleman, James S.; E. Q. Campbell; C. J. Hobson; J. McPartland; A. M. Mood; F. D. Weinfield; and R. L. York. *Equality of Educational Opportunity*. Washington, D.C.: U.S. Government Printing Office, 1966. The controversial "Coleman report," which was interpreted to mean that schools and teachers do not matter.

Congressional Budget Office. *Trends in Educational Achievement.* Washington, D.C.: U.S. Congress, 1986. Reports trends in test scores.

Coons, John E., and Stephen D. Sugarman. *Education by Choice: The Case for Family Control.* Berkeley and Los Angeles: University of California, 1978. Discusses the voucher program, arguing that a voucher system would provide better education because parents and students would have greater opportunity for educational choice.

Coons, John E.; William H. Clune; and Stephen D. Sugarman. *Private Wealth and Public Education.* Cambridge, Mass.: Harvard University Press, 1970. Developed the notion of "fiscal neutrality."

Garms, Walter I.; James W. Guthrie; and Lawrence C. Pierce. *School Finance: The Economics and Politics of Public Education.* Englewood Cliffs, N.J.: Prentice Hall, 1978. Chapter 3 discusses the reasons for government intervention in education. Chapter 4 discusses the roles of the federal, state, and local governments.

Gramlich, E. M. "Intergovernmental Grants: A Review of the Empirical Literature." In *The Political Economy of Fiscal Federalism,* ed. Wallace E. Oates. Lexington, Mass.: D. C. Heath, 1977. Reviews the literature on the effects of grants on local spending. Concludes that matching grants are more stimulative than lump-sum grants and that a categorical grant has a larger stimulative effect than an equivalent increase in private income.

Guthrie, James W. "United States School Finance Policy 1955–1980." Chapter 1. In *School Finance Policies and Practices,* ed. James W. Guthrie. Cambridge, Mass.: Ballinger, 1980. Relates the history of school finance, focusing on court cases that forced states to reform their financing policies.

Hanushek, Eric A. "Teacher Characteristics and Gains in Student Achievement: Estimates Using Micro Data." *American Economic Review* 61, no. 2 (1971), pp. 280–88. Estimates the education production function, showing that achievement depends on the general ability of teachers (as measured by scores on verbal tests) and how recently the teacher has received formal training.

————. "Throwing Money at Schools." *Journal of Policy Analysis and Management* 1 (1981), pp. 19–41. Summarizes the results of estimates of the production function, focusing on the effects of teachers on achievement. Concludes that teachers do in fact matter, with teachers of higher verbal ability doing better in terms of student achievement. Suggests that spending more money on schools does not increase achievement; argues for the development of direct performance incentives.

————. "The Economics of Schooling: Production and Efficiency in Public Schools." *Journal of Economic Literature* 24 (1986), pp. 1141–77. A survey of research on education, focusing on the production and efficiency aspects of education. Discusses the results of studies that have estimated the education production function.

Katz, Jeffrey. "The Search for Equity in School Funding." *Governing* (August 1991), pp. 20–22.

Levin, Henry M. "Educational Vouchers and Social Policy." In *School Finance Policies and Practices,* ed. James W. Guthrie. Cambridge, Mass.: Ballinger, 1980. Relates the history of the voucher proposal and describes the features of the most recent voucher proposals. Discusses the role of integrated classrooms for the promotion of occupational mobility and the functioning of a pluralist democracy, and suggests that a voucher scheme is likely to cause a stratification of the education system.

Murnane, Richard J. *The Impact of School Resources on the Learning of Inner City Children.* Cambridge, Mass.: Ballinger, 1975. Surveys the results of previous studies of the education production function, and provides new estimates of the production function. Concludes that teacher experience matters for the first few years of teaching.

————. "Understanding the Sources of Teaching Competence: Choice Skills, and the Limits of Training." *Teachers College Record* 84 (1983), pp. 564–69. Discusses the evidence about what teacher characteristics matter (verbal ability and experience) and what characteristics do not matter (formal education), and the policy implications of these findings.

————. "An Economist's Look at Federal and State Education Policies." In *American Domestic Priorities: An Economic Appraisal*, ed. John Quigley and Daniel Rubinfeld. Berkeley: University of California, 1985. Discusses a number of issues in public education, including trends in achievement scores, merit pay, the restrictive effects of state certification requirements, and curriculum reforms.

————. "Comparisons of Private and Public Schools: The Critical Role of Regulations." Chapter 4. In *Private Education: Studies in Choice and Public Policy*, ed. Daniel C. Levy. Oxford: Oxford University Press, 1986a.

————. "Comparisons of Private and Public Schools: What Can We Learn." Chapter 5. In *Private Education: Studies in Choice and Public Policy,* ed. Daniel C. Levy. Oxford: Oxford University Press, 1986b.

————. *Has Title I Improved Education for Disadvantaged Students? Evidence from Three National Assessment on Reading.* Denver, Colo.: Education Commission of the States, 1981a. Evaluates the effects of federal support programs.

————. *The Third National Mathematics Assessment: Results, Trends, and Issues.* Denver, Colo.: Education Commission of the States, 1982. Reports trends in math scores for 9-, 13-, and 17-year-olds.

————. *Three National Assessments of Reading: Changes in Performance, 1970–1980.* Denver, Colo.: Education Commission of the States, 1981b. Reports trends in reading scores for 9-, 13-, and 17-year-olds.

National Assessment of Educational Progress. *Three National Assessments of Science: Changes in Achievement, 1969–1977.* Denver, Colo.: Education Commission of the States, 1978. Reports trends in science scores for 9-, 13-, and 17-year-olds.

National Center for Education Statistics. *Digest of Education Statistics, 1982.* Washington, D.C.: U.S. Government Printing Office, 1982. Documents the differences in achievement between whites, blacks, and Hispanics.

Schiller, Bradley. *The Economics of Poverty and Discrimination*, 5th ed. Englewood Cliffs, N.J.: Prentice Hall, 1989.

Summers, Anita, and Barbara Wolfe. "Do Schools Make a Difference?" *American Economic Review* 67, no. 4 (1977), pp. 639–52. Estimates the education production function, showing that achievement depends on teacher characteristics and class size, with different effects on high achievers and low achievers.

U.S. Department of Education. *The Condition of Education: A Statistical Report, 1983, 1985, 1986.* Washington, D.C.: U.S. Government Printing Office, 1986. Reports the facts on education, including information on student performance, fiscal resources, teacher characteristics, public opinion of the schools, and governance.

U.S. Department of Education, Office of Civil Rights. *1986 Elementary and Secondary School Civil Rights Survey: National Summaries.* Washington, D.C.: U.S. Government Printing Office, 1987. Shows that classrooms are more segregated than schools are.

18 Crime and Punishment

This chapter presents the economic approach to crime and crime prevention. The economic approach assumes that both criminals and victims are rational in the sense that they base their choices on the expected benefits and costs of the alternatives. A rational person commits a property crime if the expected benefit of the crime exceeds the expected cost. Similarly, potential victims use their resources to prevent crime if the expected benefit of prevention exceeds the expected cost. The economic approach sets the stage for a discussion of the optimum amount of crime: because crime is costly to prevent, it is rational to allow some crime to occur.

Why study crime? The analysis of crime is an important part of urban economics for three reasons. First, most crime occurs in metropolitan areas, and crime rates are highest in central cities. Second, households are sensitive to crime rates, so their location decisions are affected by local crime rates. In other words, crime affects the spatial distribution of people within and between cities. Because households are attracted to areas with low crime rates, the price of housing increases as crime rates decrease. Third, the relatively high crime rates in central cities have contributed to the suburbanization of population: many households have moved to the suburbs to escape central-city crime.

Crime Facts

Most crime data come from the FBI's *Uniform Crime Reports*. The FBI collects data from local police departments on seven **index crimes**. The index crimes are divided into personal crimes and property crimes.

1. **Personal crimes.** The victim of a personal crime is placed in physical danger. For some personal crimes, the criminal's objective is to injure the victim (homicide, rape, aggravated assault). For other personal crimes, the objective is to steal property, but the criminal uses a show of force to coerce the victim (robbery).
2. **Property crimes.** Property crimes are crimes of stealth, not force. Examples are burglary (illegal entry of a building); larceny (purse snatching, pocket picking, and bicycle theft); and auto theft.

The FBI data provide a partial picture of the crime scene. Among the crimes omitted in the *Uniform Crime Reports* are disorderly conduct, shoplifting, arson, employee theft, and drug-related offenses (possession and sale of narcotics, public drunkenness, drunk driving).

Table 18–1 lists the crime rates for the seven index crimes for the last few decades. The crime rates are expressed as the number of crimes per 100,000 population. Most of the reported index crimes are economically motivated. In 1990, the four economic crimes (robbery, burglary, larceny, and auto theft) made up about $9/10$ of total reported crimes. The total crime rate rose from 1,870 in 1960 to 5,950 in 1980, and then fell to 5,820 in 1990.

Because the FBI data include only the crimes that are reported to the police, they may be deceptive. In 1986, the reporting rates were 54 percent for robberies, 46 percent for assaults, 27 percent for personal larceny, 50 percent for burglary, 27 percent for household larceny, and 71 percent for auto theft. The reporting rate for auto theft is relatively high because most people insure their cars against

TABLE 18–1   **FBI Index Crimes 1960–1990**

	Number of Crimes per 100,000 People			
	1960	*1970*	*1980*	*1990*
Personal Crime				
Murder	5.0	7.8	10.2	9.4
Rape	9.5	18.6	36.8	41.2
Aggravated assault	85.2	176.9	298.5	424.1
Robbery	59.5	187.2	251.1	257.0
Property Crime				
Auto theft	182	457	502	658
Larceny	1,024	2,124	3,167	3,184
Burglary	504	1,152	1,684	1,236
Total index crimes	1,870	3,949	5,950	5,820

SOURCE: Federal Bureau of Investigation, *Crime in the United States, 1990* (Washington, D.C.: U.S. Government Printing Office, 1990).

theft and must submit a police report with their insurance claim. Given the low reporting rates for most crimes, the FBI data may be misleading: a change in the FBI crime rate could be caused by a change in actual crime rates or a change in reporting rates. In 1988, the overall reporting rate was 36 percent, which was 12 percent higher than the 1973 rate.

Since 1973, the Justice Department has collected crime data from its semiannual victimization survey. The survey suggests that crime rates decreased between 1973 and 1988. The percentage reductions of property crime were 24 percent for robbery, 32 percent for burglary, 26 percent for larceny, and 5 percent for motor-vehicle theft.

The Victims of Crime

Who are the victims of crime? Victimization rates vary with income, place of residence, and race.

1. **Crime and income.** Figure 18–1 shows victimization rates for different income levels. The victimization rates for crimes of violence (rape, robbery, and assault) decrease as income increases: the poor are more likely to be victims of violent crime. In contrast, the victimization rates for crimes of theft (larceny) are highest at the two ends of the income

FIGURE 18–1   Victimization Rates and Income

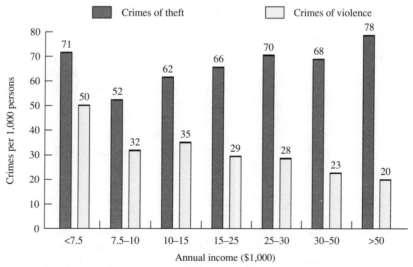

SOURCE: U.S. Department of Justice, Bureau of Justice Statistics, *National Crime Survey Report: Criminal Victimization in the United States, 1989* (Washington, D.C.: U.S. Government Printing Office, 1991).

distribution and increase with income for households with annual income greater than $7,500.

2. **Crime and place of residence.** Figure 18–2 shows victimization rates for different residential locations. Crime rates are higher in metropolitan areas than in nonmetropolitan areas, and higher in central cities than in suburbs. The largest difference in crime rates is for robbery: the central-city robbery rate is over five times the rural rate, and almost three times the suburban rate. Crime is concentrated in cities for three reasons. First, poverty is concentrated in cities. Because a large fraction of criminals come from poor households, the cities have a large supply of potential criminals. Second, wealth is concentrated in cities, and criminals are attracted by urban loot. Third, population density is higher in cities, providing criminals with a large concentration of targets.

3. **Crime and race.** Figure 18–3 shows the victimization rates for whites and blacks. For four of the six crimes shown, blacks are victimized more frequently than whites: the robbery rate for blacks is about three times the robbery rate for whites; the black burglary rate is 1.7 times the white rate; and the black auto-theft rate is 1.8 times the white rate. Whites are more frequently assaulted than blacks, but the difference is relatively small.

Crime and the Price of Housing

Crime rates vary across space, causing variation in the price of housing. Gray and Joelson (1979) studied the relationship between crime rates and property values in Minneapolis. In 1970, the burglary rate varied considerably across the city's census tracts, from 1 percent of dwellings per year in the lowest crime tract to 14 percent in the highest. A one-unit increase in the crime rate (an additional percentage point) decreased the average property value by $336. The vandalism rate varied from less than 1 incident to 30 incidents per 1,000 population. A one-unit increase in the vandalism rate (an additional incident per 1,000 population) decreased the average property by $117. In another study, Thaler (1978) estimated the elasticity of property values with respect to crime rates as −0.067: a 10 percent increase in the crime rate decreased the market value of housing by about 0.67 percent.

The Costs of Crime

Criminal activity imposes two types of costs on society. The **direct costs** are the costs incurred by the physical victims of crime: the victims of personal crimes are injured or killed, and the victims of property crimes lose their property. The **indirect costs** are the costs incurred by potential victims in trying to prevent crime: people spend money on locks, guard dogs, and other prevention measures, and also pay taxes to support society's crime-prevention programs (the police, the

FIGURE 18–2 Crime Rates and Place of Residence

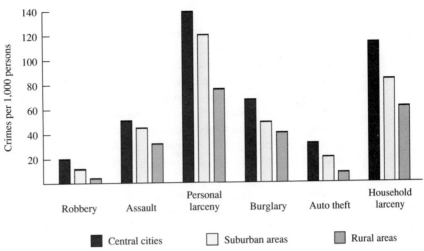

SOURCE: U.S. Department of Justice, Bureau of Justice Statistics, *National Crime Survey Report: Criminal Victimization in the United States, 1989* (Washington, D.C.: U.S. Government Printing Office, 1991), Tables 1 and 2.

FIGURE 18–3 Victimization Rates and Race

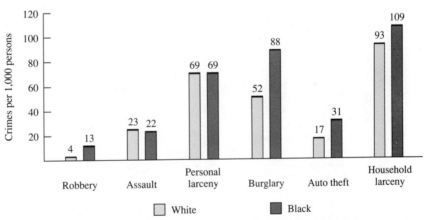

SOURCE: U.S. Department of Justice, Bureau of Justice Statistics, *National Crime Survey Report: Criminal Victimization in the United States, 1989* (Washington, D.C.: U.S. Government Printing Office, 1991), Tables 1 and 2.

court system, and prisons). The opportunity cost of crime prevention is the value of the resources in alternative uses: if there were less crime to prevent, locks could be melted into plows, lawyers could build bridges, and prison cells could be converted to condominiums.

Reynolds (1986) has estimated the direct and indirect costs of personal and property crime, using data from several sources. He estimated the nationwide cost of crime in 1983 and then divided the nationwide cost by the number of households to get the crime cost per household. As shown in Table 18–2, Reynolds estimated that the cost of crime was $2,331 per household in 1983.

Direct Costs.   There are three types of direct cost from crime: personal losses, property losses, and losses from business crime:

1. **Personal losses.** To estimate the social costs of crimes against people, one must place dollar figures on the costs of injuries and death.

TABLE 18–2   **The Costs of Crime in 1983**

	Cost per Household ($ per year)
Direct Costs	
Personal losses	
Homicide	$ 72
Rape	89
Assault	192
Robbery (cost of injury)	82
Property losses	
Burglary	93
Larceny-theft	81
Robbery (property losses)	8
Motor-vehicle theft	56
Business losses	
Arson	22
Shoplifting	300
Employee theft	125
Business fraud	600
Indirect Costs	
Protection costs	
Business	81
Households	106
Criminal justice system costs	
Police	200
Courts and legal services	87
Corrections	87
Opportunity cost of imprisonment	50
Total cost	$2,331

Reynolds (1986) assumed that the cost per homicide was $300,000; the cost per rape was $30,000; the cost per serious assault was $12,000; and the injury cost per robbery was $6,600. As shown in Table 18–2, the estimated annual cost per household ranges from $72 for homicide to $192 for assault.

2. **Property losses.** Property losses occur as a result of burglary, larceny, robbery, and motor-vehicle theft. The estimated value of property losses in 1983 was $238 per household.

3. **Business losses.** There are four types of business crimes. Arson generated losses of $1.8 billion, or $22 per household. Reynolds assumed that the loss from shoplifting was 2 percent of retail sales, or $300 per household, and the loss from employee theft was $125 per household. Business fraud, which generated total losses of $600 per household, includes credit-card theft (losses of $1 billion per year), securities theft ($8 billion), bad checks ($2 billion), insurance fraud ($4 billion), mail and bank fraud ($1 billion), deceptive practices ($18 billion), bribes and kickbacks ($6 billion), and fencing stolen property ($7 billion).

Indirect Costs.   There are two types of indirect costs: prevention costs and the costs of the criminal justice system. According to Reynolds (1986), the total indirect cost was $611 per household in 1983.

1. **Prevention costs.** Reynolds estimated that firms spent a total of $6.5 billion on crime-prevention measures in 1983. Most of this money was spent on private security guards. Households spent an additional $8.5 billion on prevention measures, so the total cost of crime prevention was $15 billion, or $187 per household.

2. **Criminal justice system costs.** Reynolds estimated that spending on police, courts and corrections facilities was $374 per household. Another cost of the criminal justice system is the opportunity cost of time spent in prison. Reynolds assumed that each prisoner could produce $10,000 worth of goods if he or she were gainfully employed. Based on this assumption, the opportunity cost of imprisonment was $50 per household. The total cost of the criminal justice system was therefore $424 per household in 1983.

The Rational Criminal and the Supply of Crime

The economic model of crime assumes that the criminal commits a crime if the expected benefit of the crime exceeds its expected cost. The model of the rational criminal is relevant for economically motivated crimes (property crimes), but not for crimes of passion and violence.

A Numerical Example of Burglary

Consider Boris, who must decide whether to spend a day planning and executing a burglary. Boris will commit the burglary if the expected net benefit of burglary exceeds the expected benefits of spending the day in some legal activity. The costs and benefits of the two activities are listed in Table 18–3.

1. **The expected loot.** The expected value of the burglary loot (EL) is the probability that Boris succeeds in the burglary (P_s) times the monetary value of the loot:

$$EL = P_s \cdot Loot \qquad (18-1)$$

   If the probability of success is 80 percent and the resale value of the stolen property is $600, the expected value of the loot is $480.

2. **Expected cost.** On the cost side, Boris faces the possibility of being sent to prison for committing the burglary. The expected value of the penalty for burglary is the probability of being imprisoned (P_i) times the opportunity cost of time spent in prison.

   a. **Probability of imprisonment.** The probability of being imprisoned is determined by the police and the court system. The probability of imprisonment (P_i) is the probability of being arrested (P_a) times the probability of being sentenced to prison once arrested (P_p).

$$P_i = P_a \cdot P_p \qquad (18-2)$$

TABLE 18–3   **Expected Benefits and Costs for a Burglary**

	Benefits and Costs
Burglary Activity	
Expected loot	
Loot	$600
Probability of success (P_s)	0.80
Expected loot ($EL = P_s \cdot Loot$)	$480
Expected cost	
Probability of punishment ($P_i = P_a \cdot P_p$)	0.02
Opportunity cost of prison time	
Daily wage (W)	$40
Expected workdays per year (D)	150
Forgone income per year ($I = W \cdot D$)	$6,000
Cost of lost freedom per year (F)	$2,000
Opportunity cost per year ($C = I + F$)	$8,000
Expected cost ($EC = P_i \cdot C$)	$160
Expected benefit from burglary ($B = EL - EC$)	$320
Legal Activity	
Daily income if employed (W)	$40
Net Return from Burglary ($R = B - W$)	$280

In the 1970s, about 16 percent of index crimes resulted in an arrest, so P_a is about 0.16 (Wilson and Boland, 1976). In the 1970s, about 13 percent of arrestees were sent to prison, so P_p is about 0.13 (Wilson and Boland, 1976). If Boris faces similar chances of arrest and sentencing, the probability of being imprisoned is about 0.02 (0.16 times 0.13).

b. **The opportunity cost of prison time.** The opportunity cost of time spent in prison equals the annual opportunity cost times the length of the prison sentence. Suppose that Boris is a relatively low-skilled worker who can find work only about 150 days per year and is paid $40 per day. For every year in prison, he gives up $6,000 in income (150 times $40). Another cost of imprisonment is the loss of liberty and freedom. If Boris values his freedom at $2,000 per year, the annual opportunity cost of prison is $8,000 ($6,000 in forgone wages plus $2,000 in lost freedom). If the prison sentence for burglary is one year, the opportunity cost of imprisonment is $8,000. The expected cost is $160 (the probability of being imprisoned [0.02] times the opportunity cost of imprisonment for burglary [$8,000]).

3. **Expected benefit from burglary.** The expected benefit from burglary (*B*) is the expected loot ($480) less the expected cost ($160), or $320.

4. **Net return from burglary.** The alternative to burglary is to spend the day in a legal job. The net return from a burglary (*R*) is the expected benefit of the burglary ($320) less the money Boris could earn in a legal job ($40), or $280. The net return is positive, so if Boris bases his decision exclusively on the expected benefits and costs of burglary, he will commit the burglary.

Morality and Aversion to Crime.   Most people have an underlying aversion to committing crime. For the typical person, crime is unattractive at any price. For other people, the net return from crime must be high enough to overcome their underlying aversion to crime. One way to incorporate the aversion to crime into the benefit-cost analysis is to estimate a person's **anguish cost**, defined as the cost associated with engaging in antisocial activity. If Gabriel has a strong aversion to crime, his anguish cost may be $10,000, meaning that he commits a crime only if the net return exceeds $10,000. If Lucifer is less averse to crime, his anguish cost is only $10, so he commits a crime if the net return exceeds $10. Returning to the example in Table 18–3, Boris commits the burglary if his anguish cost is less than the net return of the burglary ($280).

Who Commits Crimes?   The model of the rational criminal provides three reasons why some people commit crime. First, some people are relatively skillful at committing crime and escaping punishment. For such people, the expected loot is relatively large, so the expected cost of crime is relatively small. Second, some people have relatively low opportunity costs of time spent committing crime and time spent in prison, so the expected cost of crime is relatively low. For example, the poor may have lower opportunity costs because they are unemployed or earn low wages. Third, some people have less respect for society and are less averse to committing crime, so they need a relatively small net return to make crime worthwhile. For most people, the moral anguish associated with crime is large enough to make crime unattractive at almost any price.

The Crime Supply Curve

The model of the rational criminal can be used to derive the supply curve for burglary. The supply curve shows the relationship between the net return, or "price," of burglary and the number of burglaries committed.

Figure 18–4 shows a city's supply curve for crime. The horizontal axis measures the number of burglaries committed in a city per month, and the vertical axis measure the net return (*R*) of burglary. The supply curve has a positive intercept

FIGURE 18–4   The Supply Curve for Burglary

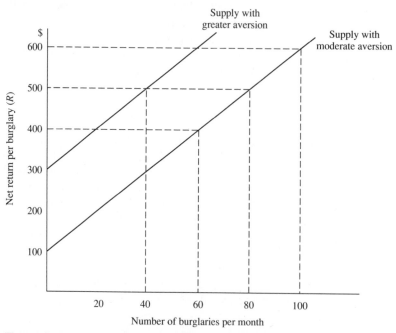

The supply curve shows the number of burglaries for different net returns (*R*) to crime. It has a positive intercept because of anguish costs and if positively sloped because an increase in the net return increases the number of of burglars and increases the number of burglaries per burglar. An increase in aversion to crime shifts the supply curve upward.

of $100 because of anguish costs: for the first burglary, the net return must be high enough to exceed the anguish costs of the first burglar ($100). The curve is positively sloped: as the net return to burglary increases, more burglaries are committed because (1) the net return exceeds the anguish costs for more potential criminals, and (2) burglars commit more burglaries per month. When the net return increases from 400 to 600, the number of burglaries increases from 60 to 100 per month.

The supply curve shows the effects of crime-fighting policies on the crime rate. Suppose that the city increases its police force and thus increases the probability of being arrested for burglary. The increase in the probability of arrest decreases the net return to burglary, so the city moves down its supply curve to a lower crime rate. The crime rate decreases as (1) each criminal commits fewer offenses, and (2) some criminals exit the crime business because the net return of crime falls short of their anguish costs. Marginal criminals "go straight" if the return to crime is not high enough to offset their underlying aversion to crime.

The aggregate supply curve shifts when the underlying aversion to crime changes. In Figure 18–4, an increase in the aversion to committing crime shifts the supply curve upward: there are fewer crimes at each net return. For example, the crime rate for a net return of $500 drops from 80 to 40. Because an individual's aversion to crime depends on age, changes in the age distribution of the population shift the supply curve. Young males commit more than their share of crimes. Therefore, a society with a relatively large number of young males is likely to have relatively high crime rates. Recent shifts in the age distribution of the U.S. population have decreased the proportion of young males. As the proportion of the population in the crime-prone years decreased, crime rates fell.

Optimum Amount of Crime

Because crime prevention is costly, the optimum amount of crime is positive. In other words, it is rational to tolerate some crime. How much crime should be allowed?

Victim Costs and Prevention Costs

The social costs of crime can be divided into **victim costs** and **prevention costs**. The victims of property crime lose property and are sometimes injured in the process. Figure 18–5 shows total victim costs as a function as the number of robberies. The victim cost curve is positively sloped and linear, reflecting the assumption that the victim cost per burglary is independent of the number of burglaries: if the number of burglaries doubles, victim costs also double.

Although society can decrease crime by decreasing the net return to burglary, crime prevention is costly. There are a number of options for crime prevention:

FIGURE 18–5   The Optimum Number of Burglaries

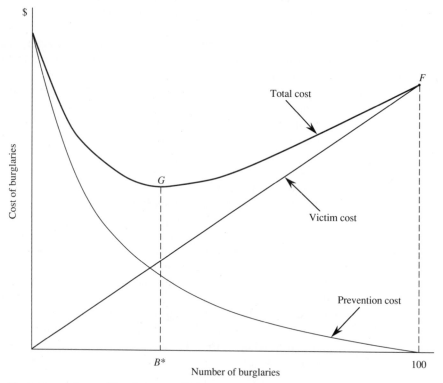

The total social cost of burglaries equals the sum of the costs incurred by victims and the cost of prevention. Victim cost increases at a constant rate if the cost per crime is constant. The prevention cost increases rapidly as the number of burglaries decreases, a result of diminishing marginal returns. Total cost is minimized at B^*.

1. **Hardening the target.** Victims can decrease the expected loot by decreasing the probability of successful burglary (e.g., by installing locks and guard dogs).

2. **Increased probability of arrest.** The police can increase the expected cost of crime by increasing the probability of arrest (e.g., by hiring more police officers).

3. **Increased probability of imprisonment.** The criminal justice system can increase the expected cost of crime by increasing the probabilities of conviction (e.g., by hiring more investigators to gather evidence on crime).

4. **Increased severity of punishment.** The criminal justice system can increase the expected cost of crime by lengthening prison sentences (e.g, by building more prison cells).

5. **Increased value of legal opportunities.** Society can increase the attractiveness of legal activity by increasing the job skills of potential criminals, thus increasing their legal wages. As the opportunity cost of crime increases, the net return to burglary decreases.

In Figure 18–5 the prevention-cost curve is negatively sloped. All of the preventive measures are costly, so the larger the number of crimes prevented (the fewer the burglaries committed), the higher the prevention cost. The prevention-cost curve increases in slope as the number of burglaries decreases, reflecting the assumption of diminishing marginal returns to crime prevention: as prevention efforts increase and the number of crimes decreases, it becomes progressively more difficult to prevent more crime. For example, it is relatively easy to decrease the number of burglaries from 100 to 99, but more difficult to decrease the number from 11 to 10.

The total cost of crime is the sum of the victim cost and the prevention cost. In Figure 18–5, the total-cost curve is U-shaped, reflecting the trade-offs between victim and prevention costs. Suppose that a city starts with zero prevention costs, so it has 100 burglaries per day and the total cost of crime is the victim cost (point F). The city could decrease the number of burglaries and decrease victim costs by spending a small amount on prevention (e.g., hardening targets, lengthening prison sentences, improving legal opportunities). By doing so, it would decrease the total cost of crime: starting from point F, the savings in victim costs would exceed the increase in prevention costs, so the city would move down the total-cost curve. The total costs of crime are minimized at point G, so the optimum crime rate is B^*.

How does the city persuade burglars to commit the optimum number of burglaries (B^*)? The city would use its crime-prevention resources to decrease the net return to burglary to the point at which burglars commit B^* burglaries per day. In other words, the city picks the point on the burglary supply curve and invests resources to bring the net return down to the necessary level.

Crime Prevention Activities

This section discusses some of the details of crime prevention, exploring the effects of various "carrot-and-stick" approaches to preventing crime. The first part of the section considers "carrot" policies: by increasing the value of legal opportunities, the government rewards people who choose legal activities over crime. The second part of the section shows how potential victims can protect themselves from crime. The final part examines "stick" policies: by increasing the certainty and severity of punishment, the government deters crime by penalizing criminals.

Increasing the Value of Legal Opportunities

One approach to preventing crime is to increase the value of legal opportunities. This can be accomplished in a number of ways, including education, job training, and government employment. Chapter 10 (Poverty and Public Policy) describes several programs that provide education and training to the poor. The discussion generated three general conclusions about the effects of the various antipoverty policies on crime rates:

1. Because crime rates are lower among teenagers who stay in school longer and get better grades, programs that increase the amount of schooling and increase scholastic achievement decrease crime rates. For example, the Perry Preschool Program increased high school completion rates and decreased arrest rates: compared to a control group, program participants had higher high school completion rates (67 percent versus 49 percent) and lower arrest rates (by a margin of 40 percent).

2. Some of the youth job-training programs (e.g., Job Corps and Youth Employment Demonstration Projects Act) increase earnings and decrease crime rates.

3. The job-training programs for ex-addicts and ex-offenders have had mixed results. For example, the National Supported Work Demonstration decreased the crime rates of ex-addicts but had relatively small effects on ex-offenders.

What is the relationship between unemployment and crime? Freeman (1983) summarizes the evidence from dozens of studies of the relationship and comes to two basic conclusions. First, although there is a positive relationship between crime and unemployment, the relationship is relatively weak. Second, the crime rates of first-time offenders are relatively sensitive to the unemployment rate. This conclusion is consistent with the results of Fleisher (1966) and Phillips, Votey, and Maxwell (1972), both of which found a strong relationship between youth unemployment and crime rates. A similar conclusion was reached by the NBER study of youth unemployment cited in Chapter 9: teenage crime rates were higher in cities with fewer legal opportunities.

Victims as Crime Fighters

Potential victims can discourage crime by decreasing the thief's expected benefit. There are two strategies for decreasing the expected loot: hardening the target and decreasing the market value of the stolen property.

Hardening the Target.   The potential victim can harden the target by investing in protective devices. Alice's options for bike protection are listed in Table 18–4. If she does not spend any money on protection, there is a 30 percent chance that her $100 bike will be stolen, so her expected loss from theft is $30 (0.30 times $100). If she locks her bike with a flimsy lock, the probability of theft drops to 10 percent; if she locks her bike with a sturdy lock, the probability drops to 2 percent. If she hires an armed guard, the probability of theft is zero.

TABLE 18–4   Protective Measures for $100 Bicycle

Protective Action	Protection Cost	Probability of Theft	Expected Theft Cost	Total Cost
No protection	$ 0	0.30	$30	$30
Flimsy lock	11	0.10	10	21
Sturdy lock	24	0.02	2	26
Armed guard	80	0.00	0	80

What is the optimum level of protection? Alice's objective is to minimize the total cost of protecting her bike, equal to the sum of protection costs and the expected loss from theft. She minimizes total cost with the flimsy lock: her protection cost is $11 and the expected loss is $10, for a total cost of $21. Although a sturdy lock would decrease the probability of theft, the marginal benefit of the additional protection (the $8 decrease in the expected loss) is less than the marginal cost (the $13 increase in protection cost). Alice tolerates a 10 percent chance of having her bike stolen because the marginal cost of additional protection exceeds the marginal benefit.

The optimum level of protection depends on the value of the item being protected. If Alice replaces her $100 bike with a $200 bike, it will be rational to upgrade her protection to a sturdy lock: the switch to the more expensive bike doubles the expected loss from theft, so the marginal benefit of the sturdy lock ($16) exceeds its marginal cost ($13). In general, people with more property to protect spend more money on protection.

How do people and firms harden crime targets? Most people lock their cars and houses, and some install burglar alarms. Purchasers of expensive car-stereo systems can buy plastic covers that make the stereos look cheap and unattractive. Most businesses keep their valuables in safes, and install alarms to deter robbers. Convenience stores keep their money in timed safes, so clerks (and thieves) have access to a limited amount of cash.

Protection and Insurance.   How does insurance affect Alice's spending on protective measures? Suppose that she insures her $100 bicycle against theft and that there are no costs associated with filing a claim (no transactions costs and no deductible payment). If so, the total cost of leaving her bike unprotected is zero: every time her bike is stolen, she collects $100 from her insurance company and then buys a new bike. Therefore, Alice will leave her bike unprotected.

This is the **moral-hazard problem**. If Alice buys insurance, she reduces her own protective measures and is more likely to be victimized. The moral-hazard problem explains why many people do not lock their cars. According to the FBI, 80 percent of stolen cars are left unlocked, and 40 percent have the keys in the ignition. The moral-hazard problem also explains why most insurance policies have deductibles: the deductible increases the property owner's expected loss from theft, encouraging the owner to invest in protection measures. Recently, some insurance companies have tried to control the moral-hazard problem by providing free home-security systems to their policyholders.

Market Value of Loot.   Potential victims can also decrease the resale value of stolen property. As the resale value of the stolen property decreases, the net return from theft decreases, discouraging crime. A potential victim can decrease the likelihood of being victimized by making his property less valuable to criminals.

The resale value depends on how easily the loot can be identified as stolen property. A person who purchases stolen property is subject to prosecution for receiving stolen goods. Given the risks associated with buying stolen goods, a consumer is willing to pay less for a good that is easily identified as "hot." The more readily the stolen goods can be identified, the lower the resale value. The typical criminal sells his loot to a fencing operation and is paid between 20 percent and 50 percent of the legal market value of the goods.

Suppose that Natasha can steal either a hundred-dollar bill or an original painting with a legal market value of $100. Which will she steal? The resale value of the painting is less than $100 because the purchaser of the painting could be arrested for the possession of stolen property. In contrast, the "resale" value of the cash is equal to its face value: given the number of hundred-dollar bills in circulation, it would be impossible to find and punish the person who "buys" the stolen hundred-dollar bill. Natasha will steal the cash, not the painting.

How do potential victims facilitate the identification of stolen goods? In the wild west, ranchers branded their cattle to discourage cattle rustling. More recently, ranchers have experimented with implanting microchips into cowhides to identify and locate stolen cattle. Many communities have developed programs under which residents mark their possessions with identification numbers (Social Security numbers, driver's license numbers) to discourage burglary. Participants in "Operation Identification" place warning labels in conspicuous places to inform potential burglars that "all items of value have been marked for ready identification."

The Police

The primary responsibility of the police is to arrest criminals. As mentioned earlier, in the 1970s, the **arrest ratio,** defined as the number of arrests divided by the number of index crimes, was about 0.16 (Wilson and Boland, 1976). In other words, only about 16 percent of index crimes led to an arrest. From the criminal's perspective, the probability of being arrested for a crime is about 0.16. Changes in the arrest ratio affect crime rates. One rule of thumb is that the elasticity of property crime with respect to the probability of arrest is about −0.50: a 10 percent increase in the arrest ratio decreases the number of crimes by about 5 percent (see Ehrlich, 1973; Wilson and Boland, 1976; Bartel, 1979; and Witte, 1980).

Police Patrol. The police spend a lot of time patrolling streets and sidewalks. The idea behind patrol is that the police should be in a position to respond quickly when crime occurs. Does patrol deter crime? A number of studies have shown that car patrol does not have a significant effect on crime rates. In a famous experiment in Kansas City, the city increased patrolling activity in some neighborhoods and decreased patrolling in others. There were no significant changes in either arrest ratios or crime rates in any of the neighborhoods, suggesting that patrolling does not decrease crime. Other experiments have come to the same conclusion (Sherman, 1983).

Why doesn't car patrol work? One reason is that crime victims are slow to report crimes to the police. According to Sherman, the typical victim takes about 50 minutes to report the crime to police. Suppose that an increase in patrolling could decrease the response time of police (defined as the period of time between receiving a report of the crime and arriving on the scene) from 10 minutes to 2 minutes. If the typical victim takes 50 minutes to report the crime, the police could arrive on the crime scene 52 minutes after the crime is committed instead of 60 minutes. In either case, the criminal's trail is already cold, so the increase in response time is unlikely to increase the arrest ratio. On the other hand, if the victim took only 1 minute to report the crime, an increase in patrolling could make a difference: the police would arrive 3 minutes after the crime instead of 11 minutes, and would therefore have a better chance of capturing the criminal.

What about foot patrol? A number of studies have shown that foot patrol can increase arrest ratios and deter crime. Police on foot patrol are constantly gathering information about the people and businesses in their territories. The foot-patrol officer knows who is arguing with whom, who is suddenly living beyond his means, and whose children are running amok. As a result, the foot-patrol officer is better equipped to prevent crimes and to solve crimes once they occur.

Police Investigation. In addition to arresting criminals, police gather information for public prosecutors and the courts. The success of investigations is measured by the **clearance rate**, defined as the fraction of arrests that result in convictions. According to Forst (1983) about 32 percent of felony arrests result in conviction. The most important investigative task is to find eyewitnesses to the crime. One rule of thumb is that if the police provide two eyewitnesses to a crime, a conviction is virtually guaranteed.

Under the traditional investigative system, crimes are investigated by police detectives rather than patrol officers. The patrol officer usually makes the arrest, prepares a report on the crime, and then hands over the investigation to a detective.

Some police forces have experimented with alternative investigative systems. Under a **community-service system**, each police officer is assigned a small territory and is responsible for both making arrests and investigating crimes. Instead of simply filing a report about the crime, the arresting officer finds eyewitnesses and gathers other evidence for prosecutors. The idea behind this system is that the local patrol officer has a great deal of information about his territory that would be useful in the investigation. There is some evidence that the community-service approach increases clearance rates.

Other cities have experimented with different incentive systems. Under the traditional system, police rewards are based on the number of arrests, not on clearance rates or local crime rates. If police were rewarded for increasing clearance rates and decreasing crime rates, they might have a greater incentive to follow up arrests by gathering information and finding eyewitnesses. The city of Orange, California, has experimented with a system under which police salaries depend on crime rates (see Reynolds, 1986).

The Court System

Forst (1983) shows how the court system handles a typical set of 100 felony arrests. His results are summarized in Figure 18–6. Only 9 of 100 felony arrests result in a prison sentence. The process by which the 100 arrests are whittled down to nine imprisonments is as follows:

1. **Juvenile cases.** About one third of the offenses are committed by juveniles, and are handled by the juvenile justice system. Little is known about the disposition of these cases.

2. **Dismissed by prosecutor.** Of the 65 cases presented to the district attorney, 25 are dropped: most cases are dropped because of weak evidence; a small number of cases are dropped because the offense is trivial. Only about 1 percent of cases are dropped because of violations of rules concerning arrest procedures and evidence.

3. **Dismissed by judge.** Of the 40 cases accepted by the district attorney, 4 are dismissed by the judge, usually because the evidence is insufficient or the offense is trivial.

4. **Disappearing defendant.** Two cases are eventually dropped because the defendant disappears after being released on bond, personal recognizance, or third-party custody.

5. **Plea bargaining.** Of the 34 remaining cases, 27 of the defendants plead guilty, usually to a lesser charge.

6. **Trial acquittal.** Of the seven cases that go to trial, two result in acquittal and five result in a guilty verdict.

7. **Probation.** Of the 32 defendants found guilty (27 from plea bargains and 5 in trials), 12 receive probation (supervised release).

8. **Jail versus prison.** Twenty convicts are incarcerated. Eleven serve time in jail (receiving sentences of less than one year), and nine are imprisoned (receiving sentences of more than one year).

Plea Bargaining.   As shown in Figure 18–6, of the 32 cases that result in conviction, only 5 cases are actually decided by a trial. The other 27 cases are resolved through the **plea-bargaining process.**

FIGURE 18–6   Typical Disposition of 100 Felony Arrests, 1974–1980

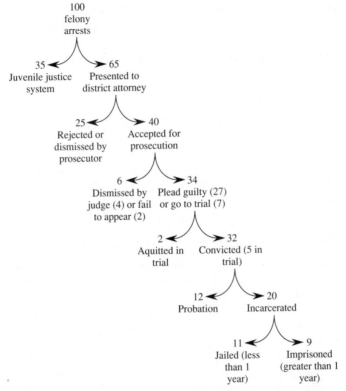

SOURCE: Brian Forst, "Prosecution and Sentencing," Chapter 10 in *Crime and Public Policy,* ed. James Q. Wilson (San Francisco: Institute for Contemporary Studies, 1983).

The district attorney has broad powers to negotiate with the accused over the criminal charge and the resulting punishment. Under the plea-bargaining process, the district attorney reduces the criminal charge and the accused pleads guilty to the lesser charge. Under a plea bargain, the district attorney gets a certain conviction and the defendant receives a relatively light sentence. In addition, both parties avoid the costs of a criminal trial. From the perspective of citizen-taxpayers, the plea bargain produces good news and bad news. The good news is that the plea bargain saves the money that would be spent on a trial, so it decreases taxes. The bad news is that the plea bargain decreases the amount of time convicts spend in jail or prison.

Proof of Guilt.   In any justice system, two types of errors are inevitable. First, some innocent people are found guilty and are punished for crimes they did not commit (a **false positive result**). Second, some guilty people are found innocent and escape punishment (a **false negative result**).

The U.S. courts have developed a set of rules that place the burden of proof on the shoulders of the prosecutors. To convict a person of a crime, the state must prove the person's guilt **beyond a reasonable doubt**. Under the reasonable-doubt rule, the accused is presumed innocent until proven guilty and close cases are decided in favor of defendants. The rule decreases the frequency of false positives (fewer innocents are convicted) but increases the frequency of false negatives (more guilty people are acquitted). In other words, the courts err on the side of innocence rather than guilt.

Other court systems err on the side of guilt rather than innocence. If the accused is presumed guilty until proven innocent, the burden of proof is on the shoulders of the accused. Under this type of rule, close cases are decided in favor of the state. The adoption of this rule would increase the number of false positives (more innocents are convicted) and decrease the number of false negatives (fewer guilty are acquitted).

The Principle of Marginal Deterrence

The penalties for various crimes are determined by legislators, prosecutors, and judges. Legislatures pass laws that establish minimum and maximum penalties, providing guidelines for prosecutors and judges. In the plea-bargaining process, the prosecutors negotiate with suspects over criminal charges and penalties, and then pass on their recommendations to judges, who usually accept the plea bargains. If a case goes to trial and the defendant is found guilty, the presiding judge sets the penalty.

In determining the penalties for different crimes, legislators and judges are guided by the **principle of marginal deterrence.** According to this principle, the penalty for a particular crime should depend on the seriousness of the crime, with greater penalties for more serious crimes.

A Numerical Example. The principle of marginal deterrence can be explained with a simple example. Suppose that a state initially has a one-year penalty for burglary and a two-year penalty for armed robbery. Robbery carries a greater penalty because robbery has higher social costs: the victims of robbery are often injured or killed, while the victims of burglary simply lose their property. Emil is a career criminal who must decide whether to commit a robbery or a burglary. He will commit the crime that provides the larger net benefit. His options are shown in Table 18–5. Robbery generates a greater expected loot ($2,000 versus $1,700) but also carries a higher expected penalty ($1,600 versus $800). The expected net benefit of burglary is $900, compared to $400 for armed robbery, so Emil will commit burglary rather than robbery.

The state's penalties for robbery and burglary provide a marginal deterrent for robbery, the more serious crime. In deciding on the level of crime, Emil weighs

---

TABLE 18-5   Marginal Deterrence

	Armed Robbery	*Burglary (1 year)*	*Burglary (2 years)*
Expected loot	$2,000	$1,700	$1,700
Probability of punishment	0.10	0.10	0.10
Prison sentence	2 years	1 year	2 years
Annual opportunity cost of prison	$8,000	$8,000	$8,000
Expected prison cost	$1,600	$800	$1,600
Net benefit	$400	$900	$100

---

the marginal benefits and marginal costs associated with upgrading from burglary to robbery. The marginal benefit of upgrading is the increase in the expected loot ($300). The marginal cost is the increase in the expected prison cost ($800). Since the marginal benefit is less than the marginal cost, Emil sticks with burglary. Society deters Emil from the more serious crime by imposing a larger penalty on robbery.

Suppose that the state passes a law that equalizes the penalties for burglary and robbery at two years. The increase in the burglary penalty decreases the expected net benefit from burglary to $100 ($1,700 − $1,600), but does not affect the net benefit from robbery. Since the net benefit of robbery now exceeds the net benefit of burglary, Emil switches to robbery. The equalization of penalties eliminates the marginal deterrent: the marginal benefit of moving from burglary to robbery is still $300, but the marginal cost of upgrading (the increase in the expected penalty) is zero. If Emil receives the same penalties for the two crimes, he commits the more lucrative crime. The equalization of penalties eliminates the marginal deterrent effect, so Emil switches to the crime with higher social costs.

The General Effects of Equalizing Penalties.   Figure 18–7 shows the effects of increasing the burglary penalty on the number of burglaries and robberies. Suppose that initially the two crimes have the same net return (R'). Given the two supply curves, there are B' burglaries and A' armed robberies. If the state increases the penalty for burglary, the net return drops to R'', decreasing the number of burglaries to B''. The decrease in the net return to burglary causes some criminals to upgrade to robbery, so the robbery supply curve shifts to the right. The net return to robbery is still R', so the number of robberies increases to A''. Because the increase in the burglary penalty weakens the marginal deterrent, some criminals upgrade to the more serious crime.

The increase in the burglary penalty decreases the total number of crimes: the decrease in the number of burglaries (from B' to B'') exceeds the increase in the number of robberies (from A' to A''). This occurs because the increased penalty causes some burglars to stop committing crimes. In other words, only some of the burglars who change their behavior shift to robbery. Is society better or worse

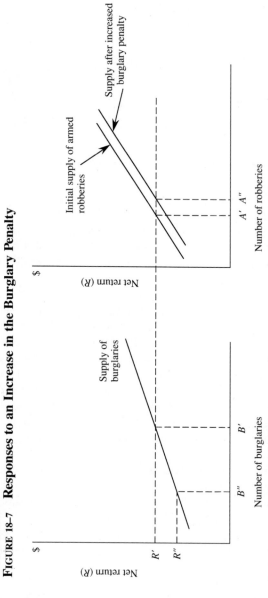

FIGURE 18–7   Responses to an Increase in the Burglary Penalty

In the initial equilibrium, both burglary and robbery have a net return of R', so there are B' burglaries and A' robberies. A decrease in the net return of burglaries to R'' decreases the number of burglaries to B'' (movement down the supply curve) and increases the number of robberies to A'' (shift of the supply curve and unchanged net return to robbery). The increase in robberies is less than the decrease in burglaries because some burglars "go straight."

off under the higher burglary penalty? It depends on the social costs of the two crimes. Because victims are often injured or killed in robberies, the social cost of robbery exceeds the social cost of burglary. According to Phillips and Votey (1979), the social cost of the typical armed robbery is about $5,400 and the social cost of the typical burglary is only about $900. In Figure 18–7, the increase in the number of robberies is about one fourth the decrease in burglaries. If the social cost of robbery is six times the social cost of burglary, the total social cost of crime increases. In this case, the increase in the burglary penalty increases the social costs of crime.

The principle of marginal deferrence generates two lessons for crime fighters. First, because stiffer penalties provide a marginal deterrent, an increase in the penalty for one crime causes some criminals to upgrade to a higher-level crime. Second, policymakers could use this approach to estimate the effects of changes in penalties on the social cost of crime. To do so, they would need information on the social costs of different crimes and the criminals' responses to the change in penalties. The principal questions are the following: How many criminals would be deterred? How many would upgrade to higher-level crime? How many would downgrade to lower-level crime?

The Prison System

The prison system has four functions. The first is the **rehabilitation** function, which is based on the idea that society can use education and counseling to persuade convicts to "go straight." The second function is **deterrence:** by punishing convicts, society makes the threat of punishment credible, discouraging other people from committing crime. The third function is **incapacitation:** prisons isolate criminals from their potential victims, decreasing crime by taking criminals out of circulation. The final function is **retribution,** or **revenge:** law-abiding citizens like to see criminals punished for their actions.

The Rehabilitation Function.   According to the popular view, society can rehabilitate convicts. The purpose of education and counseling programs is to provide convicts with the skills and the desires to become lawful citizens. The success of a particular rehabilitation program is measured by its effect on the **recidivism rate**, defined as the percentage of convicts who are arrested for another crime after they leave prison. The overall recidivism rate is about 80 percent: four fifths of convicts are arrested after they leave prison.

Do rehabilitation programs work? According to Wilson (1975), there have been over 200 studies of rehabilitation programs, none of which has been able to demonstrate that rehabilitation decreases recidivism rates. The studies evaluated the effects of several types of rehabilitation schemes, including education and job-training programs, work-release programs, and counseling programs. The rehabilitation programs did not affect the recidivism rates of either juveniles or adults. Given the results of these studies, there is good reason to be pessimistic about the prospects for using rehabilitation to reduce crime.

Why doesn't rehabilitation work? First, it is difficult to change the antisocial attitudes that make criminals relatively receptive to crime. Second, by the time a criminal reaches the rehabilitation stage (i.e., by the time the criminal is imprisoned), he is firmly committed to crime. If the probability of being imprisoned for a particular crime is 2 percent, the typical criminal has committed 50 crimes by the time he is imprisoned. Third, it is difficult to make legal opportunities more profitable than crime: crime pays, and it is difficult to increase the job skills of an adult criminal.

The **parole system** is based on the principle of rehabilitation. Under the parole system, a convict stays in prison until the parole board declares that he is "rehabilitated." The rehabilitated convict is released and serves the remainder of his prison term under the supervision of a parole officer. A parolee cannot get married or own a car, and must receive the approval of his parole officer before borrowing money or changing residence.

Most parole boards have large caseloads and base most parole decisions on simple rules of thumb. One popular rule is that a convict is released after serving either three years or one third of the prison sentence, whichever is shorter. Studies of the parole system have generated mixed results. In some states, parolees have lower rates of recidivism than convicts who serve out their entire sentence. In other states, there is no measurable difference between the recidivism rates of parolees and other convicts.

The Deterrence Function.   A number of studies have shown that the threat of imprisonment decreases crime rates. An increase in either the probability of imprisonment or the length of the prison term increases the expected cost of crime, decreasing the number of crimes.

There is evidence that an increase in the *certainty* of punishment provides a greater deterrent than an increase in the *severity* of punishment. In other words, an increase in the probability of imprisonment deters more crime than an increase in the length of the prison term. For example, Bartel (1979) estimates that the elasticity of the supply of crime with respect to the probability of punishment is about -0.30: a 10 percent increase in the chance of imprisonment decreases the crime rate by 3 percent. On the other hand, the elasticity of supply with respect to the length of imprisonment is close to zero.

Why don't longer prison sentences deter crime? Although an increase in the penalty may discourage crime by increasing the expected cost of crime, it may simultaneously encourage crime for three reasons:

1. **Hardening the criminal.** Perhaps a long prison sentence hardens the convict, making antisocial behavior more likely. In Figure 18–8, a longer prison term decreases the net return to crime from R^* to R', caus-

FIGURE 18–8   Effects of Increased Punishment on Crime

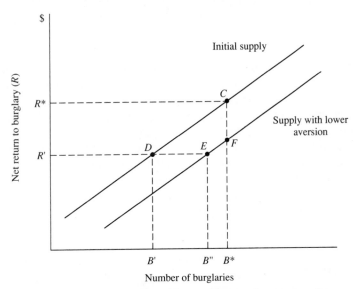

The increase in the severity of punishment decreases the net return from R^* to R', causing a move from point C to point D. If a longer prison term hardens the criminal, his aversion to crime will decrease, shifting the supply curve to the right and causing a move from point D to point E: crime rises close to its original level (B'' is close to B^*). If the criminal also learns more in prison, he will have a higher probability of success when he gets out, causing a move from E to F (increasing the crime rate to its original level).

ing movement down the initial supply curve (from point C to point D) and decreasing the number of crimes from B^* to B'. If criminals are hardened by longer prison terms, their anguish costs decrease, shifting the supply curve to the right and causing a move from point D to point E. The net effect is a small decrease in the crime rate (from B^* to B'').

2. **Prison schooling.** If prison allows a criminal to learn the tricks of the trade from other criminals, a longer prison term means more education and a more skillful criminal. The postprison probability of success increases, increasing the net return from crime. In Figure 18–8, the prison-schooling effect causes a move from point E to point F, restoring the original crime level (B^*).

3. **Discount rates.** If criminals are "present-oriented," they are more concerned with instant gratification than the long-term consequences of crime (imprisonment). The perceived cost of an additional year in prison (e.g., four years instead of three) is small relative to the benefits of

today's crime. In formal terms, if criminals have large discount rates, the perceived cost of an additional year of imprisonment is relatively small in present-value terms, so it has a relatively small deterrent effect.

The Incapacitation Function.   The third function of the prison system is to take criminals out of circulation. An obvious way to reduce crime is to lock up potential criminals. The practical policy issue is whether the benefit of incapacitation (the decrease in crime) exceeds the cost (the cost of running the prison). If each prisoner costs the state about $18,000 per year, the question is whether a one-year prison term decreases the social costs of crime by at least $18,000. If the victim cost per burglary is $900, incapacitation is worthwhile if the burglar would have committed at least 20 burglaries per year. If the victim cost per armed robbery is $5,400, incapacitation is worthwhile if the robber would have committed at least four robberies per year.

Illegal Commodities

The fact that a product is illegal does not prevent people from consuming it. Simon and Witte (1982) estimated the sales volume of a number of illegal goods and services. Their upper-bound estimates for 1974 are as follows: $11.6 billion was spent on heroin, $9.1 billion on cocaine, $5.2 billion on marijuana, $2.2 billion on illegal gambling, $3.2 billion on loan-sharking, $14.8 billion on prostitution, and $16.7 billion on other illegal goods. These figures suggest that, on average, households spent about $785 per year on illegal goods and services.

Why are some goods outlawed? First, lawmakers assume that consumers are irrational about some products: a gambler is unable to make rational choices in the heat of a gambling frenzy, and a drug user is incapable of rational thought in the middle of a drug trip. Second, the consumption of certain goods is assumed to be contagious. Society protects itself from a drug "epidemic" for the same reasons that it protects itself from a polio epidemic. Third, drug addiction is often passed from parent to child, through either physiological or psychological means. By outlawing certain drugs, the government protects children from drug dependence. Fourth, lawmakers assume that drug use leads to unemployment, poverty, and welfare dependence.

Product Illegality and Production Costs

A firm selling an illegal product differs from a lawful firm in two ways. First, there are large penalties if the illegal activity is discovered by the police. The participants may be fined or imprisoned, and the assets of the firm may be seized. Second, contracts with illegal enterprises are not legally enforceable, so creditors cannot be certain that they will be paid for services rendered. These two characteristics make the production costs of the illegal firm relatively high.

The threat of punishment increases wages. To compensate for the risk of illegal activity, the firm must pay its workers a wage premium. Just as a coal miner is paid more than a person in a safe and clean job, a worker in an illegal enterprise is paid more than a person in a legal job. In addition, the firm pays a relatively high wage to prevent "squealing." If workers earn relatively high wages, they have more to lose if the firm's illegal activity is discovered, so workers have greater incentive to conceal the firm's activities.

The threat of punishment also affects the way a firm organizes its production process. To maintain secrecy, the firm controls the flow of information about its activities. One way to control information is to segment the work force into small work groups and limit the information that passes from one group to another. For example, heroin passes through many groups on the way from the poppy field to the consumer (importer, processor, wholesaler, distributor), and each group has little knowledge of the activities of the other groups in the chain. These evasion techniques add to production costs.

The illegal activity also has relatively high capital costs. A loan to an illegal enterprise is relatively risky for three reasons. First, contracts are not legally enforceable, so lenders can never be certain that they will be repaid. Second, given its desire for secrecy, the illegal firm cannot provide the lender with financial information. Since the lender cannot assess the profitability of the illegal enterprise, the loan is relatively risky. Finally, given the risk of confiscation, the illegal firm does not have any real collateral, so the lender may be unable to collect if the borrower defaults on the loan. Because a loan to an illegal enterprise is relatively risky, the lender charges a relatively high interest rate, so production costs are relatively high.

Product Illegality and Price

Figure 18–9 shows the effect of product illegality on the market for illegal drugs. Suppose that a particular drug is suddenly declared illegal. The costs of producing and distributing the drug increase, shifting the supply curve to the left: at every price, less is supplied. The illegal status of the drug also affects its demand curve. The total cost of consuming the illegal drug equals the sum of the market price and the expected penalty for consuming the drug. For example, if there is a 2 percent chance of a $1,000 penalty for drug consumption, the expected penalty is $20 per dose (0.02 times $1,000). When the product is declared illegal, the demand curve shifts downward by the expected penalty. The penalty for drug consumption is like a tax: it shifts the demand curve by the amount of the implicit tax.

If enforcement efforts are concentrated on the supply side of the drug market, the prohibition of drugs increases the market price. In Figure 18–9, the shift

FIGURE 18–9   **Effects of Product Illegality on Price and Quantity**

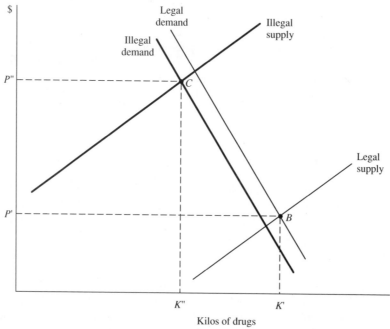

If a commodity is declared illegal, the costs of producing and selling the good increase, shifting the supply curve upward. Consumer penalties increase the net cost of consuming the good, shifting the demand curve downward. The equilibrium moves from point B to point C. The supplier penalty is large relative to the consumer penalty, so the supply shift is larger than the demand shift, so the price of the good increases from P' to P''. The equilibrium quantity decreases from K' to K''.

of the supply curve is larger than the shift of the demand curve, reflecting the assumption that expected penalty for the production and sale of drugs is large relative to the expected penalty for consumption. The price rises from P' to P'', and the equilibrium quantity decreases from K' to K''. By declaring the drug illegal, the government increases the price and decreases the quantity consumed.

What are the implications for the consumers of illegal goods? Consumers pay higher prices for the illegal goods and services. The typical heroin addict, for example, pays about $60 per day for his habit, about 30 times the amount he would pay if heroin were legal. The same analysis applies to other types of illegal goods. The patrons of loan sharks pay higher interest rates because the loan shark must be compensated for the risk of imprisonment and the costs of concealing his activities. Similarly, gamblers face lower odds (lower expected returns) because bookies face higher risks and incur large concealment costs.

Drugs and Property Crime

There is a positive correlation between drug use and criminal activity. According to Wilson (1975), between 25 percent and 67 percent of property crime is committed by drug addicts. Despite this high correlation, the causal link between drug consumption and crime is not fully understood. Although there is evidence that some addicts support their drug habits with property crime, it is unclear just how much addict crime is committed solely to support drug habits.

Will the enforcement of drug laws increase total property crime? In Figure 18–9, the illegality of drugs increases price and decreases the quantity consumed. The increase in price is relatively large because (a) the leftward shift of the demand curve is relatively small and (b) the demand curve is relatively steep (the price elasticity of demand for drugs is relatively low). Because the price rises by a relatively large amount, total expenditures on drugs (price times quantity) increase. If drug addicts support their habits with property crime, the increase in total expenditures increases property crime.

Silverman and Sprull (1977) have estimated the effects of changes in drug prices on property crime. They estimate that the price elasticity of demand for heroin is about −0.27, so a 50 percent increase in the price of heroin would decrease the quantity of heroin demanded by about 13 percent and increase total drug expenditures by about 30 percent. Because only part of property crime is drug related, the resulting increase in property crime (14 percent) is less than the increase in drug expenditures.

There are two implications from this analysis. First, there is often a trade-off between drug control and property crime. Because a supply-side policy increases total expenditures on drugs, property crime is likely to increase. Although drug-enforcement policies decrease drug consumption and thus decrease the social costs associated with drug abuse, they also increase property crime. The difficult policy question is whether the benefits (the decrease in the social costs of drug abuse) exceed the costs (increased property crime). The second implication is that demand-side policies do not have the same trade-offs. Since a demand-side policy simply shifts the demand curve downward, decreasing both the price and quantity of drugs, it decreases total expenditures on drugs and thus decreases drug-related property crime.

Summary

1. The facts on crime are collected by the FBI (from local police departments) and the Justice Department (from victimization surveys).
2. Victimization rates vary with income, place of residence, and race. Victimization rates are generally higher for the poor, for racial minorities, and for the residents of central cities.

3. The direct costs of crime include injury costs and property losses. The indirect costs include protection and the costs of the criminal justice system. According to one study, the total cost of crime in 1983 was $2,331 per household.

4. The optimum amount of crime is where the sum of victim costs and protection costs are minimized.

5. A rational person commits a property crime if the net return to crime is large enough to offset his underlying aversion to crime.
   a. The expected benefit depends on the monetary value of the loot and the probability of success.
   b. The expected cost depends on the probability of imprisonment, the opportunity cost of prison time, and the length of the prison sentence.
   c. The opportunity cost of crime is the income forgone in a legal job.
   d. The net return is the expected benefit less the expected cost and the opportunity cost.
   e. Crime is rational if the net return exceeds the anguish cost.

6. The supply curve for crime shows the relationship between the net return and number of crimes. Society determines the net return to crime, thus picking a point on the supply curve.
   a. Investments in education and job training increase the value of legal opportunities.
   b. Potential victims can decrease the expected benefit of crime by hardening the target and decreasing the resale value of the loot.
   c. The police can increase the expected cost of crime by arresting more criminals.
   d. The courts can increase the expected cost of crime by increasing the likelihood and severity of punishment.

7. The supply curve shifts as a result of demographic and social changes.
   a. As the share of the population in the crime-prone years increases, the supply curve shifts to the right.
   b. Social changes that increase the underlying aversion to crime shift the supply curve upward.

8. Police are responsible for arresting criminals and investigating crimes.
   a. The arrest ratio is the fraction of crimes that lead to an arrest, currently about 0.16. The elasticity of crime with respect to the probability of arrest is about −0.50.
   b. The success of police investigation is measured by the clearance ratio, the fraction of arrests that lead to conviction. The most important investigative task is to find eyewitnesses to the crime.
   c. Although an increase in car patrol decreases the police response time, it does not affect arrest rates and crime rates because victims are slow to report crimes. Foot patrol is more effective because the police gather information about people and potential criminals on their beats.

9. The courts are responsible for determining guilt and setting penalties.
   a. Only about 9 in 100 felony arrests result in prison sentences. Many cases are dropped because the offense is trivial or the evidence is insufficient. About one third of arrests lead to convictions, but most convicts receive probation or short jail terms.
   b. Most criminal cases are resolved through plea bargaining: the district attorney reduces the criminal charge, and the accused pleads guilty to the lesser charge. From the perspective of society, plea bargaining is efficient if the benefits (the savings in court costs) exceed the cost (the decrease in the punishment of convicts).
   c. Two types of errors are inevitable in the criminal justice system: a false positive occurs when an innocent person is found guilty, and a false negative occurs when a guilty person is found innocent. In the United States, the state must prove the case beyond a reasonable doubt, a rule that decreases the number of false positives and increases the number of false negatives.

10. According to the principle of marginal deterrence, penalties should be scaled to the severity of the crime, thus providing a marginal deterrent for more serious crimes. An increase in the penalty for a particular crime causes some criminals to switch to other crimes. An increase in the penalty for burglary causes some criminals to upgrade to robbery, others to downgrade to larceny, and others to abandon crime.

11. The prison system has three purposes: rehabilitation, deterrence, and incapacitation.
    a. Contrary to popular opinion, rehabilitation does not seem to work.
    b. Deterrence works: an increase in the certainty of punishment is a greater deterrent than an increase in the severity of punishment.
    c. Incapacitation is an efficient policy if the prisoner would commit a large number of crimes if he were free.

12. Illegal goods are relatively expensive because firms must compensate their workers and lenders for extra risks, and must spend money on concealment.

13. Policies that decrease the supply of illegal drugs increase the drugs' prices. If drug addicts support their habits with property crime, an increase in total expenditures increases total property crime, partly offsetting the benefits associated with decreased drug abuse.

Exercises and Discussion Questions

1. Consider Boris, a potential burglar who weighs the benefits and costs of burglary. Fill in the blanks in the following table:

Loot	$1,000
Probability of success	0.70
Expected loot	___
Probability of being imprisoned	0.03
Wage per day	$20
Workdays per year	100
Forgone income per year	___
Loss of freedom per year	$3,000
Opportunity cost per year	___
Length of prison term	2 years
Expected penalty cost	___
Expected benefit from burglary	___
Daily income if employed	___
Net return from burglary	___

2. Consider Boris, whose benefit-cost analysis of burglary is shown in Table 18–3. Compute the values of the following variables such that Boris is indifferent between burglary and a legal job. In computing the threshold values for each variable, assume that the values of other variables are the same as in Table 18–3.
   a. The probability of success (P_s).
   b. The value of the loot.
   c. The probability of imprisonment (P_i).
   d. The opportunity cost per year (C).
   e. The length of the prison sentence.

3. Suppose that your city has a fixed budget to allocate among 10 police precincts. You are responsible for allocating the budget.
   a. Your allocation decisions should be guided by some crime-fighting objective. What is your objective?
   b. What information would you collect, and how would you use it?

4. Suppose that Alice purchases an insurance policy for her bike. Complete the following table, assuming that her policy has a $20 deductible.

Protective Action	Protection Cost	Probability of Theft	Expected Theft Cost	Total Cost
No protection	$ 0	0.30		
Flimsy lock	11	0.10		
Sturdy lock	24	0.02		
Armed guard	80	0.00		

5. Critically appraise the following statement: "The social cost of robbery is about six times the social cost of burglary. Given the principle of

marginal deterrence, the length of the prison term for robbery should be six times the length of the prison term for burglary."

6. Consider the analysis of marginal deterrence shown in Figure 18–7. Under what circumstances (what values for the social costs of burglary and robbery) would the increased penalty for burglary decrease the total social costs of crime?

7. Suppose that Gotham City doubles the required prison sentence for burglary (its only crime). Consider the following quote from Robin: "If my assumptions are correct, the longer prison sentence will increase the crime rate."
   a. What are Robin's assumptions?
   b. Use a graph to illustrate Robin's prediction.

8. Consider the following statement: "Our drug policy is inefficient. We should legalize drugs and tax drug producers. We can set the tax at a level such that we have the same equilibrium drug consumption. By doing so, we save all the money we currently spend on the enforcement of drug laws and the prosecution and punishment of drug dealers." What are the advantages and disadvantages of this policy, which combines legalization and taxation?

9. The property losses from business fraud (white-collar crime) totaled $600 per household in 1983, compared to losses of $90 for robbery, $93 for burglary, and $56 for auto theft. Yet white-collar crime receives less attention than other types of property crime. Why do you suppose white-collar crime receives such little attention?

References and Additional Readings

Bartel, Ann P. "Women and Crime: An Economic Analysis." *Economic Inquiry* 42 (1979), pp. 29–51. The probabilities of arrest and conviction have significant deterrent effects on female property crime. The decrease in the number of preschool children accounts for over half of the increase in female property crime between 1960 and 1970.

Becker, Gary S. "Should Drug Use Be Legalized?" *Business Week,* August 17, 1987, p. 22.

Ehrlich, Isaac. "The Deterrent Effect of Criminal Law Enforcement." *Journal of Legal Studies* 1 (1972), pp. 259–76.

———. "Participation in Illegitimate Activities." *Journal of Political Economy* 81 (1973).

Fleisher, Belton. *The Economics of Delinquency.* Chicago: Quadrangle Books, 1966. Suggests that an increase in the unemployment rate increases the juvenile crime rate.

Forst, Brian. "Prosecution and Sentencing." In *Crime and Public Policy*, ed. James Q. Wilson. San Francisco: Institute for Contemporary Studies, 1983. Discusses how the criminal justice system processes a typical set of 100 criminal cases.

Freeman, Richard B. "Crime and Unemployment." In *Crime and Public Policy*, ed. James Q. Wilson. San Francisco: Institute for Contemporary Studies, 1983. Reviews dozens of studies of the relationship between crime and unemployment. Concludes that there is a negative, but weak, relationship between the crime rate and the unemployment rate.

Gordon, David. "Capitalism, Class, and Crime in America." *Review of Radical Political Economy* 3, no. 3 (1971), pp. 51–75.

Gray, Charles M., and Mitchell Joelson. "Neighborhood Crime and the Demand for Central City Housing." Chapter 3. In *The Costs of Crime*, ed. Charles M. Gray. Beverly Hills, Calif.: Sage Publications, 1979. Explores the effects of crime on property values.

Herrnstein, Richard J. "Some Criminogenic Traits of Offenders." In *Crime and Public Policy*, ed. James Q. Wilson. San Francisco: Institute for Contemporary Studies, 1983. Discusses the personal traits that predispose some people to crime.

Kelling, G. L.; T. Pate; D. Dieckman; and C. E. Brown. *The Kansas City Preventative Patrol Experiment: A Technical Report.* Washington, D.C.: The Police Foundation, 1974. Examines the effects of patrol activity on crime rates.

Levine, James. "The Ineffectiveness of Adding Police to Prevent Crime." *Public Policy* 23 (Fall 1975), pp. 523–45.

Martinson, Robert. "What Works: Questions and Answers about Prison Reform." *The Public Interest* (Spring 1974), pp. 22–54. Reviews the results of 231 studies of the effects of rehabilitation programs on recidivism rates.

Moore, Mark. "Controlling Criminogenic Commodities: Drugs, Guns, and Alcohol." In *Crime and Public Policy*, ed. James Q. Wilson. San Francisco: Institute for Contemporary Studies, 1983. Discusses the role of drugs, guns, and alcohol in criminal activity.

Phillips, Llad, and Harold Votey. *Crime and Public Policy.* Beverly Hills, Calif.: Sage Publications, 1979.

Phillips, Llad; Harold Votey; and Harold Maxwell. "Crime, Youth, and the Labor Market." *Journal of Political Economy* 80 (1972), pp. 491–504. Suggests that the crime rates of 18- and 19-year-old males are sensitive to labor-market conditions: the lower the labor-force participation rate, the higher the crime rate.

Reynolds, Morgan. *Crime by Choice: An Economic Analysis.* Dallas, Tex.: Fisher Institute, 1986. Estimates the costs of personal and property crimes.

Schelling, Thomas C. "Economics and Criminal Enterprise." *The Public Interest* 7 (1967), pp. 114–26.

Sherman, Lawrence. "Patrol Strategies for Police." In *Crime and Public Policy*, ed. James Q. Wilson. San Francisco: Institute for Contemporary Studies, 1983. Discusses the efficacy of alternative police-patrol strategies.

Silverman, L. P., and N. L. Sprull. "Urban Crime and the Price of Heroin." *Journal of Urban Economics* 4 (1977), pp. 80–103. Discusses the interactions between drug policies and property crime.

Simon, Carl P., and Ann D. Witte. *Beating the System: The Underground Economy.* Boston, Mass.: Auburn House, 1982.

Thaler, Richard. "Note on the Value of Crime Control—Evidence from the Property Market." *Journal of Urban Economics* 5 (1978), pp. 137–45. Examines the effects of crime rates on property values.

U.S. Department of Justice. *Criminal Victimization in the United States, 1985.* Washington, D.C.: U.S. Government Printing Office, 1987.

U.S. Federal Bureau of Investigation. *Uniform Crime Reports.* Washington, D.C.: U.S. Government Printing Office.

Wilson, James Q. *Thinking about Crime.* New York: Basic Books, 1975.

———. "Crime and American Culture." *The Public Interest* 70 (Winter 1983), pp. 22–48.

Wilson, James Q., and Barbara Boland. "Crime." Chapter 4. In *The Urban Predicament*, ed. William Gorham and Nathan Glazer. Washington, D.C.: The Urban Institute,

1976, pp. 179–230. Estimates the incapacitation effect for different values of crimes per offender.

Witte, Ann D. "Estimating the Economic Model of Crime with Individual Data." *Quarterly Journal of Economics* 94 (1980), pp. 57–84. Estimates deterrent effects and finds that increased certainty of punishment (larger probability of punishment) has a larger deterrent effect than increased severity (larger penalty).

Index